Mergers of Teaching Hospitals

*in Boston, New York,
and Northern California*

D1417577

Mergers of Teaching Hospitals

in Boston, New York,
and Northern California

John A. Kastor, M.D.

THE UNIVERSITY OF MICHIGAN PRESS

Ann Arbor

First paperback edition 2003
Copyright © by the University of Michigan 2001
All rights reserved
Published in the United States of America by
The University of Michigan Press
Manufactured in the United States of America
♾ Printed on acid-free paper

2006   2005   2004   2003   5   4   3   2

A CIP catalog record for this book is available from the British Library.

Library of Congress Cataloging-in-Publication Data

Kastor, John A.
    Mergers of teaching hospitals : in Boston, New York, and Northern
California / John A. Kastor.
        p.   cm.
    Includes bibliographical references and index.
    ISBN 0-472-11196-5 (cloth : alk. paper)
    1. Teaching hospitals — Administration — Case studies.   2. Hospital
mergers — Case studies.   3. Multihospital systems — Case studies.
    4. Hospitals — Shared services — Case studies.   I. Title.

RA975.T43 K374   2001
362.1'1 — dc21   2001027374

ISBN 0-472-08935-8 (pbk : alk. paper)

For Ben and Chris

Contents

Preface

In December 1993, those of us in academic medicine were amazed to learn that two of the country's premier teaching hospitals, the Massachusetts General Hospital and the Brigham and Women's Hospital in Boston, were merging. How did these hospitals, so proud of their histories and traditions and fierce competitors since the Brigham opened in 1913, ever decide to come together?

Whatever the reasons, observers predicted that other hospitals were bound to do the same, so powerful would be the example of what happened at these two hospitals and at Harvard, the medical school with which they are both affiliated. By 1997, the Presbyterian Hospital in the City of New York, the principal teaching hospital for the Columbia University College of Physicians and Surgeons, and The New York Hospital, principal clinical site for the Cornell University Medical College, came together. Later that year, the teaching hospitals for the University of California-San Francisco (UCFS) and Stanford University merged. A few others, elsewhere, did the same.

There seemed to be a story here that would interest and instruct the doctors, scientists, and hospital professionals who work in the nation's teaching hospitals and medical schools and the consultants, some of whom had advised their clients in the merging process. Perhaps other readers interested in how the leaders of these institutions are trying to assure the survival of both their hospitals and their jobs during the current turmoil would find the stories interesting. The library and the Internet offered little guidance. Interested students of academic medicine had written a few pieces over the years, and newspapers had reported the events. But often the details were hazy. So it quickly became clear that only by talking with those involved in the process at each of the hospitals and their medical schools could the events be fully understood.

This study is a tribute to the everlasting tendency of academics to talk informatively and often at length, particularly if they know their listener to be a compatriot who is familiar with the trials that they are facing. Accordingly, this study depends foremost upon the courteous and enthusiastic help of 237 faculty members, administrators, trustees, and interested observers,* several of whom were interviewed more than once.

The project took a year and a half to complete. I began interviewing in July 1998 and sent the manuscript to the publisher in February 2000. I decided not to revise and thereby slow the production of the book after that time. So, except for adding a few developments of paramount interest, the reporting ends with the events of the winter of 2000. Fortunately, that time coincided with resolution of the leadership crisis at New York-Presbyterian and the governmental dilemma at UCSF Stanford.

The book consists of eight chapters. In the first, I have written an introduction to the subject that will be suitable, I hope, for the general reader. I am an academic cardiologist, not an authority in the delivery of health care, and request that those more knowledgeable in the field will forgive my poaching on their area of expertise. None of what I describe in this chapter derives from personal research. However, I felt that, before launching into the specifics of each case, many readers would want a narrative describing why those working in teaching hospitals and medical schools have found their world so much more difficult to control during the past decade.

Two chapters are devoted to each of the three mergers. The first, in each case, describes the forces and events that led to the mergers, and the second relates what happened afterward. I chose these three mergers partly because they involved teaching hospitals that are among the most respected in the country, each directed and staffed by talented trustees, administrators, and doctors. Three seemed like a reasonable number to study if I were to finish the work relatively quickly, and as for the choices, I thought, why not work with the best? If they can't succeed at it, who can? Fortunately for the story, each of the mergers occurred in different cities, in different states, in institutions with different histories and traditions, and, most importantly, in different health care environments. A few other teaching hospitals have merged, some relatively successfully, and one disastrously, as described in the concluding chapter. Each would have provided useful information had I been inclined to include more cases.

The final chapter summarizes what I learned and what the mergers teach us. Some who read the manuscript criticized the absence of the author's opinions in the six chapters on the mergers themselves. This

---

*Forty-five of these were at Partners (Brigham and Women's and Massachusetts General hospitals), 98 at New York-Presbyterian, 79 at UCSF Stanford, and 15 unaffiliated with any of these institutions.

omission was deliberate. I thought it best to let the interviewees tell their stories without the interference of the reporter at that point.

A few words about style. During my time in academic medicine, the title of the heads of academic departments has changed from chairman to chair in many schools in deference to the discomfort among many women about the use of titles that include gender-specific words. Among the people I interviewed in Boston and New York, however, *chairman* continued to be used more often. In northern California, use of *chair* is the rule for the leaders of both academic departments and boards of trustees. Accordingly, I have employed the word that I found customary in each city.

I thank each of the people I interviewed for their participation, for without them, this work could not have been completed, let alone started. I sent to most of them drafts of the sections in which they appeared and asked them to tell me what mistakes I had made and where they would feel more comfortable not having their comments attributed to them. Hence, the interviewees did exercise some control over what I wrote but only to the extent of reducing any personal embarrassments. Everything I learned that seemed relevant is here.

Several of those interviewed read and commented on one or more of the chapters apart from the paragraphs in which they appeared. This group included: at Partners, W. Gerald Austen, Eugene Braunwald, Ferdinand Colloredo-Mansfeld, Joseph B. Martin, Samuel O. Their, and Daniel C. Tosteson; at New York-Presbyterian, Jack D. Barchas, Robert Michels, Herbert Pardes, Lewis P. Rowland, and David B. Skinner; at UCSF Stanford, Spyros Andreopoulos, Gerhard Casper, Haile Debas, Lawrence Furnstahl, Donald Kennedy, David Korn, Joseph B. Martin, and Isaac Stein. The assistance of those who reviewed portions of the text improved what you read, but what remains is my responsibility for better or worse. Drs. Braunwald and Debas, in particular, encouraged me that the study might have value, and I am deeply obliged to them for this support.

Several people facilitated the work at the different institutions. I thank, in particular, Patricia Eng at Partners, Bonnie Winters at New York-Presbyterian, and the staff in the dean's office at the Columbia University College of Physicians and Surgeons. Peter Kastor provided valuable advice on the presentation of the material.

My colleagues at the University of Maryland, Robert Barish, Patrick Breault, Robert Chrencik, and Andrew Ziskind, made useful suggestions. Phyllis Farrell provided, as always, superb assistance. I am particularly obliged to William L. Henrich, my successor in the chair of medicine at Maryland, for his many courtesies and encouragement.

This book would not have been possible without help from members of the University of Michigan Press, which took a chance on an author without experience writing this type of a book. Rebecca McDermott, editor for health policy and management, sent me the good news when the Press accepted the book for publication. Her successors, Liz Suhay and Ellen McCarthy, took the work through to completion. I also want to recognize the contributions of Marcia LaBrenz, who efficiently coordinated the copyediting, Janet Opdyke, who skillfully edited the manuscript itself, and the individuals at Twin Oaks Indexing, who professionally and promptly prepared the index.

CHAPTER 1

Introduction

This is a book about the merging of six of America's leading teaching hospitals, where the faculties of five of the country's most distinguished medical schools instruct their students and trainees in clinical medicine. The force driving the mergers was economic, and the name of the force was managed care.

Insurance for Health Care

Payment for health care on a large scale by someone other than patients began in the United States with the formation of the Blue Cross insurance plans during the Great Depression of the 1930s[1,2] as hospital income from patients and philanthropic donations plummeted.[2,3] A few doctors tried to develop prepaid medical plans, but these met with concerted opposition from the leaders of the state medical societies and the American Medical Association, which asserted that they constituted "corporate medicine,"[4] were "unethical, inferior to fee-for-service,"[4] and interfered with the private practice of the profession. Despite this opposition, the courts favored the group physicians and protected them from harassment,[2] so while the national battles raged the prepaid group practice movement continued to grow at the local level.[2]

Organized medicine saw the Blue Cross insurance programs for hospital care, which were founded in 1934,[3] as less threatening and came to accept them as the lesser of two evils compared to prepaid medical plans and their characteristic consumer control and salaried physicians.[2] Also acceptable to the state medical societies were the Blue Shield programs for doctors' fees, which some of the societies founded in the late 1930s. Blue Shield, as they saw it, prevented "the need for government . . . to pay for physicians' services."[3]

"It is doubtful," writes the medical economist Eli Ginzberg, "that private health insurance would have become a potent force if not for the boost that it received from the war [World War II]."[5] The War Labor Board, which had frozen wages to contain war-induced inflation, permitted trade unions to bargain with employers for health care,[5] and paid premiums for medical insurance was one of the benefits won for the workers.[1,3] The burgeoning postwar economy that followed allowed employers to grant health insurance to increasingly more workers. That the Internal Revenue Service exempted these benefits from federal income tax helped increase their popularity.[3,5]

By the time Medicare arrived in the mid-1960s, American doctors and hospitals had become accustomed to charging and receiving most of what the market would bear. Under the indemnity* or "fee-for-service" health insurance policies then held by most workers, doctors and hospitals rendered their charges, the insurance carriers paid most of them,† and the patients paid the rest. The reckoning began in the 1970s as corporate profits declined due to increasing competition with other economies, and the cost of medical care grew in excess of the rate of inflation for other goods and services. With their profit margins squeezed, the leaders of America's largest companies looked for a means of containing the rapidly rising costs of providing medical care for their employees.[6-8] Unlike the historical model, the revolution they fomented came from the top, not, as observers of the phenomenon suggest, "from the downtrodden — low income and disabled patients or underpaid hospital and nursing home workers."[1]

Initially, employers reduced their costs by increasing the portion of the insurance paid by their employees.[1,7] Some employers, particularly smaller ones, decided not to insure their employees at all.[1] These and other measures, however, reduced the employers' expenses relatively little. From 1960 to 1990, spending on health care grew at a rate of 6 percent per year, adjusted for inflation, more than double the rate of growth in the rest of the economy.[9]

What accounts for this extraordinary rise? "By far the most important factor," writes health care economist Victor R. Fuchs, "is the change in technology . . . used for diagnosis and treatment [which] are more expensive than in the past."[10] Many patients, only seeing their premiums rise, do not understand the reasons for this change. I am reminded of the patient who, returning for her second hospital admission and now being examined with the latest scanning device, observed that the human body must be growing more complicated if such equipment was now required to study it.

---

*Indemnity insurance provides protection against hurt, loss, or damage.

†This involved a method that those involved in the process called "retrospective reimbursement" since the payments were based on the services that had already been provided. We will see how managed care converted the basis of payment from what had been done in the past to what might be done in the future.

Managed Care and HMOs

During the 1980s and 1990s, increasingly more corporations tried to lower, or, if they could not do that, at least limit the growth of, what they spent to purchase health benefits for their workers.[7,8] Employers further reduced the benefits granted to their employees, often requiring the workers to pay a larger portion of their premiums (cost shifting)[7] and paid less to hospitals and doctors (discounted* fee-for-service). Rather than continuing to provide indemnity insurance that allowed their employees to receive care where they wished and, at least to some degree, at the price the doctors and hospitals charged, employers increasingly offered policies that required employees to receive their care from health maintenance organizations (HMOs) and similar groups. By "managing" the medical care of the employees, HMOs could successfully compete for employers' business at a lower cost than fee-for-service insurers, even when the scale of payments to the health care providers[†] was discounted. Compared with fee-for-service indemnity insurance, managed care fundamentally changes the method of reimbursing hospitals and doctors for their services. Prospective payment (dollars per patient per month) replaces retrospective payment for bills as rendered.

Managed care, in its current form, began as "managed competition," the phrase coined by Alain C. Enthoven, an economics professor at Stanford University, more than 25 years ago.[11] Managed competition:[11]

> Is based on a belief that economic incentives are the principal determinant of how patients, payers, and providers behave when they seek, finance, or render medical care. According to its proponents, if the incentives are changed and people are made to bear the economic consequences of their choices more directly, systemic reform will follow.

John Iglehart, who frequently writes on the subject in the *New England Journal of Medicine* and other publications, describes managed care as:[12]

> A system that integrates the financing and delivery of appropriate medical care by means of the following features: contracts with

---

*Discounted is a euphemism for *reduced.*

†"Health care providers" is the phrase currently in vogue for those who take care of patients — the doctors, nurses, and others, called "allied health professionals." Hospitals and nursing homes are examples of "provider organizations." These recently introduced terms reflect the influence of business consultants and writers on the terminology of health care delivery.

selected physicians and hospitals that furnish a comprehensive set of health care services to enrolled members, usually for a predetermined monthly premium; utilization and quality controls that contracting providers agree to accept; financial incentives for patients to use the providers and facilities associated with the plan; and the assumption of some financial risk by doctors.

Most organizations that provide managed care do so through HMOs, preferred provider organizations (PPOs) and the more recent invention, point-of-service plans.[12] Although what became known as HMOs had operated for several decades, the HMO movement, as such, began in 1970 when Dr. Paul M. Ellwood Jr. proposed a national "health maintenance strategy" to the Nixon administration. Ellwood, who has been described as "almost single-handedly responsible for the rapid growth of HMOs,"[2] was impressed that:[2]

The existing fee-for-service system created "perverse incentives" which rewarded physicians and institutions for treating illness and then withdrew these rewards when health was restored. . . . Ellwood believed that the health care system could be made more functional if it were restructured and incorporated genuine incentives to promote health.

When Ellwood sought to construct a more functional system, he found that it already existed in prepaid group practices. He saw that Kaiser-Permanente and similar groups were providing good care to large populations at reasonable cost.

The Health Maintenance Organization Act of 1973,[4] which followed from Ellwood's efforts,[11] represented the federal government's first real effort to develop an alternative to fee-for-service medicine.[11] The law authorized federal grants and loans to finance the creation of nonprofit HMOs that employers could offer.[11] HMOs would ideally provide incentives for doctors to keep patients well by practicing preventive medicine rather than only caring for the sick.[13] Ellwood coined the term *health maintenance organization* to describe his program with words that were "politically neutral and medically nebulous."[2] However, not everyone looked with favor on Ellwood's mission. "The most dangerous man in American medicine," he was called. "His crime: promoting a preposterous thing called competition. His weapon: a crazy idea called the HMO."[14]

One of the best-known and now the largest not-for-profit HMO in the country is the Kaiser-Permanente program. This plan, the invention of Dr. Sidney Garfield, a recently trained surgeon having difficulty establishing a practice during the Depression, began in the late 1930s for workers at Kaiser's construction site at the Grand Coulee Dam in Washington state. It expanded greatly during World War II to include the workers at the Kaiser shipbuilding plants.[2,4] Although the workers departed when the war ended, the popularity of the plan appealed to many new subscribers when enrollment was opened to the public.[2,4] Despite the development of similar plans during the next two decades, few Americans had access to them until Paul Ellwood launched the current movement in the 1970s.

Spending less on each patient by limiting the use of medical services is the essential method HMOs employ to save money.[15] They reveal their operating philosophy by calling the ratio of the money they spend on medical services to the income they derive from premiums as the "medical *loss* ratio"[16] (my italics), which is in the mid- to low 80 percent range in for-profit HMOs and somewhat higher in not-for-profit HMOs such as the Kaiser-Permanente Medical Care Program.[17,18] HMOs aim, as their name implies, to reduce disease and consequently the costs of future medical care through inexpensive preventive measures. In application, the managers of these plans emphasize cost control more than preventive medicine and improving the quality of care[19] in their relationships with doctors and hospitals.[9]

During the past decade, more than 20 years after the federal government first encouraged patients to enter HMOs, federal and state governments have rediscovered the value of the system. They now offer HMOs and in some states insist that their Medicare or Medicaid beneficiaries join them.

Managed care programs have endless variations, but there are essentially two types of HMOs: the staff or group model and the independent practice association (IPA). The staff model is the simplest and in a sense the purest form of physician organization. The HMO employs the doctors and compensates them through salaries supplemented or reduced by the skill with which the doctors manage the practice. In the group model, the physicians aggregate in independent medical groups within HMOs. In an IPA, the most common form of HMO, accounting for about half of the enrollment in the United States,[4] the HMO contracts with individual or groups of doctors to provide care at a negotiated rate per capita for a flat retainer or at a negotiated fee-for-service rate. IPAs process bills and money among doctors, patients, and insurers. In many cases, they are owned by their member doctors. The physicians in an IPA work in their own offices and may see patients on a fee-for-service basis as well as patients from other HMOs.[12]

Preferred provider organizations contract with networks or panels of physicians who agree to provide medical services on a discounted fee-for-service basis.[12] Point-of-service plans give patients the freedom to seek care from physicians not in their basic plan but at a substantially higher fee.[12]

The Effects of Managed Care on Hospitals and Physicians

Until managed care really began to bite, better-run teaching hospitals generated sizable surpluses, which their executives invested in new buildings, improved equipment and services, and professional staff. Since almost all such institutions were not for profit or owned by governments, the directors could ignore the demands of stockholders for dividends or constantly rising values for their shares.[20] However, as HMOs began to proliferate, hospital leaders and physicians were forced to recognize what others had warned, that much financial slack had developed in the American health care system and that costs, relatively uncontrolled by the market, had grown beyond what was necessary to provide good care for their patients.

More unbiased physicians and hospital executives came to realize, reluctantly, that they were partly to blame for being driven out of their fee-for-service Eden. They had eaten too many apples. Some of their charges, exaggerated by exorbitant fees, unessential procedures and tests, and excessively long hospital admissions, had helped drive up the cost of medical care and bring on the retribution of managed care. Also facilitating the growth of managed care was the excess capacity for health care in many markets, as demonstrated by a surplus of unoccupied hospital beds, underutilized expensive equipment, and a plethora of physicians in many specialties.[8,9]

Since a major cost for the payers was hospital care, the HMOs squeezed there first. The duration of hospital admissions dropped precipitously. Usually, the shorter length of stay* proceeded without particular strain, but some changes, such as the reduction in the duration of hospitalization after childbirth, caught the headlines. The immediate effect was predictable. The number of beds filled with patients,† and accordingly the hospitals' revenues, dropped. Hospitals tried to compen-

---

Length of stay is hospital jargon for the duration of an admission.

†Hospital administrators usually count the number of beds filled with patients at midnight, and this constitutes the "census."

sate for shorter lengths of stay by increasing the number of admissions. However, the HMOs opposed this solution, insisting that fewer patients be admitted and more of them treated in less expensive, outpatient facilities. Applying these reasonable economies apparently required the operation of "market forces," for most hospital leaders and doctors surely didn't implement them voluntarily.

The advance of managed care and its HMOs decreased, at least temporarily, the rate of inflation of medical costs.[8,21] The rise in expenses for national health care in 1997, the lowest in three and a half decades, was only 4.8 percent. It had been 12.2 percent in 1990.[21] "By this criterion, managed care has been a success so far," writes Victor Fuchs.[9] "Spending has been slowed in 3 ways: reduced services to patients, providing services more efficiently, and squeezing the incomes of physicians and other health care professionals."[9] The loss in their income "does not create substantial gains for society as a whole," Fuchs observes. "It is primarily a transfer from one set of pockets to another."[9]

One effect of managed care has been to increasingly disgruntle American health care providers, whose income has stopped rising, and in many cases has decreased, as they now receive fewer dollars for the same services. The annual average net income of physicians grew by 7.2 percent from 1986 to 1992 but by only 1.7 percent from 1993 to 1996.[21] "Many doctors are working harder in less fulfilling circumstances," writes John Iglehart.[22] "They are angry and unsure how to correct their situation. They see themselves in a managed care system that seems more intent on lowering their prices than in managing care."[22]

Compounding their agony, physicians and hospital executives sense that they are losing their accustomed power to protect their interests, both professional and economic, and to influence what they consider to be in the best interests of their patients.[8] Physicians, trained to regard their primary role as that of advocates for their patients' welfare, are now required to balance the patient's needs against the pressures for cost control. This transformation, it has been suggested, subtly changed their role from "advocacy to allocation."[12]

How the Teaching Hospitals and Medical Schools Use Clinical Income to Support Research and Education

For decades, teaching hospitals and medical schools have directed part of what they collected for hospital and physician services to support their academic mission. This was possible because, as a rule, most clinical faculty, who tend to be members of more highly paid specialties, accept lower salaries for the opportunity to participate in the academic enterprise than their colleagues in private practice. Furthermore, low-paid trainees, house officers* and fellows,† and unpaid medical students perform much of the clinical work in teaching hospitals.

In departments of medicine, for example, cardiologists, gastroenterologists, and their colleagues "attend" or "visit" — the latter word is still used in Boston — usually for a month at a time, on one of the inpatient services and care for all the patients there with the help of the trainees. Their departments bill for their professional services, pay their salaries, and distribute, as their leaders determine, any surpluses to support the research and educational work of the department.

This system, which educates the students and trainees through practical experience, allows the faculty members to concentrate the time they spend caring for patients. They can then work in their laboratories or see their private patients during the rest of the year and, for that matter, for the rest of the day not spent on their supervisory duties even when they are "on service." In addition, grants from agencies like the National Institutes of Health support portions of the salaries and expenses of successful investigators, relieving the departments of part of these costs.

In other departments, similar arrangements apply. One faculty anesthesiologist, for example, can "cover" two operating rooms, with resi-

---

*The term *house officer* applies to interns and residents because these "doctors in training" live in the "house" (hospital). Although now they do so by rotation — every fourth night is typical for interns in departments of medicine — several decades ago the name more strictly applied. House officers then had their own quarters in the hospital and were seldom off duty. *Internship* — which derives from the French *interne* — is the traditional word describing the first postgraduate year. A residency — "resident" in the hospital — follows and may take two to five years or even more in some of the surgical specialties. In the United States, the states license physicians to practice after they have completed their internships, but all doctors now take further training.

†Clinical fellows have completed their internships and residencies in such general clinical subjects as family practice, internal medicine, obstetrics and gynecology, pediatrics, psychiatry, radiology, or surgery. As fellows, they train further in subspecialties like cardiology or gastroenterology in departments of medicine or pediatrics, child psychiatry in departments of psychiatry, or cardiothoracic surgery in departments of surgery. Most clinical fellows no longer have quarters in the hospital, but they are often on call via telephone and pager. Research fellows are either M.D.s who have finished residencies or clinical fellowships or scientists who have recently received Ph.D. degrees. Research fellows work under supervision in scientific laboratories or with patients to prepare for careers in universities, research institutes, or industry. Trainees can spend from two to six years or even more as fellows, which can mean that some do not begin their independent careers as practitioners or investigators until as many as 10 years after graduating from medical school.

dents providing the care for each patient. The department then bills each patient's insurer for the services of the senior anesthesiologist supervising the residents in each case. The salary and benefits for one senior anesthesiologist and two trainees cost less than the cost of two faculty members.

What really makes this system work financially for the teaching hospitals and indirectly for the medical schools is the Medicare-administered educational supplement, which pays the entire salaries of the interns and residents in approved training programs. On top of the salaries, the teaching hospitals also receive money for the "indirect costs" associated with operating their postgraduate education programs.[18] In recent years the amount of support in this generous program has come under increasing pressure, providing further financial agony for the executives of teaching hospitals and the deans of medical schools.[23–26]*

This system of training and faculty development became practical only when governments began supporting the care of indigent and elderly patients. Formerly, needy patients who came to the teaching hospital seeking help were assigned to wards where their care was provided by house staff and students supervised, in degrees that varied from institution to institution, by members of the faculty. To some extent, the house staff kept the attending physicians at arm's length, thereby protecting their jurisdiction over the "clinical material."[27]†

Organized medicine and most physicians, who for decades had strongly opposed "socialized medicine," benefited greatly from the passage of the bills establishing Medicare and Medicaid. Now the federal and state governments paid doctors and hospitals to care for patients who previously had patronized public clinics and been hospitalized on free wards in community and teaching hospitals. In those pre-Medicare days, clinical faculty members, most of whom supported themselves in private practice, supervised without charge the care of these patients by interns, residents, and students for the honor of their faculty appointments and

---

*The amount paid to hospitals for their house staffs varies substantially in different parts of the country. During the federal government's 1996 fiscal year, of the hospitals in this study, Massachusetts General in Boston received $79,128 per resident, Columbia-Presbyterian Medical Center in New York City received $80,415, and University of California-San Francisco Medical Center received $58,612.[23] Effective October 1, 2000, the 1999 budget act equalizes some of these payments[25] to the detriment of New York and the advantage of California. Advocates for teaching hospitals in the cities affected by the reductions plan to propose new legislation to assure that teaching hospitals in their districts and states receive more support for postgraduate training.[24]

†*Clinical material* is doctor-speak for the indigent patients who occupy beds on the wards of the resident-run services where most students train.[27]

the privilege of admitting their private patients to teaching hospitals. A similar practice prevailed in community hospitals with house officers.

Medicare and Medicaid transformed many "service" patients, who previously had received free care from the house staff, into "private" patients. Most clinical departments in teaching hospitals now began to capture these patients for the academic enterprise by assigning their care to full-time faculty members who were salaried by the hospital or medical school. In the past, many hospitals had referred insured or well-off patients who came to their emergency departments without personal physicians to younger, private practitioners who were often recent graduates of their training programs. Many of these young doctors began their practices in this manner.

The presence of so many insured patients who had previously received their care in hospital wards and public clinics led to rapid expansion in the size of the full-time clinical faculty paid by the medical schools.[28] These physicians and their colleagues in the basic science departments, such as anatomy and physiology, now became increasingly dependent on the financial success of the clinical operations in their medical schools. If the clinical income was high, these doctors could spend more time on nonclinical academic activities, which were now partially funded by the surpluses in clinical collections, and the department directors and deans could recruit more investigators and clinicians and provide the buildings and facilities needed for their work. Obviously, any reduction in clinical income would have a potent effect on the professional lives of all salaried faculty members in the nation's 124 medical schools.

Financial pressure on the teaching hospitals also threatened the financial well-being of the medical schools and their faculty. Just as the doctors were being paid less for their work, hospitals were similarly receiving fewer dollars for their services while the costs of providing contemporary care continued to rise. As the lower payments from managed care began to influence, and in some areas dominate, the economic scene, the hospitals could less afford to support the work of the medical schools and their faculty. In addition to paying for the purchase of a new clinical laboratory, for example, teaching hospitals often paid part of the salary of the doctor who operated the laboratory and the nurses and technicians who, in addition to caring for the patients being tested, participated in the professor's research. Customarily, the hospital contributed significant amounts of money to help the school recruit department heads and well-known clinicians who would bring well-insured patients to the hospital and, by performing notable research, raise the prestige of the medical center. Lower payments thanks to managed care and reductions in the remaining fee-for-service schedules of private in-surers, Medicare, and Medicaid put all this support at risk.

Response of Teaching Hospitals and Medical Schools to Managed Care[28a]

As managed care squeezed the income of teaching hospitals and medical school clinical faculty, the leaders of the academic medical centers re-tained consultants to advise them how to respond to the "paradigm shift"[29]* in the financing of medical care. The consultants described how HMOs invaded a community in four stages from 0–10% penetration ("stage 1: unstructured market") to 50 percent penetration ("stage 4: managed competition").[32] Deans and teaching hospital executives re-viewed these data with anxiety, hoping that their regions had not as yet descended to phase four.

Clearly, however, no matter how much the leaders wished managed care would go away, they would have to deal with it. At its worst, in the eyes of academic physicians and investigators, would managed care as-sault the viability of continuous growth, one of the most cherished fea-tures of the more successful academic medical centers during the past three decades? Academic health centers and their clinical faculties have been called "unrepentant capital junkies,"[33] always demanding the latest piece of expensive computerized equipment to care for their patients and advance their research. Would these appetites go unfulfilled and plans to build new teaching hospital facilities or medical school laboratories be shelved? Would their institutions, in the managerial jargon now adopted by many leaders of academic centers, have to "rightsize" or, more omi-nously, "downsize"? Should the size of the faculty be reduced? Would their income, although generous by comparison with their colleagues in the liberal arts, drop and the quality of their professional lives, although no longer "threadbare"[34] and "genteel"[34] as in former times, diminish?

Decreasing income drives well-managed organizations to try to re-duce expenses, and teaching hospitals responded to this pressure. Deans

---

Paradigm shift, a phrase much favored during the 1990s by consultants and those writing about managed care, is used to describe, often in apocalyptic terms, the changes that managed care can bring to academic medical centers, their hospitals, schools of medicine, and doctors. (Thomas Samuel Kuhn, born in 1922, an American philosopher and historian of science, may have been among the first to use *paradigm* — meaning *a pattern, example, or model* and a word not in the vocabulary of many doctors previously — to describe fundamen-tal changes.[30] "In revolutionary science . . . researchers abandon one paradigm, i.e., Ptole-maic astronomy, and embrace another, i.e., Copernican astronomy."[31])

and their associates, however, found improving the efficiency of medical schools more difficult. Managed care did manage, however, to force the frequently competing leaders of medical schools and teaching hospitals into each other arms. Only by cooperating more closely than in the past could the institutions they were leading compete effectively with the market forces now assailing academic medical centers.

One of the methods consultants advised to meet this threat was to form "physician-hospital organizations" (PHOs) so that the teaching hospitals, medical schools, and physicians (whose clinical finances are often managed through "practice plans" within the medical schools) could counter together the assault on the income of the doctors and the hospitals. The need for PHOs might not seem self-evident. Couldn't the doctors and the hospitals simply join forces to deal with the HMOs? Part of the problem is governmental. The doctors are, in most cases, employees of the medical schools, some private, some owned by state or federal governments, whereas many of the hospitals are not owned by the schools. Furthermore, some type of organization was needed to construct contracts for the insurance carriers which combined the services offered by the doctors and the hospitals and to execute the terms of the contracts economically.

Organizing PHOs and choosing their directors can be "highly charged."[35] These organizations can become third centers of funding and administrative authority with their executives competing for resources and power with the leaders of the teaching hospitals and medical schools.

To more effectively influence the health care market in their communities, teaching hospitals acquired community hospitals, nursing homes, and rehabilitation units. Many constructed primary care networks by affiliating with community physicians or buying and then operating their practices. The *quid pro quo* is that the doctors in the hospitals and the network will favor the teaching hospital with which they are linked when their patients require referrals to an academic center for specialized medical care.

Then, as hospitals and doctors were coming to grips with managed care, based for the most part on patients employed by private companies and insured by private carriers, the federal government delivered a telling blow. Washington's desire to reduce spending through the Balanced Budget Act of 1997 hit Medicare particularly hard.[36] By 1999, decreasing payments from Medicare, the largest payer for medical care* as well as the single largest source of revenues for teaching hospitals, transformed the small surpluses many teaching hospitals had been able to

---

*$231 billion in 1998.[23]

maintain into losses,[37] some frighteningly large.* As Bob Herbert, *The New York Times* columnist, wrote in April 1999: "A deep financial crisis is spreading like a virus through the nation's teaching hospitals. It is undermining their honorable and historic mission which has been to train new generations of physicians, to conduct critically important research and to provide treatment for, among others, the poor."[39]

The academic medical centers, accordingly, faced a convergence of factors producing red ink.[40] The natural progression of medical advances means that only about five percent of the services academic centers provide to patients are unique.[41] Doctors in community hospitals can carry out, often at lower cost, most of the procedures and operations that their colleagues, and in many cases, their former teachers, perform in university hospitals. Payers, including the government, now find themselves challenged to support any longer the care of patients without insurance ("uncompensated care") or the training of house staff and students. Furthermore, to deal with their own financial exigencies, HMOs, in addition to driving down their rates, "control their cash" more effectively by paying what they owe as slowly as possible and challenging, interminably, it seems to the hospitals and physicians, whether a bill is valid.[42] And, finally, the Medicare hit. Even if hospital expenses inflate only 3–4 percent per year and revenues stay flat — a situation these days which can, ironically, make an executive "look good,"[40] — you lose money. If expenses rise more, and income drops, the hospitals and their executives find themselves in deeper trouble, and it can happen very quickly.

To respond to these challenges of falling revenues and increasing expenses, a few teaching hospitals have merged with each other.[43,44] Six of the first institutions to do this are among the nation's most famous and respected; the Brigham and Women's and Massachusetts General hospitals in Boston, the New York and Presbyterian hospitals in New York City and the University of California, San Francisco and Stanford University hospitals in northern California. Similar economic forces drove each of them to merge, but the specific steps they took to get there and the results of their actions are both similar and different, reflecting the special characteristics of each hospital, the university with which it is affiliated, and its community. Whether this course will offer these and other troubled teaching hospitals relief from their financial and other dilemmas remains to be proven.

---

*"What the guillotine was to the French Revolution," comments Dr. Haile Debas, dean of the medical school at the University of California, San Francisco (see chapters 6 & 7), "the Balanced Budget Act of 1997 is to this revolution — both deliver drastic cuts."[38]

Part 1
Partners

The following people are discussed in Chapter 2, "Formation," and Chapter 3, "Development."

(Brigham = Brigham and Women's Hospital; HMS = Harvard Medical School; MGH = Massachusetts General Hospital; MGPO = Massachusetts General Physicians Organization; Partners = Partners HealthCare System, Inc.; PCHI = Partners Community HealthCare, Inc. Most titles are those held when the individual was interviewed.)

Name	Position
Ausiello, Dennis A., M.D.	Physician in Chief, Medical Service, MGH
Austen, W. Gerald, M.D.	President, MGPO; former Chief of Surgical Services, MGH (1969–97)
Bero, Cynthia L.	Corporate Director, Information Systems, PCHI
Blumenthal, David, M.D.	Director, Institute for Health Policy, MGH
Braunwald, Eugene, M.D.	Vice President, Academic Programs, Partners; former Chairman, Department of Medicine, Brigham (1972–96)
Bray, David	Consultant; former Executive Dean for Administration, HMS
Buchanan, J. Robert, M.D.	General Director (1982–94), MGH
Burr, Francis H., Esq.	Member, Board of Trustees, MGH
Colloredo-Mansfield, Ferdinand	Former chairman, Board of Trustees, MGH and Cochairman, Board of Trustees, Partners
Connors, John M., Jr.	Chairman, Board of Trustees, Partners
DeSanctis, Roman W., M.D.	Director Emeritus, Clinical Cardiology, MGH

Fallon, John A., M.D.	Chairman, Board of Trustees, PCHI; Chief Executive Officer, North Shore Health System
Federman, Daniel D., M.D.	Dean for Medical Education, HMS
Fein, Rashi, Ph.D.	Professor of the Economics of Medicine, HMS
Fishman, Mark C., M.D.	Chief, Cardiac Unit, MGH
Gaida, John B.	Vice President, Support Services, Partners
Glaser, John P., Ph.D.	Chief Information Officer, Partners
Glynn, Thomas P., Ph.D.	Chief Operating Officer, Partners
Gottlieb, Gary L., M.D.	Chairman, Partners Psychiatry and Mental Health System
Haddad, Ernest M., Esq.	General Counsel and Secretary, Partners
Kassirer, Jerome P., M.D.	Editor-in-chief, *New England Journal of Medicine*
Lee, Thomas H., Jr., M.D.	Medical Director, PCHI
Lewin, Lawrence S.	Chief Executive Officer, The Lewin Group
Markell, Peter K.	Vice President of Finance, Partners
Martin, Joseph B., M.D., Ph.D.	Dean of the Faculty of Medicine, HMS
Matheson, David	Senior Vice President, Boston Consulting Group
McArthur, John H., Ph.D.	Dean Emeritus, Harvard Graduate School of Business Administration; former Chairman, Board of Trustees, Brigham and Cochairman, Board of Trustees, Partners
Mongan, James J., M.D.	President, MGH
Nathan, David G., M.D.	President, Dana-Farber Cancer Institute; Chief Executive Officer, Dana-Farber/Partners CancerCare
Nesson, H. Richard, M.D.	Consultant, Partners; former first Chief Executive Officer (1994–95) and President (1995–97), Partners; former President, Brigham (1982–94)
Otten, Jeffrey	President, Brigham

Parrish, John A., M.D.	Chairman, Department of Dermatology, MGH
Pieper, Jay	Vice President, Corporate Development and Treasury Affairs, Partners
Potts, John T., M.D.	Director of Research, MGH; former Physician in Chief, MGH (1981–96)
Rabkin, Mitchell T., M.D.	Distinguished Institute Scholar, HMS • Beth Israel Deaconess Mount Auburn Institute for Education and Research; former President and Chief Executive Officer, Beth Israel Hospital (1966–96)
Relman, Arnold S., M.D.	Editor-in-chief Emeritus, *New England Journal of Medicine*
Robbins, Catherine J.	Vice President, Finance, Partners
Samuels, Martin A., M.D.	Chairman, Department of Neurology, Brigham
Smith, Lloyd H., Jr., M.D.	Associate Dean, University of California, San Francisco; former Chief, Endocrine Unit, MGH (1958–64)
Thibault, George E., M.D.	Vice President of Clinical Affairs, Partners
Thier, Samuel O., M.D.	President and Chief Executive Officer, Partners; former President, MGH
Torchiana, David F., M.D.	Chief, Division of Cardiac Surgery, MGH
Tosteson, Daniel C., M.D.	President, American Academy of Arts and Sciences; former Dean of the Faculty of Medicine, HMS (1977–97)
Young, Anne B., M.D., Ph.D.	Chief, Department of Neurology, MGH
Zane, Ellen M.	Chief Executive Officer, PCHI; Network President, Partners
Zinner, Michael J., M.D.	Surgeon in Chief, Brigham

CHAPTER 2

Formation[1-3,3a]

On Tuesday, January 5, 1993, Dr. Daniel C. Tosteson, dean of the Harvard Medical School, convened the first meeting of the Harvard Medical Planning Group, a committee of 15 charged with uniting the five Boston hospitals where Harvard students receive most of their clinical instruction. Three doctors and executives — the chairman of the board of trustees, the chief executive, and a leading physician — represented the Beth Israel, Brigham and Women's, Boston Children's, Deaconess, and Massachusetts General hospitals.*

"Winds of change are blowing," warned Tosteson.[4] With each of the hospitals threatened by the transformation in the economics of American medicine, the participants already knew most of the bad news, which the consultant, selected by consensus among the chief executive officers (CEOs) and retained by the dean, reviewed for them. Although the insurance companies were still paying reasonably attractive rates for the care of patients at Massachusetts hospitals, this was likely to change quickly as fee-for-service payments dropped and capitated managed care rumbled into New England from California and the upper Middle West. The organizations that finance the patients' care, the

---

*Each of these institutions is better known in Boston medical, and to a great extent popular, parlance by their abbreviations and nicknames. The Harvard Medical School is HMS, and students are identified as HMS-I, HMS-II, and so on, depending on their year in the four-year course. The Massachusetts General Hospital is variously called the MGH, the Mass General, the General, the Fruit Street Clinic (from the hospital's street address, 55 Fruit Street), and, impiously, the Mass Jesus by those irritated by what they see as the hubris of its staff. The Brigham and Women's Hospital (BWH) has never escaped the nickname the Brigham, derived from the Peter Bent Brigham Hospital, a general hospital with medical and surgical services across the street from the Harvard Medical School. The Peter Bent Brigham had united in 1980 with the Robert Breck Brigham Hospital for patients with rheumatological and orthopedic diseases and the Boston Hospital for Women, itself a union in the 1960s of the Boston Lying-In Hospital, an obstetrical unit, and the Free Hospital for Women, mostly a gynecological service. ("The Peter Bent" was formerly in common use, but since the union one hears it infrequently.) The Beth Israel is naturally the BI, and the Boston Children's is the Children's. Only the Deaconess is usually called by its given name.

health maintenance organizations and the insurance companies, would find the Harvard hospitals too expensive. Admissions to the hospitals in the group cost 65 percent more than admission to the lowest cost community hospitals in the region.[5] Reducing costs would be vital and superb administration to make the changes essential. Beds would have to go — the region maintained about 30 percent too many — from the Harvard five as well as from other hospitals in the Boston area. Furthermore, what made the hospitals famous, their outstanding specialists, would become a burden since the HMOs sent their patients to primary care physicians — general internists, general pediatricians, and family practitioners.[4] Would the Harvard teaching hospitals, each widely known for its excellence in clinical care, teaching, and research, respond separately or as a group?

Harvard and Its Teaching Hospitals

At Harvard, unlike at many medical schools, the teaching hospitals and the faculty members who work in them are not directly governed by the medical school and university with which they are affiliated. Each of the five hospitals represented at the meetings in 1993 had its own board of trustees and cherished its independence and traditions.[6] Having no direct authority over the operation of the hospitals — whose faculties, nevertheless, proudly proclaim themselves to be teaching affiliates of the nation's third-oldest and, by general consensus, leading medical school — Tosteson knew that he could only achieve his goal by persuasion.[6]

This separation from Harvard is an old story, long fought over by university presidents, deans, hospital boards, and faculty. Dr. Joseph E. Garland, in a history of the MGH published in 1965, explained why those who favor this arrangement have long thought it wise:[7]

> Both the MGH and Harvard have reasons to be thankful that the Hospital has remained an independent institution, free from the supervision of the Medical School, while the University has escaped the burden of operating a hospital for the incidental benefit of its medical students.

Although not linked governmentally, the relationship between the hospitals and the school is close. The preponderance of Harvard medical degrees earned by the faculty, the pride of carrying Harvard academic titles and teaching Harvard students, and the overlapping affiliations of some of the board members help to secure the permanence of the marriages even though the university and hospitals regularly complain about the affiliations for various political and economic reasons.

Francis H. Burr, a longtime partner and one-time chairman of the Policy Committee at Ropes and Gray, one of the leading Boston law firms, exemplifies the Harvard connection. Burr, who earned his undergraduate and law degrees at Harvard, served on the MGH board and for 28 years as one of the seven members of the Harvard Corporation,* the smaller of the two university governing bodies, which concerns itself primarily with administration and finance.[8] In 1962, Nathan Pusey, then the Harvard president, convinced Burr to accept election as one of the 12 MGH trustees to advise him and the other members of the corporation about the university's medical establishment despite Burr's objections to joining another board because "I still have to earn a living."[8]

Tosteson's fundamental goal, according to David Bray, his executive dean for administration, was "to create a virtual alliance or quasi integration in which the hospitals would come together under a common banner to market efficiently, save costs, and advance research."[6] Thereby, Tosteson hoped to develop a structure that could successfully deal with the remarkable changes in the financing of medical care while sustaining the teaching and scholarly roles of the medical school.[9] Tosteson was the "only Harvard player who could look at the big picture even though he had no direct power or authority over the hospitals," observes Bray.[6]

The dean comprehended, as much as anyone else, that the sheer size of the Harvard medical enterprise would interfere with instituting widespread reform. Including the five largest hospitals, whose leaders were ranged around the conference table, the medical school worked with at least 18 affiliated medical institutions and included nearly 8,000 faculty members.[6] To David Bray, his captain's ship was very large and consequently could only turn very slowly.[6]

Saving money was an essential aim of the plan. "If you merge, you could save zillions of dollars," Dr. Mitchell T. Rabkin, then chief executive officer of the Beth Israel Hospital, recalls one of the consultants predicting.[4†] However, some felt the agenda was different. The possibility that the dean was trying to control the hospitals ran through many of their minds. (This is a tune long sung at Harvard and very familiar to

---

*The Harvard Corporation is officially The President and Fellows of Harvard College.

†Rabkin has succinctly and politely expressed what most leaders of teaching hospitals feel about the problems they face: "Everyone's in deep yogurt."[10]

faculty and administrators in other American academic medical centers.) A distinguished physiologist who had spent much of his career directing a research laboratory and a basic science department, Tosteson was not "one of us," not a clinician or hospital administrator. Each of the hospitals made its own arrangements with its physicians, and the medical school had little influence on how their fees were collected or dispersed.

At most academic medical centers, the financial relationship with the practicing doctors is administered through practice plans, with the deans playing important, if not dominant, roles. Practice plan administrators account for the fees generated by the clinicians and transfer them to the school or the departments in which the clinicians work. The deans levy taxes on the collections to pay for projects they want the schools to support. Harvard was unique among most American medical schools in that its dean received none of the faculty's clinical income. Consequently, Tosteson lacked the ability to support with clinical funds some of the weaker elements in the Harvard system with surpluses from the stronger hospitals and their practitioners.[6]

Although instituting such a "forced contribution" was not part of Tosteson's plan,[9] the possibility was not far from the minds of many of the participants. Tosteson knew, however, that a tax would never be acceptable at Harvard, and with physician fees being squeezed by the HMOs there would be little to take anyway.[9] Funds generated by professional fees and used in the past to support research and education would become severely limited.

Leading physicians on Tosteson's committee subscribed to his concept but not to its feasibility. They were "ready, willing, and able to explore," Tosteson explains, "but not prepared to lead. They are patriots of the school, as faculty members go, but they see their departments and its faculty as their primary responsibilities, and the clinical departments at Harvard are based in the hospitals."[9,11]* Furthermore, the younger clinical faculty members, whose acquiescence to, if not active participation in, any merger would be essential, know that individual accomplishment is the principal criterion for promotion at Harvard and that their futures would not primarily depend upon participating in cooperative, "UN-like activities," as David Bray puts it.[6]

Other committee members complained that the hospitals were too

---

*The dominant role of the hospitals in the Harvard system gives the clinical faculty members what one observer calls "One-stop shopping since their loyalty is not split with the university. The hospital gives them the space and the money, and their allegiance is to the chief [not the dean]."[11]

far apart to function effectively together. Although the BI, Brigham, Children's, Deaconess, and the medical school are strung out on both sides of an axis formed by Longwood Avenue, the MGH is more than three miles northeast of the Longwood campus and at least 20 minutes away when navigating Boston traffic on a weekday. Furthermore, members of the staff at each of the hospitals considered their institutions and their work uniquely excellent and feared that their identities would be swallowed up in an anonymous organization.[12] Representatives from some of the hospitals also worried that the MGH, as the largest hospital, would dominate the new arrangement.[4] The endowments differed greatly, with the MGH and Children's being the largest. The Deaconess was then operating deeply in the red.

Finally, Tosteson's attempt to consolidate in the medical school some of the clinical administration of the teaching hospitals faced the time-honored Harvard tradition of territoriality, which is reflected in the university's well-known modus operandi in which each department and school functions as "a tub on it own bottom." Dr. Arnold S. Relman, editor-in-chief emeritus of the influential *New England Journal of Medicine* and a faculty member at different times in his career at Harvard, Boston University, and the University of Pennsylvania, finds Harvard "the ultimate in academic autonomy. Nobody tells anybody else what to do. Getting the barons, who are supremely self-confident people, to agree on anything is very difficult."[13]

What Relman is talking about, of course, is the force of some of the egos at Harvard, not an inconsequential factor when questions of academic precedence and power arise. "There is unstated competition for leadership among the heads of the larger elements in the Harvard medical system," David Bray observes.[6] "They bring credentials and responsibilities to the table which some feel are equal to, or even superior to, those of the dean. And the fact is that at Harvard there is a higher density of top-caliber senior leadership than anywhere I have visited. Nowhere else even compares in this respect" (this is from a former executive dean who has done more than his share of consulting at other medical schools).[6]

Nevertheless, Tosteson was hopeful. He had observed at two other leading institutions, Duke University, where he was chairman of the Department of Physiology and Pharmacology, and the University of Chicago, where he briefly was dean of the School of Medicine before coming to Harvard, how valuable could be close links between the dean, the medical school, the hospitals, and the clinical faculty. Tosteson, a graduate of both Harvard College and the medical school he had led since 1977, concluded that the growing financial pressures simply wouldn't allow the tradition of "splendid isolation of this consortium of remarkable institutions from each other and from Harvard" to continue.[9]

Tosteson had begun thinking seriously about how to bring the disparate elements of the Harvard medical community more closely together during the previous summer. "Like so many of Dan's initiatives, [the process] begins with a strategic evaluation of the questions 'what is critical, what is doable?'" recalls David Bray, who has known Tosteson since they both worked at the University of Chicago, where Bray was chief financial officer of the medical center when Tosteson was the dean.[6]

As he worked out the tactics with his staff, Tosteson knew how difficult the task would be. However, the dean of the Harvard Medical School did not back away from worthwhile ventures just because they were arduous. Earlier, he had convinced the faculty to undertake a radical revision of the curriculum. This led to a plan called the New Pathway in General Medical Education in which clinically oriented conferences and small-group teaching replaced many of the lectures during the first two years of the curriculum.[14] Although the New Pathway program required that members of the clinical and basic science faculty spend more time teaching in small conferences, Tosteson pushed the program through despite resistance from some of his colleagues. The students found the new program a significant improvement, and many other medical schools adopted all or part of the Harvard curriculum.

Bray further observes:[6]

Tosteson is that rare kind of leader who is brutally honest with himself. He doesn't make decisions solely by watching the way the wind is blowing. I must emphasize that, contrary to what some of the members of the committee and other faculty members might have thought, Dan is not a "control freak."

Until recently, the staff at the larger Harvard teaching hospitals had successfully developed enough clinical and research money to fund each institution's research and educational programs and allow the hospitals to compete successfully with each other and with other schools for academic kudos.[6] Breakfasting regularly with the hospital CEOs at the Harvard Club of Boston, Tosteson had observed their rising anxiety about how the rapid evolution of the organization of clinical practice would affect their institutions and concluded that greater unity among the hospitals and the school would benefit all.[9] He saw, according to Bray, an opportunity for Harvard and its hospitals to exercise unequaled power "to leverage the market and research if they all came together."[6]

Furthermore, Tosteson feared that the hospitals on which Harvard depended for its clinical teaching might split into warring camps and perhaps even join competing health care systems.[15] John McArthur, the chairman of the Brigham board, remembers fretting about "the potential effects of 'Fruit Street' [the MGH] getting together with MIT [Massachusetts Institute of Technology]," for example.[16] Although this possibility arose several decades ago, "people remembered it as if it were yesterday," Bray recalls.[6]

The MGH and the Brigham Try to Affiliate
by Themselves

Nevertheless, the monthly meetings bogged down, as Dr. Samuel O. Thier predicted they would from his perch as president of Brandeis University in Waltham, a suburb of Boston.[17] "You'll be lucky to get two to agree," Thier told Tosteson when asked for his opinion. "They don't trust what you're doing."[17]*

Lawrence S. Lewin, a Washington-based consultant who attended a meeting of Tosteson's committee, observed, "There was something artificial at that meeting. Although the hospitals were going along with what Dan wanted, the solution would be something else. Nothing I heard was strong enough to bring them all together."[18]

One of the participants in the Tosteson committee observed: "There's a lot of wishful thinking that somehow the world would make sense again and we'll be bailed out."[19]

Another commented that everybody's natural instinct was self-preservation.[19]

Some appeared to favor the status quo if only to prevent other participants from gaining more power.[6] Many thought it best not to transfer authority from the hospital chiefs to the dean. "Better the devil you know," David Bray sensed was in many of their minds.[6]

The talk in the committee seemed endless, the inertia overpowering.[20] Five were too many entities, each hospital differed in significant ways from the others, and there were antitrust concerns.[8] Some members of the group had difficulty accepting the consultant and objected when the firm and its lawyers forbade the participants to take notes.[8,9,20,21] Sometimes as many as 30 people were in the committee room, "Much too many to get anything done," thought Dr. H. Richard Nesson, president of the Brigham. "The package of lawyers brought in by the consultants tried to control things too much, and someone was always objecting

---

*Thier will soon reappear as a principal player in this story.

to something."[21] Nevertheless, by June 14, Tosteson recalls, the members of the committee agreed to try to create an overarching entity.[9]

Meanwhile, the trustees and executives from the Brigham and the General concluded that, despite the veneer of cooperation in the committee, the dean's plan, virtuous though it was, would never work. Talking about the issue in the parking lot after a particularly frustrating meeting with the other hospitals, Dr. J. Robert Buchanan, chief executive at the General, told Ferdinand Colloredo-Mansfeld, the chairman of his board of trustees, "You know what would really energize these meetings is if we and the Brigham got together."[22] John McArthur, chairman of the Brigham board, also suggested, "Let's do it ourselves."[16] At lunch soon afterward, Colloredo-Mansfeld and McArthur agreed to try to bring their two hospitals together.

The event that, as much as anything, pushed the Brigham and MGH people forward was the dean's written proposal, which required that each of the five hospitals sign on to create a Harvard Medical Group.[16] The MGH and Brigham leaders met in the Brigham boardroom and agreed that they shouldn't commit their hospitals to join the dean's group.

A few days later, in the middle of June 1993, Burr, Colloredo-Mansfeld, and McArthur came to Tosteson's office and informed him that the Brigham and the MGH were beginning the planning process for a two-hospital association and would not participate further in meetings of what had been a five-hospital group.[9] Tosteson remembers being surprised, although their plan did not come to him totally unexpectedly.[9]

McArthur, the Brigham chairman and at the time dean of the Harvard Graduate School of Business Administration, figured that since the coming together of five business companies was virtually impossible why should Harvard's hospitals be different?[16] Furthermore, he asked how the enterprise, led by the five largest, could keep out the smaller Harvard teaching hospitals, the ones with "their noses at the window."[16] "They won't know," said someone to McArthur. "Sure," he replied, convinced that the scheme couldn't be kept from the other hospitals. McArthur had learned that hospitals have enough trouble running themselves[16] and felt strongly that the medical school should stay out of the business and continue as the "steward of the welfare of the faculty, the professional staff of the hospitals."[9]

Colloredo-Mansfeld from the General also believed that a merger of the five hospitals and thousands of doctors was impractical. He remembers thinking:[22]

Regardless of merits, regardless of the benefits to the hospitals, regardless of the benefits to the communities served by the hospitals, the perception would be generated by those outside the teaching hospital world and by those who did not understand the purpose of such a merger that the Harvard teaching hospitals would be trying to take in the patients from the community hospitals not only in the city but also in the suburban areas surrounding Boston. This erroneous perception of the "great sucking sound" of patients leaving the community hospitals for big Boston hospitals would cause a political backlash and potential challenges in the legislature and in other public settings.

The general view, erroneous perception, and potential misunderstanding of Dean Tosteson's concept would bury the project before it could get started.

The news from the Brigham and the General produced "considerable alienation"[9] from the other hospital leaders despite their having been assured that the MGH and Brigham people would report regularly about the progress of their discussions. Representatives from the other hospitals, who continued to meet with the dean, had been led to believe that the MGH and Brigham plans would lead to a solution "for all the institutions," according to Rabkin from the Beth Israel.[4]

Origins and Reputation of the Harvard Medical School

The room in which the trustees from the Massachusetts General and Brigham and Women's hospitals informed the dean of the Harvard Medical School of their plan overlooked the school's 2.5 acre quadrangle. Four large, white, three-story buildings containing the laboratories and classrooms of the medical school lined opposite sides of a grassy rectangle. Closing the south end, a fifth structure, Building A, housed the dean's office and originally the library. The north end faced Avenue Louis Pasteur, named, in the French fashion, for the most famous name in investigative medicine when the campus was built at the beginning of the twentieth century. Perpendicular to Avenue Louis Pasteur and the main axis of the quadrangle stretched Longwood Avenue, along which had developed the teaching hospitals and other Harvard educational institutions.

The Harvard Medical School was founded on September 19, 1782, and declared open as the "Medical Institution of Harvard University" on October 7, a year later.[23,24] Harvard then became the third American institution of higher learning to offer an organized program in medical education. Only the College of Philadelphia (1765), which became the University of Pennsylvania, and King's College (1767), Columbia College after the Revolution and later Columbia University, preceded Harvard in establishing medical schools.

The medical lectures at Harvard were first given in the basement of Harvard Hall and later in Holden Chapel, both of which are still in use on the Cambridge campus. In 1805, at the urging of Dr. John Warren, as much as anyone the founder of the school[25] and its first professor of anatomy and surgery, the anatomy course was moved to rooms over an apothecary shop in Boston. By 1815, the whole school had moved into a building on Mason Street, near Washington and Franklin Streets in downtown Boston,[26] completing the transfer of the medical school across the Charles River from the main Harvard campus. When the school outgrew these facilities, it moved in 1846 to the foot of North Grove Street, adjoining the grounds of the MGH, then 25 years old. In 1883, the school moved again, this time into larger quarters on the corner of Boylston and Exeter Streets in the Back Bay, midway between the MGH and the Boston City Hospital, which had been built 20 years earlier in the South End. This was its final location before the building of the Longwood campus.

Once the school left the Grove Street buildings it migrated further and further from its initial clinical home, the MGH, and finally settled, in 1906, into the "Great White Quadrangle" on land purchased from the Francis estate in Roxbury. The magnificent new home was dedicated in September by Harvard president Charles W. Eliot, who during the previous 25 years had forced the school to become a university-based academic institution. The authors of a history of the medical school described it before Eliot's changes as:[27]

> A proprietary institution run by a few families, its leaders supporting the interests of themselves and their families and friends. It was, to speak plainly, a money-making institution not much better than a diploma mill. In Eliot's words, the School was "A sort of trading corporation as well as a body of teachers."

The cost of the new school was born by the Bill Gates and Warren Buffet of the time. Banker J. Pierpont Morgan paid for three of the buildings in memory of his father, Junius Spencer Morgan, "A native of Massachusetts and merchant of Boston and London," as the fading plaque on Building C attests.[28]* Mrs. Collis P. Huntington, whose

---

*Morgan, when representatives from Harvard came to see him, said, "I am pressed for time and can give you but a moment." Shown the plans for the new medical school buildings, he moved his finger from point to point and said, "I will build *that* and *that* and *that*. Good morning, gentleman," thereby committed himself to the construction of three buildings at a cost of over a million dollars.[28]

money derived from railroads, and John D. Rockefeller paid for the other buildings.[29] Until the Peter Bent Brigham Hospital opened seven years later, much of the clinical teaching continued to be conducted at the MGH and the Boston City Hospital, neither of which was close to the new medical school.

The size and splendor of this "grand composition in white marble . . . one of the high points of Boston's turn-of-the-century Classical Revival style"[30] expresses externally the current high standing of the school. Two statistics confirm its reputation. Of 238 of the country's most competitive premedical students offered places in the class entering in the fall of 2000, 169 matriculated.[31] The faculty in the Quadrangle and at the teaching hospitals received grants worth $610 million from the National Institutes of Health (NIH) during the fiscal year ending September 30, 1998.[31] The faculty of the next most successful school in this competition, Johns Hopkins, received $225 million in support from the NIH that year.[32]

Although the scientists in the school's basic science departments, most of whose laboratories are in and near the Quadrangle, received a very credible $96 million from the NIH in 1997–98,[32] the clinical and laboratory investigators with Harvard appointments working in the affiliated hospitals generated 84 percent of Harvard's $604 million.* Since the hospital-based faculty is employed by the hospitals and not by the medical school, as is almost universally the custom in other American schools, its members apply for their grants through the hospitals and not the school. Accordingly, the NIH ranks Harvard nineteenth among the country's 124 medical schools. This anomaly allows the deans of almost 20 of the nation's medical schools to boast, incorrectly, that their institutions develop more NIH funds than does Harvard. The total amount of NIH support developed by faculty with Harvard appointments working in the affiliated hospitals and the Quadrangle exceeds by more than twice that of the next most successful school.

The Harvard faculty ranks among the most distinguished in the country. Three members of the current faculty have won the Nobel Prize, 25 are members of the National Academy of Sciences, and 91 are members of the Institute of Medicine, which honors leaders in academic medicine.[31]

---

*In 1997–98, the MGH generated $137 million and the Brigham $131 million, which would have placed the MGH tenth and the Brigham eleventh in the NIH's list if hospitals rather than only medical schools were included.[32] Together ($268 million) the two hospitals, which contribute 44 percent of Harvard's total, would have led the list, excluding Harvard, of course.

Origins of the MGH and the Brigham

As for the MGH and the Brigham coming together, here were two of the most famous hospitals in the country, with staff and officers supremely proud of the excellence and traditions of their institutions. Although these were only two of Harvard's teaching hospitals, each had the equivalent of the entire clinical structure of many medical schools.[6]

The quality of the clinical care given at the Brigham and the General was internationally respected. Each conducted research of the highest caliber, supported by industry and the most competitive granting agencies. The graduates of their training programs, the house officers and fellows, occupy chairs and senior administrative positions at Harvard and many other medical schools throughout the country. Three of the General's interns during the 1960s later won the Nobel Prize in Medicine or Physiology.

Since the Brigham opened in 1913, its doctors and investigators had competed openly with their counterparts at the older Mass General.[7,33] "The two gladiators contested each other continuously," observed Dr. W. Gerald Austen, the longtime chief of surgery at the General.[20]

From the other side of town, Dick Nesson, then the president of the Brigham and later the first CEO of the corporation combining the hospitals, said, "We were always jousting with one another to see who could attract the best students, the best residents, and well-known surgeons, etc."[34]

Dr. David Blumenthal, an authority on health care management at Harvard who has worked at both hospitals, has written that "by the 1990s, BWH and MGH had become each other's principal competition, the MGH playing the role of reigning aristocrat, and the BWH cast as the energetic upstart threatening to dislodge its senior, and perhaps complacent, rival,"[15] a point of view also held by John McArthur, the board chairman at the Brigham.[16]

The origin of America's first hospitals followed the same course as its medical schools. The Pennsylvania Hospital in Philadelphia was the first in 1756, nine years before what became the University of Pennsylvania School of Medicine opened.* Next came The New York Hospital in 1791, 24 years after the predecessor of Columbia University opened its medical school.

New England had no general hospital until the Massachusetts General, founded in 1811, admitted its first patient, a sailor, on September 3, 1821,[35] to its building on a four-acre site of a field known as Prince's

---

*Benjamin Franklin helped found both the hospital and the university.

Pasture on the bank of the Charles River in the West End of Boston.[7] The MGH was the last commission in Boston[36] for Charles Bulfinch (1763–1844), Boston's first professional,[37] and by then most eminent, architect. Bulfinch, the son and grandson of doctors,[38,39] had designed, among other fine buildings, the Massachusetts State House on top of Beacon Hill and Harvard's University Hall on the Cambridge campus. Later he would complete the design of the Capitol in Washington.

The building he proposed for the MGH cost $70,000 to build, its stonework prepared "at the state prison by convict labor."[40] Then adjacent to the Charles River, the hospital received some of its patients by boat from the river, the banks of which have been filled in over the years to house newer hospital buildings and Storrow Drive. The Bulfinch Building, a classically conceived, gray granite, Greek Revival treasure now filled mostly with hospital offices, still stands "dwarfed but not overshadowed by the great hospital complex which has risen all around it."[35]

These early hospitals, one must remember, were charitable institutions, designed primarily to care for those without a home or unable to obtain treatment through the private practices of local physicians. Doctors saw patients who could afford to pay in the patients' homes or the doctors' offices and rarely admitted patients with financial resources to a hospital. Babies were delivered and operations performed in a bed, in a chair, or on a table and without benefit of anesthesia until Dr. John Collins Warren, the hospital's founding surgeon and the son of the founder of the Harvard Medical School, performed the first operation with ether under Bulfinch's dome in the operating theater of the MGH in 1846. For the most part, the hospital was a place to avoid if one could afford to be treated at home. These were the days when a charitable citizen could endow a "free bed" in the hospital for a destitute patient.

As medical advances of the nineteenth century such as aseptic surgery, X rays, and expert nursing made hospital safer than home care, those who could choose began to favor treatment in the hospital. The General created a few private rooms, but it was not until the Phillips House, the first unit specifically designed for private patients, opened its 94 beds in 1917 that the more affluent citizens of Boston could receive the same standard of medical and surgical care offered in the wards of the hospital to those less well endowed. The MGH designed the level of comfort in the Phillips House for citizens who knew what comfort at that time meant. The rooms were large, and many had a view over the Charles River toward Cambridge, a fireplace, and in some cases a smaller room nearby for the patient's servant. Middle-class patients, able to afford more than ward care but insufficiently affluent to be housed in the Phillips House, were accommodated in the Baker Memorial for People of

Moderate Means, as the 325-bed building for this previously excluded group was formally called when it opened in 1930. An all-inclusive bill during the first years of the Baker Memorial Hospital included both hospital and professional fees and was kept moderate as the nation entered the Great Depression.[7]

From its inception, the MGH functioned as a site of education for doctors in training. The report of the committee of the legislature* recommending approval of the charter establishing the hospital in 1811 included this relevant paragraph:[41]

> The location of the proposed Hospital is intended to be such as will accommodate students in the metropolis and at the University at Cambridge.

The Brigham Hospital is a twentieth-century creation, the gift of Peter Bent Brigham, a wealthy bachelor who began his career by peddling fish on the streets of Boston and ended by owning valuable real estate and railroad investments.[42] His will specified that:[43]

> My said executors shall dispose of . . . my property and estate . . . for the purpose of founding of a hospital in said Boston, to be called the Brigham Hospital for the care of sick persons in indigent circumstances residing in the said County of Suffolk.

Here Harvard would finally have its university hospital, an ideal opportunity for a clinical teaching facility adjacent to, and largely under the control of, the medical school.[27,43] However, as Brigham's will prescribed, Harvard did not own the hospital, which opened in 1913 behind Building A but, like the General, had its own board of trustees. The university accepted this arrangement, as its president, A. Lawrence Lowell, stated in his annual report for 1910:[44] "The University has no desire to manage the Hospital, nor have the trustees of the latter an ambition to manage the School." Dean David L. Edsall later wrote to the alumni: "We have such healthy cooperation in medical education and research from nine hospitals that there would be little academic advantage to the University if it did actually own and administer them."[45]

Nevertheless, even though it was not governmentally Harvard's hospital, members of its clinical faculty came to think of the Brigham more

---

*The official name of the Massachusetts legislature is the General Court of the Commonwealth of Massachusetts.

as their university hospital than the MGH across town. Harvey Cushing, the founder of neurosurgery in the United States, who had been recruited from Johns Hopkins as the Brigham's first director of surgery, assumed that he would be working in Harvard's university hospital.[46] He only had to look out his office window to see the imposing columns of the administration building of the medical school.[46] "Our proximity," he wrote in 1922, "has from the outset obliged us to accept the unqualified role of a university hospital."[46] Consequently, as chief of surgery at what he considered to be *the* Harvard University hospital, Cushing pressed the university to be named "Head of the Surgical Department" in the medical school, the job held by his chief at Hopkins, the renowned William Halsted. This, of course, proved impossible at Harvard, which already had senior chiefs of surgery at the other teaching hospitals.[47] Rather, the department was administered by a committee of the chiefs, a system that continues.[48] Despite or perhaps as a consequence of this structure, Cushing and his colleagues competed, sometimes bitterly, with their colleagues at the MGH over resources.[47]

Although it was established by means of a charitable gift to serve the poor of the region, the Brigham from the day it opened cared for private patients. Cushing insisted on this as a requirement of his recruitment.[49] He later successfully resisted, by threatening to resign, the university's establishment of a full-time salaried structure for clinical faculty,[43] which would have limited the income he and other doctors earned by treating paying patients.[50]

By the time of the merger discussions in 1993, the Brigham had become the Brigham and Women's Hospital, larger than the elite but relatively small Peter Bent Brigham Hospital and now for the most part in new buildings.

The Brigham versus the MGH

A merger of the Brigham and the General would need to accommodate both the similarities and the differences of the two institutions. Each had the same goals, each was strong in clinical care, research, and teaching, and each was still prosperous. Although located in the same city, the distance between the hospitals — considered a problem by some members of the Tosteson committee — meant that patients came to each hospital from different areas, the MGH more from the northern suburbs, the Brigham more from those in the south and west. The MGH attracted more patients from downtown Boston where it was located, the Brigham from its surrounding neighborhoods.[5] Thus, although the doctors and the two hospitals competed with each other for academic prowess, there was less competition for patients, many of whom lived in different parts of the region.[22]

The hospitals were both busy. The number of admissions per year was almost equal, although the total number of days that all patients spent in the hospital (patient days), and consequently the number of days each patient spent in the hospital (average length of stay), was greater at the General because of the large number of short-stay obstetrical admissions at the Brigham and Women's.[5,20] The surgeons performed about the same number of procedures each year at each hospital, but at the Brigham they did almost twice as many without admitting the patients. The doctors at the General saw a few more outpatients in their offices than at the Brigham, and the General's Emergency Department treated one-third more patients. As for employees, including doctors, the General certainly was larger; there were 10,484 at the MGH and 7,235 at the Brigham.[5] The MGH had the bigger endowment.

To some degree, the atmosphere among the members of the two staffs differed.[51] The ambiance at the General was more clubby. The staff there was more self-confident, had a greater sense of its own identity, and felt more "permission to disagree" with Harvard.[51] For example, the MGH had its own Institute of Health Professions, which trained nurses and other health care professionals and awarded them MGH certificates, not Harvard degrees.[6] The General had the reputation of seeking for its staff not only doctors and researchers who were academically outstanding but also people who could work together.[51] The Brigham staff seemed selected principally for individual excellence rather than "suitability."[51]

As a rule, the hospitals chose their chiefs differently. More often than not, the General appointed its leaders and many of its administrators[11] from within, the Brigham from outside. Both of the new chiefs of medicine and surgery at the MGH led divisions there when they became department directors. Braunwald's successor as chief of medicine at the Brigham came from Stanford, although he had worked at the Brigham in the past, and the recently appointed chief of surgery was from the University of California-Los Angeles (UCLA).* As "proof" of the wisdom of the General's custom, the recent appointment of an outsider with no previous MGH experience as a division chief had proven unsuccessful and led to the chief's returning to his former institution. Not understanding the ambiance of the MGH contributed to his troubles.

---

*Braunwald had never held a Harvard appointment, nor had he worked at one of its teaching hospitals when he was appointed chief of medicine at the Brigham in 1972.

Many considered the Brigham, with its more hierarchical, business-like[11] approach and superior computer systems,[52] to be better managed,[53] raising concerns of some at the General that executives from the Brigham would dominate the merged company.[17] The Brigham, moreover, provided beds for patients of the Harvard Community Health Plan, many of whom had illnesses in the primary and secondary care categories,[54] an important feature for the managed care organizations.* However, this advantage was at risk, as the Health Plan had revoked its exclusive arrangement with the Brigham and begun to admit its patients elsewhere. Nonetheless, the Brigham clearly had more experience in dealing with managed care organizations.[53]

Another important difference between the hospitals affected the ways in which the doctors managed their clinical practices. In the Department of Medicine, characteristically the largest in any medical school, the Brigham paid nearly all its internists and specialists as "full time faculty," whereas at the MGH many of the doctors, whose admissions

---

*Primary, secondary, and tertiary care define functionally where a particular medical problem is best and most economically treated. When a patient becomes ill or needs a general medical evaluation, he or she may go to the office of a general physician or pediatrician for primary care. If the patient has chest pain, for example, and the primary care physician suspects heart disease, he or she may refer the patient for secondary care to a cardiologist, who will evaluate the patient either in the specialist's office or in the hospital, depending on the severity of the symptoms and the findings of the primary care physician. If the cardiologist decides that a cardiac catheterization is required, the patient will either be admitted to the hospital or studied as an outpatient in the catheterization laboratory. Most consider cardiac catheterization to constitute tertiary care, although the procedure, and, for that matter, the bypass operation that may follow, are performed at well-equipped community hospitals as well as university teaching hospitals. (Some also use the rather infelicitous term *quarternary care* to describe even more complicated procedures such as organ transplantation, which is almost always the purview of large university hospitals.)

New diagnostic tests and therapeutic procedures tend to be developed at teaching hospitals and then migrate to community hospitals. For example, appendicitis was first recognized, and the operation to cure it developed, at the MGH more than 100 years ago, and that is where the knowledgeable patient would go for treatment of the condition. Surgeons who had performed the operation under supervision during their training took what they had learned to the communities where they established their practices. In the verbiage of health care delivery, an appendectomy began as a tertiary care operation and became an example of secondary care.

Patients referred to teaching hospitals, and certainly to the Brigham and the MGH, require more tertiary care than is the case at other hospitals. Accordingly, the cost of caring for patients is greater than at community hospitals. Also, many staff members are specialists who are paid more than primary care physicians. Insurers would rather that patients requiring primary or secondary care be treated as outpatients or, if they must be admitted, at less expensive community hospitals.

were vital to the hospital, ran their own practices, paid their expenses, and kept what they earned. However, some of the faculty at the Brigham and Women's brought to the new hospital a tradition like that of the General. Many of the obstetricians from the former Boston Lying-In Hospital practiced privately.[55]

The General has long had a powerful clinical tradition in which the staff physicians preserve a strong sense of personal responsibility for their own patients and those referred to them, not unlike the relationship between community physicians and their patients, and delegate less authority to trainees than at many teaching hospitals. This pattern has inhibited the development of the hospitalist system at the General, whereas several full-time hospitalists currently practice at the Brigham and at a number of other foreword-looking teaching and community hospitals.[56] Hospitalists are physicians, often recently out of training since the concept is so new, who concentrate their clinical care on inpatients who are usually quite ill, as is typically the case for most hospitalized patients now. The patients' regular physicians, who see them in the office, take a back seat during the hospitalization, deferring to the hospitalist for most decisions. As one might expect, this concept does not sit well with many of the practitioners at the MGH, who see the hospitalists as directly competing for the care of their patients.[56]

Also at the MGH decisions affecting the clinical staff tend to be made by consensus, which is often associated with protracted discussion.[57] The professional units operate relatively free of high-level control, whereas at the Brigham the organization is tighter, more like the structure of the medical school.[51] McArthur thinks one reason the Brigham runs more efficiently is that there are fewer chiefs of clinical services compared to the "parliament of chiefs," as he sees it, at the General.[16] Furthermore, the clinical and administrative leaders at the Brigham are almost universally appointed, whereas some at the top of the General are elected.[55]

Brigham physician and administrative leaders can be impatient with the style of management characteristic of the General, whereas physicians at the MGH see the Brigham management as overbearing and overly controlling.[57] A reporter at the *Boston Globe* quoted "one eminent doctor, who quit the MGH for the Brigham," as saying:[58]

It's like Machiavelli, two kinds of governments, the French and the Turk. The Brigham is like the Turk. The chief is extremely strong, and everything is in order. The French style — at MGH — is all these fiefdoms, where it is easy to get things stirred up and disrupted.

McArthur and Braunwald

Buchanan's term as CEO of the General was ending and Ferdinand Colloredo-Mansfield, the MGH chairman, was ill, while the Brigham, with the strong and gifted Braunwald and H. Richard Nesson's skillful leadership, was "in full flight."[17] John McArthur, the powerful chairman of the Brigham board, known for his no-nonsense approach to meetings and reports,[11] was actively pushing the merger, some felt to establish the dominance of his hospital.

"How can we become number one when the MGH claims to be number one," Mitchell Rabkin, CEO of the Beth Israel Hospital, heard people say about McArthur's thinking at the time. "Take them over" was the obvious solution.[4]

McArthur's opinion that "everyone not with you is a competitor" had led to his convincing Braunwald to relinquish his position as chief of medicine at the BI, a job he held concurrently with the Brigham for nine years beginning in 1980.[6] The Beth Israel was not pleased.[6] David Bray heard people say that McArthur's real ambition was to become the CEO of the new corporation.[6]

A *Boston Globe* reporter described McArthur as looking like "a farm boy stuffed into Wall Street duds" when he wears a pinstripe suit and wingtip shoes.[59] "His body is barely tucked into the rumpled suit. His necktie is trying to strangle him. His hair is shaggy, his glasses slipping . . . [but] don't let the country-boy fool you."[59] The leader of the Harvard Business School from 1980 to 1995,[60] McArthur grew up in a suburb of Vancouver and studied forestry at the University of British Columbia. Not favoring life in the Yukon or rural North, he came to Harvard when his dean in Vancouver suggested that he try the business side of forestry. He joined the faculty after receiving his master's and doctoral degrees and has been at Harvard ever since.[59]

When Harvard president Derek Bok appointed him dean, McArthur discovered that his business school was supporting a large part of an ill-conceived University initiative to construct a new power plant in the medical area,[9] which, thanks to environmental activists in the community, had not opened despite having been finished.* Eventually, the hospitals "bailed out," as McArthur remembers the events, "and left the medical school holding the bag."[16] Seeing the school's financial problems as an "Exocet missile aimed at the business school," McArthur responded to

---

*McArthur acknowledges ruefully, "There are more lawyers in that area than anywhere else."[16]

Bok's request that some of his senior officials join the boards of the teaching hospitals by becoming the "designated hitter" at the Brigham.[16]

At his first meeting, sitting quietly in the back of the room as tradition dictated for a new member, McArthur remembers seeing some 90 faces and backs of heads, the combined board membership from each of the hospitals that had recently been merged into the Brigham and Women's Hospital. The new hospital had troubles. Receivables were high and cash dangerously low. Richard Nesson was trying to learn his new job as president, and the senior physicians, each a talented academic and clinician, worked dysfunctionally as a group.

McArthur was appointed chairman of the Finance Committee and began attending the department chiefs' meetings as a replacement for the ailing chairman of the board. He saw his role then as "getting Nesson and the chiefs working together. A team can beat a star anytime."[16] Although coming from an atypical background for a hospital president, Nesson soon demonstrated a unique ability to work successfully with "all kinds of people," proving himself in time "an inspired choice."[16] As for his new "hobby", which came to take as much of his time as the dean's job in the business school, McArthur saw the Brigham as:[16]

> having lost its virginity with the formation of the Brigham and Women's, and from then on we were the scrappers of Brookline. The secret weapon at the Brigham and Women's was the team of clinical chiefs and Nesson, which was closing the distance with the General.

By the early 1990s, with the economic support for clinical care in turmoil, McArthur faced the replacement of several of his clinical chiefs, who were approaching retirement. Nesson, the president, was talking about "doing something else," possibly in the public sector.[16] McArthur convinced Nesson not to leave precipitously when the chiefs changed and involved him deeply in the merger project, which would eventually lead to Nesson's becoming the first CEO of Partners, the name chosen for the corporation uniting the Brigham and the General.

One of the most influential chiefs soon to retire was Eugene Braunwald, chairman of the Department of Medicine, who exemplified the Brigham's "no-nonsense hierarchy."[58] His influence in what would become Partners alarmed some at the General. Sixty-four years old in 1993, Braunwald — the country's leading academic cardiologist, the only member of his specialty in the National Academy of Sciences, and editor of the foremost textbook on the subject — would certainly continue as an active force in Harvard medicine for many years.

Braunwald, born in 1929 in Vienna, the son of a prosperous merchant, fled the Nazis with his parents and brother after Germany attached Austria to the Third Reich in 1938.[61] After a year in Great Britain, the family moved to Brooklyn, where Braunwald's father reestablished himself in business and Gene attended the public schools and then commuted to New York University for his undergraduate and medical training. Graduating first in the medical school class of 1952, he interned at Mt. Sinai Hospital, at the time the best appointment available to Jewish medical school graduates in New York City. The next year, he conducted research at Bellevue Hospital with Dr. André Cournand, cowinner of the Nobel Prize for developing the technique of cardiac catheterization, which provides cardiologists the means with which to define precisely the anatomy and physiology of a patient's heart disease. By then married to his medical school classmate, Dr. Nina Braunwald, the country's first female cardiac surgeon, Braunwald and his growing family moved to Bethesda so that he could train further in cardiovascular research at the National Heart Institute. For the next 10 years, Braunwald studied cardiac physiology and later led the clinical and research activities of the highly productive Cardiology Branch. He concurrently completed his medical residency at the Johns Hopkins Hospital in Baltimore.

In 1968, Braunwald became the first chairman of medicine at the newly organized medical school of the University of California at San Diego and four years later accepted the chairmanship at the Brigham, widely acknowledged to be one of the premier positions in American academic medicine. From 1980 until he returned to the Brigham full time in 1989, he also directed the department at the Beth Israel Hospital, probably the first time that a Harvard medical professor concurrently administered the departments of medicine at two of the Harvard teaching hospitals. More than one observer thought, "Only Gene could have done it successfully. He's one of a kind."[33] As a physician who continued to conduct research, teach, and treat patients while leading increasingly complex organizations, Braunwald had become one of the most able administrators in academic medicine. One could easily understand, therefore, that he would take a leading role in creating what he saw as an essential reorganization of his renowned hospital in order to deal successfully with the economic changes challenging academic medicine.

Combining the Hospitals

A new committee of eight started working to unite the Brigham and the General. The members included the six representatives from the two hospitals on the Tosteson committee: board chairman McArthur from the Brigham and Colloredo-Mansfield from the General; the CEOs from the Brigham (Nesson) and the General (Buchanan); and, representing the doctors, Austen and Braunwald. An additional board member from each hospital joined the group, Richard Spindler from the Brigham and the MGH's Francis "Hooks" Burr, who had been participating in the Tosteson group because of Colloredo-Mansfeld's illness and providing particularly wise, experienced advice and a calming influence. Spindler, a retired money manager, and Burr represented the senior hospital board members and would be particularly helpful explaining a merger to the still influential Bostonians who had led Harvard institutions in the past.[16] In John McArthur's words, "We couldn't make it over the goal line if we left the previous generation behind."[16]

The committee of eight retained the Boston Consulting Group, a different firm than the one employed by Tosteson, and David Donaldson, a lawyer from Burr's office and an expert in structuring not-for-profit organizations.[8] Unlike other lawyers, Donaldson, according to McArthur, "Tries to get things done rather than finding ways why things can't be done."[16]

The most powerful force driving the union of these two giants, the committee members realized, was the potential power of the combined Brigham and MGH to influence, even dominate,* the regional market for health care.[62] Why wouldn't an insurance carrier in the region prefer to associate itself with an organization made up of what the committee members considered to be the best hospitals and most talented doctors in the region, as long as the price was right? Wouldn't patients favor even more than in the past attending one of these famous hospitals in the new consortium or selecting, for those who would have a choice, a health plan linked to the Brigham and the General that unaffiliated HMOs might not be able to offer?[8] Furthermore, the consultant emphasized, consolidating administrative and financial functions and taking advantage of the size of the new organization would save money. Most important of all, a merger would provide the hospitals with the initiative to restructure eastern Massachusetts health care in a manner consistent with the hospitals' missions — which were essentially identical. The committee members were highly cognizant of the power of leadership that the two institutions together could command.[53]

That eastern Massachusetts had a surplus of physicians and teaching

---

*Use of the word *dominate* disturbs officers at what became Partners since it may imply a purpose that could alert antitrust officials. The leaders prefer the phrase "to seek some control over our own destiny."[22]

and community hospital beds when Partners was founded compounded the risk to the doctors' and hospitals' financial health. The state had the highest ratio of doctors to citizens in the country, and many of the physicians were located in the eastern part of the state.[19] Furthermore, as David Blumenthal observed:[63]

> This excess supply of providers creates opportunities for managed care plans to pick and choose among providers and negotiate prices down. This has led to . . . competition . . . especially for the tertiary care market. A natural response on the providers' part is consolidation to increase their negotiating strength and to assure themselves a continuing flow of patients.

Favoring the Partners hospitals is what Blumenthal calls the conservative nature of the Massachusetts medical consumer.[64] Patients in Massachusetts have stronger ties to institutions such as the Brigham and the General and seem to value reputation more than do patients in other parts of the country.[19] Many well-known academic medical centers elsewhere, esteemed among their peers for superb teaching and research programs, do not enjoy the same high standing locally for clinical services and as contributors to the local economy as do the General and the Brigham in their region.[65]

As the committee members proceeded in the face of these and other issues, they had to confront some fundamental questions. "Could we develop a view of the future, a vision and strategy, for the two hospitals? Where would we like to be?" Colloredo-Mansfield remembers several asking.[22] "Can we develop a trusting relationship, an equal partnership, one that is truly 50:50, not 58:42?"[22]

Working in favor of a satisfactory outcome was the close professional and personal relationship among the physicians. For example, Nesson and Buchanan, both of whom started in their jobs as chief executives of the two hospitals in 1982,* worked together on committees of the Massachusetts Hospital Association and other organizations.[21,66] By the time the group began meeting, both had concluded that their institutions would falter by continuing to compete with one another.[66]

---

*Buchanan came to the MGH from the presidency of the Michael Reese Hospital in Chicago, at the time a major affiliate of the University of Chicago Medical School, the same institution where Daniel Tosteson briefly served as dean. A graduate of Amherst College and the Cornell University Medical College, Buchanan trained in medicine at the New York Hospital. After joining the faculty at Cornell in general internal medicine, he worked in the dean's office and was appointed dean of the college in 1969, where he served until leaving for Michael Reese in 1977.

"Fear drove it, not aggrandizement," says David Matheson of the Boston Consulting Group, who joined the committee of eight as facilitator. All saw the merger as a bold stroke, and a bold stroke was needed. "They came to realize that this was the right thing to do, and the trust among them made them decide to bring it off. A certain euphoria prevailed."[53]

Matheson and three or four of his colleagues met with the committee of eight plus attorney David Donaldson about 20 times over the course of four months to work on "issues that discomfited them or to preview what was coming up that they might have trouble with." The committee members also used Matheson and his group "to deal with their own demons and send messages" back and forth.[53]

Matheson saw it as essential that he keep the discussions "fast paced and strategic." Maintaining privacy was critical. "It couldn't happen in a fishbowl. There were enormous institutional pressures against merging which would have made it impossible to do." Furthermore, the consultant knew from his own experience that if "the word gets out, you have to do the deal in a week," which would probably kill the effort. Leaks proved not to be a problem. Furthermore, "their discretion gave us time to work out issues."[53]

Matheson remembers the Partners engagement as one of the high points of his career. Each hospital had common goals and visions, different from those of the for-profit world with which he was familiar, where creating wealth was the guiding principle. Furthermore, "the eight were so impressive. It was a privilege dealing with them." Each, however, had different strengths, and their early commitment to the project varied.

Matheson saw Nesson, the Brigham director, as "a sensitive people person who knew how to charm and guide the group through difficult passages." Nesson, to whom "getting it right" seemed vital, quickly got on top of all the detail. No other member of the group, Matheson thought, had more knowledge of all the elements. Nesson, along with McArthur and Buchanan, as much as anyone in the room, could take pride in founding the notion of merging.[53]

Braunwald, the least emotionally committed to the merger at the beginning, just wanted to get to the right answer. Matheson saw him as "coming to believe that it had to happen for his values to continue to be realized." With Braunwald onboard, the Brigham would surely follow. "Power was something you could see Gene exercise."[53]

Austen seemed to be the member of the group who was most worried about the merger. He reflected the concern shared by many of his colleagues that the new structure might endanger the MGH culture and that the conferees "must leave the two separate." When the time came to sell the project to the MGH, Matheson could count on the high respect Austen enjoyed, "but his word is not law there like Gene's is at the Brigham."[53]

"McArthur was difficult to read," and Matheson found his abilities easy to underestimate. "You would not anticipate it from his style," yet McArthur was the one who could "control a room of 20 people completely and become the architect of the conversation."[53]

The physician representatives kept their colleagues informed about the progress of the discussions. Braunwald, without whose influence Jerome P. Kassirer, editor in chief of the *New England Journal of Medicine* at the time, believes the hospitals would never have merged,[33] briefed the department chairmen at the regular meetings of the Brigham chief's council, which were attended by McArthur and Nesson.

Most of the senior physicians at the Brigham were very excited about the prospects. "We're making history," one said.[67] However, not all were sanguine about the merger. "They'll eat us for lunch," warned a concerned chief on considering the greater size and wealth of the MGH.[67] Many Brigham doctors believe that their colleagues at the General see the MGH as a fortress, dissociated because of its geography and size from the medical school,[67] which many there consider peripheral to their work.[4] Most of the Brigham faculty, however, feel themselves closely connected to the school,[4,67] which is certainly true physically since their hospital was deliberately built adjacent to the new medical school buildings almost 90 years ago.

At the MGH, Austen regularly informed influential members of his hospital's staff about the progress of the discussions. He strongly encouraged his colleagues at the General to support the merger, emphasizing that, "if we're going to join anyone, it must be only the best, and the best is the Brigham. We have the same goals."[20] Austen had favored a union of all the Harvard-affiliated hospitals, although he knew that getting them together was unlikely.[20] His brother, a renowned rheumatologist, was chief of his specialty at the Brigham and had been director of the medical service at the old Robert Breck Brigham Hospital, and Austen was friendly with many of the leaders at the medical school and at the other hospitals. A senior officer at Partners, formerly at the General, describes him as a "master politician, incremental in all he does and fundamentally conservative."[68]

Austen, who shared the details of the deliberations with his senior colleagues, says, "Frankly, we didn't know just where we were going, certainly at the beginning, and people talk."[20] Braunwald feels, from his view at the Brigham, that Austen's approach was wise.[67] Keeping the General's immense professional staff up-to-date would have been impossible, and scattered knowledge at this time would probably have impeded the work of the committee.

Finances

As the Massachusetts General and Brigham and Women's hospitals prepared to merge, the Boston Consulting Group reviewed for the planners the financial data provided by each. These were large hospitals with assets — the value of everything the hospitals owned — exceeding a billion dollars for the General and more than 800 million at the Brigham. The General was the more profitable, as seen in its larger operating margins (income from operations/total revenue). This partly reflected the MGH's better "payer mix," a phrase that refers to the distribution of the types of insurance with which patients pay the hospitals' charges.[69] More of the patients at the General had Medicare, then a "good" payer, and old-fashioned fee-for-service contracts, the best system from the financial officers' point of view. The Brigham included more patients insured with managed care HMO contracts, which paid less for the same services. This led to the Brigham's depending more on its investments to produce a positive bottom line, the "excess margin."

The debt carried by the hospitals (debt/total capital) was typical for similar hospitals, suggesting that the Brigham and MGH were neither overly indebted nor obliged to lenders less than university hospitals could typically afford. The current ratio, an indication of the hospital's liquidity or ability to meet its short-term debts, was typical for similar hospitals. Accounts receivable, the amount of billings not yet collected, was higher than desirable at the MGH but quite acceptable at the Brigham, whose better computer system probably accounted for an important part of the difference.

The Merger Accomplished

As befits a professor of finance who had spent much of his career writing the case studies for which the Harvard Business School is famous, McArthur approached this new challenge along familiar lines. "We need a process more than a plan," he suggested. "Let's, in effect, write a case study merging the Brigham and the General. We'll give ourselves from July 4 to Thanksgiving and then sell it during the next week."[16] The group kept very close to this schedule. Many feel that McArthur, as much as anyone, drove the negotiations to completion.[70]*

As the meetings continued, one of the members attended less frequently than he wished. Ferdinand Colloredo-Mansfeld, the MGH chairman, had developed a brain tumor and underwent radiation and chemotherapy during the spring and summer. Colloredo-Mansfeld, universally known as Moose, missed a few sessions, but he recovered quickly and contributed importantly to the result.[67] He hosted some of the meetings in his apartment at the Ritz Carlton Hotel, the grand lady of Boston hotels, facing the Boston Garden. Colloredo-Mansfeld's firm had financed the construction of a recent addition.

Progress was rapid. The pressures—severe financial burdens on teaching hospitals, excess capacity in the Boston area hospitals, the destructive effects of intense competition—were strong.[71] Furthermore, competing chief executives, one of the often troublesome impediments to a merger, was not an issue. Buchanan at the General was 65 and had previously announced his retirement, and Nesson at the Brigham, then 61, had already discussed with his chairman, McArthur, moving on to other work while he still had the chance.[16,70] Strong leadership from the two boards of trustees was essential. Colloredo-Mansfeld observed that "without board participation, there is a tendency to get hung up on departmental issues and historic rivalries."[72]

McArthur told Braunwald that the way Partners had developed was not how his colleagues at the Harvard Business School "taught it in Mergers 101."[67] In business, he noted, the law demands that much more planning and due diligence be performed before a deal is consummated.[16] The stockholders require that the value of each entity be precisely determined, which often results in finding out which component is the more dominant. "We didn't need or want to find out which hospital was bigger or better. In fact, doing so would kill the deal. We had to assume that the Brigham and the MGH were equal." He adds, as the expert spinmeister he had become, "The fundamental question about doing the merger was what's in the public interest, not what's best for Harvard, the medical school, or the hospitals."[16]

David Blumenthal, in a case summary about the early days of Partners, observed:[73]

> The speed and certainty with which the leaders of the two hospitals drove the process reflected in part the insights that their board

---

*Braunwald considers McArthur to be the "father" of Partners and Tosteson, who initiated the whole process, to be the "grandfather."[67]

chairmen brought from their business experiences. Both McArthur and Colloredo-Mansfeld had an exquisite sense of the vulnerability of large institutions faced with transforming environments. Colloredo-Mansfeld served on the board of a local high-tech company that had recently been forced to cut its work force from 17,000 to under 6,000 and was still struggling to stay in business. McArthur refers repeatedly to the experience of the Wang Corporation, another Massachusetts high-tech company, which went bankrupt because its leadership refused to make the changes necessary to adapt to a new environment.

The MGH and the Brigham decided to join together before their leaders had a clear idea of what, in practice, an affiliation would mean.[19] McArthur acknowledges that speed was essential. "We would announce it first, put it together later."[16] McArthur also figured that with the holidays coming opposition would subside until the beginning of the next year.[16]

By the first week in December, the committee was ready for a weekend retreat, to be held at a conference center in a Boston suburb. On Sunday, the participants decided unanimously that the two hospitals should combine. The consultant's plan for a two-week sequence of events revealing the merger to all interested constituencies[5] was superseded by the rapid spread of the news throughout Boston. By the morning of Wednesday, December 8,[74] trustees of the two hospitals had approved letters of intent to merge the institutions, and a news conference was called for that day.[71] The *Boston Globe* reported the merger in its morning editions on the day of the announcement.[70]

"Did you guys really do it?" asked a surprised Mayor Thomas M. Menino when McArthur and Nesson asked whether he would announce the merger, which he did in the presence of the principal players at the Copley-Plaza Hotel on Thursday, December 8, 1993.

Everyone has a story about the events of December 8. Mitchell Rabkin, the Beth Israel CEO, upon hearing the news from a reporter while visiting Israel, said "I don't believe it"[67] and remembers thinking that December 7 would have been a more fitting day for the announcement.[4] As a classmate in medical school of Gerald Austen, the MGH chief of surgery, Rabkin illustrates the long-standing links among the Harvard faculty, even among those leading competing hospitals.[20]

During a talk by Hillary Clinton on health care reform at the World Trade Center on the Boston waterfront on the Monday morning after the weekend retreat, Tosteson heard a rumor from a faculty member that "a deal had been cut."[9]

Later that day, McArthur and Burr informed him that the merger was going forward.[74] Francis Burr recalls Dean Tosteson, gracious as always,[8] saying "Congratulations. It's a great achievement,"[16] but he was obviously "not pleased."[8]

The dean was unaware, Austen thinks, of how rapidly and successfully the MGH and the Brigham had moved toward union, and, he adds, "this was unnecessary and unfortunate."[20]

Tosteson then reported the news to Harvard president Neil Rudenstine only to discover that the hospital trustees had "gotten there first."[9] That morning McArthur and Burr were in Rudenstine's office when he came to work. "You're kidding," McArthur remembers the president saying, "None of us thought you'd do it."[16]

In the medical school committee, with three hospitals still participating, "there was a high sense of outrage," Tosteson remembers. "I felt that the opportunity to bring the group congenially together was slipping away."[9]

Regarding the new relationship, one of the longtime surgeons at the General told Tosteson: "I was raised to hate three organizations: the Soviet Union, the Brigham, and Yale. Now all I've got left is Yale!"[9]

By a remarkable coincidence, Tosteson's long-awaited statement about a federation of the school and its affiliated hospitals, "The Harvard Medical Group: A Vision for the Future,"[75] had been mailed to the faculty at about the same time. As the *Boston Globe* reported:[74]

> The timing, many say, makes it painfully clear how little control the dean, the medical school and even Harvard University have over the hospitals . . . . "The big losers in this merger" said one prominent observer, "are Harvard and the medical school, in terms of influence and control." As one faculty member put it: "Tosteson's memo reveals one of the hidden secrets of the power distribution around here." . . . Multiple Harvard sources agree that Tosteson was totally, "out of the loop" . . . even though he may have catalyzed it [the Brigham-MGH merger] with discussions he convened among the school's five major hospital affiliates a year ago.

"Not so," responds Colloredo-Mansfeld. "We didn't run over the dean, but we did tell him that our interest in the [MGH/Brigham] process was strong and continuing."[22]

Although the merger of the General and the Brigham wasn't Tosteson's plan, his had been the initial influence bringing it about. The six months of meetings of his Harvard Medical Planning Group assembled important data about the future of clinical economics and of its effects on the hospitals. The dean hoped that "faculty glue" — David Bray's phrase — would hold the faculty together. It turned out that a firmer glue bound the doctors to their hospitals.[6] However, Tosteson could take satisfaction from knowing that his pressing for change had been productive, even though the solution wasn't the one he had envisioned.[6]

Braunwald recalls being awakened at 6 A.M. by his daughter, Karen, a clinical psychologist (Ph.D., Harvard) with training at the General, who was amazed by the story in the *Boston Globe*.[67] Braunwald and the others had discussed the merger only with those directly involved. Karen Braunwald had three questions for her father: what is the merged corporation going to be called, will the MGH go ahead with its plans for a separate obstetrical service, and what are the implications for you?[67] The answers eventually turned out to be Partners HealthCare System, Inc., yes, and a job for Gene Braunwald as vice president for Academic Programs and as member of the board at Partners upon his retirement as chairman of the Brigham Department of Medicine.

Nesson, who would become the first leader of Partners, was greeted by a "tumultuous ovation," according to the consultant David Matheson,[53] when he confirmed the announcement at a meeting of the staff and employees at the Brigham.[16] At the MGH, however, the reception to the announcement, although polite and muted out of respect for Austen, carried an undercurrent of puzzlement, if not hostility. "Why didn't I know about this?" some asked. "Many feared they had given away the store," Matheson thought.[53]

Why the difference? Matheson asked himself. The Brigham had been through several previous integrations, including the formation of the Brigham and Womens Hospital itself not long ago, and the parts were now well incorporated. Furthermore, "the Brigham was accustomed to Dick's walking in with something new and triumphant." The MGH, less accustomed to such changes, had not "folded in the same deep way" as McLean Hospital, the psychiatric unit in the suburb of Belmont, which the MGH had owned since the nineteenth century, and the Spaulding Rehabilitation Hospital in Boston.[53]

Colloredo-Mansfeld, now cured of his cancer, celebrated by joining his son-in-law, an F–14 pilot, on his aircraft carrier, the *Abraham Lincoln*, on its return from Hawaii to the West Coast. "The experience of a lifetime," he called it.[22]

Although bearing a distinctly un-Bostonian name, Ferdinand Joseph Peter Ernst Colloredo-Mansfeld has a lineage that is hardly plebeian. The family's origin was Austrian, and its name was Waldsee before a progenitor, assigned as the governor of Colloredo, a district in what is now northern Italy but was then part of Austria, adopted the name of his city. In 1784, a Colloredo ancestor married Princess Isabella von Mansfeld and, as the price of incorporating the princess's legacy into the family, adopted her name as well.*

Colloredo-Mansfeld's paternal grandfather, the last *chef du cabinet* of the Austro-Hungarian empire, represented his government as Brest-Litovsk, where in 1917 the Soviet Union, hungry for peace in order to stabilize its new government at home, withdrew from World War I. The diplomat's wife was part American, and this led to their son, our subject's father, attending Harvard College. Colloredo-Mansfeld's father married a Bostonian and worked for an international construction company, which took him to Paris, where Colloredo-Mansfeld was born. When World War II began, his parents evacuated him and his siblings to the United States, where they lived with their mother's family in Boston. His father become a pilot in the British Royal Air Force and was killed in action in 1944. His mother joined her children in the United States after the war, and, having married a Canadian, moved the family to Vancouver Island. Having lived in Britain throughout the war, survived the Blitz, and lost her first husband, she wanted "to get away from the world."[22] For school, "Moose" Colloredo-Mansfeld was sent back east to Groton, Harvard College, and the Business School and after some other jobs joined Cabot, Cabot and Forbes, a Boston real estate development firm, of which he eventually became CEO. He now directs Cabot Industrial Trust, which runs real estate investment trusts. Colloredo-Mansfeld trained for the MGH board as a trustee of a community hospital. After a successful contribution as a nontrustee adviser on real estate matters, he was elected to the 12-member MGH board.[22†]

Although the participants were greatly exhilarated by their accomplishment, the announcement was received as "incredible, shocking in this town."[67] Others in the Boston health care market perceived it as a "shot across the bow."[33] Despite their problems, teaching hospitals did not take mergers seriously "until the General and the Brigham came together."[33] Their decision would have widespread effects since what happens in Boston medicine and particularly at Harvard is closely followed at other academic medical centers throughout the country.[33]

---

*Mozart's employer, early in his career, the Prince-Archbishop of Salzburg, was a Colloredo.

†Colloredo-Mansfeld, whose father-in-law is John Lawrence, a former chairman of the board, served as chairman of the MGH board until September 1999 when he stepped aside after nine years to be succeeded by attorney Edward P. Lawrence, a nephew of John Lawrence, "just to keep it in the family," as Colloredo-Mansfeld puts it.[22]

Tosteson was quoted in the *Boston Globe* as saying, "I consider this the first in a series of constructive agreements." Asked how many hospitals would be left in three or four years, he shrugged and answered, "*Je ne sais pas*" (I don't know).[71]

McArthur added:[71]

This isn't aimed to drive anyone out of business but to get at least part of the thing moving so others would follow. If we're just sitting here with two merged hospitals five years from now, that wouldn't be much of an accomplishment.

Dr. Samuel O. Thier Becomes President of the MGH and Then Partners

While the merger discussions were proceeding during the fall of 1993, the MGH was recruiting a successor for Buchanan, someone who would direct the hospital and all its affiliates. A leading candidate was Sam Thier, the Brandeis president who had advised Tosteson that a five-hospital merger was doomed. Thier had also told Tosteson that he "missed medicine" and felt "out of the line of fire at an important time of change in academic medicine."[9] It was Colloredo-Mansfeld's opinion that "Sam wanted the job, and the more we learned the more we wanted him."[22]

The phrase "fast-track" was invented for Samuel Osiah Thier.[12] He trained in internal medicine and nephrology (kidney diseases) at the MGH and the National Institutes of Health and was appointed chief of nephrology at the General soon after finishing training — unusually early in an academic physician's career. Soon afterward, "Bud" Relman, then chairman of the Department of Medicine at the University of Pennsylvania, brought him to Philadelphia as associate director of the Medical Service and then vice chairman of the department. Five years later, Yale made Thier chairman of Internal Medicine at the young age of 37. After 11 years at Yale, he moved to Washington as president of the Institute of Medicine and subsequently became president of Brandeis in 1991. Thier, who had grown up in Brooklyn, the son of a general practitioner, graduated from James Madison High School at the age of 16, and emerged with his M.D. degree seven years later after entering Cornell as an undergraduate and studying medicine at the State University of New York Upstate Medical School at Syracuse, where he graduated at the top of his class, like Braunwald at NYU eight years earlier.

Dr. Lloyd "Holly" Smith, the longtime chairman of medicine at the

University of California-San Francisco, remembers interviewing Thier for the MGH internship when Smith was a young endocrinologist on the staff there. "In those days, several of us and the chief [then Dr. Walter Bauer] sat along one side of a long table. The finalists came in, one by one, sat down opposite us, and we grilled them on their medical knowledge. I remember Bauer leaning toward me and saying something like, 'Make short work of this Syracuse guy, Holly.'"

Smith fired questions at Thier, most of which he handled easily. "When he didn't know the answer, he admitted it and then described how he would work out a solution. A very impressive performance." Struck by his calm in what was known to be a very stressful situation, Smith asked how Thier could be so composed. "Because you're not my first choice," he replied.[76] Sam Thier became Syracuse's first MGH medical intern and was later selected to be chief resident, an appointment given to the best house officer of his year.

Thier was in some ways not a typical candidate to lead the MGH. Although an alumnus of the General, he had not graduated from Harvard and would be, if appointed, the first Jewish chief executive of a hospital founded, and primarily supported for much of its history, by Boston's established WASP families.[28] Those who knew him, however, saw in Thier the qualities of ability and leadership needed to advance the General and, as we shall see, Partners.

Relman considers Thier "an expert tactician and strategist and a very forceful person, ideal for both jobs. Sam is very much the boss. He says what he means and means what he says."[13]

A *Boston Globe* reporter found that, accordingly, Thier "can be intimidating, colleagues and underlings say, and then turn on the charm. . . . He can be a withering intellectual opponent."[12] Others allege that he is not particularly adept at listening to comments or criticism but makes up for it by being "so smart and savvy."[12]

Sometimes lost in the praise for Thier's administrative and political skills is the fact that he is an excellent doctor and a superb teacher. Even while leading the Institute of Medicine, a branch of the National Academy of Sciences that advises the federal government about health care, Thier traveled to Baltimore most Fridays to teach students and house officers at the Johns Hopkins Hospital. He continued this practice at the MGH while at Brandeis. Students and trainees have continuously praised his teaching, although to benefit from it requires a fairly thick skin. "Thier fear" is an agony suffered not only by many he has taught but also by more senior doctors and administrators with whom he has worked.

On the weekend before the retreat, Thier accepted the MGH offer,[77] and on December 9, 1993, the day after the Brigham-MGH merger was revealed, the Massachusetts General Hospital announced that Thier, then 57, would be its next president.[78,79] His title would no longer be general director, previously used for the senior officer of the hospital, because the job was now larger. Thier's new responsibilities would include, in addition to leading the general hospital in downtown Boston, the direction of all the various medical enterprises with which the MGH was involved, including the McLean psychiatric hospital.

The MGH board chairman had moved quickly to secure the appointment for Thier. McArthur remembers Colloredo-Mansfeld saying in the fall that selecting Buchanan's successor soon was vital or "the General will blow apart."[16] Colloredo-Mansfeld might not be around to finish the job; Buchanan, who had agreed to postpone his planned retirement until the end of 1993, was considering his next move; and the Partners merger was rushing forward. Colloredo-Mansfeld describes the coincidental occurrence during December 1993 of Thier's appointment at the MGH and the completion of the merger discussions as "two trains coming into the station at the same time but on separate tracks."[22]

Leaders at the Brigham were surprised when they heard that the MGH had appointed Thier[53] and did not receive his choice calmly. McArthur remembers his colleagues complaining: "That's it; we're dead. Sam's too good. No one can manage him."[16] Although Thier's recruitment to the MGH included no assurances about his role in the merger with the Brigham then being completed,[22] his presence at the General concerned the Brigham leaders.

At a tense meeting at the Brigham later in December, McArthur stated the concern at his hospital that the forceful Thier would tilt Partners toward the MGH and treat the somewhat smaller Brigham as a "stepchild."[13] The consultant, David Matheson, remembers spending several days trying to convince the Brigham people that Thier's appointment was good for the new joint enterprise.[53]

When Partners had been officially launched in the spring of 1994, the Partners board proceeded to develop a plan for the leadership of the merger. Nesson, who led the committee planning the merger,[80] would become the founding CEO. Thier would hold the title of president on a part-time basis while continuing to lead the MGH. If all went well, Thier would succeed Nesson when he retired from Partners, and a replacement as president of the MGH would be appointed.

Concern over Thier's leadership at Partners, however, persisted at the Brigham, and he agreed to postpone becoming the Partners CEO. He had plenty to do at the General adjusting the administrative structure to his liking. However, when McArthur continued to object to his succession, Thier let it be known that he had been offered the presidency of a famous university with a renowned medical center and he would take that job unless his appointment as the Partners CEO proceeded as planned.*

Accordingly, Sam Thier became chief executive officer of Partners on January 1, 1996, two years after being named president of the Massachusetts General Hospital, a title he continued to hold for a year until he and his colleagues selected Dr. James J. Mongan to succeed him. Then, with the retirement in 1997 of Partner's first leader, Dick Nesson,[66,82†] Thier became president as well as CEO of Partners HealthCare System, Inc.

McArthur and Ferdinand Colloredo-Mansfeld served as cochairmen of the Board of Directors of Partners until July 1, 1996. Then John M. Connors Jr., chairman and CEO of Hill, Holliday, Connors, Cosmopoulos, Inc., a Boston advertising agency, and chairman of the Brigham board, was elected the new chairman of Partners, thereby maintaining balance at the top, with the president from the General and the chairman from the Brigham.[16]

The contretemps with McArthur exemplifies several features of Thier's character. According to Relman, who has known Thier since he began training in nephrology, also Relman's specialty, more than 30 years ago, "Sam's character, his strength, decisiveness, and intelligence serve him well at Partners. Yes, some people are afraid of him, but they respect him, and Sam has great charm."[13] His biggest challenge, Relman believed, would come from the specialists who dominate the professional staffs at the founding hospitals, particularly the MGH:[13]

> The specialists, who are top league, are doing better than ever and, quite understandingly, they don't want to give away any of their income, whereas the primary care doctors are not doing as well as they wish and in some cases are earning less than before they joined. Partners has become the 1,000 pound gorilla, but if the M.D.'s don't do right, it could fail. Sam's got to hold the medical staffs together for the common good. The job can't be done by anyone with less backbone and gumption. If Sam can't do the job, it can't be done.

Jerome Kassirer, Relman's successor as editor in chief of the *New England Journal of Medicine*, added about the combination of Thier and Nesson leading Partners, "What a great team!"[33]

---

*It was clear, however, which position Thier preferred. He had been quoted as saying that the top Partners position was "one of the only jobs I can imagine that makes a university presidency look like playing in a sandbox."[81]

†Nesson died suddenly and unexpectedly in October 1998.[66,82]

CHAPTER 3

Development

As 1994 began, the founders of the union of the Brigham and Women's and Massachusetts General Hospitals proceeded to structure the merger and find a name for their new creation. The boards of trustees had accepted the concept of the merger early in December 1993.

The Structure

David Matheson and his colleagues from the Boston Consulting Group presented three possible structures for the new corporation: a joint venture, a holding company, or a full-asset merger producing a fully integrated entity.[1] Each had advantages and disadvantages.

A joint venture implied the least amount of consolidation, with each hospital retaining separate leadership. This solution, which the consultants clearly disliked, would allow little internal coordination, prevent jointly managed cost reduction, retain the current separate professional staffs, and present a confused message to the community. However, a joint venture would have the not inconsequential advantage of producing the least political disharmony among those working at the two hospitals.

A holding company or a full-asset merger would produce common leadership, link the professional staffs more easily, facilitate cost reduction through consolidating back office functions at the hospitals, expedite the sharing of management philosophies and tools, and make a clearer statement to the market.[1] However, the more unified the structure the greater would be the anxiety among the administrative and support personnel about their futures. The doctors would also balk at a tighter structure. Would their compensation, their administrative autonomy, and even their jobs be jeopardized if a full merger occurred? As Dr. Mitchell Rabkin, then CEO of the Beth Israel Hospital, observed at the time: "The first two letters of *merger* are *m* and *e* — what is going to happen to *me?*"[2]

The consultants warned that, while "rationalizing physician and nursing staff may offer the greatest opportunity," it would also present "the greatest challenge."[3] Gerald Austen, representing the interests of the MGH physicians, most strongly opposed this structure.[4]

From the beginning, few involved in planning the new company favored "doing it completely"[5] by creating one company with full authority. Consequently, the group concluded that a holding company was the best solution, "the only possible thing in Boston," one of the consultants agreed.[6] This would threaten the hospitals and their staffs less than a complete merger while allowing the creation of an organization that could take advantage of a coordinated management structure and compete successfully for clinical business. Each of the hospitals would keep its own officers and boards of trustees, which would report to the new corporate board and its executives. The assets and liabilities of the hospitals would not be transferred to Partners, the holding company.[7]

The possibility of fully merging was put aside for the time being. What Sam Thier would have advised were he CEO in 1994, however, is clear. As a member of the board of trustees of Cornell University and the board of overseers of its medical college, he recommended a full-asset merger and one board of trustees for the recently consolidated New York and Presbyterian hospitals in New York City, the primary teaching hospitals for the medical schools of Cornell and Columbia Universities.[8]*

Completing the Merger

The steps taken by the MGH board to bring about the new company began on December 8, 1993, with the approval of a letter of intent with the Brigham in which the two hospitals would "strive together to create an integrated health care system" and authorization to create a governing body for the newly formed system.[5] By early February 1994, the board approved the affiliation subject to a due diligence review. The trustees also accepted the concept that the new corporation would serve as the sole member of the corporations known as the Massachusetts General Hospital (MGH)† and the Brigham Medical Center, Inc. This arrangement gave the trustees of the new corporation the right to appoint the trustees of the two hospital boards and by this means exercise the control over the hospitals that the new board thought necessary.

---

*"Sam went to New York, and they took him at his word regarding how to form the merger. He didn't do it in Boston, however," notes his friend and colleague Dr. George Thibault, the Partners vice president of clinical affairs.[9] See chapters 4 and 5.

†The MGH is itself a holding company serving as the sole member of The General Hospital Corporation, The Mclean Hospital Corporation, The Spaulding Rehabilitation Hospital Corporation, and other corporate entities.

At that time, the MGH had about 250 members and the Brigham about 150. The "members" are a self-perpetuating group that functions in a not-for-profit corporation like stockholders in a for-profit company.[5] The members are present and former trustees and other citizens whom the institution wants to recognize for their contributions, financial or otherwise. They meet annually and, like stockbrokers, are often represented by proxies. At these sessions, the members approve changes in the by-laws, elect additional members and, if a vacancy develops, elect a trustee. As established by its original nineteenth-century charter from the Massachusetts legislature, the governor of the state appoints four of the 12 MGH trustees.

According to the plans for the new corporation, its membership would include all the members of the founding hospitals, who would elect the new Partners board of trustees. Although the agreement maintained the board of trustees of the two hospitals, the Partners board would be clearly and legally the dominant structure and could overrule the decisions of the individual hospital boards. This potential power that Partners could exercise was "played down big time" and left ambiguous[10] explained Ernest M. Haddad, general counsel of Partners and for 18 years general counsel to the MGH.[5] Some physicians objected to this fundamental feature of the merger; the trustees had much less difficulty accepting the concept.[5] The relative responsibilities of the boards of the hospitals and Partners would highlight the debate over governance waged during 1998.

Finally, the federal regulatory authorities and the state agencies with jurisdiction over antitrust, licensure, and determination of need had to approve the new corporation, and this was obtained without undue delay.[5] On February 11, the MGH board voted to recommend to the members that they approve the affiliation, and on March 2 the members voted to accept their board's advice. When a similar process was completed at the Brigham, the new corporation, initially called MGH/Brigham Health Care System, Inc., came into being.[5]

The Name, the Location, the First CEO, and the First Money

A planning committee,* chaired by Dr. H. Richard Nesson, president of the Brigham, decided that the title of the new company should not

---

*The same eight who put the merger together — Braunwald, McArthur, Nesson, and Spindler from the Brigham and Austen, Buchanan, Burr, and Colloredo-Mansfeld from the General — became the first members of its board of trustees and constituted the committee planning its initial organization.

include the names of the MGH or the Brigham. Other hospitals would be joining the new corporation in the future, and the Brigham and the General were well enough known already. Finally, if the names of the Brigham and General were retained in the title, some brave soul would have to decide which should come first.

At the suggestion of Robert Buchanan of the MGH,[11] the committee chose the neutral phrase "Partners HealthCare System, Inc." Partners, the committee members insisted, should be thought of more as an affiliation than a merger, which suggested to a reporter from the *Boston Globe* that "The two hospitals will retain more of their identities than was suggested in earlier statements."[12]

Rashi Fein, a health care economist at Harvard, agreed that the name made sense. "It's really a partnership, rather than a merger," he suggested.[13]

Creating a logo took more time. After one false start and two years after the affiliation was created, the executives chose a design with the word *Partners,* surmounted by three curved lines.*

The leaders decided not to locate the Partners offices at either of the founding hospitals. Originally, Nesson maintained his office at the Brigham, where he was still president, but Ellen Zane, the recently appointed CEO of the primary care network, had offices at the General as well. Meetings were held at both hospitals. In November 1994, the group moved into part of the eleventh floor of the Prudential Building, a skyscraper in Boston's Back Bay approximately equidistant from the Brigham and the General and convenient to the Mass Pike, the way home for much of the staff. Eventually, Partners took over the entire floor.

The "eleventh floor" became "an icon for everything the MGH and Brigham doctors don't like about Partners," observes Zane.[14] One of the Prudential staff said about some of the doctors and a few of the administrators at both hospitals, "They think we're sitting up here plotting against them all day."

The "Pru" offices, with their pleasant views over Boston, are functional, not palatial or glitzy. "More the Harvard way," observed one staff member.

Nevertheless, a wit, having in mind the relative comfort of the facilities, dubbed the Prudential offices "Carpet World," and to some extent the name has stuck.

As befits the chief executive of what would become a multi-billion-dollar business, the president of Partners merited a corner office. Dr.

---

*A wag of uncertain identity concluded that the logo really indicated that the new corporation was "a bridge over troubled waters."

Samuel Thier, the current president, can gaze from his aerie toward the MGH, where he trained, was briefly president, and still makes teaching rounds. In the approved spirit of an alliance rather than a merger, the conference rooms were named for leading physicians and nurses at the member hospitals.

The new board elected Richard Nesson its first chief executive officer. Nesson brought to Partners the experience of having successfully implemented the 1980 merger of the Peter Bent Brigham Hospital, the Robert Breck Brigham Hospital and the Boston Hospital for Women into the Brigham and Women's Hospital and having made the new hospital financially successful. Before Nesson's tenure, the Peter Bent Brigham Hospital had been losing money. Jeffrey Otten, the chief executive officer, succeeded Nesson as president of the Brigham and Women's Hospital.

A graduate of Harvard College and the Boston University medical school, Nesson trained to be a nephrologist (kidney specialist), like Thier, his successor at Partners. Nesson's principal professional interest, however, changed from that of a specialist in internal medicine to the delivery of health care, which he often insisted to be the right of every citizen.[15] This new vocation led him to the vice presidency of ambulatory care and community services at the Brigham and, on the academic side, to the directorship of the Division of General Medicine in Eugene Braunwald's Department of Medicine. Nesson, then working at the Beth Israel Hospital,[16] also helped found and was the first medical director of the Harvard Community Health Plan, now a large HMO known as Harvard Pilgrim Health Care. Later, as the Brigham president, he negotiated an agreement that assured that patients of the health plan needing hospitalization would be cared for at the Brigham, the first such relationship between a teaching hospital and an HMO.

To launch the new enterprise, the Brigham and the General each assigned $2.5 million to Partners.[17]

The Primary Care Network and Managing Managed Care

When the formalities of establishing Partners HealthCare System, Inc., were completed in March of 1994, Nesson set about developing a primary care network and the organization that would deal with managed care. He and his associates knew that forming close links with physicians practicing in the communities was essential if Partners was to secure contracts with the HMOs.[18] Nesson recognized that building such a network was essential, but, consultant David Matheson reminded him, neither hospital had been particularly successful so far and would probably continue to have difficulty if they "tried to gain influence over primary care" separately.[4] To lead this vital activity, he chose Mrs. Ellen M. Zane, CEO of the Quincy Hospital, a municipal hospital in a Boston suburb.

On first inspection, Zane was an unlikely person for the former president of the Brigham and Women's Hospital to employ to "build us an integrated delivery system," the charge Nesson gave her.[14] Zane was not a physician, held no Harvard degrees, and was working in a community, not a university teaching hospital. Trained in audiology (hearing) and speech pathology, she had entered hospital administration and risen to the presidency of the 300-bed Quincy Hospital. Nesson knew her through their membership on the board of directors of the Massachusetts Hospital Association.

"Many academics with Harvard M.D.'s wanted the job, and you have none of the usual tickets," Nesson told her.[14] Fortunately for Zane, Nesson wanted "a community person, not someone attached by the hip to an academic hospital."[14]

Nesson's goals for the new entity, he told Zane, were broader than just meeting the economic threat to the founding hospitals. "We have a responsibility to manage care and integrate in a manner that will enhance the health status of our population. I'm 62, and at this point in my career why should I embark on such a journey unless we can improve how health care is delivered?"[14] As someone who had spent much of his career working in and studying the delivery of primary care, Nesson had learned that much medical care is episodic and fragmented, which interferes with enhancing the overall health of patients.[14] He wanted Partners to lead the effort to reduce these impediments to first-class medical care. As for the person he had chosen to carry out these important missions, Nesson considers Zane to be "an incredibly capable person, probably the best manager I've ever known."[19]

Zane brought to Partners several specific experiences of potential value in her new position. She was accustomed to working with insured patients, local practitioners, for-profit organizations, and municipal officials. Although the city of Quincy owned the hospital, most of those hospitalized were the private patients of primary care physicians and specialists. Few were uninsured or on Medicaid since the town and surrounding region are "strongly middle class."[14] The city retained a for-profit corporation to manage the hospital, and it was the corporation that employed Zane, first as chief operating officer (COO) and then as CEO. Consequently, although the mayor appointed the hospital board, Zane, as CEO, didn't have to "pander," as she puts it, to politicians, so often the burden of executives in other municipal hospitals.[14] She also gained valuable experience working with unions in the hospital.

With Zane on board and with the help of a consultant from California, Nesson wrestled with another fundamental issue: should Partners become an HMO itself and compete directly with the organizations that were beginning to dictate where patients received their care? The leadership quickly decided that such a course was unwise — at least for now. If Partners directly competed for the income of the other HMOs, it risked losing the referrals now coming from the HMOs. Furthermore, Partners executives had no experience in the insurance business. Marketing, claims management, and product development were foreign to them. The company would have to create this complex business from scratch in its first years.[20]

Furthermore, in Zane's experience every hospital system owning an HMO has had trouble with it. Unwary executives delude themselves into thinking that they can "use it as a cash cow and make it profitable. They don't realize how much experienced administration an HMO requires to be successful."[14] For Partners to make an HMO work would probably require the company's reaching outside itself for leadership and possibly for money. To operate a successful HMO would also compel Partners to contract with competing systems in order to offer subscribers a sufficiently broad network.

So Nesson decided to concentrate on building a primary care network and the structure that could successfully contract for managed care contracts to increase Partners' share of the health care market in the Boston region. If these plans succeeded, patients requiring the complex care for which the Brigham and MGH were justifiably proud would continue to come to them rather than to other hospitals offering such services. This task required establishing close links with primary care physicians by either purchasing their practices or establishing affiliations. Partners' ability to obtain contracts from the HMOs would attract the doctors needed to sustain a steady flow of patients to their offices. Rather than approach this work from a narrow set of principles, Zane said when she was hired, "we are going to have a very flexible menu."[18]

To accomplish these vital missions, the Partners board created Partners Community HealthCare, Inc. (PCHI, pronounced "Peechee") with its own board of directors and Zane as its first CEO. PCHI stands equal in status to each of the hospitals within Partners. It is a taxable corporation because, according to Internal Revenue Service (IRS) guidelines then prevalent, to be nontaxable no more than 20 percent of the members of its board could have been "interested parties," doctors in this case. Zane and Nesson wanted to include on the board physicians from the communities as well as the Brigham and the General. In 1999, 10 (67 percent) of the 15 members were doctors, six from the community and two each from the MGH and the Brigham.[21] As for profits, which could be taxed, Zane never sees that as a problem for PCHI.[14]

Partners organized PCHI as a separate corporation to make sure that the local physicians would see it as being, as Zane describes it, "at arm's length from the MGH and the Brigham. We felt the symbolism of separateness was important. The local doctors needed a structure within Partners which would help them deal with those big places in Boston."[14] Zane remembers from her experience working in, and then leading, a community hospital how many referring physicians and their boards feared "those black holes downtown into which they send their patients never to hear from them again."[14] Not every specialist at a university hospital promptly informs the referring doctor about his or her patient's condition or sends a useful summary of the hospitalization within a few days of discharge. Local doctors also fear that the university hospital will "steal" their patients, who, dazzled by the staff and facilities of these behemoths, may conclude that their community physicians cannot provide the care they need.

PCHI would also need to provide the services that the community doctors linked to Partners needed to administer their managed care risk contracts. A management services organization—an MSO, as these structures are called—was created for this purpose. Eventually, 80 percent of the back office staff of PCHI would be working in managed care operations.[14]

To negotiate successfully with the HMOs and secure the tertiary care patients needed for the founding hospitals to prosper, Zane and Nesson estimated that by the year 2000 they must develop a network of about 1,000 primary care physicians affiliated with Partners.[14] This many doctors, they estimated, would care for between 1.5 and 2 million patients, including about 300,000 "capitated lives"—patients whose care was paid for by HMOs contracting with Partners and the doctors for a fixed amount of money per patient per month.

Buying physicians' practices was one way to do this. Nesson and Zane realized, however, that Partners could never afford to purchase hundreds of practices, as some other academic health centers were doing.[14] The cost of a successful practice in the region then ranged from $100,000 to as much as $280,000 per doctor, and the payment a doctor could expect was rising, as other organizations, particularly at that time the Lahey Clinic and local community hospitals, were bidding up the price. How much to pay for a practice could be estimated, however. Accounting firms had developed methods for determining reasonable prices, data that were available to the doctors as well as to Partners. Fundamental to the calculation were the practice's assets, both tangible, including the patient charts, and intangible. The intangible asset—the "goodwill"—is partially derived from the number of patients in the doctors' panels who stay with the practice.

However, from the beginning Zane and her colleagues decided not to employ the doctors. They would continue to own their professional corporations and operate, as in the past, with the incentives of individual, or in most cases group, practitioners. After collecting their fees and deducting the overhead costs of operating their practices, including paying the nonphysician employees and their contribution toward operating the MSO, PCHI returned the proceeds to the physicians. The doctors would then pay their malpractice insurance and distribute the balance as their income. By not paying the doctors' salaries, PCHI stimulated the physicians to do all they could to keep the costs of the practice as low as possible, thereby increasing what fell through to the "bottom line," their personal incomes.[14]

"We wanted them around the same table as us, not as our paid workers," says Zane. "We encouraged them to understand that they wouldn't receive their piece of the action until all the overhead was paid. This gave them more reason to run their practices lean and mean."[14] PCHI also avoided participating in the potentially divisive activity of deciding how much each doctor in the group received.[14] Zane did guarantee salaries for one or two years as some came onboard, but, she says, "each has come off [the guarantee] smoothly and in most cases is now earning more than before coming with us."[14]

Armed only with a secretary, Zane went about finding 100 busy physicians who would sell their practices to Partners. "I just got in my car and started visiting them," she recalls.[14] Each of the doctors with whom she spoke was first of all a primary care physician, the person whom the patient first visits for most illnesses, and not a specialist. The Brigham and the MGH had plenty of specialists.

Most primary care doctors are family practitioners, general internists, and general pediatricians, but she also included a few specialists.[22] Some community cardiologists, specialists in heart disease, work as primary care physicians in the care of their patients, seeing them for their cardiac problems but also treating their other complaints. These doctors train as general physicians before becoming specialists, and many keep abreast of advances in fields other than their areas of special interest.

Certain doctors Zane made it a point to avoid. These were physicians who, in the jargon of the business, "churned" their practices by ordering unnecessary or duplicative laboratory tests. Such studies, often performed by the practice's staff on its own equipment, constituted a handsome source of income in the rapidly departing "pay by the test" method of compensation now being replaced by the terms of the HMO contracts. Zane and Nesson consider such activity "the antithesis of taking on risk and giving the appropriate amount of care."[14] In managed care, the physician and staff must conduct their practices economically by hospitalizing, obtaining tests, and requesting consultations only for those patients really in need of such services. Some of the most success-ful fee-for-service doctors could not adapt to the managed care method of payment. "Many of the practices lead a schizophrenic lifestyle," Zane found. "Some of their members are born HMO docs, but others have great difficulty converting."[14]

Finally, the doctors she sought were successful practitioners work-ing in groups with several colleagues and not in solo practice. One-doctor practices are inherently more risky, she learned. In a few cases, however, individual practitioners agreed to form a group as a provision for joining Partners, as did 22 doctors in Framingham, a city west of Boston.

In addition to buying practices, Zane established affiliations with other groups of primary care physicians. By 1999, more than 900 doc-tors, including the 110 in the purchased practices, had assigned to PCHI the right to negotiate for them at-risk, capitated contracts with the HMOs.

PCHI contracts exclusively for all patients in the owned practices and supplies between 10 and 40 percent of the business of the affiliated practices.[14] In 1999, the PCHI doctors cared for about 200,000 patients under capitated contracts, which cost the patients or their employers premiums averaging $155 per member per month. These contracts alone were expected to generate revenue of more than $350 million during 1999.[14] The total number of residents in eastern Massachusetts whose care is provided by a PCHI doctor now exceeds 1 million.[23]

Why did so many doctors sign up with Partners as the agency that could secure the survival of their practices? The answer is simple: fear that the HMOs would direct their patients elsewhere and that they would lose further revenue from future contracting. Negotiating with HMOs is not an activity that most doctors want to undertake or are particularly skilled at doing. Having an organization backed by the reputation and strength of the region's two most famous hospitals plus Zane's, Nesson's, and then Thier's obvious abilities assured the primary care physicians that a highly competent organization would obtain HMO contracts for them and ser-vice their practices. In addition, Partners would bring a structure of shared governance to the community physicians.[24]

Richard Nesson and Samuel Thier, both of whom are strong willed as well as experienced and exceptionally intelligent, formed a highly compatible pair. Zane comments, "We would never have been able to blaze this trail if they couldn't work together."[14]

John McArthur, the chairman of the Brigham board when the merger was being planned, agrees. "Dick couldn't have done it without Sam"[25] — and this from the man who had earlier feared the effect on the Brigham of Thier's succeeding Nesson at Partners.

The doctors in the network found sending patients who required specialized care to the Partner's hospitals a reasonable request. Many thought that their patients would be impressed with their newly established association with these hospitals. Knowledgeable patients would be pleased — if a patient is ever pleased to require hospital treatment — being cared for at the Brigham or MGH for their more complicated ailments. Most of the physicians were also glad to assign much of their office work on the capitated patients, the billing and collecting particularly, to the administrative group in the MSO, built by Partners for the patients of the owned practices but available for the capitated patients of the affiliated practices as well.

"Of course, the docs are [not pleased] that managed care with capitation has replaced the old fee-for-service system," says Zane, who used a more pungent phrase to describe the physicians' ire. "Their incomes are less and at risk for the decisions they make."[14]

For administrative purposes, the physicians and their risk-bearing units are organized into 15 regional service organizations (RSOs). The two largest include the doctors at the MGH and the Brigham. The others are based on geography from New Hampshire to Fall River in southern Massachusetts.[26] In each RSO, PCHI selects an administrative "anchor group" of doctors who represent the company. Led by the anchor group, each RSO determines how the medical fees are distributed. Zane emphasizes that, "Since all health care is local, when in doubt, decentralize decision making. Only use centralized management when it adds value."[14]

Regarding referral of their patients to the Partners hospitals, Zane explains,[14] "The hub-and-spoke arrangement is not the right model. The primary care physicians should only send to us those patients who cannot be taken care of in their community hospitals. 'You decide where the gall bladder gets done,' I told them." Nevertheless, "When I say to people that the MGH and BWH are not at the hub of the network, there is a tendency not to believe it," Zane told a reporter.[27]

Is the investment that Partners has made in PCHI paying off? By the winter of 2000, Zane had spent $94 million from the $100 million target from 1994 to 2000. Each of the 110 physicians in the owned practices was by then breaking even on operations, and many were more financially productive than before Partners had acquired them.[14] Their work had grown in market share — Zane finds it difficult to compute one figure for this — and all inpatient beds at both the General and the Brigham were consistently occupied. Approximately 70 percent of all tertiary referrals from risk-based contracts in the areas where PCHI's owned or affiliated doctors practiced were coming to one of the founding hospitals. Of the 30 percent remaining, approximately 10 percent each were referred to Boston Children's Hospital, local emergency departments, or other hospitals favored by the patients, Zane's goal was to "move toward 80 percent with only a 20 percent 'leakage' to other hospitals."[14]

"Computing a classic return on investment, as one would do in a for-profit business, isn't possible in this case," Zane explains. "One can only use proxies such as studying how the at-risk business has responded."[14]

Salem Hospital and the Network Physicians

Salem Hospital, 15 miles north of Boston and now a part of the North Shore Medical Center, had long enjoyed a comfortable relationship with the MGH. Many Salem physicians referred their patients to MGH specialists, and several of the clinical services from the General rotated their trainees through Salem to gain experience working in what is often called "the real world of medical practice" at a good community hospital. Although Salem entered the 1990s a successful hospital with full beds and a comfortable financial status, many of its leaders realized that "to weather the storm ahead" a more formal link with their colleagues at the General seemed indicated.[23] Those opposed to a merger or affiliation with the MGH and then with Partners posed the usual objections. "We'd be joining this monstrously large organization, we'd lose our community mission and our autonomy, and all our patients will disappear into that 'great sucking sound' downward," recalls Dr. John A. Fallon from North Shore Medical Center.[23]

Nevertheless, the senior executives, including Fallon, and some of the other doctors and trustees convinced the remaining members of the board, and North Shore Medical Center joined Partners in 1995.[28] Most of those making the decision felt confident that the new arrangement would assure that the hospital could continue to fulfill its responsibility to provide excellent medical care to its community.[23]

Fallon, as a trustee and later chairman of the board of PCHI, represents the North Shore Health System, the physicians-hospital organization (PHO) for the doctors at the Salem Hospital. PHOs, most of which have developed in the 1990s, are independent corporations that develop clinical programs and work through issues affecting doctors and their hospitals. Fallon, who graduated from Holy Cross University and received his M.D. degree from Tufts, trained in medicine at the Boston City Hospital, where his teachers thought that he would embark on an academic career. Instead, he opened a solo practice on the North Shore in 1976 and only in 1988 finally took on a partner. In 1993, he was elected president of the Salem Hospital medical staff and began reducing the size of his practice as he became more involved in medical administration and politics. In January 1998, he stopped practicing altogether, and in May he symbolically completed the career change by receiving a master's degree in business administration (MBA). As far as his schedule was concerned, however, "I'm working harder than I ever did in practice and am out most nights at meetings."[23]

Because of its early affiliation, which occurred only one year after Partners was formed, North Shore was particularly important in the early development of PCHI. Its PHO immediately brought in more than 100 primary care physicians. Most of the secondary and tertiary care referrals continue to go to the MGH rather than the Brigham because it's closer and because of the long history of the relationship. The complicated obstetrical cases tend to be sent to the Brigham and Women's.[23]

Most affiliated doctors in the network, Fallon has found, like managing their own practices — "it's really a cottage industry" — and few use PCHI's management services organization.[23] The doctors say, "I've got someone who's really good running the office," sometimes a spouse. "Besides, I would lose even more control of my work if PCHI ran the office."[23] As it is, Fallon observes:[23]

> The practitioners feel that they are losing control of their individual practices so fast that it makes them dizzy and depressed. They are working harder and earning less, and the rising amount of paperwork is dreadful. They see more interference from the payers and the federal government and vanishing influence over what happens in their offices and the hospitals. Many feel that someone has unfairly changed the rules. The baby boomers were promised a different professional life from what they are seeing, but their kids are going to college, they need the income, and must cope. More and more of the older guys, still good docs, are quitting. The new docs don't know how it was.
>
> To add to their frustration, the doctors realize that no one is particularly interested in their complaints. Many used to take off at

least one half-day a week. That's gone. They're making $150,000 a year rather than $175,000. Still sounds like a great income to most people.

A discontented physician group troubles Fallon, Thier, Zane, and the other Partners and PCHI leaders. "Other than giving them Prozac," says Fallon, "we must try to improve their professional lives, reduce the bureaucratic pain and costs of practicing, and let them do what they signed up for in the first place — taking care of patients."

Fallon has watched Sam Thier, the power from the academic center, deal with the practitioners and their boards.[23]

> He's very good at this. Sam engages people, and he has a great sense of humor. He's a no-nonsense guy who gets to the point quickly. Sam may scare some people, but, as far as I can remember, he always lives up to his word, so most people see him as trustworthy with a capital *T,* even when he's sugar coating a problem. Sam can talk patient care and doctor satisfaction as well as the academic stuff, and the docs believe him. In many ways, he's a zealot for Partners, and particularly now that Nesson's gone, Sam's absolutely critical for us.

Partners and the HMOs

Working with the HMOs is one of Ellen Zane's most challenging jobs. She and her colleagues must try to convince them to contract with Partners at the highest obtainable price for the care their patients need, primary care through the physicians in the owned and affiliated practices and tertiary care at the MGH and the Brigham. The HMOs, acting as insurers, competitively negotiate to provide medical care for employees of companies and for governmental clients on Medicare or Medicaid. Obviously, they seek to pay the lowest amount possible for the care they must finance. The HMOs, not being health care providers in most cases, must contract with Partners and other medical groups to obtain the services of the doctors and hospitals.

"We will be market competitive but will not 'bottom fish' or be the K-Mart of health care," is how Zane describes the Partners approach. "We also learned that we must treat each market differently, even in our region. All health care is local. You can't necessarily do in Hyannis what will work in Gloucester," she adds, referring to two eastern Massachusetts communities.[14]

Formerly, the HMOs exhibited great strength in their negotiations with the providers and, as Zane sees it, "really threw their weight around."[14] But as health care providers like Partners became better organized and gained more experience in negotiating, some of the balance of power shifted toward the providers. Partners officials have made it clear that if the HMOs don't pay well and on time, Partners will create its own HMO and compete directly with those now in business. "Creating our own HMO is not something we want to do," acknowledges Zane. "We've got enough on our plate. But if we can't get a fair price, and if the HMOs continue to delay paying their bills, we may have to apply for a license and do it."

Thier acknowledges, "we don't know much about the insurance business,"[7] but adds, "if they attempt to squeeze us so tight that we can't fulfill our missions of teaching, research, and patient care, then we might be forced to become an insurer."[29] Until now, he adds, "Partners has never had a license and, for that matter, has never taken care of anybody."[8] That work is done at the constituent hospitals and by the doctors in PCHI and at the hospitals.

Some of the HMOs appear to be taking the threat seriously, since they know that Partners, with the managerial strength it has developed and the reserves of the founding hospitals behind it, could now take on this function, although not without sizable start-up funding and a large increase in its costs of operation. Furthermore, as a reporter for *Modern Healthcare* wrote:[30]

> The managed care which has evolved in the shadow of half a dozen renowned academic medical centers [in the Boston market] is not the cost-crunching, pinch-the-providers brand that has seized sections of California. . . . Hospital costs per patient day remain 40% higher than the national average. . . . HMOs with substantial market share generally have kept hard-nosed demands for cost containment to a minimum.

California consultants have been known to call Massachusetts managed care "fee for service in drag."[31]

Under most HMO provider arrangements, the HMOs police the doctor's practices to reduce the costs of practicing. Under pure capitated managed care, the physician receives a fixed amount, the infamous "dollars per member per month," to care for the patient whether ill or well. The more the doctor spends on the patient, the less the practice will earn. However, if the physician is wholly or partially employed by the HMO or if payment for care of the HMO patient is not capitated, it is the HMO that must, for its own financial success, limit the amount spent on its patients. When the practitioner, under one of these arrangements, concludes that a test or referral to a specialist is needed, the doctor must obtain the permission of the HMO, which often is represented not by a doctor or even a nurse but all too frequently by someone without professional training or experience. If the HMO representative says no, the laboratory or specialist won't be paid. Having to make one of these phone calls or fill out a form to obtain payment for the referral or test is one of the features of caring for patients in HMOs that most angers and frustrates doctors.

Partners decided fairly early in its life to take on this work itself. Zane and her colleagues believe that how the health care is provided should be Partners' job. Thus, Partners, not the HMO, disciplines those M.D.'s who churn their practices or in other ways practice wastefully or inefficiently. Partners didn't do this perfectly at the beginning. "We had our share of losses early in our experience with capitation," Zane recalls[14] — "an alarming loss in its contract with Blue Cross to care for 90,000 HMO Blue Patients," according to the *Boston Globe*.[29]

Keeping expenses down in doctors' practices costs HMOs money. Zane claims that when Partners relieves them of this job the HMOs save money and that some of these savings should be returned to the providers.[14] Some HMOs have come to favor this approach, finding it better to leave cost control to well-managed providers like Partners.[30] Zane is "underwhelmed" by the infrastructure of many of the HMOs and finds several to be "dysfunctional outfits. So it's best all around that we manage the risks,"[14] or, as Thier puts it, "move medical management out of the HMOs. If you take the risk, you have to do what it takes."[8]*

As for directing PCHI, Zane declares: "It's much more fun than running a hospital," which she did before taking on the Partners job. "Growing and managing care is more fulfilling"[14] and certainly more satisfying than spending most of her time cutting costs, the complaint of many hospital directors.

Colloredo-Mansfeld, the MGH chairman, adds, however: "If hospital CEOs can't deal with cost pressures, they should get out of the kitchen. There's going to be a permanent battle between consumers, payers, and providers. Eventually, the consumer will win, but the cost pressures won't go away."[10]

---

*HMOs are having their own financial troubles just like hospitals and doctors. Harvard Pilgrim Health Care, one of New England's largest and itself the product of mergers,[31] sustained large financial losses, lost its accreditation[32,33] at the end of 1999, and entered state receivership. The inability of an HMO to pay its bills threatens the income of Partners, other hospitals, and the physicians.

Relationships with Community Physicians:
Practice Guidelines

Improving the medical management provided by each doctor in Partners is becoming one of its leading activities. As Ellen Zane, the PCHI CEO, sees it, "Our purpose is not only to fill beds. It if were, we'd operate prohibitively expensive hospitals."[14] Partners is here "to save the missions of the hospitals, not their beds."[14]

Dr. Thomas H. Lee Jr., medical director of PCHI, coordinates much of this work at Partners.[26] He and his colleagues develop practice guidelines, which are published for all the physicians in the network. These papers suggest, in concise prose, the most contemporary and efficient methods of caring for patients with various illnesses. By recommending that most diseases be treated according to the guidelines, Partners assures that each patient will receive the best care most economically. For example, when a patient comes to a PCHI doctor with a symptom suggesting a particular diagnosis, a guideline advises how the physician can get to the root of the problem most efficiently by ordering the most appropriate tests in the order most likely to reveal the problem without "fishing" among less likely possibilities. When the diagnosis is made, the guideline describes the best available treatment.

This is information that the layperson presumes all doctors know. However, not all good physicians approach a problem in the same way. They usually get to the correct diagnosis but sometimes by unnecessarily circuitous routes, and then they may select a treatment that is less effective or more expensive than some other choice. With new information being constantly produced, Partners provides friendly counselors, Dr. Lee and his staff, who have the time to sort through the medical literature, select what is most useful, and discard material of questionable value in everyday practice. By this means, Partners hopes to bypass the influence of the pharmaceutical company representative, whose job it is to convince the doctor to prescribe the company's latest drug, even when an equally effective choice, as recommended in the Partners guideline, may suffice and for less money.

Lee represents a new breed of academic internists who have switched from the traditional specialties to study and try to improve the ways in which care is delivered. Armed with a B.A. from Harvard and an M.D. from Cornell, Lee trained in medicine and cardiology at the Brigham, where his mentor was Dr. Lee Goldman,* who like Tom Lee is a cardiologist turned health delivery expert.

---

*We will meet Goldman, chairman of the Department of Medicine at the University of California-San Francisco, in chapters 6 and 7.

Lee's academic work emphasizes cost effectiveness, quality management, and critical pathways, subjects that try to determine the most medically effective and economically efficient methods for diagnosing and treating various diseases. Richard Nesson, while the Brigham president, encouraged this work by Lee and his colleagues early in their careers to "try to make our system work."[26] Having held several competitive grants to support his research and after achieving the rank of associate professor, a not inconsequential accomplishment at Harvard, Lee has, at least for the time being, put aside writing academic research papers to apply what he has learned to Partners.

Lee, who is 47 years old, spends 90 percent of his time integrating community hospital practices with the Brigham and the General; his other 10 percent is spent in a primary care practice. This requires 70 to 80 hours per week and many 7:00 A.M. and evening meetings with the doctors. (He promises his family to be home at least one night each week.) Lee leads a "learning system" for primary care physicians who can attend weekly medical management meetings providing information that can help prevent them ever being "one-upped" by a patient who has read the latest *Reader's Digest* article on some new treatment.[26] In his role as a teacher of teachers, he warns faculty members visiting local physicians to shed, or at least submerge, any academic hubris that may alienate the community doctor. As a Chinese American, Lee has in a few cases helped community physicians from overseas deal with fears that some of the snobbery they occasionally encounter is a form of racism.[26]

Some of the issues faced by the network are complex business problems that test relationships between the teaching hospitals. For example, one 35-doctor primary care group in a Boston suburb wants to form a multispecialty group. Partners favors this plan as long as the doctors remain members of the network and participate in HMO contracts. Not so simple is the group's wish to develop tight financial arrangements for their patients with particular specialists at the Brigham and the MGH— for example, the heart patients would go to a favored cardiologist at the General and the orthopedic cases to a particular surgeon at the Brigham. As Lee explains:[26]

Neither teaching hospital wants the community doctors to commit exclusively to the other. The group in this case is large and has lots of patients—so some of the specialists at the Brigham and General insist on maintaining a free market in which community doctors can send patients to either place. On the other hand, it is difficult to forge tight bonds, including risk-sharing relationships, with specialists at both teaching hospitals, so some observers think it best that the community physicians throw in their lot with one place or the other. Any movement toward an exclusive relationship with one hospital arouses the free marketeers at the other.

To some extent, these complaints support the notion, expressed in several quarters, that the doctors at the Brigham and the General, virtuosos all, can occasionally play as a quartet but seldom as an orchestra.

Another irritant, not large in the number of patients but annoying to some of the local doctors, is the tendency for patients with a few high-profile conditions to seek treatment at one of the teaching hospitals without referral. Infertility, potentially treatable with in vitro fertilization, and cystic fibrosis are examples of medical conditions for which patients may bypass their local M.D.'s and go directly to doctors at the Brigham or the General. To the local physicians, these self-referrals mean lost business. For the teaching hospital physicians, the care of some of these patients can pay quite well, but when the patients are insured by capitated contracts it may produce large financial losses. Lee and his colleagues, continually working to eliminate such perverse financial incentives, feel far from totally successful in this part of their work.

Lee also encourages community physicians to participate in the clinical trials coordinated at Partners by Eugene Braunwald. So far, however, few trainees from the Brigham or the MGH have elected to work in the community practices, so few of the doctors there have faculty appointments. Lee anticipates that this activity will increase in the future.[26]

A Little Touch of Sam in the Night

In the spring of 1998, Dr. Samuel Thier, the Partners CEO, hosted a series of dinners with selected practitioners in the PCHI network to describe the goals of Partners, listen to their observations, and attempt to understand their problems better.* He also met with several groups of practicing physicians and surgeons at the General and the Brigham. Thier had begun to feel that his base on the eleventh floor of the Prudential Building ("the Pru") was distancing him too much from "the front

---

*As did Henry V, according to Shakespeare, to encourage his army on the eve of the battle of Agincourt in 1415 (*Henry, the Fifth,* act IV):

For forth he goes and visits all his host,
Bids them good-morrow with a modest smile,
And calls them brothers, friends, and countrymen. . . .
A little touch of Harry in the night.

lines. He needed to do his thing, as if he were on rounds," as one of his friends and colleagues said.[9]

The Partners organization had grown to include more than 30,000 employees, including physicians working at more than 30 sites. The corporate infrastructure at the Pru and elsewhere, if brought together, could easily occupy 300,000 square feet of space.[9] Thier's physical isolation did not blend easily with his personality, which has a significant element of impatience.[9] He has always wanted to see the effects of what he has decided brought to completion sooner rather than later.[9]

What Thier learned from the meetings with the physicians and through a series of retreats held at about the same time was that many of the doctors, whether doing primary care or a specialty, wanted continuing contact with the leaders at Partners and would appreciate guidance in practicing the most useful and contemporary medicine. Thier also concluded that Partners, as a clinical entity, was following and not adequately leading the profession.[9] This led him to appoint Dr. George E. Thibault, then chief medical officer at the Brigham and a longtime colleague and friend, as Partners' first vice president of clinical affairs, beginning January 1, 1999.

Partners' Vice President of Clinical Affairs

Thibault brought to this new job the experience of having attended Harvard Medical School and trained in medicine and cardiology at the General and the NIH. He had also directed the MGH training program for interns and residents in medicine and from 1988 to 1995 ran the Department of Medicine at the Harvard- and Brigham-affiliated West Roxbury Veterans Administration Hospital.

In his Partners job, Thibault works closely again with Eugene Braunwald. He had been vice chairman of Braunwald's Department of Medicine at the Brigham while directing the program at West Roxbury. He confirms what many observers report about Braunwald and Thier: "Both have strategic vision and an incredible ability to get things done."[9] Like Dr. Thomas Lee, Thibault's primary academic interest has changed from cardiology to evaluating the delivery of health care, with a strong emphasis on physician education.

"I'm the GP* for the system," is how Thibault describes his responsibilities.[9] He has made himself available to primary care doctors and

---

*GP = general practitioner. Thibault comes by the phrase honestly. Although trained as a specialist, he grew up the son of a general practitioner in upstate New York.[9]

specialists throughout the system—"house calls are in"—when they need him to deal with the type of problems they described to Thier.[9] Within a few months, Thibault and MGH and Brigham physicians began meeting with Partners community doctors for dinner at restaurants near the places where they live and work. "We talk about patient care, doctor to doctor. Finances are not the main course."[9]

With more than 6,000 physicians associated with Partners, Thibault and his Brigham and MGH colleagues can only meet with a small fraction of them, but the sessions help to keep Thibault and Thier current with what most concerns the local doctors about their relationship with Partners and its hospitals. The size of Partners contributes to some of the problems referring doctors encounter. Thibault explains, "It's what we are, but not the way we want to appear."[9]

Education of graduate physicians, one of his most important roles, fits well with one of Thibault's greatest interests. He has set up medical courses, which are held where the community physicians work, featuring "high profile talks by MGH and Brigham specialists followed by panel discussions with the local docs," and he has convinced Harvard to reduce the fees for Partners-associated physicians taking courses at the medical school.

Thibault assists Eugene Braunwald in bringing community physicians into clinical research by encouraging them to participate in studies being conducted by Harvard investigators by enrolling their patients in the trials. Thibault also takes a leading roll in publishing a Partners newsletter that "emphasizes medical rather than financial issues."[9]

In February 2000, Thibault held the first Partners "convention for all the physicians in the system. Sam updated his vision of where medicine is going, and Gene gave one of the state of the art talks on cardiology." The session, attended by over 600, was held at a downtown Boston hotel, and spouses were invited to participate.[9]

While continuing to supervise the students and house staff at the Brigham and General as an attending physician, Thibault pays particular attention to how the care is being delivered. Are the patients referred by the primary care physicians appropriate for the type of care offered at the General and the Brigham or could they be served as effectively and more economically at one of the community hospitals? Are all the facilities at Partners being properly utilized? For example, are patients being transferred to the Spaulding Rehabilitation Hospital at the right time and for the right reasons?[9]

Reflecting on his job, Thibault admits that "It's the hardest thing I've ever done. Running an intensive care unit or a medical service is much easier. The job's rather directionless, and there are few short-term measures of success." Thibault has had to modify some of his former beliefs. "I used to believe that if every patient could be taken care of at the MGH the world would be better place. Not necessarily true. I see superb care being given at our other hospitals and at less cost." Furthermore, despite what he had been warned about antagonisms between neighborhood physicians and the faculty at the teaching hospitals, Thibault has found the community doctors "hungry for more relations, not afraid of them, so long as we treat them well." He knows where Partners' standing lies. "We have these great institutions with their great reputations. It's not the Partners name on which we trade."[9]

Other Hospitals and Services

With the founding hospitals and its primary care program established as its first priorities, Partners proceeded to bring more hospitals under the umbrella. First to join, in 1996, was the Salem Hospital north of Boston, which, after incorporating other hospitals (including, a year later, the AtlantiCare Hospital) and health care providers, had become the North Shore Medical Center.[34] This affiliation came easily. North Shore had been negotiating a similar arrangement with the MGH just before Partners was formed.[35]

The Spaulding Rehabilitation Hospital in Boston and the McLean psychiatric hospital in Belmont, subsidiaries of the MGH corporation, also became constituent members of Partners. The MGH Institute of Health Professions, the successor at the MGH to its school of nursing and other educational ventures to train health care professionals, merged into Partners.

In the fall of 1998, the Faulkner Hospital merged with the nearby Brigham and Women's Hospital,[36,37] bringing Partners' market share in eastern Massachusetts to 20 percent.[36] With all of Brigham's beds frequently filled, its management hopes that the underfilled Faulkner can accommodate some of the patients that the Brigham cannot admit, particularly those not requiring tertiary care.

Also in 1998, the officers of Newton-Wellesley, a large community hospital serving the western suburbs, resumed discussions,[38] which had begun a year earlier,[39] about joining Partners, which they did early in 1999.[40] Whereas doctors at North Shore refer principally to the MGH and at Faulkner to the Brigham, Newton-Wellesley relates more to Partners as a whole rather than being primarily linked to one or the other of the teaching hospitals. Integrating Newton-Wellesley into Partners has been different than the process for each of the other hospitals.[9]

Smaller hospitals, have also formed alliances with Partners. The 24-bed Martha's Vineyard Hospital, having emerged from bankruptcy in the fall of 1998, benefits from the status associated with its affiliation with the General and the Brigham even though it receives no money from Partners.[41]

Concerning the business philosophy driving these acquisitions, Ferdinand Colloredo-Mansfield, the MGH chairman and cochairman of the Partners Board in its early years, observed:[10]

> We needed to develop a network of health care providers more than to create a typical business merger of the two hospitals. We don't see ourselves as a vacuum cleaner for all patients. They should be treated at the most convenient and appropriate locations, and this would often be in community hospitals. We were also not on a tear to buy up or merge with the community hospitals. Many would love to sell to us, particularly those which were losing money. We are obviously not interested in underwriting others' red ink.

This outline guides Jay B. Pieper, Partners' vice president for Corporate Development and Treasury Affairs. Pieper's first rule is "invest no dollars into losing enterprises now or later except when necessary for defensive purposes."[34] AtlantiCare Medical Center was such an enterprise. Its Lynn Hospital was the largest facility between the MGH and the Salem hospital, now affiliated with Partners as the North Shore Medical Center. Two for-profit hospital companies were bidding against Partners to buy AtlantiCare, which was losing several million dollars per year. Pieper computed that by integrating AtlantiCare through North Shore, Partners could save at least $4 million per year, eliminate most of the deficit, and keep out the competition. In evaluating the deal, he had to quantify the defensive question: how much was it worth to prevent the for-profit providers from entering the market? The AtlantiCare board chose the Partners offer, and the Lynn Hospital, now called Union Hospital, joined Partners as a subsidiary of North Shore.

When deciding whether to merge or affiliate with other hospitals, Pieper, Thier, and the Partners board must consider the following questions:[34]

- Will the new affiliate enhance Partners position in the health care market?
- Does the new affiliate have "operating leverage"? Will the affiliate contribute to the financial resources of Partners if not now then after the combination reduces costs?

- Will the hospital "create economic efficiency"?[5]
- Will the hospital "make the patients' stay easier and improve the quality of health care"?[5]
- Is the management of the potential affiliate ready to participate in the Partners network approach and share the Partners business philosophy? If not, cautions Pieper, "step aside — one doesn't want to join with people who will fight the Partners system every day."[34]

The merger with the large Newton-Wellesley Hospital, just west of the Brigham and serving a relatively wealthy suburban clientele, may well be Partner's last affiliation with a community hospital for a while. One of the problems with bringing Newton-Wellesley into Partners, Pieper believes, is that for primary and secondary care its "catchment area," the region from which most of its patients come, easily overlaps with that of the Brigham.[34]

Although Thier would like to add one to the south,[8] there are few unattached community hospitals that are financially healthy and far enough away from the Brigham or the General to reduce direct competition for cases well handled at good community hospitals.[34] Furthermore, limited capital constrains what Partners can now spend to merge with another hospital.[8]

With the likelihood low for merging with more community hospitals, Jay Pieper and his staff in corporate development are concentrating on developing international business and telemedicine. A few hospitals in the United States, the Mayo and Cleveland Clinics, the Johns Hopkins Hospital, and the MGH, have marketed their medical services overseas, particularly to wealthy individuals from developing countries, who in the past went to European, often English, hospitals for their care. The MGH does about 40 percent of such business in Boston,[34] but from now on the work will go forward as a Partners venture, which, it is hoped, will bring larger numbers of overseas patients to both of the founding hospitals.[34] As part of the program, MGH and Brigham specialists will travel, as some do now, to evaluate and treat patients in their own countries. Then for more complex care, the patients will be encouraged to come to Boston.

Television has been used in a rather desultory manner for several decades to transmit patient data and consultants' evaluations. Partners sees a growing application for this service as the technology supporting the program improves and the opportunity arises to charge for what had been for the most part a free service.[34]

Thier wants Partners to expand its nonacute services, such as nursing homes, home health care, and rehabilitation, beyond that now conducted at the Spaulding hospital. "We can't stop helping our patients just when they leave the MGH or the Brigham," he says.[8]

Administration

When Partners combined the back office functions of the founding hospitals, Thier realized that he needed someone to supervise these departments, which now employ 1,500 people. He hired Thomas P. Glynn with the title of chief operating officer to manage all the service departments at Partners except for those in PCHI, a separate corporation, which Ellen Zane runs. Glynn is responsible for administering the offices of communications, community benefits, development, finance, government relations, information systems, human resources, legal affairs, marketing, new business development, real estate, and treasury.[42] The employees work at several locations, some at the Brigham and the MGH and many in offices elsewhere but relatively few at the Pru.

Glynn brings varied and unusual experiences to his job at Partners. Since earning a B.A. in economics at Tufts, he has been the general manager for the World Trade Center and the Massachusetts Bay Transportation Authority in Boston and the chief financial officer of Brown University. Just before taking the Partners job, Glynn was deputy secretary and chief operating officer for Robert B. Reich at the U.S. Department of Labor in Washington. Thier heard about Glynn at Brandeis, where he had been president and Glynn had earned his Ph.D.

Glynn spends one-third of his time each on administration, managing initiatives, and the work required by his being a member of the senior management team. He is impressed that Thier, the former and present MGH doctor, has established a horizontal management structure in which decisions are usually reached by consensus. "We're not IBM," he explains.[42]

Finances

The founders of Partners anticipated significant financial savings by centralizing several of the administrative functions at the MGH and Brigham, including finance, budgeting, information systems (computers), investments, legal, and marketing. By the end of 1999, Thier and his associates estimated that consolidating functions had saved Partners $200 to $250 million.[8,43] "This equals about 2.5 percent of the adjusted cost base [expenses for clinical operations], and we've held it," says Jay

Pieper, the Partners vice president for Corporate Development and Treasury Affairs. "However," he adds, "it's not much more than inflation." The largest savings resulted from exerting the leverage of the size of Partners on vendors and reducing and consolidating the variety of items purchased.[34]

Partners, of course, has cost money over the same five years. Expenses included establishing the corporation, paying the Partners executives and staff, and renting and furnishing the Prudential offices — "an almost incidental expense compared with the others," Pieper says.[34]

Operating the parent company costs about 1 percent of operating expenses.[43] Partners looks on the sizable cost of building and developing the integrated delivery system through PCHI, the primary care network and managed care servicing unit, as a specific investment that the MGH and the Brigham might well have had to undertake if they had remained separate and not as a cost of building the merged company.[43]

The savings, spent for the most part on improving current programs and developing new initiatives, would presumably not have been available if the hospitals had continued to operate separately. "The funds also allowed Partners to establish a new governmental affairs group and invest widely in community affairs, important services which might not have been developed at all or as fully by the hospitals individually," says Pieper.[34]

Combining the endowments of the two hospitals was one of the first projects undertaken. Pieper, chief financial officer at the Brigham under Nesson since 1986, moved to Partners to direct this function. The General's endowment was larger, about $250 million versus the Brigham's $50 million.[34] Pieper found the MGH's investment policy more conservative than that of the Brigham. The MGH maintained about $500 million in cashlike securities when the hospital was then generating more than $700 million in revenue; at the Brigham $50 million was in cash when revenue was about $600 million. He ascribes this in part to the orientation of the officials in charge of this work, "more from the reimbursement side at the General and more market driven at the Brigham."[34] Furthermore, the trustees at the General tended to involve themselves more in the details of financial decisions than at the Brigham, where management was more likely to decide such matters.[34]

Partners created a four-member investment committee consisting of Peter Lynch from Fidelity Investments; Nicholas Thorndike, an MGH board member who formerly ran the Wellington funds; Glenn Strehle, the treasurer of MIT and a Brigham board member; and Jay Light, a professor at the Harvard Business School and a Brigham trustee. The members had had long and successful experience investing large amounts of money and in Pieper's view were neither particularly conservative nor "gunslingers."[34] The committee chooses areas for investment, and then Pieper and his staff execute the plan through investment pools, which are similar to mutual funds. All the money not needed for short-term liquidity is invested in longer term assets with an emphasis on equities. The program's costs are similar to what index funds charge, about 0.3 percent of capital per year.

Since this new policy went into effect, the results have been gratifying. The amount under management, consisting of the endowment of both hospitals—about $325 million at the MGH and $75 million at the Brigham—the operating funds, and the Partners retirement funds have grown from $1.9 billion in 1994 to over $3 billion in 1999.* Pieper's group directly manages $400 million in-house, and the rest is invested by outside managers.[34] Nevertheless, such an approach does have its downside. When asked about the falling stock market during the summer of 1998, Sam Thier, the nephrologist turned CEO admitted, according to the *Wall Street Journal,* "I think about it every night at about 3 a.m."[44]

Catherine Robbins, the first vice president for finance at Partners, supervises the other business departments. She is responsible for 500 people in billing, accounts payable, accounting, materials management, and budgeting, mostly in offices in Charlestown on the other side of the Charles River, north of Cambridge, where the MGH maintains a large research operation. The Brigham and the General retain their own chief financial officers, who also report to the hospital CEOs,[45] and small staffs of about 20 financial analysts. Partners does not collect the professional income for the full-time physicians at the Brigham and the MGH. Their practice corporations currently do this.

"Moving from the MGH to the Pru was quite a change," says Robbins. "I never thought I'd walk through a shopping mall on my way to work"[17] (The main corridors on the first floor of the Prudential Center are lined with shops.) As a former Mass General employee, Robbins maintains a balance with the other senior financial officer, Jay Pieper, who came from the Brigham. Robbins helps contribute to Partners the culture of the MGH—large meetings, much talk, decisions by consensus—which became the underlying theme on the eleventh floor rather

---

*Thier observes that the endowment leaves Partners "OK if we were only a hospital corporation." However, the MGH and Brigham also have large research budgets—which are administered by medical schools elsewhere—so "we're like a university," and for that purpose he sees the amount of the endowment as "marginal."[8]

than the more directed, concise style of the Brigham.[17] She believes, as a former MGH officer, that although the Brigham ran "smoother" than the General before the merger the consensus approach of the MGH works better when evaluating data leading to decisions.[17] George Thibault, who has worked at both hospitals, confirms that the representatives from the Brigham had to adjust more than those from the General to conform with the ambiance at Partners.[9]

Robbins relates that one of the intentions of the merger was to "create a new financial grandparent and, to the extent possible, leave the hospitals alone — particularly important to the General people. From the governance side, that's the way it remains."[17] The appropriate officers at the Brigham and the MGH must be brought into agreement on most substantive financial decision reached by Partners, including budgets, audits, transfers of money, and paying for new programs.[17]

The Partners financial staff develops the corporation's annual operating budget from data provided by the hospitals.[45] Partners makes the "key call," as MGH president James Mongan describes the profit margin or bottom line that each hospital must deliver, although not unexpectedly the senior hospital officials and some of the hospital board members often try to modify the target.[35] After the figures are set, the execution of the operating budget is left to the hospital executives.[45]

The annual capital allocation process, which is centralized at Partners,[45] pits the needs of each of the hospitals against each other. To partially accommodate this conflict, Partners allows each hospital to spend half of its capital budget as it thinks best without approval from the Pru.[17]

Maintaining a healthy financial picture is currently challenged by the receivables problem, a phenomenon familiar to financial officers at hospitals and practices throughout the country. The insurers have taken to "managing their cash more efficiently," a euphemism that means they are paying more slowly because of their own financial problems. At Partners, these shortfalls cause some finger pointing. Are glitches at Partners or at the hospitals also at fault? Hospital officers blame the consolidated billing office at Partners, while the Partners people claim that some of the information essential for effective billing, which the hospital people cull from the patients' records, is incomplete or inaccurate.[17] This gives the HMOs an excuse to reject claims and delay payment.

Partners made a profit (formally "excess of revenues over expenses") of $54 million in the fiscal year ending September 30, 1998, compared to $90 million during 1997. The income just from operations was $9 million in 1998 and $21 million in 1997. During 1999, despite

losing about $20 million from operations, the "bottom bottom line"*
was $55 million.[34,43] As a fraction of the total expense budget of more
than $3 billion, the loss from operations during fiscal 1999 was 0.7 per-
cent. "It's less than 1 percent," adds Pieper, "but we're still not pleased
about it. The 2000 budget requires a modest surplus on operations, and
we'll be close to it," Pieper confirmed during the summer of 2000.[34]

The corporation emphasizes the loss from operations to signal the
staff that the current financial climate for health care continues to
squeeze the hospitals and that further efficiencies are essential.[17] The
board and Thier want Partners to reverse the losses on operations and
make money. A margin of 1 percent on operations is the goal. "Otherwise, the cash goes," Thier realizes.[8]

The leading doctors deny responsibility for the red ink. "Nothing
we're doing accounts for the losses," believes Mark Fishman, the MGH
chief of cardiology. The beds at both hospitals are full, the length of stay
is down, and the staff is being reduced. It all comes from Washington,"
he says, pointing to the reductions in Medicare payments to hospitals.
"Most people here don't feel that the merger, despite the costs of setting
it up and operating it, is primarily at fault."[46]

Jay Pieper's predictions for the 2000 fiscal year proved true. The final
figures, released in December, showed a surplus on operations of $24
million, principally due to a $49.4 million surplus at the MGH.[46a] Al-
though the Brigham was also profitable ($5.2 million), several of the
community hospitals and practices owned by Partners lost money.[46a] The
turnaround from 1999 resulted, in part, from excellent volumes in the
hospitals and more favorable contracts with some of the payers.[8]

The reserves of the MGH and the Brigham have kept Partners from
losing money. By the end of 1999, Peter K. Markell, who succeeded
Robbins as vice president for finance in February of that year, could
work with more than $4.3 billion in assets, $1.5 billion in fixed assets,
and the rest in liquid assets, receivables, and cash. Total net assets were
about $2.3 billion. The cash reserve of Partners was then equal to about
200 days of operations.

Despite this extraordinary nest egg, maintaining a favorable financial status at Partners is a continual effort. During 1999, both the Brigham and the General were losing money on their managed care contracts, which paid for 30 to 40 percent of the patients at the Brigham and
15 to 20 percent at the General. "The return on Medicaid patients isn't

---

*Financial types talk about several "bottom lines." A vital one is the result of
operations, negative in the case of Partners during 1999. The "bottom bottom line" includes other income such as interest from cash and the endowment, thus increasing profits
in previous years or, in the case of 1999, reversing the loss from operations.

any better. Poor rates and the insurer's refusal to pay for services produces an average loss of 30 percent," says Markell. "It's not so much the staffing but the cost of what we use, such as drugs, implants, and blood," which are costing much more than Partners anticipated.[43] Even the census, a point of pride in recent years, is suffering. "Many beds are now filled temporarily by patients recovering from same-day surgery," Markell acknowledges. "The General is no longer saying they're full and has plenty of capacity in certain areas.[43]

"Running a hospital is not a good business," acknowledges Markell. "Most professionals in management, information systems, finances, human resources, and general operations won't go into hospital work." Markell knows that it is the doctors who drive the business. "Maybe hospitals should employ and incentivise the docs," he suggests.[43]

Information Systems

One accomplishment that most observers at both hospitals acknowledge to have been superior at the Brigham was information systems or the function and operation of the hospital's computers. Upon hiring John Glaser as the Brigham's chief information officer in 1988, Dr. Richard Nesson, then the Brigham president, told him to bring home and further develop the computer function, which was then contracted to a company outside the hospital.[47]

Glaser's preparation for this job included a Duke B.A. in mathematics (magna cum laude) and a Ph.D. in health care informatics and hospital organization from the University of Minnesota. He had written computer programs at the Research Triangle Institute in North Carolina and consulted in health care computing as the manager of the health care technology management unit at Arthur D. Little, Inc., in Cambridge. In accepting the Brigham job, he recognized that it was now time to stop traveling and do in one place what he had been advising other companies throughout the country to do.

Glaser was taking on what computer types recognize to be a difficult job. Health care, he and his colleagues believe, is among the most complicated domains for applying information systems.[47] The medical behavior of patients is variable and unpredictable and therefore difficult for computer programmers to model. Furthermore, doctors have their own ways of thinking and recording information, and few have sufficient interest in what computers can do for them to want to revise their customary operating habits.

Glaser categorizes his route to applying computer support to hospital functions into four eras.[47] Creating the function constitutes era one, in which the information people decide what it is they want the computers to do. Next comes what he calls the architectural era, designing and then building the infrastructure of equipment needed to deliver the information. Completing these steps brought the standard computer applications at the Brigham to a high level of efficiency. Because of the difficulty of convincing the medical staff to enter the computer age, Glaser and his staff first concentrated on making the Brigham's back office functions, such as finance, billing, and upgrading the ability of the hospital laboratories to report clinical results, more efficient.

Glaser's third era is the most difficult and challenging, creating sophisticated systems to serve specific clinical challenges. "Order entry" is one. Traditionally, a doctor, usually an intern or resident at a teaching hospital like the Brigham, writes by hand the instructions to administer a drug or order a test. A nurse or secretary "takes off" the order and then passes on a drug order to the pharmacy or a test request to the appropriate laboratory. Obviously, at least one step in the process could be saved if the doctor entered the order into a computer, which then transmits it automatically to the proper place while preparing a paper trail. The more developed order entry systems also advise the doctors and nurses if the patient will be receiving a drug to which he or she is allergic or if the new drug is likely to cause a dangerous reaction because of certain characteristics of the patient or a cross-reaction with another drug the patient is taking.

An even more challenging goal during the third era was creating the "computerized chart." Most or all of the narrative and data that go into the patients' charts would be entered and processed according to computer logic. It is the doctors, who would need to type in these notes, who pose the greatest obstruction to this mission, which most hospital leaders recognize to be a worthwhile project. This is seldom a problem for the younger doctors, who for the most part have mastered typing and used computers throughout their education, but how does one convert to the magic of the computer those senior physicians and surgeons who have handwritten their notes all their professional lives? The technical answer is to make the doctors dictate their notes and then instruct the computers to convert the spoken word into written words, but the systems to accomplish this are still being refined. Glaser refers to this mismatch between what the computer can do and what the doctors will do as "environmental stress." It's just another of the elements that make applying computer technology to hospitals a challenge.[47]

In the fall of 1995, Partners announced that the computer operations in the Brigham and General would combine and that John Glaser would become the first Partners chief information officer. This one was not easy. "There was much human trauma from the merging, a high early turnover," Glaser recalls about the fourth era, a process that took about two years. The first system to be consolidated was e-mail; others soon followed. More recently, attention has been directed to use of the Internet.[47]

Glaser and his staff have considered whether to integrate their system with the Partners-owned North Shore Medical Center.[47] However, since Salem Hospital sends only about 1 percent of its patients to the downtown hospitals, this didn't seem economical. However, integrating the systems at Salem with its subsidiary at Lynn and those at the Brigham with the nearby Faulkner hospital makes more sense. The Dana-Farber Cancer Institute, which Partners does not own but collaborates with through Dana-Farber/Partners CancerCare, subcontracts its computer operations to Partners. Glaser wonders if some day the Partners systems will also be connected to those of its competitors.[47]

Before the merger, about 100 employees staffed information systems at the Brigham and about 200 at the MGH. Partners now employs more than 500. Although this growth doesn't seem to fulfill the cost-cutting aims of the merger, Glaser explains that integrating the systems required bringing on more technicians.[47] Furthermore, he convinced the Partners leaders that a more aggressive, and necessarily more expensive, system would allow the hospitals to save more money through efficiencies in the departments served by the computers and would lead ultimately to better care for the patients. Glaser argues that when you skimp on the number or quality of talented people in information services departments you minimize heterogeneity and the ability to solve increasingly complicated problems. "The more aggressively you utilize the computer's ability to solve problems, the more workers and more advanced equipment you need."[47]

Accordingly, the costs of establishing and maintaining first-class information systems are high. To accommodate, among other features, order entry and the computerized record, the number of computer workstations at the Brigham, the MGH, Dana-Farber, PCHI (the primary care network), and the Partners headquarters has grown from 12,000 to 30,000. The information system budget for the fiscal year 2000 was $66 million; three years ago it was $42 million.

Glaser was accustomed to such growth in his department due to his first employment at the Brigham, where Nesson had strongly supported its computer program and subscribed wholeheartedly to the concept that computers really can make hospitals run better.[47] The Brigham management style, which Glaser describes as "command and control," led to faster and more creative development of its information systems than at the MGH.[47] Merging the systems has accelerated the pace and improved the quality of everyone's work. The computer people at the General caught the Brigham fever, and both groups have subsequently enhanced the system with similar speed and good results.[47] Nevertheless, the cost of supporting the integration of the Partners information systems was "grossly underestimated," says George Thibault. Consequently, expanding it beyond the Brigham and MGH to the other Partners hospitals will be a relatively slow process because the capital needed will not flow as rapidly.[9]

At PCHI, Cynthia Bero runs the computer operation from the network's offices in Needham, a suburb west of the Pru. Although she reports administratively to Ellen Zane, John Glaser provides the technical leadership and vision for the overall Partners information systems. "My job," she says, "is to help the community practices utilize the computer more effectively."[48] Financial and administrative functions that she has developed include registration, scheduling, and billing. For the managed care contracts, her office evaluates eligibility and the appropriateness of referrals. She helps the practitioners improve their practices by reporting to them, based on retrospective and concurrent reviews, how their patients are being managed.[48] Bero is also responsible for the infrastructure of the PCHI system, the computer stations, servers, phone lines, and the Help desk.

Materials Management

One of the classic reasons to merge hospitals is to realize savings in the purchase of the equipment and materials needed for the care of patients. The savings can be significant. An example, only atypical by the size of the difference, is a doctor's examining table. An individual practitioner may need to pay $800; a large group purchasing many can procure one for $350.[49]

John Gaida, formerly vice president for support services at Brigham and Women's Hospital and corporate director for materials management at Partners from October 1995 to July 1999, claims that Partners has saved significant amounts of money as a result of the opportunities presented to his department by the merger. The savings, however, did not come easily.[49] Doctors, as usual, were part of the problem.

A surgeon, for example, may develop an affection for the operative sutures supplied by a particular company and come to feel that only by using these products can he achieve the clinical results for which he is renowned. Another surgeon may feel the same way about a competing company and its products. Unless the surgeons agreed to standardize the sutures they use, Gaida and his staff could not obtain a more competitive price by offering to buy a larger quantity of the product from one company. This type of problem was exacerbated when working not only with many surgeons but with those at each of the two teaching hospitals. In this case, Gaida achieved an economical solution by forming a committee chaired by one of the most product-conscious doctors and charging him and his colleagues with developing a purchasing program for operative sutures that would save the most money and keep as many of his colleagues at both hospitals satisfied as possible. The committee interviewed doctors and nurses and analyzed competitive data from different suppliers. Eventually compromise won, and the issues among the doctors and nurses were resolved. As Gaida reported, "Sutures were standardized within the system, and savings were maximized."

Using this model, Gaida and his team named committees of professionals and staff members from both hospitals to work through some of the most contentious debates. He challenged the committees to compete in saving money and encouraged the members to reject the tendency "to insist on my product."[49] For the less controversial or complicated products, Gaida's group decided what to buy themselves, thereby expediting the process. Before the committees began their work, Gaida's staff had collected relevant data on the products. This process took almost as much time as that spent by the committees in examining the products and deciding which to choose.

Gaida was applying to Partners the team or committee system he had previously used when in the same role at the Brigham. He found, however, that the multiplicity of individual items needed in the contemporary hospital prevented setting up groups for each. Accordingly, the teams were charged with evaluating categories of supplies rather than individual items. Furthermore, 79 percent of the items used in each hospital were different. Gaida spent several months trying to match them but then gave up and turned the decisions over to his committees.

After all the committees had reported, Gaida sent requests for proposals (RFPs) to the largest distributors of products for medical and surgical use in hospitals along with the preferences submitted by the committees and his staff. About $75 million per year was "on the table" to purchase the standard equipment and supplies needed by the medical and surgical services at the Brigham and the MGH, although the amount assigned to the successful distributor eventually was somewhat less. Food, pharmacy, and equipment for specialty departments — such as pacemakers for cardiology — were "off the table."[49]

The distributor chosen has helped Partners save about $13 million from an annual budget of $50 million, better, Gaida claims, than the savings that would have been realized if Partners had used the consortium that serves other voluntary hospitals.[49] As a bonus, the distributor that got the contract agreed to contribute $1.5 million toward the purchase of a new information system to keep track of the inventory and, not incidentally, speed payments to the distributor.

Combining Academic Programs

"The hurricane of managed care, which was rushing eastward from its origins in California and the upper Midwest, seemed to lose some of its force as it approached Massachusetts," observes Dr. Eugene Braunwald, the longtime chairman of the Department of Medicine at the Brigham and now vice president for academic programs at Partners.[50] The number of beds in the Boston hospitals decreased, as predicted, but only temporarily at the Brigham and MGH, where admissions have risen and beds previously taken out of service are being used again.

Pressure for the amalgamation of the large clinical departments in the two hospitals also decreased as it became clear that in some cases more would be lost than gained by combining.[51] "This required much rethinking," says Braunwald.[50] As it happened, several of the most important chairs were being vacated just as Partners was formed. Rather than combine the large departments involved, individual chiefs were appointed to succeed Braunwald, the chief of medicine at the Brigham, and the chiefs of medicine and surgery at the General.

The departmental consolidations that have occurred under the aegis of Partners would best be described as "opportunistic," according to Braunwald,[50] and "pragmatic" according to Thier.[8] Describing his medical work as well as his administrative approach, Thier says: "I'm a physiologist, not an anatomist. Make it work, or we'll have one chief."[8]

Dr. James Mongan at the MGH sees Partners' avoiding the extremes, "not two totally separate hospitals on the one hand or smashing this thing together with one chair of medicine and surgery on the other."[45]

Dr. Michael Zinner, chief of surgery at the Brigham, feels that Partners has not driven clinical integration as much as he might have preferred. "I'd have broken a few more eggs to make the omelets, and I would have been wrong," he recognizes as he reflects upon the difficulties experienced at the merged Beth Israel and Deaconess Hospitals, just up Longwood Avenue from the Brigham.[52] The union of these other Harvard teaching hospitals has resulted in significant financial and administrative problems, as the two institutions are trying to amalgamate clinical services much more completely than has been attempted at the MGH and the Brigham. To the extent that programs have merged at Partners, many credit the widespread respect for the Partners' leadership as the stimulus that has brought some to completion.[17]

Psychiatry

Both opportunism and pragmatism applied in the case of psychiatry. The severe problems afflicting the financing of mental health care,[53] "a national disaster because of low reimbursement,"[50] have helped to pull the separate programs together "because each was bleeding," as Braunwald observes.[50] After a national search, Partners recruited Dr. Gary Gottlieb, the director of the Friends Hospital in Philadelphia and a professor of psychiatry at the University of Pennsylvania, to direct the psychiatry programs at all its hospitals: the Brigham, the General, McLean, and North Shore. The formerly separate residency training programs at the MGH and McLean were consolidated.[54]

The Brigham's psychiatric service had always been small, with the specialty having no beds or residency program. However, since integrating the Faulkner Hospital with the Brigham in Partners, the need for more psychiatric service has grown since the Faulkner operates an inpatient drug treatment program and a busy consultation service. The development of the Partners program has led to the promotion of psychiatry from its longtime position as a division of the Department of Medicine to departmental status within the Brigham.[54]

All this has made for a busy life for Gottlieb as chairman of the Partners Psychiatry and Mental Health System. The president of McLean and the chiefs at the MGH, Brigham, and North Shore hospitals report directly to him, and he has offices at each hospital. His administrative assistant "lives" at the General because "The MGH was the most suspicious of me," Gottlieb relates. He has to concentrate on "keeping my hands off running places like I used to," when he was CEO of the psychiatric hospital in Philadelphia. So he uses a lot of e-mail, sending as many as 100 messages on some days. He attends meetings at all the hospitals, "not just at Partners, where they think I'm conspiring against them," teases the psychiatrist with a professional understanding of paranoia.[54]

McLean, like most psychiatric hospitals, was losing money when Gottlieb took the job in 1998. It is still losing money but less of it, thanks to reforms he has instituted. Gottlieb finds that the Partners "political swagger" with the state and other groups has increased access to contracts for the care of the sickest and neediest patients with psychiatric disorders. He sees the association with PCHI as offering much potential for psychiatry, although so far relatively few new patients have been referred through the Partners network.[54]

Dana-Farber/Partners Cancer Care

Before the recent consolidation, adults with cancer received care separately and competitively at the MGH, the Brigham, and at the Dana-Farber Cancer Institute, a freestanding, not-for-profit facility with both an outpatient clinic and beds for patients with cancer on the Longwood Avenue campus. In the classic Harvard way, its own board of trustees directed the Dana-Farber, its professional staff carried Harvard faculty appointments, and its clinical and research programs provided opportunities for the training of Harvard medical students and postgraduates. Over the years, the Dana-Farber also developed extensive research laboratories strongly supported through successful fundraising by the Jimmy Fund, named for a child whose cancer was successfully treated there several decades ago.[55-57]*

Clinical and financial issues prevented Braunwald, when chairman of medicine at the Brigham, and others from transferring the adult beds at the Dana-Farber to the nearby Brigham and Women's Hospital. Concerned about operating a joint service that might interfere with their ability to apply expeditiously the results from research to the patients, the Dana-Farber physicians also feared that the service at the Brigham might not create the special environment cancer patients require. Neither the Dana-Farber nor the Brigham then had funds available to convert the Brigham service to care for patients with cancer.

A further consideration was that the Dana-Farber benefited financially from the money the insurers then paid for the hospital care of patients with cancer. This changed as the carriers reduced what they had paid in the fee-for-service system for inpatient care of patients with cancer, and capitated systems began to appear. "I tried for 10 years to create one inpatient cancer service for the Dana-Farber and the Brigham," says Braunwald. "The pressures had to get strong enough for this to happen."[50]

---

*"Jimmy" was Carl Einar Gustafson, who grew into a 6-foot, 5-inch, long-distance truck driver and businessman from New Sweden, Maine.[56,56a] In 1948, Gustafson, then 12 years old, received treatment for Burkitt's lymphoma — one of the few cancers in children that could then be cured — from Dr. Sydney Farber and his associates at the Childrens Hospital.[55] Farber, who insisted that reporters protect the boy's privacy, said in desperation when pressed for his name, "Well, call him Jimmy!"[57] Gustafson died from a stroke in January, 2001, at the age of 65.[56a]

By 1995, managed care was reducing referrals to the physicians at Dana-Farber. Beds no longer represented excess dollars and power, as they had when Sidney Farber founded the institute.[55] Insurers were paying less for hospitalized patients, driving oncologists and hospital administrators to appreciate that most care for patients with cancer could be conducted as well, if not better, in much less expensive outpatient offices than in hospital beds.* Furthermore, increasingly more patients with cancer were requiring complicated surgery and care in intensive care units which the Dana-Farber, not a full-service hospital, had difficulty providing.

An event that would bring about a change was not long in coming. On December 3, 1994, a *Boston Globe* health columnist died from an overdose during treatment for breast cancer at the Dana-Farber, a mishap that attracted nationwide attention.[58] Dr. David G. Nathan, a leading pediatric hematologist and the former chief of pediatrics at the Children's Hospital, who had become president of the Dana-Farber[59] in October of that year, was then able to negotiate a transfer of the adult beds to the Brigham (children with cancer had long been hospitalized at the neighboring Children's Hospital).[55] The Dana-Farber retained its license for 34 beds, and many of those caring for inpatients with cancer at the Brigham, including the oncologists, continued as Dana-Farber employees. Concurrently, the Brigham agreed to send all outpatients requiring treatment for cancer to the Dana-Farber.[60]

The MGH has about 40 beds for patients with cancer, but the number of oncology patients treated there is about equal to the number in the combined Brigham and Dana-Farber program. As we have seen repeatedly, the General's "system of care is more private practice oriented, and ours [at Dana-Farber and the Brigham] is more of a clinic-based team approach," explains Nathan.[2,55,61]

With these changes in place, Nathan turned to consolidating and improving the research, training, and clinical care of adults with cancer.[55] The Institute and Partners created Dana-Farber/Partners CancerCare, a joint venture and a constituent organization within Partners. Nathan, the CEO, describes the organization as a "virtual entity" with its own board of trustees, the members of which are selected by the Dana-Farber Cancer Institute and Partners.[55] The hospitals agreed to subscribe 2 percent of revenues from inpatient care to support the combined enterprise.

Dr. Bruce Chabner, chief of medical oncology at the MGH, was appointed chief medical officer of Dana-Farber/Partners CancerCare to

---

*Currently, more than 85% of patients with cancer receive their care in the outpatient setting.[55]

coordinate clinical care, research, training, and staffing in adult cancer at the General, the Brigham, and the Dana-Farber. Consolidating the oncology programs immediately provided a sufficiently large number of patients to allow the creation of subspecialty, disease management groups to study, improve, and make uniform the treatment of cancers of the lung, breast, gastrointestinal tract, and blood (leukemia and lymphoma). Nathan plans to establish other subspecialty groups as opportunities for recruiting more clinicians and investigators arise.[55]

Support for clinical trials in cancer has increased fourfold since Dana-Farber/Partners CancerCare was launched. Nathan likes to say that industry can now support research with "one-stop shopping" and obtain the expertise and facilities of "three institutions for the price of one."[55] The combined training program has become so popular that the faculty can recruit the "pick of the crop" to become Dana-Farber/Partners oncology fellows.[55] Furthermore, the consolidation, in Braunwald's opinion, has "imploded" rather than intensified the competition among the faculty at the constituent hospitals.[50] He believes that Dana-Farber/Partners CancerCare represents the best example of academic consolidation at Partners so far.[50]*

The productive alliance with Partners developed in spite of the Dana-Farber's maintaining independent governance. The officers of the Dana-Farber Cancer Institute see their institution prospering better as a "boutique" facility with its own niche — "being Switzerland," according to one observer[2] — and offering specialized care to a specific group of patients referred from a wide variety of sources.[55,63]† The Dana-Farber with its large research enterprise loses money from operations and must rely on the Jimmy Fund and its endowment to bring the profit and loss statement into the black.[55]

Neurology

"The most successfully integrated service at Partners by far," Dr. Martin A. Samuels, chairman of the Department of Neurology at the Brigham

---

*A further combination for advancing studies on cancer began in the fall of 1999 when the Dana-Farber and the medical school formed the Dana-Farber/Harvard Cancer Center.[62] This group will consolidate research and increase funding in the field among investigators working at Harvard and the MGH, the Brigham, and Beth Israel-Deaconess, and the Children's Hospitals.

†The Children's Hospital takes a similar point of view.[55] Discussions of merging with Partners in 1994 failed because of what a reporter from the Boston Globe described as "disagreement over merging the pediatrics programs [the MGH also has one] — and anchoring them at Children's.[63]

and Womens Hospital, describes his specialty. "Soon after Partners was formed, Anne [Dr. Anne B. Young, chief of the neurology service at the MGH] and I met over Caesar salads in her office and decided that combining neurology was the way to go. Sam [Thier, then president of the General but soon to take a leading role at Partners] clearly wanted this, and we figured anyone who did it in advance would benefit."[64]

Samuels, a graduate of the University of Cincinnati School of Medicine, had trained in medicine and neurology at the Boston City and Massachusetts General Hospitals. After directing the neurology service at the Brockton-West Roxbury Veterans Administration Hospital, which is affiliated with the Brigham, Eugene Braunwald appointed him chief of the Division of Neurology in the Department of Medicine at Brigham and Women's in 1988, an appointment that needs some explanation.

In most medical schools, neurology, although it often began within departments of medicine, gained independent status as it advanced and its training programs were separated from those in medicine.* At the Brigham, however, neurology, like psychiatry until recently, remained within the Department of Medicine because of the preference of its leaders to keep the number of chairmen small, only eight at the time of Samuel's appointment. This feature of the Brigham's organization had appealed to those leading the hospital from its founding and more recently to board chairman John McArthur, who saw this practice as one reason why the Brigham was better managed than by the "parliament of chiefs" he saw running the MGH.

Nevertheless, Samuels asked Braunwald to allow his specialty to be "promoted" into a department. The chairman of medicine told him "You'll have a department; it'll just take a while," and the president, Dr. Richard Nesson, agreed "if all went well." However, even the powerful Braunwald couldn't immediately deliver, and it took six years and the influence of Partners for a department of neurology to finally appear at the Brigham and Women's Hospital.[64†]

Samuels, an outstanding clinician-educator, repeatedly wins awards for his teaching skills. Nevertheless, readers familiar with the Harvard appointment system will wonder how someone not concentrating on

---

*Although most neurologists take medical internships, they then train in neurology exclusively, unlike such medical subspecialties as cardiology in which medical school graduates must complete training in internal medicine with two more years as medical residents before beginning cardiology fellowships.

†Unlike the neurologists, however, the neurosurgeons at the MGH and the Brigham have not come together. Their training programs remain separate. Even the potent Samuel Thier and Eugene Braunwald, Martin Samuels observes, haven't been able to consolidate these groups.[64]

research was chosen for such a senior position. The selection of Samuels, which has led to a sizable growth in the Brigham's neurology program in both clinical and research capacity — he's a consummate builder who understands the importance of basic research even though not doing it himself — was atypical for Harvard. Since the appointment was within an established department, the national, if not worldwide, search for the "best person in the field," the classic charge to those seeking a scholar for a tenured position at the university, need not strictly apply. Furthermore, since the funds necessary to procure such an individual were then unavailable, Braunwald stayed inside — also unusual at the Brigham — and picked a highly capable, respected colleague who frankly didn't cost too much and would accept the position without classical, permanent tenure.

"We've got this guy we like at the West Roxbury, and he's medically trained,"* Samuels imagines the departmental leadership thinking.[64] Appointing Samuels also avoided facing the almost certain demand of any candidate from outside Harvard for departmental status as a prerequisite for accepting the appointment.

Upon settling into his new job, Samuels detected a certain amount of dismay about his appointment from the other chiefs of neurology in the Harvard system. "How can you sit on the medical school's executive committee of chiefs of neurology with your record in research and your original nomination not by us but by an internist [Braunwald]," they implied.[64] Eventually, these problems passed, particularly as the service became a department and the success of his group became clear, but it took time. The merger of the training programs also added to the controversy among the neurology chiefs.

Before linking with Anne Young's service at the General, Samuels's trainees were part of what was called the "Longwood Neurology Program" since it involved the hospitals based near that street, the Brigham, Children's, Beth Israel, and the Veterans Administration (VA) Hospital some distance away. The MGH's program recruited its own residents and fellows separately. In playing the Partners card, Samuels and Young proposed breaking up the Longwood program, leaving the other hospitals, except for the Brockton-West Roxbury VA Hospital, on their own and thereby significantly reducing their attraction for the best applicants, who would no longer have the opportunity to train at the famous Brigham and Women's Hospital. Samuels was seen as more the villain than Anne Young, who was three miles away at the General. "It was a very unpleas-

---

*Samuels was certified in both internal medicine and neurology and could therefore "fit" into a department of medicine.

ant time. I don't think the founder of the Longwood program ever forgave me. Instead of taking care of his program, I killed it," Samuels ruefully recalls.[64] Finally getting it done required Sam Thier's saying, according to Samuels, "Don't worry. I'll just order them to do it."[64]

And it happened. The Partners-Harvard Neurology Program is, Samuels proudly boasts, the most competitive in the country. "We get the 12 residents we want, except for the occasional one who wants to live somewhere else."[64]*

Anne Young at the MGH, however, thinks "the jury is out" about the value of combining her residency with training at the Brigham and VA Hospitals. Working at several hospitals instead of mostly at the General, "The residents don't know all the faculty or each other. Some don't know who I am," says the chief of one of the most respected departments of neurology in academia. "A few have left because it isn't what it seemed to be." Although two of the subspecialty fellowships, in movement disorders and headache, have consolidated, four others are still administered separately at the two hospitals.[66]

Young also frets about the problems that arise because of differences in the business organizations at the MGH and the Brigham. "The inner workings of the motors at the two hospitals prevent our doing as much as we want." At the General, "we know how much we make exactly, but Marty has to negotiate with the hospital for each thing he needs," Young explains. "We can't get the businesspeople together. The bottom line is that we can't collaborate easily if we don't know where the dollars are. There are barriers to everything we try to integrate — acres of headaches."[66]

The merger hasn't meant only problems, however. Young praises PCHI for improving contracts for managed care and making the MGH and Brigham "stronger and [giving them] more clout."[66] She also sees the relationships established with community hospitals as benefiting her colleagues and the department. Most members of the faculty have specialized interests and relatively little time or desire to see patients with general neurological problems, the reason for most outpatient visits. If the patient and his or her doctor are willing, the department's access nurse will recommend a general neurologist at one of the Partners-affiliated hospitals near the patient's home. This keeps the patient within the Partners' family and assures that those who insist on being seen at the General can be accommodated more quickly. Referring from

---

*Not that the MGH program was a slouch before the merger. Dr. Joseph B. Martin, the MGH neurology chief from 1978 to 1989 and now dean of the Harvard Medical School, claims that his program was similarly attractive before the link with the Brigham.[65]

a teaching to a community hospital is not the conventional route, but it helps to cement relationships with neighborhood physicians, who will send downtown those patients with complicated problems in which the doctors at the General are expert.

Young, who earned both M.D. and Ph.D. degrees at Johns Hopkins and trained at the University of California-San Francisco, conducts research in movement disorders, the best-known example being Parkinson's disease. She has helped develop the Partners MGH/Brigham program in Alzheimer's and other neurodegenerative diseases. Such joint efforts, which she strongly supports, "could have been done without the merger," she believes, although the presence of Partners has certainly stimulated their creation. She senses that the pressure to force the merging of clinical units has decreased as experience shows how difficult this can be.[66]

Dermatology

Few departments so differed in size when Partners came on the scene than dermatology. Dr. Thomas Fitzpatrick had, over the course of several decades, developed the MGH program into one of the nation's largest and strongest. According to the current chief at the MGH, Dr. John A. Parrish, Fitzpatrick trained leaders in the specialty throughout the country and at the other Harvard hospitals, who turned to him for ultimate leadership in the specialty at the medical school.[67]

At the General, Parrish reports directly to the hospital director for the MGH dermatology service and to the dean of the medical school as the leader of one of the few Harvard-wide clinical departments. At the Brigham, dermatology remains a division of the Department of Medicine, as was neurology for much of its life.

"I helped the Brigham get going pre-Partners," says Parrish, who has succeeded Gerald Austen as a member of the Partners board of trustees. "Then, when Partners said 'come together,' Tom Kupper [the head of dermatology at the Brigham] said that he must build till 'we're as big as the General.' Since we're so big [at the General], why should he do this?" Parrish asks. On the Partners board, Parrish hears senior officers plead "'Think Partners,' but," he acknowledges, "not much happens."[67]

Cardiology and Surgical Services

One program that is holding out for its current separate fellowship program is cardiology at the MGH. Dr. Mark C. Fishman, the MGH chief, is not enthusiastic about amalgamating his unit's training program with that at the Brigham. "Of course, I would do it if ordered to do so, but that's not happened so far. We're so comprehensive that we can offer our fellows all the clinical experience they need here at home."[46]

The MGH program is one of the most competitive in the country. "We get everyone we want," he adds. "If our fellows want a research experience we can't offer, they can go to the Brigham or elsewhere, but most stay here and work in our labs."[46]

Fishman meets frequently to discuss marketing clinical services for both hospitals, research, and other topics of mutual interest with Dr. Peter Libby, his counterpart at the Brigham, and the chiefs of cardiac surgery, Lawrence Cohn at the Brigham and David Torchiana at the MGH. He describes the sessions as "more useful than you might think. They're friendly, cordial, and helpful." Fishman and his colleagues at both hospitals travel to surrounding communities to discuss with referring physicians what the Partners founding hospitals have to offer, "always two by two," he adds.[46]

Torchiana, who believes he was chosen to direct one of the General's most important programs in part because of his interest in the delivery of health care, thought that it would be the hospitals in the Longwood area that would merge, leaving the MGH on its own. So he was "quite surprised by the announcement of the MGH-Brigham merger." Torchiana joins those who have concluded that Partners "has kept us from killing each other. Numbers one and two coming together has been very helpful to both of us."[68]

As for merging clinical services at the General and the Brigham, Torchiana emphasizes those important differences in clinical practice that persist at the hospitals. The Brigham services are, to a significant degree, resident run, with faculty surgeons rotating on and off service. Clinical services at the General depend more upon the individual faculty members, who maintain greater personal control over the care of their patients than at the Brigham. "The MGH system is better for the clinician, but the Brigham and Women's is probably better for research because the faculty's time there is more protected," Torchiana believes. "These sort of differences make forced consolidations even more difficult."[68]

One surgical service that has consolidated, however, is orthopedics. Thanks to the coincidental retirements of the chiefs at both the General and the Brigham, Partners recruited a new chairman of orthopedics who directs the departments for Partners with associates leading the programs at each hospital.

Nevertheless, uniting surgical training programs has progressed slowly, which Torchiana believes reflects the "apprentice nature of surgical training." None of 15 colleagues favored combining the residencies when Torchiana surveyed them several years ago. Furthermore, despite the merger, the surgeons at both hospitals, full of pride for their highly competitive residencies, don't look with favor on sharing their residents with their colleagues and competitors across town.[68]

This attitude, so prevalent at these renowned institutions, helps to explain why little consolidation of surgical services has occurred despite the financial logic of doing so in such specialties as lung transplantation, where, because of the shortage of donor organs, relatively few procedures are performed each year at either hospital. At the Brigham, Michael Zinner, the surgery chief, says that whenever the possibility of closing one of these low-volume, high-end services arises the supporters "draw lines in the sand" and nothing changes.[52] "Perhaps if the finances really get bad," adds Torchiana, "more of these services will consolidate."[68]

The real agony afflicting the practitioners at the MGH is the sight of their incomes dropping. "Fees are in free fall," Torchiana protests, and "there's no force which can fight it." Most distressingly to doctors used to dominating hospitals like the MGH, "The worse the specialists fees become, the better for the hospitals and the primary care physicians."[68]

Further Integration of Training Programs, Departments, and Clinical Programs

Debate continues about the value of further combining training programs at the General and the Brigham into single Partners-administered units. Dr. John Potts, director of research at the MGH and former chief of medicine there, finds little enthusiasm for merging the residency programs in the large departments of medicine and surgery.[24] The trainees in these departments begin fresh out of medical school and benefit, many believe, from the support provided by one institution with long and treasured traditions.[24] In fellowships, the next step in their postgraduate education, the trainees are older, more experienced, and more mature and can utilize better the experiences of working at more than one teaching hospital.[24] Nevertheless, by the summer of 2000, 10 of 20 residency and 15 of 47 fellowship programs at the General and Brigham had merged.[50] Potts and his successor as chief of medicine, Dr. Dennis Ausiello, expect that most of the specialty fellowship programs will merge within the next few years.*[24]

---

*By the summer of 2000, Partners had integrated the residencies in dermatology, emergency medicine, medicine-pediatrics, neurology, nuclear medicine, obstetrics and gynecology, oral and maxillofacial surgery, orthopedic surgery, plastic surgery, and psychiatry, programs that include 288 (25 percent) of the approximately 1,130 interns and residents at the Brigham and MGH. The 15 integrated fellowships account for 143 (24 percent) of approximately 600 fellows training at the hospitals.

Potts, MGH president Mongan, Austen, and Braunwald see little likelihood that the large departments of medicine and surgery will soon combine,[24,45,50] although Braunwald anticipates uniting four or five more smaller departments in the future.[50] Mongan predicts closer cooperation developing at the MGH and the Brigham between what he calls the "commodity departments" of pathology and radiology.[45] George Thibault, the vice president of clinical affairs at Partners, and Mongan chair a clinical integration committee that prods the departments at both hospitals into greater cooperation, which Mongan sees as including further integration of training and research. However, he prefers that the changes occur "incrementally, step-by-step" and recognizes that, "although all departments have advanced, some are further along than others."[45] Also, some of the chairmen now feel "less under the gun," with Partners concentrating on the merged departments of orthopedics and mental health.[45] The territorial pride for its history and organization, particularly at the General, remains a continuing obstacle to more complete integration.[24]

Ausiello adds that there is little enthusiasm for converting into Partners "superchiefs" the leaders of the Department of Medicine's subspecialty divisions — or "units," as they are called at the MGH — such as cardiology, gastroenterology, and nephrology. Each of his unit chiefs see such a job as "impossible to do."[69] Ausiello obviously concurs, as is shown by the way he chose his successor as chief of the renal unit.* Rather than agreeing that the Brigham's chief of nephrology should also run the General's division, he appointed one of his colleagues to succeed him, in the characteristic MGH fashion of promoting from within. When a division at the Brigham or the General is stronger or has a more experienced chief, the senior physician may assume a leading role in the specialty at Partners and assist his more junior colleague at the other hospital,[69] but the nature of such a role has yet to be defined.

Denny Ausiello, with his ethnic heritage, beard, and stocky frame, hardly fits the model of the tall, slim, Boston Brahman previously thought to be typical of those who would fill one of the most acclaimed jobs in American academic medicine. He came to his current position with a B.A. in biological sciences from Harvard and an M.D. from the University of Pennsylvania, followed by internship, residency, and a nephrology fellowship at the MGH and scientific training at the NIH. As chief of the renal unit from 1984 to 1998, he sat in the chair briefly

---

*In nomenclature, as well as in other ways, the General sticks to its own traditions. *Renal* is synonymous with *nephrology,* which is the word used for kidney disease at most teaching hospitals, and the specialty groups, which are called "divisions" elsewhere, are "units" at the MGH.

warmed by Samuel Thier in the late 1960s. While performing basic research in kidney physiology, he prepared for his current position as John Potts's associate chief of medicine for five years before starting work in the widely respected position of physician in chief, medical service, at the General on September 1, 1996, the same day that Dr. Victor Dzau succeeded Eugene Braunwald as chairman of medicine at the Brigham.

Ausiello recognizes from his experience as an investigator that the formation of Partners has least affected the researchers. "Good science means working with others who are good wherever they are. However," he adds, "there are still too many silos.* Many who complain about Partners have never managed anything larger than an office or a laboratory and don't yet understand that academic medicine now requires much more systematic solutions to its problems than in the past."[69]

Although "thoughtful colleagues question whether we're moving too rapidly toward homogeneity," Ausiello doesn't think so. Furthermore, the forces at his hospital pushing for further rapid change have to some extent been vitiated by the prosperity that Partners has already helped bring to the MGH. The demand for beds and, until the 1999 fiscal year, the relative profitability of the teaching hospitals, both much greater than predicted when the dean first called together his Harvard Medical Group Planning Committee eight years ago, have reduced the pressure for further reform.

Accordingly, there seems to be little interest at any level in combining at one hospital the high-profile clinical programs that currently exist at both. Moreover, Partners has inhibited establishing such programs at the hospital without them. A good example is liver transplantation, which is only performed at the General. Michael Zinner and his colleagues in the Department of Surgery at the Brigham wanted to do this work at their hospital. His counterpart at the General, Gerald Austen, objected, and the Partners leadership supported Austen. Zinner has gone along, understanding that the shortage of donors limits the number of procedures that can be performed in the region. Nevertheless, he's not happy about the decision much as he understands the reason for it. "We lose training and spinoffs," he says, referring to the other medical and surgical work that necessarily accompanies such complicated procedures.[52]

There was even talk about limiting kidney as well as liver transplantation to the General. "This would have killed our nephrology pro-

---

*Silo has become a pejorative code word for faculty and staff members who continue standing on their own and reject integration.

gram," predicts Zinner.[52]* Brigham loyalists would also have had great difficulty accepting the loss of a procedure for which Dr. Joseph E. Murray of the Brigham staff won the Nobel Prize in 1990. Kidneys continue to be transplanted at the Brigham, where the procedure was performed for the first time anywhere in 1954.

What Zinner and his colleagues want most is what the leaders at both the Brigham and the MGH also want, to keep their institutions full-service hospitals.[69] "Collaboration, not combination," seems to be the motto. MGH president Mongan cautions, "Integration for integration's sake is not a plus but should occur wherever we can achieve lower costs and better care."[45] John Potts adds:[24]

No one from Sam Thier on down can force his way. To press too hard or too fast will set off a nuclear bomb since the doctors and the hospitals are so important and so strong. Most of the docs, I think, are grudgingly pleased that the merger occurred because of its ability to blunt the power of the insurers, who are seen as the real enemy now. We can't go back to the good old days for which some of the docs long, but nothing in the alliance prevents maintaining the traditions at each of the hospitals. So far, I think Sam is pacing it about right.

Although Samuel Thier would have preferred quicker consolidation of clinical services when the MGH and Brigham merged, David Torchiana from the MGH cardiac surgery unit now suspects that the CEO of Partners is not displeased that progress has been slow. Some, though not all,[16] of the amalgamation of the clinical services at the Beth Israel and Deaconess Hospitals aggravated the financial losses that merger has sustained.

Potts and Mongan confirm that the merger, so far, is relatively invisible to most physicians at the General[45] and has little influenced their work or reimbursements.[24,45] "It's the environment that has affected them, not the merger."[24]

One of the General's busiest and most respected clinicians, Dr. Roman W. DeSanctis, director of clinical cardiology emeritus at the hospital, agrees. "Partners has had little effect on my day-to-day practice."[70] He doesn't see the large cardiology divisions at the two hospitals merging but thinks it's only a matter of time before the

---

*Since one of the most important treatments nephrologists can offer their patients is transplantation, its absence at a teaching hospital decreases the attractiveness of the institution to such patients and reduces the value of training there.

cardiology fellowship program joins with the Brigham. "Let it happen," he says.[70]

Practice Plans

One of the first organizations to become a component of Partners was the Massachusetts General Physicians Organization, formed in 1994, the same year as Partners, to coordinate the practices of the full-time physicians at the General. At most medical schools, practice plans such as the MGPO operate under, or in close affiliation with, the dean and not primarily as organs of the teaching hospitals, as is the case at the MGH. The effort of Dean Tosteson to establish such an organization at Harvard in 1993 had helped to start the process, which led to the formation of Partners.

Like many of the other units within Partners, the MGPO has its own board of trustees, half of whom are doctors who also fill most of the positions on its executive and managed care committees. The MGPO bills for and collects the professional fees, acts as paymaster for much of the professional medical staff, and coordinates the administration of the managed care contracts developed by MGPO and Partners executives. Together with the hospital, the MGPO has developed global fees for physician and hospital services for such specialties as cardiac surgery, orthopedics, and radiation oncology.[35] Although most of the doctors in the organization are specialists, the MGPO has expanded existing, and has established new, primary care practices at the MGH and in the surrounding areas. The hospital had begun building and funding such practices before the MGPO was formed.[35]

Before Partners started, the hospitals negotiated directly with physician groups and other hospitals — for example, the General had almost completed a merger with the North Shore Medical Center, based at the Salem Hospital, before Partners was formed and subsequently became North Shore's parent. Now when an external organization wants to consider a relationship with the MGH or the Brigham, Partners takes over and representatives from both hospitals participate in the discussions.[35] Furthermore, Partners, when advised by the MGPO leadership as appropriate, conducts all contracting for at-risk, capitated patients. This hasn't fully eliminated occasional conflicts, which arise between the staff at the hospitals and PCHI over specific issues.[35]

The president and CEO of the Massachusetts General Physicians Organization is W. Gerald Austen, the chief of surgery for almost 30 years. Although he stopped operating several years ago and resigned his chief's job in 1997, Austen is as busy now as he ever was. His day still begins at 5:30 A.M., and many evenings are taken up with dinners and meetings.

The only slightly atypical feature of Austen's career is that his bachelor's degree comes from the Massachusetts Institute of Technology, where he has been a trustee since 1972, rather than Harvard College. After that, he followed a typical course: Harvard Medical School, surgical training at the MGH, and the usual service during the 1960s as a public health service officer at one of the National Institutes of Health, in his case, as a cardiac surgeon at the Heart Institute. As he continued to publish so that he would not perish — never a possibility for Austen — and accumulated offers to chair surgical departments at other institutions, his progress up the Harvard academic ladder accelerated. He became a full professor at the young age of 36. The clinical research of his early years brought him election to, among other usually surgical groups, the American Society of Clinical Investigation, a select association of young academic internists who seldom invite surgeons into their membership. The hospital appointed him chief of the surgical services in 1969.

Austen's long service at the hospital, during which he led most of the important national societies in his specialty, and his agreeable personality made him the only MGH doctor widely enough trusted to have brought the group practices of the independent-minded physicians and their chiefs together into a hospitalwide practice plan.[9,26] Before the MGPO started, each of the departments and several of the specialty groups administered their practice earnings independently, some well, some poorly.

The MGPO, has come to play, in both Austen's and other MGH leaders' opinions, "a central role in what happens here."[35] Accordingly, most of the important clinical issues that require high-level decisions are finally settled by Austen and Dr. James Mongan, the president. The General has not developed a formal physicians-hospital organization. It appears that Austen and Mongan function, in effect, as the hospital's PHO.

The Brigham, where a PHO has been functioning to contract with insurance carriers, is uniting the departmental clinical practices into one physicians organization. The practice plan will then become a constituent part of Partners.

Combining the practice plans, however, is not something Partners considers a first priority. As Jay Pieper explains, "We don't see a good lot of business advantage in doing so, relatively speaking. Not much can be saved, and besides there'll be a great deal of difficulty in the accomplishment." This would be the type of amalgamation in which the faculty would get deeply involved, with many looking on it with disfavor.[34]

Recruitment, Promotions, and Research

When a senior clinical job needs to be filled, the dean of the Harvard Medical School appoints a search committee which includes members from the Harvard hospitals and the medical school. The hospital in which the candidate will work contributes the most members.[71] Eugene Braunwald, as Partners vice president for academic programs, participates in each selection at one of the Partners hospitals. The Partners CEO, Samuel Thier, takes great interest in these choices and is considered "all powerful"[72] when the time comes to make the final selections, nominate the successful candidates for suitable faculty appointments at the medical school, and convince them to take the job.* At Harvard, it is the leaders of the affiliated hospitals and Partners, in the case of the MGH and the Brigham, who take the dominant role in selecting such high-level officials as chiefs of the clinical departments. At most other American medical schools, the dean decides whom the school will appoint to fill the chair of a clinical department from those nominated by the search committee. It is then the dean who recruits the finalist.

Braunwald also chairs the Partners committee that coordinates promotions and appointments for doctors at the Brigham and MGH to full professorships at Harvard. The committee, which meets monthly to review intensively the accomplishments of each nominee, assures that all the pertinent issues have been resolved before the nomination proceeds to the dean's office. Finances constitute one of the most important issues since the hospitals, and hence Partners, must guarantee the support of every hospital-based tenured faculty member.[50]

Braunwald, who still personally conducts studies in cardiology, talks with particular enthusiasm about Partners' effects on the research enterprise at Harvard. First, Braunwald consolidated the research administrative offices at the Brigham and General into his department at Partners. Two Partners vice presidents, with responsibility for either corporate or nonprofit sources of money, administer and help investigators develop financial support. Each reports to Braunwald, who proudly relates that the amount of money supporting research by investigators at the Brigham and MGH rose from $290 million in 1994 to more than $400 million.† Of this, $72 million is for industrially sponsored research. As an example of the useful links that Braunwald's office has developed

---

*The lure of a top Harvard job and the persuasive power of the leadership at Partners and the hospitals can be difficult for the most attractive candidate to resist.

†By the summer of 2000, research income was approaching $500 million, according to Thier.[8]

with industry, Partners has signed a nonexclusive "strategic alliance" for two years with the Genzyme Corporation of Cambridge, which will lead to collaboration in several different fields of medicine between scientists at the two institutions.[50,73] Partners investigators participate in advisory committees for the company, which gives Partners preferential support for research. Partners immediately benefited in the amount of $300,000, a grant from Genzyme for administrative expenses.

These numbers make research at Partners, according to Braunwald, "the largest not-for-profit, nonfederal research enterprise."[50] Thus, the research support at Partners is only exceeded by that of some pharmaceutical houses, which are for-profit enterprises, and the federally funded National Institutes of Health. Braunwald is now supervising the establishment of a Partners research building in Cambridge where investigators working in the Partners hospitals will collaborate in studying such subjects as genetics and AIDS.[50]

Braunwald also chairs the Partners Research Council to coordinate, develop, and improve present and future research initiatives.[50] The membership accords with the "Noah's ark principle," two-by-two for each topic, one from each hospital. He mentions as examples the Alzheimer's program, successfully led by a Brigham investigator despite the presence of a renowned program at the General, in which Partners funded a senior administrator. Others include the multiple sclerosis program, with $150,000 to $250,000 of Partners money per year to seed new projects; the genetics program, which Partners funded with about $200,000 for core laboratory equipment and for which it now sponsors two full professorships; and preventive atherosclerosis, a topic of particular interest to Braunwald, who is a cardiologist. In some programs, however, Partners has encountered some difficulty in deciding how to best spend its money. Immunology, for example, the Council finds too big for Partners funding to make a significant impression, although it did pay for a day's retreat for the investigators.

"The merger has had relatively little effect on the work of most investigators," says Mark Fishman, the chief of cardiology at the MGH, who leads a large basic science program at the Charlestown laboratories of the hospital.[46] "Historically, excellent collaborations have developed at many levels among investigators at the MGH, the Brigham, and the medical school."

Fishman is particularly excited about the possibilities in genetics. "The merger over the long term could be incredibly powerful in supporting studies in population genetics involving doctors at the MGH and Brigham and those in the network. Framingham redux," he adds, referring to the renowned epidemiological studies into the causes of coronary heart disease conducted for more than 30 years in that Massachusetts town.[46]

An important administrative merger within Partners affects the hospital-based institutional review boards (IRBs). These committees decide whether a research project should proceed. Their members ascertain whether the investigators' protocols fulfill the criteria for conducting humane human or animal studies and obtain appropriate informed consent from any patients entering the study. At Harvard, this work is conducted by the affiliated hospitals, whereas at most medical schools the committees report their findings to the dean. Braunwald consolidated this function, previously conducted separately at the Brigham and the General, at the Partners level, where two committees, with members from both hospitals, meet weekly at one or the other hospital to consider the applications. The united IRBs "have melded very well," he believes.[50]

Thier and Braunwald are convinced that the extraordinary intellectual resources of the Brigham and General investigators add value to purchasers of medical care from Partners. In negotiating with the HMOs, Thier and his colleagues make every effort to put Partners' competitors "on the defensive on quality the way they put us on the defensive on cost."[74]

Partners and the Harvard Medical School

"*Altitudinal* is the best word to describe how Partners affects the Harvard faculty," observes Dr. Daniel D. Federman, dean for medical education at the Harvard Medical School:[72]

> The higher you are, the more it affects you and the more you see its wisdom and value. Also, the more of your time it requires. I know chairmen of clinical departments at the Brigham and the General who spend close to 40 percent of their hours on Partners business. Unlike the medical school, organizations like Partners exist for commercial not academic purposes, and most clinical chairmen, at least at Harvard, are selected for their academic not their commercial accomplishments. This means that the chiefs have to distance themselves from their more traditional academic and clinical roles.
>
> For the many who are lower in the hierarchy, Partners means relatively little except as it requires some of them to work on new committees.

During the 1990s, members of clinical faculties at Harvard and other medical schools found themselves pressured to perform more clinical work, leaving less time for teaching. "This has worsened since Partners came into existence. Of course, it might have happened anyway with the pressures of managed care reducing the amount of money the clinicians can earn," Federman adds.[72]

Dr. Joseph Martin, who succeeded Daniel Tosteson as dean of Harvard Medical School in July 1997, brought his experience of helping to organize the merger between the university hospitals of Stanford and the University of California-San Francisco.* Unlike Tosteson, a physiologist, Martin is a clinician as well as a distinguished investigator in neurology. He had told Neil Rudenstine, Harvard's president, prior to his selection, that the times called for a dean "who wore a white coat and whom the students would see teaching at the bedside."[65] Martin regularly makes clinical rounds at the various Harvard teaching hospitals.

Martin sees Partners becoming more and more successful. "The Brigham and MGH are each responsible for their own finances and stand on their own. 'Each tub on its own bottom,'" per the Harvard organizational motto. Martin has also observed "a palpable reduction in competition between programs at the MGH and Brigham."[65] Yet the distance between Partners and Harvard remains as great as it was between the MGH, the Brigham, and the university before the merger.

"I doubt that Martin would tell Sam [Thier] what to do, but they wind up on the same page," Rashi Fein, the Harvard Medical School economist, comments. Fein, who has worked at Harvard since the late 1960s and has seen his share of deans in action, adds, "A lot of it is Martin's personality. He's tough but not dictatorial."[13]

The commercial purpose of Partners has stimulated the hospitals to try recruiting clinical faculty working at other hospitals affiliated with Harvard. "In the past, this seldom went on," reflects Federman, who has been at Harvard for most of his career since matriculating as an undergraduate in 1945. "We vigorously recruited from other institutions but infrequently tried to move an established Harvard faculty member from one hospital to another unless it came with a promotion or appointment not available where the faculty member was then located."[72] Now the Partners hospitals seek clinical faculty primarily to secure the patients who would come with the move. "Again, this activity may reflect the current climate as much as the development of Partners, but it emphasizes the importance of clinical income."[72]

---

*See chapters 6 and 7.

To regularize recruiting among the Harvard hospitals, Martin has developed guidelines for the clinical faculty. They specify that the dean and the Council of Academic Deans must review in advance any intra-Harvard recruitment by one of the hospitals to engage a candidate in a lateral career move without a change in academic rank, position, or responsibility.[75] The theory behind this rule is that any recruitment should fulfill the primary goal of creating "a net gain for the Harvard medical and academic communities."[75]

The Council of Academic Deans consists of senior leaders from the hospitals — Braunwald represents Partners — who meet with Martin regularly to discuss faculty issues, including joint initiatives and cross recruitment.[65] For other practical problems, Martin created the Harvard Medical Collaborative, Inc., a freestanding, not-for-profit working group of the CEOs of Partners, Children's, Dana-Farber, and Beth Israel-Deaconess, which meets monthly to plan, among other issues, the distribution of space among the medical school and the teaching hospitals. The discussions in this group helped to develop a new research building for the medical school, which will include some space for investigators based at the hospitals.[65]

In the summer of 1999, Martin announced that the medical school would give the teaching hospitals, including Partners, an additional $4 million per year from the school's immense endowment of $1.5 billion, the largest amount of any school at Harvard.* As long as the stock market cooperates, the school will support the hospitals with this amount for five years.[76] "Over the past year," Martin was quoted as saying in the *Boston Globe,* "we've seen that many of our best teachers are also the most busy trying to earn their living by seeing patients. . . . Each time they step aside to see students or lecture, that puts increased pressure on their livelihood."[76]

Governance

Supporting Partner's claim that its association with the member hospitals is an affiliation and not a merger, is the persistence of more than 30 boards of trustees within Partners.[45] The problems inherent in this anomaly have led to a recent reevaluation of the governance of the hospitals as they relate to Partners.[77] The basic questions in each case were which board has authority over what and what happens when they disagree?[10,35] Among the more practical issues was the complaint from many of the

---

*Harvard's total endowment was $13 billion in the summer of 1999.

senior people that attending the meetings of the multiplicity of boards was taking too much time.[10]

At the MGH, the formation of Partners created a third tier of boards. At the bottom were the separate boards responsible for activities at the general hospital on Fruit Street, the McLean (psychiatric) Hospital in the suburb of Belmont, the Spaulding Rehabilitation Hospital in downtown Boston, and the Massachusetts General Physicians Organization. Each of these boards reported to the second (or middle) tier, the 12-member board of the Massachusetts General Hospital Corporation. The top tier, of course, was the board of trustees of Partners.

Colloredo-Mansfeld, the MGH chairman, favors merging the board of the general hospital into that of the MGH Corporation, the 12-member size of which was established by the state charter establishing the hospital.[10] He also believes that physicians should fill some of the positions on the MGH board. Even though few doctors had served as trustees in recent decades, the lay trustees and the professional leadership had usually worked together closely and confidently. Now, however, he says that the doctors must have a voice at the top.[10]* This should help relieve some of the angst of the practitioners, who are joined by the rest of the professional staff in strongly believing that the MGH is, and should continue to be, an "M.D.-led enterprise."[35] Looking toward the MGH's future as well as its past, Colloredo-Mansfeld envisions a compact between the trustees and the doctors in which the role of the professional leadership will continue, as it does now, to recruit and appoint for the MGH the best physicians available, who would then "come, work, and be the best."[10] The trustees will develop the resources needed to bring this about.[10]

At the Partners-owned North Shore Medical Center, a separate board of trustees (second tier) runs this combination of the Salem Hospital north of Boston, a children's hospital, a rehabilitation hospital, and the Visiting Nurse Association of Greater Salem. Reporting to the North Shore board, a third-tier board is responsible for the Union Hospital at Lynn which had merged with North Shore in 1997.[78] The reorganization plan would merge the Union and North Shore boards.

The founders of Partners deliberately left vague several aspects of the governance of their creation,[10,35] even though the primacy of the Partners board and its executives was clearly evident to anyone who understood the situation. Some physicians, particularly at the MGH, bridled at the presumed loss of important prerogatives to the people at the Pru. "No question, there was a lot of ambiguity about how the

---

*By the fall of 1999, the size of the MGH board was being increased to 14 members, three of whom would be physicians.[10]

hospitals would relate to Partners at the beginning," Dr. James Mongan, the MGH president, observes.[45] "Many of our doctors still ask, 'Is Partners controlling or just helping?,' but no one says 'let's get out.' They want us to shape Partners, not kill it."[45]

Mongan doubts that the top hospital boards will ever disappear.[45] Several have been around for a long time — the MGH's since 1811. Although few in authority in 1993–94 wanted to fully integrate the assets of the hospitals into one corporation, this construction appealed to some trustees and executives who were prepared to "take our lumps now" during the governance debates of 1997–98.[5] Nevertheless, it seems unlikely that such a basic reconstruction of the arrangement binding the hospitals will occur.[5]

One issue that the Partners leaders must deal with is the agitation among some MGH doctors, concerned about their hospital's losing authority, who want to make sure that a sufficient number of MGH trustees serve on the Partners board. Although the General's trustees seem less concerned about this than the doctors are, the controversy illustrates the advantage of greater overlapping of trustees among the membership of the three boards — Partners, the MGH, and the Brigham.[5] The disadvantage is that some trustees would have to attend even more meetings.*

What If There Were No Partners?

By the end of 1999, Partners had been operating for almost six years. What would have happened if the MGH and the Brigham had never united? One thing that probably would have occurred is that James Mongan would not have become the CEO of the MGH. It was only because the top job at Partners was available for Sam Thier in 1996 that the presidency of the MGH opened, and who would have thought that the executive director of the Truman Medical Center in Kansas City would have been chosen to fill the slot?

Mongan is a Californian, born in San Francisco and educated at Berkeley and the Stanford Medical School. With an early but prescient interest in medical administration and public health, he interned at the Kaiser Hospital in San Francisco and, after duty with the Public Health Service, worked in Washington for 12 years at the Senate Finance Com-

---

*To comfort the doctors at the founding hospitals, the board decided that a majority of the members of the nominating committee for election of Partners trustees will be MGH or Brigham physicians.

mittee and as Assistant Surgeon General in the Carter administration. When Carter was defeated, "I had to find some real work to do,"[45] so he went to the Truman Center, the old Kansas City General Hospital and the principal teaching hospital for the University of Missouri-Kansas City School of Medicine. Later, with "no one else wanting the job,"[45] he became dean of the medical school as well.

Mongan acknowledges that he was an "unorthodox hire for the MGH. Most people in Boston think Kansas City has little to teach them."[45] Nevertheless, he seems to have absorbed the MGH mystique quickly while maintaining an appropriate reserve about its more flamboyant characteristics. An affable, experienced, and able executive, his press among the leaders and troops at the hospital and at Partners is uniformly excellent.

Mongan believes that without the merger Boston would have seen furious financial competition between his hospital, the Brigham, and the other hospitals in the region, which would have been injurious to all.[45] Furthermore, the hospitals separately could never have influenced the economics of health care in the region as effectively as when operating together. Although each hospital would have developed primary care networks separately, it is unlikely that the total result would have been as effective or as large as the Partners' PCHI program.[45] The hospitals would never have realized the savings and efficiencies from combining the back offices, and the General would not have benefited from linking its information systems to the more effective Brigham program. Of course, Mongan acknowledges, "the average doctor or staff member doesn't appreciate this. They just see the glitch in their paychecks when the amalgamation hits a snag."[45]

Gerald Austen, the president of the Massachusetts General Physicians Organization and former chief of surgery, believes few at his hospital really want to scuttle Partners.[35] "The outside things — our increased clout in the market, PCHI, the other groups which have joined us — have gone quite well." He acknowledges, however, that solving the "internal things" has been more difficult. As always, it comes back to the doctors. "Some docs just aren't too thrilled. They firmly believe that the MGH is a very special place and resist anyone having real authority over them."[35]*

Most of the privately practicing doctors at the General, few of whom underestimate their skills, see Partners as succeeding principally because the doctors are so good.[69] Dr. Dennis Ausiello, the chief of the

---

*Other observers, less circumspect than Austen, suspect that some MGH doctors hold their institution to be "God's gift to the world."

medical services at the MGH, heard one claim that Partners "brings the paper clips together, but the doctors make the system work."[69] This comment suggests that some attitudes will take a long time to change in the absence of more economic pain affecting the doctors' income. Nevertheless, "by any benchmarks, Partners has been a success," concludes Ausiello, "even though not all parts are working perfectly or even hospitably." He asks, "Assuming that there is a local culture worth preserving, can the system preserve that culture and succeed? The verdict is still out. Partners is still too young, and the pressure is not really on."[69]

Despite what a few doctors claim, business at the hospitals and for the physicians would certainly be less were it not for the creation of Partners.[8]* At the MGH, 40 to 50 percent of the referrals to specialists in the Department of Medicine now come from PCHI physicians.[69] Even though some of the doctors in the PCHI network were referring to MGH specialists before Partners was founded, many more are now doing so.[69] The bed census in the hospitals "didn't come back till PCHI was there to help," adds Sam Thier.[8]

One project that Partners does not plan to initiate, however, is a network of specialists or what Ausiello calls, somewhat incongruously, "PCHI for specialists." Rather, he says:[69]

We've recently formed an MGH subspecialty development committee to win friends among community specialists by helping all of us to better coordinate disease management. This should lead to the MGH functioning increasingly as "a hospital without walls." The mantra for this approach should be "it's the system, stupid" rather than solely "it's primary care, stupid."

---

*At the end of 1999, managed care constituted 70 percent of the market in Boston, and Blue Cross hadn't increased its reimbursement for physicians since 1991.[8]

Part 2
NewYork-Presbyterian*

The following people are discussed in chapter 4, "Formation," and chapter 5, "Development."

(Cornell = Weill Medical College of Cornell University; CPMC = Columbia-Presbyterian Medical Center; NYH = New York Hospital; NYP = NewYork-Presbyterian Hospital; NYPHCS = NewYork-Presbyterian HealthCare System; P&S = Columbia University College of Physicians and Surgeons; PH = Presbyterian Hospital. Most titles are those held when the individual was interviewed or mentioned.)

Name	Position
Al-Awqati, Qais, M.D.	Chief, Division of Nephrology, P&S
Alonso, Daniel R., M.D.	Senior Associate Dean for Medical Affairs, Cornell
Antman, Karen H., M.D.	Chief, Division of Oncology, P&S
Ascheim, Robert, M.D.	Chief Executive Officer, Physician Partners Company
Barchas, Jack D., M.D.	Chairman, Department of Psychiatry, Cornell
Beal, M. Flint, M.D.	Chairman, Department of Neurology, Cornell
Behrman, Richard E., M.D.	Senior Vice President for Medical Affairs, Lucile Packard Foundation for Children's Health, Palo Alto; former Dean, Case-Western Reserve School of Medicine
Berman, Michael A., M.D.	Director, NYP; Executive Vice President, NYPHCS

*The spelling NewYork-Presbyterian is correct. *New York* becomes one word and is joined to *Presbyterian* with a hyphen according to the latest (summer 1999) naming convention for the merger (see chapter 5).

Bickers, David R., M.D.   Chairman, Department of Dermatology, P&S

Blauer, Joanne   Associate Dean and Secretary, Cornell

Bolwell, Harry J.   Former President, PH

Burke, Daniel B.   Cochair, Board of Governors, NYPHCS

Burke, Kathleen M., Esq.   Secretary and Counsel, NYPHCS

Coleman, D. Jackson, M.D.   Chairman, Department of Ophthalmology, Cornell

Corwin, Steven J., M.D.   Senior Vice President and Chief Medical Officer, NYP

Crystal, Ronald, G., M.D.   Chief, Pulmonary Division, Cornell

Daly, John M., M.D.   Chairman, Department of Surgery, Cornell

DeBuono, Barbara, M.D.   Chief Executive Officer, NYP Healthcare Network; Executive Vice President, NYPHCS

Dick, Harold M., M.D.   Former Chairman, Department of Orthopedic Surgery, P&S

Driscoll, John M., Jr., M.D.   Chairman, Department of Pediatrics, P&S

Edelman, Isidore S., M.D.   Director, Columbia Genome Center; former Chairman, Department of Biochemistry, P&S

Emond, Jean C., M.D.   Director, Center for Liver Disease and Transplantation, P&S

Farber, Saul J., M.D.   Dean, School of Medicine; Provost, Medical Center; Chairman, Department of Medicine, all at New York University

Farrell, Nancy L.   Chief Administrative Officer, Cornell Physician Organization

Fein, Oliver T., M.D.   Associate Dean, Network Affairs, Cornell

Feinberg, David A.   Vice President, Marketing, NYP

Ferguson, A. Hugh   Director, Doctor's Offices, NYP, Presbyterian campus

Fischman, Donald A.   Professor of Cell Biology, Cornell

Gersony, Welton, M.D.   Director, Pediatric Cardiology, Babies and Children's Hospital

Gotto, Antonio M., M.D., D.Phil.   Dean, Provost for Medical Affairs, Cornell

Greenberg, Maurice	Member, Board of Governors, NYPHCS; former Chairman, Board of Trustees, Presbyterian
Grusky, Morton	Deputy Vice President for Budget and Finance, P&S
Hedge, Arthur J., Jr.	Member, Board of Governors, NYPHCS; former Trustee, PH
Hirsh, David, Ph.D.	Chairman, Department of Biochemistry and Molecular Biophysics, P&S
Hogstrom, Harold	Senior Vice President, Hospital Financial Services, NYP
Hyman, Allen I., M.D.	Chief of Staff and Chief Development Officer, Public Relations, NYP
Isom, O. Wayne, M.D.	Chairman, Department of Cardiothoracic Surgery, Cornell
Kelly, Robert E., M.D.	Chief Operating Officer, Presbyterian; former Chief Medical Officer, NYH
Klein, Arthur A., M.D.	President, New York-Presbyterian HealthCare Network; Vice Chairman for Administrative Affairs, Department of Pediatrics, Cornell
Kligfield, Paul, M.D.	Professor of Medicine, Cornell
Knowles, Daniel M., MD	Chairman, Department of Pathology, Cornell
Lavan, John	Executive Vice President, Finance, NYPHCS
Leahey, Michael E.	Director, Clinical Trials Unit, PH
Ledger, William J., M.D.	Chairman, Department of Obstetrics and Gynecology, P&S
Leiman, Joan M., Ph.D.	Executive Deputy Vice President for Health Sciences, P&S
Lewis, Linda D., M.D.	Associate Dean, Student affairs, P&S
Libby, Dan, M.D.	President, Society of Practicing Physicians, Cornell
Lieberman, James S., M.D.	Chairman, Department of Rehabilitation Medicine, P&S
Lobo, Rogerio, M.D.	Chairman, Department of Obstetrics and Gynecology, P&S
Lodge, Henry S., M.D.	General internist, P&S
Lory, Marc	President and Chief Executive Officer, Eastern Connecticut Health Network,

	Inc.; former Chief Operating Officer, PH
Mack, John J.	Cochairman, Board of Governors, NYPHCS; former Chairman, Board of Trustees, PH
Martin, Kathryn	Senior Vice President, Hospital Operations, NYP
McGillicutty, John F.	Co-Chairman, Board of Governors, NYPHCS
Michels, Robert	Dean (1991–96), Cornell
Miller, Edward	Chief Executive Officer, Johns Hopkins Medicine; Dean of the Medical Faculty, Johns Hopkins University School of Medicine
Morrell, Martha J., M.D.	Director, Columbia Comprehensive Epilepsy Center, P&S
Morris, Marcia C., Esq.	Former General Counsel, PH
Morris, Thomas Q., M.D.	Vice Dean, P&S
Mundinger, Mary O., DrPH	Dean, Columbia University School of Nursing
Nachman, Ralph L., M.D.	Chairman, Department of Medicine, Cornell
New, Maria, M.D.	Chairman, Department of Pediatrics, Cornell
O'Donnell, Kathleen D.	Associate Dean, P&S
O'Quinn, Marvin	Chief Operating Officer, New York Hospital site; former Chief Operating Officer, PH
Pardes, Herbert, M.D.	Dean, Columbia University College of Physicans and Surgeons
Pedley, Timothy, M.D.	Chairman, Department of Neurology, P&S
Perales, Cesar A.	Senior Vice President for Community Health Services, NYP
Pile-Spellman, John	Director, Interventional Neuroradiology, PH
Prager, Kenneth M., M.D.	Clinical Professor of Medicine, P&S
Puchner, Peter, M.D.	Former President, Society of Practitioners, P&S
Quaegebeur, Jan M., M.D.	Director, Pediatric Cardiac Surgery, NYP, based at Babies and Children's Hospital

Reuter, Louis	Executive Vice President, Administration, NYPHCS
Rose, Eric, M.D.	Chairman, Department of Surgery, P&S
Rowe, John W., MD	President and Chief Executive Officer, Mount Sinai NYU Health
Rowland, Lewis, M.D.	Former Chairman, Department of Neurology, P&S
Rubin, Moshe, M.D.	President, Society of Practitioners, P&S
Scalzi, Guy L.	Senior Vice President, Information Services, and Chief Information Officer, NYPHCS
Schley, W. Shain, M.D.	Chairman, Department of Otorhinolaryngology, Cornell; President, Medical Board, NYP
Schwartz, Allan	Director, Cardiac Catheterization Laboratories, PH
Serfling, Aubrey	Chief Operating Officer, Columbia-Cornell Care
Shelanski, Michael L., M.D.	Chairman, Department of Pathology, P&S
Silverstein, Samuel C., M.D.	Chairman, Department of Physiology and Cellular Biophysics, P&S
Skinner, David B., M.D.	Vice Chairman and Chief Executive Officer, NYP and NYPHCS; former President, NYH
Smith, James, M.D.	Clinical Professor of Medicine, Cornell; Medical Director, Columbia-Cornell Care
Smith, Leighton B., M.D.	Primary Care Medical Director, Physicians Organization, Cornell
Solomon, Robert A.	Chairman, Department of Neurosurgery, P&S
Sostman, Dirk, M.D.	Chairman, Department of Radiology, Cornell
Sparer, Cynthia N.	Executive Director, Babies and Children's Hospital
Speck, William T., M.D.	President and Chief Operating Officer, NYPHCS and NYP; former President, PH

Spivey, Bruce, M.D.	President and Chief Executive Officer, Columbia-Cornell Care
Tapley, Donald F., M.D.	Senior Deputy Vice President, P&S; former Dean, P&S
Tenenbaum, Joseph, M.D.	Assistant Chairman for Clinical Affairs, Department of Medicine, P&S
Thompson, Keith, Esq.	Chief Legal Officer, NYH
Vecchione, George	President and Chief Executive Officer, Lifespan, Inc.; former Executive Vice President and Director, NYH
Wang, Christopher M., M.D.	Director, Family Medicine Service, NYP
Wazen, Jack J., M.D.	Associate Professor of Clinical Otolaryngology, P&S
Weisfeldt, Myron L., M.D.	Chairman, Department of Medicine, P&S
Williams, David O., M.D.	Director, Interventional Cardiology, Rhode Island Hospital; Professor of Medicine, Brown University
Wolk, Michael J., M.D.	President, Cornell Independent Practice Association

CHAPTER 4

Formation

The view through the windows in the office of Dr. William T. Speck on the fourteenth floor of the Atchley Building* of the Columbia-Presbyterian Medical Center faces the broad expanse of the Hudson River and New Jersey to the west and the length of Manhattan Island to the south. The view to the north showed Speck his deeply troubled responsibility, the Presbyterian Hospital in the City of New York, which he had led as president since 1993. To survive and continue its missions of healing, research, and education as the principal teaching hospital of Columbia University's renowned College of Physicians and Surgeons, Speck firmly believed that Presbyterian, one of the largest and most famous teaching hospitals in the country, could no longer stand alone.[2]

Financing Medical Care in New York City

The market in which Speck was working and worrying differed from most others. Managed care had barely invaded Manhattan compared to much of the rest of the country. Eli Ginzberg, the Columbia University health care economist,[3] ascribes this to the absence of manufacturers who employ large numbers of workers needing health insurance, the cost of which HMOs can reduce by decreasing payments to hospitals and doctors.

"We have many affluent corporations," says Ginzberg, which "don't care much about the costs of health care because they have so few employees" compared to what the companies earn. "Among our largest employers are nonprofits like Columbia and NYU," both of which run large medical establishments, and whose leaders, Ginzberg has found, "don't push this business. Furthermore, the hospitals have been full, so the local HMOs have not been as able to successfully lean on them."[3]

Furthermore, compared to other communities, Manhattan has been slow in developing offices unassociated with the teaching hospitals,

---

*The Atchley Building was long known as the Atchley Pavilion. It contains doctors' and administrative offices and the Irving Cancer Center.[1]

which can offer advanced care to outpatients less expensively than hospitals.[3] "The real estate values are prohibitively high," explains Ginzberg, which discourages doctors and medical administrators from opening such projects.[3]

Manhattan, the borough where the hospitals discussed in this part of the book are located, abounds in sophisticated, well-educated people who are often quite rich. "They demand high-class medical care from their physicians and hospitals," says Ginzberg, without the cut-rate, often inconvenient features that may accompany managed care. Consequently, "We have a very high proportion of M.D.s, particularly specialists and subspecialists, many of whom work in the academic medical centers that enjoy high prestige.[3] We're very big spenders compared with other places," Ginzberg adds.[3]

New York devotes 20 percent of its economic power to health care compared to about 13 percent of the gross national product of the country as a whole. Despite its financial problems, however, Ginzberg finds New York City's medical finances "an acme of stability compared with Boston or Philadelphia."[3]

Deregulation: Speck to the Rescue

For decades, a New York State agency had sustained hospital rates, which prevented the market from lowering rates as was happening elsewhere. However, on January 1, 1997, New York would stop this practice, and Presbyterian's income would drop further as the insurers, now free to negotiate rates, paid less for care at the Columbia-Presbyterian Medical Center.[4] "There will be competition, conflict and war between the academic centers. They won't all survive — and I worry none will survive," Speck told a reporter in one of his more gloomy moments.[4] "Nobody likes to use the word 'closure' [for the closing of hospitals] — they talk about re-engineering, consolidation. I worry that we will end up with a group of mediocre institutions."[4]

Would deregulation ravage the academic supremacy of the medical center as the Peloponnesian wars devastated the ancient Athenian culture, Speck, the classical Greece aficionado, wondered?[4] "I have heard him fret that without a merger Presbyterian could be on the slippery slope to bankruptcy," remembers a colleague.[5]

"Merging was almost a religious principle with him," recalls another.[6] "Bill felt Presbyterian had to be part of a 10-ton gorilla to fight off the inevitable."[6]

At Presbyterian by the early 1990s, the red ink was flowing broadly. To repair its predicament, the hospital trustees had consulted with Harry

F. Bolwell, a Cleveland manufacturer who had been chairman of the board of trustees at the University Hospitals there. The presidents of Presbyterian changed, not for the first or last time — one lasted only three months — and finally Bolwell, then in his midsixties and retired from being CEO of his billion-dollar business, was hired as president for a limited term. In 1992, Bolwell recruited Speck, whom he knew from Cleveland, as Presbyterian's chief medical officer, executive vice president, and candidate to succeed him as president.[7,8]

Speck, a distinguished academic pediatrician, graduated at the top of his class at Bowman Gray School of Medicine in North Carolina in 1968 and obtained one of the highly competitive residency positions at the Babies Hospital of the Columbia-Presbyterian Medical Center. "As an intern, he knew everything about every patient on his service, even those for whom he wasn't directly responsible," remembers Dr. Allen Hyman, Speck's faculty supervisor in the intensive care unit.[2] "He was a crew-cut, red-haired* workaholic, a tough chief resident but superb, and everyone had tremendous respect for him."[2]

After completing his training, the Department of Pediatrics gave Speck one of the cherished faculty appointments at P&S. He performed research in infectious diseases at Columbia and later at Rainbow Babies and Children's Hospital of Cleveland, where medical students at the Case-Western Reserve medical school train in pediatrics. In 1982, Speck became chairman of the Department of Pediatrics at Case-Western Reserve, where his dean, Dr. Richard Behrman, was pleased with his leadership, seeing Speck as "an effective chairman."[9] Two years later, Speck was appointed CEO of the Rainbow hospital, reporting for this function to the president of the University Hospitals of Cleveland.

In New York, two other senior executives besides Speck were competing to become Presbyterian's CEO. Members of the faculty at Columbia saw Bolwell and the board "setting it up for the three to 'duke it out,'" recalls Dr. Edward D. Miller, then chairman of anesthesiology at Columbia (1986–94) and now dean of the Johns Hopkins University School of Medicine.[10] "The board was made up of hard-nosed businessmen who saw the Presbyterian leadership as unable to make decisions. The faculty to them were just employees."[10] This way of doing things, Miller adds, "was an anathema to the Columbia culture, particularly when compared with the tenure of Tom Morris, who represented what Columbia-Presbyterian Medical Center was all about."[10†]

---

*Speck's hair is now pure white.

†Dr. Thomas Q. Morris, vice dean of the medical school, was president of Presbyterian from 1985 to 1990. Dr. Herbert Pardes, the P&S dean, describes Morris as "honor and truthfulness personified."[11]

"Miller had this place figured out," believes Dr. Michael L. Shelanski, chairman of pathology at P&S. "He realized that Presbyterian should become a 700-bed institution, not 1,100 as we are now. If we'd done what was necessary, we wouldn't have had to merge," Shelanski believes.[12]

Bolwell interviewed many well-known executives to succeed him in running one of the country's most prominent teaching hospitals. For one reason or another, each was either found inadequate or, if offered the job, turned it down. Then one morning, Bolwell recalls, "I went into the office at 7 A.M. feeling rather badly. The next thing that happened was bypass surgery, and someone had to be appointed."[8] Speck was there and rapidly learning the job under Bolwell's tutelage,[8] and he was chosen. Thus, a year after moving back to New York City from Cleveland, William Speck became president and CEO of Presbyterian and inherited the leadership of a famous hospital in dire financial straits.

History of the Presbyterian Hospital and the College of Physicians and Surgeons of Columbia University[13]

The Presbyterian Hospital in the City of New York, despite its celebrated reputation, is not a particularly old creation. On January 2, 1868, James Lenox, the inheritor of a fortune made by his father, a Scottish immigrant, sent a letter to 32 other prominent New York citizens, observing that:[13] "The City of New York has many General Hospitals . . . but the large and influential body of Presbyterians has no such institution of this kind under its care." This pleading led to the formation of a Board of Managers for the building of a hospital "under the auspices of Presbyterians . . . for the Poor of New York without regard to Race, Creed, or Color."[13] Lenox, whose personal collection of books would later constitute a major part of the New York Public Library, donated the land, originally bought by his father, between Madison and Fourth (now Park) Avenues and 70th and 71st Streets on which to build the new hospital. From its opening on October 10, 1872, with 36 beds, the Presbyterian Hospital would remain on the east side of Manhattan until the building of the Columbia-Presbyterian Medical Center in the 1920s.

The medical school with which the name of the Presbyterian Hospital in the City of New York — there are Presbyterian Hospitals in many other American cities — would become irrevocably linked began as part of King's College in November 1767. Only the College of Philadelphia's medical school, founded two years earlier, was older. Early graduates of the two schools received bachelor's degrees. In 1770, after further study, Robert Tucker, one of the original King's College graduates, was awarded the colonies' first doctorate in medicine, which subsequently became the standard degree awarded to medical graduates in America.* When King's College, which closed during the Revolution, reopened as Columbia College, few medical students matriculated, and, after several decades of haphazard function, the medical school closed.

Meanwhile, in 1807, the Medical Society of the County of New York received permission from the legislature and the regents of the State University to incorporate a College of Physicians and Surgeons as a proprietary medical school owned by its founders. Four years later, the new school absorbed the faculty of the medical college of Columbia College, marking the end of medical instruction at Columbia for 80 years. In 1860, P&S, the name by which the school has long been known, severed its relationship with the regents, gained the right to grant degrees and elect its own trustees, and allied itself nominally with Columbia College. The presidents of both P&S and Columbia signed the graduates' degrees.

When P&S made overtures to Columbia for a genuine affiliation in 1878, the majority of the Columbia trustees, fearing that the financial demands on the college would be too great, refused the offer.† Finally, in 1891, Columbia College's desire to become a university prompted its agreeing to absorb the medical school. P&S transferred assets of $1,653,000 to Columbia, which assumed full financial and legal responsibility for the medical school. P&S reserved the right to nominate its own staff and refuse to admit women, a restriction that continued until 1917.

Before the link with Columbia was completed, the Vanderbilt family, heirs to the New York Central Railroad fortune, offered in 1884 to fund a new medical school building and construct for P&S a women's hospital, bearing the name of a son-in-law, William D. Sloane, and an outpatient clinic with the Vanderbilt name, all on a large plot of land at Tenth Avenue between 59th and 60th Streets on the west side of Manhattan. Attempts by P&S to associate with Roosevelt Hospital, located across 59th Street from the medical school, failed when the Roosevelt board, influenced by members who strongly opposed opening the hospital to students, rejected the overtures in 1908 and again in 1910 by the narrowest of margins. If this connection had developed, as historians of the period have observed, the renowned establishment in upper Manhattan would be known as the Columbia-Roosevelt Medical Center.

---

*The M.D. degree was, and remains, in English universities a graduate medical degree awarded after preparing a thesis based on research.

†More recently, Columbia would reject the opportunity of owning Presbyterian Hospital for the same reason.

The union of P&S and Presbyterian was principally due to the influence and resources of Edward Stephen Harkness (1874–1940),[14] an heir to the immense fortune in Standard Oil of one of the early partners of John D. Rockefeller, Sr. Harkness had been one of the leading Roosevelt Hospital trustees pressing for the connection with P&S, and, when this failed, he resigned from the Roosevelt and joined the Presbyterian board. After presenting a detailed plan for affiliation to his new associates and offering to fund the construction of buildings Presbyterian needed, Harkness prevailed. The terms of the connection gave the P&S faculty the right to nominate all members of the Presbyterian professional staff — a fundamental feature of the relationship between most medical schools and teaching hospitals but, as we shall see, a topic of continuing and recent controversy.

Basic to Harkness's plan was the eventual physical union of the medical school and the hospital, then on opposite sides of Manhattan, with Harkness money as an important stimulus. After considering property between 66th and 67th Streets along the East River — just south of the land on which the buildings of Presbyterian's eventual partner, the New York Hospital, would rise — and a location near the Columbia University campus on Morningside Heights, Harkness and his associates settled on an "up-and-coming neighborhood"[15] called Washington Heights on the site where the team that became the New York Yankees once played baseball from 1903 to 1912.[16] The space obtained was large enough to fulfill Harkness's current dreams and allow future expansion. To further cement the relationship between P&S and Presbyterian, Harkness arranged for Columbia to own some of the hospital's land and Presbyterian some of the property of the medical school. Furthermore, the agreement included no provision allowing for a divorce of the institutions.[17] This was "all part of Harkness's genius," according to Dr. Lewis P. Rowland, chairman of the Columbia Department of Neurology from 1973 to 1998. "This has prevented the hospital from pulling out as it has tried to do over the years."[17]

Harkness chose the architect James Gamble Rogers to design his medical center. Rogers's first commission for Harkness was a mansion for his family built in 1908 at the corner of Fifth Avenue and 75th Street in New York City and now the headquarters of the Commonwealth Fund, which Harkness founded. Subsequently, Gamble designed a large dormitory complex and tower* that the Harkness family had contributed to Yale University, their mutual alma mater.

---

*The Harkness Memorial Quadrangle at Yale now includes Branford and Saybrook Colleges.

Gamble's design for the medical center was unique for its time. Hospitals, until then, had been "low, sprawling complexes organized around a central core in which each ward occupied its own wing."[18] Gamble devised the first skyscraper hospital. The north wing, which faced 168th Street, housed the medical school. The south wing, in a higher tower of 21 floors, contained the 400 beds of the Presbyterian Hospital. A "stem," originally containing doctors' offices, connected the hospital and medical school buildings.

After much delay, the country's first medical center opened in 1928 with P&S and the Presbyterian Hospital, the Sloane Hospital for Women, and the Vanderbilt Clinic physically linked to each other. Babies Hospital, a large pediatrics hospital, and the Neurological Institute, for neurological and neurosurgical patients, also joined the center. Later, the Institute of Ophthalmology, endowed by Edward Harkness (1933), and the New York Orthopedic Hospital (1950) were added.[19] The state of New York built a Psychiatric Institute staffed by the medical school's psychiatrists and researchers adjacent to the main structure. In honor of the family that had led the effort, the pavilion for private patients bore the Harkness name, where for decades the wealthy and famous from New York and elsewhere came to be treated.[18]*

Leading a Hospital in Desperate Financial Condition

Presbyterian Hospital had lost money over the years, but contributions from Harkness and other wealthy donors usually made up the deficit, and the losses were petty compared to the deluge of the 1980s. Critical to the new financial problems was servicing the huge debt acquired to construct the long overdue replacement of the 1920s hospital with the Milstein[†] Hospital Building for inpatients, which opened in December 1988[1] across Fort Washington Avenue from the original structure. The building had cost about $500 million and was $100 million over budget.[20]

Furthermore, even though managed care was only approaching New York, the Diagnosis Related Group (DRG),[21] or prospective payment system, established in 1984, dramatically changed how Medicare

---

*The Harkness Pavilion for Private Patients at the west end of the complex allowed, as the author of a book describing the architecture of the medical center wrote, "a direct entrance from the more quiet Fort Washington Street for the more genteel patients" compared to bustling Broadway to the east, which the public clinic faced.[18]

†Pronounced as if it were spelled "Milsteen."[1]

reimbursed the hospital for the care of its patients.[20] Instead of paying for each individual service provided to a patient, the DRG system paid a fixed amount for each hospitalization, depending on the patient's diagnosis.[22] This method of reimbursement set prices for various diagnoses and procedures[4] at levels that were less than Presbyterian needed. Presbyterian's doctors and staff had difficulty reducing the amount of time patients were spending in the hospital to the levels dictated by the payment schedules for particular diagnoses. Besides, "New York State was months behind in paying its bills for patients on Medicaid," Harry Bolwell remembers.[8]

Nevertheless, competition, which would have lowered rates further, was buffered by New York State's continued regulation of what hospitals were paid, insulating hospital executives to some degree from paying adequate attention to wasteful operations[23] while pressure from HMOs was growing since the regulated rates applied only to traditional insurers.[4] The growing losses led to the appointment of five chief executive officers, four chief operating officers, and five chief financial officers during "five years of total chaos."[20]

The hospital that Dr. William Speck was called on to lead in 1993 had lost more than $20 million per year for more than five years and more than $56 million in 1992 alone.[7,20] The hospital was in technical default of its mortgage, no more borrowing seemed possible, some vendors had stopped delivering supplies, vital repairs were postponed, and the employees faced the threat of payless paydays.[7] At one point, the hospital had $35,000 in the bank while confronting a $10 million weekly payroll.[20] The hospital was "in a desperate situation — days from closing," according to Dr. David B. Skinner, then president and CEO of the New York Hospital, the principal teaching hospital for the Cornell University Medical College on the east side of Manhattan and eventually Presbyterian's partner.[24] Actual closure was unlikely in view of Presbyterian's critical functions in the community, but the possibility existed that the state of New York or the federal Department of Housing and Urban Development, which backed the debt, would take over the hospital and appoint its own management.

Speck hired a new senior management team — seen as the sixth by critics in the hospital and medical school.[20]* "The job actually was less difficult that it might have seemed," according to Harold Hogstrom, whom Speck had recruited as his chief financial officer from a similar job

---

*"We changed administrators as often as the people change socks," jests Dr. James S. Lieberman, chairman of the Department of Rehabilitation Medicine and associate dean for clinical services at P&S.[25]

at Long Island Jewish Hospital.* This was not the first time that Hogstrom had considered working at Presbyterian. Two years before, one of the former CEOs has approached him about taking the same job, but friends had advised him not to proceed "because of the mess."[20] This time, however, Speck's enthusiastic approach to fixing what had eluded others convinced Hogstrom to move uptown as one of two executive vice presidents.[20] "What I most like about Bill [Speck]," explains Hogstrom, "is his extraordinary vision; he spends much of his time thinking about the future."[20]

Dr. Robert A. Solomon, the chairman of neurosurgery, agrees. "Speck's certainly a visionary, and he turned the place around."[5]

"What had to be done was obvious," says Hogstrom.[20] The largest savings came from reducing the work force by about 10 percent. Almost 500 employees were laid off, the total reduction equaling 771 workers.[20] Refinancing the mortgage and the outstanding short-term loans at lower interest rates also produced substantial savings.[7] The receivables then served as the collateral for an additional loan.[20]

As his chief operating officer, Speck recruited Marc Lory, then CEO of University Hospital in Newark. "The board gave us a clear mandate: 'Get the financial bleeding under control,'" remembers Lory.[26] One of his more unpleasant tasks was saying no to the clinical chairmen when they asked for hospital funds to support programs they favored. "The hospital had become the playground of the medical school, and we could no longer afford it."

Lory and Hogstrom — "we worked arm-in-arm," remembers Lory — restructured the way the employees "reported into the system. The organization had lost control. No one knew who had authority for what.[26] We gave the administrators of the Milstein building, Babies Hospital, and the Allen Pavilion [Presbyterian's community hospital] targets for reductions and told them to ask the question, 'If we eliminate it, how would it affect revenue?' We created a vacancy committee, which reviewed all positions which opened up to see how much attrition could help us."[26] The unions posed less of a problem than was feared. "We sat down with their leaders to work out how to avoid losing new workers who were good," says Lory. "With unions, seniority rules. You just have to work within the confines of the contract."[26]

---

*Hogstrom had come to Speck's attention through Cynthia Sparer, Speck's chief operating officer at Rainbow Babies and Children's Hospital in Cleveland. Sparer knew Hogstrom through her position as administrator of the Children's Hospital at Long Island Jewish. Speck would later appoint Sparer administrator of the Babies and Children's Hospital at Columbia-Presbyterian.

The hospital proceeded to subcontract* services such as food ser-vice, housekeeping, and parking to independent vendors.[7] The hospital's unions prevented more extensive outsourcing, and consequently the amount of money saved from this action was relatively small.[20] New invest-ments in administrative departments were limited to those that would pro-vide a quick return such as improved billing systems and more effective methods of collecting money owed to the institution.[7] Billing and collect-ing had become particularly serious problems. For example, bills couldn't be processed for New Jersey Medicaid because the 1970 era computer sys-tem could not accommodate the code required for patients from that state, which was one number longer than that for New York residents.[20]

"Those were great days," remembers Allen Hyman, Speck's former teacher, whom he appointed Presbyterian's chief medical officer. "The quartet, Marc [Lory], Harold [Hogstrom], Bill [Speck], and I, met three times a day. We got it done. My job was to bring the doctors on board."[2]

Lory took a leading role in increasing the hospital's income. "We were losing market share to New York Hospital and Mount Sinai [Hospi-tal]. Even first-class community hospitals in Westchester County and New Jersey were taking business away. We had to increase market pene-tration," he recalls.[26] "We went to the medical staff, and they helped us identify where the community doctors were sending their patients. To pull this off, we had to form a network."[26]

Networks at the Presbyterian and New York Hospitals

Presbyterian had no formal arrangements with community hospitals when Speck and his team took charge in 1993.[2†] The deals he arranged were "soft," what Allen Hyman calls "handshake affiliations,"[2] confirm-ing that the hospitals shared the same values — "rather like apple pie."[2] Typically, Presbyterian would dispatch one of its doctors, a medical spe-cialist or pediatric surgeon, for example, to perform a consultation or operation at the community hospital. The affiliated hospital or the patient would pay on a fee-for-service basis. The arrangement promoted good-will between the institutions and led to some referrals to Presbyterian. However, no money passed between the community and university hospi-tals and Presbyterian had no authority over the community hospitals, unlike the tighter arrangements that New York Hospital was developing.[2]

---

*The term would be *outsource* in current business parlance.

†P&S had teaching relationships with Harlem and St. Luke's-Roosevelt hospitals in Manhattan, but Presbyterian was not a part of these arrangements.

"We decided to link up with higher quality hospitals, those that were strong clinically and financially," says Harold Hogstrom, Presbyterian's chief financial officer at the time.[20] "Such hospitals were secure enough on their own not to need being taken over by places like us." We couldn't afford then to invest in troubled hospitals with financial problems anyway."[20] Lory adds, "In any event, we spent a lot less in developing our networks than New York Hospital had to."[26]

"The biggest challenge [in developing the network] was dealing with the medical school," Marc Lory found. "Even though Pardes [Herbert Pardes, the P&S dean] was supportive, it was often difficult to convince our doctors to go to the community hospitals in the numbers they wanted. We were, however, able to convince some departments to sign contracts with the hospitals and deliver circuit riders from their faculties. When this happened, our market share rose."[26]

At New York Hospital, David Skinner began building his network in the early 1990s. He appointed George A. Vecchione to lead the project. "Quiet and amiable,[27] a beacon of sanity,"[25] Vecchione "served as the glue which made many of Skinner's projects work,"[27] Presbyterian officers recognized.[25,27] Skinner had hired him as executive vice president and director of The New York Hospital from a large medical-school-affiliated community hospital in suburban Westchester County where Vecchione had been president and CEO for 12 years.

"The network was fundamental to our need to rebuild the hospital," remembers Vecchione, now president and CEO of Lifespan of Providence, Rhode Island, which owns several large hospitals, including the principal teaching hospitals for the medical schools of Brown University in Providence and Tufts University in Boston.[28] New York Hospital was about to build a new inpatient building, analogous to the Milstein inpatient facility at Presbyterian.

"To convince the board to accept the debt that the new construction would require, David and I had to demonstrate to the governors that the project would be relevant to the health care needs of the year 2000 and beyond. We all felt that the link to the community hospitals had to be more solid than in the past — a corporate long-lasting relationship."[28] In the beginning, the hospitals that the team approached wouldn't sign on. "Then the Booth opportunity came up."[28] The Salvation Army, which owned this community hospital in Queens, wanted to divest itself of its hospital activities. "So we replaced the Salvation Army as its sponsor.* Other hospitals took note and started to show interest."

The successful Methodist Hospital in Brooklyn, with more than 400

Sponsor is the euphemism New York Hospital uses for *owner*.

beds filled with patients, desired stronger academic ties through under-graduate and graduate teaching programs so as to upgrade its status. Its CEO also "felt that 'stand alones' couldn't continue to stand alone, and he wanted to pick his partner" rather than be picked, remembers Vecchione. New York Hospital brought in the Flushing Hospital (now New York Flushing Hospital) across the East River to protect its "flag-ship" in Queens with 500 beds less than one mile away.[24] The United Hospital Medical Center of Portchester in Westchester County also joined, wanting to relate to a system that would provide several benefits, including a strategy for dealing with managed care.[29] Building its new hospital partially on the site of the venerable Payne-Whitney psychiatric pavilion required that New York Hospital purchase the Gracie Square Hospital to provide facilities for patients formerly treated at Payne-Whitney. When these patients returned to New York Hospital and its new Greenberg Pavilion in 1998, Gracie Square remained within the network.[29]

Looking for a method "of forming *real* connections with the commu-nity hospitals, Skinner convinced them to accept a sponsored relation-ship with New York Hospital," remembers Dr. Arthur A. Klein, a pedi-atric cardiologist who joined Vecchione in 1995 to help develop the network.[29]* The New York Hospital became the sole member of the community hospital boards — a change not requiring regulation from New York State — which gave the New York Hospital the right to appoint the board members of the sponsored hospitals. However, in each case most of the community hospital's trustees remained in place, with the addition of a few members from the New York Hospital's board "for communication."[29] Skinner and his team told the community hospitals' leaders, "We believe in local autonomy with the community board run-ning its hospital, and we won't interfere."[29] Although theoretically New York Hospital could replace the members of a community hospital board if they headed "in the wrong direction," Skinner realized that the news of doing so would quickly get around and reduce the likelihood that members of other boards would agree to take their hospitals into the network.[29] The "common bond" formed among members of the boards at the sponsored and teaching hospitals has facilitated banding together for managed care contracts.[29]

What did the leaders of the community hospitals anticipate in be-coming a sponsored hospital of the New York Hospital network?[29] Many

---

*Klein is also executive vice chairman of the Department of Pediatrics at the Cornell University Medical College, which is connected to the New York Hospital as P&S is to Presbyterian.

needed capital, and New York Hospital could supply this. Involving New York Hospital's administration in some of their administrative and financial operations could produce savings because of the size of the larger operation. Joining a winning, prestigious, medical institution like New York Hospital-Cornell increased the community hospital's prestige and also allowed it to establish academic relationships with educational and public relations value. And, of course, a recurring reason for such unions was the opportunity to obtain managed care contracts negotiated by a large organization able to obtain more competitive rates than the smaller community hospital could negotiate.

New York Hospital acquired the relationship with most of the sponsored hospitals without directly investing capital. In the cases in which funds were transferred, most of the money was loaned. Many of the network hospitals consolidated at New York Hospital such services as financial analysis and planning, plant and materials, telecommunications, food, legal, and consulting. "We price these services slightly below what the community hospitals would have to pay on their own, but the volume makes them profitable for New York Hospital, something up to $10 million per year," Klein calculates.[29] As time passed, however, the connection between the teaching and the community hospitals became increasingly "about relationships" rather than specific services, Klein has observed.[29]

The chief financial officers at each of the sponsored hospitals report to John Lavan, Skinner's chief financial officer, as well as to the CEOs of their hospitals. Lavan and members of his staff also serve on the finance committees of the sponsored hospitals. This allows Skinner and his officers to closely monitor the finances at each of the network hospitals as revenues drop and "we enter the white waters," as Arthur Klein describes the coming financial problems.[29]

New admissions of about 4,000 patients per year have increased the annual income at New York Hospital by $30 to $40 million thanks to referrals from doctors, particularly those paid on a full-time basis, at the sponsored hospitals who previously sent their patients elsewhere.[29] "These patients have complicated problems where we can really help," Klein observes, "and they're very profitable for the hospital."[29]

Other successes of the sponsorship program include improved local financial stability at both the community and university hospitals, enhanced competence of the medical staffs, and enriched graduate medical education. *Outcomes,* the trade word for "results of treatment" are beginning to improve.[29] So far, however, the integration has been more horizontal than vertical, there has been little assimilation among the doctors, and the main discussions continue to center on bricks and money.[29] Financial management remains more decentralized, and the entities still act more independently than the difficulties of the future may require.

The network, and later the merged hospitals, would support Skinner's vision in which his hospital must convert from an academic medical center, which concentrates on treating each patient, to an academic health system, which would also change the health status of an entire population.[30]

At Presbyterian, meanwhile, Marc Lory, the chief operating officer, and Bill Speck concentrated on building their affiliated hospital program. "We looked for high-quality, cost-effective community hospitals. We felt that owning hospitals, as George [Vecchione] and David [Skinner] were doing at New York Hospital, was not the way to go," says Lory. "First of all, we didn't have the capital to repair other places. Although you may call it a loan, the medical center has to supply the cash to bail out the hospitals it sponsors, and several in the New York Hospital network were financially marginal at best. Of course, when we started, New York Hospital was in better shape than it had been and than we were and could afford to invest. It was quite a time," he remembers.[26] "We'd come out of the [community hospital] CEO's office and there in the waiting room were David and George or the people from Sinai."

Even after working in the New York market for six years, Lory still doesn't see the advantage of sponsorship. "The nature of the ownership does not change the physicians' referring patterns, and you can always use joint ventures to link up programs."[26]

Community Patients

Reflecting a long-held conviction, Speck reached out to potential patients of the local community, thought in the past to be a liability, and worked to convert them into an asset. Washington Heights, the northern strip of Manhattan immediately surrounding Presbyterian Hospital, had long been home to recent immigrants: Irish and Greeks in the 1920s and 1930s, Jews throughout the twentieth century and particularly during the 1930s and 1940s,* Puerto Ricans and Cubans in the 1950s and 1960s, and Dominicans beginning in the 1970s. Many came to the emergency departments and clinics of Presbyterian and Babies hospitals on the Columbia-Presbyterian campus for their medical care.

Comfortably middle class when the Columbia-Presbyterian Medical

---

*The presence of so many refugees from Hitler's Germany led to the region's acquiring, at one time, the nickname "the Fourth Reich."[31]

Center opened, Washington Heights had increasingly become the home of an economically deprived population "overwhelmed by HIV, crime, and drug dealers."[32] Fortunately, the neighborhood had recently improved, and the burden of offering medical care to the most indigent and deprived had lessened.[32] By the 1990s, the typical Presbyterian Hospital clinic patients were young, fundamentally healthy, hard-working immigrants, mostly living in families, employed, and upwardly mobile.[2,32] All too many, however, were very sick ("train wrecks"[2] in medical jargon) and uninsured.

The hospital sponsored its own Medicaid HMO and enrolled many of the local residents. Speck claims that by vigorously applying the principles of preventive medicine Presbyterian doctors reduced the incidence of adolescent pregnancy, AIDS, tuberculosis, and admissions to the hospital for asthma to levels not matched in any similarly sized area in New York City.[7]

To receive approval from New York State to replace the hospital, which had been designed in the 1920s and was woefully outdated, Presbyterian agreed to construct a second hospital to serve the local population. The Allen Pavilion, Presbyterian's community hospital, opened in 1988 north of the medical center just across the Harlem River from the Bronx on land owned by Columbia University and near its football stadium, Baker Field.[33] With the Milstein Hospital Building replacing the original hospital, Presbyterian would have about 1,100 beds, 300 of them at the Allen Pavilion.[34]*

The Allen Pavilion had not prospered. The state, which then set the rates hospitals could charge, had allowed Presbyterian to include in its charges funds needed to repay the mortgage, providing, of course, that the hospital's beds were filled. Throughout the 1970s and 1980s, each of the community hospitals in the area was forced to close, leaving the Columbia-Presbyterian Medical Center as the only source of hospital and clinic care for most of what was becoming an increasingly poverty stricken population. Before then, the local hospitals relieved the medical center of much of this responsibility so the faculty could get on with their academic work. Now the financial turmoil brought many more desperately poor patients to Presbyterian's doorstep.[27]

Despite these environmental changes, the Allen Pavilion remained underutilized.[33] A division of Presbyterian Hospital,[17] with medical

*In January 2000, the Columbia-Presbyterian campus operated 723 beds in Milstein and 212 in the Babies and Children's Hospital. There are 206 at the Allen Pavilion.[34] The New York Hospital on York Avenue operates about 770 beds and the Westchester Division about 230 beds for psychiatric patients.[24]

center house officers and students working there, the community hospital did not attract enough patients, many of whom continued to prefer the medical center for their care.

Treating patients in teaching hospitals — as we have seen in Boston and as is the case elsewhere — whether in beds or in emergency departments and clinics, was becoming very expensive compared to caring for them in freestanding outpatient clinics and community hospitals. The advent of managed care for Medicaid patients threatened further reductions in the amount the hospital could collect for the care of these patients. Speck was determined to reduce these inappropriate costs at the medical center and believed that in doing so he could simultaneously improve the care of the local population. To manage this effort, he hired Cesar A. Perales as his senior vice president for community health services and president of the hospital's ambulatory care network corporation.

Perales, a lawyer, not a doctor or hospital administrator, had spent most of his career in government service. He had been President Carter's assistant secretary for human development services, later commissioner of the New York State Department of Social Services under Governor Mario Cuomo, and, before coming to Presbyterian, deputy mayor for health and human services in the Dinkins administration. The founder, president, and general counsel of the Puerto Rican Legal Defense and Education Fund, Perales earlier in his career had been a neighborhood legal services lawyer.

Perales increased the number of community health centers from the three small clinics set up when the Allen Pavilion was built to eight larger and better-equipped units augmented with health education, family planning, and the information systems needed to link them together.[33] New York State helped by raising the Medicaid rate as an incentive for hospitals to develop more community-based facilities for outpatients. To deflect the more acutely ill patients from the overcrowded and expensive emergency departments at the medical center, he created an urgent care center two blocks away. Perales staffed the center and the clinics with emergency medicine and primary care physicians dedicated to working in the community, whom he paid on a full-time basis. Many were recent graduates of the highly competitive Presbyterian and Babies hospitals' residency training programs.[33]

Perales next attacked the dismal situation at his community hospital. He aimed to convince the residents of the community to look on the Allen Pavilion as "Presbyterian outside Presbyterian,"[33] their local hospital, which they could choose for the care of most of their illnesses with Presbyterian always available for their more complicated problems.[33] To be successful, he would have to treat an unhealed wound, continuously reopened by conflict between the hospital and its medical school, which would appoint the professional staff of the Allen Pavilion, a subsidiary of the principal teaching hospital for P&S students.

From the earliest days of their association, only physicians on the P&S faculty nominated by the medical school could receive one of the prestigious, highly valued positions on the staff at Presbyterian. Now the hospital's financial need to associate with the local physicians conflicted with the medical school's desire to limit membership on the faculty to doctors whose training and accomplishments could be authenticated at medical schools and hospitals known to the school's leadership. The private physicians in the area declined to care for more poor patients, even though by the 1960s these patients were eligible for Medicaid, because the program, then and now, reimburses physicians poorly.[35] This was not the case for the hospitals where Medicaid paid reasonably well. Consequently, the Medicaid population flooded the clinics and emergency rooms of the medical center, eventually the only hospital remaining in the area.

The private physicians who had remained in the community were for the most part graduates of foreign medical schools* whose credentials might not have ordinarily been seen as adequate for them to admit and care for their private patients at the esteemed Presbyterian Hospital. Nevertheless, these were the doctors who were providing the care for many of the patients whom Perales wanted hospitalized at the Allen Pavilion. A compromise was reached. The better-qualified local primary care physicians were given admitting privileges to the Allen Pavilion with the understanding that they would turn over the care of their patients who required specialty care or hospitalization at Presbyterian to members of the full-time staff.[36] Meanwhile, the patients at the Allen Pavilion would benefit from the assistance of the Presbyterian house staff and the full-time clinic physicians working there. To further improve relationships, the hospital created a Presbyterian Hospital Physician Service Organization through which physicians from the community meet regularly with Perales and other members of the hospital staff to develop means of supporting their office practices.[33]

Another contention between the school and the hospital involved the management of the clinics. Traditionally at Columbia-Presbyterian, the medical school's departments supervised, often poorly according to

---

*American-trained physicians, among others, often call foreign medical graduates *FMGs,* sometimes used as a derogatory term. The currently favored and more "correct" term is *IMGs,* meaning "international medical graduates."

hospital officers, many of the activities in the clinics. The Vanderbilt family had endowed these clinics for P&S before the school became affiliated with Presbyterian. When several of the hospital's clinics moved out of the medical center buildings, Perales's department took over their management. Any problems that now occur in these clinics can bring onto Perales the wrath of physicians from the relevant academic clinical departments.

From 1993 to 1998, visits by community patients to the expensive emergency departments at Presbyterian and Babies hospitals dropped by 25 percent. Admissions of community patients, more economically cared for at the Allen Pavilion, also decreased at Presbyterian and Babies.[33] At the Allen Pavilion, growing numbers of patients, most of whom were admitted by the community physicians and the increasingly busy full-time staff in the Presbyterian-owned clinics and urgent care center, filled most of its beds. The finances at the Allen Pavilion changed from losing money to breaking even.[33]

Presbyterian benefited from the state's decision to delay deregulating the rates Medicaid was paying for the care of outpatients. Soon, however, the effects of managed care — bringing a potential $10 million loss to the hospital if fully instituted[37] — would also be applied to this group and would put another strain on the hospital's financial ability to treat its community patients. Furthermore, as the care in the clinics and Allen Pavilion improved, the patients' length of stay in the hospital shortened, putting at risk the pavilion's recently achieved high census. To counter this painful but desirable development, which was also occurring at Presbyterian, where the length of stay had been longer than at many of the other New York City teaching hospitals, Perales and his colleagues looked to the nearby lower Bronx, where he launched a marketing effort to attract new patients to the Allen Pavilion. Proud of what he and his associates have accomplished, Perales says, "We have something to teach the folks at New York Hospital [which would later become Presbyterian's partner] about delivering primary care to the residents of lower income working communities."[33]

Another feature of Speck's commitment to provide effective primary care for the residents of the Presbyterian community was his establishment of a family medicine program in the hospital. Family practice or family medicine is the successor to the general practitioner of distant memory. Family physicians train in approved residency programs for three years in the medical and psychological care of entire families, including adults of both genders and children. Many also deliver babies. Family physicians, therefore, consider themselves the primary care doctors of families.[35]

Although family medicine, as an organized form of medical work, has had difficulty establishing legitimacy in some of the older, private medical schools like Columbia and Cornell, as of the end of 1999 all but nine of the country's 124 medical schools had departments or divisions of family medicine.[35]

Many patients now turn to family physicians for their primary care. HMOs actually favor family practitioners in this role, since they tend to treat their patients more efficiently from the HMO's point of view, which sees them as ordering fewer tests and requesting fewer consultations than physicians from other disciplines.

Speck selected Dr. Christopher M. Wang to direct his new Presbyterian-sponsored program in family medicine.[35] Educated at Amherst College and the Boston University School of Medicine (M.D., 1980), Wang trained in a residency in social medicine and family medicine at the forward-looking Montefiore Medical Center in the Bronx. Beginning in 1990, he directed the residency training program in family medicine at the Catholic Medical Center of New York before coming to Presbyterian four years later. In 1996, he received a Master of Public Health degree in health policy and management from the Columbia University School of Public Health.

Wang and his 11 physician colleagues work in a community office site north of the medical center and supervise house officers training to become family physicians. The first class completed its three-year residency in June 1999. Patients requiring hospitalization are usually admitted to the Allen Pavilion, where the group supervises the care of 10 to 20 patients throughout the year. The family physicians also have admitting privileges at Presbyterian and Babies hospitals.

For his clinical work, Wang reports to Dr. Walid Michelen, the director of ambulatory care for the hospital, and to the dean of P&S on the academic side. In the absence of a department of family medicine at the school, he and his colleagues hold academic appointments in the Department of Medicine. This somewhat anomalous administrative structure, in which the family physicians report primarily through the hospital rather than the medical school for their clinical work, reflects the greater desire of Speck, at the time, to bring such a program to Presbyterian than the desire of the leaders of the school to establish a department of family medicine or for the departments of medicine or pediatrics to emphasize primary care.[35] In the future, Wang plans to operate more than one community site; improve the quality and increase the size of his training program, which now admits six residents each year for the three-year program; institute electronic medical records for his group; advance his group's research abilities — three of his colleagues are now funded—and, of course, achieve departmental status in the medical school.[35]

P&S versus Presbyterian

Although the interconnected Presbyterian Hospital and Columbia University College of Physicians and Surgeons separately own most of the land and buildings they occupy, they share many services such as steam, the telephone system, and the backbone of the computer system. The school and hospital are jointly rehabilitating the original Neurological Institute building, which Presbyterian owns, into administrative offices and research laboratories. The Milstein Hospital Building now receives the inpatients formerly hospitalized there. The state of New York, which recently built a stunning new Psychiatric Institute overlooking the Hudson River,[16] sold to Columbia its old building, which is being converted to house the School of Public Health.[16]

Even though these two renowned institutions have been locked in a physical and functional embrace for more than 70 years, skirmishes between them seem to have been a relatively frequent occurrence. When in 1944 the hospital director, claiming that the neurology and neurosurgery services were "not being administered satisfactorily," forced the single department to split, the dean at the time, Dr. Tracy Putnam, resigned. The gist of his complaints sound familiar: "All who are familiar with the situation of the Administration of the hospital to take over functions of the University such as nomination to staff positions and supervision of research . . . ."[38]

Dr. Charles A. Flood, in his unpublished history of P&S, written in 1989, reports that: "The hospital tried to change the [appointment] arrangement in 1946 and 1950. The University did not agree, and the original plan was maintained."[38] In 1948–49, Presbyterian wanted to consolidate at Presbyterian the pathology laboratory at Babies Hospital. The chairman of pediatrics, Dr. Rustin McIntosh, wrote a letter to university president Dwight D. Eisenhower objecting to the change and enclosing his resignation. According to Flood, "Apparently this was followed by diplomatic activities at the highest level."[38] The lab stayed where it was, and McIntosh withdrew his resignation.

Presbyterian presented a fundamental solution to these perpetual conflicts in 1995 when its leaders offered to sell the hospital to Columbia University. "I went to Henry King [the chairman of the Columbia board] and told him it was his for a dollar," remembers John J. Mack, a leading member of the Presbyterian board.[39] "We'll [the Presbyterian board] resign, and you can appoint a group from your board to run the hospital." However, worried that taking on the Presbyterian debt might lead to invasion of the university endowment, the Columbia trustees backed away, and the sale never materialized.[39]

"It wasn't packaged right," believes Michael Shelanski, the P&S pathology chairman. "The problem was that, although the Columbia endowment could have been legally protected from hospital losses, could the university as a good citizen of the city avoid bailing out the hospital if that became necessary?"[12]

Speck's administration as Presbyterian CEO, while it rescued the hospital from financial losses, disaffected some of the P&S faculty. Although Speck's sometimes abrasive personality accounted for some of the problems, "Anxiety about the coming of managed care was more important in alarming the medical school leaders about where the hospital was going," believes Lewis Rowland, then chairman of the Department of Neurology.[17]

Among those troubled by Presbyterian's progress was Dr. Edward D. Miller, the chairman of anesthesiology and vice president of the Executive Committee of the hospital's Medical Board, who objected to Speck's attempt to give admitting privileges to hospital nurses in 1993. Feeling that he was being "pushed aside" and prevented from influencing the future of the medical center, Miller responded quickly to an offer to become chairman of anesthesia at Johns Hopkins, a lateral career move.[10] To try to convince him to stay, Herbert Pardes, the P&S dean, took Miller to the university offices in the Low Library on Morningside Heights to meet with the president and the chairman of the Board of Trustees of Columbia University. Despite three hours of talk, as Miller remembers it, he decided to leave, "an easy choice for me; I didn't feel part of where Speck was leading Presbyterian."[10] Three years later, Edward Miller became dean of the Johns Hopkins School of Medicine and CEO of Johns Hopkins Medicine, which made him the leader of the Johns Hopkins Hospital as well as the medical school.[10]

After Miller left, Presbyterian did grant admitting privileges, as requested by Dr. Mary O. Mundinger, dean of the Columbia School of Nursing, to selected advance practice nurses without objection from other service chiefs.[40] Mundinger observes that Miller "might have had a high antibody level about admitting privileges for nurses because of the traditional controversy among [physician] anesthesiologists versus nurse anesthetists."[40] Presbyterian hospital continues to employ nurse anesthetists.[40]

Washington Heights versus Morningside Heights

For decades, the leaders of Columbia University, 50 blocks south on Morningside Heights, controlled the finances of the medical school while providing relatively little support to the dean of P&S.[41] The university kept downtown the comptroller function, the tuition income, and, most importantly, the indirect funds that granting agencies paid for the underpinnings of the laboratories — the heat, light, cleaning, telephones, computing systems, and other services needed by the investigators to perform their work.

The departments at Columbia's College of Physicians and Surgeons had long flourished as decentralized, entrepreneurial enterprises,[42-44] much as at the Massachusetts General Hospital, admired by many P&S leaders as a model of successful academic independence.[44] Since the P&S deans found themselves unable to support, in substantial amounts, the plans of the department chairmen and their colleagues to develop faculty and programs, departmental success depended upon the faculty's developing this highly independent administrative culture.[45] Fortunately, the quality of the professoriat and the work performed by the investigators were sufficient to win support in increasing amounts from the granting agencies, while the reputation of the medical center attracted well-insured, and in some cases wealthy, patients to help finance the clinical departments and pay the practitioners.

Downtown, the university administrators — as the P&S people saw it — concluded that the success of the medical center faculty allowed them to spend some of the surplus generated by the overheads to support university-based programs such as the graduate faculties.[44] At the medical center, the faculty and the chairmen, necessarily raising most of their own funding, became used to hustling for their resources without the help or dominance of the university or the dean.

When Pardes took charge in 1988, the physical plant was aging,[16] the school was spending more than was wise from its endowment, and a restless faculty knew that too much of the school's income was "going south" to the university.[41] Pardes was able to dismantle this arrangement by insisting, when he accepted the deanship,[11] that within three years the medical school would obtain greater autonomy from the university.[41,45] The tuition income and the overheads would then stay uptown, with of course the obligation to pay for the services formerly covered by the university from this income. Also, the new dean's tax on clinical income and an assessment Pardes imposed on gifts would not be detoured downtown.[45] The effect of these changes, and the success of Pardes's fund-raising efforts during the 11 years of his deanship — the endowment grew from $230 to $804 million and the number of endowed professorships from 43 to 96[11] — has allowed the school to recruit more talented faculty, repair and renovate some of the facilities, and further develop educational and clinical programs.

Pardes also became the senior university official on the Washington Heights campus. As vice president for health sciences, the deans of the schools of dentistry, nursing, and public health report to him. "An improvement,"[44] reflects Dr. Donald Tapley, dean of P&S from 1973 to 1984, since formerly conflicts inevitably arose between the dean and the vice president, who could be caught between the politics of the school and those of the university.[46,47]*

Similarly, it is difficult to find much criticism of Herbert Pardes, the current P&S dean, among members of his faculty and staff, even when they are given the opportunity to speak off the record. He is seen as an optimistic, energetic, and dynamic leader, an effective consensus builder and administrator who actively participates in such external organizations important to the medical school as the state government in Albany an various federal agencies. Pardes has led the three professional organizations to which doctors in his position belong: the American Association of Chairmen of Departments of Psychiatry (president, 1986), the American Psychiatric Association (president, 1989–90), and the Association of American Medical Colleges, the "dean's club" (chair, 1995–96).

"For all his strengths," one of his admirers observes, "he's not seen as someone who really understands science. I'm not criticizing. That's not his career." Pardes's Brooklyn days may explain why a close colleague describes him as being "street smart, a real scrapper and hard fighter."

Pardes first came to P&S in 1984 as chairman of the Department of Psychiatry and director of the Psychiatric Service at Presbyterian Hospital and the New York State Psychiatric Institute. He earned his B.S. degree at Rutgers University and his M.D. at the State University of New York College of Medicine in Brooklyn. He then trained in psychiatry at King's County, the immense municipal teaching hospital in Brooklyn, and in psychoanalysis (1965–70) at the New York Psychoanalytic

---

*Tapley suggests that the loss of income from P&S indirect costs was one of the reasons why Columbia University sold the land under Rockefeller Center, which it had owned since the university moved there in the nineteenth century before building the Morningside Heights campus 100 years ago.[44] Tapley, who died on December 16, 1999,[47] is much admired by the senior faculty who worked with him. One characterized him as "an excellent dean, the model of the aristocratic WASP"[73] thought characteristic of the P&S clinical faculty in those days. A basic scientist describes Tapley as "devoted to Columbia, with a strong commitment to science, which is the engine driving everything around here."[46]

Institute. In 1972, at the age of 38, he was appointed to the first of four chairman/director positions at his own medical school (chairman of psychiatry, 1972–75), then at the University of Colorado (chairman, 1975–78), the National Institute of Mental Health (director, 1978–84), and finally Columbia (1984–).

"Herb's very good at making deals. After all, he's a psychiatrist," observes his colleague, James Lieberman.[25] Again, perhaps because of his training, "Herb can say no and make you feel good about it," observes Dr. David R. Bickers, the chairman of dermatology.[48]

Seen by others as a "political animal," not a "detail man," Pardes micromanages to the extent that "all power is retained by Herb," according to one of his admirers, which may account for his keeping the psychiatric chairmanship while also serving as dean. His colleagues don't talk much about this anomaly, although one member of the senior faculty observed, "Herb's not giving up psychiatry defies me. It's not healthy, but no one makes a big deal of it."

Despite his keeping the two jobs, his administrative colleagues praise his ability to delegate effectively.[41] The P&S faculty particularly admire Pardes for his fundraising, for engineering the transfer of fiscal authority from the university to the medical school, and for being "the most accessible dean in the country."[12]

For whatever reasons, Pardes and his medical school have filled many of its recent openings for departmental chairmanships with inside candidates, which, as we have seen, is the custom at the Massachusetts General Hospital, so admired by many Columbia faculty. Does this practice, however, reflect in part inadequate resources to attract candidates from elsewhere, and consequently does it reduce the opportunity of bringing in leaders who might, as Michael Shelanski, who came to P&S from the outside, suggests, "shake things up"?[12]

Speck Looks for a Partner[49]

To complete his merger, Speck knew that he had to make a more compelling case to his board than "I, Bill Speck, want to merge."[50] Accordingly, he engaged consultants and hired Marcia C. Morris as general counsel to help develop a persuasive strategy.[50] Morris, who had recently completed a degree in health care administration at Harvard's Kennedy school, had previously worked as a lawyer and executive in the for-profit sector. She enjoyed, however, one distant connection to the challenges she faced at Presbyterian. While attending Boston University law school in the early 1970s, Ernest Haddad, later general counsel to the Massachusetts General Hospital and now Partners, was an associate dean.[50]

Although capitated fees were yet to invade Manhattan in appreciable amounts, most hospital administrators anticipated the problem arriving soon.[32] Speck and the consultants he hired further believed that only by merging could Presbyterian finally bring its costs under control by unifying administrative and financial operations.

Presbyterian and NYU

One of the first teaching hospitals with which Speck tried to merge was the Tisch Hospital, an important site for training medical students and house officers at the New York University (NYU) School of Medicine, whose largest affiliate is the city-owned Bellevue Hospital. Tisch, formerly called the New York University Hospital, had been renamed for the wealthy family dominant in NYU affairs.

Dr. Saul J. Farber, who, as NYU's dean and provost, then led both the medical school and the Tisch Hospital, was greatly attracted to the prospect, particularly if the deal included some form of affiliation between the two medical schools.[51]

"I myself was very much in favor of it," he recalls. In 1969–70, when P&S left the divisions at Bellevue, which the school had long directed, "Columbia sold us the Cournand labs in the C&D Building.* It was a very cordial goodbye."[51] Though an NYU loyalist through and through, Farber had long admired Columbia's academic accomplishments.[2,51] "Our faculty has a lot of respect for Columbia — hardly anybody around here would have objected to a meaningful connection with P&S."[51†]

The referral patterns for the two hospitals did not conflict. Tisch Hospital is on the far east side of Manhattan in the thirties, and looks toward lower Manhattan, Brooklyn, Queens, and Long Island for its patients, whereas referrals to Presbyterian, at the northwestern end of Manhattan, tend to come from the west side of the borough and from New Jersey and New York's Westchester County. The combination could lead to domination of a large share of the market.

The consultants advised that NYU should transfer the Tisch Hospital, which the University owned, into a holding company created with Presbyterian[51] — a structure similar to that at Partners. They recommended integrating the subspecialty services but retaining separate major

---

*Drs. André Cournand and Dickinson Richards had performed the work in these laboratories, which brought them a Nobel Prize in 1956.

†This statement contrasts with the conflict that developed not long afterward when a merger of the NYU and Mount Sinai medical schools was contemplated, but that's another story.

departments and chairmen at each school.[51] The deal would "make money and save money," Farber remembers the consultants predicting.[51]

However, getting the "boards on board,"[20] proved impossible. Presbyterian's financial statements, although improved from the nadir of 1992, still didn't look particularly strong to the businessmen at NYU.[45] Many at Presbyterian and P&S, however, think that what really scuttled the merger was the preference of Laurence A. Tisch, the powerful NYU board member, to join the hospital with his family's name on it to Mount Sinai Hospital, where one of his sons was a member of the board.[20,23,39,45] "Not true," says Farber.[51] "The reason was strictly financial. Our board and its hardheaded businessmen just didn't want to take on the debt Presbyterian had developed for the Milstein building and other capital improvements. They had less trouble with the operating losses."(The NYU endowment was said to be invested very conservatively, mostly in bonds.)[51] Farber adds, "If anyone on the hospital committee dealing with the merger thought differently, no one told me about it."[51] Farber's explanation of the breakup, however, never reached the ears of the Presbyterian leaders, according to John Mack, cochairman of the Presbyterian board.[39]*

The NYU board's decision, which terminated a year's negotiations, from January 1995 to February 1996, disappointed Saul Farber. "No one was going to close Presbyterian despite its problems, and something would have been done about the debt. The members of the Presbyterian board whom I met were fine people, and we developed very good relationships. Bill Speck and I got along extremely well. A hospital merger with Presbyterian could have been excellent, and I looked forward to close ties, short of a medical school merger, developing with Columbia."[51]

Speck felt the same. He liked the idea of merging Presbyterian with Tisch and had a "high comfort level with Saul and the management team at NYU," Marcia Morris remembers.[50] "We invested a lot of time in this effort, and it seemed that they [the NYU board's committee for the Tisch Hospital] were enthusiastic. We presumed the committee and the parent board were talking to each other until the end, when the board said no."[50]

Pardes was said to be less enthusiastic; he didn't look on the NYU School of Medicine as equal to P&S. "Not so," says Pardes. "I would have been very comfortable with an NYU relationship." He adds, as a warning, "This was the first time that the two schools–one hospital concept reared its head."[11]

---

*The Tisch and Mount Sinai Hospitals merged in 1998.

North Shore, Mount Sinai, and
St. Luke's–Roosevelt Hospitals

The North Shore Hospital,* a large, successful institution on western Long Island, had also figured in the discussions between Presbyterian and NYU, but "it became clear early in the discussions that North Shore wasn't ready to affiliate," Farber recalls.[51] Thus, efforts by Presbyterian to forge a union with another large hospital had failed.[2]

Although no connection developed, a merger between Skinner's New York Hospital and North Shore, which had long been affiliated with the Cornell University Medical College,[52] seemed more natural. North Shore was built on land from the estate of the Whitneys, the wealthy New York family that had generously supported the New York Hospital for decades. North Shore is "where our Bellevue program went when the Cornell services left the city hospital in the 1960s," recalls Dr. Robert Michels, the Cornell dean from 1991 to 1996. "North Shore dominates Long Island medicine, and our students always like going there."[53]

"The leaders at North Shore wanted parity with New York Hospital, like the Brigham and MGH with Harvard," recalls Dr. Donald A. Fischman, a basic scientist at Cornell then working in the dean's office.[54] "They saw North Shore becoming an academic medical center and wanted their department chiefs to acquire equal standing with the chairmen at New York Hospital. Cornell wouldn't accept this premise. The North Shore people wouldn't accept what they saw as a subordinate role if they became a sponsored hospital in the New York Hospital network."[54] Fearing that the network would encircle them,[54] the North Shore leaders broke off their academic relationship with Cornell in 1996.[55,56] North Shore would later merge with the Long Island Jewish Hospital and in 1999 would form a joint venture with the Mount Sinai and Tisch hospital combination.[57]

Up at 168th Street, a consultant retained by Columbia University advised Dr. Herbert Pardes, the P&S dean, "Don't put all your eggs in one basket."[50] Accordingly, concerned that the financially strapped Presbyterian Hospital might someday no longer be able to provide adequate clinical training for P&S students,[17] early in 1995, Pardes held preliminary talks, initially without the knowledge of the Presbyterian officers,[2] with Dr. John Rowe, the CEO of the Mount Sinai Medical School and Hospital, about some sort of "broad alliance"[11] between the schools and the Mount Sinai Hospital. Before the Sinai medical school opened in

---

*This facility is on Long Island, not near Boston, the location of the North Shore Medical Center and Medical System, a component of Partners.

1964, Mount Sinai Hospital had been affiliated with Columbia and some of the physicians there then held faculty appointments at P&S. "Collaboration has been in the air in New York for a while," explains Pardes,[11] but nothing concrete developed. "Jack Rowe was convinced that divided administration wouldn't work."[11]

"Bill [Speck] and his group were never enthusiastic about merging with Sinai," recalls Tom Morris, the former president of Presbyterian.[36] "They saw Sinai as an aggressive competitor and therefore not the ideal partner."[36] Another Columbia observer suggested that the P&S-Sinai talks were doomed from the start because Rowe wanted to preserve an independent medical school and that, if the hospitals merged, neither Rowe nor Speck would have accepted a secondary position.

Next, during the winter and spring of 1996, P&S asked Presbyterian to look at St. Luke's–Roosevelt Hospital, which had put itself in play as a candidate for a merger and which the P&S dean feared New York Hospital might buy.[2] Pardes's anxiety was well founded. Skinner saw St. Luke's–Roosevelt as fitting well with his hospital[53] since each was on opposite sides of Manhattan. Michels, the Cornell dean, also liked St. Luke's–Roosevelt.[53] Here was a real teaching hospital for Cornell students in contrast to the community hospitals — many of which were "dog and pony hospitals," as the medical college viewed them from the academic point of view[53] — that Skinner and Vecchione were bringing into the New York Hospital network.

P&S had long sent its students for training to St. Luke's–Roosevelt,[58] itself a union of two older hospitals.[45]* Such a combination,[59] its proponents suggested,[20] could provide the merged hospitals with a dominant position in the market for patients on the west side of Manhattan, much gentrified in recent years and no longer the violent neighborhood of *West Side Story.* Speck, his colleagues, and members of the Presbyterian board[45] concluded early in 1996, however, that joining with this institution, despite its connection to the medical school, was unwise.[2] Many of the patients in the region were young — "great for obgyn and sports medicine" but not a likely source of older patients with the complex medical problems in which tertiary hospitals like Presbyterian specialize.[50] Furthermore, St. Luke's–Roosevelt was "not a financial win," as a Presbyterian officer put it.[20] The hospital was losing money,[4] and Presbyterian, just beginning to recover from its losses, had much to do at the medical center and would not be able to invest the funds or manpower that St. Luke's–Roosevelt required.[20] The faculty at

---

*Roosevelt was the hospital that almost became the major affiliate of P&S early in the twentieth century.

St. Luke's–Roosevelt, it was rumored, found Speck overpowering,[32] while Speck saw St. Luke's–Roosevelt as a competitor rather than a potential partner.[53]

The failure of Presbyterian to join with St. Luke's–Roosevelt disappointed many of the Columbia leaders.[17,39,42] Michael Shelanski was not alone in thinking that St. Luke's–Roosevelt would have been a better fit for Presbyterian than New York Hospital, with which it eventually merged.[12] Senior members of the P&S faculty also saw it as a first step to be followed by a merger with hospital on the east side of Manhattan.[36] At NYU, Saul Farber envisioned a comprehensive merger of the Presbyterian, St. Luke's–Roosevelt, and Tisch Hospitals.[51,60]

As it happened, the Beth Israel Hospital* eventually bought St. Luke's–Roosevelt by offering "real money," as Bob Michels remembers the deal,[53] whereas David Skinner at the New York Hospital could only contribute prestige.[53] Although Beth Israel, on the lower east side of Manhattan, is affiliated with the Albert Einstein College of Medicine in the Bronx,[45] students from P&S continue to train at St. Luke's–Roosevelt, much to the relief of members of the dean's staff charged with providing sites for the clinical training of Columbia students[61] and those doctors at the affiliate who are P&S loyalists.[61]

In analyzing the reasons why these merger attempts failed and why P&S and Presbyterian seemed to be walking down different streets during many of the projects, Marcia Morris, the Presbyterian counsel, cautions: "The health care industry really isn't a single industry. There are many different pieces. In academic medical centers, the teaching hospital and the medical school often have different goals. The overlapping interests between them are dropping. For example, in New York the deregulation of the rate structure affects the hospitals much more than the doctors who are employees of the schools."[50]

Several Columbia-Cornell Attempts at Merging: The Cornell–New York Hospital Suit

Speck, at this point, appeared to his friend, Allen Hyman, to be "quite low."[2] Convinced that, despite its size, Presbyterian's future depended upon its joining with another leading hospital, Speck and P&S had failed to find a partner in NYU, Mount Sinai, St. Luke's–Roosevelt, North Shore, and now The New York Hospital. Historically, Presbyterian,

---

*This is the New York City Beth Israel Hospital, not the one in Boston, a Harvard teaching hospital discussed in chapters 2 and 3.

New York Hospital, and their medical schools had danced around a merger or some form of association for decades. In the archives of The New York Hospital is a copy of a letter written on January 27, 1917, by Jacob Gould Schurman, president of Cornell University, to Nicholas Murray Butler, the Columbia president, about a "union of our medical colleges and hospitals."[62]

By the early 1980s, the precarious financial condition of the Cornell University Medical College led the deans of P&S and Cornell to consider combining their schools. Dr. Donald Tapley, then the Columbia dean, remembers that the Cornell administration in Ithaca saw its medical school—200 miles south, a trip taking five hours by car or more quickly on the one flight per day then available[63]—as a definite, though distant, financial burden.[44] The medical college needed investment in both its aging physical plant and its faculty to rise to a standing among medical schools comparable to that which Cornell University held as one of the nation's leading research universities.[44]

A preliminary plan for the combined school called for the first two years of instruction, when the scientific basis of medicine is taught, to be conducted on the P&S Washington Heights campus.[44] A new laboratory building would be constructed for the Cornell basic science faculty across Broadway from the Columbia-Presbyterian complex where new P&S research buildings now stand.[16] The clinical courses would be taught at both the Presbyterian and New York Hospitals. The name being tried out for the new school was the College of Physicians and Surgeons of Columbia and Cornell Universities.[44] Skinner remembers being told that both faculties warmed to the idea.[24]

However, fundamental questions were never settled. Who would own the school? How would the Cornell alumni respond when they saw their school partially swallowed by Columbia, and how would the P&S alumni react to the new name? Would the alumni in either of the schools contribute to the new school?

A meeting on the project between the two university presidents, Frank Rhodes from Cornell and Michael Sovern from Columbia, was unsuccessful. Sovern insisted the endowments be merged and was worried about the financial implications of taking on the salaries of all the full-time Cornell faculty members, particularly those who were tenured.[54] Rhodes, it was said, felt "put down."[24,36,44]

The second attempt to combine the schools had failed. In view of what followed, one should bear in mind that the 1980 plans only involved the medical schools, although Tapley had reviewed the project with Dr. David Thompson, then the director of the New York Hospital.[44]

In 1986–87, Thompson and Tom Morris, then the president of Presbyterian, initiated some early discussions about associating their institutions. During the next years, however, "both of our hospitals fell on bad economic times," Morris remembers. "By the time Dave Skinner arrived downtown [at New York Hospital in 1987], both of us circled the wagons to save ourselves and merging was no longer discussed."[36]

Morris, who directed the hospital during a particularly difficult time, exemplifies the P&S loyalist whom the faculty admires. Since graduating from Notre Dame, Morris has only worked at Columbia, except for two years in the Air Force. He received his M.D. from P&S in 1958, trained on the Columbia services at Bellevue Hospital, and then settled in at the Washington Heights campus, where he has served as associate chairman of the Department of Medicine twice, acting chairman of the department for four years, associate dean for academic affairs from 1982 to 1984, and, since 1994, vice dean of the Faculty of Medicine.

By the late 1980s, the time was distinctly out of joint. For several years, Cornell had been suing New York Hospital.[2] The medical college wanted to construct a new building for laboratory research. In the process of working up the project, the ownership of the land on which the building would rise came into conflict. Both New York Hospital and Cornell University claimed it was theirs. With the hospital insisting it owned the land, the university sued "as the only way to get the hospital's attention since we were approaching the end of the statute of limitations on our claim," according to Joanne Blauer, a lawyer who is associate dean and secretary of the medical college.[63]

Nancy L. Farrell, a veteran administrator at the medical college and now the chief administrative officer of the Cornell Physicians Organization, remembers people threatening to lock the doors between the adjacent institutions.[64] The dean at the time saw the hospital engaged in "open aggression" with the medical school.[64] The politics tended to divide the doctors and administrators into "hospital people and medical college people."[64] Finally, in 1992, the boards of the hospital and the university settled the dispute, realizing that the conflict would prevent raising money and building the new hospital, which involved resolving the problem over air rights in particular.[53] The university accepted a 225-year "evergreen" lease on the property it occupied, evergreen because the duration of the lease would be perpetually extended. The New York Hospital "kept its face," but the college got what it needed.[63] The conflict cost both parties substantial legal fees.[64]

Worried about the survival of the still debt-ridden Presbyterian, its leading teaching base, P&S leaders turned again to the white tower on the east side with the hope of securing another principal affiliate.[2] This latest iteration in the long history of a possible Columbia-Cornell union began in January 1995 when Herbert Pardes and Robert Michels first discussed bringing their schools together over breakfast during a meeting in San Diego at the same time that the leaders of Presbyterian and NYU's hospital were beginning their merger discussions. The deans — who are both psychiatrists for whatever that adds to the story — strongly favored uniting their two schools. Michels had had a long-standing connection with P&S. He had trained at the Presbyterian Hospital–New York State Psychiatric Institute, studied psychoanalysis at the Columbia University Center for Psychoanalytic Training and Research, and was a member of the Columbia faculty for 10 years until being appointed chairman of the Department of Psychiatry at Cornell in 1974. Through such a development, P&S and Cornell would respond to the widely held belief at the time that the country had too many medical schools.[53]

The discussions that followed were "hot and heavy," according to Pardes,[11] and constituted "a very serious venture," as Michels remembers them.[53] "Both Columbia and Cornell are Ivy League universities," Michels adds. "Few students admitted to either medical school choose to go to another in New York State."[53] Of those given the opportunity to choose between the two schools, about half come to Cornell and half go to P&S."[53,65]

Accordingly, "the quality of the student body is comparable," observes Dr. Daniel M. Knowles, chairman of pathology at Cornell and a former P&S faculty member.[66]

Although accountants inspected the schools' finances and the deans engaged the faculty in the process, a potential merger of the schools raised all the expected complications inherent in uniting two faculties and groups of alumni, each proud of its traditions. Among the more touchy problems was the feeling among some P&S faculty members that many of their colleagues at Cornell weren't up to Columbia's standards. Rather aggressively, some Columbia faculty members caustically asked, "Why should we give tenure to a faculty, many of whom couldn't get jobs here as postdocs or chiefs?" Another Columbia loyalist puts it this way: "The doctors at New York Hospital are filled with 'P&S envy.'"

P&S officials who, along with their faculty, take pride in their school's longtime dominance of academic medicine in New York City,[67] look with unmasked competitive pleasure at the National Institutes of Health (NIH) pecking order, which is determined by the amount of NIH grants received by the nation's 124 medical schools. In 1999, Columbia stood seventh nationally* and first in New York State. Cornell

---

*It ranked eighth if one includes Harvard, which is number one. Harvard's standing in this particular list only includes the grants held by its basic scientists and not by members of the faculty who work in its teaching hospitals (see chapter 2).

ranked thirty-second nationally* and in the fifth position in New York State behind Columbia, Albert Einstein College of Medicine, Mount Sinai, and NYU.[68][†] Furthermore, P&S has five members of the highly selective National Academy of Sciences and nine Howard Hughes Investigators, a particularly competitive award for medical scientists.[11] Cornell's medical college has only one member of the academy[69] and no Hughes Investigators.

To support research, Columbia, compared to Cornell, has twice as much space assigned to investigators, "an important indication of which schools produce the most research," according to Dr. Donald A. Fischman, who, as dean of the Graduate School of Medical Sciences and senior associate dean of the medical college at Cornell from 1992 to 1997, studied research space allocation at leading medical schools. "NIH dollars show a direct correlation with laboratory space."[54]

When Daniel Knowles left P&S in 1994 to become chairman of pathology at Cornell, some of his friends at Columbia tried to convince him to stay, admonishing him, "but it's Cornell," just as they had "felt bad for me when I took a job at NYU earlier in my career. There's no doubt that P&S people feel that 'this is Columbia' and there's nothing else in New York. They like to compare themselves with Harvard."[66] Knowles adds, "If you put all the Columbia chiefs in one room, each would say that he's more accomplished than his counterpart at Cornell because it's Columbia, even though it's clear that the reverse is true in some cases."[66] Some senior faculty members believe that the P&S culture favors its faculty being "more introspective and self-critical" than at Cornell and suggest that this may also help to account for its academic leadership.[70]

These and other differences and conflicts never had the opportunity to be played out. The new Cornell president, Hunter Rawlings, previously the president of the University of Iowa, which has a distinguished medical school on the same campus as the rest of the university, insisted on a quick decision and rejected a prolonged dialogue.[53] By September

---

*It ranked thirty-third if one includes Harvard.

[†]Other lists raise the standings of both medical schools. The large number of grants held by Columbia's Department of Psychiatry, which Dean Pardes chairs, is not counted in the NIH list because applications are submitted through the Institute of Psychiatry, a state entity. Similarly, the grants held by investigators with Cornell titles at the Sloan-Kettering Cancer Institute and Rockefeller University do not appear in the NIH medical school list. Cornell leaders point out that the work of the scientists in the York Avenue axis — the medical school, Sloan-Kettering, and Rockefeller — more fairly characterizes the accomplishments of the larger Cornell enterprise compared to the science at Columbia's medical complex at 168th Street.[53]

1995, the deans, a joint committee of the trustees of the two universities, and their attorneys called off the effort.[53] Rawlings was not upset. The story went around that when asked why he didn't push to combine the schools, Rawlings replied, "If I didn't have a medical school, I'd be nothing but Princeton."*

Many university presidents, however, have found their medical schools difficult to encompass. A story that seems particularly relevant was making the rounds when previous merger talks were in the air: Frank Rhodes, then the Cornell president, asked the devil what heaven is. "One medical school," he was told. And what is hell? "Two medical schools."[52]

Within a year, Skinner, Speck, and their boards had decided to merge the Presbyterian and New York hospitals. What followed was exactly what Herbert Pardes, the P&S dean, least wanted; rather than one medical school and two hospitals, he would soon have to contend with two schools and one hospital,[2] with the potential scenario of the hospital playing the schools off against each other. "The most prevalent pernicious fear is that a merger would further marginalize the medical schools, which can less successfully influence the policies of a single hospital," warns Dr. Paul Kligfield, a Cornell cardiologist with a special interest in such matters due to his studies in the history of medicine and specifically in the founding of his medical school.[71]

Basic Science

Although not directly involved in the operation or merging of the teaching hospitals, the members of the medical schools' basic science departments, scholars not devoid of strong opinions, will have their say. The American medical school course ordinarily takes four years, although some students stay longer, usually those taking Ph.D. as well as M.D. degrees. The faculty's principal object during the first two years, the "preclinical years," is to teach the students the scientific, as opposed to the clinical, basis of their profession. Most of the courses, among them anatomy, physiology, biochemistry, and pathology, are taught by members of the basic science departments, most of whom hold Ph.D. not M.D. degrees. A few physicians populate these departments, but they seldom engage in clinical practice other than running clinical laboratories in, for example, pathology or microbiology. Although small-group conferences and symposia have replaced part of the lecture-laden cur-

---

*Despite its many virtues, Princeton University has no medical school.

riculum of former years, the amount of strictly clinical information imparted during this time is limited by the wealth of scientific knowledge that the faculty of each basic science department believes it must teach its students.

To the faculty member of a basic science department, most of his or her effort is directed toward research. Despite the educational purpose of medical schools, the primary reason why most biological scientists seek and obtain appointments in such departments is to advance rather than impart knowledge. The more scientifically oriented schools also sponsor training programs for Ph.D. candidates in which the basic scientists gladly teach, more at home in the instruction of pure scientists than preprofessional students, who, incidentally, or perhaps not incidentally, will eventually earn more money than their teachers. The faculty members of the basic science departments competitively recruit to their laboratories the most capable recent Ph.D. graduates to take postdoctoral fellowships, an essential step for budding academic scientists before admission to the ranks of the faculty. The help of the "postdocs" is often critical to the success of a professor's research.

Since few members of basic science departments support themselves by earning clinical fees, the financial underpinnings of these departments must come directly from the school of medicine or from grants obtained from governmental agencies, foundations, and industry. We have seen how the deans and senior faculty of American medical schools look anxiously at the scorecard issued annually by the National Institutes of Health to see how their schools compare in the race to obtain grant support from this important source. To a reasonable degree, the more support its faculty wins from the NIH the more successful is the science of the school, or so it is thought by those to whom this race matters.

Partly accounting for P&S's higher standing in the NIH sweepstakes is its size. The classes of future M.D.'s and Ph.D.'s are larger at Columbia than at Cornell, as are the number of faculty members, particularly in the basic science departments, for the development of which Cornell desperately needed more space and money. When Columbia and Cornell were talking about merging in the 1990s, the medical college accounted for about 25 percent of the total research budget of Cornell University, whereas P&S's investigators brought in about 50 percent of Columbia's research money.[53]* The endowment at Columbia's health campus was twice that of Cornell's medical college.[53]

Maybe some type of collaborative arrangement or even a union

---

*In 1999, P&S brought in 65 to 70 percent of Columbia's total research money.[11]

between the schools, Robert Michels, the Cornell dean at the time, remembers thinking, could help relieve, at least to some degree, Cornell's need to raise money for more faculty and laboratories in the basic sciences.[53] This was before the Weill family gave the medical college $100 million in 1998,[72] part of which will be spent on recruiting 30 new basic scientists, creating new laboratories, and "building the scientific base of the school," according to Antonio Gotto, the current Cornell dean.[65]

Before the Weill gift[72] and the deanship of Gotto, P&S investigators believed that one reason Cornell could not recruit more and better basic scientists was because of the influence of New York Hospital and the clinicians in the administration of the medical college.[43] This problem is long standing. Donald Fischman, chairman of the Cornell Department of Anatomy and Cell Biology from 1982 to 1998, still remembers a comment of the distinguished scientist Don Fawcett when he left Cornell to become chairman of anatomy at Harvard several decades previously: "This place will never be great till it gets out from under The New York Hospital."[54] In comparing his institutions to P&S, Fischman senses that the Columbia medical school is not run by Presbyterian.[54] "From this a lot follows. That place looks upon itself as a great academic center, so the hospital cannot dominate it. The resolution of the suit here supports how the hospital controls our center."[54]

Daniel Knowles, the Cornell chairman of pathology, confirms that "up there [at P&S, where he trained and was previously a member of the faculty] the medical school is dominant, down here the opposite."[66] Put another way by Dr. Paul Kligfield, a senior full-time Cornell cardiologist, "The medical school serves the needs of the hospital at Cornell. It's the other way around at Columbia."[71]

As a prime example of the ascendancy of The New York Hospital and its clinicians, the critics point to David Skinner, who was, and is seen as, the most powerful figure at New York Hospital and Cornell.[73] Knowles confirms that Skinner, a cardiothoracic surgeon, "thinks like a surgeon. He's jovial and collegial but tough, a real leader and definitely in charge."[66]* At Columbia-Presbyterian, "the hospital administration was bloated and poor, disorganized and unstable, a revolving door."[66]

When the merger between the Presbyterian and New York Hospitals came about, these concerns alarmed many of the researchers at Presbyterian, as executives at New York Hospital were appointed to several of the choice positions in the merged institution. "That's the reason for

---

*Skinner's influence on the Cornell search committee was considered critical in the choice of Antonio Gotto as the medical college's current dean.

our anxiety," commented one senior P&S clinician-investigator, who then added with partisan exaggeration, "New York Hospital has never been academic."

"At New York Hospital, they believe they practice the best medicine, but since the Libby Zion case* the legal side has become very strong. There're buttoned down and believe that things are mostly OK," observes Michael Shelanski, who was chairman of New York University's Department of Pharmacology (1978–86) before taking the pathology chair at Columbia. "I think that the P&S faculty would have made a better match with NYU than with Cornell."[12]

Dr. John Pile-Spellman, the director of interventional neuroradiology at P&S, agrees about the nature of the two faculties. "People at New York Hospital think things are great. They're Princeton, white shoe, stiff upper lip, don't complain, don't explain.[74†] Here there's much complaining. We're more 'in your face.' People will tell you four things are bad before they tell you one thing is good." Pile-Spellman believes that these characteristics at P&S "go along with Columbia being more multicultural. We have among the largest number of black M.D. and Ph.D. students at any non-traditionally-black medical school plus many Jewish students and faculty members, certainly more than at Cornell, it seems to me."[74‡]

When the possibility of merging the two medical schools arose again in the 1990s, most members of the Cornell clinical faculty "weren't strongly for it and acquiesced rather than pushing it," Dr. John Daly, chairman of surgery there, remembers, "but most of the faculty in the basic science departments opposed merging with Columbia."[76]

On the other side of town, Dr. Isidore S. Edelman, director of the Columbia Genome Center and former chairman of the Department of Biochemistry at P&S, agrees. "There's no compelling reason to put

---

*The deaths, under questionable circumstances, of Libby Zion, the daughter of a journalist, who publicized the event and sued the hospital, and the artist Andy Warhol created much unfavorable publicity for New York Hospital.

†Dr. Jack Barchas, the chairman of psychiatry at Cornell, adds that this traditional image has its advantages by emphasizing New York Hospital's excellent doctors, those white-coated superclinicians. Furthermore, Cornell warmly and kindly welcomes the members of its relatively small medical school class so that "once you're joined Cornell, you're really a member of the family."[75]

‡This is not true according to former Cornell dean Robert Michels. "Cornell has the greater number, despite the small class size, and the highest percentage of underrepresented minorities in its medical school," he says, "of any medical school in New York State." He adds that the misconception persists that Cornell University Medical College and New York Hospital are primarily populated with WASPs, a false impression that hasn't been true for many years.[53]

together basic science departments. Size doesn't make great departments. It's the quality of the scientists which counts. The best basic
scientists want to build their own groups and work best in smallish
enterprises."[46] As for a hospital merger, "Most basic scientists here have
a neutral view," according to Edelman, a board certified internist who
prides himself on "making it to 57 without becoming a chairman" and
plans to retire from directing the Genome Center in 2000 when he
reaches the age of 80.[46]

Dr. David Hirsh, chairman of the Department of Biochemistry and
Molecular Biophysics at Columbia, agrees. "Most good science is conducted on a small scale. As one of my colleagues told me, 'We collaborate all around the world anyway without combining schools.' Our work
is driven by topics and scholarly interest, not in corporations." On this
subject, Hirsh speaks from experience. For five years, he directed research at a biotech company in Colorado. "I favor cottage industries for
discovery science," he adds.[77]

Clinical scientists feel similarly. Dr. Karen H. Antman, director of
the Cancer Center and chief of the Division of Medical Oncology at
P&S, observes, "We're more like Microsoft than a bank merger. Major
companies which are high on intellectual capital don't operate the way
many members of the board might expect based on industry mergers.
I did comment to Dan Burke [then cochairman of the New York-
Presbyterian board] that if we're going to merge teams had to stay small
and encourage 'ownership' by team leaders and members."[78]

Antman presents three options. "Look at it this way. If you have an
'A' person coordinating the whole program, you can only get 'B' people
at each site, and it's more expensive because you need three directors. If
an 'A' person directs the program and runs the service at one hospital,
you'll only be able to recruit a 'B' person for the other site. However,"
and Antman clearly thinks this is the best solution, "let each academic
program run independently at each site, and you can obtain two 'A'
people.[78] An administrator can coordinate the programs to take advantage of economies of scale."

Although Isidore Edelman finds that so far "dropping clinical income has had little financial effect [on P&S basic scientists] since most of
our money comes from research grants,"[46] reducing hospital support to
the clinical departments indirectly affects the teaching of basic science
by forcing clinicians to see more patients. This gives them less time to
teach clinical correlations in the basic science courses, a popular feature
of the otherwise relentlessly scientific character of the first two years of
medical school.[43]

"As the hospital's financial problems reduce support which flows into salaries and other expenses of the clinical faculty, the dean has less money to assign to those expenditures of the basic science departments which are not paid by grants,"[43] observes Dr. Samuel Silverstein, chairman of the Department of Physiology and Cellular Biophysics at P&S. "The basic scientists fear loss of their autonomy, the more this occurs." These anxieties reflect the effects on the medical school of the financial pressures that afflict all teaching hospitals more than any specific consequences of the hospital merger itself. The basic science departments at Columbia "are rather diffuse and function very much on their own," says Silverstein. "We are not the sum of our parts, even though we are very collegial. One thing we do together is convince our best people not to accept recruiting attempts from other places."[43]

Speck and Skinner Meet

At first, the auguries for a merger between the principal teaching hospitals of Columbia and Cornell were poor. Bill Speck, diligently searching for a partner, was quoted in a New York newspaper as saying that the most natural fit for Presbyterian was with New York Hospital.[24] Knowing nothing about what was in Speck's head on this matter, Skinner phoned him and suggested that they really ought to get together to discuss Speck's plans for Skinner's hospital.[24]

The two met for the first time in January 1995. Their talk about merging Presbyterian and New York Hospital progressed sufficiently to convince them to take the prospect to their boards. However, a meeting attended by Skinner, Speck, and senior board members from each of the hospitals—Maurice "Hank" Greenberg and David Wallace from New York Hospital and Seymour Milstein and Daniel Burke from Presbyterian—"didn't go very well," as Skinner remembers.[24]

"The timing was wrong," recalls John F. McGillicuddy, a member of the New York Hospital board.[79] Milstein and the Presbyterian people feared that The New York Hospital could not successfully fund its replacement hospital, then being built, and New York Hospital representatives looked with anxiety on Presbyterian's operating losses.[80] This effort having failed, Speck continued talking about merging with NYU and considered St. Luke's–Roosevelt, though neither effort succeeded. Meanwhile, Skinner, as well as Speck, tried to merge with North Shore Hospital, but nothing came of that possibility for either of them.

A year later, however, the prospects for a Presbyterian and New York Hospital merger brightened. Presbyterian was finally in the black, only slightly profitable but no longer losing money. The New York

Hospital's new inpatient building was coming in under budget, and the hospital's financial circumstances had improved sufficiently to assure that the debt for the new structure could be funded.[24] The referral patterns at the two hospitals had always seemed favorable for a merger. The New York Hospital draws from the east side of Manhattan, Brooklyn, Queens, Long Island, and Connecticut, and Presbyterian, as noted during the merger discussions with NYU, draws from Manhattan's upper west side, southern New York State (including Westchester County), and northern New Jersey.[81]

"The historical connections also fed some of the discussions," Dr. Ralph Nachman, chairman of the Department of Medicine at Cornell, believes. "It all started in the eighteenth century when Samuel Bard founded both The New York Hospital and what became Columbia's medical school. In addition, we have many cultural and Ivy League connections."[82]

On April 22, 1996, Skinner and Speck got together again, at the River Club, with Hyman and Vecchione in attendance.[2] Speck, Hyman remembers, was uneasy about what would follow.[2] He had been warned, a *Wall Street Journal* reporter wrote, that Skinner is "an old grizzly bear, who's not quite as tough as he used to be, but you don't want to get into his embrace."[83] He feared that Skinner would dominate the meeting and never agree to equal representation of both hospitals on the prospective board.[2] Speck recognized that "the financial capital is at New York Hospital," but, ever the loyal P&S professor and former Presbyterian resident, he firmly believed that "the intellectual capital is at Columbia."[7] He was not alone in this opinion. Dr. Myron Weisfeldt, chairman of the Department of Medicine at P&S, confirms that many colleagues at both centers acknowledge that New York Hospital is more potent clinically, while Columbia leads in research.[32]

Keeping the principal agenda for the dinner at the forefront, Skinner displayed a map of how their union would affect the New York area medical market. Claiming that his hospital was the more dominant clinical institution, Skinner insisted, as Speck had anticipated, that a majority of the trustees of the new board should come from the New York Hospital board. Speck countered that he could never sell such a proposal to his board. Skinner was dominating the evening,[28] as Speck had assumed he would.[2] As a final reminder of who was in charge, they were dining at Skinner's club.[2]

Described as "a defining personality,"[84] "the great salesman,"[85] and "supremely confident,"[86] Skinner was used to taking over.[28] He is a tall, large man who conveys the impression that he's in charge and knows how to run other people's lives.[2] And he is a surgeon[2,73] — a specialist whom other doctors, as well those outside the profession, often consider more forceful and decisive than, for example, most internists, pediatricians, or psychiatrists.

Born in Joliet, Illinois, raised in Cedar Rapids, Iowa, he came east for his undergraduate work at the University of Rochester and for medical school at Yale, where he won the prize as the top student of his year, as had Samuel Thier and Eugene Braunwald of Partners at their medical schools. Next came a choice appointment as an intern and resident in surgery at the Massachusetts General Hospital. In 1972, after four years on the faculty of the Johns Hopkins Hospital, Skinner was appointed chairman of the Department of Surgery at the University of Chicago. He was only 37 years old, the same young age as was Thier when he became chairman of medicine at Yale. As a surgeon, Skinner developed a reputation for performing the difficult operations required for treating diseases of the esophagus.

When the New York Hospital needed a new CEO, the trustees turned to Skinner, whom they had come to know through his membership on the Board of Visitors of the Cornell University Medical College. After 15 years as chairman of an academic clinical department, Skinner moved to New York City as the president and CEO of the Society of the New York Hospital and the director of the country's second-oldest hospital.

History of the New York Hospital and the Cornell University Medical College[87]

The hospital David Skinner was now to lead came into official existence on June 13, 1771, when King George III granted a royal charter to the Society of the New York Hospital and its board of governors. One of the founders was Dr. Samuel Bard, who had also helped establish the medical school of King's College four years previously and whose name is preserved in the title of the professorship held by the chairman of the Department of Medicine at Columbia's College of Physicians and Surgeons. The first governors were "merchants almost to a man, and numbered among them not only a DeLancy but two Livingstons, a concentration of the wealthiest men in the Colony."[87] With the opening delayed by fire, riots, and the Revolution, the hospital finally admitted its first patient 20 years after its founding. The New York Hospital's first building, the Old Hospital as it came to be called later, was a two-story (plus a basement and attic) gray stone structure facing east toward Broadway between what are now Worth and Duane Streets in lower Manhattan. A third story and additional wings were added later. In October 1782, attendance at lectures at New York Hospital became a requirement for students at the soon to close Columbia medical school.

By the middle of the nineteenth century, the hospital had long outgrown its original building, then downtown and far from where the citizens were migrating. A site between Fifth and Sixth Avenues and 15th and 16th Streets was obtained, and the second hospital, a structure in red brick and iron with a mansard roof, opened in March 1877, five years after Presbyterian inaugurated its first building further uptown on the east side of the city. Although medical students had attended lectures and physicians' rounds at New York Hospital since its founding, the hospital was not officially connected with any of the city's medical schools until 1912, when Dr. Lewis A. Stimson acquired $250,000 "for the purpose of effecting an affiliation between The New York Hospital and Cornell Medical College."[87]

Lewis Atterbury Stimson had begun work as a businessman like his father, but when his young wife became ill he sold his seat on the stock exchange and took the family to Europe to study medicine. Returning to New York, he worked on the surgical staff at the recently opened Presbyterian Hospital until resigning 12 years later to join The New York Hospital. Stimson also became a teacher at the medical school affiliated with New York University, then a proprietary, not a university, school. In 1895, the NYU chancellor proposed to Stimson and his colleagues that the medical college become part of the university in fact as well as in name. When conflict arose over the terms of the agreement, most of the faculty members resigned and joined the recently established Cornell University Medical College just as the faculty of the short-lived first version of Columbia's medical school had transferred their allegiance to the newly formed College of Physicians and Surgeons at the beginning of the nineteenth century.

Cornell had tried and failed three times to create a medical school in New York because, among other problems, the distance from its main campus at Ithaca was then thought to be too great. Now, with the NYU faculty suing its university, Stimson, his friend Oliver Hazard Payne, rich from his association with John D. Rockefeller Sr. in the Standard Oil Company, and Dr. William Polk, professor of obstetrics and gynecology, joined with Jacob Schurman, the Cornell president, to establish a new medical college with the initial faculty consisting of most of the disaffected NYU teachers. Payne offered to fund a new laboratory building for the school, to be designed by the noted architect Stanford White, across First Avenue from Bellevue Hospital, where the students would receive some of their clinical training.

The New York Hospital trustee who provided Stimson with $250,000 in 1912 to link Cornell and The New York Hospital, George F. Baker, can be compared to Edward Harkness, who led the effort to connect Presbyterian Hospital to P&S and conceived the medical center. Unlike Harkness, however, Baker, a trustee of The New York Hospital from 1899 to 1931, had not inherited his wealth. He began work as a clerk in the New York State banking department and rose to leadership in the New York community by directing the First National Bank. His mentor in the affiliation process was his friend Lewis Stimson, whose name is honored in the professorship held by the chairman of surgery at Cornell, but it was Baker's vision and money that helped complete the process. Under its terms, Cornell would nominate more than half of the New York Hospital staff. If the hospital should terminate the agreement, it would have to return the $250,000.

The two institutions continued on their related but physically separate courses until the need to replace the hospital, now in a deteriorating neighborhood, arose for the second time in its history. Familiar with Harkness's plans for the Columbia-Presbyterian Medical Center, the leaders of The New York Hospital considered a similar arrangement. Now Oliver Hazard Payne, and in the next generation his nephew and heir, Payne Whitney — his uncle's bequest made him one of the richest men in America — became major influences. It was Payne Whitney who purchased the land along the East River between 68th and 70th Streets on which the medical center would rise.

As had the Sloane Hospital at Columbia-Presbyterian, another medical institution, the Lying-In Hospital of New York, joined the east side complex to provide obstetrical service.* The Society of the Lying-In Hospital, founded in 1799, was almost as old as its counterpart, which owned the New York Hospital. Its greatest benefactor was J. Pierpont Morgan, who paid for and endowed the Lying-In building on Second Avenue between 17th and 18th Streets in 1902,[88] the last site it occupied before joining the new medical center. This was the same man who paid for three of the buildings at the Harvard Medical School.[†] The Rockefellers, who had joined Morgan in the construction of the Harvard quadrangle, contributed to building the current Lying-In Hospital.

Lying-in was the felicitous word that a more genteel age used in referring to a woman's "confinement," the time preceding, during, and following childbirth.

[†]At the time, rumor attributed Morgan's support of the hospital to his interest in taking care of all the pregnancies for which he was responsible.[88] The real reason was less lurid. He wished to support the work of the obstetrician James W. Markoe, who had become Morgan's principal medical adviser.[88] Markoe was assassinated in 1919 by a man who mistook him for Morgan's son Jack (John Pierpont Morgan Jr.).[89]

A plaque in the entrance memorializes Laura Spelman Rockefeller, wife of John D. Sr.

Construction of the medical center began in 1929, and despite the Depression, which soon followed, it was completed three years later, although somewhat reduced in scope. The name given to the magnificent structure with its 25-story central tower was The New York Hospital–Cornell Medical Center. The institution whose name came first was clearly the dominant partner.

Now physically combined, the hospital and the medical college retained their independent governance with the Society of The New York Hospital in charge of the hospital and the dean of the medical college reporting for most administrative decisions to senior officials on the main Cornell campus at Ithaca. The inconveniences caused by the distance between the campuses and the reality that medical schools require particular attention led the university in 1980 to create a board of overseers for the medical college with representatives from the university board of trustees, other community leaders, faculty members, hospital officials, and students.[63] Originally developed to encourage fundraising, the overseers acquired important administrative duties and now are empowered to give final endorsement to academic and senior administrative appointments, including the granting of tenure and approving the budget of the medical college.[63] The dean holds the title of provost for medical affairs and is equal in status to the provost at Ithaca. Consequently, Dr. Antonio M. Gotto Jr., the current dean, reports directly to the university president.[63]

To resolve any disagreements that might arise when the medical center opened, the governors of the hospital and the trustees of the university created a joint board, described as "a discussion group with little power."[53] When important differences arose, the protagonists often went around the president of the medical center, who chaired the joint board, to members of the hospital or university boards for support and resolution.[53] After the merger, the boards of the hospital and the two universities created a conjoint board with four members each from the boards of Cornell and Columbia and eight from the New York-Presbyterian Hospital.[63] Whether the conjoint board will prove to be more effective than its predecessor remains to be seen.

The striking hospital building, whose outline dominates the skyline along the East River in mid-Manhattan, looked much more handsome on the outside than the inside. The single integrated medical center, 55 years old when Skinner became CEO, had rested on its architectural laurels. Only 200,000 of 2 million square feet of space had been renovated, and little had been spent on maintenance.[30] A modern hospital was needed to replace the handsome but aging buildings, which were almost as old as the original buildings at the Columbia-Presbyterian Medical Center.

In the 1960s, hospital planners had considered expanding west of York Avenue, but the local community "became outraged," according to Fritz Reuter, the architect who would supervise construction of the new building. Local activists insisted that the hospital "can't be allowed to take over a residential area," he remembers being told.[30]

Since a new structure was clearly needed, building east of the original hospital over Franklin D. Roosevelt Drive adjacent to the East River seemed to be the best solution. Obtaining the air rights was crucial. The New York Hospital and the adjacent Hospital for Special Surgery and Rockefeller University accomplished this with the proviso that any building had to be completed within 20 years. The other two institutions began building in plenty of time, but the New York Hospital dawdled and would have lost this vital provision if the regulation hadn't been extended. Construction would have to begin by 1993, a deadline the hospital barely met.

"Building this way was very expensive," Reuter says, "and then the place went broke" in the mid-1980s. Skinner arrived in 1987 "to put the hospital on a sound financial footing, build the network, and replace the old hospital," Reuter remembers. "We had to navigate through many shoals. There was the financing, of course, but also we had to obtain a CON [a certificate of need for the construction, which state agencies had to approve], and there were the falcons." A group of these endangered birds had taken to nesting near the top of the New York Hospital tower. The construction could not imperil these creatures, environmentalists insisted.[30]

"Because we were building over the FDR Drive and the river, the federal and state departments of transportation and the Coast Guard got involved."[30]* Finally, the project had to overcome opposition from those who insisted that what was not needed in the New York City of the 1990s were new beds.[53]

---

*Building over the drive required the fabrication of thirteen 900-ton, custom-built, steel trusses by an ironworks in Toronto, Canada, and transporting these immense structures across Lake Ontario, through the Erie Canal system, and across the Hudson River to New Jersey, where they were assembled. The units were then floated down the Hudson and up the East River to The New York Hospital. An immense crane on a barge, guided by tugboats, lifted the trusses over the drive to create a trestle from which the hospital construction would rise. This scheme enabled the project to avoid creating additional vertical barriers to the traffic on the drive. This process took two months because officials would only shut down the FDR Drive from midnight to 6:00 A.M. and the weather had to be perfect, with no wind, no waves in the river, and appropriate tidal conditions.[30] The truss project cost $40 million but saved six months and, along with other savings, helped bring the cost of building the new inpatient facility down to about $750 million.[30]

The original estimates approached $1 billion. Subsequent revisions would temper the enthusiasm to spend that much. "We had to raise one-third of it in cash, not pledges, and the rest in debt," Fritz Reuter recalls. "Finally it came together, and we broke ground in 1993," just within the deadline established for the air rights.[30] By 1997, when all the inpatients had been moved into the new building, there was surprisingly little unassigned space left in the old structure, but 60,000 square feet in the Whitney Pavilion was available to be turned over to Cornell for renovation into research laboratories.

The Merger Proceeds

David Skinner's claim to be leading the more successful hospital in 1996 had merit. Although there were more patients in the beds of Presbyterian, Babies and Children's, and the Allen Pavilion, the New York Hospital had the better location, the larger network, and the bigger endowment, about $700 million, partly derived from a large tract of land surrounding its psychiatric hospital in suburban, wealthy Westchester county. Just the appearance of its institutions spoke to the New York Hospital's classier standing. Located on the choice east side of Manhattan and clad in an award-winning limestone and light gray brick facade with an imposing tower, it looked like the Hollywood image of a great medical center. Presbyterian was grittier, sited in what had become a low-income community at the northern end of Manhattan, far from the apartments and offices of the city's leaders. To many observers, the New York Hospital's greatest advantage was its address and Presbyterian's greatest liability was *its* address.[53]

Speck, of course, speaks up for Presbyterian's location, far from other teaching and community hospitals.[7] He emphasizes the greater opportunity his hospital and staff have to serve the residents of a relatively deprived community in need of first-class medical care contrasted with the New York Hospital in its more economically favored part of the city and surrounded by several other large university and community hospitals.[53] Michels, the former Cornell dean, counters that the New York Hospital also serves its community well. "It just happens that our local community is comparatively rich. In many fields, such as mental health, neonatalogy, kidney dialysis, and burns, we serve the entire metropolitan area."[53]

As when Speck took over at Presbyterian six years later, Skinner, the new CEO of the New York Hospital, also faced a flood of red ink. In the year before his arrival, the hospital had been losing $1 million a week. The accounting system couldn't even tell the executives where the money was going.[30] The cuts dictated by the Diagnosis Related Group method of payment had been delayed by waver until 1987–88, but now, just as Skinner took over, its effects were added to the hospital's woes.[30]

Skinner quickly assembled a team of senior executives. George Vecchione as executive vice president, John Lavan in finance, Kathryn Martin in operations, Fritz Reuter in administration and construction, and Keith Thompson in legal affairs joined him in turning the financial mess around, running the hospital more effectively and eventually building the network and the new hospital.[30] He was greatly helped during this learning period by the advice of leading members of the New York Hospital board, particularly the chairman, Maurice "Hank" Greenberg, CEO of the American International Group, an insurance company.[55] The new hospital would be named for Greenberg, who led the fundraising and contributed greatly with extensive support from the C. V. Starr Foundation and its board of directors.[24]

"Hank taught him his job," recalls Thompson. "They must have talked with each other daily. David needed this kind of advice. New York Hospital had become a very big business."[55] As a result of the help he received from his board and his own intuitive abilities, Skinner fulfilled what he told P&S dean Pardes were his fundamental criteria for a good executive: appoint good people, skillfully work out the problems one faces, and represent the institution successfully to the general community outside the hospital.[11] Within four years, the hospital was breaking even, which was essential, of course, if the banks were to loan the money needed to build the new hospital.[30]

By the spring of 1996, New York Hospital's financial situation had improved. The new building was going up, private contributions had helped reduce the projected debt, and Skinner had developed with Vecchione a network of hospitals, nursing homes, and physicians, which was larger and more dominated by its parent than Presbyterian's network.[86] Even with its extensive network, however, New York Hospital could never command as much influence in negotiating with the managed care companies as could a corporation containing, in addition, a hospital the size of Presbyterian.[76]

Irrespective of how Speck and Hyman perceived the psychology of the dinner meeting, this time, in contrast to their earlier meeting, the value of merging seemed "synergistic," as Skinner remembers.[24] The accomplishments of the two hospitals together would exceed the sum of what each could do separately. "Side by side, they just slid into each other," Skinner says.[24]

"As they say, you always come back to your first love," said Speck to *The New York Times*.[80] "It took us a lot of dates with others and lots of talking with multiple parties to realize that we belonged together."[80]

"It was a positive step for both institutions," James R. Tallon, president of the United Hospital Fund, observed.[80] Nevertheless, a perception persisted that Presbyterian had benefited more from the merger by acquiring a "powerful and important partner." The New York Hospital, somewhat less imposingly, had gained "a positive presence on the west side."[80] The *Times* reporter added that the merger would bring to New York Hospital "Presbyterian's academic clout."[80]

The merger was presented to leading members of the boards of the two hospitals. Their enthusiasm rekindled after the unsuccessful attempts to join with several potential partners[24] — including North Shore, where the negotiations had consumed much time and effort[52] — the new board leaders, Presbyterian's Daniel Burke and John Mack and New York Hospital's Frank Benack and John McGillicuddy, each described as "a merger maven,"[24] supported the idea. The leaders of the two boards traveled in similar circles. "We mutually respected each other. Nobody was playing games. It wasn't one hospital bailing out the other," remembers McGillicuddy.[79]

Skinner emphasized to his board the costs that could be saved by merging. With the doctors, he took another approach, stressing that the merger would allow the combined hospital in which they worked to become the best in the country, no longer just in the city.[85]* The boards resolved the problem of representation by agreeing that each of the two hospitals would have an equal number of seats on the new board. Skinner would emerge as vice chairman and chief executive officer of the new corporation, and Speck, six years younger, would become president and director of the combined hospital with the expectation of succeeding Skinner on his retirement. Speck understood that Presbyterian needed the New York Hospital more at that point than Skinner's hospital needed his.[45]

John Mack, the Presbyterian board cochairman, who had recently completed a merger of his bank, Morgan Stanley, with a leading brokerage house, Dean Witter, observes: "Social issues — who's the CEO — kill

---

*These pledges produced what Dr. Bruce E. Spivey saw as "a big-league dissonance" in what the board members and the physicians came to see as the principal aims of the merger. We will meet Spivey later as CEO of Columbia-Cornell Care, the organization that contracts for managed care support of the clinical work of the doctors from the two medical schools.[85]

90 percent of merger attempts."[39] Mack knows. He accepted the number two position in his merger to make it work.[39,90]*

In addition to the financial and clinical considerations of the merger, some of the Presbyterian board members envisioned a slight personal advantage.[2] Now they and their families could attend the more conveniently located New York Hospital for their care without appearing disloyal to the hospital they served.[†] The Presbyterian board trekked up to 168th Street only once or twice a year for their meetings, favoring for most of their sessions the boardrooms of the large corporations their members led or more recently Presbyterian's downtown clinical center on East 60th Street.[2] As one administrative leader put it, "They could meet at the hospital without going to the hospital."[27] The members of the New York Hospital board, however, usually met in their hospital's boardroom, lined with wood from the first building of the 1770s, which reminded those attending of its 200-year history.

In June 1996, both boards decided to combine in a full-asset merger, and the plan was announced on July 24.[80,91] The Presbyterian and New York hospitals and their boards would become a new hospital with one board of trustees. Even the royal charter establishing the Society of the New York Hospital more than two centuries before would be legally scrapped. During the remainder of 1996 and throughout 1997, the many legal, administrative, financial, and regulatory issues were worked through, and on January 1, 1998, the New York and Presbyterian Hospital,[92] later renamed the NewYork-Presbyterian Hospital, came into being. Ten days later, in a public relations event similar to the Boston mayor's announcement of the formation of Partners, officials from the new hospital presented a personalized white doctor's coat to Mayor Rudolph W. Giuliani,[92] who observed, "I can wear the same one at either place."[93]

Enthusiasm reigned. In a news report referring to the new hospital as a "colossus," Bill Speck said, "This is the big bang—the other mergers in this city and around the country have been pops. . . . It's like merging Coke and Pepsi,"[94] said the man whom most agree was the driving force behind the merger.[39]

---

*Mack resigned as president of Morgan Stanley Dean Witter on January 24, 2001, less than four years after he had led his former company into the merger. No reason was given.[90a]

†Although in its halcyon years, before the neighborhood deteriorated, many of the leaders on Wall Street and other wealthy New Yorkers came to the Harkness Pavilion at the Columbia-Presbyterian Medical Center for their care, they now found The New York Hospital and other nearby institutions more convenient and agreeable.[28]

"Our goal is to construct the single best medical facility in the United States, if not the world," exclaimed Skinner about the union of "the city's two premier"[95] teaching hospitals.[24] "'Why,' one of the board members asked me, 'should B-level cities like Boston [the Partners hospitals] and Baltimore [Johns Hopkins Hospital] take patients from New York City?'"

Rivaling, and perhaps surpassing, "Harvard Medical School, its affiliated hospitals and Johns Hopkins in national standing,"[94] and thereby establishing New York-Presbyterian Hospital as the "best in the world,"[24] led Speck's[7] and Skinner's[24] lists of priorities. Perhaps the merger would reverse the impression that P&S, Cornell, Presbyterian, and New York Hospital had never really made it to the top.[52]

Skinner further blessed the union by telling a reporter from the *Times* that the merger "assured that the Columbia-Presbyterian Medical Center will be there for the next 100 years."[92] Speck's reaction to this comment was not reported.

CHAPTER 5

Development

Having accepted the concept of merging their institutions in June 1996, the governors of the Society of the New York Hospital and the trustees* of the Presbyterian Hospital in the City of New York and their executives spent the next 18 months clearing up the many legal, financial, and regulatory requirements for the new hospital. The founders eschewed hiring consultants, unlike the MGH and the Brigham, which had retained the Boston Consulting Group when Partners was being created. Several were called in, consultant David Matheson remembers. "They picked our brains, but didn't choose any of us."[2] The trustees had said to Skinner and Speck, "You've got the best consultants on mergers right here on the board."[3]

By November, a temporary holding company had been formed with a board drawn from both hospitals, "which gave us a legal relationship together," explains Marcia Morris, then the counsel to Presbyterian Hospital.[4] The holding company became the sole member of the Presbyterian Hospital and acquired the right to approve many of the decisions of the New York Hospital, a provision necessary because of the legal character of the royal charter. With this development, "neither of the boards could go out on their own."[4] Throughout 1997, the two hospitals began to function as one enterprise while the staff worked out the technical details of forming the single company.

The Boards

On January 1, 1998, the statutory merger went into effect, and the corporations previously known as the Presbyterian Hospital in the City of New York and the Society of the New York Hospital were "extinguished by operation of law and merged into the parent corporation."[4] The members of the boards of the former hospitals resigned and became the members of the board of a new corporation, the NewYork-Presbyterian Healthcare

---

*The original term, *managers,* had been changed in 1945.[1]

System, Inc. This new board consisted of 66 governors with an equal number from each of the founding hospitals, their titles adopted from the names of the members of the board of the New York Hospital.[5] Included were two appointed from each of the boards of Columbia and Cornell universities plus one physician from the medical staffs of each of the former New York and Presbyterian hospitals.

The NewYork-Presbyterian Hospital was constituted as a separate corporation led by a board of trustees identical to that of the system, with their titles in this role adopted from the Presbyterian board.[5] Although functionally acting as one, two corporations with two boards were required for legal and financial reasons.[5] For example, it is the hospital, not the system, board that the state of New York had authorized to direct the NewYork-Presbyterian Hospital.[5]

This membership was "frozen"[3] for three years, after which time new members would be appointed, who, David Skinner, CEO of both corporations, hopes will think of themselves less as representatives of a Presbyterian or New York Hospital constituency and more as leaders of single enterprise.[3]

Eventually, John McGillicuddy, the board cochairman, predicts, the titles of cochair, developed immediately after the merger to ease the transition for the trustees still attached to Presbyterian or New York hospital and now used for the leaders of the board and its committees, will be replaced with the more standard names of chairman and vice chairman.[6,7] The size of the board, which all agree is too large, will shrink as those members who are older than 70 become life members. Many of these, having retired from their jobs, wish to continue to contribute to hospital work. As life members, they can work and vote on board committees but no longer vote on issues coming before the board itself.[7,8]*

The boards and officers of the system and hospital corporations also created several subsidiary corporations to administer endowments, real estate, and other functions. Members of the parent boards serve on the boards of the subordinate corporations.[7]

Combining all these enterprises made the NewYork-Presbyterian Healthcare System, Inc., one of the largest of the nation's teaching hospital complexes, encompassing two famous medical centers, their networks, and endowments. Depending on how one counted, the board, its executives, and the medical staff were now responsible for the care of

---

*The board approved these changes in December 1999 and created an executive committee of 12.[8] McGillicuddy then became the chairman of the board and John Mack the vice chairman.

about 2,000 inpatients.[9] Despite some shaky financial history, the hospitals brought into the new corporation about $900 million in assets, of which about $350 million were unrestricted.[10]

One Director for Each Administrative Department:
The Joint Commission Review

Skinner's desire for "a single academic center"[11] would require, as he was heard to say, "making one business entity out of two."[12] Accordingly, the same departments at the New York and Presbyterian hospitals would need to be combined, and the duties of one or both of the two administrative departmental directors at the highest levels of the organization would need to change. In the beginning, according to Fritz Reuter, the executive vice president for administration, "everybody was a 'co-something,' so no one was in charge of anything."[12]

One of the leaders most affected was Kathryn Martin, who would become the senior vice president for hospital operations for the combined hospital. Martin faced a daunting task in bringing together the day-to-day functioning of the two physically separate medical behemoths. Preparing for review by the Joint Commission for the Accreditation of Healthcare Organizations (JCAHO) in the fall of 1999 provided the impetus for completing the amalgamation quickly.

The joint commission is a certifying agency whose approval is required for hospitals to receive Medicare and Medicaid funding. The commission's reviews for the Presbyterian and New York Hospitals could probably have been conducted separately, at least for a while, as in the past.[13] However, "to force the pace,"[3] Skinner instructed Martin to prepare for a combined review the next time either component was scheduled for one, thereby "uniting us against a 'common enemy,' the commission."[13] This meant consolidating hundreds of clinical and administrative practices, often differently conducted at each hospital. As David Skinner's chief operating officer at The New York Hospital, Martin had led a highly successful JCAHO review of it in December 1997. On thinking over what had to be done to bring about the consolidation and survive the next review, she mused, "I was penalized for doing a good job" by being given this assignment.[13]

Martin established joint working groups from each hospital to review and rewrite clinical and administrative policies. In many cases, the changes needed were "just around the edges,"[13] but in others the differences were so fundamental that the participants eventually wrote a new set of policies for the combined hospital. Infection control was a particularly controversial subject. The specialists at Presbyterian and New York hospitals, all well known in their fields, had developed over decades detailed methods for preventing contagion from developing and spreading to other patients. Although each group began the meetings thinking their methods were best, the process forced the participants to reexamine whether this was really true and whether some practices at the other hospital might be superior. Eventually, after much prodding, the two hospitals' experts produced a set of policies that most concluded were superior to the guidelines each hospital had followed separately.[13]

This exercise, Martin believes, "creates an infrastructure upon which quality patient care programs will develop regardless of the site and each patient will receive the same quality of care wherever hospitalized."[13] However, a mock review in the winter of 1998–99, conducted by the JCAHO to help the executives learn where problems persisted, was "pretty bad"[12] due to differences in standards and procedures still remaining.

As a result of Skinner's basic directive, the responsibilities changed for many of the senior executives with similar titles at each of the hospitals when they were separate. Most frequently, the person with the senior title and greater responsibility appeared to be the New York Hospital administrator. "Understandable," says Marvin O'Quinn, chief operating officer at Presbyterian for six months before the merger. "Skinner's team had been together much longer than Speck's people."[11]

Columbia doctors complained that "They've replaced all our middle managers with their middle managers"[14] while acknowledging that the New York Hospital people are well qualified.[15]

The changes strongly affected the amount, as well as the character, of the work of several of the senior executives. For example, Harold Hogstrom, recruited by Speck in 1993 as Presbyterian's chief financial officer to help reverse its losses, found himself by 1999 without much to do, although nominally he is the chief financial officer of NewYork-Presbyterian Hospital. Few people report to him, and those who do are New York Hospital people with longtime relationships with John Lavan, executive vice president for finance of the parent corporation and Skinner's former chief financial officer at New York Hospital.[16]

After the merger, Marc Lory, formerly Speck's chief operating officer, who developed the Presbyterian networks, reported to George Vecchione, the network chief at the former New York Hospital. "It seemed do me that the Presbyterian executives were being sacrificed to those from New York Hospital," he remarked.[17] Later he was put in charge of information services, then materials management and long-term care. In April 1998, Lory left to become CEO of the Eastern

Connecticut Health Network, Inc. "I pulled the trigger. You know when it's time."[17]

With amalgamation, Kathryn Martin assumed the direction at both hospitals of over 35 operating units, including such basic services as clinical laboratories, design, emergency rooms, engineering, food, housekeeping, human resources, nursing, materials management, medical records, operating rooms, pharmacy, and purchasing, each of which was operating as a single unit by the fall of 1999. Marvin O'Quinn, senior vice president for program development and clinical services, directed, among other functions, the administration of the behavioral health network—in effect, the psychiatric services of the combined hospital—the community health system, which includes the Allen Pavilion, Presbyterian's community hospital at the northern tip of Manhattan, ambulatory and home care, and graduate medical education (the interns and residents). O'Quinn's associate, Cesar Perales, adds about the community health programs, "at this point [1999], the merger has not affected our operation."[18]

Accordingly, Martin and O'Quinn's previous duties have been divided "horizontally, not vertically"[13] with each performing part of the work at both hospital sites for which O'Quinn was previously responsible at Presbyterian and Martin at New York. This plan, some observers suggest, was partly designed to give all those formerly employed at each hospital something to do even though the assignment in each case didn't make perfect sense. "One can only deal with ambiguity for a while," suggests one of those affected, and it "might have been better to shoot one." As in Boston, the enemies are the "silos," separate, nonintegrated, vertically organized structures in each of the formerly separate hospitals.[19]

Coordinating all these efforts is Dr. Michael A. Berman, executive vice president and director of the New York-Presbyterian Hospital.[9] Unlike most of the other senior directors, Berman is new to both hospitals. Speck, who recruited him, knew Berman through pediatric and other professional organizations to which they both belonged. Like Speck, Berman had been chairman of a department of pediatrics, in his case at the University of Maryland in Baltimore, from which post he came to New York in October of 1997 as the first chief medical officer of the combined hospital, reporting to Speck, president and chief operating officer of the New York-Presbyterian Hospital and System. Speck told Berman that he would become Speck's number two when Speck succeeded Skinner.

For Berman, this happened sooner than expected. When George Vecchione, executive vice president and director of the hospital and system, left in the spring of 1998, Berman was promoted to hospital director, reporting to Skinner and Speck. Four senior vice presidents — O'Quinn, Martin, Harold Hogstrom (for hospital financial services), and Cynthia Sparer (for the children's health network), report to Berman, as do the physicians who direct the clinical services, most of whom also chair the clinical departments at P&S and Cornell.

By early in 1999, the changes inherent in managing the new hospital had discouraged many of the doctors who direct hospital departments.[20-22] Dirk Sostman, chairman of the Department of Radiology at Cornell, found that "the new merged hospital has totally lost its focus," unlike the formerly independent New York Hospital, which was well manged.[21] "Then you only had to state the case and you got a solution. Now you can't even find the right person to talk to when there's a problem."[21]

Dr. William J. Ledger, chairman of the Department of Obstetrics and Gynecology at Cornell, agrees: "We ran short of scrub suits in the labor and delivery suite [and] couldn't find the person who was responsible. David's [Skinner] very good people here used to respond quickly to complaints. Now the junior people have to get approval from higher up, and the senior administrators are running back and forth between the hospitals. There are too many generals and not enough majors."[22] Ledger adds, "David's no longer a presence here [at the New York Hospital site], and Speck and Berman seem to spend more time at Presbyterian. We need another Kathryn Martin just for this hospital."[22]

Other Cornell faculty, such as Wayne Isom, chairman of the Department of Cardiac Surgery, agree[23] and believe that Martin herself is frustrated by the difficulty of directing operations at both campuses.[23] "David's out of it [day-to-day hospital management]," Isom regrets.[23]

"Skinner's team of Lavan, Martin, and Vecchione were first class, and the people under them were dedicated to the hospital and tried to do a good job." says Daniel Knowles, the chairman of pathology at Cornell. "They were so good, in fact, that the place appeared to run itself, and Dave seemed to have nothing to do. Not true, of course, but he did have time to meet individually with each of the service chiefs monthly, which we very much appreciated. He met with me weekly soon after I started, which was very helpful." However, since the merger, Knowles adds, "Now, with these good people splitting their time, things are better there [at Presbyterian] and worse here. You can't get through to the administrators. The communication has weakened. I may have to take a taxi to Presbyterian and spend over an hour in transportation to meet with Kathy [Martin] for 30 minutes about a problem down here."[24]

At Presbyterian, however, some of the chiefs find the new approach heartening. Dr. Myron Weisfeldt, the medicine chairman,* feels that "the hospital is running better than it has ever run now that the New York Hospital people are directing things. The churning of executives has stopped—the chief operating officer of the Milstein Building [the inpatient facility] changed every year. Now the leadership is consistent, and you know where to go to get an answer." He particularly praises Arthur Klein for the network and Kathryn Martin in operations.[25] "Kathy really makes the trains run on time," adds Jean Emond, the liver transplant surgeon.[26] Weisfeldt ascribes the improved management to the long period of time in which the New York Hospital executives have worked together, the trust among them, and their obvious competence. "A single management is certainly helping Presbyterian," he and some of his colleagues believe.[25] Knowles, however, has heard former colleagues at Presbyterian complain that, although they didn't like their former administration, "at least they were ours."[24]

Information Service and Communications

"He who has the data will win" says Executive Vice President Fritz Reuter in explaining the importance NewYork-Presbyterian places on information technology and the willingness of management to invest capital in improving the computer and communications systems.[12] The job of directing these enterprises falls to Guy Scalzi, chief information officer and senior vice president for the NewYork-Presbyterian HealthCare System, who began consolidating the computer services for the New York Hospital's network before the merger.

"We combined information services for Methodist [in Brooklyn] and New York Hospital. We closed their data center, moved their 40 people and $4 million per year operation here [the computer center on East 38th Street], and gave their mainframe back to IBM. The Methodist operation now costs half as much to run. One large mainframe and its software costs less than two."[27] Although some jobs were duplicated, Scalzi didn't fire anybody. "Natural attrition took care of a few, but frankly we needed most of the staff from both hospitals. Finding a job in computer technology in the New York market is pretty easy now."[27] Using this model, Scalzi next consolidated information services at Queens Hospital and the Community Hospital of Brooklyn. "Our focus then became the Greenberg Pavilion [New York Hospital's new inpatient facility] and Presbyterian.

---

*Weisfeldt holds the Samuel Bard Professorship of Medicine at P&S, named for one of the first faculty members of the medical school of King's College.

My staff thinks of themselves as network people, so Presbyterian simply becomes just another network affiliate as far as our work is concerned."[27]

Since the Greenberg Pavilion is almost two city blocks from the radiology department of New York Hospital, "We would have had to build a new radiology department in or near Greenberg if we stayed with a film system and its darkrooms. That helped convince management that we had to go 'filmless,'" Scalzi says.[27] A picture archiving and communication system (PACS) provides this service at a cost of more than $10 million for each of the teaching hospitals. PACS renders all radiological images into computer language and then displays the pictures on screens throughout the hospital. Doctors and trainees can review their patients' X rays without going to the radiology department where the films were formerly displayed. Gradually, the old films are being scanned into the computer system, so that eventually few films will be retained.[27] About $2 million per year will be saved just in purchasing and processing the film, and eventually staffing the film library will become unnecessary, a further saving.

Furthermore, when the radiology department becomes fully computerized, films can't be lost, a common problem at hospitals. Many X-ray films "travel," never to be seen again when signed out of the film library for conferences or review elsewhere in the hospital. In addition to being unavailable for comparison with later studies, lost films can complicate the defense during malpractice conflicts.

"The merger fostered PACS," Scalzi suggests. "We were nowhere near putting it in Presbyterian Hospital. The money was not budgeted, and we couldn't justify the expense. The concept of one radiology department helped to rationalize doing it."[27] Presbyterian will soon have its PACS. Already Scalzi has closed the Presbyterian mainframe computer and consolidated its work into the large unit on 38th Street. "We will recoup the capital costs in two years and save a couple of million a year in operating expenses."[27] His motto is "If it can be standardized, the bigger the better."[27]

A paperless hospital record has been the goal of hospital information directors like Scalzi for more than a decade, but now the necessity of it has become more and more apparent. At New York Hospital, all the nursing documentation and about one-quarter of the physicians' notes are entered into the computer, which, in generating the patients' hospital records, makes them available to any appropriate health care worker in the office, laboratory, or clinic. The paperwork from each discharge and visit for ambulatory care since 1997–"the whole damn chart," as Scalzi puts it—has been scanned into computerized medical records, though "so far we haven't had the courage to destroy the old records."[27]

Complying with the increasingly complicated requirements of the insurance carriers for documentation becomes much more reliable when the writer must conform to a predetermined list of required information presented on the computer screen.[27] Presbyterian's computerized repository of clinical information, which allows those needing information to obtain it through the Internet, is being integrated into the system for both hospitals.

Scalzi's department is also combining the telephone systems at both hospitals—there are 35,000 telephones at NewYork-Presbyterian and the two affiliated medical schools—into one "switch," or telephone exchange, a process to be completed in the fall of 1999.[27]

Recruiting and retaining first-class computer programmers and other technical employees plagues those who direct information technology programs in not-for-profit hospitals. The best eventually leave, often to form or participate in private companies that can offer better compensation, including stock options. To counter this problem, NewYork-Presbyterian announced, in November 1999, the formation of an outsourcing venture with First Consulting Group, Inc. (FCG), a California health care consulting firm, which the hospitals will pay to run their information technology and telecommunications departments. NewYork-Presbyterian will own 15 percent of FCG Management Services, a new company, and the consulting group will provide most of the capital and employ the technical personnel, many of whom will be the current members of Scalzi's department, including himself, to assure that the NewYork-Presbyterian culture pervades the new company.[12,27,28]

Scalzi's current administrative position reflects the comprehensive nature of his job. He reports to Fritz Reuter, Executive Vice President for Administration of the NewYork-Presbyterian HealthCare System, whose boss is David Skinner, and not to one of the other executive vice presidents such as Michael Berman, the hospital director, or Barbara DeBuono, the network director. "I have to recommend which computer services need to be funded. As a rule, John Lavan [executive vice president for finance] gets what he needs—you have to collect the dollars—but sometimes there's competition between Mike and Barbara for computer equipment and time."[27] For such problems, he must ask Skinner, which tells Scalzi that the system needs an active chief operating officer to whom he can turn for resolution of similar issues rather than running to the CEO every time.[27]

The consolidation of information services at NewYork-Presbyterian under one director did not present the usual "two persons for one job" problem that developed in other departments. Scalzi and his counterpart, Mark Anderson at Presbyterian, were simultaneously recruited for the position of director of information at Yale. Since he lived in Connecticut, Anderson decided to take the Yale job, and Scalzi thus became director at NewYork-Presbyterian.

Financial Consolidation

The merger required the consolidation of many financial components formerly handled separately. The mortgages held by each hospital, $550 million by the New York Hospital and $450 million by Presbyterian, were so large that they constituted the two biggest loans retained by the federal Department of Housing and Urban Development (HUD), the lender of last resort in this market. New York State institutions held 90% of the HUD portfolio of debt.[4] Both hospitals had exhausted further lending opportunities.[10] The new corporation with its two major campuses would be responsible for servicing the debt on both loans, which together equaled $1 billion. The New York health care market appeared more fragmented than in Boston to those planning the merger, and consequently the financial position of many of the hospitals was precarious.[4]

A single investment committee replaced the two committees, which were managing about $450 million at New York Hospital and $400 million at Presbyterian. The policies at the two hospitals were similar, with both endowments invested primarily in equities. Presbyterian concentrated on large capitalization growth stocks, whereas the New York Hospital's investment committee was somewhat more aggressive and included some hedging.[3] The new committee, as had the old committees, chose the investment strategies and then selected money managers known for particular styles of investment to carry out its decisions. The board also appointed a single finance committee with one set of financial statements. The audit committee selected a single auditor by competition based primarily on price.[10]

New York State required that the hospitals receive a full certificate of need to merge. Their representatives must convince a commission that the change would serve the public good in their region.* This application was approved with little difficulty and surprisingly quickly.[10] Similarly, obtaining a tax exemption for the new corporation from the Internal Revenue Service posed no problems. However, consolidating the

---

*To prevent the market from becoming oversaturated with unnecessary and expensive resources, CONs must be obtained whenever a hospital wants to acquire or expand an important facility.

foundations, which constitute an important part of the endowments, was delayed. The office of the New York State attorney general had to establish that the intent of each donor is satisfied, including those whose gifts are reserved for specific programs at the former Presbyterian or New York Hospital.[10]

"Saving costs by consolidating back office functions and clinical programs constitutes the principal goal of the merger," believes Dr. Ralph Nachman, chairman of the Department of Medicine at Cornell, "under the rubric of improving patient care."[29] So far, John Lavan has combined the two finance departments into one unit, which serves the hospitals and the networks of the corporation.[10] His group and the members of the Information System Department work in the East 39th Street building, not at either of the major hospital campuses.

So far, the combined finance office has saved about $10 million per year compared to what the two finance offices would have cost operating separately. With annual corporate income of about $1.5 billion, financial expenses have been reduced about 0.7 percent. "Not that much," comments Lavan, "but helpful, nevertheless."[10]

Marvin O'Quinn confirms that hospital mergers in general have produced fewer savings than their supporters had predicted by consolidating various functions.[11] Nevertheless, since the consultants projected that the merger could save $60 million,[30] members of the hospital board prod Skinner and Speck to tell them "where's the $60 million?"[12]

Increasing its share of the market, one of the primary reasons for the merger, looks rather favorable when one considers that the New York-Presbyterian Hospital and its network of affiliated hospitals account for 22 percent of the discharges from hospitals in New York City and the three-state surrounding area.[9] However, the medical center hospitals, whose beds are 90 percent filled most of the time, discharge only about 6 percent of those hospitalized in the city.[11]

So far, the consolidated hospital has spilled no red ink, an accomplishment of which Skinner is understandably proud.[25] He recognizes, however, that the large medical centers face large financial deficits as the effects of lower Medicare and Medicaid payments joined the squeezing of revenues by managed care.[25]

Whole Asset Merger versus Holding Company

Once the discussions between the leaders of the two hospitals became serious, the decision that the founders of Partners struggled with seemed like no decision to Skinner and Speck. Little consideration was given to creating a permanent holding company, the Partners model, and all parties became wedded early to merging into one new corporation all the assets of the two hospitals, including their networks and endowments. They believed that this structure would best achieve a common vision, culture, and bottom line for the new hospital.[4] A united entity would also more easily enable the executives to avoid duplicating investments in equipment and people at each site. As Marcia Morris remembers Skinner and Speck saying, "We need to become indifferent to the campuses and concentrate on what serves the interests of the patients first."[4]

Those founding Partners thought that the holding company structure would avoid some of the conflicts among the executives and physicians at the hospitals that a whole asset merger would cause.* Dr. Samuel Thier, the CEO of Partners and a member of both the Cornell University Board of Trustees and the Board of Overseers of the medical college, advised a full asset solution at Presbyterian and New York Hospitals. Thier, who had not participated in the Partners structural decision, described the difficulties that the less hierarchical features of the holding company had caused him in Partners' early years.

Explaining the effects of making this decision, Keith Thompson, chief legal officer of the New York Hospital during the merger talks, adds, "The full asset merger is less important than having one board. From a legal point of view, the asset merger and one board are not necessarily equal. It was the one board responsible for the single hospital that we wanted in order to avoid competing interests between separate boards for the main hospitals, as we see possible in the Boston arrangement."[5] Thompson also saw that the board members and executives chose the full asset merger rather than the holding company approach "less for legal than for psychological and political reasons."[5]

Thompson, who joined the New York Hospital as its first general counsel soon after Skinner arrived, observes that "Merging [in not-for-profit enterprises like the Presbyterian and New York hospitals] is where American business was at the end of the nineteenth century. There's no personal financial incentive for the executives or board members to bring about such changes — no stock options for them. It took economic stress and the effects of managed care to overcome the essentially conservative nature of the charitable boards which run these institutions."[5]

Skinner and Speck decided not to create a corporate headquarters apart from Presbyterian and New York Hospitals such as Partners had in the Prudential Building. Skinner felt particularly strongly that "to be-

---

*See chapter 3.

come the best, we had to function as one" and that the creation of a third center of authority would interfere with this process.[3] He and Speck also wanted "to keep their hands on operations" and "not to be distant" or allow a separate, top-level administration to continue at each hospital.[12] At the corporate level of the NewYork-Presbyterian Healthcare System, Skinner, the vice chairman and chief executive officer, and Speck, the president and chief operating officer, direct from a single administrative office, according to the January 1999 table of organization, with four executive vice presidents — for the NewYork-Presbyterian Hospital (Dr. Michael A. Berman), the network (Dr. Barbara DeBuono), the corporate office (Fritz Reuter), and finance (John Lavan) — reporting to them. Skinner explained that the occupants of the administrative box containing him and Speck would act presidential. "Regal is more like it," countered one of their critics.

This plan requires a lot of traveling over the six miles between the two hospitals, which are separated by 100 blocks north and south and the entire width of Manhattan Island. Driving over highways along the East River, where the New York Hospital sits, west at the level of the George Washington Bridge to New Jersey, and then briefly south along the Hudson River to Presbyterian takes from 20 minutes, at the best of times, to more than an hour, depending on the time of day and the direction of the traffic. Add the time getting to and from one's car and the frustration of traffic at bad times — for those less favored souls without drivers — and many conclude, as has Fritz Reuter, one of the architects of the current modus operandi, that "travel will drive you nuts."[12] Others agree.[20,31]

A common phrase characterizing the travel burden is "a real drag."[32] A clinician at Cornell offered the most extreme complaint: "We're in the most unlikely of marriages. It's almost easier to get to Philadelphia than Presbyterian."[33]

To reduce the sense that "everybody's living in a tent"[12] and ease the burden on the most peripatetic of the staff, who tend to be the higher-level executives, "sit-in" offices have been created at both hospitals so that each traveler has a home at each hospital regardless of where his or her base office is located. A few have moved their bases. Speck, the former Presbyterian CEO, transferred his principal office to the New York Hospital, a change that added further substance to the impression that the east side troops have taken over Presbyterian and are really running things.[34] The senior officers for finance (John Lavan), operations (Kathryn Martin), administration (Fritz Reuter, whom disaffected Presbyterian officers call "Dave's spy"), board affairs (Kathleen Burke), the Allen Pavilion (Elizabeth Nelkin McCormick, former director of ambulatory nursing programs at the New York Hospital), and the whole operation (David Skinner, the CEO) all come from the New York Hospital. Some faculty members at P&S continue to believe that the former New York Hospital trustees dominate the new board and that eventually the composition will numerically favor the east side campus.[34] They consider the origin of Michael Berman, the hospital director, neutral since he came from another medical school after the merger was formed.

"It's very complicated dealing at both sites," acknowledges Dr. Robert E. Kelly, who directs quality and medical management at both campuses. "A chairman from one of the schools attends a meeting at the other site, and he's still made to feel like a subordinate." When an administrator tries to work at the other campus, "The docs and the staff see you as a 'marauder.' It's paranoia associated with the merger."[35] Furthermore, Kelly observes, "It's very difficult to get busy people to take the time to travel back and forth for frequent administrative or academic meetings."[35]

Despite attempts at teleconferencing, leaders recognize that often only face-to-face meetings will work.[20] "New Yorkers need a lot of body language to communicate," finds Dr. Michael Shelanski, chairman of the Department of Pathology at P&S, and teleconferencing can't provide this input.[36] "The merger has taken so much of my time attending unproductive meetings that it has made seriously consider resigning the chair," Shelanski adds. "It has compromised my research. The endless number of meetings must pass."[36]

Daniel Knowles, the Cornell chairman of pathology and formerly a member of Shelanski's department, agrees. "We talk most of the time about the merger, not what we need to do here. I must spend at least five or six hours per week on it at one of the countless meetings or on the phone."[24] And the result: "Despite the merger, nothing has happened. From a medical point of view, we're not better from having combined."[24]

Dr. Maria I. New, chairman of pediatrics at Cornell, adds: "When we do meet, the old intimacy of the clinical chiefs' meetings at New York Hospital, where we all knew each other and we used to work out day-to-day clinical problems, is gone. Now the meetings are very large, and there's a whole additional layer of administrators present. Who are they?"[37]

Flint Beal, the chairman of neurology at Cornell, sees the merger as creating even more meetings for people with his responsibilities. "The clinical chiefs from the two hospitals meet every week at 7:00 A.M. with David and his staff at one or the other campus, plus the frequent sessions for us as departmental chairman with our dean."[38]

"A child used to ask his father going to work, 'Are you going to operate, Daddy?' Since the merger, it's become, 'Are you going to a meeting, Daddy?'" reflects Wayne Isom, the Cornell cardiac surgeon.[23]

Marvin O'Quinn, who has participated in community hospital mergers, albeit in the different surroundings of the Pacific Northwest, wonders if the absence of a separate corporate office is wise.[11] Not having one, he suspects, can cause the senior executives to overlook, or at least deemphasize, the larger system.[11] Or, put another way, the lack of separation between "hospital-think" and "corporate-think" can lead to too much "hospital-think."[11] O'Quinn recognizes that not being a physician he is less likely to feel the difficulty, if not the pain, of leaders working in a corporate headquarters when they have spent most of their careers in clinical work, as an academic pediatrician in Speck's case and a surgeon in Skinner's.

Just as difficult seems to be the fact that Skinner and Speck have fully delegated the management of the New York-Presbyterian Hospital to those charged with this responsibility. The hospital director, Dr. Michael Berman, who is appreciated by leaders at P&S as a fair, reasonable, problem solver, knowledgeable about practice plans,[39] able to communicate skillfully with doctors[40] ("a doctor's doctor"),[40] having good "people skills,"[21] and so far with "no scars from previous battles,"[21] appeared to some to be watching rather than leading during 1998 and early in 1999 and deferring to Skinner or Speck. He was seen as "trying to dance fast in a very difficult situation."[41] Perhaps, O'Quinn and others suggested at that time, his reticence reflected the fact that the two senior leaders were too close physically, and possibly emotionally, to hospital operations.[11] He also seemed to be overwhelmed by the problems of his new responsibilities and looking for quick solutions.[36]

Furthermore, in O'Quinn's experience, vertically integrated systems such as Skinner, Speck, and Berman are trying to develop at New York-Presbyterian Hospital work better in the fully capitated environment he had experienced in Oregon. Most of the hospital's market is not yet capitated—if it ever will be—so, he wonders, is this the right place to copy this model?[11] An interested observer suggests that Berman had become politically vulnerable in his current position and might have done better by remaining chief medical officer, from which he was promoted into the position vacated by George Vecchione as hospital director when Vecchione left to become CEO of another large hospital corporation.

From the financial point of view, John Lavan, the chief financial officer, in comparing his institution's full asset merger to the holding company structure at Partners, believes his system will in time permit more money to be saved by, among other improvements, preventing duplication of expensive facilities at both hospitals.[10] Unfortunately, the difference in union representation—many of the workers at Presbyterian are members of unions,[11,13] whereas at the New York Hospital few are—will prevent as much consolidation as has developed in other hospital mergers, where most of the employees either are or are not unionized.[10] This disparity precludes significant savings from the economies of scale[11] resulting from combining the administration of the nursing services, billing operations, and many of the laboratories and support services on the two campuses.[10,11,13]

O'Quinn sees the Skinner-Speck business plan as being based on the model developed for the mergers of community hospitals, the type of institution where most hospital mergers have occurred.[11] Whether this model is applicable to the NewYork-Presbyterian Hospital must take into account important differences between the structure, character, and function of community hospitals compared to teaching hospitals. First of all, there is size. Academic hospitals tend to be larger, much larger in the case of Presbyterian. Furthermore, the leaders and doctors working at community hospitals have no or relatively little contact with medical schools. The staff at NewYork-Presbyterian must work with the leaders of not just one but two medical schools. These differences make it difficult to predict whether combining the functions of the basic hospital departments—apart from the "back office" divisions—under one executive at two such disparate sites will improve the finances and the operational and clinical functioning of the new hospital beyond what was present at each hospital before the merger.[11]

Some members of the hospital's board of trustees—called "a very New York board, with top leaders in banking, law, and the arts"—are active in overseeing and stewarding the development of the new hospital and not completely happy with the pace of the merger.[42]

Practice Plans

Medical schools jealously guard the collection of the clinical income generated by their full-time faculty and do their best to keep the teaching hospitals at arm's length from this important source of revenue. The schools claim this right since they pay the clinicians' salaries, except, as we have seen, at the hospitals affiliated with Harvard. At most schools, deans play a major role, participating in, if not directing, the organizations that administer this function as practice plans.

Many practice plans first developed in departments and divisions. A chairman of surgery or chief of cardiology, for example, may have formed a legal entity to bill and collect the fees for the doctors in his group. Some ran efficiently, some quite ineffectively. In time, most deans forced these departmental plans into schoolwide entities, both to consolidate the various, dissimilarly administered plans under competent administration in their offices and to make sure they could efficiently collect a tax levied on the physicians' income for the support of their administration and the academic programs in the medical schools.

However, as Dr. Herbert Pardes, dean of the Faculty of Medicine at P&S since 1989, knew from his view as chairman of psychiatry, he would be leading a school without a coordinated practice plan that collected no dean's tax. The tradition of rugged individualism at P&S and the power of the surgical chairmen, in particular, had prevented these policies from developing.[43] Pardes could take consolation, however, in reflecting that at Harvard,* the school to which he most likes to compare P&S, the dean collects no tax on the income of his clinical faculty either.[†]

Despite the agony he knew it would involve, Pardes was determined to join most other medical schools by forcing a dean's tax through despite the opposition of many members of the clinical faculty and their leaders. "It almost got me killed," he remembers.[45] As a compromise, he had to agree that the amount of the tax from 1991 to 1995 would grow from 1 to a maximum of 5 percent of gross collections.[46] "The tax was exceedingly unpopular, and some of the departments fought Herb tooth and nail, even though at 5 percent (about $9.5 million in 1998) it's lighter than at many other schools," according to Dr. James S. Lieberman, chairman of the Department of Rehabilitation Medicine and senior associate dean for clinical services at P&S.[47] "Nevertheless, some of the clinical departments still feel some animosity about it."[47]

A few of the more senior practitioners were grandfathered out of the tax, but all clinical faculty members now appointed on a full-time basis are required to pay it.[46] Never a man to back away from a battle he thinks is in the interest of P&S, Pardes is currently trying to form a schoolwide practice plan, which, if it had been consolidated in 1998, already would have collected more than $250 million on behalf of 815 members of the clinical faculty.[32] A committee is trying to develop a plan that Pardes wants to be mandatory for all full-time faculty members.

"It's quite controversial because, in the traditional P&S way, the departments like doing most things on their own," says Lieberman.[47] "We do not share facilities or standards of care and have no centralized billing, scheduling, or referrals. And then there's the financing. The

---

*See chapter 2.

[†]As the Harvard dean looks at his charge, he sees "a two-year school," Donald Tapley, the former Columbia dean, suggested with a smile.[44]

school doesn't want to give the money, and the departments don't want a further tax."[47]

Cornell in the 1960s developed a practice plan for its full-time faculty, now called the Cornell Physicians Organization (PO).[48] Since Cornell University is a private institution, the plan could be organized within the medical college and not as a separate corporation, as is required in state-owned schools.[48]

The chairmen of the clinical departments run the physicians organization with the dean and representatives of the New York Hospital on its operating board. The dean does not, at least at this time, play a direct, day-to-day role in the decisions taken by the organization,[21] but he does take an important share of the earnings through a taxing structure that now includes:[48]

- A Medical College assessment of 7.25 percent made up of a dean's tax of 5 percent and an administrative overhead charge of 2.25 percent. The hospital took half of the dean's tax until the 1990s, when Skinner allowed his portion to stay with the dean. The hospital didn't lose, however. It subsequently reduced funds paid to the departments for faculty services.
- Administration of the practices, including billing: 2.5 to 7 percent, the amount varying among the departments in proportion to the billing activity — fewer bills per dollar collected for surgery, more bills per dollar collected for medicine and pediatrics.
- A Physicians Organization Development Fund of 3 percent now being spent for the expansion of primary care, information technology, and Columbia-Cornell Care, the joint venture, managed care company for the doctors at both universities.

With 13 to 17.5 percent of gross collections leaving the departments before the chairmen levy their own assessments[49] or begin to pay their physicians' salaries, the full-time clinicians at Cornell look with some envy at the 5 percent taken by Pardes.[20,48] Of course, at P&S the departments themselves must still pay for the practice expenses partially covered by the 2.5 to 7 percent at Cornell.

In view of the lower Columbia tax and the looser management of the practice plan, Cornell faculty members believe that being full time at P&S must be less burdensome or onerous than at their school.[20,48] Despite their presumption that Columbia's full-time system seems more agreeable, the Cornell clinicians can take satisfaction in knowing that their practice plan generated $230 million in the year ending June 30, 1999, which is about 48 percent of the college's income, a significantly higher fraction than at P&S. The difference may reflect in part the greater income from grants generated by the Columbia investigators.[48]

A portion of the Cornell practice plan taxes has been assigned to develop offices for the primary care of patients who come to the New York Hospital when they require hospitalization. In charge of this activity is Dr. Leighton B. Smith, medical director of primary care for the Cornell Physicians Organization. Smith is, as far as he knows, the only family medicine physician on the Cornell faculty. Since Cornell does not have a department of family medicine, Dr. Leighton Smith's academic appointment is in the Department of Medicine, even though he is not certified in that specialty. He was hired, almost in spite of his professional training, because of his broad experience operating similar practices, chairing the Department of Family Medicine at the University of Illinois, and directing a hospital, all in the Chicago region.

Smith, who came to Cornell in June 1997, has developed several practice offices in parts of the city distant from the New York Hospital. One is in the prosperous upper west side of Manhattan, "right across 72nd Street from the Dakota."* Another is at 80th Street and Third Avenue.[51] In this respect, these Cornell primary care sites serve patients with rather different economic opportunities than do the centers established by Presbyterian in Washington Heights. Smith's department also staffs an urgent care center in a blue-collar section of the Bronx that is near the Westchester Square Hospital, a part of the hospital network.

"We're there because the PO decided it had to create a primary care program," explains Smith. "Establishing a site costs about $3 million." Between eight and 10 doctors, internists, pediatricians, and obstetricians work at each location, which has about 12,000 square feet of office space. "We anticipate collecting about $2 million per year per site in the startup year, which should generate $10 million in downstream revenue to our specialists and up to $20 million in annual billings for the hospital," Smith estimates.[51] The doctors at the Cornell primary care sites accept managed care patients.[51]

Smith also has a point of view about New York's HMOs: "The managed care payers are the most difficult I've worked with in any market. Delays are the norm for getting doctors credentialed."[51]

Up the hall from the medical college, David Skinner, the New York Hospital CEO, looked with unfeigned interest at the Cornell practice

---

*This handsome apartment building, still home to some of New York's most illustrious citizens, opened in 1884. Its builder named it for that remote territory because the structure's location was then far from the center of the city where most New Yorkers lived.[50]

plan and its sizable cash flow. Although some think that he offered to buy the practice plan[52] and thereby bring the full-time doctors' billings and much of their activity under the hospital's administration, Skinner denies this.[3] Many doctors felt strongly that they wanted to keep the organization a PO, not a PHO—the *H* stands for *hospital,* as in the New York Hospital, which, they feared, would dominate the organization.[53] "David's a maneuverer," Dr. D. Jackson Coleman, chairman of ophthalmology at Cornell observes, "but we still trust him. I think it might have been better if we could have formed a PHO together with the hospital."[53]

Full-time status, despite the taxes, need not severely limit the income of those doctors, who can still generate sizable fees.[49] "Private practice in drag," Dr. Dirk Sostman, chairman of radiology and associate chief medical officer of the Physicians Organization, has heard the system called, for full-time doctors keep only what's left after their expenses and taxes are paid.[21] This custom is also practiced at the proudly academic College of Physicians and Surgeons of Columbia University. Dr. Edward Miller, the former chairman of anesthesiology there and now dean at John Hopkins, remembers: "I set my own salary so long as I could generate the money."[53a]

Although members of other, less well compensated specialties grumble, the New York Hospital supports the work of these big-practice admitters, who are employed full time by the medical college but earn almost as much as they could in private practice. Sostman and others predict that if and when capitated managed care bureaucratizes New York and the fees drop, these operators will join their other full-time colleagues in the amount of their earning power as well as in their status.[21]

Unrecovered debt to the Physicians Organization is a loophole through which some departments slide to better their financial positions. Sometimes the red ink has accumulated because of ineffective management, other times because no one has insisted that the departments make the PO whole. Staying in debt to the practice plan means that the department in effect is receiving a grant to support its activities.[21] Paying it back would almost certainly reduce the physicians' income, at least temporarily. Financially squeezing a doctor whom The New York Hospital relies on to admit well-paying patients, and thereby potentially driving him or her away, hardly appeals to executives trying to keep the hospital solvent. The hospital's need, therefore, can substantially influence decisions, even though theoretically whether or not to pay the debt should be the exclusive decision of the Physicians Organization, a medical college entity. That "the hospital has the majority of the power because it has the majority of the money" is a fact of life, observes Sostman.[21]

Chairmen such as Dr. W. Shain Schley of otolaryngology (popularly ENT, for ear, nose, and throat), who is also vice president of the medical board, often remark that "the merger's pretty terrific" after acknowledging that it has "had little effect on the average practitioner."[49] However, as physician income flattens or falls, Schley and others will find it increasingly difficult to convince their colleagues to donate time to work in the hospital clinics, supervise the trainees, or lecture.[49]

Physician Issues

The chairman of each clinical department in American medical schools also directs the relevant clinical service at the principal teaching hospital. Only at Harvard, where there are no clinical department chairmen in the conventional sense, is this organizational precept of academic medical centers not observed. Thus, Dr. Myron Weisfeldt, chairman of the Department of Medicine at P&S, is also chief of the Medical Service at Presbyterian. Similarly, Dr. Ralph Nachman, professor of medicine and chairman of the Department of Medicine at Cornell, is chief of the Medical Service at the New York Hospital.

Most affiliation agreements at academic medical centers require that the medical school nominate every attending physician on the staff of the principal teaching hospitals. For more than 15 years at P&S, only doctors accepting employment as full-time members of the faculty received such nominations and consequently privileges to work at Presbyterian Hospital,[39] where the full-time faculty admits more than 90 percent of the patients.[32] The department's practice plan handles all the financial consequences. This requirement concentrates the work and loyalty of the doctors at the medical centers and not in private offices or at other hospitals.

At New York Hospital, Cornell must also nominate those attending at the hospital — all physicians now and not the half required under the original affiliation agreement of 1912. Cornell, however, does not oblige those attending and teaching at New York Hospital to be full-time members of the faculty. The half who are "volunteers" run their own private practices, receive little if any of their income from the school, and admit 50 to 60 percent of the patients at New York Hospital.[32]* Many members of the voluntary staff attended the Cornell University Medical College

---

*In this respect, New York Hospital–Cornell appoints more like the Massachusetts General Hospital and Columbia-Presbyterian more like the Brigham and Women's Hospital.

or trained in New York Hospital.[48] Intensely loyal to the school and hospital, they teach students, interns, residents, and fellows and participate in committee work.[48]

Potential conflict arises when a physician, usually one who has developed a flourishing practice, wants to leave full-time status, run his or her own practice as a volunteer, and continue to enjoy the advantages of a faculty appointment at the medical school and admitting privileges at the teaching hospital. This is not a problem at New York Hospital, where the executives favor, and the Cornell University Medical College does not interfere with, doctors' becoming volunteers and opening private offices, often across York Avenue from the medical center.[32,48] As far as the hospital is concerned, what counts is that the new volunteers don't admit their patients elsewhere. Less pleased with such conversions are the full-time department chairmen and division chiefs. They paid many of the volunteers on a full-time basis[48] during those unprofitable years before their practices were sufficiently large to prompt the decision to leave the full-time system.

"We pay back the investment in us as full timers by the fees retained by the departments for our unpaid assignments as consultants and attendings and by our teaching," says Dr. Daniel Libby, a pulmonary specialist now practicing as a voluntary physician at New York Hospital. "Besides, the hospital benefits by our admissions."[54]

At Columbia-Presbyterian, the opposite is true. Just as P&S will not appoint clinicians to other than full-time status, the school will not approve the conversion of medical-center-based full-time doctors to volunteer status. A few senior clinicians who were appointed before the school began enforcing the full-time rule have been "grandfathered" and allowed to continue working at the medical center as volunteers. Most, however, contribute funds that are comparable to what the department and dean deduct from the collections of the full timers.[43]

Recently, the chairman of a surgical department at P&S had to demand the resignation of a colleague who was operating at community hospitals on weekends and keeping the fees.[43] "It's my time, I'm not on call at Presbyterian, so why can't I do it?" he asked his chairman.[43] Despite the intervention of Speck, who contacted the chairman of the hospital board, whom the doctor in question had treated and who offered to "negotiate the surgeon's activities," the department chairman, with Dean Pardes's support, forced the surgeon to leave when he refused to abide by the policies for full-time employment.[43]

In another case, Speck's intervention proved more effective. Dr. Jack J. Wazen, an otolaryngologist with special interest in surgery at the base of the skull and previously director of otology-neurotology at Presbyterian, opposed his chairman's practice model, which consolidated the departmental staff and space, because the plan deprived the surgeons of their offices and personal secretaries.[55] Wazen saw this design as decreasing the effectiveness of his work and interfering with his patient care. After the chairman refused to restore his previous arrangements, on July 1, 1998, Wazen had to leave the full-time staff, on which he had served since 1984. However, wanting to continue to practice at Columbia-Presbyterian, for which he feels much loyalty and affection, Wazen went to Speck, who instructed Hugh Ferguson, the hospital administrator in charge of the doctor's offices, to find Wazen space outside that allotted to his department.[56] Wazen, who continues to operate at Presbyterian, now sees patients two days per week in a small office in the Harkness Pavilion and downtown on 77th Street the rest of the time. The chairman, according to Ferguson, was "livid" about this special arrangement.[56] Although his colleagues in otolaryngology told him that what he did was "bold and courageous," they no longer refer patients to him, and the chairman proceeded to recruit a replacement for him.

"I'm forever grateful to Speck," says Wazen. "He helped me stay at Presbyterian. The hospital should continue to keep and support senior faculty and physicians who are good for the hospital. The whole dichotomy between hospital and medical school is unnecessary. The hospital has two goals, patient care and resident education. The school has another, the pursuit of its academic mission. I am also fortunate that the dean's office finally approved my switch to take place. I could not have survived this without Speck's backing and the dean's approval."[55] Wazen belongs to Columbia-Cornell Care, the university organization that contracts with HMOs on behalf of the clinical faculty and accepts most managed care patients and assignments from Medicare.[55]

Speck and the leaders of the combined hospital favor the schools' adopting one policy, the Cornell policy.[32,39,46] They fear the potential loss of the admissions of doctors going into private practice elsewhere and would like to decide who can admit to Presbyterian regardless of the wishes of the medical school.[57] The dean of P&S and his colleagues see the full-time system as the "backbone of the medical school."[41] They anticipate losing control over the administration of the clinicians' practices if the school allows doctors to convert to volunteer status. So far, "P&S has not caved on this."[39]

Consequently, each school will continue its current practice, "sovereign on its own campus," as Dr. Joan Leiman, chief administrative officer in the P&S dean's office, puts it.[39] Clinical faculty will continue to have one primary academic appointment to the faculty at either P&S or Cornell. Those who work at both campuses can receive adjunct appointments at the other school so that they can treat patients at both teaching hospitals,[46] a process said by many to be quite prolonged.

Obtaining hospital appointments is also "a very slow process," Dr. Michael Berman, the hospital director, admits, "because each of the hospitals has different criteria. We've finally decided to adopt the New York Hospital's rules throughout since they're the more rigorous." The pediatrician in Berman smiles: "New York Hospital requires that all doctors provide proof of vaccination for all the usual preventable diseases — not easy to prove if one got a measles shot as a child."[9]

Losing outstanding clinicians to other institutions or private practice elsewhere because of political differences concerns the leaders of the schools and the hospital. For this reason, if for no other, "two sets of physicians are needed," observes Tony Gotto, the Cornell dean. Concerning the growing pains between the schools and hospital, he warns, "We mustn't let this force our best people out."[58]

Consolidation of Clinical Programs

With the administrative consolidation of the two hospitals, should a single chief of service, who may or not be a chairman, reign over the appropriate clinical service at New York-Presbyterian Hospital, just as a single senior vice president, Kathryn Martin, now directs hospital operations at both campuses? John Mack, an influential hospital trustee, thinks this has to occur as financial pressures squeeze the hospital's ability to keep out of debt.[59] "Why," he asks, "should Presbyterian replace its retiring chairman of orthopedics when the chief at the Hospital for Special Surgery [which provides the orthopedic services for the neighboring New York Hospital] could do the job for both? We don't need two clinical chiefs in everything at both places."[59] John F. McGillicuddy, the board cochairman agrees, "Combining departments over time is essential."[6]

This solution comes from hospital executives and board members and not from chairmen or deans. Herb Pardes, the P&S dean, is "not that intrigued about combining chairs."[45] Tony Gotto at Cornell doesn't "take a firm position against one chair or appointing joint heads as a policy. We'll cross that bridge when we come to it."[58] Consolidating clinical departments "faces daunting challenges in combining fiercely competitive and autonomous medical departments," observed Dr. James A. Block,[30] president and chief executive officer of the Johns Hopkins Health System when the New York merger was announced and formerly one of William Speck's bosses in Cleveland. "How well it will work depends upon how it is executed. There are many, many people involved, multiple departments."[30]

"Both campuses are full-service providers of care, and they serve different constituencies," Skinner told a *New York Times* reporter.[60] This implies that both campuses of the New York-Presbyterian Hospital will offer most or all of the clinical services usually found at large university teaching hospitals and will seldom combine programs at one site or the other. As we shall see, Skinner's statement for the most part remains true and the consolidating that has occurred has been limited to special situations.

There are practical problems in combining clinical services. Dr. Ronald G. Crystal, who directs the pulmonary and critical division at Cornell, observes, "One person can't run ICUs [intensive care units] at both campuses."[31] Crystal, a distinguished investigator who came to Cornell from the NIH several years ago and has developed an experimental gene therapy program at New York Hospital, "talked to Mike Weisfeldt [chairman of medicine at P&S] about combining the pulmonary divisions. Presbyterian backed away from it. We may be able to combine the fellowships, but not so far. As for consolidating activities in general, I've seen a wall of opposition at Columbia."[31]

Whether combining clinical programs between the Presbyterian and New York campuses will save money by preventing duplication remains, as we have seen in Boston, a controversial issue.[31] The possibility concerns many of the department chairmen at both schools.[20,22] "I have to trust that 'overmerging' will not occur," says John Daly, chairman of surgery and the Lewis Atterbury Stimson Professor at Cornell. "If I was no longer chairman, would the hospital try to force the schools to accept one chairman of surgery for both campuses? I hope not."[20]

Dr. M. Flint Beal, who was recruited back to Cornell, where he took part of his house staff training, as chairman of neurology in 1998 after working at Harvard and the Massachusetts General Hospital for 20 years, senses that almost all of the chairmen at both medical schools oppose melding the residency training programs.[38]

Amalgamation is primarily an issue for full-time faculty members, since it is they and not the volunteers who are appointed chairmen and division chiefs. Nevertheless, volunteers have their own concerns about such reorganizations. Dr. Michael Wolk, a busy voluntary cardiologist and fundraiser for the Department of Medicine and Division of Cardiology at Cornell, reflects the opinion of his colleagues that the New York Hospital branch must remain a full-service hospital with none of the important medical services performed only at the Presbyterian site.[40] So far, unlike Partners, few of the fellowships have become integrated either.[24]

Cynthia N. Sparer, the director of Babies and Children's Hospital on the Presbyterian campus and a supporter of amalgamation of services whenever possible, has come to the conclusion that, in view of the angst associated with even the possibility of most clinical combinations, "Rather than force-feeding these amalgamations, let's work on less troublesome issues."[42] Based on what he was seeing, Marc H. Lory, chief operating officer of Presbyterian when Speck was its chief executive officer, agrees: "Stay away from the medical staff until restructuring the internal management is completed."[17] Faculty members understand. "Academics can get in the way of the business mission." acknowledges Jack Coleman, who has been a professor of ophthalmology at both Columbia and Cornell.[53]

Liver Transplantation

"Developing the liver transplant program would not have been possible without the merger," believes Dr. Eric A. Rose, chairman of surgery at P&S.[61] "Even if we could recruit a real headliner in the field, could he develop the referrals and successfully compete with the only program then in New York City at Mount Sinai?"[61] The merger with New York Hospital created an "enormous virtual network that would make it go."[61]

For example, hospitals in the New York Hospital network now send patients and donated organs for operation at Presbyterian, which "couldn't have happened before the merger because neither hospital had a liver transplantation program then," adds John Daly at Cornell.[20]

Rose had tried for more than two years to convince Presbyterian to support liver transplantation, which he estimated would cost $12 million over five years to establish. Speck and his associates saw this as a lot of money to build a sophisticated, low-volume, clinical program from scratch, which would have to compete with a well-established enterprise at another of the large New York City teaching hospitals. "Understandable sticker shock," comments Rose, "but we drove through the goalposts and made it happen three months before the merger was finalized."[61]

With the resources pledged by the hospital, Rose was able to recruit Dr. Jean Emond from the University of California-San Francisco to direct the program, which will be conducted only at the Presbyterian campus. Will liver transplantation develop into a self-supporting project? "The volumes are growing, and we're developing a nice research program," says Rose.[61]

Organ transplantation is one of the "high-margin, high-profile, high-financial-risk," advanced medical procedures usually carried out at university hospitals, explains Jean Emond. It is "a particularly suitable activity for the merged hospital. Transplantation services are expensive, and they shouldn't be provided at every hospital. The conflict arises when the egos of the institution's leaders and the ambitions of the academics" conflict with the economic realities.[26]

Kidneys, the most frequently transplanted organs, are transplanted at both the New York and Presbyterian sites. Hearts and lungs are transplanted only at Presbyterian and pancreases only at New York Hospital.[20]* Livers are transplanted only at Presbyterian, and the hospital executives have no intention of paying to duplicate transplantation capabilities at sites where they do not now exist.[19]

In addition to directing liver transplantation at Presbyterian, Emond says "I became the first coordinator of transplants on both campuses — the first successful service line. We ought to build more programs like this."[26]†

As for the merger itself, Eric Rose advises, "Since it exists, let's go with it. We should all be worshipping at the same temple."[61] He sees the liver transplantation program as a good example of what the merger can do. All clinical projects that New York-Presbyterian Hospital supports should be "interdisciplinary and approached with a thematic perception," Rose advises. "The program, not primarily the person, should be the basis for the recruitment."[61]‡

Medical Board[49]

Every hospital has a medical board made up of senior doctors and administrators, which is responsible for establishing professional standards

---

*The pancreas is the organ lying behind the stomach, which, among other functions, manufactures insulin, the absence of which produces diabetes.

†Born in Venezuela, Emond went to college and medical school at the University of Chicago and trained in surgery at the University of Illinois's services at Cook County, the Chicago region's immense public hospital. After fellowships in liver surgery and transplantation in Paris and at the University of Chicago, Emond joined the Department of Surgery there when David Skinner was chairman of surgery. Beginning in 1992, five years after Skinner went to the New York Hospital as CEO, Emond worked at the University of California-San Francisco. He was recruited to P&S in July 1997.

‡Rose's commitment to Columbia-Presbyterian is long-standing. A graduate of Columbia College, P&S, and cardiothoracic surgical training at Presbyterian, he joined the faculty in 1982, became director of the Division of Cardiothoracic Surgery in 1990, and in 1994 chairman of the department with the doubly endowed title of Valentine Mott and Johnson & Johnson Professor of Surgery at P&S. In 1996, he passed on the division director's job to a colleague, "one of the best things I've done" (not every new chairman has the wisdom to appoint a successor into the division he led before his elevation).

throughout the institution and assuring the adherence to them of the doctors and staff.

With the merging of the Presbyterian and New York Hospitals, the separate medical boards from each institution were united. During the fall of 1997, committees from both boards developed and adopted one set of bylaws. The new medical board of the New York-Presbyterian Hospital consists of 20 members, 10 from each campus. It includes the chiefs of the two largest services, medicine and surgery, and the president and vice president of executive committees operating at each site. The staff at New York Hospital and Presbyterian each elect six physicians. Drs. Speck and Berman, representing the senior hospital executives, became voting members. In response, the hospital's board of trustees agreed to make the president and vice president of the medical board voting members of the hospital board. Executive committees of the united medical board continue to operate at both campuses.

The presidents of the medical board during this process, Dr. John M. Driscoll Jr., chairman of pediatrics at Presbyterian, and Jack Coleman, chairman of ophthalmology at Cornell, agree that this effort demonstrated that the physician leaders of both schools can work together successfully.[53,62]

Pediatrics

Although all medical schools have departments of pediatrics, the size and complexity of the hospital services where they train students, residents, and fellows can vary greatly. Some, particularly those in independent or specialized children's hospitals, are comprehensive, with strength in most if not all of the medical and surgical subspecialty divisions. For the most part, this is the case at Babies and Children's Hospital on the Presbyterian campus. The department at New York Hospital is smaller, with fewer beds and one-quarter as many faculty members as at Columbia, which helps to explain Cornell's difficulty in fully staffing each division.

Consolidations in teaching hospitals, many observers have suggested, are more likely to succeed in activities regarding which one unit is strong and the other weak. "The most difficult departmental mergers," a senior pediatrics professor explains, involve those "when both programs are similarly strong."[63] The motivating forces then impeding consolidation are "the fear factor and loss of autonomy."[63]

"The Babies and Children's Hospital can be seen as a microcosm for the whole merger," suggests Cynthia Sparer, the executive director of the pediatric component on the Presbyterian campus.[42] Founded in 1887 and eventually settled into two houses at 56th Street and Madison Avenue in Manhattan, Babies Hospital moved into a new building at the Columbia-Presbyterian Medical Center when it opened in 1928. The new Babies Hospital — expanded in 1976 — quickly confirmed its standing as the premier pediatrics service in New York City and was the hospital where the young Dr. William Speck served his residency in the specialty. The name of the hospital evolved from Babies for most of its life to Babies and Children's Hospital of New York in 1996.

An independent legal entity when it moved to the medical center, Babies and the Neurological Institute were formally incorporated into Presbyterian in 1943, but the original names "were still to be used and every effort made to foster the interests and traditions of the separate institutions," according to Dr. Albert R. Lamb of the Presbyterian staff in his authoritative 1955 book on the history of the hospital and medical center.[1] "The one corporation," Lamb continues, "would make for economy and efficient administration and should result in better integration of the administrative and professional staffs."

Soon after the merger between the Presbyterian and New York Hospitals was announced, a nurse in the neonatal intensive care unit at the New York Hospital called a nurse at Presbyterian to request information on managing newborns with heart disease. This innocent professional question led to some Presbyterian nurses assuming that nurses from the New York Hospital would soon replace those at Babies. "Scabs," Sparer remembered hearing them called.[42] "Most employees do not understand why the merger happened. They ask 'what value does the merger have for me?' We still haven't lived the merger," Sparer believes.[42] "The hardest thing to preach is that the enemy is not within but without. People still feel locked in competition with New York or Presbyterian hospital."[42]

As the leaders work to consolidate some of the pediatrics services between the two sites, the New York-Presbyterian Hospital will invest major capital at the Presbyterian campus. A new, 9-story addition to Babies and Children's, budgeted at $120 million, will begin rising along Broadway just south of the current buildings. A fund drive to pay for the hospital is under way, with large pledges already received.[64] The new structure will contain 100 standard beds and 67 in the intensive care units, a total bed capacity similar to that in the current hospital. "We don't see the census falling, but the patients we treat will be sicker," predicts Cynthia Sparer.[42] The older buildings will gradually be renovated into outpatient, doctor's, and administrative offices and research laboratories, as was the space vacated in the old Presbyterian Hospital when the Milstein Building opened.[42,64a]

Eighty percent of the beds in the new pediatric hospital will be surgical, a distinct change from the former distribution when the medical and surgical services shared the care of inpatients almost equally. As Sparer explains, "Childrens hospitals which succeed rely on surgical admissions; they need children who require transplantation or operations for cancer, trauma, and other special problems. Those heavily involved in medical care fail."[42] Pediatric medical services used to be filled with children with respiratory illnesses. Now most patients, in particular those with asthma, can be treated as outpatients and never admitted.

Pediatric Cardiology

Babies and Children's Hospital dominates pediatric cardiology in New York City. The chief there is Dr. Welton Gersony, who has led the Babies program since 1971. Gersony, one of the best-known clinicians in the field, was named director of the combined program at both campuses in November 1997 and was, accordingly appointed adjunct professor of pediatrics at Cornell in addition to his primary professorship at P&S.

The most positive aspect of the combination has been the merger of pediatric cardiology training at the two sites. "The Cornell clinical program had dwindled, particularly after their surgeon quit. This left their fellowship program barely viable it was so small," observes Gersony.[63] Although officially directing the specialty at both campuses, Gersony was not particularly welcome at the Cornell campus during the first 18 months. However, by the fall of 1999 he was actively directing the program there. He convinced an experienced pediatric cardiologist at the North Shore Hospital on Long Island to move to Cornell and begin building as he had done at Presbyterian. Gersony now visits the New York Hospital site two half days a week, teaching and seeing private patients there.[63]

One plan Gersony would like to see develop at Cornell reflects one of his most satisfying initiatives at Babies and Children's. "In 1985, we started a program involving our former fellows who had taken jobs at nearby community hospitals. We gave them Columbia faculty appointments and treated them as full-time members of the department — *part time* is not in my vocabulary. Each of them spends one or two days a week at Babies, seeing patients in the clinic or working in the clinical labs. The key is making them feel they are part of Babies."[63] The practical result, of course, is that these doctors—there are now 14 of them working with 20 others based geographically at Babies and Children's—bring their sick children to Presbyterian and help to maintain the large clinical program at the medical center. After completing their treatment at Babies, the children return to the care of pediatricians in the community.

When asked why he bothers at this stage of his distinguished career to involve himself at another medical center on the other side of Manhattan Island when he has plenty to do at the Washington Heights campus, Gersony responds simply, "The hospital says it's a financial must." It is clear that pediatric cardiology would never have been united at the Babies and New York hospitals without the strong influence of the leaders of the NewYork-Presbyterian Hospital, which provided the impetus and money for what Gersony is accomplishing. "It would have been reasonable to have only an outpatient presence at New York Hospital, but politically it would have been unacceptable to Cornell."[63]

To further the collaboration, Gersony has formed a center for pediatric cardiology and cardiac surgery through which the hospital directs the funds for development. Thanks to this help, Gersony has arranged that an adult cardiologist at Presbyterian, who took some of his training with Gersony's unit, will establish a new service at both sites for adults with congenital heart disease, a relative new subspecialty, which has developed as children whose lesions have been successfully corrected become adults and need care that the average adult cardiologist is not experienced in handling.[65] Gersony has also successfully recruited a leading expert from another well-known East Coast medical school to direct the pediatric catheterization laboratories at both sites.[63]

The chairman of pediatrics at Cornell, Dr. Maria I. New, a distinguished endocrinologist and the only member of the active faculty who is a member of the National Academy of Sciences, "had little luck finding a successor to Mary Allen Engle," the chief of pediatric cardiology for several decades, "partly because the clinical program was so relatively small."[37]

Dr. Arthur Klein, vice chairman of the department, explains: "We have special problems. Our area is not child rich compared with Presbyterian's, where the families are younger and have more children. I understand that Gersony receives money from the medical school, but we don't. As a rule, the clinical departments at Cornell have to make it on their own financially."[66]

Klein is referring to Columbia's greater tolerance for departments' temporarily running cash deficits while building programs, an accommodation that Gersony has utilized to develop pediatric cardiology at

Babies. "Cornell won't allow this," he has heard, "which inhibits building programs there."[63]

"On the research side," says New, "I'm looking for a molecular cardiologist, very rare in pediatric cardiology, to work from the Engle endowment," which was established to honor the former division chief.[37] "My imprimatur is to make our department more academic. We have the biggest pediatric clinical research center [an NIH-sponsored group of beds and laboratories where investigators study the mechanisms of disease] in the country. The way to help children is to advance research."[37]

Welton Gersony is optimistic. He sees NewYork-Presbyterian Hospital having the proper setting for consolidation in his specialty. "Putting medical and surgical pediatric cardiology together here at Babies — it's difficult to get over saying 'here' and 'there' — and at New York Hospital makes sense since one program is strong and the other less so."[63]

Pediatric Cardiac Surgery

A program the consolidators discuss with particular satisfaction is pediatric cardiac surgery, one of the few clinical services that has completely merged.[58] Putting it together was relatively easy. The cardiac surgeon who operated on children with heart disease at the New York Hospital left for another job, and no one there was skilled in this highly technical field. The pediatricians were referring patients who required surgery involving all but the most routine procedures to other hospitals, sometimes as far away as the Boston Children's Hospital and seldom to Presbyterian.[67]

At Babies and Children's Hospital, the director of the pediatric cardiac surgical service of the Columbia-Presbyterian Medical Center, Dr. Jan Modest Quaegebeur, described by a colleague who chairs one of the surgical departments at P&S as "the best in the world,"[68] was running the most successful program in the region. Born in Oostende in the Flemish-speaking part of Belgium, Quaegebeur had trained in Belgium, the Netherlands, with Dr. Michael deBakey in Houston, and then in pediatric cardiac surgery in Leiden, a renowned center for this specialty, where he wrote his Ph.D. thesis on a particularly complicated, then new operation for congenital heart disease. In the late 1980s, Columbia-Presbyterian recruited him from Erasmus University in Rotterdam, where he had been appointed professor of pediatric cardiac surgery and chief of service to succeed the retiring Columbia surgeons who had developed a well-known clinic for children with congenital heart disease. Quaegebeur brought to New York particular skill in operating on newborns and infants. "It was an offer I couldn't refuse,"[67] says Quaegebeur, and he began working at Babies Hospital in February 1990.

By the time the merger occurred, Quaegebeur and his colleague were operating with excellent clinical results on 400 to 450 babies and children each year. Asked to also work at New York Hospital, he introduced the technical protocols that had helped him operate so successfully at Presbyterian by inviting the New York Hospital nurses, anesthesiologists, and perfusionists, who operate the heart-lung machines essential for these operations, to observe and work with him at Columbia.[67] When Quaegebeur felt that each was properly trained, he began to operate on the east side of town. In a recent year, he and his team treated 90 patients there with results comparable to those at Columbia-Presbyterian.[67] He and his colleagues now operate on all the New York Hospital patients there except for the sickest neonates, whom he transfers to Babies where his team has had more experience handling these delicate cases.[67] This practice has "caused some dissatisfaction" on the New York Hospital campus, but Quaegebeur believes that for now he and his team can treat these babies more successfully at Presbyterian.[67]

Quaegebeur's program dominated the region even before the merger, with the surgeons in the second-largest program in New York City performing less than half as many cases per year. He projects that the combined New York-Presbyterian program will treat more than 600 cases annually within three years with a staff of four or five surgeons.[67] The economics of the program shows that the payer mix is better at Presbyterian, where Medicaid in New York State, at least so far, pays quite generously for the treatment of sick children from poor families. The majority of cases in the combined program continues to come from pediatricians accustomed to referring to the service at Babies. In accordance with Quaegebeur's reputation, 60 percent of the patients are neonates or infants.[67]

Since the referral patterns that bring children to the two hospitals do not overlap geographically, Quaegebeur sees his program's leadership in the region growing. To accomplish this, he must recruit two associates, one of whom will base his work at the New York Hospital site. Complicating such a recruitment is the reality that if there's no business at the hospital a surgeon is less likely to come, and if there's no surgeon there'll be no business and the entire pediatric cardiology enterprise will remain underdeveloped. Here the merger may help. The surgeon based at the New York Hospital can operate at Babies until the program builds at the east side site, thereby keeping him busy and helping to integrate the team.[63] When a next surgeon does arrive, Quaegebeur will operate mostly at Babies but continue to help out at the New York Hospital campus while supervising the work at both places as he does now. Conferences are now held alternately on both campuses.

Although many believe the presence of Quaegebeur's team at the New York Hospital has improved the care of the sick children who are brought there, the arrangement is not working perfectly. Although they are "trying to keep out of politics," Quaegebeur senses that the adult cardiac surgeons at the New York Hospital see them as "those guys from Columbia doing some cases here"[67] and keeping the money at P&S.[22] One cause of this feeling may have been a misunderstanding, subsequently repaired, between the Cornell and Columbia deans over financial distributions of fees earned by the Presbyterian surgeons working at the New York Hospital.[67]

Dr. O. Wayne Isom, chairman of the Department of Cardiac Surgery at Cornell, acknowledges Quaegebeur's skill. "However," he says, "Dr. Quaegebeur's time is stretched very thin when you consider he is the only pediatric cardiac surgeon covering both campuses." Since traveling from one campus to the other can take from 20 to 90 minutes, "the time spent devoted to post-op care or talking to families becomes very limited," Isom adds.[23]

Isom, who beguiles with his Texas-inherited "good old boy" manner of speaking,* postponed hiring a replacement for a pediatric cardiac surgeon who was leaving while the merger was being completed, and the hospital wasn't inclined to support pediatric cardiology at the New York Hospital site then. The educational program at the New York Hospital, however, suffered because the physical separation of the Presbyterian and New York sites made "presenting cases to the groups of interns and residents from both campuses almost impossible."[23]

More recently, the hospital's interest in supporting Isom's program

---

*Isom was born in Lubbock, Texas, in 1940 and received his M.D. degree and trained in surgery at the University of Texas Southwestern Medical School in Dallas — universally called Southwestern and generally accepted as the leading medical school in the Texas system. Its principal training hospital is Parkland, well known in academic medicine for its excellence and renowned as the hospital to which President Kennedy was brought when he was shot. Isom learned his cardiothoracic surgery at New York University, where he later joined the staff led by Dr. Frank Spencer, the department chairman and a nationally recognized cardiac surgeon. In 1985, the New York Hospital and Cornell recruited Isom uptown with the carrot that he would become chairman of a new department of cardiothoracic surgery. At most schools — Stanford, which we will look at in chapters 6 and 7, being one of the few exceptions — the chief of cardiothoracic surgery leads a division within the department of surgery.

has increased. "Mike Berman has really helped me, so we've recruited a new pediatric cardiac surgeon who will be based at New York Hospital. Also the Columbia campus has recruited another pediatric cardiac surgeon to be chief up there. Dr. Quaegebeur will remain overall chief of both programs. All three of the pediatric cardiac surgeons will be able to cross cover for weekends and vacations as we expand both programs."[23] Isom also praises the recruitment of another pediatric cardiologist for the Department of Pediatrics at the New York Hospital.

In the spring of 1999, Isom believed that, from the patient care point of view, the merger was failing, but, more recently, "as the merger has matured, the likelihood of success has risen, though the jury is still out as to what the real advantages will turn out to be."[23]

Pediatric Surgery

After much delay, a search committee selected Dr. Charles Stoler of Babies and Children's Hospital as the chief of general pediatric surgery at both campuses.[9] "This wasn't easy," recalls Cynthia Sparer, the Babies Hospital director. "When the recruits came in, the docs at New York Hospital, which never developed pediatric surgery — the head of general pediatric surgery there had departed for greener fields elsewhere — complained 'woe is us. You'll be dazzled by uptown [Babies and Children's] and not pay attention to us.'* Merger politics at play."

Stoler received academic appointments at both Cornell and Columbia with equal status, not one primary and the other adjunct, but he is only tenured at Columbia, the campus of his major employment. "He'll recruit an associate chief at the other campus. The dollars will flow into a black box. Taxing is still being worked out," says Dr. Michael Berman, the hospital director. Confirming the complex aspects of such a recruitment, five people — the two deans, both surgery chairmen, and the director of the NewYork-Presbyterian Hospital — signed the offer letter.[9]

Pediatric Endocrinology

Dr. Maria New has been appointed the superchief of pediatric endocrinology at NewYork-Presbyterian. "Most of the staff at Presbyterian trained with me," she says "so I hope that soon the two endocrine programs will work closely together."[37]

---

*There were 10 pediatric surgeons at the Presbyterian site and one at the New York Hospital.[42]

Recent Consolidations

In 2000, the departments of rehabilitation medicine at the two sites combined under the leadership of James Lieberman who is based at Presbyterian.[45] During the same year, the residency in otolaryngology merged.

Nonconsolidation of Programs

Adult Cardiology and Cardiac Catheterization Laboratories

At the meetings of the American College of Cardiology in the spring of 1998, several of his friends approached Dr. David O. Williams about a job leading invasive cardiology and helping to unify the cardiac catheterization laboratories at the Presbyterian and New York Hospital campuses.[19,69] In cardiac catheterization laboratories, cardiologists define specific features of patients' heart disease and open closed coronary arteries with balloons, stents, or drugs. Pediatric cardiologists can repair congenital heart lesions through cardiac catheterization, often avoiding cardiac surgery for these children. This work is often referred to as "invasive" or "interventional" because the operators can "intervene" in the process that produces heart attacks or angina (chest pain from disease of the coronary or cardiac arteries).

Williams was then quite comfortable as director of interventional cardiology at the Rhode Island Hospital and professor of medicine at Brown University. "But why not," he thought, and came to New York for "exploratory discussions."[69] When he arrived, Williams asked for a job description. None existed. He then asked how his superiors would judge his performance. What was he expected to accomplish in, say, two or three years? No one could say. Who would be his boss? This was unsettled, although one executive heard that Bill Speck favored Williams reporting directly to him. "I was getting a lot of mixed messages," is how he summarizes the experience.[69] "The hospital was ready for a united job, but the faculty wasn't."[69] Subsequently, the chief of cardiology at Cornell asked Williams to consider leading the clinical and research programs at the cath lab just on the New York Hospital campus, but the NewYork-Presbyterian Hospital, holding the purse strings, would not support this approach. By the summer, Williams told the New York people that he would stay in Providence.

"The attempt to merge the cath labs was undertaken without adequate thought about how this would work with the two schools and their faculties," remembers Dr. Allan Schwartz, the director of the cardiac catheterization laboratory at Presbyterian.[14] "Top-notch people were invited, but the process was hideously embarrassing. The good side of it was that it got us talking with the people downtown [at the New York Hospital]."[14]

Dr. Sheldon Goldberg,* who also looked at the position in the winter of 1998 agrees.[70] "There seemed to be much mutual suspicion, hostility, even backbiting between the cardiologists at Columbia and Cornell, and the reporting structure would be very unusual in my experience. Dr. Speck told me that I would report directly to him. Regarding the details of the job, the place seemed to be totally disorganized."[70]

At Presbyterian, Dr. Milton Packer leads one of the nation's most respected programs in the treatment of congestive heart failure, the condition that develops when the heart has been severely affected by heart attacks or the destructive process known as cardiomyopathy. It is these patients, and the number of those who survive is increasing as the treatment of patients with heart failure improves, who become candidates for cardiac transplantation. The NewYork-Presbyterian Hospital suggested charging Dr. Packer to direct the congestive heart failure services at both sites. The physician leaders at Cornell objected, saying that such a relatively common and important illness needs strong independent programs at both campuses.

Despite this controversy, patients with end-stage congestive heart failure at the Cornell campus all go to Presbyterian for cardiac transplantation. Formerly, the cardiologists at the New York Hospital would send many of these patients elsewhere.[20] "The docs wouldn't have been so cooperative without the merger," predicts John Daly, the Cornell chairman of surgery. "They're beginning to act like cousins rather than competing neighbors."[20]

Complicating this subject is the desire of Eric Rose, Columbia's chairman of surgery and a cardiac surgeon himself, to organize "an absolutely top cardiac center" involving both hospital sites and medical schools.[61] This vision came to him as he turned down the opportunity to succeed one of the most famous cardiac surgeons in the country at a particularly wealthy teaching hospital — with "tons of resources" — in another part of the country. "I decided that I preferred staying here at home but only if I could help build an interdepartmental and interinstitutional

---

*At the time, Goldberg was director of the Center of Excellence in Interventional Cardiology at the Massachusetts General Hospital. He was previously chief of cardiology at the Jefferson Medical College in Philadelphia.

unit which would be a champion, not the playoff candidate we are now."[61] At this writing, Rose is working hard to pull together the departments, faculty, and funds to "beat the Cleveland Clinic, my model of such an enterprise."[61] He will have to resolve all the issues already raised and others yet to surface to accomplish this ambitious goal.

As a final complexity, Dr. Michael Berman, the NewYork-Presbyterian Hospital director, began negotiating with leading cardiologists in Washington and New York to bring their programs to his hospital. One of the prospective recruits runs one of the largest and nationally best known catheterization-based cardiology programs in a large community hospital and would clearly, if he comes to New York, dominate the invasive cardiology work at both the Presbyterian and New York Hospital sites. Observers found it interesting, and some faculty members troubling, that this recruitment was being conducted by a hospital official, albeit a former chairman of pediatrics and a cardiologist himself, rather than by one or both of the directors of the departments of medicine or the cardiology divisions at Columbia or Cornell.

The recruitments did not come about, and P&S medicine chairman Weisfeldt chose Allan Schwartz, the director of his cardiac catheterization laboratories, as the new chief of cardiology at Presbyterian.

Neurosurgery and Neurology

Another clinical service ripe for possible consolidation was neurosurgery, but it didn't occur. Both campuses were simultaneously looking for new leaders. The chairman of neurosurgery at a leading academic center in another city was brought in as a potential chairman for both schools and director of the clinical program at both hospital sites. The schools and hospitals never made a unified offer, and the candidate stayed where he was.

Presbyterian then began its own search in the fall of 1997 when the New York and Presbyterian Hospital, then its name, was only a few months from formally beginning unified operations on January 1, 1998. The committee's choice was Dr. Robert A. Solomon, a P&S professor known for his operative work on cerebral aneurysms, which are vascular abnormalities within the brain.

Presbyterian had great strength in neurology and neurosurgery due to its famous Neurological Institute. At Cornell, however, neurosurgery was a division of the Department of Surgery, not an independent department, a status the specialty had long enjoyed at Columbia. From Solomon's point of view, the quality of the academic work in neurosurgery at Columbia far exceeded Cornell's,[68] an analysis with which Dr. Lewis

Rowland, the former chairman of neurology at P&S,[57] and Dr. Timothy Pedley, the current chairman,[71] not unexpectedly agree.

When the division chief at New York Hospital retired and other neurosurgeons transferred to voluntary status,[3] Solomon proposed that he direct a combined program at both campuses with a site chief on the east side of town. However, Antonio Gotto, the Cornell dean, quashed the proposal and proceeded with the recruitment of Cornell's own chairman of a new department of neurosurgery. David Skinner, of course, is paid to keep his hospital full and has been heard to say about the neurosurgical search, "Don't bring me someone who can't bring me a New York practice."[68] Nevertheless, Skinner continues to favor the "Solomon solution."[3]

Gotto doesn't "take a firm position against one chair or appointing joint heads as a policy: We'll cross that bridge when we come to it."[58]

Solomon, who strongly approves of the merger of the hospitals despite the events in his specialty, believes, like Bill Speck, that there are too many medical centers in New York City and that only by coming together can some of them survive and prosper.[68] However, although the merger was billed as producing a unified medical center with "everybody rowing the same oar," the universities appear desirous of retaining their own programs.[68] Deans do not intuitively favor, Solomon has observed, giving up the direction of their departments, certainly the large and successful ones, to another medical school, even one linked through a merger of the principal teaching hospitals. The leaders and some of the faculty at each school of medicine perceive the appointment of a chief from the other campus to direct a large program at their site as constituting a dangerous and threatening precedent to the status and authority of their school. "Here's the invasion we're all worried about," he thinks some have concluded.[68] "There's still lots of suspicion. Everybody's resisting a real merger. I suspect we will continue to be competing entities."[68]

Rowland sees the one-chairman thesis as "unnatural."[57]

"Combining neurosurgery at the time seemed logical," suggests Rogerio Lobo, Solomon's colleague as chairman of obstetrics and gynecology at P&S, "except that Cornell wants parity with Columbia and is looking inward, filling in where we're strong. I see the medical schools actually pulling further apart, if that's possible."

Neurology also presented an opportunity to appoint one director for both campuses. Following the retirement of Lewis Rowland at P&S and Fred Plum at Cornell, both eminent academic neurologists who had been chairmen at their schools for decades, a candidate from a West Coast school was brought in to look at both jobs. "Although the hospital wanted him, the deans decided that neurology departments were too important to the schools to have them combined," says Dr. Timothy A. Pedley, the Columbia professor who succeeded Rowland on January 1, 1998.[71]

Eighteen months later, Flint Beal from the Massachusetts General Hospital succeeded Plum, who observed to a reporter from the *Wall Street Journal* that a merger "would degrade the productivity" of both.[72] He added, "derisively," the reporter wrote, "They could cut him [a single neurology chairman for both schools] down the middle and on Monday, Wednesday and Friday the right side of his body could go uptown [Columbia-Presbyterian], and then on Tuesday and Thursday his left side could come down [New York Hospital–Cornell]."[72] The West Coast applicant withdrew.

Pedley complains about his lack of success in forming a unified program in epilepsy built around Dr. Martha J. Morrell, a West Coast specialist he successfully recruited who had "built the Stanford program so well that she drove University of California-San Francisco out of business."[71,73]* All Cornell would accept is a common ambulatory facility for these patients in midtown. "We have to help Cornell," he was told. "We're not building on our strengths. The merger's failing because the leadership has not been able to meet their objective of streamlining the high-resource, high-end stuff."[71]

Morrell adds, "The size of our epilepsy program is as large as many well-known academic neurology departments."[73] Morrell, the head of the Epilepsy Foundation and a nationally admired leader in the field, moved east to show nationally what could be done for clinical epilepsy in New York. But she has been frustrated in trying to develop the clinical program promised to her when she left Stanford. "Although P&S is very strong in epilepsy research, we can't increase patient care because of our poor outpatient facility, and the hospital won't support it because of what Mike Berman and Steve Corwin [who directs the service line project] call 'political effects.' The hospital won't give me the money for Presbyterian alone, but Cornell won't let me set up a combined program. Meantime, the competitors are rising, and we could lose our preeminent status since NYU has developed a huge and very responsive enterprise."[73]

Morrell has had to deal with three different administrative teams since she arrived in September 1998. "The latest administrator is a nice enough person, but she's inexperienced and insensitive to doctors. She's

---

*"Not quite," says Morrell, "but we did build up a large and very well regarded program."[73]

straight out of her MBA and administration internship and already in charge of neurology at both sites."[73] All this is very familiar to Morrell. "At Stanford, there was much talk about one merged epilepsy program with me in charge of it, but the UCSF guy wouldn't agree. I came here because I thought this merger would work."[73]

Berman explains that when Pedley began recruiting there wasn't a chairman of neurology at Cornell to settle the deal and that by the time Morrell was appointed the hospital had not yet agreed to develop one epilepsy program under her direction.[9]

Obstetrics and Gynecology

"I'm not resigning the chair so that the chief at Presbyterian can run both departments," declares Dr. William J. Ledger, chairman of the Department of Obstetrics and Gynecology at Cornell. Recently feted for his 20 years of leadership, Ledger has seen that attempts to share faculty have "come a cropper. If I were offered the combined chair, I couldn't do it. It would take years just to learn the practical things and the customs at Presbyterian while also trying to run the department here."

The Cornell pathology chairman, Daniel Knowles, agrees. "I was offered a chair at another medical school with two hospitals which were widely separated. I turned it down, didn't think it was doable."[24]

Ledger finds too many differences between the institutions for such arrangements to flourish, and, besides, "P&S is arrogant about the quality of their programs." The strength of the merger, Ledger believes, is in "the size of the two places. We should concentrate on making them both better. The reality is that the two medical schools don't want to be one; the programs should continue to compete with each other."[22]

The merger was driven by the boards, he believes, "and a few of the senior hospital executives. The medical leadership and staff were never asked." Ledger served on a committee that questioned each of the Cornell chairs about the effects of the merger. "All were concerned about turf and losing control of what they did."[22]

Ledger also reports a worry that the talk about a merger aroused in many of the Cornell faculty members. "Would the New York Hospital, which was the 800-pound gorilla versus Cornell before, now become an even bigger problem?[22] At least we have our practice plan [the Cornell Physicians Organization], which, as a strong independent entity, can counter some of the hospital's power."[22]

When David Skinner arrived in 1987, Bill Ledger admits, "I wanted to get rid of him. He and the dean at the time, who had recruited me, were at loggerheads, and David seemed to have no compunctions in running over the medical school. My point of view turned 180 degrees. He took care of the million-dollar weekly losses. I came to like him, particularly because you know where you are with David and he's dedicated to doing things right."[22] Since the merger, however, "He's deeply missed, having been bumped to a higher level."[22] If the reorganization dictated by the merger falters or the financial savings don't materialize, Ledger predicts that "the board will look for a scapegoat. They'll want someone's head, but it won't be Skinner's. He's too well liked, and he's done too much."[22]

By the fall of 1999, Ledger had become, if anything, even more pessimistic about the value of the merger. "We have nothing to show for it. We're less efficient, losing money, and have less market share. We're too big and getting no savings." Ledger emphasizes the distance between the board of trustees and the doctors. "We think the board doesn't get it, and I suspect they think we don't get it. David sold them a fantasy, and they're acting on it."[22]

Ledger decided to retire from his chair in September of 1999, having lost enthusiasm for fighting unsuccessfully for the services and support his department needs. "I'm much happier this way," he says. Ledger received assurances that Cornell would appoint a successor and his department would not be directed by a common chairman from Columbia.[22]

Dr. Rogerio Lobo, who chairs the Department of Obstetrics and Gynecology at Columbia, fundamentally agrees with Ledger's point of view about joining the departments. "The hospital executives floated a plan that when Bill [Ledger] retired I would be responsible for both campuses. I knew this would never work at Cornell, which wants its own department. Bill told me that Gotto [Antonio Gotto, the Cornell dean] agreed.[74] We might bring together some of our divisions like gyn oncology [cancer of the female reproductive organs] or fetal medicine or possibly prepare a common hospital budget. But we need on-site autonomy and shouldn't combine our residency training programs." Lobo has found that "This lack of clinical integration is consistent with every other merger. Everybody wants his own thing."[74]

Pathology[24]

With Daniel Knowles, the former Columbia faculty member, now at Cornell as chairman of the Department of Pathology, collaborating within the merged hospital seemed like a natural development. Knowles, an acknowledged expert in the field of hematopathology, the study of diseased blood cells, suggested to his former chairman, Michael Shelanski at

P&S, that the specimens in this area be brought to the New York Hospital for study and diagnosis. In return, Knowles would send his kidney pathology to Columbia, which had greater strength in this field. The proposal fell through because Dr. Karen H. Antman, the chief of oncology at Presbyterian, insisted that P&S have its own hematopathologist, a field that includes leukemia and lymphoma, cancers in which medical centers specialize. "You've got to trust your pathologist," Antman says.[75] "Leukemias are emergencies. You can't be sending smears and biopsies off campus and waiting hours for an answer." She offered to help Shelanski hire a replacement for Knowles at Presbyterian, and that is what happened.[24]

The routine clinical laboratories offer a less controversial opportunity for potential amalgamation in the future. The New York Hospital is installing a highly computerized, robotized, and very expensive ($12 million) clinical laboratory, with greater capacity than can immediately be utilized locally. The savings in personnel costs that the laboratory's equipment will provide should pay for the investment in three years. This period could shorten if the lab takes on work from Presbyterian and the network hospitals. Their samples might be processed at the New York Hospital more economically despite the need to transport the specimens. One of the issues to be worked through is a feature of the union contract at Presbyterian that prohibits moving certain samples to a non-unionized laboratory. Shelanski is optimistic that consolidation of the clinical laboratories will occur relatively soon.[36]

Thanks to these developments, Shelanski's and Knowles's programs have arranged to support three or four residents in clinical pathology who will train jointly at both the Presbyterian and New York Hospital sites, an opportunity that would not have been possible without the merger.[36]

Psychiatry

Before the New York–Presbyterian merger, the leaders of psychiatry at Columbia, Cornell, and the Catholic hospitals based at St. Vincent's Hospital in Manhattan were putting together a partnership to develop their clinical programs. They planned on promoting a common 800 telephone number for patients requiring psychiatric care and developing a unified approach to contract for managed care. "This effort fell apart once our hospital's merger with Presbyterian came about," says Dr. Jack D. Barchas, the Cornell chairman, "much to the disappointment and anger of our colleagues at the Catholic hospitals."[76] The New York–Presbyterian merger was "not necessary as far as we're concerned and has actually slowed up what we could have done in psychiatry such as arranging common care at Presbyterian and at our services down-town and in Westchester County," where the New York Hospital long operated a large psychiatric hospital and clinic in White Plains."[76]

Barchas is disappointed by the efforts of various organizations to obtain managed care contracts in his specialty. "John Lavan's people are so slow in developing contracts [the system's finance office, which con-tracts for hospital services] and CCC [Columbia-Cornell Care, the uni-versities' organization that solicits managed care contracts on behalf of the faculty] is almost irrelevant for us. In many of their contracts, psychi-atric services are not included."[76]

Despite these reservations about the help he receives in obtaining managed care patients, Barchas praises Marvin O'Quinn, the hospital officer in charge of mental health services. "He's a magnificently cap-able guy, extraordinarily articulate and an excellent advocate for psychi-atric services."[76]

Barchas does not support the "single best hospital" thesis which motivated many of the most enthusiastic merger-makers. "I think it's a naïve thought."[76]

Clinical Trials

P&S and Presbyterian are proud of their joint office of clinical trials, which coordinates clinical research with various granting agencies and companies that manufacture drugs. "During the most recent year, the unit has supervised studies worth about $36 million," says Michael I. Leahey, director of the Office of Clinical Trials at the Columbia-Presbyterian campus. Leahey, who brings both academic and business experience to the trials office, reported to a committee of investiga-tors and administrators from Columbia and Presbyterian before the merger and now to Columbia and NewYork-Presbyterian Hospital and its network.

As members of the university clinical faculty, some of whom for-merly participated in clinical trials, respond to the pressure to spend more time practicing to generate adequate incomes, Leahey and his investigator colleagues have increasingly turned to community physi-cians associated with hospitals, many in the network, where he finds "outstanding clinical practitioners anxious to partner with academic thought leaders. To meet the demand for high-quality, well-trained sites, the office of clinical trials recently created a new division, which partners with Columbia, Cornell, and NewYork-Presbyterian."[77]

Using a formula the administrators and investigators have agreed to, P&S and the hospital distribute the proceeds from the trials, all of which is reinvested to support clinical research. "Pardes had the leadership and vision to assign money to the unit," says Dr. David Bickers, chairman of the clinical trials committee.[78] "We've been able to convince the departments to share some of their authority with the unit and help the investigators comply with what the sponsors require."[78]

The unit also succeeds by offering pharmaceutical houses "a modern business office with standardized budgeting for them to deal with."[77] The reputation of the group has spread. "We've been visited by more than 100 medical centers and universities," Leahey reports.[77]

Leahey comes from a medical family — his father was a surgeon and his brother a cardiologist — and consequently "is not intimidated by doctors," according to Bickers.[78]

Although both medical schools are now partners in the network portion of the unit, Leahey's group does not represent research taking place exclusively at the Cornell campus. "Gotto wouldn't budge despite the efforts of Pardes and Skinner," Leahey remembers. "Cornell would have shared in the overheads [the indirect costs charged by academic institutions for research], but they wanted their own unit."[77]

Bickers, who also chairs the Department of Dermatology at P&S, believes that "running the unit as a seamless operation across departments was too radical for Cornell to take on. Some of the old paranoia at work — here comes Columbia-Presbyterian again."[78]

Discord with the merged hospital over Leahey's unit emerged when a large pharmaceutical company wanted to develop and pay for a 36-bed inpatient service at Presbyterian, where patients would participate in trials of drugs for the treatment of cardiovascular diseases. Acquiring suitable space for the unit brought Bickers into conflict with executives at NewYork-Presbyterian Hospital: "They were giving us the runaround."[78]

Coincidentally, in March of 1999, trustees John Mack and Daniel Burke invited Bickers to have lunch with them for a wide-ranging discussion of hospital issues. Bickers, who had been recruited to Presbyterian from Case-Western Reserve in Cleveland, was a friend and close associate of William Speck in several of the Presbyterian merger attempts. "We met in a private dining room at Morgan Stanley Dean Witter [where John Mack is the president] and got around to discussing how the two schools could cooperate better. I told them about the drug company sponsored inpatient unit and that it would pay off for the hospital and could be the first of several such deals."[78]

The next thing he heard about the issue was an irate phone call from David Skinner. "How dare you go around me and discuss this with trustees," he shouted at Bickers. One had called Skinner about the problem. "I've got space down here [the New York Hospital site] for this," he told Bickers.[78] Skinner was holding the Presbyterian space Bickers had his eye on for possible use by Babies and Children's' Hospital if it could not fund its new building.

"He showed me the space in the old New York Hospital. 'Look at the beautiful views!'"[78] But the drug company didn't want the views. It wanted the participation of Dr. Milton Packer, a leading investigator of drugs for treatment of heart disease, and Packer, a professor at Columbia, was based at Presbyterian. Skinner kept pushing to build the unit at the New York Hospital. "David didn't get it that this was a scientific issue. 'It's just real estate,'" Bickers remembers Skinner telling him. Michael Leahey checked with his contact at the drug company, who confirmed that they wanted Packer with the beds at Presbyterian and had no interest in the New York Hospital.

"John Mack called me for a progress report. I said we were working on it." Bickers didn't want to anger Skinner again by further involving a trustee.[78] By the time NewYork-Presbyterian had found space at Presbyterian acceptable to both Bickers and Skinner, the drug house had replaced the executive who favored the project with someone less enthusiastic. Bickers fears the scheme is probably dead.[78*]

In view of all these difficulties in pulling clinical programs together, Eli Ginzberg, the Columbia economist, finds NewYork-Presbyterian "a make believe merger, with absolutely no commitment for heads of clinical departments to buy in."[79]

Service Lines

The hospital leadership favors combining clinical programs into "service lines," organized groupings of such medical and surgical specialties as cardiology, geriatrics, neurology, oncology, transplantation, and women's health. "In 10 years, only service lines, which are much better for patients, will exist. Departments are anachronisms," Tim Pedley remembers Speck saying.[71]

Dr Steven J. Corwin, a cardiologist based at the Presbyterian campus, leads this effort at both sites, reporting to Marvin O'Quinn and through him to Dr. Michael Berman. Corwin's job before the merger was chief medical officer at Presbyterian. "How and where should one build clinical programs?" Corwin asks. "The old department structure

---

*Skinner remembers the episode somewhat differently. "First, I didn't shout or say 'how dare you.' Not my style."[3]

misses something. It's based on shaping the product by constantly adding ornaments to the Christmas tree rather than by buying the right tree.
We should proceed along disease management, rather than organizational, lines."[19]

This concept cuts to the heart of the traditional departmental arrangements at academic medical centers and exemplifies, as Corwin and
others explain, "the basic power struggle between the dean of the medical schools and the directors of the hospital in choosing which clinical
programs to develop and, almost more fundamentally, which faculty to
hire and support."[19]

Traditionally, the chairman and his senior associates leading the
subspecialty divisions recruit faculty to fill specific clinical or research
slots that they determine the department needs and can fund or develop
the means to finance. The chairman's priorities, however, may not
equate with those of the hospital director, who may want to recruit
someone to run a disease-oriented program such as, for example, a
comprehensive program in neurological illnesses. The individual selected to direct such an enterprise should, from the hospital's viewpoint,
be responsible for all the clinical work in adult and pediatric neurology
and neurosurgery, currently the purview of as many as eight doctors
directing these activities in three independent medical school departments — neurology, neurosurgery and pediatrics — and on two campuses.
Such an approach would consolidate the subject even more comprehen-
sively than just bringing together the discipline of neurosurgery under
one director, a project that, as we have seen, the two schools and the
hospital could not accomplish.

The first efforts to establish these service lines were "extremely
disruptive," Corwin admits, "both academically and operationally. The
faculty didn't see any compelling strategic reasons for doing this, so the
hospital backed off. Actually, everyone understands that the hospital
has to change to compete successfully, and many" — Corwin may exaggerate here — "accept that the service line concept is the way to go, but
people are fearful about the leadership issues."[19]

Corwin and his associates are now defining what they mean by
service lines, what their governance should be, how they should be
managed clinically, what the cost implications are, and how much should
be invested in each. The hospital leaders are working to develop such
integrated programs in cancer, heart disease, and neurological disease at
both the Presbyterian and New York Hospital sites.[19]

In attempting to carry out this ambitious program, the hospital enjoys a fundamental advantage over the medical schools. Only it has
the beds and clinic space to allocate and the money to buy the equipment

and recruit and pay the doctors, nurses, technicians, and supporting personnel. Consequently, Berman and Corwin, backed by Skinner and Speck, can approve and fund those projects that support the consolidated service-line-oriented approach and not fund those programs at both campuses whose proponents want to develop or expand them under separate administration at only one site.[19]

Bringing clinical programs together, however, must resolve a fundamental difference between the sites. Columbia and Presbyterian have more academically admired, specialized programs, but they tend to be less well structured and more loosely run. At Cornell and the New York Hospital, the management is more effective and the programs more coherently administered, but the academic strength of many of the programs is less potent.[19] To some extent, therefore, the doctors at each site think those at the other site are taking over, administratively by the New York Hospital contingent and academically by those at Columbia-Presbyterian. David Skinner was heard to say that "The merger must be working. Both sides say they're being taken over."[14]

But whether or not the service line concept will succeed is uncertain. Aubrey Serfling, the chief operating officer of Columbia-Cornell Care, which we will next discuss, sees Skinner tied to service lines: "When they fail to achieve what he had hoped for them,* David will want to save face, and Mike Berman will get the blame for not executing it."[80]

Contracting for Managed Care: Columbia-Cornell Care[81]

Even before the Presbyterian and New York hospitals merged, groups at the medical schools were forming to obtain contracts from the local HMOs. Columbia-Cornell Care (CCC) is the most comprehensive.

Fearing that capitation would "arrive tomorrow," Kathleen O'Donnell, Pardes's deputy vice president for medical center affairs at Columbia, and James Berardo, then the administrator of the Cornell Physicians Organization, "slammed together a business plan"[32] in the spring and summer of 1996 to create an organization that could meet the threat on behalf of the doctors, as Dr. Bruce E. Spivey, later the president and CEO of CCC, tells the story.[82] With the university presidents encouraging its formation,[41] Columbia and Cornell quickly allocated funds for the new organization.[21]

---

*Serfling's skepticism is based in part on the failure of service lines in the UCSF-Stanford merger. Serfling worked for many years at UCSF's most potent local competitor, the California-Pacific Medical Center. (See chapters 6 and 7.)

Columbia-Cornell Care was founded just as the hospitals were pre-paring to launch their merger,[21,32] which was "the private reason for its formation," according to Spivey.[82] "The public reason was managed care, but a parallel motive was the anxiety that the merger would lead to such a consolidation of power by the hospital that the schools would be at a disadvantage if they did nothing."[82]

Mike Weisfeldt at P&S and Darracott Vaughan, chairman of urol-ogy and director of the Cornell practice plan, acted as interim CEOs until Spivey took over on October 1, 1997.*

Spivey's first job was converting what was essentially a conceptual premise for the organization into a formal business plan.[80] Then he got to work convincing managed care organizations to choose Columbia and Cornell faculty members to care for their patients. By the end of 1999, Spivey and his associates had contracted with 16 HMOs to send their patients to his new colleagues for professional services. "There is no insurance provider in New York who can exclude Columbia, Cornell, and our hospital," says James Lieberman of P&S. "We're still the pres-tige operation. The other big hospitals can't cut it for many of the executives on Wall Street, for example. Consequently, the contractors have to play ball with us."[47]

Each of the agreements so far developed by CCC is based on dis-counted fee-for-service payment, and none is capitated, emphasizing that the Manhattan market is not yet attuned to accepting "at-risk con-tracts," which hold the provider financially responsible if the costs of caring for the patients exceed the amount agreed upon in advance. "The New York market is five years behind Philadelphia, 10 years behind California," estimates G. Aubrey Serfling, Spivey's colleague and succes-sor at California-Pacific in San Francisco.[80†] Spivey adds that the

---

*A newcomer to the New York medical scene, Spivey, an ophthalmologist and a high school classmate of David Skinner, was educated at Coe College in Cedar Rapids, Iowa, and the University of Iowa College of Medicine, where he trained in his specialty and later joined the faculty. For 20 years beginning in 1971, he worked at the Pacific Presbyterian Medical Center in San Francisco, first as chairman of ophthalmology and from 1976 as CEO and president of the Board of Trustees. Pacific Presbyterian (now called California Pacific), a large community hospital catering to the carriage trade of San Francisco, was the teaching hospital for Stanford's medical school before its clinical programs moved to Palo Alto. For much of this time, Spivey was also executive vice president and CEO of the American Academy of Ophthalmology, the professional organization for his specialty. In 1992, Northwestern Healthcare Network in Chicago recruited Spivey to become president and CEO from which position he was engaged to direct Columbia-Cornell Care.

†Serfling, who came to work with Spivey again at Columbia-Cornell Care as its chief operating and financial officer, had previously been employed by a medical network based at a large Philadelphia suburban hospital.[80]

local HMOs have decided that they can make more money by squeezing the providers with discounted fee-for-service contracts than with capitation, at least for now. "Besides, it's not to the advantage of the insurers to see the big places fail."[82]

Columbia-Cornell Care contracts for more Columbia than Cornell doctors. This difference reflects the size of the clinical faculties and the contrast between the full-time and volunteer arrangements at Cornell and P&S. With a few exceptions, the practitioners at P&S are full-time employees of the school. However, at Cornell only about half of the clinical faculty members working at the New York Hospital campus are full time. The others are self-employed, usually with offices near the medical center.

Spivey's annual budget at Columbia-Cornell Care is about $7.5 million. Cornell funds its portion through the 3 percent development fund tax on the fees generated by the full-time clinicians, from loans backed by the clinical departments, and by means of funds provided by the dean and the university.[48] At Columbia, the CCC contribution comes from university and dean's funds and not directly from the doctors or their departments, a difference that produces some grousing among the Cornell doctors.[40,48] Spivey estimates that at least five years may be required before CCC breaks even.

Although Spivey reports to a policy board from the medical schools, "The reality is I have to keep the world happy. It is my opportunity to work with two university boards, two university presidents, two medical school deans, two faculties, the merged hospital, and the network hospitals and their physicians. My job is to get two faculties who would prefer to be working alone to work together and to do something no one wants to do—managed care."[82] At this time, he outsources data warehousing, claims payment, and some aspects of medical management because he is hampered by a shortage of physicians skilled in outcomes management in New York compared to the larger number in Boston.[82] He is building a staff to handle capitation when and if it arrives in the market where his doctors work.

To deal with medical management, Spivey hired Dr. James Smith, a Cornell clinical professor, as chief medical officer for Columbia-Cornell Care on April 1, 1999. Described by Serfling as "a trusted, respected insider—Jim Smith won't let bad medicine be practiced." Smith will lead the effort to convince the doctors serving HMO patients to follow the most clinically and financially efficient practices.[80] Despite his new position, Smith is one of the many Presbyterian and New York Hospital doctors who, at least till now, do not accept managed care patients nor

accept assignments from Medicare. Smith, Spivey, and Serfling are recruiting a specialist in medical management to assist Smith.[80]

Spivey has proposed, and the universities have accepted, forming a
new initiative he calls Columbia Cornell Network Physicians (CCNP) to
obtain contracts for doctors who are not members of the groups based at
the medical centers but are linked to the universities through faculty
appointments or the hospital network. Community physicians are sign-
ing up to participate in this venture, "putting to rest the claim that
academic and community docs can't work together when it's in their
interest to do so," observes Aubrey Serfling.[80]

From meeting with representative community physicians to find out
"what it will take to bring them in," Spivey has learned that the doctors
want to have a major role in operating such an entity and do not favor
taking direction from the universities or the hospital.[82]

Why did the two universities come together so quickly to create
Columbia-Cornell Care when they had suffered such a tortured history
of unsuccessful attempts to merge in the past? Spivey, who was not there
at the time, thinks that the medical schools had both "offensive and
defensive reasons."[82] Their leaders knew that they needed a professional
organization to obtain the clinical business increasingly becoming available only through HMO contracts.

"Each of us is concerned about contracting," acknowledges Herbert
Pardes, the P&S dean, who adds, "so we decided to craft a physician
alliance."[83]

Defensively, both schools feared themselves becoming "vulnerable
to being picked off one at a time — divide and conquer" by the hospitals'
executives, who could "play one school off against the other," Spivey
assumes.[82] "Considering how quickly CCC was put together, one can't
help concluding that the hospital merger was one of the driving forces,"
says Smith.[84] It was "a defensive ploy to the merger," adds Jim Lieberman, a close advisor of P&S dean Pardes in practice affairs.[47] Nevertheless, the force of the HMOs and the potential for capitation has led some
observers, such as Morton Grusky, Pardes's deputy vice president for
budget and finance at P&S, to conclude that Columbia-Cornell Care
might have developed even if the hospitals hadn't merged.[46]

Thus, CCC became the vehicle for the universities "to maintain a
balance of power between the new hospital and their faculties," Serfling
believes.[80] The word on the street was that the university leaders who
developed Columbia-Cornell Care intended to merge the Cornell and
still to be formed Columbia practice plans within it, a plan that makes
some of the leaders of both physician groups uncomfortable. Despite

these bureaucratic anxieties, however, both the Columbia physician network and the New York–Cornell Independent Practice Association have appointed Columbia-Cornell Care their exclusive contracting agent for managed care.[20,21]

In 1993, about 600 full-time and 400 Cornell voluntary clinicians formed an independent practice association, the legal entity required by New York State to contract with HMOs for managed care contracts for doctors.[21] The New York–Cornell IPA is an independent organization, not a part of the medical college or the New York Hospital.[21,40] As the hospitals prepared to merge, the activity of the IPA slackened, and, upon the arrival of Spivey, Columbia-Cornell Care assumed most of this function.[40] Dr. James Smith, prior to joining the leadership at CCC, and Dr. Michael Wolk, both members of the volunteer faculty, cochaired the New York–Cornell IPA.[40]

One of the creators and early leaders of the New York–Cornell IPA was Dr. Robert S. Ascheim, a cardiologist on the voluntary staff at the New York Hospital. In the fall of 1996, Skinner suggested that Ascheim develop an organization that would contract with physicians not working primarily at the medical center. "You've complained so much about needing an M.D. network, I want you to form one for the hospital, and I'll pay you for it," Ascheim remembers Skinner telling him.[85] This led to the formation of another entity, the Physicians Practice Company (PPC), which was designed to develop IPAs at the community hospitals affiliated with the New York Hospital and obtain HMO contracts for the physicians there.

Clinicians at the home base were not pleased. "Our project was alien to the New York–Cornell IPA," a colleague at the medical center told Ascheim. "The medical college thought of me as Skinner's stalking horse. If I stepped in with the network docs, they saw me getting in the way of their referrals."[85]

Many of the Cornell doctors objected to PPC because they saw it as a hospital initiative.[48] They felt that the activities of the contracting office provided further evidence that the hospital "doesn't have another vocabulary than running everything and dominating any joint ventures."[48]

"When we tried to form an MSO [medical services organization], it should have been done with the hospital, but the hospital went its own way," recalls Michael Shelanski, the P&S chairman of pathology, who was then chairman of the medical board.[36]

Nevertheless, Skinner continued to support Ascheim's project and agreed in the fall of 1998 to let PPC become independent. Ascheim and his associate, Dr. Susan Spear, became the sole owners of a new, for-profit Physician Partners Company with a consulting arrangement with

NewYork-Presbyterian Hospital. The PPC only develops at-risk contracts for community doctors, including some who are not associated with hospitals in the NewYork-Presbyterian network.[85]

"Where's Ascheim coming from?" asked Aubrey Serfling from the competing Columbia-Cornell Care.[80] "Most of his adult life he was a loyal Cornell doctor," actively participating in the college's practice activities but, Serfling emphasizes, not accepting managed care patients in his "Harley Street practice."* "Now he's linking up with the 'revenge of the primaries,'" the effort of primary care physicians to gain the political control that the specialists have appeared to exercise in the past.[80]

Despite all this controversy, Ascheim is an enthusiastic supporter of the merger and thinks the potential is "enormous." He believes, however, like trustees John Mack, Arthur Hedge, and others, that ultimate success might depend upon the medical schools also coming together.[59,85,86]

Columbia-Cornell Care is not the only organization within the schools that contracts with HMOs. In 1994, before the hospitals merged and Spivey's company was formed, several of the P&S clinical leaders, spurred by Myron Weisfeldt, the medicine chairman, formed the Columbia Presbyterian Physician Network (CPPN), a "virtual organization," according to Joan Leiman of the dean's office,[39] formed to negotiate for managed care contracts for P&S full-time doctors.[15] CPPN, which retains contracts for Columbia University employees and members of the hospital unions, has ceded to Columbia-Cornell Care verification of credentials, contract compliance, and most negotiating with large managed care companies.[15]

As Columbia-Cornell Care prospers, the extent of CPPN's future activities has become uncertain; a P&S administrator sees it "withering into Columbia-Cornell Care."[32] Dr. Joseph Tenenbaum, the Department of Medicine's assistant chairman for clinical affairs, suggests that CPPN should retain the role of representing the P&S faculty in dealing with issues arising from managed care.[15] Not unexpectedly, competition persists between CCC, Weisfeldt's CPPN, and Vaughan's Physicians Organization at Cornell.[41]

Why are several entities within the hospital and its medical schools separately contracting with HMOs? "David [Skinner] thought Columbia-Cornell Care would be too specialized with just the academic doctors at Columbia and Cornell and not the network physicians. He also believed that the universities taxed CCC too much and that it wouldn't work,"

---

*"Harley Street practice" identifies a medical practice consisting of genteel, wealthy patients seen by consultant physicians and surgeons in handsome, formerly family homes in, and adjacent to, the famous street in North London.

believes Arthur Klein, president of the network.[66] "Bruce [Spivey] is only beginning to achieve credibility with the hospital and competes with Lavan [the chief financial officer of the hospital, whose office contracts with HMOs for hospital services]."[66]

Many of the chairmen at Cornell feel quite cynical about the presence of several organizations at the hospital and medical schools competing for the contracts.[21] Dirk Sostman from the Cornell Physicians Organization suggests that the force necessary to "focus the mind" on effective joint contracting may not exist as long as New York continues to escape capitation.[21] Antonio Gotto, the Cornell dean, has been heard to say that the contracting function must be united.[87] Other observers comment:

> I don't see cooperation coming soon, though it's essential.[47]
> CCC versus Ascheim just provides another level of controversy.[88]
> The hospital won't recognize CCC as representing the physicians group.[62]
> David's a poker player, PPC is David's chip.[53]
> A recipe for disaster.[17]

The executives at Columbia-Cornell Care agree that David Skinner is the problem. "David is wedded to the multiple physician approach in the contracting business," Aubrey Serfling believes. "It's almost as if the hospital were pleased so long as the doctors are fragmented."[80] Spivey and Serfling have tried, so far in vain, to convince Skinner to let this activity consolidate.[80] Nevertheless, Bruce Spivey is confident that marketing the services of both doctors and hospitals together, preferably at his company, would benefit all and that eventually such an operation will replace the current system.

During the 1998 academic year (July 1, 1997–June 30, 1998), establishing joint contracting was much in the air again, but as of the winter of 2000 the parties had not risen above their mutual suspicions[21] and the hospital and the medical schools continue to market separately for managed care contracts.[48]* David Skinner had verbally supported a physicians-hospital organization that would conduct activities beneficial for both entities, but "he never allowed it to evolve," according to Spivey.[82] Reflecting the clinicians' uneasiness about the hospital's participation in any collective venture, Dr. Michael Wolk of the volunteer

---

*This differs from Partners Community HealthCare, Inc., in Boston, which contracts for the doctors, the MGH, the Brigham, and the other hospitals in the Partners network. Like PCHI, Columbia-Cornell Care is located in an office building, not at either of the medical schools or on the hospital campuses.

staff observes, "We are always concerned that the *P* in PHO should also be a capital letter, not only the *H*."[40]*

The Society of Practitioners of the Columbia-Presbyterian Medical Center

The clinical faculties have embraced Bruce Spivey's Columbia-Cornell Care with some skepticism.[41] The Columbia[89] and Cornell[40] practitioners, disappointed by the amount of money paid to them through some of the contracts Spivey has obtained, complain that he doesn't bargain adequately with the HMOs. "If CCC were more forceful, it would do better," believes Dr. Moshe Rubin, president of the Society of Practitioners of the Columbia-Presbyterian Medical Center. "Many of the practitioners didn't join CCC because they felt the dean and chairman didn't intend to let them participate in its management."[89]

Rubin is obviously critical of Columbia-Cornell Care, on whose board he serves by virtue of his office in the society. "Frankly, I see the CCC officers skimming dollars off the top to support themselves."[89]

The size of the budget at CCC and the annual salary of Spivey, assumed to be somewhere between $750,000 and $1 million, has aroused many complaints from various quarters. "It's bloated," says Dr. Leighton Smith, who directs the Cornell primary care initiative and has worked for most of his career in the Midwest.[51]†

David Skinner is reputed to have told some of the clinicians, "If Spivey can do contracts for you as well as he did for himself, you'll do just fine," a comment that Skinner denies making.[3]

Despite his reservations, Rubin regularly attends the meetings of the board of Columbia-Cornell Care. Why does CCC retain this critic on its board? "To provide diverse representation, so long as the minority doesn't rule," explains Aubrey Serfling.[80]

The leaders at Columbia-Cornell Care and at the hospital hear

---

*"Columbia-Cornell Care is definitely not a PHO," James Lieberman explains. "It's actually a managed care contracting organization, not even a physicians' centralized practice organization."[47]

†Spivey has compared the costs of Columbia-Cornell Care with similar organizations and finds that "we're in the national ballpark and probably low when one considers what New York's expenses are." As for the estimates of what he is paid, Spivey says, "I wish the rumors were true, but they are not."[82]

"The money which the universities have already invested in Columbia-Cornell Care tends to assure its survival," believes Jim Lieberman of P&S, who predicts that "CCC will continue unless the merger breaks up."[47]

clinicians like Rubin — he is only 43 years of age — pleading, "Give us the past — the sixties, the seventies, the eighties — not the future. Let's build the barricades and defend the doctors and their medical centers. What we do is important, and dollars should be made available. Cost should not be a consideration. How dare we allow the HMOs to run things?"[42] In other words, health care should be exempt from limitations on spending. "Unrealistic, of course," replies Aubrey Serfling of CCC, "socioeconomic movements like managed care can't be avoided. The docs don't want to acknowledge the failures of the current system. It's just denial."[80]

Another reflection of the medical economics prevalent in the unusual New York City market is the hope of many doctors, as expressed by Dr. Peter Puchner, former president of the Society of Practitioners, that "managed care may well not survive."[90]

"This type of thinking persists in a significant number of New York City doctors," explains Serfling, "because they haven't yet felt real pressure from managed care."[80] The good economy has slowed employers' reaching for managed care. "When corporations are profitable, the cost cutters have less control."[80]

Accordingly, quite a few physicians, particularly the well-known specialists at the medical centers, still rely solely on fee-for-service patients and can afford to refuse to see those who will pay only through HMO contracts, according to Dr. Kenneth M. Prager,[91] a busy specialist in lung diseases based at the Presbyterian site. "I don't belong to any HMO other than the one which provides care for our faculty and employees and haven't joined CCC. The merger has had zero affect on my practice and teaching so far."[91]

Dr. William P. Lovejoy, an all-Columbia product since playing football for Yale in the 1950s — "I'm paying the price; I see my orthopedist too often now"[92] — is a senior cardiologist who joined the faculty as an old-time Columbia volunteer before the 10 percent tax system. "The merger hasn't affected me. I can still make it on fee-for-service patients and haven't joined CCC, but retirement is what I'm thinking about now."[92]

Serfling understands. "In California, the more senior doctors let themselves retire by taking only fee-for-service patients. Gradually, or not so gradually, they find themselves working three, then two, then one day and finally stopping. Relying on non-managed-care payments can only continue for a while. Most of the younger docs here will eventually come up against a lack of patients willing or able to buy fee-for-service contracts or pay from their own pockets."[80]

Despite Serfling's concerns, Lovejoy is not the only cardiologist who avoids patients who only pay through HMOs. Allan Schwartz, the Presbyterian chief of cardiology, has "dropped out of CCC. Enough patients are willing to pay my usual fee to see me so that I don't have to take the HMO rate, which has fallen to 50 percent of what I charge." One aspect of the managed care payment schedule that really bothers Schwartz and other experienced physicians like him is that "The HMOs pay the same amount for a procedure to an operator who has just finished his fellowship and to someone with years of experience like me. I refer the HMO patients to my younger colleagues." Schwartz was worried that his decision to restrict his practice to non-HMO patients might not provide him with enough work. "Actually, my referring docs like that I'm sticking it to managed care. I'm busier that ever, and I think I could continue my practice like this indefinitely. I'm still an old-fashioned doc. My patients get the same doctor at night whom they saw in the daytime."[14]

The doctors having the most difficulty are those who depend upon what is called "evaluation and management" by the billing department. These are the generalists, the primary care physicians, and specialists such as psychiatrists, endocrinologists, and rheumatologists without the more lucrative procedures of Dr. Schwartz and his colleagues. "They take it on the chin," observes Dr. Michael Wolk at Cornell,[40] "as do the 'twofers,'"[40] doctors who supplement their nonprocedure specialties with general practice.

As for the specialists with their procedures, "The problem hasn't become sufficiently personal yet," Warns Serfling. "Just wait till some of Moshe's patients leave him for doctors who accept payment from the HMOs."[80]

Moshe Rubin, a P&S gastroenterologist, leads the Society of Practitioners, an organization of about 500 Columbia clinicians, each of whom pay annual dues of $125. The members meet monthly, and the minutes are distributed to university and hospital executives and board members. "We're democratically run, unlike the medical school," he adds. The society's goals include "interfacing with the hospital, so that we can continue to practice in a high-class way, and with the university, almost as a union, to prevent the school's forcing coercive contracts on new clinicians."[89]

Dr. Kenneth Prager, a member of the society's executive committee, chairs a subcommittee that is looking at the contracts offered to new clinical faculty members. "Some of them exploit the young appointees," he and Rubin believe.[91] The chairman of a major department "presented a new contract to the members of his department and in a rather arrogant fashion," as Prager and the officers of the Society of Practitioners saw the offer. "We hired lawyers to help the practitioners, and the chairman backed off."[91]

"The hospital people are very happy with us, the school less so, but we're not out to hurt the medical school," says Rubin.[89]

Prager believes that he reflects the opinion of many members of the Society of Practitioners in saying, "The school has less sympathy for our needs than the hospital, which is more understanding and accommodating." On issues of importance to practitioners, "I'd rather talk to Speck than to Pardes."[91]

What bothers Rubin and his colleagues causes many doctors to question why they continue to work in their profession as faculty members in a medical school. Among other motives, many men and women choose to become doctors because they want to run their own professional lives,[89] an aspiration increasingly restricted by the financial and administrative problems that are more and more an annoying feature of their work. Although practitioners know that they will further lose some of their much-desired independence by joining the faculty of a medical school, a few manage to retain a strong spirit of independence within the walls of academe. They enjoy the collegial nature of the work and the prestige associated with being a member of a fine medical school but dislike, in varying degrees, some of the elements inherent in structured organizations.[32] Given their choice, these intermittently disaffected faculty doctors would prefer to "keep the dean and the hospital administration out of their lives."[32,89] At P&S, such physicians share their frustrations through membership in the Society of Practitioners.

The Society of Practitioners was formed in the 1970s by a group of "old-type volunteers to protect themselves from being eliminated as the school began appointing only full-time faculty members."[89] The society is now being led by members of the clinical full-time faculty as the volunteers are retiring.[90] "Regardless of their status as volunteers or full-time faculty," observers Peter Puchner, "the clinicians at Columbia see themselves as quite independent and more entrepreneurial than in many other full-time academic centers."[90]

Almost all clinicians appointed to the P&S faculty and the Presbyterian staff receive their salaries "through checks from Columbia University, the essential feature of full-time employment at P&S," according to Tom Morris, vice dean of the medical school.[41] Many of these clinicians pay 10 percent of their collections to their departments and, as full-time members of the faculty, receive Columbia University benefits, including the valuable college tuition benefit for their children. They must pay all the expenses of their practices such as office rent, secretaries' salaries and billing as well as part of the cost of their university benefits. Cornell officials point to this arrangement as ersatz full time and functionally similar, except for the 10 percent tax, to their volunteer classification.[48]

Leaders at P&S suggest that their system encourages academic productivity from all clinicians and helps to account for the higher academic standing the Columbia school enjoys.

Moshe Rubin, who graduated from Queens College (Phi Beta Kappa) and the Yale University School of Medicine (Alpha Omega Alpha, an honorary scholastic society for medical students similar to Phi Beta Kappa for undergraduates), sees most of his patients at Columbia-Presbyterian East, a large and well-furnished group of offices on 60th Street between Fifth and Madison Avenues. There's no question about his admitting to New York Hospital–Cornell, where he took his internship and residency and which is much closer to his office than is Presbyterian. For all his differences with P&S and Columbia-Cornell Care, the disadvantages of the commute, and the problems at Presbyterian, Rubin is deeply loyal to Columbia and proud to be an associate clinical professor there, where he trained in his specialty. "I work with a homogeneous group of first-class doctors, all collegial people, at the city's best hospital. The academic setup is very enjoyable, and the flow of patients is great."[89]

His predecessor as president of the society, Peter Puchner, a professor of clinical urology at P&S who joined the faculty in 1970 as an unencumbered volunteer like Bill Lovejoy in cardiology, admits: "We're very inbred, but we're happy with it and are here to give, not to take. We like the people we work with. Our best friends are here."[90] Like many of the doctors in the Atchley Building, Puchner takes on significant teaching responsibilities, including administering the training in urology for the medical students.

Physically "binding the practitioners to the area"[90] is their office building, the Atchley Building, across Fort Washington Avenue from the old Presbyterian Hospital and adjacent to the Milstein Hospital Building, the new home of the inpatients. Owned by Presbyterian, the Atchley Building, a 14-floor tower that opened in December of 1968[93] and where 300 P&S doctors practice,[56] is named for Dr. Dana Atchley, a renowned Presbyterian internist who raised much of the money for its construction from his wealthy patients.[56,90]

The Atchley Building enables many of the Presbyterian clinicians to see their patients on the campus and not, for example, in suburban Westchester County or downtown on Park Avenue, where most of the Presbyterian clinicians maintained their offices in the past. When the medical center opened in 1928, and for many years afterward, most of the practitioners stayed where they were near the old Presbyterian Hospital in the east seventies between Park and Madison Avenues and came up to the new hospital to treat their private inpatients in the Harkness Pavilion and to teach the P&S students.[90] Life had its perks in those days. Peter Puchner was told that some of the doctors had their own drivers to ease traversing the city from office to medical center.[90]

In those early days of the medical center, P&S encouraged physicians on the Presbyterian staff to move their offices uptown so they could spend more time teaching and avoid the commute from the downtown offices.[56] "Space was found, which quickly became filled. We found more so that, although in the early days 80 percent of the doctors practiced downtown, by the beginning of the 1940s it was fifty-fifty," according to Hugh Ferguson, who has administered the Presbyterian practice offices for 35 years, "an interesting job placing me right in the middle between the hospital administration and the doctors."[56]

Ferguson began working at the hospital in 1954 soon after graduating from Princeton University.* "We promised our doctors in the war [World War II] that they could have offices at the medical center when they returned. So when most of the big admitters moved up here we developed more space but still needed an office building for them. Originally, what became the Atchley was to have only six stories, clearly not enough."[56,94†]

By the 1970s, Ferguson remembers, the medical school and its departments began hiring as clinicians "only those who would agree to be full time. Gradually, they replaced almost all of the volunteers, so that now 93 to 95 percent of the staff is salaried. There's something of a backlash now. The Society of Practitioners believes the doctors should have the right to drop their salaried arrangements and still stay on the Presbyterian staff."[56]

As for the long-term benefits of the merger, Ferguson says, "We don't know yet. At least it brought about an improvement in our telephone service" when Presbyterian adopted the superior New York Hospital system.[56]

The "urge to merge," Dr. Peter Puchner confirms, "was pushed primarily by the hospital. Very few of the practitioners were initially involved. They weren't too enthusiastic about joining NYU because few of them knew the practitioners there. However, there were many relationships between the docs at Presbyterian and New York Hospital. There were no hostilities as far as anyone could see." Puchner and other Presbyterian clinicians, nevertheless, either can or could see important differences between their institutions. "Their full-time group is smaller

---

*Princeton, also founded as a Presbyterian institution, has provided the premedical training for many a P&S medical student.

†Nor is it enough now. The contemplated building of a hotel in a parking lot adjacent to the hospital may include additional office space for the doctors.[94]

and less flexible than ours, and the New York Hospital is seen as more hierarchical than here. Their volunteers are more closely tied to their Park Avenue and Fifth Avenue offices."[90] He sees the Columbia practice plan that Dean Pardes is trying to facilitate as successful if it is: "loose, entrepreneurial, encouraging rather than controlling clinical practices, and has a low tax base, unlike Cornell, where it is high and potentially repressive."[90]

To remedy the separation between faculty and hospital trustees and to acquaint the members of the Presbyterian board of trustees with the aims of the Society of Practitioners, Puchner, other hospital and school leaders, and a group of trustees met for dinner several times each year at a club across the street from Columbia-Presbyterian East, where many of the P&S clinicians see some of their patients. Several of the departmental chairman also attended the sessions, although "the chairs can't really represent the practicing docs and have to walk a fine line between us and the hospital."[90] These dinners, Puchner believes, "were very useful. The trustees really learned what was on our minds. We tried joint meetings after the merger, but it didn't work."[90]

A P&S general internist who seems to walk a line between the advocacy of the Society of Practitioners and the policies of the medical school is Dr. Henry Sears Lodge — from Boston, of course — schooled in geology at the University of Pennsylvania and in medicine at Columbia.[95] "The society is," Lodge suggests, "in some ways analogous to the AMA.[95]* Whenever the dean makes a proposal, the society's leaders have to first consider 'how could it hurt me?' The financial structure of the relationship between the physicians and the medical school locks the society into a reactive, protective approach rather than being progressive. Its more senior members won't have to deal with managed care; they'll retire before it really hits us."[95]

Lodge was planning to take an oncology fellowship when the dean at the time asked if he would like to take over the practice of Dr. Richard Stock, a general internist on the Columbia faculty who was planning to retire. Lodge said yes because "General medicine is not unlike oncology in that you have to take care of the whole patient in both cases. Cancer and the treatments we use affect all parts of the body and the mind."[95] So ten years ago Lodge moved into Stock's office at 72nd Street and Park Avenue only to discover that his partner had decided "not to hang it up after all."[95]

Like Stock, Harry Lodge developed a "Harley Street" practice,

---

*The American Medical Association, the doctor's "union," was long renowned for its opposition to governmental interference in the practice of medicine.

seeing 10 to 12 patients per day. This is a number that, if he collected only what managed care reimburses, would hardly pay the bills of most general physicians, let alone provide the means of living in an apartment, albeit rent stabilized, at the corner of Central Park West and 85th Street and privately educating one's children. It can work, however, if you don't accept payment from HMOs and your patients are sufficiently affluent to pay healthy fees — "a very enjoyable, higher income practice," as Lodge describes his work. Lodge and his colleagues net between $150,000 and $200,000 per year, not an extravagant amount as Manhattan practices go. He does represent, however, a surprisingly large number of clinicians at both medical centers who can and at least for a while continue to successfully operate what Robert Ascheim calls "boutique practices,"[85] based upon serving the affluent patients which Manhattan, fortunately for these doctors, seems to generate.

Three years ago, Lodge and a group of colleagues, now 10 internists and four obstetrician-gynecologists, many with long-standing downtown Columbia-Presbyterian practices, organized New York Physicians, P.C., a multispecialty group practice of which Lodge is the chairman and CEO. They rented space in an office building on Madison Avenue between 59th and 60th Streets, close to Columbia-Presbyterian East, the complex for P&S practitioners in which Moshe Rubin works. Why don't he and his group work there? "It's too expensive. We pay half as much where we are, and we're here all the time. Many of the docs at Columbia-Presbyterian East are there part time. We're one of their biggest outside referral sources."[95]

How about admitting to New York Hospital? "A few of our group are Cornell people and do, but the rest of us are not planning to make the ultimate push — keep the 10 percent and go to New York Hospital/Cornell. Loyalty and collegiality keep us at P&S. It would be a really wrenching experience to leave," acknowledges Lodge. "Almost no one admits to both hospitals; haven't figured out how to do it."[95]

Despite his allegiance to P&S, Lodge thinks that "the Cornell system's more oriented toward growth. Herb Pardes [the Columbia dean] is looking toward a different future. The medical school plays on the loyalty of his faculty — I'm taxed on my altruism. The school will never lose control over the clinicians, but retaining control will cost it tremendously in terms of sustaining a competitive, world-class, clinical faculty."[95]

Rogerio Lobo, the P&S obstetrics and gynecology chairman, agrees with Lodge about admitting to New York Hospital. "Some of our people, suspicious about the merger, thought about moving there, but it hasn't happened."[74] He doesn't believe that the dean and the medical school will ever stop dominating the P&S clinical programs.

As for his relationship with Columbia-Cornell Care, on the operating board of which he serves, Lodge wants to be thought of as "the credible, quasi-loyal opposition. Although Bruce [Spivey, the CCC CEO] is very good politically, he misread the timing of managed care's movement toward risk in New York. He's consumed much more money than he needs to build an infrastructure to handle discounted fee-for-service contracting, and it is uncertain whether there is a mission that justifies the current CCC."[95]

Has the merger affected the practice of Lodge and his partners? "Not much. The hospital politics are distant from a predominately outpatient practice such as mine. Actually, the hospital has little to help us with except dollars, and that's out. The merger has generated a new set of turf wars. A lot of institutional energy has gone into this. On the positive side, I think Presbyterian is being run somewhat better now."[95]

The Association of Practicing Physicians

New York Hospital/Cornell also has its organization of clinicians, called, at Cornell, the Association of Practicing Physicians, which has functioned for about 25 years. Its president in 1999 was Dr. Daniel M. Libby, a specialist in pulmonary disease and recently promoted to clinical professor of medicine at Cornell. "The merger has not affected my practice on a day-to-day basis," he believes, "but then neither has managed care."[54]

Libby does not accept payments directly from HMOs for treating patients with these plans. He bills such patients directly, and they then collect what they can from their plan. Libby observes that the most popular product that the Oxford Health Plan sells, "though it costs more, lets you go where you want. It's really a cheap indemnity plan."[54] He also directly bills patients with Medicare and lets them collect from the government, usually an amount that is less than his fee. This means that he does not "accept assignment," the amount that the insurer pays, except when specifically requested to do so by the referring physician. "When I tried taking managed care payments directly, my income dropped — no surprise. So I stopped working this way. I lost some patients, but my income rose. Managed care pays me so poorly that if I saw 40 percent as many patients at my usual fee, I'd actually make more money."[54]

Being able to perform such tests in his office as blood counts, urinalysis, electrocardiograms, and pulmonary function tests — an important study for a doctor with his specialty — "pays the office expenses. Without them, I couldn't stay in practice in New York, where rents are so high."[54] Some managed care plans severely limit payments for testing.

In 1983, Libby and his partners bought the small apartment building near the New York Hospital where they work. "We love our independence; that's the main thing. We have to run the office very efficiently to make it work financially. There's no direct financial relationship between us and the hospital or medical school. We like it that way."[54]

Like Moshe Rubin and Harry Lodge, Libby serves on the board of Columbia-Cornell Care. Also like Rubin, he is not a supporter of CCC, which he finds "too big and too expensive," and along with the merger functions as "catalysts for the promotion of managed care. What CCC does is anathema to what I do. There are few general internists among the clinical faculty at Cornell and Columbia, although that is whom Bruce Spivey wants to promote. Most of us are specialists. The population my colleagues and I see are reasonably well off and sophisticated. They want to see specialists. I don't think the people at CCC know New York."[54]

Both Libby and Rubin criticize the amount of financial support that CCC requires. "It's still deeply in the red, will need more than 50,000 covered lives to cover the overhead and infrastructure. I'm dead set against what Bruce is doing there." As for influencing what CCC does, "I go to the meetings [of the CCC board]. They ignore my advice." Will managed care ever really come to New York City? "Possibly if the economy turns real bad, but up till now they're been consistently wrong predicting what will happen."[54]

As for the more academic side of the merger, Libby finds useful the new combined case conferences for the pulmonary physicians at both campuses, which are held monthly at either the New York Hospital or Columbia-Presbyterian East, the midtown outpatient offices for the P&S physicians on 60th Street. This location lets most of the physicians avoid the long trek to and from 168th Street.

Networks

On November 1, 1998, 10 months into the merger, Dr. Barbara A. DeBuono, the former New York State commissioner of health, became executive vice president for the network of hospitals, nursing homes, and other health care agencies at the NewYork-Presbyterian Hospital.* Described in the *Wall Street Journal* as "a scrappy Bronx-born specialist in infections diseases"[96] and by the *New York Times* as "both blunt and

---

*DeBuono's tenure directing the network was short. She left NewYork-Presbyterian at the end of 1999. Dr. Arthur Klein succeeded to DeBuono's responsibilities in March 2000.

politic,"[97] De Buono had supervised the deregulation of rates that the insurance carriers were required to pay to the hospitals in New York State,[97] a change that presented severe challenges to all hospital leaders in the state, including Skinner and Speck, the two executives to whom she would now report.

One of the issues that she and her colleagues would soon face was making sense, in some manner, of the fundamental differences between the structures of the networks built by the formerly independent New York and Presbyterian Hospitals. George Vecchione, who had led the network development for David Skinner, did not offer the type of informal, affiliated relationship that Bill Speck favored for Presbyterian. The board of trustees of each of the sponsored hospitals in the New York Hospital network contains at least one member from the parent board, which legally controls the community hospital board. Skinner's policy of decentralized management, however, means that New York Hospital's control is gently exercised.[66] Many of the nonclinical services in the community hospitals have come to be performed by the New York Hospital departments.

The risk of taking on sponsored hospitals is of course that they will drain the NewYork-Presbyterian coffers. This concerns board members, particularly those who were formerly associated with Presbyterian like Arthur J. Hedge Jr., an IBM veteran who, during 34 years with the corporation, rose to senior positions. "The finances at some of the sponsored hospitals are rocky and need significant capital investment. The affiliates [the Presbyterian approach] have strong balance sheets, but we have a place for both models."[86]

Although the executives at the combined NewYork-Presbyterian Hospital favor the Skinner approach, they do not insist that the affiliated hospitals convert to sponsorship.[66] The new corporation did maintain, however, that the affiliated hospitals in the former Presbyterian network agree to accept a common information system and offered them the integrated business services that the sponsored hospitals used. Dues of about 0.075 percent of operating revenues were also assessed for the first time on the affiliated hospitals. The sponsored hospitals paid slightly more, about 0.1 percent.[66] NewYork-Presbyterian is taking a pragmatic approach in its relations with the affiliated hospitals but clearly hopes that most will eventually decide to join the sponsored system.[66]

Although the hospital takes a proprietary interest in the network, the medical schools have begun to participate more fully than in the past. Cornell and Columbia, though not partners in the network arrangements, are "certainly interested parties," Arthur Klein explains, "and academic linkage always follows."[66]

At each sponsored hospital, its physicians are offered faculty appointments, the usual status for members of the New York Hospital network before the merger. New members of the hospitals' staffs are vetted through the medical college's standard system for evaluating faculty appointments.[66] Search committees of local physicians with representatives from the New York Hospital and the medical college, including the relevant department chairmen, are now formed for all major appointments, such as directors of clinical services, at each of the sponsored hospitals. The local physicians predominate on these committees, but the doctors from the medical center give the process, as Klein observes, its "academic imprimatur."[66]

Dr. Oliver T. Fein coordinates the Cornell medical college's relationships with the hospitals of the NewYork-Presbyterian network.[87] A general internist who worked at P&S for 17 years before moving downtown in 1995, Fein is now an associate dean at Cornell and directs the Office of Network Affairs. Tony Gotto (the Cornell dean, who supports this work strongly) and Fein have visited most of the hospitals in the network to emphasize the importance of the connection to the education of their students.[87] Fifty to 60 percent of the students work with network doctors in the introduction to clinical medicine courses during the first two years. During the third year, half take at least some of their clinical clerkships—the assignment when medical students first participate in the day-to-day work with inpatients and outpatients—at the network hospitals.

"The children's network wouldn't have been possible without the merger," Cynthia Sparer, the director of Babies and Children's Hospital at Presbyterian, firmly believes.[42] "We could have done it from Columbia-Presbyterian Medical Center alone, but the network would have been smaller, less comprehensive, and we wouldn't have looked like such a strong partner for New York City."[42] Developing the pediatric network occupies much of Cynthia Sparer's time since she sees it as vital to the health of the hospital she leads. "Our Children's Health Network doesn't compete with the pediatrics units at the network community hospitals," where inpatient units are closing as care of children moves increasingly to the outpatient offices and emergency departments. "We offer improved access to the medical, surgical, and mental health programs, which they can't provide and we specialize in. We try to convince them that we at the academic center mean to be their helper and not their competitor."[42] Babies and Children's recently contracted to operate the neonatal services at three of the affiliated community hospitals. Sparer sees the pediatric network as aiding many of the other departments. "Concentrate services on young married women, and in addition to her you get her husband, parents, and children and thereby make contact with the community outside the medical center."[42]

When counted at the beginning of 2000, the network, including the New York and Presbyterian branches of the parent hospital, consisted of 32 hospitals, of which 11 were sponsored. The NewYork-Presbyterian Network also includes more than five specialty institutes, 17 nursing homes, 11 home health agencies, and 103 satellite clinics and primary care centers.[3]

On March 25 and 26, 1999, the CEOs, board chairs and senior physicians from each of the institutions in the network, met with the leaders of the NewYork-Presbyterian Hospital and officers of the medical schools in a two-day retreat to review and discuss the operation of the network and the merger of the teaching hospitals. After hearing from David Skinner and network director Barbara DeBuono, the leaders from the network hospitals got their chance to press for changes and improvements, and they had several of them. The network hospitals particularly wanted the public to recognize that they were tightly associated with NewYork-Presbyterian Hospital and their affiliated medical schools.[66] Other important desires included more involvement in network decision making, help for network physicians in managing their practices, a policy statement that the schools favored education and not only research, seeding of their staffs with graduates of Columbia and Cornell training programs, help in recruiting interns, greater participation in clinical trials, and faster processing by the medical schools of faculty appointments, which can take years, some claimed.[66]

Arthur Klein has concluded that what the doctors in the affiliated hospitals most want are "academic linkages and branding—a leg up in the market place—contracting, and access to capital."[66]

One Hospital and Two Schools: Dr. Gotto

To trustee John Mack, one of the country's leading bankers and president and chief operating officer of Morgan Stanley Dean Whitter, the current structure of two schools and one hospital trying to succeed together and apart cannot continue forever.[59] Mack, the son of a Lebanese grocery wholesaler from North Carolina, began at Morgan Stanley as a bond salesman in 1972 and, according to a profile in the *Wall Street Journal,* "won a reputation as a sharp trader."[98] As one of the officers who put together a merger of one of America's most famous investment banks with a large brokerage house, Mack sees NewYork-Presbyterian Hospital's working with two medical schools as inherently unstable.[59]

"There's lots of turf involved," says John F. McGillicuddy, cochairman of the hospital board. "There's so much external pressure on the hospitals, doctors, and medical schools. Add internal troubles, and functions get hit quickly." He finds more institutional loyalty among doctors in medical centers — "there's real passion there" — than among executives in the financial services industry. McGillicuddy knows. He was involved in three mergers, the first in his thirties when Manufacturer's Trust Company, where he worked after graduating from Princeton and Harvard Law School and serving two years as a naval officer, merged with the Hanover Bank to form Manufacturers Hanover Trust. He became president in 1971 and chairman and CEO in 1979 of "Mannyhanny," the popular name for the bank, and emerged intact with the same jobs when it later merged with Chemical Banking Corporation. Retiring in 1993, he observed his bank's later amalgamation with Chase Manhattan. "During mergers in my business, I found that you tend to look at things through your own glasses. You miss the people you know, not the people you don't know. The other guy's the odd man out."[6]

McGillicuddy and his colleagues on the NewYork-Presbyterian board have learned that "mergers can't be done as easily in teaching hospitals as in our businesses." Nevertheless, difficult thought it may be, he feels that "integrating operations within the hospital is an economic necessity."[6] This should be less difficult than it appears, he suggests. "There's a great deal of compatibility between Presbyterian and New York Hospital. The docs in each place respect each other, and of course the doctors are the institution."[6]

No fundamental organizational change will occur, trustees John Mack[59] and Arthur Hedge[86] suspect, until the hospital starts losing significant amounts of money. The pressures are not yet strong enough.[59] Someday, the institutions will find a way to emulate Johns Hopkins, which recently combined its separately governed hospital and medical school, or Duke, Mack's alma mater, where the two components are united under one executive.[59]* Asked if he would like to run the NewYork-Presbyterian Hospital, Mack responds cryptically, "It's an interesting job."[59]

"Some of the board members," an observer with information from all camps believes, "see the schools as the problem and not as the asset that they can be."[80]

---

*It was John Mack, acting on behalf of the Presbyterian trustees, who suggested that Columbia buy the hospital and adopt in Washington Heights the Duke and Hopkins model as the governing structure of the Columbia-Presbyterian Medical Center.[59]

Paul Kligfield from Cornell suggests that "members of hospital boards may be looking for solutions with which they are familiar from where they work but which can't be found in academic medical centers. One of the reasons for this thinking may be that the mission of a hospital is simpler to state than the purposes of medical schools. Some of us fear," he adds, "that a few of the people on the hospital board think that the academics of the medical schools operate outside the real world, which is limited to their businesses, where the fundamental rules and purposes are different."[33]

Dr. John Driscoll, a voting member of the board by virtue of his being president of the hospital medical staff, regrets to observe that "Too many of the businessmen just don't understand how we work."[62]

Dr. Qais Al-Awqati, a senior investigator and chief of the Nephrology Division in Weisfeldt's Department of Medicine at P&S, warns about the potential intellectual disadvantages of merging institutions like teaching hospitals and medical schools. He strongly believes that "great institutions must maintain their individuality. Loss of particularity is not good. We can't afford the loss of diversity" that such melding can bring about.[34]

Antonio Gotto and Herbert Pardes, the deans at Cornell and Columbia, see each other weekly, when the two of them are in town, partially, according to a senior P&S investigator, "so that the merger does not bury the schools."[34] Once a week, Dr. Thomas Morris, the vice dean at Columbia, convenes a meeting of the Columbia-Cornell Joint Executive Committee, which is attended by the deans and their staffs, to work on issues affecting the schools and the hospital.[99] Dr. Michael Berman usually represents the hospital.

"The merger has caused the two schools to deal with each other much more. Some of this has been very good. Unity is needed so as not to be picked off by the hospital," observes Oliver Fein, the Cornell associate dean, who has worked at both schools.[87]

"Granted that the merger is mostly about hospital issues, dollars, and practice plans," says Dr. Daniel R. Alonzo, a pathologist who is senior associate dean for academic affairs at Cornell, but "we have seen relatively little stimulus so far for the education people [at the two schools] to get together."[100] The Cornell dean, with whom Pardes has developed what he calls a "love feast,"[45] is, according to Fein, "a southern gentleman, one clever guy, certainly able to hold his own."[87]

"The quiet voice is Tony's," comments Jack Barchas at Cornell, in discussing how Gotto, with a personality distinctly unlike the fast-talking New York types who populate the faculty at both schools, injects a soothing personality into the problems he faces. Unlike many others, "He's not fighting with the hospital," Barchas adds.[76]*

Cornell recruited Gotto to become dean and provost for medical affairs in 1997. Members of his faculty praise his leadership and only complain that his many national and international responsibilities take him away from Cornell more than they would wish, although, as Oliver Fein observes, "I'm surprised how in touch he is despite his travels."[87] Described as smart and committed and very active behind the scenes in fundraising and putting out fires, Gotto gives good advice but allows the chairs to do what they do without interference. The only consistent complaints are that one may have to wait weeks to see him and he is usually late for his appointments.

Names

One thing that Dean Antonio Gotto of Cornell learned from a recent survey about the newly structured hospital that trains his medical students is that, although the names and reputations of the medical schools of Columbia and Cornell universities are widely recognized, the title of the NewYork-Presbyterian Hospital is "poorly understood."[58]

The faculty at both campuses would not be surprised. Presbyterian people regret the loss of the name Columbia-Presbyterian Medical Center, which for more than 70 years identified the country's first medical center with its renowned medical school and teaching hospital. Those at the New York Hospital, who have long suffered from confusion of the name of their institution with New York University's medical school and hospital,[101] and with the New York Medical College,[100] feel just as deprived.

The name NewYork-Presbyterian Hospital has no meaning for this place, believes Jack Barchas, the Cornell psychiatry chairman, "and ads

---

*Born in 1935 in Nashville, Tennessee, Antonio M. Gotto Jr. received his B.A. and M.D. degrees at Vanderbilt University and a D.Phil. in biochemistry as a Rhodes Scholar at Oxford, which uniquely awards this degree, which other universities call a Ph.D. Gotto then trained in internal medicine at the Massachusetts General Hospital, where Samuel Thier, the CEO of Partners, was one of his chief residents and David Skinner had just finished his surgical training. Next he performed research in lipid biochemistry with Dr. Donald Fredrickson, a leading investigator in the field, at the National Institutes of Health in Bethesda. In 1971, Gotto joined the faculty at the Baylor College of Medicine in Houston, Texas, and six years later he became chairman of the Department of Medicine there. Through his work, constantly supported by grants from the NIH, Gotto became a national spokesman for the prevention of heart disease and in 1983 was elected president of the American Heart Association, the leading professional society in cardiology.

won't help." Many there see the name as identifying in what city Presbyterian hospital is located, an ironic development in view of the feeling of many at Presbyterian that the merger was actually a takeover by The New York Hospital.

"When a patient tries to find the phone number of New York Hospital," says Cornell cardiac surgeon Wayne Isom, "he gets Presbyterian.[23] We've both lost our name identification. One hospital's fine for managed care, administration, and finance," he argues, "but not for taking care of patients. For the patient's sake, we should have kept our separate identities. Look at it like General Motors," he suggests. "Because the company's so big, they can buy cheaper and better steel, rubber, and computers than the other automakers, but they still maintain healthy competition and name recognition between the different automobile divisions. If they put it all together as a 'Chevropontiocadillac,' what would you have?"[23]

Michael Wolk, cochairman of the Cornell IPA, is also concerned about loss of identification for his institution as a result of the changes in the name of the combined hospital. This is a problem, he suggests, particularly for the voluntary doctors, whose affiliation, in his case with New York Hospital, a name that has been around for 200 years, brings patients to see him.[40]

"When corporations merge, the executives name the new company and design its logos, style book, and even its business cards before the public announcement," according to David Feinberg, the marketing expert who directs this function for NewYork-Presbyterian Hospital.[101] None of these steps had been taken when Feinberg arrived in December 1997 just before the public announcement of the merger. Specifically selected to bring a professional approach to an industry with which he was unfamiliar — he had previously worked for pharmaceutical companies and advertising agencies — Feinberg entered "a tremendous political battle, which was preventing the leaders from coming to a decision about the name."[101]

Feinberg began by questioning 800 consumers in the tri-state region (New York, New Jersey, and Connecticut) about their awareness of the medical centers. Asked about the standing, on a scale of one to 10, of Columbia-Presbyterian, New York–Cornell, NYU, and Mount Sinai, they saw no significant differences. "The academicians asked, 'Don't they know our school is better, that students prefer coming to us?' The survey tells me that nobody cares" about these criteria, so important to those on the inside. "This means that these four academic medical centers are not differentiated from each other as far as most people are concerned. Even Columbia-Presbyterian, the one I had heard the most about, was not that much better recognized," Feinberg learned. As for the merger itself, a poll conducted in December 1998 showed that only 20 percent know anything at all about hospital mergers. When asked to name one, only 5 percent could do so, and barely 3 percent had heard of the NewYork-Presbyterian merger.[101]

Furthermore, the study revealed that New York Hospital was perceived as an upper-crust, silk stocking institution where rich people came to die. Many still associated it with the widely publicized deaths of Libby Zion and Andy Warhol, which the press had suggested were due to less than perfect care. The principal baggage carried by Columbia-Presbyterian was its location.[101]

Accordingly, Feinberg faced developing marketing plans for two institutions that, despite their high standing in the medical and academic communities, most potential consumers poorly recognized or understood. He also had to devise his program within the fundamental strategy of creating one hospital where there had been two rather than taking the Partners' approach of leaving the names of the teaching hospitals as the public had long perceived them. "We need one name because we are one hospital with one license, one set of standards, and one tremendously high level of medicine," he was told.[101] "The Partners solution and the General Motors naming strategy were rejected from the get-go, never on the table."[101] This would require selecting and marketing, from scratch, a new name, which, of course, consumers would not yet recognize. To have picked one of the existing names would have been "off strategy" and contravened one of the marketing profession's fundamental principles.[101]

Feinberg retained a marketing consultant to help the hospital apply sound "branding" principles, which dictate that the name be memorable, as simple as possible, and easy to understand. Now consumer research and politics faced each other. The name selected, before Feinberg arrived, was The New York and Presbyterian Hospital. New York Hospital people were deeply wedded to the definite article, a part of their hospital's name since its founding. The use of *and* avoided the implication that *New York* primarily identified where Presbyterian was located.

"They're arguing over nothing," thought Feinberg. "Consumers will drop both words, much as Federal Express has become FedEx, and besides the *and* implies two institutions, distinctly off strategy." After much discussion, *the* and *and* were dropped.

While the debate raged, Feinberg raised the possibility of selecting a new title that would not include the names of either of the hospitals. That "would have been the best political solution," he thought. "This didn't appeal either, perhaps too much like the Partners solution."[101]

Next came the question of how to connect the hospital to the famous universities with which they were associated. In April 1998, the consultants first advised using a subtitle, The University Hospitals of Columbia and Cornell.

"The hospital people loved it," remembers Feinberg. "The university people didn't. They fundamentally wanted to retain the separateness of the two campuses—the Partners solution."[101] "What happens to our beloved Columbia-Presbyterian Medial Center or New York Hospital–Cornell Medical Center?" the university advocates complained. Furthermore, the hospital people insisted that the word *medical* be removed because it implied separateness.[101]

Dr. James Smith, a senior Cornell professor, said, "I'm losing my parent, New York Hospital–Cornell Medical Center, but I'm an old orphan and I'll survive."[84]

Another senior faculty member who was relatively unaffected is Dr. Rogerio Lobo, chairman of obstetrics and gynecology at Columbia, "Most people here don't like the names being lost. It matters less for me since I'm from California."[74] Lobo, an authority in reproductive endocrinology and infertility, was recruited from the University of Southern California in Los Angeles and had never trained or worked in New York City.

Someone suggested identifying the two campuses by their locations overlooking Riverside Drive, in the case of Columbia-Presbyterian, and on York Avenue for New York Hospital–Cornell. "This went over like a lead balloon," remembers Feinberg.[101] Gotto objected that no one would contribute to "York Avenue."[101] Eventually, the campuses would be identified as the Columbia-Presbyterian Center uptown—a solution the Columbia people insisted upon[53]—and the New York Weill-Cornell Center on the east side.

Battling over the names occupied many meetings and lasted until December of 1998.[101] Accounting for part of the delay, Feinberg suspects, was the fact that no one person could make the final decision. Names interest trustees, and they had to be consulted before any titles became final. Dean Pardes was heard to say, "I can't make the decision alone, even if I wanted to, which I don't."[101] Some wondered whether part of the delay on the Columbia side reflected greater differences between Speck and Pardes than between Skinner and Gotto at Cornell. Eventually, they all decided on New York-Presbyterian, the University Hospital of Columbia and Cornell, and this is how the institution was identified in an advertising campaign that was launched in the spring of 1999.

But the story wasn't over. In the summer of 1999, several of the New York Hospital chiefs resumed pressing for a name that would make *New York* appear less like an adjective. They favored the General Motors solution, with each site retaining its long familiar designations as at Partners in Boston and the recent Mount Sinai–Tisch (NYU) hospital merger. But Skinner and the board would not accept this and insisted that the hospital name reflect the unified operational reality they had envisioned from the beginning. In the face of this decision, David Feinberg proposed dropping all the spaces, as in DaimlerChrysler. With this approach, the name would become NewYorkPresbyterian, but the doctors weren't immediately impressed, and when the marketing committee of the board would not resurrect the "and" solution, as in New York and Presbyterian, they agreed to the "hyphen" solution, "New York-Presbyterian."* Feinberg's DaimlerChrysler suggestion was resurrected, and the solution became NewYork-Presbyterian. The board accepted this name, which then became official for the hospital and the corporation, NewYork-Presbyterian Healthcare System, Inc., in September of 1999,[101] that is, until it is changed again.

Settling on a name for Columbia-Cornell Care produced similar angst. Which name should come first? After the usual debate, the namers decided to toss a coin. Cornell won but not for long. The Columbia trustees threatened to pull out if Columbia wasn't first.

Then there was the replacement of the hundred-year-old name of the Cornell University Medical College with Weill Medical College of Cornell University in recognition of the family's $100 million gift. Changing the medical college's name in the midst of the hospital merger and its naming problems added to the difficulties faced by those trying to develop means by which the public could identify the institutions.[76]

The Cornell change displeased many at the medical college. "It was easier for them to give away the name," concludes one senior physician, referring to the president and dean, "because they were new to Cornell." Although senior officials[3] confirmed that it was they who presented the idea for the title to Weill, for according to the provisions of the gift the family name must precede that of the university, "no one believes that story," according to more than one skeptic.

It is said that Weill hopes people will eventually associate his family's name with the medical college as they do the Wharton name with the University of Pennsylvania's business school. Members of the Cornell faculty agree that this may happen. "In time, Weill may become the familiar name for the medical college, pushing Cornell out of the picture," fears another faculty member. "If we don't keep the Cornell name prominent, Columbia will further come to dominate."

Columbia faculty members say that such a change could never happen at their institution, "Shows their desperation," adds one of them.

Have these plans helped the public's recognition of the hospital?

---

*As Feinberg suggested about the hyphenated solution, "You see it, but you don't say it."[101]

The New York Times, that beacon of journalistic accuracy in the city, was still confusing the names as 1999 ended. When a former mayor was admitted for treatment of chest pain in the summer of 1999, the hospital was identified on three different days as "New York Weill Cornell Center of *Presbyterian Hospital*" [my italics].[102–4] A few days later, the same newspaper referred to a research investigator at the New York Presbyterian Medical Center,[105] and a month later, in reporting on a potential nurses' strike at the Washington Heights Campus, it wrote about "the 1996 merger of New York Hospital and Columbia-Presbyterian Medical Center"[106] and "New York Hospital, now renamed the New York Weill Cornell Center of Presbyterian Hospital,"* a mistake repeated in early September.[107] As the year ended, when one of the presidential candidates developed an arrhythmia, his doctor was identified as associated with the Columbia-Presbyterian Medical Center, which no longer officially existed.[108] By the first month of 2000, the *Times* almost got it right, identifying the place where a television celebrity received his coronary artery bypass graft surgery as the New York Weill Cornell Center of New York Presbyterian Hospital. The editors couldn't quite bring themselves to drop the space between *New* and *York* or use the hyphen before *Presbyterian.*[109†]

The naming fiasco convinced David Feinberg that if the founders had been required to settle on a name for their enterprise beforehand, the merger attempt would have collapsed.[101]

The Succession: Skinner and Speck

One of the principal topics of discussion during the winter and spring of 1999 was whether Bill Speck would succeed David Skinner as CEO of the NewYork-Presbyterian HealthCare System when Skinner retired on December 31, 2000. Speck's acceptance of the number two position when the merger was negotiated in 1996 came with the implied assumption that he would inherit the job. "I have three years to convince the board I can bring the hospitals together, increase the quality of care and reduce costs," he told a reporter in November 1997.[111]

---

*The uptown partner that joined the merger was the Presbyterian Hospital, not the medical center, and the correct title for the merged hospital is the NewYork-Presbyterian Hospital.

†Someone at NewYork-Presbyterian did reach the authors of the 1999 edition of the *New York Times Manual of Style and Usage* in which the centers are correctly named and identified as part of New York Presbyterian Hospital (including the space and minus the hyphen.)[110]

"The job was his to lose," a Columbia supporter said.[71]

Skinner's setting his retirement date when the merger was negotiated seemed most unwise to his close friend and colleague, the New York Hospital's chief operating officer, George Vecchione. "I advised him that announcing this in 1996 would be devastating," Vecchione remembers.[88] "You run the risk that the heir will tell people that he's now the one who counts, and your effectiveness will be diminished. But he made the announcement anyway and then bent over backwards to show that he and Bill were a partnership. He divided up the CEO job with Bill as Mr. Inside and he as Mr. Outside. This upset the Cornell chiefs, who could no longer get David's attention to their issues."[88]

Vecchione left New York in June of 1998 to become president of Lifespan. Speck, now number two in the merged hospital, was on track to succeed Skinner, not that Vecchione thought he had a chance for the job as a nonphysician. "I wanted to move on with my career," he says, "and Lifespan presented me with that opportunity."[88]

About "the magic of David Skinner," supporters say: "He has us in the palm of his hand."

"He's so good, we salute even though we know he is only telling us only some of the truth."

"He says what's on his mind but will then say something childish with a wink and a joke."

"A very capable communicator, very effective at one-on-one meetings, elegant, the image of a hospital CEO to the trustees."

"Very impressive the way he apprehends issues and comes up with solutions."

"He's positive, friendly, imperturbable, avuncular, very smart, and won't lie to you."

"He has tremendous energy, is an unstoppable force."

"Confidence in what he does, delegates, is a quick study, very smart."

"The new hospital wouldn't have been built without him."

Critics, and he has some, find Skinner "headstrong, like a middle linebacker. I suspect he sometimes creates a problem so he can solve it."

Another senior faculty member observes, "Both Skinner and Speck can be ruthless, but David disguises it better."

Severer critics find him "carnivorous, a command and control kind of guy, inconsistent, can't be trusted."

And, most galling of all, "He doesn't use e-mail."

Bill Speck, seen by many as "a visionary, a very bright guy who cares about the right things, a product of a financial savvy era," is credited with "saving Presbyterian by coming in when the hospital was on the brink of receivership, lopping off expenses appropriately, and putting the place in the black."

"He was good for us, did things long overdue at Presbyterian. We only became a potential merger partner because Bill cleaned us up."

"Bill knew and articulated that the salvation of Columbia-Presbyterian depended on the local community, built bridges to the Dominican population and local doctors, and improved the Allen Pavilion," thereby contributing "to the decrease in crime and the number of drug dealers in the area."

"Most of his predictions have been borne out."

Unfortunately for him, Speck suffers in some respects when compared with Skinner. His critics complain that when he "says what's on his mind" he's "less cool and less soothing" than Skinner, without Skinner's "sensory input — he doesn't listen as well."

"Whereas Skinner will talk to the janitor, Bill just doesn't deal as well with people."

"Bill's a brilliant guy who works at a different level from everyone else."

"He makes more enemies that he needs to."

"He's very candid, sometimes brutally so."

"His intimidating style can cause people to be afraid of him and not tell him the truth, but you can change his mind if your case is good."

"There's no gray with Bill."

"He certainly cares about the right things, the academic mission and the community, but he's easy to demonize by the New York Hospital people opposed to the merger."

A board member who admires him admits that Speck can be, "brutal, dogged, and intimidating in getting things done — a bull in a china shop," a phrase also used by others.*

"His caustic, intimidating tough guy [nature] is posturing when he's insecure."

Speck was seen as hiring people like him, "big picture thinkers, who flew at 30,000 feet" while Skinner hired people different from him, "who walked on the ground."

Unlike Skinner, the macromanager, Speck tended to micromanage and encouraged staff members to report to him outside the usual chain of

---

*Dr. Richard E. Behrman, now senior vice president for medical affairs at the Lucille Packard Foundation for Children's Health in Palo Alto, appointed Speck to be his successor as chairman of pediatrics when Behrman became dean at Case-Western Reserve School of Medicine in Cleveland. "Bill is a very bright and capable man but can be a bull in a china shop," said Behrman without prompting.[112]

command. Speck came on rather strong at the New York Hospital, antagonizing some leaders there, more so than Skinner did at Presbyterian.

Analyzing Speck's skills and shortcomings, one senior P&S faculty member suggests that when Speck became Presbyterian's CEO the hospital needed "Attila the Hun, someone with steel balls," but the characteristics that served him well while repairing Presbyterian's financial state were not ideal for his next role. "He's a good brinksman, necessary then, but not a good statesman, necessary now."

Another observer, close to Speck, observed, "Bill had trouble reporting to David. When you've been in charge, it's difficult not to be in charge."

Finally, unlike just about every other faculty member at either campus, Speck wears a short white coat, the type traditionally reserved for medical students or trainees — if they wear them at all these days. It "differentiates him," and the comment was not intended as a compliment. Skinner, like most of the faculty who wear white coats, favors the full-length laboratory variety.

On March 23, 1999, Skinner met with the directors of the clinical departments from both campuses at Presbyterian, confirmed the date of his retirement from the CEO position on December 31, 2000, and announced that he had asked the hospital board to begin a search for his successor. He raised the possibility that perhaps two jobs would be developed, with a businessman leading the NewYork-Presbyterian HealthCare System and a doctor in charge of the NewYork-Presbyterian Hospital, an option that trustee John McGillicuddy saw as feasible.[6]

During the previous weeks, Skinner and Speck had individually lobbied senior faculty to support their positions with the board, either the plan later announced by Skinner or Speck's desire to succeed him. "It's a breach of contract," Speck told one.[71] Faculty members also gave their opinions to the board members they knew, who in some cases were their patients.

Speck implied that if he didn't become CEO, Presbyterian "will be lost."

Skinner told one of the chairmen privately that the board had asked Speck to leave — an ultimatum Speck denies receiving from the board — but he did not confirm this at the meeting.

"The merger won't happen until we're both gone," one chairman heard Skinner say.[61] The statement aggravated the rumors that the hospital would tread water for 21 months until Skinner left and the new CEO took over.[61,71]

As for Bill Speck's realizing his ambition to lead the hospital he was so instrumental in creating, one observer noted, "Speck's a survivor. Will he pull a rabbit out of the hat again?"[25]

Speck sees his problems as having begun when Skinner told him to restructure the organization, by putting aside his line responsibility for the NewYork-Presbyterian Hospital, and prepare for his role as CEO.[113] Skinner describes the process as Speck's becoming "more presidential, more of a delegator, and more involved with the network and the national organizations that represent teaching hospitals."[3]

As the fall of 1998 advanced, Speck began to feel more and more out of the loop and less and less involved in key decisions.[113] Then, while Speck was on vacation, Skinner held his meeting notifying the clinical leadership about the search.

"I suddenly got calls from my friends. 'What was going on?' I couldn't tell them," remembers Speck.[113] "I had no warning this was coming and got no apology afterwards."[113] As for this time in his life, Speck acknowledges, "It's been terrible."[113]

"Bill's usually infallible radar wasn't working," believes Cynthia Sparer, the executive director of Babies and Children's Hospital and a longtime friend and associate of Speck from Cleveland days.[42] "It didn't pick up what was going on. Why? I think Bill looked on Dave as a father figure and believed that it would be like Clinton and Gore. As soon as Dave began pushing Bill to restructure, Bill should have seen what was coming and not relieved himself of everything operational."[42] Sparer continues, "Throughout the winter [of 1999], David started ignoring Bill and didn't invite him to important meetings. He could come if he wanted, but he wasn't notified."[42]

Speck's new role was never really defined, several observers believe,[9] which was regrettable because, Guy Scalzi, the chief information officer believes, the corporation "badly needs a real number two as chief operating officer."[27]

"Dave did a number on me," a P&S chairman remembers Speck telling him.[71] His friends see him as constantly shooting himself in the foot. Political wags suggest that he was committing suicide and that Skinner was his Kevorkian.

"I'm not sure just when David concluded that Bill shouldn't succeed him," reflects George Vecchione, his former colleague at the New York Hospital.[88] "Probably, few people know. David's a very good chess player. At the beginning, David told me that he could mentor Bill and get him there."[88]

Others agree. James Smith, a senior Cornell clinician long involved in practice issues, observed, "Dave and Bill looked genuinely in league with each other. Dave was not down on Bill, and the relationship looked good at the start."[84]

Cynthia Sparer concludes, "This [the succession fight] hurts us and helps Jack Rowe.* The infighting prevents energy being directed to the challenges outside where it should go. The problem can even get in the way of our new Babies and Children's Hospital. David's ready to act as its patron saint but only if Bill doesn't run it."[42]

Tim Pedley, the neurology chairman at P&S, agrees. "We've merged, but we're basically treading water, very bad in this competitive environment. The Skinner-Speck controversy has been quite divisive. To succeed, the process mustn't drift," Pedley warned.[71]

"Everything's in limbo now," observes Dr. David Bickers, the P&S chairman of dermatology who has known Speck from their association in Cleveland and participated with him in some of the merger attempts.[78] "The executive group of chairs meets monthly at New York Hospital or here. It's like adjusting the deck chairs on the *Titanic*. No one wants to address the real issues. I've given up going to some of the meetings." The effects of the inaction worry him. "If you stand still, you fall behind. In this market, you can fall off the cliff."[78]

The succession conflict reached beyond the NewYork-Presbyterian Hospital. "The network hospitals have found the succession squabble very dissembling," adds Oliver Fein, who coordinates network relations with Cornell.[87] "Network executives and leading doctors hope for a speedy resolution."[87]

These events also alarmed the P&S clinical chairmen, who, putting aside their previous differences with Speck, now began supporting him. Feeling that the merger of equals had gone "down the tube" and that Presbyterian was being taken over by the people at the New York Hospital, most of the clinical chiefs at Presbyterian signed a letter to the hospital board on March 17, 1999, which read:[114]

> As clinical leaders of the Columbia-Presbyterian Medical Center, we write to express our concerns regarding the New York Presbyterian Hospital. We perceive a leadership vacuum characterized convincingly by a lack of cultural understanding and an absence of strategic direction for our hospital campus. We have witnessed the wholesale replacement of our administrative hospital leadership with personnel from our sister center. Most recently our concerns have been aggravated by our sense of the impending abandonment of the hospital leadership succession plan which we considered to symbolize the construct of a merger of equals.

To complicate matters further, those with their ears to the ground began detecting signals about consolidating the medical schools — again.

---

*Dr. John Rowe, CEO of the combined Mt. Sinai and Tisch (NYU) hospital.

When Antonio Gotto, the Cornell dean, was asked about this at the March meeting at which David Skinner announced the latest political developments for the hospital, he replied that "at this time," no one was considering merging the schools.[25] This was enough to start rumors that what he really was saying was that the deans were talking about doing just that.[25] As one of the senior faculty member observed, "There is obviously tremendous reluctance to merge, but if the financial pressures become impossible, you can never tell."

Dr. Leighton Smith, the director of the Cornell primary care program, who, unlike most of his current colleagues, spent most of his career at other institutions, believes that "Merging medical schools is a pipe dream."

A senior member of the P&S faculty suggests, "Cornell is trying fiercely to stay independent. They must feel equal to Columbia before joining up."

By Friday, April 9, 1999, the newspapers had learned about the controversy, and articles describing the problem appeared in *The New York Times*[115] and the *Wall Street Journal*.[116] Speck's going quietly seemed unlikely and inconsistent with the feisty character he had developed on the streets of Newark, where he grew up. He "had to work very hard all the way," according to an admirer on the P&S faculty.

An unnamed administrator, who attended a meeting Speck called at Presbyterian to discuss, among other matters, the price of conformity, concluded: "The message was clear. . . . He's going to put up a fight."[115] "Bill's supporters on the board will say, 'A deal's a deal,'" another observer suggested.

His friend and colleague Allen Hyman recalls, "There were three givens when the merger came about: (1) a full-asset merger, everything would get scrambled; (2) it would be fifty-fifty, a merger of equals; and (3) first Dave, then Bill, not first Dave and then we'll see. Without all three, it wouldn't have happened."[117]

"The 'Bill thing' could fractionate the board," predicted others. But it didn't, and on April 14 the board decided that it would undertake a national search for Skinner's successor.[72,118] "A few of us from the old Presbyterian board met with Bill," said one of the trustees who has been a longtime Speck supporter and admirer. "It was Bill who suggested that the best solution might be to bring in someone entirely new. Bill might have hoped that we would disagree and insist he stay, but his suggestion was the right one. It's ironic. If it hadn't been for Bill, the merger would never have happened."

"I think it was considered best for all to let Bill make his own break and move on to cap off a very successful career," said George Baker, cochairman of the merged board's investment committee and before that a longtime board member of New York Hospital, which his family had served for a century; the first George Baker became a trustee in 1899. "I think the feeling is that down the road we really have to bring these institutions closer together and in order to do that we have to create a new culture. We have got to accelerate the process more than has been done in the past. . . . The merger [has] definitely slowed down. It may mean a new team of executives."[118]

Trustee Daniel Burke, the retired president and CEO of Capital Cities/ABC, confirmed this conclusion when he met with the P&S chairmen to explain that Speck would not succeed Skinner. "The merger's not working" was the reason.[78]

The board quashed suggestions that the merger might come apart and emphatically reaffirmed its support of the combined structure,[6] relieving Tim Pedley's concern that "I hope things are not driven apart before we know whether it [the merger] will succeed."[71]

John Driscoll, the P&S pediatrics chairman, agrees. "We'd be fools if we missed it. The merger must be preserved, but we'll continue to struggle so long as the schools, the hospital, and the doctors insist on fighting among each other."[62]

Board cochairman John McGillicuddy suggests that the recent controversy served as a catharsis for the board and forced it to resolve this and other fundamental questions.[6] "Boards [of university hospitals] seem to be less willing to come down on a CEO than in industry. I think this is partly because he's often a doctor, and doctors are special people with skills we're somewhat in awe of."[6] But the scene may be changing. Today's teaching hospital CEOs "are under a lot more financial pressure than previously."[6] The governance of these institutions helps to explain why some of the CEO-board interactions differ from those seen in industry. McGillicuddy explains, "In most businesses, the CEO is the chairman of the board. We seldom see a nonexecutive chairman in the for-profit sector, as is the case in the hospital."[6]

In spite of the board's ringing endorsement of the merger, the recent events caused some of the medical school leaders to wonder whether it was a good thing in the first place. "The whole planning process left much to be desired," someone said, "and the physician leadership should have been involved. If they'd anticipated the troubles we've had, the Partners model might have been better. Should the merger have happened?" he asks himself. "I'd like to be optimistic and say yes."

In retrospect, another observer suggests, the founders "should have used consultants. The professional managers and some members of the board advised this. That's the way we do it in business, but the physician leadership turned it down. 'Why would we need consultants?' they asked. Because consultants ask the necessary questions."

Michael Leahey, director of the clinical trials unit, who has worked in the private sector, observed, "In a business merger, there would have been better developed short-term and long-term plans with analysis of capital investment. This merger seemed to depend primarily upon the 'visions' of the leadership. There are huge cultural differences, and inadequate attention was paid to how the cultures could coexist."[77]

"The personal animosity between Speck and Pardes highlighted the problems we were having. One of them would say no almost automatically," observes Dr. James Lieberman from Columbia. Now that Speck was going, would it get better? "Not necessarily. There's so much paranoia about each move. Unless we can get past this, we'll sit here squabbling for 10 years like a bad marriage. At least our Ivy League aura helps us survive despite the mess. To the outside, we both still look like 500-pound gorillas."[47]*

Speck offered no comments about the decision. He was said to be negotiating a severance package[118] to replace his salary, reported by the *Wall Street Journal* to be $1.2 million per year.[120] (Skinner made $1.5 million, according to the same source.)[120] Speck's wife, Phoebe, was less reticent and said to a reporter, "Of course, he would have liked to have stayed on and fulfill his vision. But you give birth to this, and then do you sacrifice yourself or do you sacrifice your child?"[118]

"Skinner's back in charge," his close friend and associate Fritz Reuter, exclaimed,[12] and Jim Smith at Columbia-Cornell Care adds, "This could be David's finest hour."[84]

Nevertheless, these events seemed to have taken their toll on Skinner. Dr. Jack Barchas, the chairman of psychiatry at Cornell, saw him "walking the stage as a stricken king, all powerful but without power,"[76] and David Bickers from Columbia found him "under stress. He looks tired and not well. He's out to pasture."[78]

Skinner, another observer commented, "had been beaten down by the Speck thing and the loss of some of his associates. He took a battering we didn't fully appreciate and doesn't have the energy to go on."

---

*The unlikely union of these two famous, competing institutions, each with long and different traditions, led Dr. Thomas Delbanco, a professor at Harvard and a leading scholar of primary care, to observe at a lecture he recently gave at Columbia, "If I'd said that Presbyterian and New York Hospital would merge when I worked here 20 years ago [as a Presbyterian resident], I'd have been admitted to PI [the Psychiatric Institute]." His audience received the comment with prolonged laughter.[119]

"It seems that the executive committee of the board has begun to personalize the merger, and many of us may well go off into the sunset at the end of 2000 when David retires," Fritz Reuter says.[12]

The process had already begun by the summer of 1999. Kathryn Martin, the director of operations, announced that she was moving across York Avenue to Memorial Hospital, the renowned cancer center, into a similar job.* Martin had had to concentrate on Presbyterian's operations, and New York Hospital leaders had missed her attention. In her absence, other mangers had had to leave the "well-oiled ship" downtown to improve operations in Washington Heights. Had Martin left, people wondered, because of the impossibility of managing the operations of such a large enterprise? "Her departure was a real blow. . . . She knew the finances and knew operations, but felt she was always being second-guessed," someone told a reporter for *Crain's New York Business.*[121]

It was also said at this time that, in addition to Martin, John Lavan, the executive vice president for finance, had let his name circulate under the presumption that a new CEO would want to bring in his or her own people.† To push this scenario further, if a successor is quickly chosen, Skinner could leave his post before his planned retirement date of December 31, 2000.[118]

To replace Kathryn Martin, Michael Berman appointed Marvin O'Quinn, the former chief operating officer at Presbyterian, to direct operations at the New York Hospital site and Robert Kelly, the former chief medical officer at the New York Hospital, as operations chief at Presbyterian. These appointments recognized the difficulty of one person's directing all operations at both sites. Speck and Skinner's concept of single direct management of operations at both centers wasn't working and needed modification. The size of the places, the presence of two

---

*Martin goes to what one observer sees as "an easier job at the same location for more money and greater security." It will include, however, ambulatory services and network development, not part of her assignment at NewYork-Presbyterian. After the immense scale of her responsibilities at NewYork-Presbyterian, Martin looked forward to working in the smaller Memorial, where she sees her responsibilities as being similar to those she had as director of operations at the New York Hospital before the merger.[13] When she decided to switch, she did not know who would be CEO at either her new or her old hospital. The new head of Memorial turned out to be Dr. Harold Varmas, director of the National Institutes of Health and a Nobel Prize–winning scientist previously at the University of California-San Francisco.

†In the spring of 2000, Lavan became the leader of NewYork-Presbyterian Health Care Ventures, a new enterprise to develop revenue beyond the usual clinical sources. Phyllis R.F. Lantos from Yale University School of Medicine was appointed chief financial officer of NewYork-Presbyterian.[45]

medical schools, and the necessity of keeping so many clinical directors as content as possible conspired to create a job description unworkable even for someone as capable as Martin. Drawing on her recent experiences, Martin has concluded that "certain functions need to be done at the local level, particularly the issues of greatest importance to doctors. Two such different environments require separation."[13]

Berman reversed the loci of O'Quinn's and Kelly's assignments so that they would bring to their new sites features learned where they had originally worked and avoid encouraging unwise patterns to persist.[9] The talents of O'Quinn and Kelly differed and seemed to fit better with their new assignments. Kelly, trained in the Skinner and Martin mold, emphasizes organizational discipline and close attention to detail, skills needed at the larger and more diffuse Presbyterian campus.[25] O'Quinn, hired originally by Speck, favors program development, suitable to the smaller New York Hospital where a well-managed structure was already in place. Whereas Presbyterian's buildings needed fixing and investment, Kelly's strength, the P&S faculty had developed strong academic programs. At the New York Hospital, the place ran better and its clinical plant was new, but the Cornell programs needed attention, which fit O'Quinn's skills and interests. These differences between the two campuses reflected the priorities of the people at the top — Skinner, the surgeon, on infrastructure and Speck, the pediatrician and classicist, on programs.

As expected, the staff at New York Hospital, deprived of Martin, now complained about the loss of Kelly, as did people at Presbyterian about the transfer of O'Quinn. "I'm seen as the eighth chief operating officer in nine years," says Kelly, but he was welcomed at Presbyterian, which he found starved for local leadership and discipline. Although he knows the doctors to be excellent at both sites and very proud of their hospitals and schools, "they feel more deprived at Presbyterian and disenfranchised from the administration." Kelly expects his honeymoon to be short. "My bubble will burst as soon as the cuts start. Then I'll be the marauder from the south, like a Hunter person."[35]*

The two retained former assignments common to both centers such as mental health, the outpatient clinics, human resources, and the Allen Pavilion by O'Quinn and facilities, including food, plant, and laundry, by Kelly.

Arriving at The New York Hospital, O'Quinn confirmed some fundamental differences between Presbyterian and his new assignment.

---

*The Hunter Group is a hospital consulting firm often retained to reverse financial losses and improve management. We will see it in operation in the merger of the teaching hospitals of Stanford University and the University of California-San Francisco in chapter 7.

"There's more stability downtown, more of a sense of itself," which he ascribes to the skills of the team David Skinner built there. Richer staffing in nursing helped produce a higher level of comfort for patients, and the absence of unions contributed to a calmer atmosphere for the administration. At Presbyterian, "it was more of a high-wire act thanks to Bill [Speck]." Despite the merger and the changes in which he is participating, O'Quinn sees a minimum of clinical integration by the fall of 1999.[11]

As the financial pressures built during the latter part of 1999, hospital director Michael Berman and his staff planned to reduce expenses, mostly though cutbacks in personnel, needed to continue to avoid a deficit in operations, which, if nothing is done, could reach $120 million by December 31, 2000.[9] All feared the arrival of consultants, specifically the Hunter Group, to make the cuts at NewYork-Presbyterian. Berman assured the chairmen and the board that he and his team could do what Hunter was being employed to do elsewhere.[9]

Should the Merger Continue?

The executive and search committees of the board of NewYork-Presbyterian now faced two fundamental issues as they worked to find a successor for David Skinner. Should the new CEO be a layman, not a physician? Would the business executives who led the board of trustees agree with a nonphysician administrative leader from P&S who held that "Hospital and university people don't understand each other. We need more corporate types and fewer doctors running things."* Second, and of more basic importance, the board had to consider, partially in response to recent events in the merger of the teaching hospitals of the University of California-San Francisco and Stanford,[86]† should the merger continue? Some of the more senior trustees, who were among the largest donors, suggested that this was the time to look again at the value of the combined structure.

A business publication implied that the hospital was in trouble, "rocked by management turmoil, [facing] mounting deficits . . . and

---

*As for the faculty's opinion of the process of finding the next David Skinner, one senior member with experience at other medical centers believes that, "The [trustees'] search committee has no comprehension of the academic life. They're a group of wealthy people without intellectual love in their bodies." He regrets that neither of the university presidents serves on the committee.

†See chapter 7.

failing to swiftly consolidate operations between the two hospitals," its reporter wrote. "Far from being the crown in Chief Executive Dr. David Skinner's health care strategy, the massive merger appears to have overpowered its creator."[121]

Was the merger becoming unbalanced? Presbyterian needed more capital than the New York Hospital site — about $30 million per year for six years was estimated — and was taking significantly more of management's time. With income falling further behind expenses, would the necessary cuts be better administered and tolerated if they were instituted at smaller entities rather than throughout the immense NewYork-Presbyterian Hospital? Finally, charitable contributions had decreased slightly in 1998, and some of this seemed due to reduced enthusiasm by members of the board for the merged entity than for the separate hospitals.[12] Skinner reports that contributions subsequently increased during 1999.[3]

On Wednesday, November 3, the search committee and the board of trustees held extended meetings. The trustees resolved to continue the merger and put to rest, for the second time in less than a year, speculation that the hospitals might return to independent status. Leading members of the board concluded that the merger had benefited the Presbyterian and New York Hospitals, which, if they had remained separate, would be losing large amounts of money rather than remaining "marginally in the black" on operations, as described by Arthur Hedge, a former Presbyterian trustee and now a member of the executive committee of NewYork-Presbyterian.[86]

The large endowments contributed to NewYork-Presbyterian by its founding hospitals produced enough income to more than offset any unanticipated losses by the end of the year. However, the board will expect the new administration to so manage the hospital that operations breaks even at least, difficult though this may be. The endowment and its income must be protected for future improvements and development.

Although Presbyterian, an older and more sprawling institution, needed a greater allotment of capital funds and administrative attention now, the downtown site would need money later, and the high census at Presbyterian had helped to float the greater depreciation generated by the new Greenberg Building at the New York Hospital.[86] The board continued to maintain that in time the "branding" of the name, NewYork-Presbyterian, would take effect and lead to recognition that the hospital had become truly a world-class institution. Hedge[86] joined others[101] in pointing with satisfaction to the standing of NewYork-Presbyterian as number 11 on the honor roll of the nation's 13 "best hospitals" in the July

19, 1999, issue of *U.S. News and World Report.*[122] As individual hospitals, neither Presbyterian nor the New York Hospital had ranked so high in recent surveys.*

The Choice

The members of the search committee decided that, in the best of all worlds, a physician successor to Skinner would be their first choice. This approach appealed to one of the senior Cornell doctors, who also preferred that the winning candidate have specific medical experience. NewYork-Presbyterian needed, in his judgment, "someone now running an academic center, preferably a doctor. It helps to have flown a plane if you're head of the Air Force."

However, the committee also resolved to try to recruit the best leader available regardless of professional training and indicated that preferably an outside choice would be best. As a rival hospital executive suggested to a reporter, "If the board really wants to see the merger blend, they need a neutral person, not someone identified as a partisan."[124] Skinner's retirement and the appointment of a leader not associated with either of the hospitals would support his prophesy that both he and Speck might have to depart for the merger to reach completion.

The committee retained Dr. John H. Moxley III, a physician and managing director of the academic health sciences group at the firm of Korn/Ferry International, to assist in the search. Moxley presented a list of 10 outside candidates but also advised considering Dr. Herbert Pardes at P&S. The committee decided that since it would be considering one inside candidate it should look at other possibilities from within NewYork-Presbyterian.

The prospect of Pardes being selected became public relatively quickly and aroused anxiety at Cornell, where some were concerned about the effects of such a Columbia partisan leading the merged hospital, not unlike how the Presbyterian faculty had felt about the New York Hospital's Skinner being the first CEO. Some of the external candidates informed the committee that if Pardes was being seriously considered they wanted to withdraw their candidacies.

Leading trustees from both Presbyterian and the New York Hospital interviewed Pardes and, rather early in the process, told their col-

---

*In the July 17, 2000 listing, the magazine did not include NewYork-Presbyterian among the 15 hospitals in its "Best Hospitals Honor Roll."[123]

leagues, "He's our man." The committee's opinion coalesced around Pardes quickly, as his winning character swept all before him. The trustees came to realize that the hospital was experiencing increasing internal trouble[121] and a leader was needed quickly. Pardes's nomination was presented to Columbia University trustees and officials for approval and to leaders at Cornell, where some objections arose. However, Dean Antonio Gotto and trustee Sanford Weill supported the choice, and the Cornell officials agreed to Pardes's selection.

On December 15, 1999, nine months after Skinner had announced that a search for his successor would begin, the trustees of the NewYork-Presbyterian HealthCare System elected Dr. Herbert Pardes as the second CEO of the hospital and system.[125,126] The board had concluded, according to an informed observer, that "Herb will be a healer."

Pardes's appointment pleased the Columbia-Presbyterian contingent, which had continually felt that people from the New York Hospital had dominated the merger. One of his strongest uptown supporters finds Pardes, "a natural leader, with a distinctive style. At a meeting, unlike some people, he listens and watches the dynamics,* then crisply summarizes, crystallizes, and shapes the salient points. He respects the people he leads, who don't leave disaffected if Herb's decision isn't the one that was wanted."[42]

All Columbia faculty members interviewed regretted losing Pardes's skills as dean — "the best dean in the country," said one — and sympathized with his taking on such a difficult job. At Cornell, his fellow psychiatry chairman, Jack Barchas, was also happy about the choice. Long favoring Pardes for the job, Barchas says, "He can run very complex systems. This would combine Columbia and NewYork-Presbyterian Hospital."[76]

Dirk Sostman, the Cornell chairman of radiology, calls the appointment "a fabulous choice." With respect to Pardes's being an internal selection, Sostman adds, "We don't have the time to let an outsider learn the job. Herb can hit the ground running."[21]

Because of Pardes's age — he would be 65 when starting the job, nine months older than Skinner — speculation when his appointment first surfaced suggested, falsely, an "interim" appointment.[127] A leading member of the board said, "Herb's got the energy of a man 20 years younger."[59]

The new position required Pardes's relinquishing his administrative responsibilities at Columbia, which would now undertake searches for a dean and a chairman of psychiatry. Until a permanent successor is appointed, Thomas Morris agreed to serve as acting dean for the clinical

---

*This is suitable, one can't help but note, for a psychiatrist.

departments and David Hirsh, the chairman of biochemistry and molecular biophysics, as acting dean for the basic sciences.*

Pardes took over as the CEO of the NewYork-Presbyterian Health-Care System on January 3, 2000, with the comment, "David [Skinner] gets us through Y2K, then I take it for the rest of the century."†
Stressing that "the battle is with the outside," Pardes plans to emphasize his well-recognized skills of bringing people together into "a harmonious effort. I understand the relationship between the schools and the hospital and will be evenhanded with the Cornell faculty."

"Herb knows how to play the docs," a Cornell faculty member observed.

"A team has to be fashioned," Pardes adds, "which is genuinely collaborative."[45]

Pardes looks forward to "getting a high head of steam up" to improve philanthropic support and wants to see the hospital become a "beacon for national policy in health care. New York has always had the perspective of being the best," the New Yorker in Pardes says. "Our center is the best positioned to become the best, but it'll be a five to 10 year process. The whole institution is an elaboration of the basic doctoring and caring instinct that brought us into medicine."[45]

The interregnum of the past year at NewYork-Presbyterian would now end. The prolonged search had "opened up a Pandora's box of bitching, with everyone looking out for himself," as one observer described the mood.

Optimistic predictions followed. "The atmosphere has completely changed. There's more hope that the merger can now reach its potential." "A 'we can do this' feeling will return. People need to believe."‡

---

*On December 5, 2000, Columbia University announced the selection of Dr. Gerald D. Fischbach, director of the National Institute of Neurological Disorders and Stroke at the National Institutes of Health, to succeed Pardes as dean of the Faculty of Medicine and vice president for health and biomedical sciences.

†The hospital board named Skinner president emeritus for life and gave him a new office and all the secretarial assistance he needs. He professes great satisfaction for his new life, which includes membership on several boards and work for his many professional societies. "And I don't have to attend all those 7:00 A.M. meetings," he adds.[3]

‡When interviewed in the summer of 2000, seven months after taking over, Pardes asserted that the "acrimony between the constituencies would now be hard to find," collaboration had greatly increased, and "the inside tension has gone."[45]

Part 3
UCSF Stanford

The following people are discussed in Chapter 6, "Formation," and Chapter 7, "Development."

(Stanford = Stanford University School of Medicine; UCSF = University of California, San Francisco School of Medicine; UCSF Stanford = UCSF Stanford Health Care. Most titles are those held when the individual was interviewed.)

Name	Position
Abel, Michael E., M.D.	Chief Executive Officer, Brown and Toland Medical Group
Andreopoulos, Spyros	Director Emeritus, Office of Communications, Stanford University
Arenson, Ronald L., M.D.	Chair, Department of Radiology, UCSF
Ascher, Nancy L., M.D.	Chair, Department of Surgery, UCSF
Atkinson, Richard C., Ph.D.	President, University of California
Bauer, Eugene A., M.D.	Dean, Stanford
Behrman, Richard E., M.D.	Member, Board of Trustees, UCSF Stanford
Bishop, J. Michael, M.D.	Chancellor, UCSF
Bloem, Kenneth D.	Former Chief Executive Officer, Stanford University Hospital
Blume, Karl G., M.D.	Director, Bone Marrow Transplantation Division, Stanford
Boyden, Jaclyne W.	Vice Dean for Administration and Finance, UCSF
Byerwalter, Mariann	Chief Financial Officer, Stanford University
Casper, Gerhard, Ph.D.	President, Stanford University

Cohen, Harvey J., M.D.   Chair, Department of Pediatrics,
                                    Stanford
Cohen, Neal H., M.D.   Vice Chair, Department of
                                    Anesthesia, and Director, Intensive
                                    Care Unit, UCSF
Cox, Kenneth L., M.D.   Chief, Division of Pediatric
                                    Gastroenterology, and Chief
                                    Medical Officer, Lucile Packard
                                    Children's Hospital, Stanford
Dawes, Christopher G.   Chief Executive Officer, Lucile
                                    Packard Children's Hospital,
                                    Stanford
Debas, Haile, M.D.   Dean, UCSF
Esquivel, Carlos O., M.D.   Professor of Surgery and Associate
                                    Chair, Department of Surgery,
                                    Transplantation Service, Stanford
Fuchs, Victor   Professor of Economics Emeritus,
                                    Stanford University
Furnstahl, Lawrence   Senior Vice President and Chief
                                    Financial Officer, UCSF Stanford
Garzio, Catherine   Administrator, Clinical Cancer
                                    Center, UCSF Stanford
Glantz, Stanton A., Ph.D.   Professor of Medicine, UCSF
Glaser, Gary M., M.D.   Chair, Department of Radiology,
                                    Stanford
Gold, Warren M., M.D.   Chief, Pulmonary Division, and
                                    Chair, Faculty Association, UCSF
Goldman, Lee, M.D.   Chair, Department of Medicine,
                                    UCSF
Goldstein, Avram   Professor of Molecular
                                    Pharmacology Emeritus, Stanford
Goodell, Brian, M.D.   Senior Vice President, the Hunter
                                    Group
Gregory, Peter B., M.D.   Chief Medical Officer and Senior
                                    Associate Dean, Stanford
Hanley, Frank L., M.D.   Chief, Division of Cardiac Surgery,
                                    UCSF
Harris, Edward D., Jr., M.D.   Medical Director, International
                                    Medical Services, and former Chair
                                    (1987–95), Department of
                                    Medicine, Stanford

Hauser, Stephen L., M.D.	Chair, Department of Neurology, UCSF
Hellman, F. Warren	Trustee, UCSF Stanford
Holman, Halsted R., M.D.	Guggenhime Professor of Medicine, and former Chair (1960–71), Department of Medicine, Stanford
Hunter, David	Chief Executive Officer, the Hunter Group
Jamplis, Robert, M.D.	Former President and CEO, Palo Alto Clinic
Kane, John P., M.D.	Professor of Medicine, UCSF
Kennedy, Donald, Ph.D.	Former President, Stanford University
Kerr, Clark, Ph.D.	President Emeritus, University of California
Kerr, William B.	Chief Operating Officer, UCSF Stanford; former Chief Executive Officer, UCSF Medical Center
Korn, David, M.D.	Former Dean (1984–95), Stanford
Kornberg, Arthur, M.D.	Professor of Biochemistry Emeritus, Stanford; Nobel Laureate, 1959
Krevans, Julius R., M.D.	Chancellor Emeritus, UCSF
Lane, Alfred T., M.D.	Chair, Department of Dermatology, Stanford
Laros, Russell K., Jr., M.D.	Vice Chair, Department of Obstetrics and Gynecology, UCSF, and Chair, UCSF Practice Plan
Luft, Harold S., Ph.D.	Director, Institute for Health Policy Studies, UCSF
Macleod, Karen	President, University Professional and Technical Employees Union, UCSF
Margaretten, William, M.D.	Vice Dean for Academic Affairs, UCSF
Mark, James B. D., M.D.	Professor of Surgery Emeritus, Stanford
Martin, Joseph B., M.D., Ph.D.	Dean of the Faculty of Medicine, Harvard Medical School; former Chancellor (1993–97), UCSF

May, G. Brian

Senior Vice President, Information Technology, UCSF Stanford

Mcafee, Thomas V., M.D.

Executive Vice President and Chief Medical Officer, Brown and Toland Medical Group; Vice President of Primary Care Services, UCSF Stanford

Melmon, Kenneth, M.D.

President, Faculty Senate, and former Chair (1978–84) Department of Medicine, Stanford

Melnick, David, Esq.

Chair, Mount Zion Hospital Advisory Committee

Miller, Ronald D., M.D.

Chair, Department of Anesthesia, UCSF

Mitchell, Malinda S.

Chief Operating Officer, Stanford University Hospital

Perry, Patricia E.

Senior Vice President, Strategic Development, UCSF Stanford

Polan, Mary Lake, M.D., Ph.D.

Chair, Department of Obstetrics and Gynecology, Stanford

Reitz, Bruce A., M.D.

Chair, Department of Cardiothoracic Surgery, Stanford

Ring, Ernest J., M.D.

Associate Dean for UCSF–Mount Zion Medical Center

Rizk, Norman W., M.D.

Director, Intensive Care Units, Stanford

Rockafellar, Nancy M., Ph.D.

Director, Oral History Program, UCSF

Rudd, Peter, M.D.

Chief, Division of General Internal Medicine, Stanford

Schindler, Robert A., M.D.

Chair, Department of Otolaryngology, UCSF

Schrock, Theodore R., M.D.

Chief Medical Officer, UCSF Stanford; former Chair, Department of Surgery

Schroffel, Bruce

Former Chief Operating Officer, UCSF Hospitals

Shapiro, Larry J., M.D.

Chair, Department of Pediatrics, UCSF

Showstack, Jonathan A., Ph.D.

Professor of Medicine and Health Policy, UCSF

Shumway, Norman E., M.D.

Professor of Cardiothoracic Surgery

	and founder and former Chair (1974–92), Department of Cardiothoracic Surgery, Stanford
Smith, Lloyd H., Jr., M.D.	Associate Dean and former Chair (1964–85), Department of Medicine, UCSF
Stein, Isaac, Esq.	Chair, Board of Trustees, UCSF Stanford
Stone, John B.	Interim Chief Operating Officer, UCSF Hospitals; Senior Vice President, the Hunter Group
Swain, Judith L., M.D.	Chair, Department of Medicine, Stanford
Van Etten, Peter W.	Chief Executive Officer, UCSF Stanford; former Chief Executive Officer, Stanford Health Services
Wilson, Charles B., M.D.	Professor of Neurosurgery and former Chair (1968–97), Department of Neurosurgery, UCSF
Wintroub, Bruce U., M.D.	Chair, Department of Dermatology, UCSF; former Chief Medical Officer, UCSF Stanford
Yamamoto, Keith, Ph.D.	Chair, Department of Cellular and Molecular Biology, UCSF

CHAPTER 6

Formation

In April of 1995, Gerhard Casper, president of Stanford University, and Dr. Joseph B. Martin, chancellor of the University of California-San Francisco, took their renowned "walk in the woods."* Casper and Martin, who were attending a meeting of the California Business Higher Education Forum in Palm Springs, discussed how they could share more and compete less, challenges that would lead to the merging of their teaching hospitals, which are among the most admired in the country.[1,2]

"We can't succeed with this arms race with such marginal bottom lines," Martin remembers telling Casper. "We're going to kill each other if we don't find a way to work together."[1]

California, a Different Country

The California health market, described by Casper as a jungle,[2] "has undergone the most advanced switching to managed care."[2] The use of indemnity insurance had virtually disappeared, constituting only 1.5 percent of all support by 1998.[3] HMOs continued their penetration of the San Francisco market, with a 59 percent share in July 1998 compared to 50 percent in 1996.[4] By consolidating,[4] HMOs further increased their ability to make providers accept lower payments.[5] Although pressure from providers had begun to force HMOs to raise some of their rates, those paying less tended to accumulate more of the market. This pattern caused the better-paying HMOs to lose business, vitiating the effect of increasing rates and continuing the downward pressure on revenues, which one observer described as "incredible."[5]

---

*"The use of *woods* was metaphorical," Casper explains (one would have difficulty finding woods in Palm Springs). "It alluded to an episode during arms control talks in Geneva in the 1970s. Actually, it was the desert."[2] One can't help but observe how different were the locations where the initial discussions about the mergers described in this book took place — in Boston in a parking lot, in New York at a club, and in California in the desert.

"People are comfortable with HMOs and don't see them as rapacious bad guys," says Harold S. Luft, a health care economist and director of the Institute for Health Policy Studies at UCSF. The public's acceptance of HMOs partially explains why hospitals and physicians in California have such difficulty securing what they consider to be adequate compensation for their services. "Kaiser has been active in the Bay Area for some 50 years and has developed long-standing relationships with unions," adds Luft. "That's three generations of Kaiser families."[6]

"Furthermore," explains Luft, "California is a state of immigrants. Very few people have been here for a generation, so many come without their doctor relationships, unlike in New York or Boston. Potential patients seem more willing, even happy, to accept organized plans, which provide them with physicians and hospitals, which, as newcomers, would be foreign to them."[6]

Large employee purchasing groups, such as CalPERS[7]* and the Pacific Business Group on Health, have developed in California and successfully pressure the insurers to charge less, thereby driving down further what the HMOs pay to hospitals and doctors.[4]

Although "no one has satisfactorily answered the question 'What makes California different?'" Stanford health care economist Victor R. Fuchs suggests that at least one factor is that patients spend less time in California hospitals, where the length of stay has been shorter than in other parts of the country for many years. "The patients and the staff want to go home on weekends, the weather's so nice, and the doctors aren't used to working seven days a week."[8] In addition, California has been closing hospital beds for over a decade because of excess capacity.[9] Not as an explanation for California but more as a general observation, Fuchs says, "Health care is a locally produced resource."[8]

Complicating the situation further is the relative lack of standing that teaching hospitals enjoy in the West compared to their prestige in the Northeast.[10] "Payers and patients in California have little use for teaching hospitals," believes Dr. Michael J. Zinner, chair of the Department of Surgery at the University of California-Los Angeles School of Medicine from 1988 to 1994 and now surgeon-in-chief at the Brigham and Women's Hospital in Boston.[11] Furthermore, Medicare pays significantly less for the education of graduate physicians — the interns and

---

*CalPERS is the California Public Employees' Retirement System, which describes itself as the largest public pension system in the nation, with nearly $155 billion in assets providing retirement and health benefits to more than a million state and local public employees, retirees, and their families from more than 2,400 employers.[7] Small wonder that its ability to reduce payments to health care providers can be sizable.

residents so vital to the operation of teaching hospitals — in California than in other parts of the country.[12]

Reasons for the Merger

Most believe that the core issue[13] prompting the merger was the desire to release the two academic centers in northern California from competition over "high-end"* work. A new corporation could more easily stabilize the prices that the insurance carriers paid to the hospitals and prevent the "volumes"† from going elsewhere.[14]

Acting separately, Stanford and UCSF "would be in a death spiral against each other," explains a senior UCSF chair. "We'd fight with other people rather than ourselves, and, we assumed, new collaborations would arise among the two faculties."[14]

"We had become locked in deadly competition with Stanford and California-Pacific‡ for the high-end work," says Dr. Theodore R. Schrock, chief medical officer at UCSF and former chair of surgery there. Stanford had recently recruited the entire liver transplantation team from California-Pacific, and "this meant big trouble for us."[15] The liver transplant program was one of UCSF's leading high-end activities.

UCSF officials also thought that Stanford had its own reasons for wanting to transfer the ownership of its hospital. "Stanford felt that their hospital enterprise was the tail that wagged the dog and needed more money than the university wanted tied up there," William Margaretten, from the UCSF dean's office, remembers hearing."[16] Stanford, UCSF officials understood, was considering a merger with the for-profit hospital chain, Columbia-HCA, and they feared that if the Stanford hospital "went private [for profit]"[15] competition would intensify further, driving down what the carriers would pay UCSF for similar care.[16,17]§

It was easy, however, in the enthusiasm of the moment, to overemphasize the impact of the merger on specialized care. "Although we did

---

High-end is the approved jargon for medical conditions requiring highly sophisticated, complex (also called tertiary or quarternary) care and usually generating large fees for the hospital.

†*Volumes* is medical administrative jargon for the number of patients admitted.

‡California-Pacific Medical Center is UCSF's principal competitor in San Francisco for tertiary care. Most of the patients who patronize California-Pacific, which is located in Pacific Heights where houses cost a small fortune, are well insured, and many are wealthy.

§Although UCSF observers thought a merger between Stanford and Columbia-HCA was possible, Stanford officials regarded such an association as "unthinkable or a solution of last resort.[17] Casper confirms that "we never discussed a merger with Columbia-HCA.[2]

80 percent of the organ transplants in the region, we only accounted for about 11 percent of the tertiary care and only 1 to 2 percent of all levels of care in Northern California," explains Dr. Bruce U. Wintroub, chair of dermatology and one of the senior UCSF faculty members intimately involved in the process leading up to the merger.[18] "We aren't Kaiser; we're not in the 'wellness' business. We're in the severely ill business. An additional reason for UCSF's joining the merger was to free us from the cumbersome relationship with the state."[18]

"If UCSF and Stanford merged," thought Margaretten, "cost savings through bigger buying power would result, and our fees in high-tech procedures would be maintained because we would not compete with each other."[16]

"We thought that the merger," remembers Haile Debas, the UCSF dean, "would provide us a strong position for quality complex care and allow us to develop innovative programs across the two campuses. There was real excitement about developing the best center in the country. The possibilities captured all of our imaginations."[19] The deans, in particular, saw the merger assisting them with their educational responsibilities by consolidating training for students, residents, and fellows and enabling the two schools together to provide training and research in specialties too small to permit full development at each school.[20]

Almost two years would elapse before the merger finally went into effect. Although "the idea of the merger was superb, it had great complexity," explains Debas. The unions representing some of the UCSF employees strongly opposed the merger, which, their leaders argued, would reduce members' benefits and diminish the union's authority, particularly if the new hospital corporation were private, as Stanford was bound to require. In addition, some of the faculty and concerned citizens opposed it for other reasons.[19]

With the Stanford hospital private and UCSF owned by the state of California, the legislature would become involved. "It would be the first public-private merger," says Gerhard Casper, who realized that the scheme was "very ambitious." As for the schools, also one private and one public, "We saw it as foolhardy to merge [them], a pragmatic decision, for that would kill us with the faculty."[2] Casper suspected that any significant academic merger would take five to 10 years. "The culture issue," he recognized, was a core subject.[2] Nevertheless, "The highest quality teaching, research, and medical care was shared, which should, in the long run, be more important than the differences."[2]

"This is the most difficult thing I've ever done in my life, let me assure you," he told a reporter.[21]

"No wonder it took two years to complete," Debas adds.[19]

Thus, the strongest stimulus for joining together was economic, specifically, the pressures causing "Both medical centers to feel themselves in jeopardy because of the extraordinary changes occurring in the market," explains Peter Van Etten, then CEO of the Stanford University Hospital and later of the merged entity with UCSF. "HMOs and health care entities were consolidating, and most hospitals in California had become part of some system or other."[22]

Enthusiasm and Skepticism

Soon after Martin and Casper's walk, the Stanford president met with Van Etten and his medical school dean, Dr. Eugene Bauer. He described his discussion with Martin and asked, "What do you think of this?"[22] "All of us, including Gerhard and Joe, were skeptical," remembers Van Etten,[22] but the group determined to pursue the discussions.

On April 1, 1995, the Stanford leaders joined their UCSF contemporaries.[22] From San Francisco came Dean Haile Debas and the chief medical officer and executive vice dean, Bruce Wintroub. The Stanford group included Eugene Bauer, the new dean, and Dr. Peter Gregory, the chief medical officer. The meal was lunch, and the site was San Mateo, "neutral territory" between San Francisco and Palo Alto.[22] The date was April Fool's Day, Wintroub remembers.[18]*

"I introduced Bauer to Debas," recalls Bruce Wintroub. Like Wintroub at UCSF, Eugene Bauer had been chair of dermatology at Stanford. "We started talking about how to do it. Everyone looked fascinated. The two schools could leverage their synergies,† and this drove a lot of it. It was a very sexy idea."[18] The San Francisco group was prepared. Wintroub remembers discussing just such a project with Debas before Martin and Casper had told them about their plans. "Nevertheless, I was worried because it was so glamorous that it might take us

---

*Bauer recalls that it was on that same April Fool's Day that his appointment as dean of the Stanford School of Medicine took effect.[23]

Eugene A. Bauer received his undergraduate and medical degrees from Northwestern University and trained in medicine and dermatology at Barnes Hospital and Washington University in St. Louis. After 17 years on the Washington University faculty, Stanford recruited him to become chairman of the Department of Dermatology in 1988. Bauer is an authority on bullous diseases, a group of potentially serious illnesses that are associated with fluid-filled collections in the skin and elsewhere in the body.

†"Leverage their synergies," means approximately "to gain the advantage of combining the separate entities to produce a result that is greater than could be achieved if the two parts acted separately," a good example of management jargon adopted by academic physicians engaged in business ventures.

away from acquiring access to specialty programs in San Francisco and looking at other possibilities."[18]

So there were concerns, even at the beginning. "It seemed improbable that these two places, which competed so strongly with each other, would get together," Peter Van Etten remembers thinking.[22]

Dr. Neal Cohen, vice chair of anesthesia and former chief of staff at UCSF, recalls, "Faculty who knew the Stanford model feared we would adopt a model that we did not think would maintain the strength of the School of Medicine or that we would be required to support Stanford. At that moment, UCSF was doing well. Many concluded the promised cost savings could not be realized and feared setting up a costly infrastructure. And then there were many who were concerned about losing our culture and success."[24]

Most of the UCSF faculty, however, seemed removed from the process. John Kane, a senior professor at UCSF, found many "disengaged, blasé, you might say, taking the point of view most of us take about earthquakes. They're hanging over us, but we can't do anything about it."[25]

The UCSF community, however, had confidence in Joseph Martin, the chancellor; Haile Debas, the dean; and William Kerr, the hospital CEO.[16] Martin held town meetings with the faculty to describe why he and Gerhard Casper, the Stanford president, thought the merger was needed.[18]

"We had very positive relationships with the school and the faculty," claims Kerr, and most people at UCSF confirm this. "The campus being only health related helped this."[26]

Most of the UCSF faculty liked Kerr, who is described as bright, a quick study, and agreeable. Kerr liked being part of an academic medical center and encouraged the hospital to support the missions of the medical school.[24]

The group retained Larry Lewin, a consultant, "to develop a compelling case for it," as Wintroub recalls.[18] Lewin led the leadership group for three or four months, working through the advisability of the merger. As the group came to accept that the merger made sense, they concluded, in Peter Van Etten's words, "What didn't make sense was merging the schools. To do so would have meant rejecting the state aid to UCSF each year."[22]

The committee also decided not to develop an integrated delivery system (IDS).* "No one could make it work in our market because the

---

*An integrated delivery system includes the primary care physicians in practice outside the medical center. These doctors refer patients to the specialists, who constitute most of the clinical faculty at medical schools.

price the HMOs pay for care is so low," says Bruce Wintroub. "Our developing a network [of primary care doctors] would be suicidal. We were even less prepared than some others because we lacked the managed care skills needed to run a price-competitive IDS."[22]

"Or the capital," adds Martin.[27]

"Integrated groups don't please anyone and don't add value. Most doctors want to run their own lives. You can lose at least $50,000 on each doc you employ," says Wintroub.[18]

"Thank goodness it never happened," concludes Van Etten.[3,22] In this respect, UCSF and Stanford shared a common view of their roles in the delivery of health care, "quite different from Partners or New York."[22]

The founders and their consultants also rejected merging with community hospitals. "There was a lack of suitable candidates," Martin says, "and we felt very strongly that this would limit referrals."[27]

Van Etten summarizes the approach that the merger took. "We saw ourselves as niche players, focused to succeed in a competitive environment as a tertiary provider."[22]

Stanford versus UCSF

The leaders of these two famous northern California medical schools and teaching hospitals saw what they were contemplating as an exciting, productive scheme to combat the economic threats to their continued success. The institutions involved, however, substantially differed from each other. As time passed, these differences would interfere with completing and then sustaining the merger.

"Our institutions have always been big competitors going back to undergraduate days of 'Cal' [University of California-Berkeley] versus Stanford," Bill Margaretten, the UCSF vice dean, recalls.[16]* "With world-class leaders at both, one would be skeptical about Stanford being subservient to UCSF or vice versa."

The rivalry extends far beyond the football field and is more deep seated within the different cultures of each university.[28] "UCSF is a very collaborative, friendly place," says Jonathan Showstack, a sociologist in the UCSF Institute of Health Studies on the Laurel Heights campus.† "Stanford is much more insular."[29]

---

*Yes, you recognize the name. Margaretten's grandfather and great uncle founded the company renowned for its kosher foods and wines.

†Thanks to a scarcity of space on the main UCSF campus on Parnassus Avenue, several nonclinical programs have moved into the former headquarters of an insurance company in Laurel Heights, one of the wealthiest areas of San Francisco. "Look out the window and you'll see 100 lawyers," says Showstack.[29]

"Here there's a history of unusually good feeling between the hospital administration and the faculty," says Dr. Larry Shapiro, the UCSF chair of pediatrics. "At Stanford, the relationship is more typical of what I've heard it is at other places, not quite so congenial."[30]

Neal Cohen adds, "This is a very participatory school. It's managed from the bottom up rather than from the top down." Cohen sees Stanford as very different. "There the clinical faculty relate primarily to the hospital, at UCSF to the school. The 'fund flows'* are different. Clinical income here is controlled by the chairs after the dean's tax [has been extracted]. At Stanford, the professional fee income flows through their clinical enterprise,† and such hospital expenses as rent are deducted from it."[24]

A San Francisco–based consultant interviewed by a reporter from the *San Francisco Chronicle* emphasized another pertinent difference between the two institutions. "Stanford has rich alums accustomed to giving, UCSF does not." She suggested presciently that if the hospitals were to merge, "Stanford . . . might want to protect its assets against this starving inner-city facility."[31]

Chancellor Joseph Martin heard University of California regents described Stanford as "a country club place, second rate and worse than you know. Why do we need that mediocre place?"[1] Cal alumni, it was said, feel that Stanford is arrogant and overfed; Stanford alumni think that Cal is populated with rabble.[28‡]

Down the peninsula in Palo Alto, Stanford elicits many emotions, but one is clearly affection. Dr. Bruce Reitz, chair of the Department of Cardiothoracic Surgery, says, "I love the place, the people, the environment. It's smaller, more open than Hopkins, which is so big and has so many other big departments that one can't exercise much influence there."[33§]

Fund flows, a relatively new term in academic medicine, is used to explain in what direction and through which entity money is directed.

†In addition to a physician-hospital organization, the august-sounding *clinical enterprise* is often used in academic medical centers to describe entities that incorporate the clinical work of the faculty, the medical school, and the university hospital.

‡These stereotypical portrayals that some graduates, faculty members, regents, and trustees at the University of California and Stanford hold about each others' institution are no longer true if they ever were. "They remind me," says former Stanford president Donald Kennedy, "of the frequent characterization of the Stanford [undergraduate] student body as rich and privileged, Cal's as poor and striving. In fact, the median family incomes of the two student bodies are nearly identical."[32] Nonetheless, the merger would exacerbate bad feelings between the faculties of the two medical schools.[80]

§Reitz was chief of cardiothoracic surgery at the Johns Hopkins Hospital in Baltimore when he was recruited back to Stanford to succeed Dr. Norman Shumway, the renowned pioneer in cardiac transplantation, who had trained him.

Dr. Kenneth Melmon, president of the Faculty Senate at the Stanford medical school and chair of the Department of Medicine from 1978 to 1985, praises the entrepreneurial culture and small size of Stanford. He adds, "We like being small."[34]

Dr. Edward D. Harris, another former chair of medicine (1987–95), who came to Stanford after spending all of his previous career at East Coast institutions, adds, "It's a terrific place. You're part of a superb, major university, but because we're relatively small much of the senior faculty can have contact with undergraduates and people in law and business. With our very strong basic research, it's a wonderful platform on which to have a clinical center." Harris sees distinct advantages to being at Stanford rather than the school in San Francisco. "UCSF also has superb basic science, but it's not a complete university. The overriding difference, of course, is that we're private and UCSF's state."[35]

Dr. Judith L. Swain, the current chair of medicine, also praises the Stanford environment. "People love it here, the weather,* the ambience, the intellectual climate. Even the high cost of living is worth it." says Swain, who, although she grew up on the West Coast, trained and started her faculty career at East Coast schools.[37†] In addition to directing Stanford's largest department, Swain also runs a research laboratory and like many of her colleagues is a partner in a private company. This speaks to Swain's extraordinary ability to use her time productively. In addition to chairing the Department of Medicine, running her lab, and guiding UCSF Stanford Health Care (the name adopted by the merged hospitals), of which she is a member of the board, she regularly commuted to the East Coast, while her husband, Dr. Edward W. Holmes, was the dean of the School of Medicine at Duke.[‡] "We're a part of a campus, a real community," Swain emphasizes. "The medical school is closely tied with other parts of the Valley. Actually, Stanford played a major role in the genesis of Silicon Valley."[37]

Swain praises Stanford's policy of revealing as much financial information as possible. "All data is shared. We're explicit about subsidies and not afraid to see the information. The chairs know how much the hospital gives to each department. On the practice side, each department knows

---

*President Casper has said, "If you can't live in Tuscany, this is the next best place."[36]

†Swain received her M.D. degree from the University of California-San Diego and trained in medicine and cardiology at Duke University in North Carolina. Before coming to Stanford in 1996, she was chief of cardiology at the Hospital of the University of Pennsylvania in Philadelphia.

‡Holmes is now (2001) dean of the school of medicine at the University of California, San Diego.

all.[37]* The culture here is entrepreneurial, the Silicon Valley culture," says Swain. "If you have an idea, one is expected to act on it, maybe form a company."[37]

"Everything done at Stanford is small, not big," says Swain, who has previously worked at large private medical schools. "We have a lot of funded PI's [principal investigators on competitive grants] and small space. We're not the biggest in NIH grants, but we're the best," claims Swain. "To get a faculty job here is tough. Our promotion policy is very rigorous."[37]

In San Francisco, too, promotion does not come easily. In addition to the usual criteria, candidates "must show that they have given service to the university and the public," according to Dr. Stanton A. Glantz, a professor in the Division of Cardiology. "Public service is important, and we have a long tradition of this." Conversely, being governmental subjects the administration and faculty to the open meeting laws, "a colossal nuisance," says Glantz. "However, we're more insulated from state politics than some other parts of the University of California. UCSF tries to protect us when these problems arise."[38]

Although forming companies may be less common at UCSF than in the departments throughout Stanford University, the San Francisco faculty believes they are just as entrepreneurial. "The culture here," says Larry Shapiro, chair of the Department of Pediatrics, "emphasizes that departments and chairs, who have more responsibility than at Stanford, be entrepreneurial. If I run a deficit, I can ask the dean for a loan, but I must pay it back. Any subsidies come to us indirectly. At Stanford," he has seen, "there's an intricate system of cross-subsidies and very tight accounting ever since the 'scandal.'† 'We'll take it away from you and then give some back,' seems to be the way they operate. So their overhead is higher than here, but they get program support to make up for that."[30] Comparing the two departments of pediatrics, Shapiro says, "Although Stanford has more endowments, we have the state money. We're much bigger, twice the faculty size, five times the NIH support."[30]

The San Francisco school is clearly larger. UCSF has almost twice

---

*Soon after he became permanent dean in 1995, Bauer disclosed to the leadership "for the first time all the sources of their support." Bauer feels strongly that dysfunctionality follows lack of knowledge and "the faculty wasn't going to buy in" if important information continued to be kept from them.[23] He does not discuss, however, how much support he gives to the basic science departments.

†The "scandal" occurred when the federal government accused the university of improperly employing the indirect funds recovered with grants. "The government absolved Stanford without qualification," according to Gerhard Casper.[2]

as many medical students as Stanford. The total amount of NIH support in the fiscal year ending September 30, 1999, was $218 million at UCSF compared to Stanford's $167, which places Stanford four slots below UCSF in the NIH pecking order.[39] The number of full-time faculty members at UCSF exceeds 1,200, three times as many as at Stanford. After applying some arithmetic, however, one can understand Stanford's claim that on the average each of its faculty members develops significantly more grant support than does each professor at UCSF.[9] UCSF loyalists counter that a larger fraction of the Stanford full-time faculty members are investigators and thereby are more likely to receive NIH support. Relatively few of the full-time faculty at Stanford spend most of their time taking care of patients. Much of the clinical work is performed by community physicians on the part-time or voluntary staff, whereas most clinicians at UCSF are full time and not competitive for NIH grants because of their clinical obligations.

Risk is a feature of medical school life about which faculty members at each school seem to take pride, each assuming that life at the other place is more secure. "Here [at Stanford] everyone is ready to take risk. There's no one to bail you out," says medicine chair Judith Swain. At a state school like UCSF, the financial risks are less "because the state is always there."[37] Kenneth Cox, the chief of pediatric gastroenterology at Stanford agrees, saying, "We don't have a crutch."[40]*

UCSF people, however, think that the Stanford faculty's support is more stable. "Here," says Charles Wilson, the former chair of neurosurgery at UCSF, "all sorts of people are on soft money,† even those with state salaries. At Stanford, 80 percent of their salaries are guaranteed — they feel entitled."[41]

Members of the Stanford clinical faculty, under constant pressure to support their salaries and expenses, would find this "guarantee" a fantasy. Wilson's statement reflects a common misunderstanding at one of the schools about the security of the medical faculty at the other.[17]

"The Stanford hospital has a more pleasant environment for patients, and the infrastructure is wonderful," acknowledges Dr. Nancy Ascher, the chair of surgery at UCSF, "and they have beautiful flowers."[42]

---

*The state, however, was not the crutch the Stanford faculty assumed it would be, and UCSF officials hoped it would be, when the merged hospital faced severe financial difficulties in 1999.

†*Soft money* refers to income based on grants, which can disappear if the grant is not renewed. Hard money comes from a source guaranteed to pay except under the most extraordinary circumstances, such as the state's allotment to the school of medicine, tuition, or income from permanent endowments.

She knows that the "payer mix"[43]* of patients at UCSF is not as favorable as at Stanford. "We sure are a low-cost, low-income place."[42] Consequently, Stanford can afford to offer more of the comforts a paying patient desires, as can California-Pacific, the San Francisco community hospital that many well-insured and wealthy patients favor over Moffitt-Long, the UCSF hospital. "They have more dark wood there," explains Ascher. "However, I think we do better with referring docs, who see Stanford as more of a 'black hole'† than us."[42]

Lawrence Furnstahl, who would become the chief financial officer of the merged hospitals, can see important differences between the institutions without the prejudices of longtime faculty members or administrators at one or the other. Furnstahl had spent the previous 15 years in Chicago as a senior financial officer of the University of Chicago Hospitals and most recently as chief financial officer of the University of Chicago.[5] One difference that Furnstahl, coming from a private university, was unprepared for was that whenever problems developed at UCSF the public and press were likely to get involved. At Stanford, administrative difficulties, such as those that arose in 1994 when the faculty's practice plan was merged with the Stanford University Hospital, seemed to be handled more quietly.

Reluctantly, Furnstahl also came to believe that the different organizational styles of UCSF and Stanford might prevent the merger's succeeding.[5] "UCSF worked by Bill Kerr's talking to the chairs. You would turn to Suzy or Joe to help you rather than rely on the organizational structure. It was almost 'Mom and Pop' at UCSF versus the corporation at Stanford," which, Furnstahl discovered, ran more "by due process than by relationships. Stanford studied issues with consultants" that UCSF solved more informally.[5]

Moreover, the fundamental operating premises of the UCSF and Stanford hospitals differed. Kerr, who had spent 30 years with the UCSF hospital on Parnassus Avenue and 20 years as its CEO, ran his charge very economically as "a lean, cost-effective, low-cost" institution.[26]

Observers from Stanford saw UCSF's infrastructure as "very thin."[22] With an inadequate capital budget, the UCSF hospital's information

---

*Payer mix, more jargon employed by hospital administrators, refers to the distribution of a hospital's revenue by insurer.[43] A good payer mix has many well-insured patients. The patients who produce a bad or poor payer mix are uninsured or covered by low-paying insurance. Until the Balanced Budget Act of 1997 began to severely reduce what Medicare pays to hospitals, a good payer mix included many Medicare patients.

†Black holes are institutions into which patients disappear, never to be seen again by their referring physicians.

system was underdeveloped just when the most contemporary computer technology was needed to track data on the patients and keep the executives aware of the hospital's financial status.[22]

Furthermore, "The merger with Stanford was not the type of enterprise to which UCSF could easily adjust," Furnstahl believes. "Stanford was more used to it." In 1994, Stanford had created, with some difficulty, Stanford Health Services and had survived intact the politics of incorporating the Lucile Packard Children's Hospital three years later.* These actions "required solving corporate and governance arrangements and developing complicated formulas," suggesting to Furnstahl that Stanford was more likely than UCSF to apply a systematic approach to change.

Despite having gone through the experience of acquiring Mount Zion Hospital in the early 1990s, a deal requiring the management of complex structural change, UCSF, in Furnstahl's view, lacked "the tool kit to deal with the pressures the merger would produce." UCSF had thinner middle management, although its senior leadership, compared to Stanford's, enjoyed remarkable continuity, William Kerr having been first appointed the director of the UCSF Medical Center in 1977.[5†]

UCSF's hospitals had survived in the past, Furnstahl found, by operating cheaply and "leveraging for systems from the university and not having to pay for other basic services. The University of California capital structure is strange, at least as far as the hospitals are concerned. The chancellors‡ have great power and can decide most matters locally, but to borrow money they have to go to the regents, and chancellors don't want to go to the regents."[5]

"We could spend up to certain limits locally, but large expenses did involve the regents," explains Bill Kerr. "When necessary, we were prepared to go to the regents."[26]

With UCSF priding itself on making do with less, Furnstahl predicted that the campus would be "unprepared for the drops the market was bringing. It wouldn't have survived a great deal of change and would have fallen off the cliff due to year 2000 computer problems without help." Anxiety after the merger was formed that UCSF "would tank led to almost unbearable north-south strain that no one was prepared for."[5]

---

*The Packard Hospital, adjacent to the Stanford University Hospital, accommodates Stanford's clinical programs in pediatrics.

†Peter Van Etten became CEO of Stanford Health Services in 1994.

‡Chancellors are the chief executives of each of the University of California campuses.

"The handicap of being part of a public enterprise was exaggerated," Kerr believes. "I got what I needed in time. The state built the Long Hospital,* and other improvements came from cash flow and philanthropy." Accordingly, Kerr and his colleagues became accustomed to succeeding within the UCSF system, which "distances operations of the medical center from the Board of Regents."[26] Kerr reported directly to chancellors, who were physicians with distinguished academic careers adverse to involving their bosses, the president of the University of California and ultimately the Board of Regents, in their decisions.

Although avoiding interference from one's chief has its charms, there are disadvantages. This method of operating deprived the executives of whatever guidance individual regents could provide. Furthermore, since the medical center was a public not a private entity, no members of a board of trustees of community leaders devoted just to the hospital — the regents are responsible for all the University of California campuses — were available to provide disinterested and regular advice on subjects within their areas of expertise such as management, finance, and organization.[†]

Consistent with Kerr's financial philosophy, the Parnassus hospitals had taken on little debt. "I was more fiscally conservative than most and definitely very debt adverse," Kerr acknowledges.[26] However, by not petitioning the regents to borrow money, the UCSF chancellors, Kerr, and the other senior executives at UCSF missed opportunities to obtain the resources required for such capital expenses as information systems at a time when other not-for-profit teaching hospitals were turning to the bond market to fund their expansions.[‡]

---

*The Long Hospital opened in 1983, physically connected to the older Moffitt Hospital, which was built in the 1950s.

†We have seen how at the New York Hospital insurance executive Maurice Greenberg, the chairman of the board, helped the academic surgeon David Skinner learn how to manage the immense hospital and how John McArthur, dean of the Harvard Business School, counseled CEO Richard Nesson at the Brigham and Women's Hospital in Boston.

‡William Kerr's long tenure as CEO of UCSF gave the institution a greater degree of organizational stability than at Stanford, where the terms of deans and CEOs were shorter. A YMCA social worker after graduating in sociology from Loyola University in Chicago, where he had grown up, Kerr decided early to enter the medical field. He obtained a master's degree in hospital administration in 1969 and, keenly interested in urban issues, worked briefly at New York City's municipally owned Bellevue Hospital and with its commissioner of the Department of Hospitals. He was then recruited to UCSF as assistant to the director, whom he succeeded in 1977 at the young age of 34. Kerr's accomplishments as the longtime director of one of the nation's leading teaching hospitals brought him election to membership in the Institute of Medicine, the component of the National Academy of Sciences for leaders in academic medicine.

Conflicts with the State of California: Martin Leaves

In 1995, "I told the regents that fall what we were doing and got their permission to proceed," remembers Joseph Martin, the UCSF chancellor. The group hired an accounting firm to help it prepare a business plan. "It was positive, and most of the regents agreed to go forward."[1]

Before they did so, however, those opposed to the merger tried to derail Martin's plans. Chief among the opponents were the leaders of the unions representing UCSF hospital workers, who feared that the not-for-profit private corporation the founders of the merger contemplated would lead to loss of jobs and retirement benefits for their members. "The regents' haste to privatize is immoral, illegal and a disservice to UCSF patients and employees," said an attorney for the unions to a reporter from the *San Francisco Examiner*. "We are confident that this case will shine the light of day on this profit-motivated scheme and that the people of California will defeat this move to commercialize patient care."[44] Martin countered by pledging that 95 percent of UCSF hospital employees would be offered employment in the merged hospital,[45] a promise that would come to haunt the managers later.

In June 1996, the regents entered the dispute. Frank Clark, an attorney from Los Angeles who would strongly oppose the merger, said, "We really don't understand this. Everything about the transaction remains a great mystery. Some of us are very queasy about this."[46] In a memorandum sent soon afterward to University of California president Richard Atkinson, Clark wrote that the UCSF hospitals would complete the 1996 fiscal year on June 30 with a surplus from operations of $15.4 million compared to a "history of extremely large operating losses" at the Stanford Hospital. "How such a [surplus] can be reconciled with the present drastic action being proposed by the administration is totally inexplicable to me."[47]

Peter Van Etten, then the Stanford hospital CEO, countered that his hospital's financial performance had substantially improved.[47] The irony of Clark's observations will be evident to those familiar with the comparative finances of the two hospitals two and a half years later.

Senior state politicians also criticized the effort to push through the merger quickly. Gray Davis, then the lieutenant governor, said during a meeting of the Regents' Health Services Committee, "I'm always getting nervous when I'm asked to make a decision under pressure, especially when we don't have all the facts before us. We represent a public institution, and we have a fiduciary responsibility to the taxpayers."[46]

Part of the pressure to get on with it was being applied by Gerhard Casper, Stanford's president. Casper, an academic lawyer, insisted that the new, not-for-profit corporation be private and not wholly or even partly governmental. "Rather than enter into a quasi-state entity," he wrote to Atkinson on June 24, 1996, "Stanford would end the negotiations and remain separate."[48] Casper persisted with this point "because the flexibility of a private organization is fundamental to success in the current marketplace."[48]

The contents of the letter quickly leaked to the newspapers. "I can't say that I didn't expect it to be leaked," Casper said of his correspondence with Atkinson, "But I didn't expect it to be leaked in what seemed to be minutes of its arrival."[21] Casper was unaccustomed to operating in the highly charged political world of the regents compared to the almost invisible role that Stanford trustees play.[21]

Casper set a mid-July 1996 deadline for an agreement in principle,[49] which the regents met on July 19 when they approved, 14 to four, the governance structure demanded by Casper. The new board of the merged hospitals would have 17 members, six each from Stanford and UCSF plus the chief executive officer and chief medical officer of the hospital and three outside directors.[50] Gray Davis, believing that the University of California should not cede majority control to a private board, proposed that the regents maintain 50 percent control. Strongly opposing Davis's proposal, Joseph Martin, the UCSF chancellor, threatened to withdraw the merger proposal if the motion passed.[51] It was defeated 13 to five.[50]

During the summer and fall of 1996, unexpected events occurred, which many thought would adversely affect, if not destroy, the merger. On July 8, 1996, Neil Rudenstine, the president of Harvard University, asked Chancellor Martin whether he would like to succeed Daniel Tosteson as dean of the Harvard Medical School.[1] For the previous four months, Rudenstine had retained Martin as a consultant on the university's search to fill this widely respected position.[1] If Martin became dean, he would be returning to Harvard, where he had been chief of the neurology service at the Massachusetts General Hospital from 1978 to 1989.*

---

*Joseph Boyd Martin's origins were not as lofty as the positions he came to occupy in academic medicine. Born in 1938 in Bassano and raised in Duchess (population 325, "324 after I left"),[67] both in Alberta, Canada, he attended Eastern Mennonite College, now University, in Harrisonburg, Virginia, and received his M.D. degree from the University of Alberta. After two years of medical internship and residency at the University Hospital in Edmonton, he trained in neurology in the Case-Western Reserve system in Cleveland. Research he performed at the University of Rochester led to a Ph.D. degree in 1971. When the MGH selected him, Martin was chair of the Department of Neurology and Neurosurgery at McGill University in Montreal. Martin was the first chair appointed by Daniel Tosteson, the Harvard dean, who had just arrived from the University of Chicago

At the June, 1996 meeting of the regents, Martin had been accused of covering up matters relating to the proposed merger. The Harvard opportunity was looking more and more attractive. During August, he negotiated the terms with Rudenstine and, by October, agreed to become Harvard's next Dean of the Medical Faculty. On November 8th, he told the regents and announced publicly that he would leave UCSF by July, 1997.[52] "This came a year too soon," Martin commented, "But the opportunity to be dean of Harvard Medical School doesn't come up very often. The dean there has been doing it for the last 20 years."[52]

The news displeased many in San Francisco. "Some of the faculty felt betrayed by his leaving" just as the enterprise he helped invent was finally being formed, says Jaclyne Boyden, the vice dean for administration & finance in the School of Medicine.[53] Martin was recognized as one of the principals involved in the UCSF Stanford merger and a leader whom the UCSF faculty depended upon to make it work.

Regent Roy Brophy, a Sacramento developer who had voted for the merger in July, said, "I frankly believe it is time to push the pause button. No one can step into his place and continue the work he is doing."[52]

The other principal, president Gerhard Casper of Stanford University, wonders, four years after the "walk in the woods," whether he would have persevered with the merger had he known that Martin, in whom he had "complete trust that together we could solve future issues," would leave.[2]

The announcement of Martin's departure did not prevent the merger, although "it certainly had a negative overall effect."[2] Only a week later, on November 15, 1996, the regents of the University of California voted 14 to two to create a new, nonprofit, public benefit corporation called UCSF Stanford Health Care to operate the UCSF and Stanford hospitals.[4] The board of Stanford Health Services and a delegation of Stanford trustees unanimously adopted similar directives.[54] Of vital importance, as we shall see, the merger agreement permitted either UCSF or Stanford to petition for an involuntary dissolution.[54]

Almost two years had elapsed since Martin and Casper's first discussions, and the leaders sounded euphoric. "I believe this will be seen, when we look back in five or ten years, as one of the most important things that happened in American academic medicine in the 1990's," said Martin.[54]

---

the year before.[1] In 1989, Martin moved to San Francisco as dean of the school of medicine and four years later became chancellor of UCSF, the chief executive for all the health care schools on Parnassus Heights and the Moffitt-Long and Mount Zion Hospitals.

Peter Van Etten, the Stanford Health Services CEO, hailed the votes as creating "one of the nation's premier medical centers."[54]

The History of UCSF[55-58]

The two medical schools, whose principal teaching hospitals were preparing to merge, are among the nation's most respected. As West Coast schools, they are younger than two of the three already discussed in this narrative, and one of them differs from each of the other four in being publicly owned. Like the original College of Physicians and Surgeons in New York City, they started as proprietary schools, each founded and owned, in the case of the California schools, by one person.

The medical school of the University of California-San Francisco, the oldest medical school in continuous operation in the state, was founded in 1864 by Dr. Hugh H. Toland, who had arrived in San Francisco 12 years earlier and become the city's foremost surgeon, managing what was reportedly the largest practice on the West Coast. The original school, opposite the San Francisco City and County Hospital, was built on Stockton and Steiner Streets in the North Beach section of the city. In 1870, Toland proposed giving his medical college to the two-year-old University of California, but the university balked at his insistence that the school retain his name. Eventually, Toland relented, and three years later the regents accepted the Toland Medical College as the Medical Department of the University of California. In 1874, the medical school admitted its first woman student, who became, two years later, the first woman to graduate from a medical school in California. The governance of the school remained proprietary until 1899.

In the 1890s, the medical, dental, and pharmacy departments and the School of Veterinary Medicine moved to their current location an Parnassus Heights thanks to Mayor Adolph Sutro's gift of 13 acres, reputedly the result of his admiration for his daughter's medical education. The city established a temporary hospital on the site during the emergency that followed the earthquake and fire of 1906. To accommodate a permanent hospital, which opened in April 1907 in medical school buildings, the preclinical departments moved to Berkeley, the site of the main university. With the faculty in anatomy, biochemistry, and physiology teaching their courses in Berkeley and the clinical work centered in San Francisco, the school took some pointed criticism in 1910 from Abraham Flexner in his influential report on American medical schools for separating basic science from the clinical programs. The University of California medical degree in those days was awarded from Berkeley, not San Francisco.

Pressure to consolidate the school in Berkeley also came from the Rockefeller Foundation, which during the 1920s was funding medical schools if they would adhere to Flexner's principles, which were based to a great extent on the practices of the Johns Hopkins Medical School and Hospital. The regents, however, influenced by the powerful clinicians associated with the medical school, insisted that the school remain in San Francisco. Since the foundation would not agree to support a school that was separated from the university at Berkeley, the funding went elsewhere, as did other philanthropic support then being directed to improve American medical schools and teaching hospitals. The school suffered not only the loss of the money. Several of the best members of the full-time faculty left for more attractive positions at other schools.

The school, however, did advance in the years between the two world wars, particularly due to the efforts of Dr. Robert Langley Porter, who became dean in 1927. The Departments of Bacteriology and Pharmacology transferred from Berkeley to Parnassus in 1928, a clinics building was constructed, the Neuropsychiatric Institute, named for Langley Porter, was built, and a department of psychiatry was initiated. In the 1950s, a new hospital, honoring former dean Herbert C. Moffitt, and the Medical Sciences Building went up, and finally, in 1952, half a century after moving to Berkeley, the remaining departments returned to Parnassus Heights.

By 1964, the university had established the office of chancellor to direct the entire Parnassus campus, which then consisted of the expanded medical school, the other health-related professional schools, and the hospital. Then, in 1970, the site became the University of California-San Francisco, the only health sciences campus in the University of California system. The chancellor of UCSF was now equal in rank to the chancellors of the other campuses such as those at Berkeley and Los Angeles.

The organization of a campus solely devoted to the health sciences avoided competition for funding between, for example, a biochemistry department in the medical school and a chemistry department in the faculty of arts and sciences.[59] Furthermore, the medical school received a greater number of salaried faculty positions per student than did the other campuses. The leaders decided to assign a disproportionate share of these positions to the basic science departments on the presumption that the clinical departments had income from the care of patients not available to the basic scientists to help pay their faculties.[59]

"For its first 90 years," according to Dr. Lloyd H. "Holly" Smith, chair of the Department of Medicine from 1964 to 1985 and associate dean since then, UCSF was "a solid, regional school dominated by local practitioners."[60] The events of the 1950s and 1960s were vital to the school's rising to its current eminence. "Basic science moved back to Parnassus into new buildings. We obtained the status of a separate campus. Stanford got out of town and went to its natural habitat on the farm.* The NIH dollars lifted all ships."† Smith[60] was not alone[59,61] in believing that the arrival on the scene of the jet aircraft was critical. "Now faculty could conveniently visit schools on the East Coast and the NIH to attend meetings, and recruiting top people became more practical. The sense of isolation was gone. Finally, being in San Francisco didn't hurt.

"Around here, we refer to 'B.C.,' before Comroe, and 'A.C.,' after Comroe,'" Smith remembers. Comroe was Dr. Julius Comroe, who was recruited from the University of Pennsylvania in 1957 to develop what became "the splendid CVRI [Cardiovascular Research Institute], which quickly attained national standing.[62]‡ Comroe was brilliant, a brooding person with a tremendous sense of people, but he wasn't very diplomatic and suffered fools badly."[60,63]§

Another person critical to the early development of the modern UCSF was Dr. William Reinhardt,[59] who was appointed dean in 1961, "unsung but very important, a quiet, saturnine person with a steely will," as Smith remembers him. "For the first time, the school undertook national searches," no longer relying solely on the local faculty for its leaders.[60]

Among these new leaders was Dr. J. Englebert "Bert" Dunphy, a

---

*The Stanford medical school conducted its clinical activities in San Francisco until the 1950s when it consolidated all its activities on the Palo Alto campus. Until then, UCSF had to share the facilities at the San Francisco General and Veterans Administration Hospitals with Stanford. Stanford's immense property is often called "the farm" or "the ranch."

†During the 1950s and 1960s, the NIH was so generous that most good, and many not so good, grant applications were funded.

‡One of the "bright young people"[56] in Comroe's unit was Dr. Isidore Edelman, now director of the Columbia Genome Center and former chairman of the Department of Biochemistry at the Columbia University College of Physicians and Surgeons (see chapter 4). As chair of the committee on educational policy of the UCSF Academic Senate, Edelman was a member of the cabal (see below) that brought about the modernization of the medical school.[62]

§"No one here knew about the NIH before him," Nancy M. Rockafellar, Ph.D., director of the Campus Oral History Program at UCSF and a historian in the Department of the History of Health Sciences, has been told about Comroe.[63]

surgeon trained at the Peter Bent Brigham and recruited from the surgery chair at the University of Oregon, and Smith, then 40 years old, from the Massachusetts General. "I came out here, and they offered me the job [chair of the Department of Medicine] during the first visit," Smith remembers. "I accepted immediately and told my wife, 'Pack.' I was afraid to look more carefully. Under the oil immersion lens, I would have seen mediocrity among other problems. Under the dry lens* I could see a great public university, a great city, good support, and a small number of very good people."[60]

A few years after arriving in San Francisco, someone from the MGH asked Smith if he was interested in being a candidate for the chair of medicine at the MGH and the Jackson professorship at Harvard. "I said no. Couldn't leave what I had just started. A good decision."[60] Later, when the possibility of the deanship at Stanford was raised, "I considered Stanford's reputation for administrative disorder and concluded that I'd rather be mayor of Beirut."[60] By staying at UCSF, Smith's career did not suffer. As the fame of his department and the school increased, he became president of most of the professional organizations to which leaders of academic internal medicine belong.[†]

Soon after arriving in San Francisco, Smith found himself "a member of a cabal" of newer faculty dedicated to removing the chancellor. "It was to be a quiet, donnish affair, as it would have been in Boston, but here it quickly got into the newspapers. So we found ourselves in the office of one of Clark Kerr's principal associates.[‡] We made our case, and, although the alumni opposed us, Kerr agreed with us."

Kerr, the president of the University of California, had come to

---

*An oil immersion lens of a microscope allows the viewer to see specimens at high magnification. A dry lens doesn't magnify as much as an oil immersion lens.

†Except for white hair, Lloyd Hollingsworth Smith Jr., 75 years old in 1999, looks and acts much as he did when he took the chair in San Francisco 35 years ago—tall, articulate, and dominating. The accent he acquired from growing up in South Carolina persists. A summa cum laude alumnus of Washington and Lee University in Lexington, Virginia, Smith entered Harvard Medical School, graduating magna cum laude in 1948. He was an intern and resident at the MGH, served in the army for two years, and was then appointed a member of the Harvard Society of Fellows, a select group of young academics who pursue research without specifically working for a graduate degree. He also performed research in laboratories at the Public Health Research Institute of New York City and the Karolinska Institute in Stockholm. After six more months of residency at Presbyterian Hospital in New York, Smith returned to the MGH as chief resident in medicine. By 1958, he was chief of the Endocrine Unit there, one of a group of young academic internists whom Walter Bauer, the MGH chief of medicine, was then appointing to lead the specialty groups in the Department of Medicine.

‡This was the university's executive vice president Harry Wellman.[56]

look on the medical school, as did Smith and his fellow conspirators, "as a regional medical school, not a national medical school or international medical school, and really more sensitive to the profession in San Francisco than to the university. . . . San Francisco was more concerned with what the local medical association said than what the university said."[56]

"So there we were," remembers Smith. "We had won, but the school still included many tenured faculty not attuned to the national goals we had for the place. Well, 'while there's death, there's hope,' as a local cynic said to me about tenure."[60]

Smith chaired the search committee for the new chair of biochemistry. "In those days, a school's academic clout depended primarily on the people in medicine and biochemistry. We were able to recruit two outstanding investigators, William J. Rutter and Gordon Tomkins, who had splendid taste in people, to run the department and build the basic sciences."[60]

Vital to the development of UCSF science was "the interest in recruiting young, budding stars," according to Dr. David J. Ramsay, senior vice chancellor for academic affairs in the 1980s and early 1990s and now president of the University of Maryland, Baltimore."[59] Two of those brought to UCSF, according to this plan, were Michael Bishop and Harold Varmus, who were to win the Nobel Prize in 1989 for their work on cancer-causing genes.*

"The basic sciences here operate like a syncytium,†" Smith says. "The walls between the departments are porous. They pick their graduate students together. For its size," Smith believes, "they are the best in the country. They look on Harvard College and MIT [Massachusetts Institute of Technology] as their competition."[60]

William Kerr, the longtime CEO of the UCSF hospitals, remembers the faculty as "racehorses. We just had to feed them to make their programs grow. They had come in part because they liked each other. In New York City," where Kerr had worked before moving to San Francisco, the faculty "spent much time one-upping each other. Not here, a very different gestalt than back East, and then they had the weekend outdoor pleasures here."[26]

Moffitt-Long Hospital, the university's hospital on Parnassus Avenue, forms only part of the UCSF clinical teaching and research enter-

---

*Bishop, now chancellor of UCSF, is a great supporter, as one can imagine, of the new UCSF scientific campus about to be built at Mission Bay (see chapter 7).[64] Varmus, the former director of the National Institutes of Health, is now the CEO of the Memorial Sloan-Kettering Cancer Center in New York.

†*Syncytium* refers to the biological fusion of cells into one functioning organism.

prise. "We introduced the concept of three coequal university hospitals, one owned by the federal government [the Veterans Administration Hospital], one by the city [San Francisco General Hospital], and one by the state [Moffitt-Long Hospital]," Smith explains.[60] In the Department of Medicine, Smith and his successors developed strong academic programs at each hospital. "A decade ago, we had more young Turks* at the VA," he claims, "than P&S [Columbia University College of Physicians and Surgeons] had in its entire department."[60]

"The amount of research grants in just our Department of Medicine exceeds that in two-thirds of the country's medical schools," former dean and chancellor Julius Krevans adds.[61] "Why is UCSF UCSF?" Krevans continues in the same vein as Smith. "Jet airplanes, national searches, and San Francisco, although the city became somewhat of a burden when housing became so expensive." William Kerr, as head of the Moffitt-Long Hospital, "didn't report to me, although that was the official arrangement, so much as worked with me as a colleague."[61]

Krevans, who came to UCSF from Johns Hopkins, found that preeminent patient care, so much a feature of the famous Baltimore hospital, wasn't as high a priority at his new institution. "The basic science programs were growing more rapidly than the clinical programs." As the volunteer physicians who filled most of the beds at Parnassus retired, few members of the full-time faculty took their places as senior practitioners. "Presbyterian [now California-Pacific Medical Center] was more clinical and had a better clinical reputation in San Francisco."[61]

In 1999, the school ranked as one of the most successful in the country. In NIH grant funding, it stood fourth behind Harvard, Johns Hopkins and the University of Pennsylvania.[39†] Its faculty includes three Nobel laureates, 25 members of the National Academy of Sciences, and

---

*Young Turks is a nickname — as in "He's a young Turk" — for members of the American Society for Clinical Investigation, a professional association of young academic investigators, mostly in departments of internal medicine, who have shown precocious success in research. The sobriquet, which was first applied about 90 years ago, comes from the name of a group of young Army officers who opposed the Turkish government. "Old Turks," in academic internal medicine parlance, are members of the Association of American Physicians, founded in 1886 by William Osler and others,[65] which elects its members when they are further along in their careers. Many old Turks are previously elected young Turks.

†This was quite different from the twentieth position UCSF held in an unofficial telephone survey of medical schools conducted in 1966. Harvard and Hopkins were ranked then exactly as the amount of their NIH grants places them now, first and second.[60] The official NIH list places Harvard nineteenth because it excludes the grants generated by investigators in its teaching hospitals (see chapter 2).

41 members of the Institute of Medicine.[66] The school's current endowment exceeds $500 million.[67]

UCSF admits the most competitive college seniors; the mean grade point average (GPA) of the 153 students in the class of 2002 was 3.78. Eighty-one percent of the class are California residents—they pay $10,080 in tuition; the out-of-state students pay almost twice as much—and 60 percent are women. Of the applicants also accepted by other medical schools, most come to UCSF, except when the other school is Harvard. About one of three of those admitted to UCSF and Harvard choose UCSF.[60]

The school is also proud of the quality of its postgraduate trainees in clinical medicine and research. According to Department of Medicine chair Lee Goldman, "Our principal competition for interns and residents in many of our departments are the Brigham and the MGH, not," he emphasizes, "Stanford."[14]

Mount Zion Hospital[68]

UCSF owned more than one hospital. On Parnassus Avenue, William Kerr directed Moffitt-Long, a general hospital, and the Langley Porter Psychiatric Institute. In the Western Addition district of San Francisco, about 2 and a half miles north of the Parnassus hospitals, is Mount Zion, a community hospital acquired by UCSF in 1990 to increase space for the work of the UCSF faculty.[18,19] "Since I came here in 1971," Julius Krevans, the former dean and chancellor says, "our major problem, then and now, has been a shortage of space. We've never had enough of it for our clinical or research work."[61] Mount Zion Hospital, now called the UCSF-Mt. Zion Medical Center to remind people who owns it, offered the leaders of the cramped facilities on Parnassus much needed opportunities for expansion.

Mount Zion opened in 1899 to provide medical care for immigrant Jewish patients and professional opportunities for Jewish doctors prevented by anti-Semitism from training or practicing at other hospitals.[69] During more recent decades, however, most of the cultural reasons for building such sectarian hospitals were passing. Many formerly indigent Jews and their descendents had prospered, moved away from the district surrounding Mount Zion, and attended other hospitals when they became ill. Wealthy Jewish families now contributed to other institutions, as their money was found to be just as valuable as that of other supporters. Other hospitals and medical schools, both locally and nationally, now welcomed Jewish physicians.

"Mount Zion had a better reputation than Moffitt for the care of patients in the fifties and sixties," senior physicians told Dr. Ernest J. Ring, associate dean for the UCSF-Mount Zion Medical Center.[70] "All the bright young Jewish docs were there then." By the 1990s, however, the patients using Mount Zion had become increasingly impoverished. Many were quite sick and elderly[15] with inadequate insurance coverage for their care. Except for recent immigrants who had settled near the hospital, progressively fewer were Jewish, thereby decreasing the commitment of their prosperous coreligionists to support the hospital.[71] Furthermore, many of the local physicians who admitted to Mount Zion referred their patients needing work not performed there to other community hospitals — California-Pacific, UCSF's principal competitor for well-insured patients is nearby — not to "the hill," the pejorative name for the UCSF campus on Parnassus Heights.[15] Despite the poverty of many of its current clientele, Mount Zion's location showed promise. On Divisidero Street between Sutter and Post, the hospital was located near the wealthy Pacific Heights district, and real estate values were rising in the surrounding area.

"We had had a longtime working relationship with Mount Zion," remembers Krevans, "but the trustees there didn't want to put their toes further into the water — afraid of losing their autonomy. Throughout the 1980s, however, they saw big-league problems coming, and we agreed to plan together for the future."[61] Then when the hospital "was going under," recalls Krevans, "its board finally said 'Take us over.'"[61]

"The Jewish community breathed a sign of relief when UCSF took over," recalls Warren Hellman, a San Francisco investment banker whose family has had a long association with the hospital.[72] The financial state of the hospital was so precarious that a clause in the agreement stated that if Mount Zion lost money for two consecutive years or if the UCSF Medical Center lost money for one year, Mount Zion could be closed.[72]*

A UCSF committee advised against the acquisition despite the campus's space problems. "We didn't need the community problems we had previously had," Krevans remembers the committee members warning. Many recalled the conflict that had erupted a decade earlier when the community around the medical campus forced the administration to agree to limit its expansion there. All too many in the community characterized the campus as "that place on the hill," a cold, elite establishment with little interest in local patients, a point of view shared by some UCSF faculty members.[70] "Not true, of course," counters Krevans, "but Mount Zion had the opposite image."[61]

More meetings were held, and finally in 1990 the regents of the

---

*As we shall see, Mount Zion continued to lose money throughout the next decade, but UCSF kept it open anyway.

University of California acquired Mount Zion Hospital, which was incorporated into UCSF. William Kerr and his associates at Parnassus assumed responsibility for operating the community hospital. As Mount Zion Hospital boosted the impression that UCSF could provide sympathetic community care, it also provided much needed space for several important clinical and research programs and additional opportunities for training students and residents. Two UCSF buildings, one for patients with cancer and another with research laboratories, rose on Mount Zion land.[26]

The History of Stanford University[73-75] and Its Medical School[17,74,76-79]

About 35 miles south of UCSF, on the peninsula that ends on the north at the Golden Gate, has risen one of the country's leading private universities with a medical school, which, despite its propinquity, has different traditions and cultural distinctions compared to its famed neighbor in San Francisco.

The birth of Stanford's medical school preceded by 26 years the founding of the university it eventually joined. As at the University of California-San Francisco, Stanford's school began as a proprietary institution, founded in this case by Dr. Elias Samuel Cooper in 1859 when 13 students assembled in his office for their first class. In 1864, two years after he died, his school closed. Some of the Cooper faculty joined Hugh Toland's new school, many of whose first students had been attending the now defunct school.* Six years later, Cooper's nephew, Dr. Levi Cooper Lane, resurrected the school, which in 1882 was named the Cooper Medical College in recognition of the gift by Dr. Lane of a new building and hospital at Clay Street between Webster and Buchanan in Pacific Heights. In 1908, Lane transferred ownership to Stanford at no cost. The school's buildings had survived the fire that followed the earthquake of 1906. The university now had a "Department of Medicine" — its name would change to School of Medicine two years later — but it was in San Francisco, 30 miles north of the main campus in Palo Alto. The hospital became known as the Stanford-Lane Hospital, acknowledging the university and the donor.

---

*The failure of Cooper's school allows UCSF to call itself the oldest medical school on the West Coast in continuous operation. Note the similarity to New York half a century earlier, when the faculty of the failing Columbia medical school, which was soon to close, joined the new College of Physicians and Surgeons (see chapter 4).

The Leland Stanford Junior University, still the official name for what we now routinely call Stanford University,[38]* owes its origins to typhoid fever, an infectious disease that doctors could do little to cure when it killed the 15-year-old son and only child of Leland and Jane Lathrop Stanford on March 13, 1884. The boy's father was one of the country's richest men, in part due to the Central Pacific Railroad, which he and his partners built to provide the western link of the first transcontinental railroad and of which he was president. Born in 1824, one of five sons of an upstate New York "farmer, woodcutter and one-time innkeeper,"[75] Stanford read law and later joined his brothers in the California gold fields as a shopkeeper. He helped to organize the Republican Party in California and supported the election of Lincoln. He was elected governor at the age of 37 (in 1861) and a U.S. senator 24 years later.

In 1876, Stanford purchased a 650-acre section of a ranch south of San Francisco† and built a large home and an elaborate horse-breeding operation there. In time, he acquired 8,000 acres, which extended from the foothills of the Santa Cruz range to El Camino Real, the old Spanish Trail, now California Route 82. This immense property would provide Stanford with one of its most valuable possessions, land, an asset unavailable to most other universities.

From the loss of the Stanfords' son grew what was to become one of the nation's premier universities. Unlike the seventeenth- and early-eighteenth-century creations in the East, which were founded when the country was neither independent nor rich, Stanford started with a magnificent campus. The founder selected Frederick Law Olmstead, the country's preeminent landscape architect and designer of Central Park in New York City; Francis A. Walker, president of the Massachusetts Institute of Technology; and the 28-year-old architect Charles Atherton Coolidge from Boston to build his university. They chose the Romanesque revival architectural style, with more than a touch of the Spanish rather than the collegiate Gothic then fashionable in the older universities. The first class was admitted on October 1, 1891.‡

---

*"Why go to a junior college?" jokes Stanton Glantz, a UCSF loyalist, who despite the jibe earned his doctorate at the "junior college" to which he refers.[38] We'll hear more from Glantz, one of the merger's most stalwart opponents, later.

†In a region known as Rancho San Francisquito, identified by a sentinel redwood tree called El Palo Alto, literally "the high stick." The town of Palo Alto developed across the Southern Pacific Railroad tracks from the ranch.

‡One of the members of the founding class was Herbert Clark Hoover, president of the United States from 1929 to 1933, a longtime trustee of the university, and an important supporter of Stanford's medical school at a critical time in its early development (see below).[74]

The endowment that Stanford provided for the university, said to be the largest in the country at the time, permitted the students to attend without paying tuition during its first 28 years. The university was coeducational from the beginning, but Mrs. Stanford, who took a leading role in university affairs from the time of her husband's death in 1893 until she died 12 years later, had ruled that the number of women be limited to 500 to prevent the university's becoming a women's college, hardly, she felt, an appropriate memorial to her son. The trustees revoked this restriction in 1933.

Until World War II, Stanford remained a good regional school, described by one longtime faculty member as "a rich boys' playgound"[80] and by another as "an ingrown, nice-guy, boys club" populated with second- and third-generation Stanford graduates.[81] Stanton Glantz, the UCSF investigator with an engineering Ph.D. from Stanford, saw it as a "backwater [until] during the war the engineering school, like the Massachusetts Institute of Technology, was energized by important governmental work in radar and electronic countermeasures."[38]

When peace returned, J. E. Wallace Sterling, president of Stanford from 1949 to 1968, Provost Frederick E. Terman, the former dean of the school of engineering,* and their successors recruited superb faculty, constructed new buildings, and substantially increased the endowment. Although the university wasn't, when Sterling and Terman began their work, "endowment rich, it was space rich," observes Dr. Halsted Holman, the first chair of the Department of Medicine after the move from San Francisco.[80†] "The notion was that the university could vault itself into the first class by emphasizing engineering and science, including medicine, and make some money by leasing space on the campus to new companies."[80]

"Creation of the Stanford Industrial Park characterized the very strong entrepreneurial force at the university," says Glantz. Industrial support became the "defining karma at Stanford. Professors are almost expected to create businesses on the side."[38]

By its centenary, Stanford ranked among the country's leading institutions of higher learning, a university with outstanding professional and graduate schools and the college of choice for many of the country's most able high school seniors.

The medical school participated in this improvement but not until it

---

*Terman knew how to pick his students. Two of them were William Hewlett and David Packard,[38] the founders of the Hewlett-Packard Company and substantial supporters of many of Terman's and his successors' plans for Stanford's development.

†The university's charter prevented it from selling any of the founder's land.[38]

migrated from San Francisco to Palo Alto in 1959. During its early days, Stanford almost lost the school. Financial problems led the university president in 1913 to propose to his board that the school merge with UCSF.[82] The trustees of both Stanford and UCSF placed provisions on the merger that the other school couldn't accept, and the first attempt to combine medical care at the two universities failed.[83]*

The school struggled on, gradually gaining a local reputation for its clinical faculty. According to former dean (1984–95) David Korn, the school had become "a quality medical school to train well-off, mostly white men to become doctors. Some of the San Francisco faculty became well known for their clinical scholarship but not for science. The basic science faculty on the campus wasn't too much."[9] The student body was "quite inbred in those days," and many had obtained their undergraduate degrees at Stanford.[80] Each class studied the basic sciences on the Palo Alto and San Francisco campuses and then trained in San Francisco hospitals during the third and fourth years.

Rather than invest in the sizable renovations needed for the San Francisco campus, the president, provost, and Stanford trustees decided in 1953 that the school should be consolidated in Palo Alto, "the single most important decision to build medical science during Stanford's rise to research eminence," according to former Stanford president (1982–92) Donald Kennedy.[32] A few members of the faculty in San Francisco, including Henry A. Kaplan,† chair of radiology; pharmacologist Avram Goldstein; and Robert H. Alway, chair of pediatrics, who would become dean in 1958, strongly supported the move south.[81]

---

*Stanford trustee Herbert Hoover, a close friend of the dean, Dr. Ray Lyman Wilbur—class of 1896, one year after Hoover's—strongly opposed the university's losing its new medical school. John C. Branner, the president at the time, with the support of much of the nonmedical faculty, tried to convince the trustees to dispatch the school by claiming that its large and increasing costs could "swamp the university."[74] The Hoover-Wilbur contingent won, and Stanford retained its school of medicine. Wilbur, again with Hoover's support, succeeded Branner as Stanford's third president (1916–43).

In comparing the first UCSF-Stanford merger attempt more than 80 years ago with more recent events, Spyros Andreopoulos, director emeritus of the Office of Communications at the Stanford Medical Center, observes, "The more things change, the more they are the same."[82]

†"A giant of a man, though not a particularly good colleague," according to David Korn,[9] Kaplan developed the first successful treatment for Hodgkin's lymphoma, a previously almost universally fatal cancer of the lymphatic system. Morton Meyer, a well-known UCSF internist, tells the delightful and possibly apocryphal story that Kaplan, rebuffed because of his efforts to move the school to Palo Alto—he was accordingly not the most popular person on the San Francisco campus—was flying to Boston to accept the chair of radiology at one of the Harvard hospitals. When Stanford president Sterling heard this, he sent him a telegram, which read "Get back on the plane and come out here. We're going to move down on the farm."[56]

"Stanford was a third-rate place," remembers Goldstein when he was recruited from Harvard in 1955 to develop a department of pharmacology at the new medical school in Palo Alto. "Henry Kaplan helped to convince me that things were going to change. The school was going to be about research. We were going to build a first-rate institution with strong scientific departments, both in science and clinical. Students would come not because of family connections but because of their interest in research."[81]

Pharmacology, Goldstein's new charge, microbiology, and pathology were taught in San Francisco. Since the school had no department of biochemistry, the lectures for that course were given by a member of the Department of Chemistry at Palo Alto.

"Biochemistry was where molecular biology was starting," Goldstein explains. "Creating the department came to a showdown with the dean, who didn't understand. Kaplan and I separately saw Sterling and advised making a clean sweep and changing the dean."[81] They were prepared to leave if a contemporary chair of biochemistry wasn't recruited. The president followed their advice and appointed as dean Robert Alway, who didn't want the job, according to Goldstein.

The trio of Alway, Kaplan, and Goldstein now ruled the medical school as a cabal.* The change, however, left much bitterness, some of which persists to this day among retired professors. "One wife still won't talk to me," says Goldstein, who, although he retired from Stanford in 1989, continues working in addiction, his field of interest throughout his career.[81]

"We all felt that Arthur Kornberg was the country's leading biochemist," says Goldstein.[81] Kornberg, a medical doctor who worked as a basic scientist, then directed the Department of Microbiology and Immunology at Washington University in St. Louis. He was about to win the Nobel Prize in Medicine or Physiology with Severo Ochoa of New York University, with whom he had trained in 1946, for their discovery of the mechanisms underlying the formation of two of the basic chemicals of the cell, deoxyribonucleic acid (DNA) and ribonucleic acid (RNA). "He responded to the offer, as did most people we contacted," remembers Goldstein: "Where? Stanford?"[81]

Cabal is Goldstein's word and the same one that UCSF Department of Medicine chair Holly Smith used to describe the group that convinced University of California president Clark Kerr, seven years later, to replace the chancellor at UCSF so that contemporary first-class scientists could be recruited to that school.[60] Stanford loyalists can thus take satisfaction in their school's conversion to a scientifically based institution before their competitor to the north.

Although he had vacationed in the West, New York–born (1918) Arthur Kornberg had never considered working there. He had attended the local schools and took his undergraduate degree at the City College of New York. He was one of only five premedical students in his class to be accepted into medical school, in his case at the University of Rochester. Most of the 200 who had applied were rejected, almost certainly because most of them were Jewish.[84]*

"Washington University had seduced me to leave the NIH in 1953," remembers Kornberg, "despite the bare light bulbs and old sinks," and chair the department as the youngest member of the school's executive committee — he was only 35 years old at the time.[85] Kornberg knew the institution. In 1947, he had been a fellow at Washington University with Nobel laureate Carl Cori. "Washington University had a very distinguished faculty, but we were teaching students few of whom cared about science."

Kornberg visited Stanford, which was about to begin its new building project on the campus. "I was taken by the plans and the setting." He decided he would move but only if he could bring his whole department with him.[85]

"We said OK," remembers Goldstein, "and he did."[81]

"St. Louis was called the Gateway to the West. I took it literally," Kornberg says. "There was no review of [his colleagues'] appointments at Stanford. I set their ranks." Six of the original members of the group are still together 40 years later. It was a unique department. It started small and stayed small so that we could talk with each other." The research Kornberg and his colleagues emphasized remained narrowly focused on nucleic acids and proteins.[85]

Kornberg's recruitment led directly to Stanford's acquisition of another Nobel laureate, Joshua Lederberg of the University of Wisconsin, who had won the year before Kornberg for his discoveries about genetic recombination and the organization of the genetic material of bacteria. "When you recruit Arthur, come talk to me," he told Goldstein.[81]

"Joshua and I had known each other from the late forties," remembers Kornberg. "When I moved, he wanted to join my department, but we all agreed that Lederberg should have his own department."[85] Accordingly, Stanford created a Department of Genetics, the first in the country at a medical school, according to Goldstein, for Lederberg to chair.[81]

"Kornberg became the intellectual leader of the school," former

---

*Kornberg discusses his career, including the effects of anti-Semitism on his life, in an informative, insightful memoir, *For the Love of Enzymes: The Odyssey of a Biochemist.* The paperback edition, published in 1991 by Harvard University Press, is still in print.[84]

dean David Korn recalls. "He personally checked every promotion to senior rank. If Kornberg disagreed, it died. 'I do not believe this is a distinguished appointment,' he would say."[9]

Kornberg's influence continued even after he relinquished the chair of biochemistry after 10 years to his colleague Paul Berg. "I didn't enjoy the meetings any more," he admits. "Being a chair is not a life sentence." Kornberg now believes that basic science chairmen should hold their jobs for only about five years.[85]

With Alway now the dean, the chair of pediatrics was open, and the cabal recruited Norman Kretchmer* to build a strong research department and David Hamburg from the NIH in psychiatry. "I wanted biological psychiatry to begin here," says Goldstein. The specialty "was in the doldrums of Freudian analysis."

Goldstein became a traveling salesman for Stanford, but he could offer little money. Everyone who came would have to develop support from the NIH. "What we could offer was space."[81]

Pressured by Kaplan, the university commissioned the noted architect Edward Durell Stone to design the new hospital and medical school to be built "in the middle of a eucalyptus grove on an isolated part of the Stanford campus," remembers Dr. Donald Harrison, faculty member for 25 years and chief of cardiology there from 1967 to 1986.[87]

Stone had wanted to build a high-rise, vertical structure for efficiency, but the university trustees required that no building on the Stanford campus exceed the height of the Hoover Tower.[17] Consequently, the medical center is a long, horizontal, three-story building. Given these restrictions, according to Avram Goldstein, "Stone sketched his grill and then gave the job to his people to work out the details.[17†] He

---

*Dr. Norman Kretchmer, who studied childhood nutrition and diabetes, led the Department of Pediatrics at Stanford for 10 years and then the National Institute of Child Health and Human Development at the National Institutes of Health. From 1981 until his death 14 years later, Kretchmer conducted research and treated children and adolescents at UCSF.[86]

†The grill was a characteristic feature of the exterior of his embassy in New Delhi and other Stone buildings at the time. University President Sterling, besieged by complaints about how the hospital worked, was heard to joke, "The medical center is a place where you go to have your passport renewed."[17] Among those who opposed, unsuccessfully in this case, the style of the architecture was former President Herbert Hoover, a constant feature of Stanford life beginning with his freshman year in its first class in 1891. Nevertheless, he agreed to serve as honorary chair of the committee to raise the funds to build the new medical center.[83] Stone, too, recognized the limitations of his design. He wrote to Henry Kaplan, "The patients of this and future generations won't curse the Stanford trustees. They will curse Edward Durrell Stone." Stone omits discussing the Stanford University Medical Center in his autobiography.[17]

had little interest in functional architecture. A wheelchair couldn't pass through some of the doors." The maze of corridors made it difficult for patients to find their doctors' offices, and the examining rooms were too small. The designers almost adhered to the trustees' dictum that all Stanford buildings had to have red-tiled roofs, as on the original university buildings, by settling on crushed red stone.[81]

The result was "architecturally magnificent, functionally marginal," the description David Korn applies to the beautiful new home for medicine at Stanford.[9]

The name of French biologist Louis Pasteur was adopted for the street leading to the new medical center. Whereas Harvard Medical School faces Avenue Louis Pasteur, Stanford is approached via Pasteur Drive.

The enthusiasts for the new medical center grossly underestimated the costs. A figure of $3 million was suggested. "Way too low," remembers Goldstein. If the trustees had known that the cost would exceed $20 million, "they wouldn't have done it."[81] The effect of this larger than expected expenditure was to delay the construction of other buildings needed for academic development and to assign the responsibility for further growth and continuing support for operations to the medical faculty, thereby placing even greater pressure on its entrepreneurial activities.

Since most members of the clinical faculty stayed in San Francisco,* few of the beds in the new hospital or appointments in the clinics would be filled until a new clinical faculty was recruited. Accordingly, local physicians were encouraged to admit their patients to the new hospital at Stanford, which was jointly owned equally by the university and the city of Palo Alto. From the beginning, the system didn't work well. David Korn saw the community as "constantly fighting with the university."[9]

Although "Palo Alto wasn't the rich city it is now," remembers Donald Harrison, now senior vice president and provost for health affairs at the University of Cincinnati Medical Center, "The horizons were unlimited. A world of young people were attracted there."[87] Harrison was typical, trained at a highly competitive East Coast hospital, in his case the Peter Bent Brigham, and at the NIH. Halsted Holman recruited him to be chief resident, and two years later Harrison became chief of cardiology at a hospital with few patients. Of the faculty's services in those days, one medical student observed, "There are more people in

---

*Stanford turned over its hospital facilities in San Francisco to the Presbytery of Northern California, which called its new acquisition Presbyterian Medical Center. It was renamed the California-Pacific Medical Center in the 1990s.[88]

white coats than patients." The staff contracted with Kaiser to care for its patients for what turned out to be an early example of a discounted fee-for-service contract.[87]

Alway's successor, Robert J. Glaser, dean and vice president from 1965 to 1970, together with leading members of the faculty, convinced the university to buy the half of the hospital owned by the city of Palo Alto. Having worked at Harvard, the Brigham, Barnes Hospital in St. Louis, and the University of Colorado, where he had been dean, Glaser was certain that "You can't have a split university hospital."[89]

Finally, on July 1, 1968, after prolonged negotiations that took two and a half years, Stanford University fully owned its own university teaching hospital on the campus.[9,89] The hospital remained dependent on the community doctors, however. Any physician demonstrating proper qualifications — "competence, character, and ethics were the exclusive criteria allowed," according to Korn — could joint the medical staff and admit to the hospital.[9] The chiefs of each service would be Stanford faculty members and community doctors the vice chiefs. The only clinical department that was "closed" and solely staffed by Stanford faculty was pathology, a provision Korn insisted upon when he was recruited from the NIH in 1967.[9]

Preeminence of Biomedical Science at Stanford

Thus, the move to Palo Alto from San Francisco was driven mainly by the promise of scientific advancement at Stanford. "It was a humongously important decision pushed by a few visionary faculty and a very courageous university president based on the great potential in biomedical science," says David Korn. Hope was high that the medical school faculty would relate closely with scientists in the rest of the university and "benefit from cross-fertilization."[9]

In important ways, this approach refounded the Stanford University School of Medicine. The leadership's commitment to science reduced the supremacy of clinical practice, previously predominant at the school. Clinical leaders in San Francisco were told that if they came south they would not continue in leading positions and that those looking toward such opportunities in the future would not advance to authority if their primary dedication was to clinical practice rather than biomedical science. Accordingly, few moved, and the full-time clinical departments were created almost from scratch.[80] The Department of Medicine is a good example. Ordinarily, the largest department in schools of medicine, there were only eight members to greet Dr. Halsted Holman when he arrived from the Rockefeller Institute in New York in 1960 to build a contemporary department based on scientific investigation.

Surgeons familiar with the history of their specialty will recognize the origin of "Hal" Holman's unusual first name. His father, Emile F. Holman, chief of surgery at the Stanford Hospital in San Francisco, was the last resident trained by William S. Halsted, the renowned founder of the Department of Surgery at the Johns Hopkins Hospital.[90]* The younger Holman, whose mother was a pediatrician at a time when few women were doctors, grew up in Richmond and entered Stanford in 1942, the year after America entered World War II. The navy took him into its V12 program, which paid for his education in preparation for military service as a doctor. Transferred to UCLA and rushed through his undergraduate education, Holman applied to medical school in his freshman year, was accepted at Johns Hopkins and Yale, and was sent to New Haven by the government two years after beginning college and without a bachelor's degree.

Holman did not immediately enter an internship but accepted a research fellowship in the Carlsberg laboratories in Copenhagen. After this experience he worked with the International Union of Students in Prague, among other European cities. He was then appointed to a medical internship at Yale–New Haven Hospital, but when the university officials learned about his work with the union, they withdrew the position. Anticommunist hysteria was strongly affecting America at that time, and Holman's participation in the union was suspect. "I'm sure there were communists in it," Holman explains. "I succumbed on the rocks of the cold war."[80]

Holman's politics — "I'm a political radical," he proudly acknowledges — did not prevent Montefiore Hospital in the Bronx from giving him an internship and then residency and chief residency (1952–55).[80] Montefiore, in the early 1950s, was not a primary university teaching hospital; it would later become one with the creation of the Albert Einstein College of Medicine. Holman then returned to the laboratory and worked with Dr. Henry Kunkel, a leading protein chemist at the Rockefeller Institute for Medical Research,† on the scientific causes of rheumatoid arthritis and systemic lupus erythematosus.

---

*A Stanford undergraduate, Emile Holman received his medical degree at Hopkins after a Rhodes Scholarship at Oxford. Characterized as the original Halstedian disciple in the Far West, the senior Holman pioneered an academic surgical program at a time when there were few others west of the Mississippi.[90]

†This later became Rockefeller University, located on the east side of Manhattan just south of the New York Hospital–Cornell Medical Center.

This is the background that the group building the new Stanford Medical School wanted in the chair of its Department of Medicine, a 35-year-old assistant professor whose primary interest was laboratory investigation. "The people who picked me didn't want a clinician as much as a scientist," Holman explains. "I expect the choice was helped by Norm Kretchmer, the new head of pediatrics, who was my roommate at Montefiore and knew me."[80] Holman was almost totally inexperienced in academic administration, but he was greatly helped by the mentoring of William Greulich, the chair of anatomy, "an older man who taught me how to behave in this crowd."[80] So in 1960 Holman moved back to his home state to chair Stanford's miniature Department of Medicine. The university bypassed the associate professor rank and named him Guggenhime Professor of Medicine, a title he still holds.

Holman's first priority was building the faculty. "We recruited from Boston, New York, and the NIH. I didn't favor trainees from Hopkins or Duke because they were being principally prepared for clinical care, not science. I also didn't like the restrictions on freedom traditional in their training programs. When the interns got a haircut at Hopkins, they had to do it at one shop, which was wired to the hospital in case they were needed. I've always been against hierarchies and wouldn't establish one at Stanford."[80]

The scientific quality of Holman's faculty made them highly competitive for grant support from the NIH, so much so that in the beginning the department didn't bill for the professional services rendered by its faculty to patients. "We focused on building the specialty services. The NIH was paying for specialty training since at the time it was thought that that's what the country needed. We also didn't want to compete with the local doctors, many of whom were generalists, so there was no emphasis on general medicine in the full-time faculty. In the early days, the house staff, which was small, only worked on the university service and the community doctors cared for the patients on their service," Holman explains. The department received little money from the school. "The dean and I settled our arrangement with an hour's meeting once a year and a handshake."[80]

The controversy over the country's participation in the Vietnam War reached into the medical school during the 1960s and 1970s. "Many of us were opposed to both the war and to Stanford's involvement through its engineering work with the Defense Department. The administration didn't particularly appreciate what I was doing." In 1971, with the appointment of a new dean, Holman presented his resignation. "I did it routinely. If my new boss didn't want me, I didn't want him."[80]

Unexpectedly to Holman, the dean accepted the resignation, and his 11-year chairmanship was over.[17]* Deciding that humoral immunology, his scientific specialty, was "falling out of fashion"[80] and being replaced with molecular biology, in which he was not trained, Holman changed his field. Since then, he has conducted research on the organization and delivery of health services. He continues to care for patients in rheumatology and general medicine.

In addition to the emphasis on research, new to the Stanford medical school, the cabal and the other pioneers planned a radical change in the education of the students Stanford trained, a proposal that has not met with the same degree of success. To accomplish this, the size of the Stanford classes has been kept small, about 65 when the school first moved to Palo Alto in 1959 and about 85 students currently, fewer than at other medical schools with which Stanford competes. After the move south, the students were selected to favor those who wanted to do research since the new leaders of the faculty were not primarily interested in training practitioners. "There ought to be one school that does this," is the way Avram Goldstein describes the attitude of his colleagues in those halcyon days.[81]

To assure that each student had a meaningful research experience, for several years after the consolidation in Palo Alto Stanford required that each student spend five years in obtaining the M.D. degree.[81] During this extra year — the conventional curriculum is four years — the students could elect to study any relevant subject, including topics taught outside the medical school such as anthropology. Most students, however, worked in basic science, leading to the local joke that Stanford then offered the "DNA degree."[79] The program reached its peak in the 1960s and 1970s, Goldstein remembers.[81] More recently, however, the students, many laden with large debts from their undergraduate and professional educations, have chosen to get on with their careers, usually in practice, and the dream of primarily producing academic clinicians and investigators has eluded Stanford, as it has almost every other medical school.

By the mid-1970s, the curriculum had become totally elective.[81] "Students were of course required to take a certain number of course credits but were not required to take any course they chose to omit,"

---

*The university president had charged the new dean with emphasizing the clinical focus of the school. Holman had been hired to create another Rockefeller University Hospital, which was designed primarily to facilitate clinical research with a few patients rather than deliver a broad range of clinical services to many patients.[17]

says Goldstein. "To the best of my knowledge, this Stanford plan was unique — and colleagues elsewhere thought we were nuts!"[81] Under Goldstein's leadership, the Faculty Senate "restored a required core curriculum . . . returning structure and discipline to our curriculum."[81] One observer has called this period "the Goldstein revolution."[17]

Concerned about the preponderance of research in the school, Stanford leaders decided that the clinical programs must grow, one of the changes assigned to Dean Robert J. Glaser (1965–70) and his successors.[89] During the 1980s, new construction included not only a building for the expanding programs in molecular and genetic medicine but an expensive enlargement of the hospital and clinics and a new children's hospital. The school of medicine continued to operate the outpatient clinics and the faculty's practice plan.

The Deanship of David Korn

David Korn, who served as dean in the 1980s and the first half of the 1990s, brought to Stanford, eight years after the school moved from San Francisco to Palo Alto, distinguished scientific accomplishments, although not quite as illustrious as those of Kornberg and Lederberg. A graduate of Harvard College and Medical School and trained in pathology at the Massachusetts General Hospital, he began his research career at the NIH. In 1967, Stanford asked him to take over the Pathology Department, again, like Holman, primarily as a physician-scientist rather than a clinician. As for the next step, which occurred 17 years later, after he had built a highly respected department, Korn says "I didn't intend to be a dean, but I was pushed into [it]. The president [biologist Donald Kennedy throughout most of Korn's tenure as dean] told me who the other two candidates were. I didn't think that I could work for them, so I took the job defensively."[9]

Kennedy had returned to Stanford as provost in 1979 after serving for two and a half years as commissioner of the U.S. Food and Drug Administration in the Carter government. One year later, the board elected him Stanford's eighth president. Kennedy's training in biology had naturally led him to demonstrate a greater interest in medical center affairs than had his predecessor. Throughout most of his presidency, Kennedy chaired the board of trustees of the Stanford University Hospital.[32]

Korn's term coincided with several troubling events in the university and in medicine. "The turbulent town-gown relationship with the local doctors had waxed and waned since 1960 and was continuing, the hospital's occupancy was falling, price competition was growing fierce, and hospitals throughout California were being seen as potential disasters."[9]

Then in March 1991 "the indirect cost crisis hit," as Korn describes this particularly troublesome period for the university and the school.[9] The federal government accused Stanford of misusing some of the indirect payments it had received to administer and support federal grants.* The inquiry led to a reduction in federal indirect cost payments to the university, significantly decreasing the school's discretionary income.

"The university's and our budgets were heavily dependent on indirect cost recoveries, and our data projected a close to $80 million cumulative deficit over five years," says Korn. "'What are you, David, going to do about this?' the trustees asked me." The university insisted that the school break even or show a surplus. "We patched together a new projection, reasonably credible, but had to do draconian things to stop the school's losses." It was operating in the black again by 1995.[9]

The other "hit," as Korn describes the trauma of his deanship, was the rapid advance of managed care in California, which put severe pressure on the hospital's bottom line and forced the leadership to make severe annual cuts in its projected operating budget. The financial problems affecting the hospital and the school exacerbated his differences with the CEO, Kenneth Bloem.[32]

During the spring of 1993, Korn invited Chancellor Joseph Martin from UCSF to dinner in one of the San Francisco airport hotels midway between the schools.[9] "I told him we'll be killed by managed care and should present a common alliance, partnership, some kind of relationship to the insurers. I didn't know what mechanism this should take but felt that we had to do something so they won't chip away at us." Martin raised the antitrust possibilities. "I said that our places had very smart people. They'd figure out something that works. He never got back to me."[9]

Kennedy's presidency was ending, and Korn knew that his close relationship with those at the top would probably change. At an early meeting with Gerhard Casper, the new president, Korn talked about the meeting with Martin. "That's the last I heard about it. Then Casper and Martin had their walk in the woods. I wasn't involved." Korn knew what was coming. "Casper told me he wanted someone new as dean, someone

---

*Peter Van Etten, later the CEO of Stanford Health Services and UCSF Stanford Health Care, became the university's chief financial officer in 1991 and helped to resolve these disputes.

who would be less dominant on the scene." Did his department leaders support Korn? "No, the chairs went into survival mode." Korn continues, "I don't think Casper wanted strong deans as Stanford had had. He wanted them to be more docile, as at Chicago."[9]*

"For me, he may have been right," Korn reflects. "I had appointed 23 chairs, many of them major investigators from outside Stanford." Although the school ranked seventh[†] in the NIH listing of support to American medical schools, "the amount of grant support per faculty member has been consistently at the top despite our being the smallest medical school in our peer group.[23]‡ I had become confluent with the job and wasn't happy."[9] Korn took early retirement from Stanford and moved to Washington, DC, where he is now senior vice president for biomedical and health sciences research at the Association of American Medical Colleges (AAMC), the Washington-based voice of academic medicine.

Clinical Services at Stanford

"Stanford's a sensational research place, but during my 29 years there they never considered building a clinical medical school," Korn allows.[9] "The plot was that the university people would do research and teaching and the local docs would do the clinical work. A sterile barrier should exist [to separate] pure intellectual activity from the messy, clinical business."[9]

Several of the clinical departments, Korn thought during his time,

---

*Casper, who had been dean of the law school and provost at the University of Chicago before coming to Stanford, differs with Korn's analysis of his preference in deans and the character of his choice to become Korn's successor. "Any sound university president wants strong deans, especially medical deans. I have appointed strong deans at Stanford, and which president would want to run the medical school? All I did was to apply to David what I have applied to myself twice: my '10-year rule'" (the maximum amount of time Casper thinks university officials should hold senior administrative jobs).[2]

†It ranks eighth if Harvard is included.

‡In the AAMC's 1997–98 report, each basic science faculty member at Stanford generated an average of $671,159 in grants, the largest amount among the country's 125 medical schools. The clinical faculty in this race was only beaten by that of the University of California-San Diego. UCSF was third in both heats.[91] "On a one-to-one basis," says a leader in academic medicine who has worked at several eminent medical schools, "Stanford is the strongest academic institution I've seen. It's an elite community of scholars wedded to academic excellence." In the summer of 1999, the Stanford medical school faculty included two Nobel laureates, 24 members of the National Academy of Sciences, and 36 members of the Institute of Medicine.[23]

"were spotty.[92]* Henry Kaplan developed an outstanding radiation oncology service but didn't care much about diagnostic radiology or nuclear medicine.[†] Shumway was also an exception thanks to his building a first-class clinical service, having a thick skin and not taking guff from anyone."[9]

Norman Edward Shumway is a name known throughout cardiac surgery, cardiology, and transplantation, for it was he, more than any other American, who developed the field of cardiac transplantation. In doing so at Stanford, he founded one of the few very strong clinical programs there, but its origins were in the research that he and his colleagues performed.

Wanting relief from the winters of Minnesota, where he had trained as a surgeon and received his Ph.D. for experimental work on transplantation—Vanderbilt University had given him his M.D. in 1949—Shumway moved to San Francisco in 1958 to what was then known as the Stanford-Lane Hospital as a cardiothoracic surgeon in private practice. "I frankly wasn't making much money, and with Frank Gerbode [the leading cardiac surgeon in the city] the only academic surgeon in the place, staying there, I thought moving to Palo Alto was a great opportunity."[93]

Shumway found the Surgery Department at the newly constructed hospital "not particularly distinguished, not up to the science the university did."[93] The only cardiac surgeon in his department, Shumway began the experimental and clinical research that led to his eventual dominance of the cardiac transplant field. Shumway received a contract with Kaiser in the 1960s, which helped develop his early practice. "The Department of Medicine was a research department, so I didn't get many patients from there." Eventually, thanks to the reputation of his work, "They began to come from all over." The department created a division for him in 1964, and 10 years later, when UCSF tried to recruit him, Stanford elevated cardiac surgery from divisional to departmental status

---

*Stanford president Donald Kennedy (1980–92) confirms Korn's impression: "Stanford built its reputation on basic science, not the clinical side." Kennedy believes that Stanford has had few great clinical departments due to "lingering problems from the move from San Francisco" and the local clinical competition from the Palo Alto and other private clinics.[32] Dr. Daniel D. Federman, who must have appeared stressed at times while leading the Department of Medicine in the mid-1970s, was asked by a colleague. "Aren't you sleeping well?"[92] "Fine," responded Federman. "I sleep for an hour, and I cry for an hour." Federman, who returned to Harvard (see chapter 3) after five years at Stanford, was heard to quip that his goal was "to make Stanford number two."[92]

†Diagnostic radiology, "reading the films," and nuclear medicine, in which nuclear agents and special cameras are used for diagnosis and treatment, are both part of the responsibility of most chairmen of departments of radiology.

with Shumway as chair. "Frankly, I didn't want to leave Stanford," so the solution was agreeable to most, even the chair of surgery, who didn't fight the loss of Shumway's division.[93]

In 1992, Shumway turned over his department to one of his trainees, Dr. Bruce Reitz, then director of the division of cardiac surgery and professor of surgery at Johns Hopkins. Although he no longer operates, Shumway, now in his midseventies, remains an active member of his department. His legacy is a very successful cardiac surgical program, significantly more successful, as it has been for decades, than that at UCSF.

Stanford University Hospital

"Scientifically, going to Stanford was almost like entering the Garden of Eden, but clinically, it was broken, flawed." That was what Kenneth D. Bloem thought when Stanford president Donald Kennedy invited him to become president and CEO of the Stanford University Hospital in September 1989.* "The West Coast's so trendy. I didn't really want to go there. Stanford's one of the few academic centers in suburbia. It's not surrounded by large populations and is afflicted with a tremendous amount of managed care."[94] Nevertheless, he was intrigued by the possibilities and took the job.

"The medical school had been harnessed to the NIH, but there had been little planning for the clinical programs," Bloem saw. "Little thought had been given to managed care, even though it was taking 40 percent of our business when I arrived in 1989. Our alliance with the Palo Alto Clinic and the other docs in town was very fragile, which was ironic since Stanford had trained many of them."[94]

The Palo Alto Clinic[95,96] is a multispecialty group of physicians with their own extensive outpatient facilities, now being consolidated in a new campus across El Camino Real from the Stanford sports fields. Founded in 1929, the group has grown to include more than 150 physicians, who perform most of their procedures in their own outpatient facility and use the Stanford University Hospital for the relatively few patients who need hospitalization. Clinic doctors, most of whom hold Stanford voluntary clinical faculty appointments, constituted almost the entire clinical faculty of the school during its first years after the move from San Francisco.

---

*Bloem, like Gerhard Casper, Kennedy's successor as president, and Lawrence Furnstahl, UCSF Stanford's chief financial officer, had come to Stanford from the University of Chicago, where Bloem had been executive vice president and chief executive officer of the University of Chicago Hospitals.

Recognizing that the first priority of the professors in the clinical departments was research, Bloem nevertheless hoped that the practitioners could be brought closer together with the full-time faculty and the university. "We also needed to elevate Stanford Hospital's appeal from regional to national."[94] Consequently, Bloem saw his biggest jobs to be "Dealing with managed care, the unstable town-gown relationship, and reversing the declining margins,* which Kennedy and the board were seeing."[94]

Bloem, like many other hospitals CEOs at this time, instituted an "operations improvement" program. "That's a euphemism for 'cost cutting,' which continues, I suspect, to this day. Managing and reviewing utilization, particularly by reducing length of stay, appealed to the insurance companies."[94]

Bloem, seen by senior doctors such as cardiothoracic surgical chair Bruce Reitz as "very physician friendly,"[33] enlisted several of the faculty to visit current and potential referring doctors to "detoxify the climate. Ted Harris [the chair of medicine during most of Bloem's tenure] and Gene Bauer [then chair of dermatology, later dean] were terrific." Bloem found some of the surgeons and the doctors who specialized in performing procedures less helpful. "We saw the top people at the Palo Alto Clinic and really 'loved them up.'"[94]

University president Donald Kennedy and his board had restructured the governance of the medical school and Stanford University Hospital by creating a separate corporation for the hospital to shield the university from direct financial responsibility for future hospital losses. The hospital director thereby gained independence from the dean and reported to a separate board of trustees, which was largely composed of representatives from the community, with only three Stanford trustees, even though the university still fully owned the hospital. The dean continued to report to the university president.[32]

Critics saw this change as eroding the authority of the dean and the faculty in hospital affairs and even changing the school's original missions of research and education when it moved to Palo Alto "into a by-product of the medical practice business."[97]

Primary Care

During the early 1990s, "The lack of a primary care mechanism was asphyxiating the medical center," Bloem believed. This is a point of view

---

*For *margins,* read *profits.*

Bloem continues to hold for UCSF Stanford, although he had left the West Coast before the merger was completed.[94]

"Stanford had at least two possible strategies. The wiser one, I thought, was to build alliances with Stanford alumni and local health care providers" to assure that the hospital would be filled and the academic mission accomplished. This implied that clinical operations would need to grow.[94] "The other approach involved the cartel strategy, the one they chose," with which the merger with UCSF would fit. Bloem wondered if such a tactic made economic sense since a relatively small portion of the tertiary care market went to either of the hospitals before or after the merger. Furthermore, he feared that political and operational forces would reduce the ability of the executives to focus on day-to-day business operations when they were also obliged to maneuver in such a large enterprise. In particular, he did not favor the exclusive use of the cartel strategy. "There are times when there're so many changes occurring that you need several arrows in your quiver."[94]

Bloem was not alone in favoring a role for primary care within Stanford. Van Etten's commitment to building Stanford Health Services and then UCSF Stanford Health Care as a "specialty boutique" — "outsource" primary care, he has been heard to say — distressed those members of the faculty with an interest in this work.

"This pattern is not new," observes Halsted Holman, the immunologist turned health services researcher and chair of the Department of Medicine at Stanford from 1960 to 1971. He sees many of the successors to Sterling, Terman, and Alway, the president, provost, and medical school dean who initiated the scientific supremacy of Stanford, as caretakers rather than problem solvers. "They wouldn't push primary care despite my pushing them. A science place like Stanford should do this also. I look on us as nouveau riche. We did unusual things at the beginning, but, even though Stanford is now established, we don't have the traditions of the East Coast schools, which let them take risks."[80]

If Stanford was to take a role in primary care, Bloem wondered, "could we pull the Palo Alto Clinic into Stanford? Kennedy, the politician, wanted to do it. Others were opposed, David Korn particularly so. It was like Horatio at the gates. 'I won't allow this,' I remember him saying. David considers himself an economic realist and believed that we couldn't afford to share our revenues with the community. 'Just wait till next year when the income drops further,' he warned."[94]

Dr. Robert Jamplis, then the president and CEO of the clinic, remembers the discussions. "Stanford wanted us to do primary care for them, but we're a multispecialty group, and, besides, our cultures are quite different."[96]*

Korn reflects that "over the years the Palo Alto Clinic leadership always seemed to have more influence on the Stanford University leadership and especially the Hospital Board than did the Stanford faculty, a fact widely known and resented. I strongly opposed the deal, which did not involve the faculty and was designed by consultants whose report I, and many other faculty, found quite off the mark and frequently offensive." Korn felt then, and continues to feel, that if an appropriate arrangement had been developed a union between Stanford and the clinic presented "a great opportunity that might well have transformed Stanford's clinical enterprise and changed the course of medical practice and politics in the South Bay."[9]

Korn's point of view carried the day, and the university broke off negotiations.† Within three weeks, the Palo Alto Clinic was talking to the Sutter Group."‡ Not long afterward, the clinic became an affiliate of Sutter in return for Sutter's investing in a new outpatient facility.[95,96] After this failure, Bloem and Korn talked to other groups and did eventually purchase the Menlo Clinic, a highly respected group of doctors with a carriage trade, "most of whose physicians were long time members of the voluntary clinical faculty and had very warm relationships with the medical school," Korn says.

In retrospect, however, Bloem questions the value of the acquisition. "It worked out not to be a great strategic move. We had all the usual problems converting hardworking private docs into full-time salaried employees." In buying the clinic, Stanford was competing with Sutter for "the last classy clinic in the region. So we overpaid for it."[94]

Stanford considered forming its own HMO. "We would have needed

---

*Jamplis told Spyros Andreopoulos, a perceptive student of Stanford medical policy and history, that "When you have students involved in patient care, they gum up the works, slow down the whole process and cause inefficiency."[17] All academic leaders recognize this, though they seldom talk about it. Students must be taught, and most medical schools spend little money specifically on teaching. Consequently, a private organization such as the Palo Alto Clinic, when it takes on the teaching of medical students, can expect little financial assistance from the school, which may have long depended on volunteer faculty members to help with this responsibility. As clinical income has decreased, managers of such clinics and practicing community doctors increasingly find teaching an activity they can no longer afford to do.

†Kennedy remembers "a high hostility level between Stanford and the Palo Alto Clinic preventing a deal between the hospital and the clinic."[32]

‡The Sutter Group, a not-for-profit corporation based in Sacramento, owns several hospitals and physician groups in northern California.

at least 50,000 lives just to break even," Bloem computed.[94] Most of the patients in the region were already connected to Kaiser and the other clinics, so creating an HMO was shelved. "We talked to everyone, even tried to do something with Kaiser. We wanted an institutional relationship. They just wanted service lines. Nothing happened."[94]

After all this, Bloem was frustrated. "I went to Kennedy and then Casper after David [Korn] had killed the Palo Alto Clinic project and said, 'This is dysfunctional. The CEO wants to go right, the dean wants to go left. Get a vice president for health affairs or Korn reports to me or vice versa. I'm willing to give up my job. Life is too short to fight for another three years.'"[94]

Stanford Health Services

This brings this story to Isaac Stein, a Palo Alto lawyer, corporate manager, and venture capitalist with law and business degrees from Stanford. A director of the Stanford University Hospital since 1988 and then chair of its finance committee, Stein had just sold one of his businesses and was available to help Gerhard Casper develop a strategy in response to the issues Bloem and others had raised.[98] "It was 1993. Gerhard had just arrived and needed help with the hospital, the Clintons were trying to change the country's medical system, and I had some spare time," Stein remembers.[99] His salary would be a dollar a year. "The amount hasn't increased, and as a matter of fact he hasn't seen the first dollar yet," says Casper.[2]

The relationship between Casper and Stein is close. Dr. Victor Dzau, then chair of medicine at Stanford and much involved in hospital affairs at the time, describes Stein as "a major driving force behind what was happening at Stanford, and Gerhard trusts him. Stein is a great proponent of using business methods to run hospitals. Something was needed, Stein felt, to protect market dominance and the brand name of the university."[98]*

On the job as Casper's personal consultant on health matters, Stein set up a small committee consisting of the president, medical school dean (David Korn), university chief financial officer (Peter Van Etten),

---

*During the winter and spring of 1995–96, Dzau was considering succeeding Eugene Braunwald as chair of the Department of Medicine at the Brigham, where he had worked before moving to Stanford as chief of cardiology. He accepted the Brigham job in April. "I wouldn't have left [Stanford] for any other job, but Gene [Braunwald] was my mentor."[98]

and the CEOs of the University (Kenneth Bloem) and Lucile Packard Children's (Lorraine Zippiroli) Hospitals. "We met regularly at 7:00 A.M. with Gerhard in the chair and me as vice chair. We agreed at the beginning to concentrate on the university hospital, not the children's hospital."[99] Did the group consider selling the hospital, something many thought the university wished to do?* "Never," says Stein. "Kaiser came to us — we didn't go to them — to discuss some sort of deal to use our beds for them so that they wouldn't have to build a new hospital. At the time, our census was down." That failed as Kaiser went through several management cycles, including deciding how it should run its hospitals, nationally, regionally, or by states. "That possibility stopped with a whimper," Stein remembers.[99] Columbia-HCA, the mammoth for-profit hospital-owning corporation, "talked to us, but that was meaningless. They were invading the Bay Area, bought Good Samaritan Hospital in San Jose. We felt insufficiently confident about shared visions" to go further.[99]

"Korn and Bloem were at each other's throats," remembers Casper. "The debate would stop if we could align the interests of the faculty closer to the hospital. We might be making the wrong decisions if we kept the services separate [the school versus the hospital]."[2] Consequently, the committee decided to create a Stanford-operated, not-for-profit "clinical enterprise," consisting of the adult hospital with its inpatient services, the outpatient clinics, then run by the clinical departments of the School of Medicine, and the practice plan of the Stanford faculty. Surprisingly to some, David Korn approved transferring the practice plan, then in the medical school, to the new clinical enterprise under the direction of a chief executive to be identified by means of a national search. In fact, he had advised the committee and Casper to consider making just such a decision.[9]

The trustees named the new entity Stanford Health Services, with Stanford University as its sole member, assuring university control of the

---

*Observers on both the Stanford and UCSF campuses presumed this was the case. UCSF economist Harold Luft says that "Stanford identifies itself more with engineering and high technology, not with hospitals, which gobble up space and are financially risky." Luft also suggests that the rest of Stanford University was uncomfortable with the influence and potential votes of all those full-time clinicians, who "didn't think like history professors."[6] Former dean David Korn believes that "The Stanford board and the leadership never understood why the university should own a hospital with its icky, sick people."[9] Carlos Esquivel, the transplant surgeon at Stanford, was told, "The university had to dump the hospital so its losses wouldn't hurt the university."[100] And Neil Cohen of UCSF remembers hearing that "Stanford was concerned that the hospital would bleed the university and wanted to get rid of it."[24]

clinical enterprise. Casper decided not to chair the new board of trustees as Donald Kennedy, Casper's predecessor and a biologist with an academic interest in medical issues, had chaired the Stanford Hospital board. Instead he appointed Stein. "Not being chair would give me a greater ability to watch over things," explains Casper.[2]* The new corporation commenced operations on September 1, 1994.

Stein wanted a business-oriented board for the new entity, which would meet frequently and direct the operation. "I can't think of another industry where so little has changed organizationally in a field which itself is changing so much. Therefore, we needed professional leadership," businessman Stein says. "Stanford runs a shopping center [a high-end establishment on Stanford property adjacent to El Camino Real]. We don't send law school professors and graduate students to run it. It's purely a business. We also run a history department, which is purely academic. The medical center is the one part of the university that combines business and academic issues. It is larger than a shopping center and competes with people who have nothing to do with academics, but we run it mainly to support the academic missions of the medical school. Hence," Stein continues, "faculty must be involved, but we can't operate it like a history department.[99]

"The adult hospital, adult practice plan, and the children's hospital each had a different strategy," Stein observed. "There were no harmonies among them, with each part and each department having different views and making different assumptions of what was going on." Then there were the differences in the financial results among the specialties. "Obgyn was losing money on the medical school side but making money for the hospital."[99] In assembling the parts, Stein saw Stanford "rationalizing the Byzantine arrangements and deals" operating among the hospital, the clinical departments, and the school. "It was as complex and unworkable as the tax code. We wanted to get the faculty more involved in the functioning of the hospital and making strategic decisions.[99]

"We decided at the outset to concentrate on what we do best, perform tertiary care for the region," explains Stein. "If we tried to compete in the primary care market, we had a serious scale problem since our clinical faculty was half the size of our peer institutions, and the faculty mix [strongly skewed toward specialty care] would have to change."[99]

---

*Comparing the attention the presidents gave to the medical enterprise, Kenneth Melmon, who chaired the Department of Medicine during Kennedy's presidency, often saw the president at the medical center. Kennedy "ran the hospital," he remembers. Now, although the hospital has taken much of Casper's time and attention, he does this work at a distance and, according to Melmon, "doesn't set a foot in the place."[34]

Stanford had considered and rejected buying the Palo Alto Clinic. "We couldn't successfully compete with them or with Kaiser for primary care, just weren't large enough or competent enough to do so, and I didn't think we would even learn how to run such practices economically."[99]

Dr. Judith Swain, chair of the Department of Medicine, agrees. "Primary care is not a mission for Stanford. We're not under state mandate for this [as is UCSF]. We ought to be up front that we train specialists and academic physicians."[37]

Kenneth Bloem, then the CEO of the soon to be integrated Stanford University Hospital, was offered, but declined to accept, the job as the first CEO of Stanford Health Services. "I decided that I didn't want to stay in academic medicine at that time, and I would have had to commit for at least three more years. I had been at Stanford for five years, the best years of my life, but I was tired of fighting with the dean. A friend had offered me the chance to run the Advisory Board Company [a research and consulting enterprise in Washington], which was very appealing."[94] Accordingly, Bloem resigned from Stanford in April 1994, five months before Stanford Health Services began operating.[101] A senior Stanford faculty member speculated that Casper may not have been heartbroken by Bloem's decision. "He wanted his own person."

Then, when David Korn's deanship ended—Casper announced on August 24 that Korn would retire from the position in a year[102]—the president first tried to recruit a vice president for health affairs to direct the School of Medicine and Stanford Health Services and interface with the Lucile Packard Children's Hospital and the community.[33,98]* Unable to find the right person or convince those he favored to accept, Casper discarded the vice president idea and in February 1995 confirmed that Peter Van Etten, his former chief financial officer, who had been acting as CEO since Bloem left, would lead Stanford Health Services.[103] Casper also decided to appoint the dean from within Stanford and chose Eugene Bauer,[103] chair of the Department of Dermatology, to succeed David Korn.

---

*Kenneth Bloem reflects that most vice presidents for health affairs are former deans and not hospital CEOs. "It is the academics and not the clinical enterprise that most interests them." Casper, distressed at having to expend so much of his effort on medical affairs,[33,98] hoped that a vice president would allow him to devote more time to his other responsibilities as university president. Bloem remembers him saying, "I'm spending 70 percent of my time on medicine, and that's not all I'm here for."[94]

The figure's obviously an exaggeration, but Casper acknowledges that "There were intense periods when I have come close in a given month, but that was the exception."[2] The merger, when it came, did not relieve him of his responsibility but rather created more work for him.

"Gene has excellent perception into situations," comments Dr. Alfred Lane, whom Bauer had recruited to Stanford and who now succeeded him as chair of dermatology.[104] "He's excellent at looking at options, helping people work things through if there's time. Otherwise, he can decide himself."

"A bright man, quietly effective, Gene enjoys the respect of the clinical and scientific chairs," says Dr. Edward Holmes, who watched Bauer in action as senior associate dean at Stanford before leaving to become dean of the medical school at Duke University in 1999.[105]

Compared to the climate at Stanford when Korn was dean, Alfred Lane adds, "Under Gene, things are much more calm than previously when everybody was fighting. He's always accessible and has tried to open things up. I see other department's financial statements."[104] A senior faculty member adds, "Gene Bauer wants to be liked. Korn couldn't care less."

With Bauer appointed, the leaders from Stanford were now in place who would assemble and then operate the merger with UCSF. Stein would be the chair of UCSF Stanford and Casper,[106]* Bauer, and Van Etten members of its board. Van Etten would become the first CEO.

The Lucile Packard Children's Hospital: Pediatrics

The pediatric service at Stanford operates in the Lucile Packard Children's Hospital, a 214-bed facility for the care of children that originated as the Stanford Home for Convalescent Children. In 1970, it was renamed the Children's Hospital at Stanford, located about half a mile from the adult hospital. Then, in 1986, David and Lucile Packard gave the first of a series of donations that led to the construction of a new hospital adjacent to the Stanford University Hospital, which opened in 1991. It is described as a carpeted "hotel for children," with beautiful facilities.[104] Named for Mrs. Packard, who had died four years earlier, the Lucile Packard Children's Hospital was separately governed when it

---

*The close attention Casper gives to medical affairs at Stanford reflects the large part this component of the university plays in its operation not because of the profession he chose.[106] Although married to a psychiatrist, Dr. Regina Casper, Gerhard Casper is an academic lawyer. Born in Hamburg, Germany, in 1937, he studied law at the Universities of Freiburg, Hanover, and Yale. After two years (1964–66) on the faculty at the University of California-Berkeley, Casper taught and wrote scholarly papers and books at the University of Chicago for 26 years. He also administered the law school as dean from 1979 to 1987 and was provost of the university from 1989 until becoming Stanford's ninth president on September 1, 1992.

was founded but in January 1997, under pressure from the likely merger with UCSF, it merged with Stanford Health Services,[107,108] a change not popular with many members of the pediatrics faculty, who feared losing their special identity with the children's hospital.[40,109]

Stanford now had what Dr. Larry Shapiro, chair of pediatrics at UCSF, says is a "bone fide children's hospital, no longer one that was predominately for children with chronic diseases."[30]

The negotiations leading up to the affiliation, however, had not been easy, Donald Kennedy, the Stanford president at the time, remembers. "How do we move both the dollar-positive neonatal intensive care unit and the dollar-negative rest of the pediatrics service from the Stanford hospital to the [then independent] Children's Hospital?"[32] Furthermore, the new hospital included few doctors' offices, no emergency or operating rooms, no radiology — Stanford insisted that this work be performed at the adult hospital — and no dedicated pediatric surgeons, anesthesiologists, or radiologists.[30] Admissions depended upon community pediatricians, and the university's full-time Department of Pediatrics was small.

This is what Dr. Harvey Cohen, head of pediatric oncology at the University of Rochester, would face when Stanford offered him the chair of pediatrics in 1993.[110] Fortunately, he had great friends to support his goal of developing a first-class pediatrics service at Stanford in the David and Lucile Packard Foundation and, after 1996, the Lucile Packard Foundation for Children's Health. He received $20 million from the foundations for his work in the first years of his tenure.

With the faculty in pediatrics and pediatric surgery underpopulated, Cohen decided to organize the department's clinical and research programs separately. Cohen charged the chiefs of his clinical specialty divisions, such as cardiology and oncology, Cohen's special interest, with concentrating on the care of patients. He then pooled his investigators into programs such as molecular genetics, immunology and transplantation biology, developmental biology, cancer biology, and health services research and disease prevention. Cohen encouraged the directors of these programs, who held administrative rank in the department comparable to that of the division heads, and their colleagues to collaborate with scientists in other clinical and basic science departments of the medical school and elsewhere in the university. By 1999, Cohen's department had 80 full-time faculty members, 25 of tenure or tenure-track rank and appointed to perform successful, fundable research. However, Cohen explains, "The department is leveraged toward clinical, nontenure faculty."[110]

At UCSF, Shapiro sees the market better for pediatrics than for adult medicine "because the competition is less, only Stanford and Oakland Children's." Other hospitals like the California-Pacific Medical Center, "without much else in pediatrics, tried to develop boutique programs such as liver transplantation. They couldn't compete. The surgeons went to Stanford, and the program folded," says Shapiro. "The problem for us is not the market. About 20 percent of our patients come from the city, which has only about 100,000 children. Forty percent come from other places in the Bay region and another 40 percent from elsewhere." Shapiro worries more about his costs. "They're so high. The illnesses of our patients have a very high level of complexity."[30]

Practice Plans: Brown and Toland

The UCSF School of Medicine established its practice plan to consolidate, administer, and develop the professional earnings generated by the full-time clinicians in 1986 in response to managed care, which was developing in California. "The insurers didn't want to deal with the departments separately," remembers Dr. Russell K. Laros Jr., chair of the practice plan and vice chair of the Department of Obstetrics and Gynecology.[111] The plan's billing service eventually represented about 80 percent of the full-time physicians. Some of the departments, however, continued to employ private agencies outside the medical center. The funds flowed through UCSF to the departments where the services had been rendered. The costs for centralized billing were deducted, and the dean taxed the collections from about 4 to 8 percent. The hospital charged for use of the offices where the patients were seen.[111]

On January 1, 1997, 10 months before UCSF Stanford began operating, the physicians at UCSF joined an independent practice association of doctors practicing at California-Pacific Medical Center to form what they renamed the Brown and Toland Medical Group,[112-15]* "a subspecialty cartel," a consultant called it.[116] The UCSF leaders had decided that they couldn't efficiently build their own primary care business alone through the usual academic medical and pediatric routes. The

---

*Brown and Toland derived its name from two people important in the founding of the hospital and the medical school, with, an observer noted, "just a touch of political correctness." Dr. Charlotte Brown, one of the first woman physicians to practice in San Francisco, founded the Children's Hospital, which, by the time it merged with Presbyterian Hospital to form the California-Pacific Medical Center, had become a general and no longer a pediatric hospital. Dr. Hugh Toland created the medical college that eventually became the medical school at UCSF.

other University of California hospitals had had relatively little success doing so, and the attempts were always expensive.

"We were two marquee groups and would gain better leverage with payers," explains Patricia E. "Patty" Perry, senior vice president for strategic development at UCSF Stanford.[115] Brown and Toland would only seek fully capitated contracts from the HMOs and in some cases would share the risk with the hospitals. "We say we've got the best 1,500 docs, with UCSF providing much of the specialty business and California-Pacific most of the primary care. The wall between the hospitals has come down, so the patients go back and forth."[115]

When Brown and Toland was formed, UCSF brought in 28,000 subscribers and California-Pacific 138,000.[114] In addition to reducing competition between the two institutions, Brown and Toland consolidated administrative costs and provided "pull-through" business,* which the faculty performs on the California-Pacific patients.

In the Bay Area, the HMOs would rather contract with physician groups like Brown and Toland than with individual physicians.[6] Thus, coupling specialists at UCSF with the primary care convenience of California-Pacific is "very attractive in this market," according to Dr. Thomas V. Mcafee, who coordinates the UCSF piece of Brown and Toland.[114†] Most of the contracts HMOs send to Brown and Toland are capitated, as is most managed care in the region. The medical group often deals with the doctors through discounted fee-for-service arrangements.[6]

At Stanford, Gerhard Casper transferred the faculty's practice plan from the School of Medicine to Stanford Health Services when it was formed in 1994. The leader of the practice plan now became the CEO, a hospital administrator, and no longer the dean, a physician. Many faculty saw this change as unwise. "What we learned from Stanford Health Services' running of the practice plan was that the hospital didn't have a great handle on professional practices," says Dr. Gary M. Glazer, chair of the Department of Radiology at Stanford and of the finance committee of the practice plan. "They brought in someone from American Express. It was a disaster, poorly run, poor customer satisfaction. Billing on the M.D. side is very different from billing on the hospital side." Most of the full-time clinicians, Glazer felt, were not involved in the new

---

Pull-through business in this case refers to medical examinations and procedures, often performed by specialists in hospital facilities, that result from a patient's having come into a doctor's office for primary care.

†Dr. Michael Abel, the CEO of Brown and Toland, believes many subscribers who favor the plan think, as does his wife, "I don't want to go to university for my own care, but if my child is sick I don't want to jump through hoops to get there."[112]

clinical enterprise, "and then, with the practice plan not worked out, the merger came."[117]

Van Etten explains that, although "there were significant problems in SHS [Stanford Health Services] billing, independent reviews concluded that physician and patient satisfaction with clinical care improved following their inclusion in SHS."[22]

The Steps Leading to the Merger

"The merger process went on for two years," Dr. Bruce Wintroub of UCSF remembers. "Haile [Debas, the dean], Bill [Kerr, the hospital CEO], Lee [Goldman, the chair of medicine], and I spent each Tuesday meeting with the Stanford people putting it together. We were a good, practical, working group and could make decisions fast."[18]

"I thought, if we were going to do this, we needed to really do it together, not like the holding company at Partners," says Van Etten, then the CEO of Stanford Health Services. "We would do it differently. One CEO, one CMO [chief medical officer]. But, we whispered, 'one chair for each.'"[22]

Peter Gregory, the Stanford chief medical officer, remembers the discussions well. "The merger was driven by the mantra 'We won't be like Partners.' We wouldn't create two operating pieces. We would be one." Gregory feels that not being another Partners drove many of the fundamental organizational decisions for UCSF Stanford.[109]

John McArthur, former dean of the Harvard Business School and now cochair of Partners, came to visit, and members of the group talked with Dr. Richard Nesson, the first Partners chief executive.[22] An accounting firm proposed a business plan. Opposition came from the UCSF unions, which lobbied Democrats in the state legislature. San Francisco businesspeople, however, favored the plan, and they talked with legislators sympathetic to the business community.[22]

In the midst of the process, the University of California commissioned a "third-party report" to determine whether creating what became UCSF Stanford was a sound business decision. President Atkinson asked Warren Hellman, a San Francisco investment banker, to chair the committee, which retained the management consulting firm of Bain and Company to develop the data needed to answer the charge given to him and his colleagues. In addition, Hellman consulted with Dr. Samuel Thier,[118]* by then the CEO of Partners, and with McArthur.

---

*Thier halved the financial projections, "and even at that thought it's optimistic," but he advised that they should "go ahead."[118]

The committee concluded, in their report published on November 8, 1996,[119] that the merger was a sound business decision for the University of California and that the UCSF Medical Center would prosper more under Newco, the name adopted for what became UCSF Stanford, than by continuing to stand alone. During the 1999 fiscal year (July 1, 1998 to June 30, 1999),* a particularly important year, as we shall see, the committee projected that without merging UCSF would probably lose money on operations but could expect to make about the same amount as part of Newco. The report also projected that much of the cost of activating the merger would come from Newco's having to assume the pension contributions and health benefits previously the responsibility of the University of California and not the UCSF campus.[119]

Other observers feared that the Hellman report projected too rosy a picture. "I would describe [the report] as mere cheerleading for the advocates of privatization," said an attorney representing the unions. "They can't possibly reach the conclusion that this is a sound business decision with all the questions it leaves open."[120] Another union critic said, "The report might satisfy some bean counters who are working for the regents, but it doesn't answer the real questions. Is it legal? Is it fair? [What will be] the effect on patients."[120]

Furthermore, Jonathan Showstack, a UCSF sociologist who studied the origins of the merger for his Ph.D.,[121] firmly believes that "The founders didn't have the data necessary to fully evaluate what they wanted to create. For example, the accounting firm refused to audit the practice plan because the data were inadequate to be audited."[29]

Showstack sees the process as beginning in the minds of "a neurologist [Joseph Martin, chancellor of UCSF] and a lawyer [Gerhard Casper, president of Stanford]. They conveyed great excitement when first meeting with their colleagues. This is what we'd like to do, they said. Let's go. The leadership group then proceeded without a lot of questioning or analysis," Showstack believes. "They accepted what the consultants told them without personal expertise, and the consultants told them what they wanted to hear. Was there ever a real marketing analysis done in those days?" Showstack asks. "They had data suggesting that the four hospitals controlled about 10 percent of the local market. 'If we could raise this to 12 percent, a 20 percent increase, that would be great,' they thought."[29]

"The data illustrated the problem," Showstack continues. "The Bay Area has a lot of competition for much of tertiary care, and I don't think the leaders were really admitting that to themselves except to conclude

---

*It was assumed that the fiscal year of Newco would begin on July 1, when the university's fiscal year begins.

that the distribution reduced the problems raised by charges of monopoly. As it turned out, the new cases that came to UCSF after the merger were the 'wrong patients,' very sick medical cases for whom Medicare pays poorly when compared with surgical cases. The claim that we're unique, and therefore Medicare should pay more, is no longer the case. True, the situation was different at Stanford."[29]

In the middle of November, soon after release of the Hellman report and, despite the objections to it, the regents and Stanford created UCSF Stanford Health Care.

Selection of a CEO

By early January 1997, the members of the new board for UCSF Stanford Health Care had been appointed. From the University of California Board of Regents came Tirso del Junco, chair of the board, Richard Atkinson, president of the University of California, and Howard Leach from the regents' Health Services Committee. The UCSF appointees were Chancellor Joseph Martin, Dean Haile Debas, and Chair of Medicine Lee Goldman. The Stanford trustees were all members of the board of Stanford Health Services: Woodrow Myers, Denise O'Leary, and Isaac Stein, the chair, who was also a university trustee. From the Stanford administration came President Gerhard Casper, Dean Eugene Bauer, and Judith Swain, the chair of medicine. The three independent directors were Richard E. Behrman, managing director of the Center for the Future of Children of the David and Lucile Packard Foundation; Richard Rosenberg, retired chair and CEO of BankAmerica Corporation; and investment banker Warren Hellman.[122] Eight of the 15, more than half, were physicians: Bauer, Behrman, Debas, del Junco, Goldman, Martin, Myers, and Swain. The new board elected Stein the first chair.

The board of UCSF Stanford then mounted a search for the corporation's first CEO, with William Kerr and Peter Van Etten the obvious internal candidates. Kerr and Van Etten, who had worked closely together on the merger, agreed, as the Hellman Committee had recommended,[119] that cochiefs should be avoided, that there had to be one chief executive and one chief medical officer.[22]

Joseph Martin, the UCSF chancellor would soon be leaving for Harvard, and rumors were about that Haile Debas, the UCSF dean, might resign to found a medical school in Eritrea, where he was born. To combat the line at UCSF that "Peter's a Stanford person" and "if it's Van Etten, Stanford'll take us over" and to maintain balance at the top — Isaac Stein, from Stanford, was chair — the CEO had to be a San

Francisco person. UCSF insisted, it was said, that Kerr, its hospital director, must be chosen, and failing this UCSF would withdraw. Hence, an independent search for the best recruitable candidate for CEO wasn't really possible.

Accordingly, on Thursday, February 13, 1997, the board of UCSF Stanford Health Care named William Kerr chief executive officer of the new corporation, effective March 1.[123] The next day, however, Kerr informed the board that he preferred not to take the job, that he didn't like what he would have to do as CEO[41] and was better suited to the position of chief operating officer.[124] The board then met again and appointed Peter Van Etten as the first chief executive officer.[125] At this point, further searching simply wasn't practical, a Stanford participant observed.

"I was skiing in Utah," Van Etten remembers. "I phoned to check in — I think it was Valentine's Day — and was told to call Stein immediately. 'You won't believe what's happened,' he said and told me about Bill's decision. 'Will you do it?' I said yes,"[22,126] and Peter Van Etten became the first president and CEO of UCSF Stanford Health Care.[125]*

Kerr's withdrawal and the appointment of Van Etten just as UCSF Stanford Health Care was about to be launched were not received calmly at UCSF. "A huge letdown," remembers Charlie Wilson.[41] "People were blown away by it," says Jonathan Showstack.[29]

At UCSF, Van Etten was seen as responsible for setting up Stanford Health Services, which combined the hospital with the practice plan. Another Stanford loyalist, Isaac Stein, was chair of its board.

---

*Raised in New Hampshire — "in a big white house with a barn" as he told a reporter[126] — a music and international relations major at Columbia University — Peter Van Etten started his career as a branch manager and loan officer at a Boston bank. After graduating from the Harvard Business School in 1973, he returned to banking in Boston but thought better of it. "I suppose it was a question of values, ultimately. I wanted to work in the nonprofit sector."[126] Van Etten then began a series of jobs at teaching hospitals, first as chief financial officer of Boston University's hospital (1976–80) and then as chief financial officer and executive vice president at the New England Medical Center, Tuft University's leading teaching hospital (1981–89). This experience led to the positions of CEO at the University Hospital and deputy chancellor for management and finance at the University of Massachusetts Medical Center in Worcester. In 1991, Van Etten joined Stanford University as its chief financial officer with the primary task of helping to resolve the university's dispute with the federal government over the use of overheads. Three years later, he returned to health care as president and CEO of Stanford Health Services, the corporation that manages both the Stanford University Hospital and the faculty's practice plan. This was Van Etten's second chance to lead Stanford's hospital. Donald Kennedy had considered him for the position in 1989, when he chose Kenneth Bloem as president and CEO. This introduction to Van Etten led to Kennedy's appointing him the university chief financial officer one year before Kennedy stepped down as president.[32]

"The practice plan's business manager reported to the hospital, not the dean, and Stanford Health Services was failing," Neal Cohen, the UCSF vice chair of anesthesia, remembers. UCSF faculty were very concerned about the Stanford Health Services model.[24]

Although Van Etten's first action was to appoint Kerr chief operating officer and number two in the administration of the merged hospitals, "the UCSF faculty was quite distressed by Bill Kerr's not taking the top job," Jaclyne Boyden, the dean's senior administrator, remembers.[53] "Haile [Debas, the UCSF dean] called each chair and explained why Bill wasn't taking the job and why we'd be OK."[53] Boyden continues, "There was an emergency meeting with Bill, the chairs, Haile, and me. Bill explained why 'I don't want to do that job.' Haile got the senior faculty behind him continuing the merger. They felt he would look out for them, make the right decisions, and keep the academic mission paramount. 'If there's a problem,' he said, 'I'll fix it.'"[53]

UCSF radiology chair, Ronald Arenson, who particularly admires Kerr, thinks he made the right decision in turning down the CEO job, that it wasn't right for him. "Bill didn't like the PR stuff like going to the regents. He had great comfort just running the hospital."

An independent observer also concluded that the recent events were fortunate. "Kerr couldn't do it without Van Etten," and Van Etten was unlikely to stay "in a lesser role because he has been courted by other institutions," according to "sources at Stanford" interviewed by a reporter for the *San Francisco Chronicle*.[124] Both Van Etten and Kerr were elected members of the UCSF Stanford board, bringing the total number of trustees to 17.

As expected, regent Frank Clark was not pleased. "The chair [Stein] and the lead executive officer [Van Etten] will now be from Stanford, and that's a problem. I'm not at all comfortable that the whole deal is going to get through."[124]

UCSF's Dean Haile Debas

The man who calmed the faculty when Kerr said no to becoming UCSF Stanford's first chief executive is widely hailed as an excellent leader at UCSF. Among the comments his colleagues make about Haile Debas, all agree that "First and foremost, he's a gentleman, and he knows right from wrong."

Others observe, "You just want to do things for him. Anything he does would seem to be in your own best interest, though this can't always be true."

Debas, all agree, has excellent interpersonal skills. "He's a joy to watch," an admirer comments, "So much of it is natural. He may not be the best public speaker, but you feel the humanity in him."

Jaclyne Boyden, his senior administrator, says, "As a dean-administrator, he can make the tough decisions, can tell people no and not obsess about it afterwards. He's a very good negotiator, never boxes himself in.[53]

"When making tough personnel decisions," Boyden, who has watched this process, says, "he tries to allow the person to maintain his or her integrity and prevent embarrassment." She finds some of those so affected "relieved. Although these are tough decisions, none would say he was unkind or didn't give them a soft landing."

The creation and management of the merger has taken much time from the dean's schedule, already fully booked. Boyden estimates that Debas "must spend at least 20 percent of his time when in San Francisco" on the issue.[53] During its creation, "several of us spent one full day per week on it," she recalls.[53]

"The merger has worn him down," believes Dr. Ronald D. Miller, the longtime chair of anesthesiology at UCSF. "Some people have suggested that he's lost his dedication to UCSF, that he's not as much on the job. No one doubts his integrity or intelligence. Haile enjoys enormous respect, but I believe that his family is right in telling him he needs a break."[127] After several postponements, he finally scheduled a sabbatical leave during the summer and fall of 1999, when, as we shall see, the future of the merger became problematical.*

Debas has given much thought to the reasons that impelled him and his colleagues to create UCSF Stanford Health Care and asks why the economics of teaching hospitals is so particularly difficult in California and specifically in the San Francisco Bay region. Debas finds the

---

*Haile T. Debas was born in 1937 in Asmara, Eritrea. After college in Addis Ababa, he studied for his medical degree at McGill University in Montreal and trained as a general surgeon and investigator at Ottawa Civic Hospital, the University of British Columbia in Vancouver, the Western Infirmary of the University of Glasgow in Scotland, and the University of California-Los Angeles. His plan to return to practice in Eritrea was prevented by the civil war with Ethiopia, and he spent a year in private practice in the Yukon Territories and British Columbia. In 1970, he returned to the University of British Columbia as a member of the faculty until taking faculty positions at UCLA in 1980 and the University of Washington five years later. In 1987, UCSF recruited him as chair of the Department of Surgery, the first African or African American to be appointed to such a position at an American medical school not traditionally designed for the training of African Americans physicians. Six years later, he was chosen dean. During 1997–98, following the departure of Joseph Martin, Debas served as the UCSF chancellor while the UCSF-Stanford merger was created.

purchasing pools, organizations of the "biggest banks and industrial companies — all the big mucky mucks — with over 3 million employees," important factors in the local problem.[19] "The business groups are very organized. We get paid less to care for a capitated patient who is a Bank of America employee than a Medi-Cal [Medicaid in California] patient."[19] In 1995, he remembers, "the pools asked for a 15 percent reduction in the premiums they paid for health care. The insurance companies accepted this and passed it on to the hospitals and doctors. Some doctors being recruited at Davis [near Sacramento, another of the University of California medical centers] saw six wonderful houses, all vacated by cardiologists leaving for the Midwest."[19]

Will the large employers providing insurance for health care continue to control the market? "The next thing that may happen is that the companies will say [to their employees], 'Here's some money, you get your own insurance,'" Debas predicts. "There'll be a big public outcry and then major reform. If this happens in the next two years in California, you'll see a single-payer system in this state, the first step in a major revolution in health care."[19]

More Troubles

One might think that the activation of USCF Stanford Health Care, planned for July 1, 1997, could then proceed as planned by its board and executives. This was not to be the case. In March, state senator John Burton raised the question of public knowledge. At a meeting of the state Senate Judiciary Committee, which he chairs, Burton criticized the merger because, although half the assets of the corporation would come from UCSF, a public entity, the corporation would be a private, not-for-profit entity.[128] Burton then introduced a bill requiring that hospital corporations that had state assets transferred to them be subject to the California Public Records Act, in effect forcing UCSF Stanford to act as a public corporation, a status unacceptable to Stanford.[129] "The only way the organization can succeed is if its business plans aren't open to its competitors," a Stanford administrator said.

"You can't tell everyone what you're going to do and expect to compete against them,"[128] Casper added. "We would not be able to survive in the marketplace" as a public hospital.[130]

San Francisco assemblywoman Carole Migden introduced a second bill, which would require that the new entity be subject to oversight by the legislature. Migden's bill produced another "line in the sand," according to Casper, who declared, "We'll accept some review but not full exposure."[2]

Despite Casper's threats to pull Stanford out if some compromise couldn't be reached and Van Etten's assertion that UCSF Stanford Health Care was exempt from disclosure laws,[131] by May 22 both bills had passed through one of the chambers, Migden's in the Assembly and Burton's in the Senate.[132] To stave off final passage of either of these two bills or any other similar one, Casper, Atkinson, and Van Etten proposed that UCSF Stanford should "be required to hold periodic meetings to consider issues of greatest concern to the public."[133]

All this political activity postponed the planned start of the merger. What the *Palo Alto Weekly* had described as "an overload of administrative work"[130] had already led Peter Van Etten to state that the activation date would be advanced from July 1 to September 1. On July 10, the regents announced that they would postpone for two months a final vote on merging UCSF.[134]

By August 26, UCSF Stanford had agreed that the meetings and records of the new hospital would be made public "except for collective bargaining or other contract negotiations, sale of property worth less than $5 million, pending lawsuits and the terms of health care contracts."[135]

This satisfied Senator Burton, who claimed, "The public's right to know basically prevailed."[135] The compromise assisted the progress toward passage into law of a bill agreeable to Burton and the hospital.[136]

Just how far the agreement would keep the plans of UCSF Stanford confidential when required was left to be determined. "The reality of so-called 'Sunshine Laws,'" the *Chronicle* editorialized, "is that they are not terribly stifling since few reporters or citizen gadflies have the time or temperament to sit through long meetings or pore through file drawers full of documents."[137] The interest of the politicians and the press in the hospital's coming turmoil, however, suggested that not much of importance would be shielded from public view.

But this wasn't the end of it. Both houses had approved Carole Migden's bill allowing the Legislature to review the state's assets in UCSF, which would be transferred to UCSF Stanford under the merger plan. Governor Pete Wilson, saying that the bill "goes beyond what is prudent in protecting the public interest," vetoed it on September 2.[138]*

Casper, among others, was greatly relieved. "We got through in a form we could live with, a measure of how much we wanted to make it work."[2]

---

*Wilson is a Republican, and each of the leading proponents for public review of UCSF Stanford was a Democrat.

Bolstered by a report from the California state auditor that UCSF Stanford should "make the partners fiscally stronger,"[139] the regents of the University of California, on Friday, September 19, 1997, approved the merger of the hospitals of the University of California-San Francisco with Stanford Health Services.[140] Four of the regents, including Lieutenant Governor Gray Davis and Los Angeles attorney Frank Clark, voted against the merger. Davis, then competing for the Democratic nomination for governor, had voted in favor of the merger previously. Now he was no longer convinced that the arrangement would provide the economic benefits originally projected.[140] The Stanford University board of trustees gave its approval three days later.[141]

Suits brought by unions and civic organizations failed to block the merger,[142] and the state Fair Political Practices Commission ruled that the new hospital corporation would not be subject to the conflict of interest laws that apply to elected officials and officials of public agencies.[143] On November 1, 1997, the UCSF and Mt. Zion Medical Centers in San Francisco and the Stanford University and Lucile Packard Children's Hospitals in Palo Alto would officially begin operating together as UCSF Stanford Health Care.*[141]

---

*The Langley Porter Psychiatric Institute and Clinics, however, remained part of UCSF.

CHAPTER 7

Development

Before the merged corporation was officially established on November 1, 1997, UCSF Stanford Health Care had acquired headquarters of its own but not at either UCSF or Stanford. "There had to be firewall between UCSF and the UCSF Stanford, which mustn't be viewed as a shadow of the University of California," says Bruce Wintroub, the recently appointed chief medical officer for UCSF Stanford Health Care.[1] Furthermore, "siting the central core at either university would have been unacceptable to the other," says Robert Wachter of UCSF, "despite the schlep factor of traveling."[2]

Executive Park

Van Etten and his colleagues had chosen Executive Park in the 3Com Center[3]* and located the executive offices and several of the business functions there.[4] Executive Park is 10 miles from the Parnassus buildings. The trip takes 15 to 20 minutes when the traffic is reasonable. Stanford is 25 miles or about 35 to 40 minutes away.

Based at Executive Park are the general counsel, the contracting officer, the marketing director, the director of materials management, the chief information officer, and the offices of auditing, compliance, and the chief financial officer with his divisions of budgeting, accounting, and accounts payable. Most of the billing functions remained at the hospital sites. Human resources, though integrated, is for the most part conducted at the hospitals. The university continues to handle personnel issues for those San Francisco employees who remain on the UCSF payroll. A former Stanford employee directs human resources, and a former UCSF executive is head of strategic contracting. New employees,

---

*The center is located next to 3Com Park, formerly Candlestick Park or "the Stick," where the San Francisco 49ers football team plays and the San Francisco Giants baseball team used to play until it moved to the new Pacific Bell Park downtown in 2000. Candlestick Point, where the stadium is located, is said to have been named for a bird that used to populate the region.[3]

not from either site, direct finance and information systems. Throughout 1998, William Kerr, the chief operating officer of UCSF Stanford Health Care, supervised operations for each of the hospitals — UCSF, Stanford, Lucile Packard Children's, and Mount Zion — through chief operating officers at each site.

Despite the reasons for creating Executive Park, the corporate headquarters aroused much criticism. Jonathan Showstack, the UCSF sociologist who studied the process leading up to the merger in his dissertation,[5] sees it as adding "a huge increase in administrative costs and people."[6] He finds the 3Com facility "awful. It's not close to where anyone lives and is a physically unpleasant place with poorly designed space."[6]

"You can't run an institution like ours from Executive Park," says UCSF neurosurgeon Charles Wilson. "There's a huge geographical problem. People there get out of touch, less interested in the day-to-day problems. You get easily isolated and not smell the smoke."[7]

In addition to the problems of working at 3-Com, the distance between UCSF and Stanford proved to be a major distraction. "The 40 miles between the two campuses really makes a difference for doctors and patients," finds Lee Goldman, the Department of Medicine chair at UCSF. Although some arrange to do it, "It's barely manageable for most doctors to work at both campuses on the same day."[8,9]* The former Harvard professor believes that the distance interferes more with uniting faculty of the two schools than does the lesser geographical separation between the principal components of Partners or New York-Presbyterian Hospital.[8]

The separation, however, did have at least one political advantage. "The faculty realized that the 40 miles made it virtually impossible for most of the departments to integrate despite the talk about putting together high-end services," says Dr. Robert Wachter, associate chair of the Department of Medicine. Realizing the unlikelihood of merging clinical units, many UCSF faculty members felt less inclined to oppose the merger "because it would not hurt their fiefdoms or autonomy."[2]

Chief Medical Officers

One of the first administrative steps taken by UCSF Stanford Health Care was the creation of a chief medical officer for the merged entity

---

*"I got caught by a Giants baseball team playoff once," remembers Carlos Esquivel, the Stanford transplantation surgeon. "I just gave up and went back home. We tried telemeetings, wasn't the same. Once at a televised board meeting the TV went dead."[9]

to assure the highest quality for all clinical activity conducted in each of the hospitals.[10] The selection of Van Etten from Stanford as CEO made essential that the CMO appointment came from UCSF—the "Noah's Ark, two-by-two" policy—and Bruce Wintroub from UCSF was chosen.[2]*

"The original concept was to have one CEO and CMO," Wintroub explains. "My job was to herd both faculties into one medical group, although the one-CMO notion was poorly defined and there was no history of such an organization to draw upon. I was to be an associate dean at each school but not the associate dean for clinical affairs. So my dean's titles didn't have much function."[1]

The faculty at UCSF, where he was known, accepted Wintroub's new role. But at Stanford "it didn't work. My friend Gene Bauer[†] backed up my accountability, but I was always 'the UCSF guy' to the Stanford faculty. They would never fully trust me. Besides, I didn't have the power of the purse. It was a terrible job."[1]

Before the roof fell in on him, Wintroub did manage to establish a combined medical group led by a physician's board of about 20 doctors who met weekly. "It was designed to be an M.D.-run organization, but it never functioned well."[1] The group served principally to receive information disseminated by UCSF Stanford leaders, deliberated little, and had minimal authority. Eventually, attendance decreased. "We might as well have used e-mail," one of the members said. "It just faded away."[11]

The hospital also had a traditional Medical Board, and some of the functions of the two groups overlapped. A fatal mistake, Wintroub feels, was "never viewing the $300 million [the combined revenue of all the full-time doctors at both schools] as a separate core business" to be developed and improved. The members of the group "were more concerned with running the hospitals than practicing medicine and paying adequate attention to the practice plan," Wintroub believes.[1]

---

*Wintroub, like many UCSF faculty, had trained at the most competitive places— B.A. from Amherst College, M.D. at Washington University in St. Louis, medical internship and residency at the Brigham, and dermatology training and a junior faculty position in the Harvard system. In 1982, he was recruited to UCSF and became the chair of the Department of Dermatology four years later. Wintroub had been the university's point man as associate dean for the Mount Zion Hospital connection when UCSF acquired the community hospital in 1990. Through this work, he developed an interest in helping UCSF respond to the changes in health care.[1] As UCSF executive vice dean and one of the senior faculty members helping to develop the merger, he became the first, and so far the only, chief medical officer for the merged hospitals.

†Eugene Bauer, the Stanford dean, is also a dermatologist and had chaired the department at Stanford when Wintroub chaired the department at UCSF.

It became clear that Stanford and UCSF needed individual chief medical officers, if for no other reason than "each dean wanted his own CMO," Wintroub saw.[1] "But my job really blew up over financing the losses," which suddenly appeared in the winter of 1999. With dollars short, "a third person as overall CMO didn't make sense,"[1] and the position, in which he had served from November 1997, was discontinued in April 1999.

Wintroub, who sees himself as more of "a strategy than an operating guy," came to accept the change as best for him. After the early pain passed, "I went on leave and my golf game improved significantly." In January 2000, he returned to the chair of dermatology, which had not been filled while he was chief medical officer, and to a job in the dean's office.

The conflict over Wintroub's position pained Dean Haile Debas. "Haile doesn't like having a faculty member unhappy," which Wintroub knows from having observed him closely as a chair and then in the run-up to the merger.[1] The episode taught Wintroub one vital lesson for his future career: "I'll never be a dean or hospital CEO. No point having another job with such a limited upside and large downside."[1]

"Bruce took the fall for this one," Dr. Theodore Schrock observes. "He favored the integration and service line concept and then took the blame for the failure."[12] Schrock, the former chair of surgery at UCSF, became CMO for the San Francisco hospitals after Wintroub's job collapsed. "The job [of unified chief medical officer] was ill defined and not doable," Schrock believes.[12]

Schrock describes his current job as "the UCSF physicians' advocate in the management team of the merged hospitals. I run committees to standardize materials for efficiency and try to free up ICU [intensive care unit] beds clogged with patients who don't need to be there."[12] He reports to Peter Van Etten, CEO of UCSF Stanford Health Care but also carries a title in the dean's office "so that I can interact with the faculty in the school better." An administrative realist, Schrock understands that "this CMO job is high risk" and adds that, if he fails in it, "I may have to go back to taking care of patients."[12] Even with his current responsibilities, he operates one and a half days per week.

In Palo Alto, Dr. Peter Gregory, a member of the Department of Medicine at Stanford for almost 30 years, was directing the practice plan when he was appointed the first chief medical officer of Stanford Health Services, the entity established in September 1994 that combined the Stanford University Hospital, the Stanford outpatient clinics, and the school's practice plan. In this role, Gregory participated in much of the planning for the merger. When the UCSF candidate,

Bruce Wintroub, was chosen to be the single chief medical officer for UCSF Stanford, Gregory moved temporarily back into the dean's office, where he had worked previously.

Gregory comments about the problems that often accompany an academic physician who works in the hospital's executive office. "I became isolated from the chairs and the faculty and was perceived as 'just another suit,'" he says. "Even after I was no longer the CMO, I think some of the faculty saw me as soiled by working for the hospital."[13]

When the CMO position returned to the sites, however, Gregory accepted reappointment for Stanford along with Schrock at San Francisco. Gregory works with the executives at 3Com and with Malinda Mitchell, the Stanford chief operating officer, and links them to the Stanford clinical chiefs. As for Wintroub's old position as CMO for all of UCSF Stanford, Gregory agrees with Schrock and calls the job "Impossible. A CMO from outside has to have trouble. He doesn't know the docs. The way the job was constructed, the chiefs were supposed to go to the CMO. That's not the way it works. They went to the CEO."[13]

Furthermore, says Ernest Ring, an interventional radiologist who is associate dean for the Mount Zion-UCSF Medical Center, "UCSF Stanford never used the power that a CMO should have." In Ring's department, the faculty went home when their work was completed at the end of the day, and the residents covered after 5 P.M. The chair had tried unsuccessfully to convince at least one faculty member to remain in the hospital till 11 P.M. "A strong CMO should have made this happen," says Ring. "We're talking about a clinical enterprise having to compete in a different way [than has been traditional in academic medicine]. The people we have trained stay here because this is a great place to live and compete right against us because northern California is a small place."[10]

At Lucile Packard Children's Hospital, Dr. Kenneth Cox, chief of the Division of Pediatric Gastroenterology, is the chief medical officer. With Wintroub gone, Cox now reports directly to the hospital CEO for his hospital work. Not an associate dean in the medical school like Gregory, Cox reports to Bauer through his chair. He's losing interest in the job. "I attend 35 committees, if you can believe it," he says. "I'm getting burned out."[14]

Computers and Information Systems

Information technology, the application of computers to the management of the hospitals, presented major difficulties to UCSF Stanford. Although the systems at both Stanford and UCSF had shortcomings, the

UCSF computer program was woefully inadequate. "The data center at UCSF was a mess, cables hanging from the ceiling and lying on the floor," G. Brian May discovered when Van Etten recruited him in the spring of 1997 as senior vice president for information technology at UCSF Stanford. "The setup was so old, and no one was coordinating it. UCSF didn't have a chief information officer, just a consultant."[15]

"We took pride in having computers 10 years old," says Dr. Ronald Arenson, the chair of radiology at UCSF, whose particular academic interest is the application of computers to medical care. "Stanford prided itself in having up-to-date information systems."[16]

Why was the UCSF system so undernourished? California had suffered a severe recession during the early 1990s when computer updating at UCSF might have been carried out, and funds from the state for such projects were scarce.[17] The organization of UCSF, May believes, also accounted for part of the problem. Information systems falls under the purview of a campus vice chancellor, and the hospital purchases the services from that office. "The hospital did not develop what its needs were, and medical schools and hospitals don't always have the same ideas about what the needs are."[15]

Furthermore, William Kerr, the UCSF CEO at the time, had great difficulty competing with the Silicon Valley firms for good computer people to work at the hospital. "No one on the campus, or in the school, or I, for that matter, was expert in it, and we didn't have the capital to invest in a first-class operation," says Kerr."[18] So the people who were there tinkered with the systems to make them at least adequate, but when the time came to integrate with Stanford the UCSF system was incompatible and no longer standard thanks to the changes the technicians had made.[15]

May learned that the state bureaucracy limited whom you could hire as chief information officer and how much you could pay, unlike at Stanford. The previous chief information officer at the UCSF Medical Center, May discovered, "was a 'go-along, get-along' guy under no pressure to keep the system current." May also saw the state financing system as contributing to the dysfunctional operation of the campus's computers. "If you get some dollars, you spend them," rather than striking out with a plan for a system and then obtaining the support for it, and it wasn't only because UCSF was owned by the state of California. "Other state hospitals have made appropriate investments in information systems," May knows from his own experience.[15] The future without a major investment seemed bleak. The UCSF computer problems "would have come home to roost," May believes. "They would have tried to do it on the cheap, and that couldn't be done."[15]

"The campus's information systems should have been redone 10 years ago," says Jonathan Showstack, the UCSF sociologist. "Being so far behind created terrible problems. For example, UCSF's information system is balkanized. Patients don't have a uniform identification number" for their visits to the outpatient clinics or when they are hospitalized. "UCSF paid $20 million and enormous staff time to bring in a system for billing and uniform patient tracking, which had to be totally scrapped when a Y2K problem in billing surfaced." UCSF Stanford then "had to devote money and time to putting in a new billing system." To complicate matters further, Showstack discovered, "If you try to put in one comprehensive computer system in an academic health center, you get something which satisfies no one."[6]

When the necessity to support UCSF information technology became clear early during the merger, the flow of money to this project led some at Stanford to tell Brian May, "All we hear is that 'sucking sound' from the north."[15] But Stanford, which May discovered had survived with an acting director of information technology for years, was not perfect in computer technology either. "Stanford had a hodgepodge system, though still light years ahead of UCSF. To some degree, they were willing to spend money and spread the envelope, but we still had to replace the e-mail system there because there were multiple separate systems." Without the investment UCSF Stanford is making in information technology, about two-thirds of which is going to UCSF, May predicts that by January 1, 2000, neither Stanford nor UCSF "would have been able to care for patients or send them bills."[15]

As for the role of physicians in hospital computer technology, May believes, "You need physicians to help in planning your computer programs. They should be real, practicing docs who want computers to help with their work but have not become primary computer people. 'Medical informatics docs' stop practicing and lose their credibility." Moreover, warns May, "avoid the 'propeller heads,' the hackers, and tinkers. Don't let them plan your computer strategy."[15]

May considers adequate computer programs so important today that he lists an information technology conversion that didn't go well as one of the reasons hospital administrators lose their jobs.[15]

Practice Plans

When the teaching hospitals of UCSF and Stanford merged, the practice plans of both schools of medicine became part of UCSF Stanford Health Care. Stanford's plan had been transferred from its medical school to the newly formed Stanford Health Services in 1994, and the UCSF plan along with all medical group activity joined the merger when UCSF Stanford began operations on November 1, 1997. This was not foreign territory for the UCSF leaders either since their practice plan and the UCSF Medical Center would have formed a physicians-hospital organization if the merger had not intervened.[19]

When the hospital had been part of UCSF, the state had paid the physicians' malpractice insurance from a separate account, an advantage many a dean and chair at other schools would have envied. After the merger, UCSF Stanford agreed to share this new expense for which the state no longer assumed responsibility.[12]

With the merger in place, the two schools formed a joint contracting committee from both sites. Peter Gregory led the Stanford delegation, as did Dr. Russell Laros for UCSF. The executive who had coordinated managed care contracting for UCSF now took on the job for UCSF and Stanford. Collections flowed into UCSF Stanford and then to the two deans, who distributed the proceeds to the departments.[19]

After the merger, direction of the combined practice plans was theoretically assigned to an 18-member committee, nine from each school. In fact, a leadership group of the most senior officers from each school and the hospital made the important decisions regarding dollars. The leadership group began their work by trying to settle disputes by consensus to assure that each campus would be treated fairly. "You get one, we get one," is how Peter Gregory from Stanford describes the process.[13] Equality was the basic theme of so much at UCSF Stanford that when differences between the sites appeared, as they inevitably did, the group had great difficulty developing satisfactory methods of distributing the proceeds, allocating the strategic support, and dealing with losses.[13]

The agreement establishing the merger required that by September 1, 1999, the faculty from the two schools, through their practice plans, must agree to share the risks of contracting for managed care in order to avoid antitrust complications. They would have to develop a method of deciding how to divide the profits or losses. The faculties would not meet this deadline, putting future contracting at risk.

Marketing for Managed Care Business

"Eighty percent of the reason for the merger was to deal with the market and 20 percent to save money," says Lawrence Furnstahl, UCSF Stanford's chief financial officer.[20]

Patricia E. "Patty" Perry, senior vice president for strategic development, agrees. "The single market position has been the most important factor in the merger. We've increased our return and prevented further reductions in what we're paid.[21] Here at UCSF Stanford, we contract on behalf of all four hospitals. Eighty-five percent of our business is with HMOs. There's virtually no indemnity insurance left here."[21] Perry's office was managing 400 contracts with HMOs on behalf of UCSF Stanford in the summer of 1999. "The industry is still very dispersed here. Blue Cross, the biggest, has only 10 percent of the business," she says.[21]*

The Merger's Effect on Administration in the UCSF School of Medicine

"How has the merger affected my operation?" asks Jaclyne Boyden, vice dean for administration and finance at UCSF.[22] "For starters, the professional fees now come directly to the dean rather than through the UCSF hospital," as was previously the case, adding work for the dean's office, which must now track this activity.[22] Previously, Boyden was only responsible for watching the money flow from UCSF to the departments.[19] Now she and her staff must administer the faculty's collections. "The departments don't like it because the data are less satisfactory."

"I have had to set up a leased employee office," says Boyden, since the school must now provide an administrative home for 1,000 of the 5,000 hospital employees who have remained on the university payroll.[22]

"The relationship with the hospital is different now," Boyden reports. Formerly, "we got along extremely well with Bill [Kerr, the CEO], Bruce [Schroffel, the operations director], and their financial people. There was trust and respect both ways." If Boyden needed something, "I just called them up."[22] Recruitments were collaborative. Faculty and administrators from both school and hospital served on search committees for either entity.[22]

"There was tremendous pride in the institution," Boyden remembers, "because of the excellence of the place and the wonderful long-term relationship between the basic scientists and the clinicians. Space was so tight that it was tough to have fiefdoms."[22] Since the merger, "this has changed," she says. "Initially, flexibility was taken away. Bruce

---

*Before switching to UCSF Stanford, Perry had worked at UCSF for 17 years, most recently in charge of planning and marketing in addition to directing the managed care operation. Previously, she had had responsibility for UCSF's operating budget and government reimbursement programs. After receiving her bachelor's degree from Yale, she had worked for the Harvard Medical School and several agencies of the federal government before moving to San Francisco.

[Schroffel, who succeeded William Kerr as the top administrator at the UCSF hospitals] didn't have the war chest Bill had." Department leaders, as well as Boyden and her colleagues in the dean's office, felt that "the new corporate people were very bottom-line related and didn't have a feel for the school. We were losing the mutual respect that we had before. When we need space for a program, they'd reply, 'It won't help my bottom line.' Previously, the hospital people would say, 'Let's try it if it helps our academic mission.'"[22]

Boyden also finds the people in the new corporation less forthcoming about information, often saying, "You don't need to know about that." Boyden adds that whether or not these impressions are real or only perceived doesn't matter "because it has the same effect."[22]

The change affected the personnel in Boyden's department. One of the departmental business managers left "because of having to deal with the new medical center." As a replacement, she told Boyden, "You need to hire someone who doesn't know how it used to be because it's breaking my heart."[22]

Academic Affiliations and Service Lines

As at New York-Presbyterian Hospital, the leaders of the UCSF Stanford merger saw several advantages in coordinating clinical programs and constructing service lines. In addition to allowing more effective marketing, service lines, as described by Peter Van Etten, would "establish multi-institutional programs, integrate professional and institutional activities, and achieve integration across sites."[4]

"Let clinical functionality rather than departmental structure be the organizing units," the advocates of service lines insisted.[23] Such thinking implied that some of the services would be centered at UCSF, others at Stanford. Besides the inherent institutional forces obstructing such developments, would the patients cooperate? "Just like San Franciscans don't want to leave the city for their medical care, why should most Palo Altons desert Silicon Valley for San Francisco?" Lee Goldman wondered.[8]

Pediatrics

The work of the Departments of Pediatrics at UCSF and Stanford has shown the greatest promise of benefiting from the merger. Before the merger, the Lucile Packard Children's Hospital at Stanford "was starting to raid UCSF," remembers Neal Cohen, vice chair of anesthesia and former chief of staff at UCSF. "This was not a good thing. They would have to either compete more aggressively or stop competing and fight managed care together."[24]

Financially, children's hospitals and services suffer because so much of the care, in many cities, is given to children without many economic resources. Yet the hospitals need expensive information technology, equipment, and trained personnel.[25] Except for those working in a few services like neonatal intensive care, most pediatricians have difficulty generating generous incomes from their practices. "To generate $150,000 to support a doctor's salary," says Kenneth Cox, "we must bill at least $1,000,000." For each dollar billed, his unit collects an average of only 33 cents, the collection rate reduced by Medi-Cal, in particular, which pays 19 cents on each dollar charged. "You can't survive on this," Cox adds. Further reducing what is available for salary are the various internal tax, overhead, and benefit costs charged against the collections.[14] Since most of his colleagues, including himself, must spend much of their time seeing patients, few are in the tenure track, membership in which at Stanford requires significant research productivity. Even Cox, a full professor, division head, and recognized expert on the tumors that the drugs required to prevent rejection of transplanted livers in children can produce, does not have Stanford tenure.

Stanford's difficulty in recruiting pediatric specialists reflects the reality that the number of such faculty in most departments of pediatrics is relatively small and depth or "critical mass" in many of the subspecialties is difficult to achieve. This prevents chairmen from developing enough strength to provide specialized care and perform research for each of the many, but often uncommon, illnesses that can afflict children. "Together with UCSF, we could get there," says Dr. Harvey Cohen, chair of the department at Stanford.[26] Accordingly, the leaders of pediatrics at the two schools went about forming one of the few successful academic affiliations at UCSF Stanford.

Cohen and Dr. Larry Shapiro, his counterpart at UCSF, saw several areas in which they could collaborate. "Early in the merger discussions, Larry, the pediatric surgeons, the CEOs, and I looked at our strengths and weaknesses. We had a good program in eating disorders, UCSF in access to health care. In rheumatology, we had recruited a superb clinician. UCSF had very good science. Each of us had small programs in pediatric cardiac electrophysiology and only one electrophysiologist at each place."*[26]

---

*Electrophysiologists are cardiologists who diagnose and treat arrhythmias, disturbances of the heart's rhythm, with drugs, pacemakers, and defibrillators. Few pediatricians specialize in this work.

Cohen and Shapiro applied successfully for a grant to support a "center of excellence" in pediatric rheumatology at both schools. Either school alone might not have won the award. Pooling resources and the potential at the two locations, the chairmen successfully recruited Dr. George Van Hare, a leading pediatric electrophysiologist from Case-Western Reserve University in Cleveland, who probably wouldn't have moved if Stanford or UCSF alone went after him. Van Hare chose to be based at Stanford but also works in San Francisco. Now the two institutions have three arrhythmia specialists between them. Van Hare and his wife, a pediatrics infectious diseases specialist at UCSF, live in San Mateo, about halfway between the schools. The chairmen are now searching for a common chief of their pulmonary divisions.[27]

Cohen and Shapiro have combined some of their training programs.[27] The two institutions offer single fellowships in academic general pediatrics, genetics, and pediatric gastroenterology. "It's filled for the next four years," crows Ken Cox about the success of his division in recruiting pediatric gastrointestinal (GI) fellows.[14]

Why has academic collaboration at UCSF and Stanford flourished in pediatrics while floundering in other departments? Cohen thinks there are several explanations, starting with his observation that "pediatricians are intrinsically less competitive and more collaborative." They need not, however, lack ambition.

Cohen hopes the combined enterprise will someday become the best pediatric program in the country. Cohen also cites Shapiro's and his style of leadership. "Larry and I saw collaboration as good, that it would help us provide better care for children, our primary goal."[26]

Children's services account for 30 to 35 percent of the admissions at both Stanford and UCSF. "By combining our work, we assure that care for children doesn't get marginalized at either location" says Cohen, who remembers that not that long ago pediatrics at Stanford was not a major player in the science-rich medical establishment there, nor did it provided much clinical strength to the hospital or the school.[26] The merger increases the likelihood that the pediatrics service at Stanford will remain busy, Cohen believes. "There're not enough children here to build a large program. Besides, you can only afford to live here if you have no children," he almost seriously observes. "Without the merger, we would have to compete again. When I was recruited here, I was told to beat UCSF. Each of us would have been bloodied. We'd be fighting for patients in Monterey" and other communities where each center would like to recruit patients.[26]

Shapiro adds, "Since we're the only places south of Seattle who do bone marrow transplants, the insurers played us off against each other, one year here, the next year, if the price was better, there."²⁷

But what will really make the collaboration in pediatrics between UCSF and Stanford work is the Packard money, "the golden carrot," as Larry Shapiro of UCSF calls the commitment of the Packard charities to children's health. In 1996, just before Stanford Health Services absorbed the Lucile Packard Children's Hospital, the newly established Lucile Packard Foundation for Children's Health received the reserves of about $65 million from the hospital.²⁸ The new foundation would support projects to improve the health of children in the region and not specifically in Palo Alto.

When the UCSF Hospitals merged with Stanford Health Services, all agreed that the pediatric services on both campuses would be named the Lucile Packard Children's Health Services, described, on the services' web site, as "two, strong complementary pediatrics programs, supported by two of the nation's top universities and leading medical schools. . . . It is the Foundation's vision to make the Bay Area the healthiest place in America for a child to be born, to live, and to grow."¹⁹ Stanford and UCSF Stanford also decided that the foundation would direct all fundraising for the Lucile Packard Children's Hospital and Stanford's pediatric programs.

The UCSF Stanford merger pleased the leaders of the Lucile Packard Foundation for Children's Health because an organization was now in place that would allow it to fund the development of a superb children's health program with the participation of the combined hospital and the two schools.* "The [Packard] family had been disappointed by their investment in Stanford," says Shapiro of UCSF. "Maybe their expectations were unrealistic in hoping to compete with Boston Children's or CHOP [Children's Hospital of Philadelphia, the pediatrics affiliate of the University of Pennsylvania]. They had been unable to recruit key surgical leaders in general pediatric surgery or neurosurgery. They really bought into the vision of the merged pediatric program and pledged a lot of money to it," says Shapiro,²⁷ but the support almost certainly wouldn't have materialized without the merger, Cohen firmly believes. Both chairmen fear that if the departments at UCSF and Stanford fail to pull together or if the merger breaks up the special funding may stop,²⁶,²⁷ and, Shapiro suspects, "The foundation will do no

---

*The pediatric services at UCSF and the Lucile Packard Children's Hospital at Stanford have as many beds together, about 300, as does each of the children's hospitals in Boston and Philadelphia.²⁷

more than just support the Stanford children's hospital at its historical level."[27]

Dermatology

"The merger's a natural thing for dermatology," says Dr. Alfred T. Lane, chair of the department at Stanford, "although we've had a long-standing relationship with UCSF which precedes the merger."[29] For years, the Stanford and the UCSF dermatology for faculty and community dermatologists had been gathering quarterly at San Francisco Dermatological Society meetings held at San Francisco and Stanford, where cases are discussed, guest lecturers give talks, and business subjects are reviewed. The two chairmen of dermatology, Wintroub at UCSF and, previously, Bauer at Stanford, had good relations and encouraged productive research interactions. The residencies at the two schools are still separate, but some of the trainees electively train for limited periods at the other hospital.

"We've seen some contracting by UCSF Stanford, which has helped us leverage prices," says Alfred Lane, but bringing the children's services closer together has been very beneficial. "We've integrated genetic diseases of children, and of course, the Packard Foundation money has put teeth into this work, so I think it's critical that the merger survive. It will help us work together."[29]

Pediatric Cardiac Surgery

Dr. Frank Hanley at UCSF dominates this specialized field. He personally operates on more than 500 children each year, similar to the number of patients treated by Dr. Jan Quaegebeur at Babies and Children's Hospital in New York, and Hanley's team treats about twice as many. The surgeons at Stanford, who handle about 100 cases per year, "were struggling and having less than ideal results," observes Dr. Theodore Schrock, the UCSF chief medical officer and a surgeon himself.[12] Consolidating the program in San Francisco seemed to be one of the most appropriate service line maneuvers once the merger was in place. However, says Schrock, "The leaders at Stanford and its children's hospital insisted that a congenital cardiac surgery program was essential at their institution. How else could Children's hold up its head as a contemporary pediatric hospital?"[12]

At UCSF, says Hanley, "We were doing many more cases than Stanford. I pushed the plan to do all the cases at UCSF all the way to the dean's office, but with two medical schools there's added complexity and academic issues came up. How could Stanford fulfill its teaching mission if they didn't do pediatric cardiac surgery? The hospital administrators didn't care, but the academics at Stanford didn't want to lose the patients."[30] Eventually, "from on high," as Hanley puts it, the decision came down that unless there was mutual agreement there would be no action.[30]

So, having to accept that Stanford would continue to have a pediatric cardiac surgery program, Hanley volunteered to guide the work there. He now operates one day per week at Packard, in addition to supervising the program and personally operating at the Oakland Children's Hospital across the bay and at Valley Children's Hospital in Fresno, also one day per week at each. Hanley juggles his schedule by living in Berkeley, which is adjacent to Oakland. "It takes 30 minutes to get to UCSF when I drive there," says Hanley,[30] whose day, like that of most surgeons, begins early. For the two and a half hour drive to Fresno, Hanley hires a driver and does paperwork or reads during the journey. Hanley puts up with the trip because Fresno, in California's Central Valley, is the fastest-growing region in the state and a potent source of patients.*

Hanley's operating at several hospitals does not particularly appeal to UCSF loyalists, who would rather see the cases sent to San Francisco and treated by Hanley and his team there.[12] Hanley doesn't disagree in theory. He would prefer to do all the surgery at UCSF or Stanford, but if he didn't help the other hospitals personally, he has told Theodore Schrock, they would hire their own surgeons and not send their cases to UCSF anyway.[12]

The merger, however, may not be the only impetus for Frank Hanley's peripatetic life. Larry Shapiro, chair of pediatrics at UCSF, sees Hanley's motives as "ego driven, not merger driven."[27] Hanley developed his arrangements with Oakland Children's and in Fresno before UCSF Stanford was formed. The arrangement at Stanford is new, however. Although Hanley is the nominal head of pediatric cardiac surgery at Stanford, most of the cases there are now handled by Dr. Michael D. Black, a recently recruited former trainee of Hanley. Bruce Reitz, chair of the Department of Cardiothoracic Surgery at Stanford, who recruited Black, sees Hanley's roll there as "window dressing, not functional."[31]

---

*Hanley is an example of the UCSF-trained doctor who went elsewhere — in his case Boston Children's and Harvard Medical School — but returned to the West Coast. "Haile called, and I came back to run the section of pediatric cardiac surgery in the Division of Cardiothoracic Surgery here at UCSF, even though I had some ambivalence because my career in Boston was quite promising," Hanley says.[30]

Hanley strongly favors the merger. Without it, he would never have been brought into the Stanford orbit, which he considers important to developing the comprehensive clinical and research program he envisions. "We have 1,200 cases per year at the four hospitals. Can you imagine the opportunity this gives us for clinical research to advance the field?" As for the politics, he adds, "Without the merger, UCSF and Stanford would never have gotten together in pediatric cardiac surgery, but despite the merger we can't consolidate the work at one place."[30]

Hanley also understands how collaboration between the two pediatric departments is essential to obtaining the continued support of the Packard Foundation. "The Packard people made it clear that unless the pediatrics merger works neither place will get the money for the Children's Health Initiative. The dollars are designed to create a permanent children's program."[30]

Adult Cardiology and Cardiac Surgery

Thanks to the pioneering work of Dr. Norman Shumway, "Stanford has long dominated heart and lung transplants in this region," admits Theodore Schrock, the former chair of surgery at UCSF.[12] "Bruce Reitz [Shumway's successor] wants to bring all of these patients to Stanford. UCSF thinks it must do heart transplants to be a great place and wants Reitz to help recruit us a team."[12]

Schrock admits that UCSF has "never been strong in adult cardiac surgery* for as long as anyone can remember." He explains, "CABGs [coronary artery bypass graft operations] in San Francisco are done at the community hospitals, particularly at California-Pacific," where Frank Gerbode, a pioneering cardiac surgeon, reigned supreme for decades. "The surgeons here blame the cardiologists for being too academic and not referring them cases. The cardiologists complain that UCSF has never had a real headliner in adult cardiac surgery."[12]

Frank Hanley, UCSF's pediatric cardiac surgery star, is also director of the adult program, although he only treats children. Previous efforts to import a leading adult cardiac surgeon had failed. When the most recent chief of cardiothoracic surgery, to whom Hanley reported, left, Haile Debas, who had not filled the chair of surgery for two years after vacating it to become dean, promoted Hanley to his current position. Why didn't the school recruit a top leader for this high-end specialty? Hanley suspects that the coming of the hospital merger and other

---

*UCSF treats about 250 cases per year, a relatively small number for a university hospital.

political events about which he is not privy deflected the leadership from UCSF's previous style of searching for the best and the brightest.

Shumway's, and now Reitz's, adult cardiac transplantation program at Stanford dominates the Bay Area. "We do five times as many transplants as UCSF," says Reitz, "so why not do all the operations here? With the merger, there should be a chance to do something, but UCSF decided to recruit another transplant surgeon."[31]

"If we can't rationalize transplants at Stanford, why have we merged?" asks Karen A. Rago, the service line administrator for cardiac programs on both campuses. "Dr. Ascher [Nancy Ascher, chair of surgery at UCSF] was heard to say that if the merger failed where's heart-lung transplantation at UCSF? It's a self-fulfilling prophecy."[32]

Kidney and Liver Transplantation

Haile Debas, the UCSF dean, wanted Dr. Nancy Ascher, the director of liver transplantation at UCSF and a leading surgeon in her field, to manage liver transplantation at Stanford as well as at UCSF as part of the service line concept. Stanford, where Dr. Carlos Esquivel directs the "below the diaphragm"[9]* transplant program, wouldn't agree.[1]

As Esquivel tells the story, "Nancy and I tried meeting every Tuesday. We made little progress on creating a service line with one service chief. Stanford didn't like having Nancy as the chief, and UCSF felt the same about me."[9] Someone suggested compromising by placing Ascher in charge of the adults and Esquivel in charge of the children. "But two-thirds of my patients are adults," says Esquivel. "Let's try two co-directors," Esquivel suggested. "Let time build trust in the two divisions. The administrators liked the idea but not Nancy."[9]†

Eliminating competition between UCSF and Stanford was one of the principal purposes of the merger. In transplantation, "It hasn't happened," acknowledges Esquivel. "Nancy and we continue to compete with each other. A service line in liver transplantation at UCSF Stanford never got off the ground."[9] No progress has been made, either, in merging the subspecialty training programs in transplantation of the departments at UCSF and Stanford.[9]

---

*Kidneys, livers, and pancreases are organs that lie "below the diaphragm." Hearts and lungs are above the diaphragm and the province of cardiothoracic surgeons.

†Lee Goldman, who chaired the joint committee working on service lines for UCSF Stanford, says that the support for Ascher's leading the program was unanimous among the UCSF members. The Stanford leadership, he remembers, said no to the project.[8]

Esquivel had founded the liver transplantation program at Presbyterian [now California-Pacific] in 1988, and "we ran neck and neck with UCSF," Esquivel says.[9] When California-Pacific suffered its own financial problems in the early 1990s, the CEO decided to close the pediatric programs.[14] Stanford came calling, and Esquivel—"my claim to fame was pediatric livers"—moved south in 1995 along with Kenneth Cox's pediatric gastroenterology group.[9,14] Esquivel's program at Stanford has done well. "We're one of the largest liver programs, number three or four nationally, and Medi-Cal pays very well for liver transplantations at Packard."[9]

At UCSF, "The liver transplantation program has been very successful here in keeping costs down and getting contracts partly because transplant is a 'carve-out'* area," Nancy Ascher explains. "Before the merger, we were successfully selling our high-end, carve-out products to the health plan people. The merger threatened to mess up the contracts since now everything is supposed to be set up as a combined program." However, she adds, "Since we've returned to operating with a site-specific bottom line [as a response to the financial losses in early 1999], we're not really a merger anyway."[33]

In the winter of 1999, the University of Pittsburgh offered Nancy Ascher the chair of surgery. Retaining Ascher at UCSF was important to Debas not only because of her surgical skills and the importance of the program she directed but also because "he felt vulnerable not having a woman chair at UCSF," Bruce Wintroub believes.[1] The chair of surgery then was Dr. Theodore Schrock, a renowned colo-rectal surgeon and UCSF veteran since entering medical school there in 1960.

"I suggested to Haile that I get out of the way. He didn't ask me to do it," Schrock explains,[12] and that's what happened. Ascher took over the department, and her husband, Dr. John P. Roberts, also a transplant surgeon, succeeded her as chief of transplantation at UCSF.[12] Schrock, who holds the Dunphy Professorship of Surgery, endowed for the founder of full-time surgery at UCSF, then took on the position of chief medical officer for UCSF.

The appointment of the chair of the Department of Surgery raises the question about whether UCSF still had the resources or the will to recruit the best people in the country to its senior as well as its junior

---

*"Carve-outs" are programs not covered by the more comprehensive managed care contracts because they are seldom performed and usually expensive. Consequently, hospitals that specialize in such high-end treatments as organ transplantation can negotiate for their support separately and usually obtain relatively attractive rates.

positions.* After becoming dean, Debas delayed for two years selecting his successor. A colleague suggests that with Debas's great love for clinical surgery he couldn't part with his former job. Schrock, however, describes the situation differently. "Haile wasn't sure he wanted to be dean; he loved leading the Department of Surgery." When Joseph Martin vacated the deanship to become chancellor, "Haile agreed to take the job for three years and asked me to be acting chair for the same period."[12] Then came the effort to merge with Stanford. Debas decided to keep the dean's job, and Schrock was appointed the permanent chair after a comprehensive, national search.

The basic scientists, one of UCSF's most powerful and successful constituencies, "played a important role in recruiting me to UCSF in 1987," Debas recalls.[36] Later, the basic sciences chairs had joined with the clinical chairs in making sure that Debas was appointed dean in 1993. "Each of them was a personal friend. Indeed, I have always found it as easy to deal with the basic science chairs as the clinical chairs."[36] However, he told one of his colleagues, "Compared with clinicians who are pretty straightforward, those basic scientists and their deals with biotech companies—that's quite a thing."

Medicine

Although no merging between the departments of medicine, the largest in the schools, has come about, the departments are suffering less than might be feared. At UCSF, research grant support during 1999 was 19 percent greater than the previous year and the size of the faculty continues to expand, Lee Goldman proudly reports.[8] The department's

---

*Ronald Miller, the chair of anesthesia, joins some who fear that UCSF may be losing its edge. "There's been some slippage in recruitments," he says. "We've got major problems, our resources are not great [not enough space for basic science laboratories being one of the most troublesome], and people are beginning to say [when recruiting for open positions] 'Let's stay inside.' I'm worried that we're no longer going after the best people in the country."[34] Recruiting from outside UCSF, however, may be less necessary now than during the school's earlier days before it had achieved its current academic standing. "Appointing chairs from within works well," says Dr. Keith Yamamoto, chair of the Department of Cellular and Molecular Biology," who emphasizes that they "know our culture." Despite national searches, most junior appointments in the basic sciences have been scientists who earned their Ph.D. or M.D. degrees or took research fellowships at UCSF. "Why not?" says Yamamoto, "They're the best in the country. Even so, the new chair of pathology comes from Harvard."[35] Lee Goldman, who disagrees that UCSF is losing its edge in convincing faculty to come, has recently recruited four of his division heads in the Department of Medicine from other schools.[8]

finances remain sufficiently agreeable so that faculty salaries, which had not grown for several years, began rising faster than the rate of inflation with Goldman's arrival in 1995. However, Goldman observed in the summer of 1999, "The losses are so new that it's too early to tell" how they may affect his department in the future.[8]

Only half of the full-time faculty members in clinical departments such as medicine work at the Moffitt-Long Hospital on the main campus. The rest care for patients, teach, and carry out their research at the San Francisco General Hospital and the San Francisco Veterans Administration Hospital. Although the merger talk clearly made some at the San Francisco VA Hospital "nervous and asking 'What's my role?'" according to former dean and chancellor Julius Krevans,[37] Goldman sensed that most felt that the merger and its problems were not directly relevant to them.[8]

Members of the faculty relish comparing the leaders of the departments of medicine at UCSF and Stanford. "Judy's [Swain, the Stanford chair] a bulldog, not nuanced. She gets from here to there and will run you over to get there." What her colleagues are saying, according to a longtime member of the department, is that Swain "is able to make the hard choices." Unlike some of her predecessors, Swain realizes that she can't be loved by everyone, which helps make her "a real leader. She's incredibly open, honest about everything, communicates all the time." She is seen as an able businessperson in research as well as practice, and "she's a scientist" in the Stanford tradition.

About Goldman, who (with Swain) is a member of the board of trustees of UCSF Stanford, observers say, "Lee's a better politician; he sees the big picture." But "Lee's work has taken a hit along with everybody else" who led the effort. "He's the *éminence grise,* although too obvious for that," suggests a senior member of his department, who adds, "I have compassion for him. He got into a fast-flowing stream which couldn't be anticipated." Goldman's intellect holds many "in awe of him. He's incredibly articulate, a good showman."*

---

*Born in Philadelphia in 1948, Goldman obtained the degrees of Bachelor of Arts, Master of Public Health, and Doctor of Medicine at Yale. He first worked at UCSF as an intern and junior resident, was then a senior resident at the Massachusetts General Hospital, and, after training in cardiology at Yale, joined the Harvard faculty at what was then called the Peter Bent Brigham Hospital. Before returning to San Francisco, Goldman was professor of medicine at Harvard, vice chairman of Eugene Braunwald's Department of Medicine, and chief medical officer at the Brigham and Women's Hospital. Goldman's research has produced several admired studies on the methods, results, and costs of delivering health care to patients with heart disease.

Obstetrics and Gynecology

Only in gynecological oncology has any merging occurred in the Department of Obstetrics and Gynecology. The two centers engage in joint outreach to develop referrals to both UCSF and Stanford, and they share a joint fellowship in the subspecialty. "Neither of us had a fellowship before the merger," explains Dr. Mary Lake Polan, the chair of the Department of Obstetrics and Gynecology at Stanford, "so it wasn't difficult to appoint a single fellow each year who splits assignments between the north and the south."[38] At Stanford, the full-time gynecological oncologists face stiff competition from "a very powerful oncology group with eight to 10 docs," says Polan. "We have two attendings at each site and are recruiting a fifth. They practice with the same protocols at both UCSF and Stanford."[38] The two hospitals tried to bring their gynecological oncology groups together in the past, but lawyers advised them of possible antitrust problems. "The merger was needed to let us come together."[38]

No other joint programs have yet developed in obstetrics and gynecology between the two hospitals, where the economic status of the patients differs significantly. Many of the patients hospitalized at UCSF are indigent and insured by Medi-Cal, much as one would also find at municipal hospitals such as the San Francisco General. Most well-insured and affluent pregnant San Franciscans seek medical care and delivery at community hospitals like California-Pacific, which offer a friendlier atmosphere in more accessible and agreeable parts of town. To combat this tendency, the department at UCSF has established off-campus outpatient offices closer to where potential patients live or work to attract more women into the UCSF system.[19]

A reality that the UCSF obstetricians find difficult to refute is that Moffitt-Long Hospital loses money on most deliveries[12] because so many of the cases are high risk, and hence expensive, and supported poorly by Medicaid.[4] Accordingly, the executives at the UCSF hospital don't see this business as profitable despite the pull-through work that accompanies complicated cases. The medical staff is further distressed by reductions in hospital support for the primary care that obstetricians, as well as other physicians, perform.[19] The leaders of the Obstetrics and Gynecology Department at UCSF, where the full-time staff performs or supervises all the deliveries, are doing what they can to make deliveries more efficient and less expensive.[19] At Stanford, the community obstetricians deliver 75 percent of the babies, and the university obstetricians there deliver about the same number as the full-time staff at UCSF.[38]

Despite these difficulties, the UCSF obstetricians along with their pediatric colleagues dream as creatively as other specialists. It is the hope of those who deliver babies and care for children that someday, with the generous support of the Packard Foundation, a women's and children's center will rise on the site of the Mount Zion Hospital. "San Francisco must be one of the few large cities without a dedicated children's hospital," says Russell Laros, vice chair of obstetrics and gynecology at UCSF. If the women's and children's service should transfer to a new facility, the Parnassus medical center would evolve into predominately a medical and surgical hospital.[19]

Oncology

In May of 1998, deans Debas and Bauer and UCSF Stanford chief medical officer Wintroub appointed Dr. Charlotte DeCroes Jacobs, director of the Clinical Cancer Center at Stanford, to coordinate all clinical cancer services at the merged hospital.[39] The assignment did not constitute direction of a service line because financial direction of the project was excluded and consequently no pooling of the money occurred. Although based at Stanford, Jacobs spends about two days each week in San Francisco, usually at Mount Zion Hospital, where much of the UCSF cancer work is conducted. She developed a leadership group to coordinate clinical cancer programs at both centers, facilitated joint clinical research projects and the sharing of clinical data, and helped initiate the beginnings of common training programs.[39]

No consolidations, other than Jacobs's job, have developed in oncology. Each center continues to have its own directors. Before Jacobs came onboard, an effort to assign bone marrow transplantation to one director for both campuses failed, and, Jacobs has found, some dissention persists among the principal doctors involved. Despite these difficulties, which we have seen throughout UCSF Stanford, Jacobs found the assignment particularly agreeable. She had trained at UCSF as well as at Stanford and had participated in the long history of cooperation and good feeling among the oncologists at the two institutions. As for the merger's effects on her colleagues, Jacobs finds "the vast majority of the 150 faculty involved in cancer work at both places unaffected. What they are affected by is the national problem" of payers continuously reducing the amount they compensate providers.[39]

Charlotte Jacobs's associate, Catherine Garzio, administrator of the UCSF Stanford Clinical Cancer Center, adds, "It's very hard to convince the docs at UCSF that California-Pacific, not Stanford, is the clinical competition. They've been competing with Stanford since medical school for publications and research grants and contracts."[40] For many patients, however, California-Pacific, a few blocks away, is a more attractive option than the distant hospital in Palo Alto. Similarly, Stanford competes with its regional hospitals much more than with UCSF to attract patients with cancer to its program.

Mount Zion Hospital has increasingly become the UCSF center for research and treatment of patients with cancer. There, according to Garzio, "The patient mix* mirrors the city; the employees mirror the local community." Many of the patients coming to the center are seeking second opinions from the specialists about the course their treatment should take.[40]

Two years after purchasing Mount Zion in 1990, UCSF moved the obstetrics service to Parnassus to develop space for the outpatient program in clinical oncology, which had been transferred to Mount Zion in 1994. A new clinical center for outpatients with cancer opened in October, 2000.[10] Radiation oncology, which remains at Parnassus, a significant inconvenience for the patients who need this increasingly important treatment, will be consolidated at Mount Zion when new construction, funded by bonds already approved, is completed.[40]

The research building at Mount Zion, which opened in 1997, houses the scientists who recently successfully applied to become one of the highly competitive National Institutes of Health Comprehensive Cancer Centers.[42] This designation brings government funding and prestige to the medical school. "The Stanford people are disappointed that their school didn't get one," Garzio has heard faculty members there say. The award is clearly an achievement of the UCSF medical school, not UCSF Stanford.[40]

Other Specialties

Special problems have contributed to the lack of cooperation in other fields. For example, UCSF chief medical officer Ted Schrock admits, "Pediatric neurosciences is moribund. We don't have strength at UCSF, and the neurosurgeon running the program at Stanford left for a more attractive opportunity."[12]

"The neurosurgeons at Stanford and UCSF have little use for each other," says Charles Wilson, the former chair of the department in San Francisco. Maybe the next group [of chairmen] could make it happen."

Patient mix is a general term that most administrators use to describe the hospital's patients from a clinical point of view.[41]

The phrase we have heard before in reference to change in academia reappears: "Where there's death, there's hope."[7]

An opportunity for academic consolidation presented itself in anesthesia when the chair at Stanford opened. Dr. Ronald D. Miller, the UCSF anesthesia chair, doesn't expect anything revolutionary to happen in his specialty, and he wonders about the advisability of having single departments anyway. "It is difficult to imagine that integration could be successful," he observes. "The antagonisms between UCSF and Stanford are worse now than before the merger."[34]

Dermatology was another specialty in which a single chair might have been appointed. At UCSF, Bruce Wintroub had left the chair to become executive vice dean and chief medical officer of UCSF Stanford, and Stanford had appointed Eugene Bauer, the chair there, as dean. However, Bauer elected to appoint a new chair at Stanford to succeed him, and a common chair for the two medical schools was never established.[1]

Development of Service Lines Halted

"Service lines were not a good kickoff [for the merger]," says UCSF neurosurgeon Charles Wilson,[7] for in the winter of 1999, when UCSF Stanford reported severe financial losses, the service lines were shelved, victims of the need to curtail spending for the personnel needed to develop and administer the project.

Program development returned to the individual hospitals, "where it probably should have stayed when the merger began," believes Isaac Stein, the UCSF Stanford board chair. "Perhaps we would have been more successful if we had developed the service lines on a local basis first before trying to do it in the two places."[43]

Few leaders at either campus mourned the loss of the service lines. Although initial enthusiasm had defined seven of them, "none really came together. There are prima donnas at each place," explains Bruce Wintroub.[1]

Gary Glazer, chair of radiology and a leader of the practice plan at Stanford, sensed that "the faculty was skeptical. They saw it as adding cost and not much else." Glazer points out that "If you couldn't do it for transplantation, you can't do it. There's a small, high-end thing, but they're big people at both places" who won't join together. "The job of service line director wasn't attractive, and few were interested in it."[44]

Peter Rudd, the general internal medicine chief at Stanford, saw the service lines as producing "parallel hierarchies" and causing additional expense. "Middle management would be needed, and to whom would they report?" he asks.[23] Whenever the leaders tried to "go beyond the kernel of the merger—reducing competition for high-end work and some economies of scale—one runs into trouble." It's very difficult, he finds, to motivate faculty into accepting joint programs as part of a merger. "Could meetings at expensive hotels really lead to a magical interplay? That didn't happen." There was "much talk about generalities, but few were prepared to really do it. The promise was much greater than the reality." The exception was pediatrics "because of the personalities of the leaders involved, fewer egos getting in the way."[23]

Karen Rago, the service line administrator for the adult cardiac programs on both campuses since January 1, 1998, was achieving some success in coordinating the programs, but with the end of the UCSF Stanford service lines "I was out of a job."[32] With the departure of Van Etten and Rago, Bruce Reitz, chair of cardiothoracic surgery at Stanford, resigned as the service line director for UCSF Stanford. Rago transferred back to the Stanford University Hospital, where she had previously worked, to administer clinical programs in adult cardiac services and in the Department of Surgery at Stanford.[32]

Dr. Ronald Arenson, the UCSF chair of radiology, opposed service lines at the beginning of the merger and continues to do so. "Financially commingling services won't work. Everybody looks at service lines as a means of making money at someone else's expense."[16]

A "bad tactical decision" is what Jonathan Showstack, the UCSF sociologist, believes about UCSF Stanford's effort to develop service lines. "Neither side was willing to give up its prerogatives. Service lines were ill before the financial losses of 1999 were known," he believes. "The red ink only provided the coup de grâce."[6]

Aubrey Serfling, chief operating officer of Columbia-Cornell Care in New York and for many years an executive at California-Pacific Medical Center in San Francisco, wasn't surprised when he heard that UCSF Stanford had dropped service lines. Although financial losses were the immediate cause, Serfling thinks that "the duality in department chiefs makes it almost impossible to consolidate. There are so many ways they can block it. If you can't merge the staffs and the leaders, you can't merge the functions."[45] Serfling adds that the voluntary nature of the effort also dooms it. "Only a mandatory reorganization, improbable, perhaps impossible, in the presence of two first-class medical schools, could bring about such consolidations."[45]

Some regretted that the concept never received an adequate chance. "We were encouraged by the board and administration to do the things

that Partners supposedly hadn't the guts to do," remembers Lee Goldman, who then acknowledges, "perhaps they were right. So far, we
haven't had the opportunity to see if service lines would work."[8]

However, just because Partners didn't set up service lines hardly
stopped the consultants from recommending that UCSF Stanford use
them. "There were zillions of committees and consultants — many of
which were MBAs from Boston — pushing service lines," Ronald Miller,
chair of anesthesiology at UCSF, remembers. "I asked them, 'Why are
you pushing service lines while the MGH and the Brigham didn't?'" The
consultants replied that Partners had taken the safe position, but that
UCSF Stanford shouldn't. "Now I know what MBAs are for — to give
smart answers to questions like that!" says Miller.[34]

Opposition at the Schools

From the time that Joseph Martin revealed what he and Gerhard Casper
were planning, faculty members started objecting to the proposed
merger. Among the most vociferous has been Stanton Glantz, an investigator in the cardiology division at UCSF. An activist in the fight against
the use of tobacco since 1978,[46] Glantz was "against the merger from the
beginning. UCSF and Stanford have completely different realities. I
know Stanford." Glantz earned his Ph.D. in engineering there. "UCSF
is a public institution. We have a commitment to the public, one of the
things which made UCSF great."[47]

Glantz believes that the marketing advantages touted as one of the
primary reasons for forming UCSF Stanford could have been solved
with joint agreements between the hospitals and schools rather than a
merger. "I expected that back office savings would work but not well
enough to warrant the merger."[47]

As to why the merger went through, Glantz, who is not a physician,
believes that "doctors are conservative and prone to accept authority.
Everybody deferred to Haile [Debas, the UCSF dean] and the leadership. Jon Showstack told me 'It will cost more than suspected.' Right.
'We'll struggle through.' Wrong. I wish it would work, but it won't."[47]

Consistently critical of the merger has been Dr. Norman Shumway,
the pioneer in cardiac transplantation who developed a highly successful
and respected cardiac surgical program at Stanford. He explains his
point of view with characteristic gusto. "Such a dumb idea from the get-
go. We're similar but different schools — UCSF's state, we're private —
40 miles apart. We could have done it by some sort of understanding and
have avoided the huge new administrative staff. We had a friendly but

stimulating competition, which is important. Pride in one's unit has been destroyed. With that gone," he adds, "it takes away one of the motives for fundraising. Now we're all angry at the administrators who alienated the faculty at both."[48]

Shumway's successor, Bruce Reitz, wonders, "Despite what the lawyers told us, was it really necessary to merge to contract together successfully?" Reitz is reminded of what a colleague told him when discussing the merger: "You don't have to marry someone to get into bed with them. This is the 1990s."[31]*

Ronald Miller, the leader of one of the country's most respected departments of anesthesiology and a UCSF veteran since beginning his residency there in 1965, says, "If one took a vote when the discussions were ongoing, 80 percent [of the faculty] would have voted against it. Those of us who supported it at the time did so because of our faith in Joe [Martin, the chancellor], Haile [Debas, the dean], and Bill [Kerr, the hospital CEO]. Without them, it wouldn't have happened." But Miller's optimism faded after Kerr turned down the CEO job of the combined hospitals, Martin left for Harvard, and people feared that Debas might go to Africa to start a new medical school. "I lost confidence in the leadership." At a black-tie dinner held in honor of Martin, Miller expressed quite strongly that the chancellor had instituted a change in the culture of UCSF and then left before the change could be implemented. "That's wrong."[34]

Organization partially explains why UCSF Stanford has not meet the goals expected of it, believes Dr. Robert A. Schindler, the former chair of ENT at UCSF. "Academics is horizontally organized. To move forward requires consensus building. Groups of experts, who think they know best, run the organization, but actually no one wants to be responsible for making decisions." Schindler sees an inherent conflict when this type of bottom-up authority meets the corporate model, which requires top-down management. Referring to himself and his colleagues on the faculty, he says, "We talk, we lecture. The best businesspeople listen. Our culture breeds poor business models. Ours was a very naive attempt to do the right thing." Schindler finds the fallout from the merger "demoralizing." He fears that the academic mission "has been damaged, not assisted. Revenue and time have been taken away from the departments. The time factor is easy to ignore. One can gloss it over."[50]

"The bulk of the faculty don't want it. The merger has little rele-

---

*Gerhard Casper, the Stanford president, objects to the assumption by many members of both faculties of what is required to jointly contract. "The full integration model resulted . . . from antitrust concerns, which played a large role."[49]

vance for most of them," says Kenneth Cox at Stanford. "Pockets, many in my department, are supporting it."[14]

A poll conducted in the fall of 1999 by the UCSF Faculty Association, whose leaders, like Warren Gold, have consistently opposed the merger, found that 52 percent of faculty members reached by e-mail wanted it to end and only 23 percent favored continuing.[51] By the fall of 1999, as many as 90 percent of the faculty at Stanford favored dissolution, Peter Gregory suspected.[52]

Concerning the demands of time required from those working to create and manage the merger, Larry Shapiro, the chair of pediatrics at UCSF, agrees with Schindler. "A major cost of the merger is having so many senior people spending so much time on it. During the past three years, I estimate that I have had to spend 30 to 40 percent of my time on the merger."[27] Many others concur about the discouraging temporal demands of the merger.[43,53]

Unions

Many of UCSF's hospital departments are unionized, mostly by politically active municipal worker unions that have consistently opposed the merger. Stanford, when the merger was being contemplated, only had a local professional nurses' union.[43]

The new private corporation required that most of the hospital workers at UCSF resign from their state jobs and reapply for positions in UCSF Stanford Health Care. Many of those affected were union members. The leaders of some of the unions contest that the new jobs are less attractive and the employees enjoy fewer benefits, including the former right to transfer within the University of California system. The hospital allowed the more senior employees, about one-quarter of the total, mainly nurses and leading technicians, to remain on the state payroll and continue to receive richer pension and holiday benefits. UCSF Stanford Health Care leases their services from the state.[54]

As president of the University Professional and Technical Employees shop at UCSF, Karen MacLeod, an animal technician in neurosciences, believes that the principal purpose of UCSF's merging with Stanford was "to get out from under public scrutiny. A major factor was to deunionize." By giving the state's assets in the hospital to UCSF Stanford, "They robbed the taxpayers."[55]*

---

*The state of California still owns the land under the former UCSF Medical Center and leases it to UCSF Stanford for a dollar a year.

MacLeod objects strenuously to the cost of the Executive Park offices, "with lots of space available elsewhere such as Laurel Heights" in San Francisco, where UCSF owns a large office building. She also objects to the executives' salaries now being hidden from the public and to the outsourcing of several functions "without competitive bidding."[55]

MacLeod joins others in concluding that the merger is failing because "You take two competitive faculties and put them together, and you get trouble. Dealing with the distance between the two wasn't feasible from the beginning."[55]

Red Ink

In the year after the merger began, opposition both within and outside the hospitals was muted. Few articles appeared in the local newspapers, and all seemed relatively calm. Behind the scenes, however, the executives feared the storm they saw coming over future financial losses. Then, early in 1999, the red ink surfaced for all to see.

"When the big losses suddenly appeared last winter [1999], it was a big shock. Since the merger was planned to save money, these results seemed strange at best," remembers Kenneth Melmon, president of the Faculty Senate at Stanford, who reflected the surprise of many of his colleagues.[56]

Lee Goldman acknowledged, "The two hospitals were breaking even before the merger. Now we're projected to lose $50 million this fiscal year,* all in the UCSF hospitals, which have been profitable for the past five years. We were told last January [1999] that we were making $1 million per week, a week later that we were breaking even, the next week that we were losing $1 million per week. The people doing the counting counted wrong. Since then, the fire drill has been to sort it out and develop a rational plan.[8]

"One of the fundamental premises of the merger had not come to pass," Goldman says. "The hope of the original business plan of drawing in the tertiary volume has not worked out."[8] The UCSF hospital has a highly successful kidney transplantation program, larger than its program in coronary artery bypass graft surgery, a standard tertiary care service at university hospitals. "The high-end penetration was already substantial. Those cases were already coming here, and not much more is left to capture."[8]

---

*The loss from operations grew to $78 million by the end of the UCSF Stanford fiscal year on August 31, 1999.

With the UCSF and Stanford hospitals not competing with each other, however, the merger had helped to maintain the price that the insurance carriers paid for such procedures as kidney transplants. "The fear that the prices for the high-end cases would fall hasn't happened," says Goldman. "We have the Kaiser northern California contract for about 100 cases per year. If Kaiser could do the work cheaper, they would." He then asks, "Where else could they go for pediatric surgery [a specialized field that UCSF dominates]?"[8]

It is ironic that in the midst of the financial turmoil the Moffitt-Long Hospital at UCSF was busier than it had been for years. The number of admissions to the medical service at UCSF had grown by 30 percent during the past four years.[2] The anomaly can be explained by realizing that many of the additional cases are very sick patients with complicated illnesses often involving many systems of their bodies.[2] Such patients frequently require long hospitalizations and expensive diagnostic and therapeutic measures. These are just the patients university hospitals specialize in treating, but they can be financial losers, the management of their illness costing more than their insurance, frequently inadequate for their problems, can pay. Furthermore, many of these patients cannot contribute to the cost of their care from personal funds.

"We never scrutinized that the train wrecks* transferred to us cost so much to take care of," explains Robert Wachter, chief of the medical service at Moffitt-Long Hospital.† The inadequate coverage and the poverty of these deprived, very ill patients are often underlying reasons that other hospitals transfer, more pejoratively "dump," such patients to "institutions of last resort" such as university, municipal, or federal hospitals. Not admitting that the patients' financial resources are important considerations, doctors and administrators at referring hospitals often explain the transfer by saying that the patients will receive better care for their severe illnesses by the scholarly full-time house staff and faculty and in the special facilities large teaching hospitals tend to have.

Finally, another almost hidden reason for the cost is fundamental to the education of medical students and postgraduate trainees. These young physicians and students, inexperienced in the most economical

---

Train wreck is doctors' jargon for a severely ill patient with many diseases.

†In many academic clinical departments, clinical chairmen also direct the relevant services at the principal teaching hospital. At UCSF, Lee Goldman followed the local custom by delegating this responsibility to his number two, Robert Wachter. "This was purposeful on his part," explains Wachter. "He also needed time to be associate dean for clinical affairs," a position not usually held by a chair but one Goldman accepted upon being recruited for the chair in 1995. "This makes Lee first among equals at the top table when clinical matters are discussed," says Wachter.[2]

ways of managing patients, order more tests than would senior doctors. Furthermore, many young physicians are inclined to solve every problem that afflicts the patient, an activity to be praised from the medical and humane points of view but expensive as revenue for medical care drops.[6]

As for the main cause of the red ink, "Everyone tried to pin the tail on Medicare," Robert Wachter adds, "but that accounted for only about one-fifth of the projected $50 million loss that year."[2]

Lawrence J. Furnstahl, senior vice president and chief financial officer of UCSF Stanford, explains further, "The merger was approved after a two-year political campaign but then slammed together very quickly. Getting the merger approved was a stunning achievement, but the political distraction prevented fully developing the details." And there were other reasons why the true status of the parties, particularly the UCSF hospitals, was unknown when the corporation was created on November 1, 1997. "It was the party line that there were no clouds on the horizon, which was ridiculous considering the clouds on the horizon."[20]

The leaders at Stanford and UCSF had to assume that they were building a merger of equals, whereas "that simply wasn't true," Furnstahl continues, "and each party doubted that it was true." An accounting firm submitted projections that Furnstahl found "unbelievable rosy." The founders couldn't admit any weaknesses and accept a realistic plan because "if you showed losses, it wouldn't be a merger of equals, and no one considered the transactional costs of this incredibly complex conversion."[20]

From the beginning, the UCSF hospitals, in Furnstahl's view, were the more vulnerable, and events proved this to be correct. "I suspect that some of the UCSF leaders knew that big trouble was coming but couldn't talk about it. The projected losses they anticipated helped to push them into the merger."[20]

Costs of Transferring Ownership of the UCSF Hospitals

When the merger began, UCSF appeared to be the more financially successful enterprise. During the last year before they merged, the four hospitals reported making $36 million on operations, with UCSF earning $27 million and Stanford $9 million. The apparently superior status of UCSF, however, included subsidies from the state of California, which would disappear with the transfer of ownership of the UCSF hospitals to UCSF Stanford Health Care. Contributions to the pensions of UCSF employees* would constitute the largest new obligation. This had cost Stanford $17 million that year. The UCSF campus provided legal and auditing functions worth about $6 million per year, and as a private corporation UCSF Stanford would have to accrue money for paid time off, which had cost Stanford $6 million in its last independent year. Because of its older and undernourished plant, UCSF paid $18 million less in depreciation than did Stanford. Capital would need to be spent in San Francisco to upgrade deficient systems — the amount would be much larger than estimated — and greater depreciation would then appear on the books.[57] The total of these costs to Stanford equals $47 million per year. If it had had to pay all these amounts, UCSF would have theoretically lost about $27 million during the last year of its separate operation rather than earning $20 million.

"We totally underestimated the effect of the loss of the University of California's support and services,"[13] says Stanford chief medical officer Peter Gregory, which Lawrence Furnstahl, who came to UCSF Stanford five months after the merger had begun, confirms. "Many of these figures were known in advance, but it appears that not much attention was then paid to them."[20]

"We hoped," says Stanford president Gerhard Casper, "we would do well enough to overcome the state money we no longer received.[49]

The effect of these data was to convince people at UCSF in 1997 that their hospitals were in better financial shape than were Stanford's and that the two campuses had not entered the merger as financial equals. Actually, from the beginning, as we have seen, UCSF's finances were more fragile than those at Stanford when one adjusts for the funds to be lost by the separation from the University of California and the infrastructure improvements needed in San Francisco. In view of these data, critics claim, the coming losses could have been predicted.

In addition to losing the money and services previously provided by the University of California, the new corporation would have to integrate various functions formerly conducted by the San Francisco and Stanford hospitals separately. "All hell broke loose when we ripped UCSF at its roots from all the systems and processes of UC [University of California]," Lawrence Furnstahl describes, "the financial information, payroll, supply, distribution, and information systems without the staff to support the work. Many of our best accounting people, worried

---

*Actually, the University of California was not paying into the pension fund because it was overfunded at this time. However, most hospital employees left the University of California umbrella with the merger, and the new corporation would now have to pay for their pensions.

about keeping their jobs, had left. We had to create a new payroll system," a process that Furnstahl estimates usually takes about 18 months.[20] "We had to do it in six months, and no firm would even bid on the job with that time limit. The team that was developed had to do it suddenly, and it went horribly. It was so complex. We went live with payroll uninterfaced with the general ledger system."[20] The conversion also required changing the tax identification and billing numbers for each account. "Our cash receipts dropped $30 million during the first months," Furnstahl remembers. "We eventually got it back, but it cost $10 to $15 million to do it."[20]

The changeover for the personnel at UCSF from state to private was a "nightmare of complexity," Furnstahl was told. "We had to change everyone's benefit policies."[20] Paychecks did not appear on schedule, and some were inaccurate, contributing to the tendency to blame the merger for all the problems afflicting the hospitals.

Although there were problems with coordinating materials management at the two centers,[20] "We saved a fortune by just using Stanford's rather than the state's contracts," says Brian May, the senior vice president for information technology. "Stanford's private and doesn't have all the restrictions state institutions have. Besides, the Stanford system was much more businesslike than UCSF's."[15]

The staff had made few preparations for the inevitable conversions required by the merger "because no one knew if the merger would go," says Furnstahl.[20] The political crisis of the spring and summer of 1997 had raised the real possibility that the hospitals would not merge, and then, when approval was obtained in late September, the new corporation had to begin operating quickly, just two months later. "No one understood the complexity of the process, and a lot of people had left, which contributed to the mess. There was also great pressure at the start to try to do everything as cheaply as possible," says Furnstahl.[20]

John B. Stone, a consultant from the Hunter Group, which was called in to help reduce the losses, looks back to analyze why Furnstahl had such difficulties. "Lawrence is not trained to be an operations guy and didn't have adequate assistance in doing the immense job he was given. The magnitude of the operations problems was so immense that I, an operations guy, would have needed assistance." Stone sees Furnstahl having to fix the Y2K problem very quickly as well as consolidating many other functions. This made it very difficult to concentrate on the most essential projects first, which ideally would have been the best course.[58]

As for the transactional costs, "We underestimated them," acknowledges William Kerr, as apparently everyone did, including the state audit and the accounting firms the hospitals retained to advise them "It was the most investigated merger known to man," Kerr recalls. "All said go ahead, though the amount of money people thought was involved varied. No one really asked, 'Where's the money?'" In summary, he says, "We just blew it."[18]

Growing Losses

Despite the new expenses, the unexpected growth in admissions, which developed before any specific efforts to build admissions by the new corporation could take effect, permitted UCSF Stanford to earn $20 million during the 10 months of its first fiscal year (November 1, 1997, to August 31, 1998). These favorable financial reports lulled observers not privy to the data that Furnstahl was developing into thinking "we had to be making money."[20] However, the leaders already knew that losses were soon to come, despite the deficiencies in the reporting structure that delayed the audited financial statements for the 1998 fiscal year, which ended on August 31, from being presented until January of the next year.[20]

"We recognized early in 1998 that we faced rising costs and flat revenues, that the lines on the graph would cross into negative territory and we had to cut costs," explains Furnstahl. "We knew that we faced a huge problem, losses up to $1 million a week in fiscal 2000, but overestimated the time we had to perform the repairs. It hit six months before we expected."

Furnstahl blames the surprise on poor data systems providing necessary information too slowly. "We showed the terrible graphs during the summer and fall of 1998 and that [without taking action] we couldn't close the gap." One of the actions that management suggested was bringing in the Hunter Group to help quench the losses, and "we began discussing this in late August 1998," remembers Furnstahl.[20] But it was hard to get people to pay attention. When Furnstahl presented the data he had accumulated, he was told:[20]

"We're so busy. How could we be losing money?"

"We always made money on unexpectedly high volumes."

"We had to say that all will be well to get it [the merger] approved."

"We don't want headlines about losses."

"We promised we wouldn't cut staffs."

"You're just drawing lines [on a make-believe graph]."

"You CFOs [chief financial officers] do this [present ominous financial news about the future] every year."

A national union was organizing service and maintenance workers at the Stanford and the Packard Children's hospitals, and the executives of UCSF Stanford Health Care, fearing that revealing the potential losses would unfavorably influence the ballot, did not announce Furnstahl's projections in the summer or fall of 1998. Keeping quiet about the coming red ink failed to influence the election as management wished — the union won the election with 62 percent of the vote[59] — and increased the assumption by critics that the leaders were ignorant of what was coming until the last minute.[20]

A favorite accusation when the losses became known was that UCSF Stanford Health Care had bloated itself with new staff when one of the reasons for the merger was to save money by consolidating functions. Peter Van Etten joked, when he could still smile, that "every patient will have his own accountant."[47] Critics on the faculties and in the legislature and reporters at the newspapers held the merger to be at least partly to blame for the financial losses and the expansion in staff.[60-65]

Increased admissions required that more clinical staff be employed, particularly at UCSF. Then even more were hired to approximate the staffing patterns at Stanford. The formerly state-owned hospital in San Francisco staffed its patient care units and clinics more frugally than did Stanford, which provided greater comforts and a higher ratio of staff to patients for its more affluent clientele. With the merger, UCSF executives and doctors looked forward to emulating their more patient-friendly partner to the south and "staffed up" accordingly without understanding how much this would cost.[38,66] "There was much concern about achieving equity north versus south," says Furnstahl. "With the great increase in volume, it was easy to overshoot hiring by thinking that receipts for the new patients would cover all the additional costs."[20]

"Us too creep," Kerr calls it.[18]

"Wholly ill advised," says Stanford president Casper.[49]

Many of the new recruits were needed in the administrative departments to solve the operational problems introduced by the exceedingly rapid and complex amalgamation of the state and private hospitals, the whole process greatly complicated by inadequate information services at both hospitals, particularly at UCSF. Furnstahl explains that, despite the problems, the process improved operations throughout UCSF Stanford, which now had one accounting and one budget department where there had been two of each. "The people are better, the systems are better, and professional discipline has improved."[20]

Other costs adding to the red ink at UCSF Stanford included greater support to the medical schools promised as part of the negotiations leading to the merger before anyone recognized how stressed the finances of the new company would be. Costs for UCSF Stanford to comply with local, state, and federal regulations were more than for each of the hospitals separately, as were audit, legal, administrative, and insurance expenses during the first year.[57]

By the beginning of the 1999 fiscal year, UCSF Stanford officials knew that expenses would have to be seriously cut back, that draconian measures might be necessary to stop the losses. With the help of the Hunter Group, which arrived in December 1998, UCSF Stanford began reducing the number of personnel, swollen by the clinical and administrative challenges faced by the administration. Of the more that 1,000 people added to the payroll, clinical personnel made up about 600, finance 130, information technology 100, and administrative areas the remainder.[57]

Efforts to reduce other expenses often met with strong opposition. One of the most vigorously opposed economies became the "laundry issue."[60] UCSF was the only University of California hospital that did its own laundry. All others obtained this service from private vendors at significantly lower cost, but because of political pressure UCSF had not previously made the change. "We just did it," a senior administrator says about what UCSF Stanford, but not the previously state owned UCSF, would undertake, an action that saved $6 million per year but led to the discharge of about 100 reasonably well paid, unionized, minority employees. The hospital also closed its San Francisco pharmacy for low-income patients on Medi-Cal or Medicare, which accounted for $500,000 in annual losses.[67] Even savings that appeared minimal were applied. Pay stubs for employees whose salaries were directly deposited to their bank accounts had been delivered by hand to their offices. Now they were mailed to the employees' homes.[20]

An important reason for the increasing losses was that revenue was not rising as much during 1999 as it had during 1998. Admissions to the hospitals were growing more slowly, and the payers were squeezing. Medi-Cal froze its rate of payment for adults, mergers in the local HMO market allowed payers to reduce reimbursement rates further — HMO premium rates in 1998 had dropped 9 percent below rates during 1993 — payer mix was deteriorating at the San Francisco hospitals, and then the Medicare reductions dictated by the Balanced Budget Act began to bite.[57]

Brown and Toland

Not only was UCSF Stanford losing money. The city's largest medical group, Brown and Toland, which represents 50 to 60 percent of all the doctors in San Francisco,[68] was having trouble. Brown and Toland, an independent practice association, had been formed in 1997 to link the physicians at UCSF with the California-Pacific Medical Center for joint contracting with the HMOs. The UCSF doctors came to receive about 10 percent of their clinical income from Brown and Toland.[69] They benefited more from the arrangement than did their hospital, which received highly discounted payments for its services.[70]

Despite being rated one of the best medical groups in the state by the Pacific Business Group on Health,[71] Brown and Toland lost $9.8 million on operations in 1998, most in its physician-owned medical service organization and much of the rest through physician overspending. "The physicians just blew their budgets," according to the CEO, Dr. Michael E. Abel, a California-Pacific-based surgeon.[69] Brown and Toland thereby joined most California physicians' groups by ending the year in the red.[70]

To ensure that the UCSF doctors would receive payment for their services in 1998 and, Abel believes, to keep the physicians satisfied with Brown and Toland,[69] UCSF Stanford stepped forward and paid the UCSF faculty $900,000[72] before the merger was fully aware of the losses it was facing. Management cut expenses, including physicians' salaries, and reapproached the health plans for higher rates, enabling Brown and Toland to break even during 1999. "Our P&L [profit and loss statement] is now ok," says Abel, "but our balance sheet looks awful."[69]*

With the UCSF Stanford merger in place, "it seemed a no brainer to add the Stanford doctors and open up the south of San Francisco market," according to Abel, but it didn't work.[69] The leaders of the Stanford physician group, recognizing that they worked in a market that was clearly different from the San Francisco market, knew they must compete with the local community hospitals. Furthermore, they weren't benefiting from referrals and other clinical business derived from the patients signed up by Brown and Toland. As Abel recognized, Stanford didn't want to increase its contracted business since most of its patients still held fee-for-service contracts.[69] Also, many at Stanford were concerned about other deleterious effects of Brown and Toland's expansion down the peninsula.[70]

Brown and Toland had overestimated Stanford's willingness to work in a capitated managed care environment. "They really didn't want the business," says Abel. "We recognized we were unwelcome there and shouldn't be there."[69] So the Stanford doctors and Brown and Toland,

---

*Except during 1998, Brown and Toland and its predecessor had made money each year since it was founded in 1992.[69]

who had joined together on January 1, 1999, began the process of separation, to be completed by December 31 after only a year's association.

By the summer of 1999, Brown and Toland was serving 200,000 patients in San Francisco.[70] Tough negotiating with the health plans by large providers like Brown and Toland[68] has helped increase rates in the Bay Area by as much as 10 percent,[70] leading optimists to hope that the financial pressures on providers in northern California may have peaked.

Mount Zion Hospital

The merger brought into UCSF Stanford Health Care the Mount Zion Hospital, a constituent part of UCSF. Since its acquisition in 1990, Mount Zion had provided UCSF with much needed additional space for clinical programs, research, and training. The problem with Mount Zion was that the hospital consistently lost money, bringing to mind the suggestion of Holly Smith, the former chair of medicine: "Why didn't we try to marry the rich girl, Presbyterian,* rather than the poor girl, Mount Zion?"[73]

For most of the 1990s, no one worried much about the annual losses, although they had grown from about $15 to $30 million by 1997.[18] The hospital on the main campus was sufficiently profitable — making as much as $50 to $70 million during several of these years[36] — to swallow Mount Zion's deficits and still produce a surplus.[12] "I told the regents," explains William Kerr, then CEO of the UCSF hospitals, that "I saw Mount Zion as the sixteenth floor of Moffitt-Long.† Since we were operating as a fully integrated institution, there was no purpose in developing separate bottom lines for the two hospitals." UCSF had subsidized Mount Zion with more than $200 million during the decade.[74]

Its financial problems don't reduce the affection for the hospital held by many of its staff, including Charles Wilson, chair of the Department of Neurosurgery at UCSF from 1968 to 1994. Wilson had so successfully developed his specialty at UCSF that for many years, except for normal deliveries, patients with brain tumors constituted the most frequent diagnosis of patients admitted to the Moffitt-Long Hospital.[10]

To accommodate his growing service, Wilson had moved part of his program to Mount Zion in his search for more operating rooms and intensive care unit beds than the Parnassus hospital could provide.[7] "We have three full-time people there, and that's where we do all our

---

*Presbyterian is the prosperous general hospital, now called California-Pacific Medical Center, located in a high-rent district of the city.

†Moffitt-Long Hospital has 15 floors.

spine work. It would be a disaster for our program if it closed," says Wilson. "The Jewish community would feel betrayed. Besides, Zion's an incredible safety net." Other hospitals want it to stay open lest the patients, mostly Medi-Cal and uninsured, come to their emergency departments. "Much of Mount Zion works like another city hospital, and so we need help for its indigent load. I love the place and truly hope that it survives."[7,75]

Despite this paean to the virtues of the hospital, Mount Zion doesn't make much money when Wilson works there. An operation by him or his associates costs almost as much to perform at Mount Zion as at Moffitt-Long, but the hospital collects appreciably less when they work at Mount Zion. Part of Mount Zion's operational losses are caused by the insurance carriers, which pay less there for the identical medical care provided at Moffitt-Long Hospital. They compensate on the incorrect assumption that a particular procedure or admission is less expensive to perform at the community than at the university hospital.[6] Thus, the expectation for increased revenue from high-end work proved less than predicted as losses of revenue from the pressures of managed care and then Medicare reductions proved greater than predicted.[37]

"As the reimbursement rates in the Bay Area fell so low, UCSF became no longer profitable," UCSF dean Debas explains. "The surpluses at Moffitt-Long quickly vanished, and the losses at Mount Zion appeared for all to see."[36]

"We don't want to make money, but we can't lose $60 million a year," said Peter Van Etten, who would consistently advocate methods to reduce Mount Zion's financial drain on UCSF Stanford.[76] "Contrary to popular belief," he explains, "Mount Zion did not have a higher portion of Medi-Cal and uninsured patients. It did have more Medicare patients. The primary financial problem was to support the infrastructure of an increasingly complex patient base on very low volumes."[4]

The executive team came to look on Mount Zion as an acute financial burden they could no longer carry in its current form and spoke of closing the inpatient and emergency departments.[77] Looking ahead, furthermore, the hospital faced large capital expenses. Between 2001 and 2008, Mount Zion would have to comply with safety regulations should another earthquake like the devastating events of 1989 strike San Francisco again. An engineering firm presented estimates of $25.4 million for improvements or $53.2 million for replacement.[78]

These problems convinced many at Stanford that UCSF had made a mistake in buying the financially strapped hospital and bemoaned the lack of understanding of its losses when the merger was being constructed. Edward Harris, the former chair of medicine there, who now coordinates the International Medicine Program at Stanford as former chancellor Julius Krevans does at UCSF, criticizes the amount of "due diligence in advance of the merger. If Zion's losses were understood, the principal of equality wouldn't have applied and I think the merger wouldn't have happened."[79]

Not unexpectedly in San Francisco,* the threat of closing Mount Zion's inpatient and emergency services aroused community activists, who feared its effect on the health of the local population. The mayor, Willie Brown, who once lived near the hospital,[80] city supervisors,[76,80] state legislators, regents of the University of California,[81] patients,[82] employees,[82] and union officials,[83] several of whom have always opposed the merger,[81,83] joined the fray. The newspapers printed editorials and articles pleading for the hospital's preservation.[84,85] Mayor Brown said, "I'll lobby like hell . . . and see if can gets the feds or the state to step in and make it a community-based hospital."[80]

"Where would the patients go for their care?" the patient advocates asked. A Mount Zion social worker, when interviewed by a reporter from the *San Francisco Examiner*, explained, "These are not popular patients at Cal-Pacific or St. Francis," San Francisco hospitals where most patients are well insured and prosperous. They are "fairly low-reimbursement high-maintenance patients with complex medical problems."[86]

"It would be the final straw after several other hospital closures," explains Neal Cohen, recently the UCSF chief of staff. "The one hospital in an African American neighborhood, serving African American and Russian immigrant patients in a city with an African American mayor — no wonder it's hard to close. The city and state government, employees, and others perceive us laying off low-paid, union workers. They say, 'There's been mismanagement. Get rid of the executives. The rich medical centers should support us.'"[24]

In addition to its affect on the community, the closure of parts of Mount Zion would also influence UCSF's academic programs. Other sites for training students, house officers, and fellows who now work at Mount Zion would need to be found, and in all likelihood the number of postgraduate trainees in UCSF programs would be reduced.[12] The state had mandated that in all California teaching hospitals half of the postgraduate training positions must be filled with doctors going into primary care. Of all the state teaching hospitals, "only UCSF isn't in compliance," Neal Cohen says. UCSF still trains more specialists than generalists. "Most of the training slots at Mount Zion were primary care slots. If

---

*"San Francisco," UCSF health care economist Harold Lust observes, "is a union, liberal town with a rabble-rousing press." The campus also has its Faculty Association to keep the water boiling.[68]

Zion closes, how will we maintain the primary care speciality balance?" he asks.[24]

Closure of Mount Zion might also affect referral patterns, so important for UCSF, with the former Mount Zion physicians directing their patients to hospitals other than UCSF. Twelve faculty members and 12 residents from Nancy Ascher's surgery department are based at Mount Zion. Closing the hospital could be a "huge deal for the surgeons there and may drive faculty away," she fears.[33] A portion of the surgery department's cancer program has been developed at Mount Zion, but "as a cancer center it was incomplete. I don't see it ever working as a Memorial," she says comparing the UCSF cancer program at Mount Zion Hospital to the famed cancer hospital in New York City.[33] Although most patients with cancer in the UCSF system come to the doctors' offices and same-day operating rooms at Mount Zion for treatment, which does not require overnight admission, much of the inpatient cancer surgery, including the bone marrow transplantation work, continues to be performed at Moffitt-Long.[2]

"I think Mount Zion is a scapegoat," says Ronald Arenson, "it's only a small part of the problem. If we close the inpatient service, we'll lose many of the outpatients." An orthopedist he knows who admits many patients to Mount Zion "will go to California-Pacific. He's part of the community, a big-time practitioner, not an academic."[16]

Attorney David Melnick and his colleagues on the Mount Zion advisory board, the successor to its board of trustees before ownership passed to UCSF, presented a vigorous case for retaining the services that UCSF Stanford was discontinuing.[87] The Mount Zion Health Fund pledged $5 million in what the *Examiner* called "a last-ditch effort to keep the hospital from being partially closed."[88]

After listening to the pleas of many Mount Zion supporters at an open meeting, the regent's health committee deferred to the UCSF Stanford board for a resolution.[89] On July 23, 1999, the board of UCSF Stanford decided not to decide, at least for the moment, and postponed resolving the future of Mount Zion Hospital.[90] The strong desire of the UCSF contingent to find some way of saving the threatened services greatly alarmed their Stanford colleagues, who feared the effect of continued losses at Mount Zion on their university.[66]

Mission Bay

In the midst of the financial and political turmoil attendant on Mount Zion's closing, the scientific supremacy of UCSF seemed about to climb to new heights with the groundbreaking of the Mission Bay complex on October 25, 1999. "There's an obvious symbolism in these two events," Warren Gold, president of the UCSF Faculty Association and scourge of UCSF Stanford, told the *Chronicle,* "The medical-discovery side of the campus is extremely healthy, but the medical-delivery side is sick."[91]

"Our scientific groups need to grow," says Holly Smith, who as associate dean has been one of those planning the Mission Bay project for UCSF, "and there's no space on Parnassus. Fortunately, we received a gift of 43 acres in Mission Bay," where the school will build a new research campus.[73]* "We will put our most fundamental science there,[97] like the science in the Harvard quadrangle with other programs at the MGH."[73]

Originally, many members of the basic science faculty were concerned that the move would disrupt the close relationship between them and the clinical scientists.[6,73] "It's not best to have such a separation, but one can't moan. Now scientists are competing to get into the beautiful buildings we're putting up there," says Smith. "Eventually, I mean in 20 or 30 years, the hospital may move there also."[73] Smith sees the Mission Bay project as more important to the School of Medicine than the hospital merger. Others agree.[98] "We've probably benefited more from the merger than has Stanford," adds Smith, "but without the merger, we

---

*More space for science has challenged UCSF chancellors for several decades. "When I became chancellor," says Joseph Martin, "relationships between the university, city, and neighborhoods were nothing short of disastrous."[94] Martin learned through meetings with local groups that efforts to further expand on Parnassus would not succeed.[94]

UCSF has considered three sites for a new campus, Alameda, Brisbane, and Mission Bay, the latter in the former rail yards of the Southern Pacific Railroad south of Market Street at the foot of Third to Sixth Streets overlooking the San Francisco Bay.[92,93] After negotiations with the mayor[94,96] and major corporate entities[94] to keep the project within San Francisco, Mission Bay was chosen, a selection made easier when the university received donations of 13 acres from the city and 30 acres from the Catellus Development Corporation, which now owned the property.[50,92]

In obtaining Mission Bay to build its new research laboratories, UCSF avoided the community action by members of what one UCSF official called "a scientifically illiterate population." Community action had prevented expansion at Parnassus and the Laurel Heights campus, where the activists, afraid of science, responded as Luddites, as one UCSF investigator saw it. He remembers a story in the *Chronicle* about a woman who feared being chased down California Street by the worms some of the faculty would be investigating there. (*Luddite* referred originally to people who viewed new methods of manufacture as a cause of unemployment and low wages. It derives from the name of a probably mythical figure named Ned Ludd, in whose name early-nineteenth-century English workmen destroyed labor-saving machinery in the textile industry.)[95] At Mission Bay, there were few residents to object, and for those who were there "we played the population better," one senior UCSF faculty member said.

would have faced, alone instead of conjugally, the same problems, which are generic everywhere."[73]

The job of selecting which projects should move to Mission Bay has been assigned to Dr. Keith Yamamoto, chair of the Department of Cellular and Molecular Pharmacology. Yamamoto, a Princeton Ph.D. in biomedical sciences, assembled a committee of 44 members to determine how to populate the new buildings. "We decided that we had to move a critical mass. The group had to include some of our best researchers but not leave Parnassus a purgatory of second-class people," explains Yamamoto.[35] The group concluded that the new buildings should include new scientific projects, not just be used to enlarge existing laboratories, and that entire departments or subjects would not move.* Most important was that flourishing collaborations between basic and clinical science groups must not be broken up.

Yamamoto remembers that, when he was writing his first grant applications in the 1970s, "we dreamed up relationships to clinical medicine [to sell the projects to the NIH]. Not so now. What's changed? We know better how things connect. Basic science is much more a continuum with clinical medicine." Yamamoto observes basic scientists crossing administrative boundaries and becoming sufficiently familiar with clinical issues to engage their colleagues in meaningful discussions and work. Similarly, clinical scientists seek out basic scientists to improve their work and expand their scientific horizons. Accordingly, Yamamoto sees that traditional departments and programs "make less and less sense." Referring to the union of basic and clinical science, he says, "It's a tremendous victory."[35]

As a leader of the basic scientists at UCSF, Yamamoto observes that the UCSF Stanford merger hasn't yet affected them very much. However, "I do fret that managed care and merger mania, over which we have little control, may affect the quality of the interplay between basic and clinical science." Can the clinical departments continue to retain good investigators who will want to work with their colleagues in basic science "or will [economic and administrative forces] put such pressure on them that they can't do this?"[35]

Dr. John P. Kane, a senior investigator-clinician in the Department

---

*The "first wave" of people moving to Mission Bay when the first buildings are completed in August of 2002, according to Yamamoto, will number about 1,000. The projects that will probably move include structural biology, computational biology, cell and molecular biology, and the beginnings of developmental and neural biology and human genetics. Eventually, he predicts, Mission Bay will house about 80 percent of UCSF's basic science.[35]

of Medicine who holds both M.D. and Ph.D. degrees, thinks that his basic science colleagues may be insufficiently concerned. The merger's trouble "impacts everything," he believes. "If we lose money, Mission Bay may suffer, so the basic scientists are involved, though they don't realize it yet."[98] Others believe, more optimistically, that the addition of the campus at Mission Bay implies that, regardless of how much the clinical programs may be stressed, the research enterprise will continue to grow.

Kerr Returns to UCSF

Following the bad news of January 1999, the board decided that William Kerr, then chief operating officer of the entire UCSF Stanford Health Care system, should return to his former job and resume direct management of the San Francisco hospitals, where the money was being lost. "We must organize patient care on the north campus that is cost effective," said Kerr. "UCSF has to return to profitability or Stanford will not want to go forward."[18]

By returning to Parnassus, Kerr would displace Bruce Schroffel, who had risen to the senior operating job on that campus. Kerr asked Schroffel to revert to his previous position of number two, and Dean Debas tried to convince him to do so,[22] but with the steady progress of his career interrupted Schroffel decided to resign. "I didn't see that [job] as a good move for me."[99]

An eight-year veteran of the Parnassus campus, Schroffel was the most senior hospital administrator to lose his job at that time. From 1991, when he arrived at UCSF from a large teaching hospital in New York City, Schroffel had advanced from director of operations to chief operating officer, the senior administrator of UCSF and Mount Zion in the merged UCSF Stanford Health Care system.

"I had come to heaven," Schroffel reflects in comparing the atmosphere at UCSF with that of his previous employer, with whom "I had profoundly different perspectives, making it difficult to work together."[99] In contrast, Schroffel found that "UCSF is very collegial, a real partnership between the school and the hospital. The UCSF leadership was very stable. Kerr had been the CEO for 20 years, and most people at the school were happy about this."[99]

Schroffel does not think that these characteristics were as representative of Stanford.[99] Although a governmental hospital, "UCSF took an entrepreneurial approach clinically—just the opposite of what one would think."[99] His UCSF colleagues sympathized. "Schroffel took the fall for UCSF's losing money," says one.[12] "Bruce was the scapegoat," agrees another.[24]

The spring of 1999 was an uncomfortable time for Schroffel and for Bruce Wintroub, the chief medical officer of the combined hospital, who agreed to relinquish his post when the goals of the position couldn't be realized. Their similar distress, same first name, and the stature they shared prompted one to characterize the two of them ruefully as "two short, Jewish guys named Bruce in the same fix." By January 1, 2000, Wintroub had returned to the chair of dermatology and a job in the dean's office.[1] Schroffel is consulting for UCSF at its Fresno affiliate.[99]

Will It Last?

As the financial losses and the pressure from politicians, unions, and the newspapers mounted during the summer of 1999, members of faculty and administration who had supported the merger at the two universities and UCSF Stanford Health Care reconsidered their positions. Most hoped that a resolution of the difficulties would include maintaining the merger in some workable form. Others decided that the dream had failed and each of the institutions should return to its former status. The minority who had opposed the merger from the beginning said, "I told you so."

In San Francisco, Jackie Boyden from the UCSF dean's office kept her enthusiasm for UCSF Stanford. "In bringing two top 10 hospitals together, we were building something fabulous. Now," she pauses, "it depends on whom you talk with." Boyden feels that the senior leaders did not adequately drill into everyone "what the mission was — to create a wonderful complex of hospitals delivering the best care in the world. Nevertheless," she says "I'm still a believer, although some things have to change for a dream to become a reality."[22]

Ted Schrock, who also hopes that the merger will not dissolve, says "If we pull apart, we're left with the same problems. Separation could only lead to the university bailing out the hospital as it has had to do at Irvine and San Diego."[12]*

Robert Wachter wonders whether the merger itself, which is receiving all the bad press, is really responsible for the problems now besetting it. "Mount Zion Hospital had been losing money for years before UCSF Stanford was formed. The shared core services and the marketing are

---

*Irvine and San Diego are two of the other University of California teaching hospitals that suffered losses.

benefiting everyone, but, nevertheless, I think the merger has little credibility now. The basic mantra, 'We're trying to preserve the academic mission,' hasn't changed, however."[2]

In the UCSF Department of Pediatrics, where the Packard funding may depend on the preservation of the merger, Larry Shapiro says, "Personally, there's a level of disappointment. I did, and still, believe in the merger and want it to survive in this market." However, despite his anticipation of collaborating with Stanford under the umbrella of the Packard money, Shapiro has been having second thoughts. Several years ago, Boston Children's tried to recruit him from San Francisco. "Joe* shared his vision with me about things that were coming at UCSF and convinced me to stay. However, if I knew then what I know now . . ."[27] Shapiro doesn't finish the sentence.

At Stanford, pediatrics chair Harvey Cohen speculates, "Suppose the merger does collapse. The adult services return to competing and pediatrics wants to cooperate — a big disconnect. It would be a real tragedy if it breaks up, something that doesn't have to happen."[26]

Ronald Arenson, says, "People are angry. They see the service lines dead, and we're losing money rather than saving it. So they say, 'Why continue the merger?' The problem is that separation will be costly. We would need assurances that UCSF would go back to the state with advantages. Maybe the answer is a holding company in fact as well as in practice."[16]

Kenneth Melmon, president of the Stanford Faculty Senate and former medicine chair there, sees many of the problems afflicting the merger as not due to dishonesty but to a lack of adequate competence to handle extremely complicated financial and administrative issues. He takes issue with medical people who are not businesspeople making decisions of the type that a high officer of General Motors would be called on to make: "We pretend we know what we're doing." Another problem, Melmon says "is that academic medicine is difficult for even such competent businesspeople as Isaac Stein and Warren Hellman [the investment banker who is a member of the UCSF Stanford board] to fully comprehend." He sees what is happening at Stanford and UCSF as "a national issue, an experiment which hasn't failed or succeeded. It's too early to tell."[56]

"A marriage in trouble with separate bedrooms and counseling," is how Gary Glazer, the Stanford radiology chair, now saw the merger. "Divorce, however, is expensive. Only the lawyers and consultants win.

---

*The reference is to Joseph Martin, dean and later chancellor at UCSF and now dean of medicine at Harvard, who had brought Shapiro to UCSF.

Then there's the sadness that the leadership has not lived up to the standing of the two great universities."[44]

At Executive Park, where the storm has been most acutely felt, Patty Perry, who directs managed care contracting for UCSF Stanford as she did for UCSF before the merger, believes that the preeminence of the medical schools in the governance of UCSF Stanford is a problem. Favoring the schools at the expense of the hospital "will kill the goose which laid the golden egg. There's too much strength on the school side, so the board is not saying what's in the interest of UCSF Stanford but what's in the interest of each school," she says, reflecting on the presence on the board of the Stanford University president, the UCSF chancellor, and the dean and a department chair from each school. "This approach might work if the market were more forgiving."[21]

Perry sees the pattern of "tit for tat, spend a dollar here, spend a dollar there," whether or not the expenditure was wise, making everybody jealous and angry, "the UCSF people about money going to Stanford for faculty support and the Stanford people for money spent on information technology at UCSF." Stanford patriots noted with irritation that as UCSF went into the red their hospital continued to be profitable. The lower paying insurance held by patients in San Francisco explains much of the difference. More UCSF than Stanford patients had Medicare or Medi-Cal, and many held capitated contracts that paid poorly. Perry is forced to conclude, "It can't stay together the way it is. There's no arbiter in the middle."[21]

Despite the problems, chief financial officer Lawrence Furnstahl feels strongly that the merger was wise. He theorizes about what's keeping it going in the midst of the financial debacle: "80 percent the cost and other problems of divorcing and 20 percent the concern that contracting against each other again would ruin one or both of them. Unfortunately, the unequal losses may kill it."[20]

At the top, Isaac Stein said, "If the merger goes away, UCSF's problems don't," and, he wonders, "can they get back the state subsidies? I don't think we need equal profitability, but UCSF can't be in the red." Stein insists that eliminating academic support to the medical schools is not the solution. "This would negate what we do and what gives us our competitive advantage," he believes. "It would be like a company eliminating its R&D [research and development] to make a profit. It works for a while but eventually fails."[43]

On July 14, 1999, the regents of the University of California reaffirmed their commitment to the merger. "Let's stay the course for a while," regent Sue Johnson told the *Chronicle*. "Give it a chance to work. The reasons for the merger are still there, and I fully support it."[100]

The stay of execution, however, seemed short-lived. Three weeks later, the two presidents, Richard Atkinson from the University of California and Gerhard Casper from Stanford, wrote the regents that they were appointing a committee to conduct a review of the merger and to report their recommendations by October 1. The press release stated that, despite the merger's "valuable aspects," it didn't have the "flexibility" to meet both UCSF and Stanford's needs.[101] UCSF dean Haile Debas, his sabbatical at Oxford interrupted, summarized his conflicted thoughts about the merger's status in an e-mail to the faculty: "The events of the last three weeks have . . . had a decided effect on my feelings about the merger."[102] The *Chronicle* speculated that one of the reasons for the reassessment was "an apparent attempt to save Mount Zion Hospital."[103]

The Future for the Leadership

As expected, the red ink put the jobs of the UCSF Stanford officers at risk. First to be discussed during the inevitable gossip on the subject was Peter Van Etten, the CEO. A statement in May by Richard Atkinson, president of the University of California, that "We failed badly in the management of the operation"[81] couldn't have cheered Van Etten. Nor could William Kerr, the chief operating officer and longtime director of the UCSF Medical Center, have been pleased by the criticisms of Stanford observers who had been told that "UCSF had reason to hide things, so there was lots of obscurity. Independent directors couldn't believe UCSF's bad management."

The previous jobs held by Van Etten and Kerr account for part of the problem, Robert Schindler of UCSF believes. "Peter and Bill lived in academic centers developing systems which they understood, but they didn't know how to run what was envisioned for UCSF Stanford. We really considered only two candidates for the CEO job, both very fine, ethical men, but neither had experience with mergers or how to build hospital systems." Schindler deeply regrets that Van Etten has been "so terribly vilified because our leaders aren't villains, just good people who don't have the knowledge or experience to do it right. The real villain is underfunding Medicare. The [failure of the] Clinton health initiative actually helped the private insurers to squeeze us more since government was unable to solve the problem."[50]

Recognized as thoughtful, intelligent, responsive, and committed to the merger by his supporters, Van Etten also has his critics, mostly at

UCSF, who question his leadership skills and ability to inspire confidence. They find him "misguided" and "a better strategic planner than manager" and described him as "Casper's hired gun."

"Here," a senior UCSF faculty member said, "the rank and file don't like Stanford, don't want to be associated with Stanford, and don't like Peter. They hold him responsible for the big increase in people [and] his outrageous projections about savings we knew couldn't happen. Peter simply has to go, and not because he's from Stanford. . . . His top-down view of management, which he instituted from day one, isn't the way we like to do it here."

At Stanford, Van Etten has many friends and admirers. Donald Kennedy, who, while Stanford president, hired Van Etten to be the university's chief financial officer, calls him "a very fine person."[104] Judith Swain, who as chair of medicine and a member of the UCSF Stanford board has watched Van Etten at close hand, concludes, "Peter's done a good job, and he didn't cause the losses at UCSF. The purchase of Mount Zion was a bad financial decision, and the lack of good information systems there isn't his fault. The people at UCSF increased the costs when they tried to do what Stanford does. They're a city hospital; we're not. Someone has to pay for the lack of infrastructure there," says Swain, who then adds what many of her colleagues say, that "Stanford can't subsidize UCSF any longer."[53] If the Stanford faculty had known in advance about the losses to come at UCSF, Swain believes, "we'd never had gotten into it."[53]

Another Van Etten supporter at Stanford is Kenneth Melmon, who believes that "If Peter can't succeed, no one can."[56] Nevertheless, "People began to think that he couldn't survive," remembers Peter Gregory, the Stanford chief medical officer. "Peter's blamed single-handedly and unremittingly by the North for the problems."[13] Among the most ominous observations then heard both within and outside UCSF Stanford was that "Peter's been hanging on by his fingernails for months."

Van Etten and Kerr Leave

On Monday, August 9, 1999, a week after the two presidents announced that the future of the merger would be reviewed, Peter Van Etten and William Kerr resigned as chief executive officer and chief operating officer of UCSF Stanford Health Care.[105] The UCSF Stanford board had met in executive session on Thursday, August 5, and decided, according to an informed observer quoted by the *Chronicle*, that "This was the right time for Peter and Bill to leave. They were lightning rods for the whole thing."[105]

The usual neutral statements accompanied the changes. According to a story in the *Chronicle*, Isaac Stein, UCSF Stanford Health Care's chair, said "Peter and Bill wanted to facilitate any organizational changes resulting from the study requested last week."[105]

Van Etten had lobbied strongly for closing Mount Zion Hospital's inpatient services, a decision with much financial and administrative logic, but one that aroused a public storm much greater than he or his colleagues had anticipated. "Stanford had become very uncomfortable with the public process surrounding Mount Zion," Van Etten says. With Mount Zion playing an important role in its academic programs, "UCSF was unwilling to make the decision [that Van Etten had recommended], and Haile wanted the state money back," which, Van Etten suspects, will almost certainly require restructuring UCSF Stanford. Furthermore, the retention of Van Etten and possibly Kerr might interfere with UCSF Stanford's receiving financial aid from the state for Mount Zion whatever happens to the future structure of the merger. Van Etten continued to think that revising Mount Zion's role is critical to solving UCSF's financial problems but acknowledges that the Mount Zion question was "one of the most destabilizing issues."[4]

What had happened to Van Etten's support, observers wondered? Donald Kennedy, who had hired him as the university's chief financial officer to help Stanford deal with the overhead scandal, regretted the loss of Van Etten to Stanford and believed that "he took the fall" for problems not entirely of his own making.[104] Gerhard Casper, who inherited Van Etten from Kennedy, had appointed him CEO of the newly established Stanford Health Services. Was this done partially to move him out of the president's office, some of those involved now wondered? Did Casper and Isaac Stein, Casper's friend who chaired the UCSF Stanford board, now conclude that Van Etten had to be sacrificed to reduce the heat the merger was taking? And, if Van Etten had to go, did the same hold for Kerr, so as to maintain "balance" between the campuses in discharges as well as appointments?*

"Bill became a different person when he moved to UCSF Stanford," observed a friend on the UCSF faculty. "He seemed to take a backseat, no longer the take-charge Bill we knew and loved. We had had

---

*This would be the ultimate example of merger-driven equality between the two schools, "the Noah's Ark approach."[44]

a very close relationship with our hospital executives, like a community, a family."[16]

Although his UCSF colleagues consistently praised Kerr for his leadership of the UCSF hospitals before the merger, he was criticized for the problems that UCSF Stanford brought. A colleague and admirer at UCSF said, "Bill's not a tough manager. He would have had trouble with trouble."

Another said, "In a hospital with lots of money coming in and political problems, Bill flourishes. Given five chairs and five opinions, Bill will develop one conclusion. However, the times turned away from Bill. He was OK for the seventies and eighties but not for the nineties," which is a rather harsh comment considering how well the UCSF hospitals met the challenges of the 1990s before the merger.

People remembered that Kerr had publicly accepted and then rejected the CEO position when it had been offered to him in February 1997. The board had then turned to Van Etten. Thus, the management team, as one observer put it, "involved much compromise, and, therefore, no one really loved anyone."

Van Etten says that the decision to leave was his, although "several members of the board wanted my resignation."[4] After the presidents' letter appeared announcing the study on restructuring the merger, he concluded, "I didn't want to take apart when I had spent four years putting together." He then asked himself, "Do I resign now or after the restructuring?" and decided, "better for all of us that I leave now." His ability to lead the organization, clearly about to change, would be limited. "There wasn't really a role for me" during the restructuring process.[4]

Van Etten's boss, board chair Isaac Stein, while decrying the "political diatribes against Peter," recognizes that he became "the embodiment of the decisions, and when a manager becomes the symbol of the problem, he has to go."[43]

"Criticism of top management on both campuses and among the larger public," an observer commented, "made it impractical to think that a solution could be found that included Van Etten and Kerr. Their resignation was indeed an indication that UCSF Stanford Health Care was not ready to throw in the towel."

"We hospital administrators have to be prepared to take the heat," says John Stone of the Hunter Group, adding that these jobs are not designed for the faint of heart who want sinecures.[58]

The posture assumed by Van Etten during this difficult time in his career is characteristic of how most changes in high-ranking personnel are presented to the public. "The more senior, the more mature the fired person, the less he fights it," says Kenneth Bloem, the former Stanford hospital CEO. "He thinks of his career, of the faculty in a case like this, of the institution. Such an approach is embedded in the genetic code. You're a member of the club, and fighting [the discharge] is a career threat."

Bloem also described what the person who has to carry out the discharge should say: "You've gone a grade A job. We're forced to make a change because of external factors. We'll take care of you. All the severance you need. Good references." As for the reason why Van Etten and Kerr had to leave when they did, Bloem adds, "You need a symbolic change to head in a new direction."[106]*

Bloem also speculates about the dynamics of the critical meetings of the UCSF Stanford board that led to the change in management. "There must have been much gnashing of teeth and complaining that it's not getting better, members mentioning people and groups who are saying this. Then off line [in executive session], the issue of leadership comes up again. They get input from Hunter. Should they recruit someone quickly or give it to Hunter?"[106]

The Hunter Group Takes Over

They went with Hunter. As interim CEO to run the system until completion of the reorganization plan in the fall, the UCSF Stanford board appointed David Hunter, a former hospital executive and the CEO of the Hunter Group of St. Petersburg, Florida, the consultants called in during the fall of 1998 to help control the financial losses.[107] The board rejected the advice of Hunter and his colleagues, who favored retaining Van Etten and Kerr since "They're doing our plan."[66,108] "We saw it more difficult to do our job if they weren't here," adds John Stone, the Hunter officer who had arrived in April to help implement the recovery plan.[58]

Hunter's company, founded in 1988, is the first such organization to assist distressed, originally community, and, more recently, teaching hospitals to restore financial solvency.[109] The group only advises not-for-profit hospitals and academic medical centers. "They have a wide breadth of focus, and their boards are invested in their communities," explains David Hunter. "For-profits never focus off financials."[108]

---

*In January 2000, Van Etten became the president and CEO of the Juvenile Diabetes Foundation in New York City. Kerr joined the Hunter Group as a senior vice president in October, 2000.

Recognizing that more than the external environment may have caused a hospital's red ink provides part of the angst for executives when Hunter comes calling. A hospital chief executive officer who has experienced the Hunter approach says, "You bring in the Hunter Group because you've pretty much abdicated your responsibility to your institution. . . . It reflects a failure on the part of the owner or the governing body to have done their job in the first place."[110]

"Hunter is making the hard decision that must be made," observes Warren Hellman from the UCSF Stanford board. "They use common sense and have experience with troubled hospitals."[111]

"By the time we're called in," says Hunter senior vice president David Coats, "It requires serious surgical intervention.[110]

"We're there," adds David Hunter, "because, like alcoholics, they don't recognize they're in trouble. We force people to understand that they've got a problem."[108]

Described by their critics as tough minded, heartless, and cold hearted in carrying out their mission, the executives of the Hunter Group have been characterized in a trade journal as "consultants that specialize in scorched-earth hospital makeovers."[112]

As for the work they do, a consultant described it as being "like Civil War surgery. There's not a lot of artwork here. Boards have difficulty dealing with management failure," and that's why Hunter is hired.

"They're tough, tough guys," says the board chair of a hospital that received the Hunter treatment. "They don't take prisoners, and they make some wrong decisions, but at least they're making them."[110]

The group's advice often leads to large layoffs and sometimes to the closing of hospitals owned by the corporations retaining the group. When executives leave, the boards of the troubled hospitals may hire Hunter officers until permanent replacements are recruited. Not unexpectedly, most hospital administrators wince when their board members say, "If you can't fix things, the Hunter Group will."

UCSF would not be the first University of California hospital to experience the ministrations of the Hunter Group. In 1996 and 1997, the group reversed the losses at the principal teaching hospital of the University of California-San Diego (UCSD) by cutting 500 positions and reorganizing the administration.

"We needed changes in the way we did business," a spokeswoman from UCSD told a *Chronicle* reporter. "They came in with the outside expertise and worked with us."[105]

In UCSF's own territory, the Hunter Group had reversed "a

$34 million shortage" at California-Pacific Medical Center in 1994 "by temporarily taking over operations and carrying out a sweeping cost-cutting plan, including the elimination of 1,000 positions," according to the *Chronicle*.[105]*

During July 1999, while UCSF Stanford was going through its own trials, the University of Illinois-Chicago[105] and the illustrious Hospital of the University of Pennsylvania in Philadelphia,[113] both losing millions, retained the Hunter Group. Previously, the Allegheny Health, Education, and Research Foundation, George Washington University, the University of Massachusetts, and the New England Medical Center, among others, had turned to the group to restructure their organizations and/or eliminate their red ink.[66]

As interim chief financial officer of UCSF Stanford and interim chief operating officer of the San Francisco hospitals, David Hunter appointed his colleague, John Stone. Thus, Lawrence Furnstahl, the UCSF Stanford chief financial officer for almost two troubled years, also lost his job, although he was retained temporarily as a "financial advisor, available to assist the University of California and Stanford University as they re-evaluate the future of the merger," according to the e-mail that David Hunter sent to UCSF Stanford employees.[114]

"For the past few months, I've come to work expecting to be fired," Furnstahl says.[20]† He had come in for his own share of criticism, some unfair. One of the UCSF departmental chairmen complained, "He's taken decision making away from the departments and removed financial things from here to 3COM." This, of course, was the job he was hired to do, combining at UCSF Stanford the financial operations of the two campuses.

"Kerr did a great job making people feel good so that UCSF didn't know its own troubles," a Stanford faculty member suggests. "With all infrastructure at UCSF underdeveloped, Lawrence did what he had to do and shouldn't be blamed." A consultant described Furnstahl as "hon-

---

*A doctor who worked at California-Pacific Medical Center when Hunter was there says, "Their modus operandi is to flatten and take out senior management. Hunter takes away the spirit of the place and leaves it decimated. When they depart, FTE creep follows."[69] FTE (full time equivalent) creep means increasing the number of employees, which critics of the Hunter Group claim follows Hunter's cuts after they leave.

†Another casualty was Patricia Perry, senior vice president for strategic development and the director of managed care contracting. She wrote to her colleagues, "I have proposed to David Hunter that we eliminate my own position. . . . I have been prompted to reconsider [the] organization in light of the need to make additional budget cuts in overhead departments so that we can reduce the burden of cost reductions borne by patient care . . . . Last spring I told my own staff in Strategic Development that the next budget reduction would be my own position. I don't think they believed me."[115]

est, a genius in health care, a brilliant strategist but a naive young man and not trained as an operations person."*

Although Hunter announced that William Kerr "has agreed to work for the UCSF campus during the evaluation of the merger,"[114] there was no mention of a transient position for Peter Van Etten, who, Furnstahl observed, "looks greatly relieved, best I've seen him in six months."[20] Despite Debas's stated desire that Kerr return to run the Stanford hospitals he had led for 20 years, Kerr decided not to become a candidate for his old job, saying that "new blood" was needed.[116,117]

At the Stanford Hospital and Clinics, Malinda S. Mitchell, chief operating officer, and Peter Gregory, chief medical officer, remained in place, as did Christopher G. Dawes, chief operating officer, and Kenneth Cox, chief medical officer, at the Lucile Packard Children's Hospital.

Lawrence Furnstahl was not alone in expecting a return to on-site management. "After disavowing knowledge about what the reviewers will decide," David Hunter wrote, "I anticipate that . . . it will involve giving more accountability and responsibility to the campuses."† As a final note, Hunter added, "It is vital that our patients continue to receive the highest quality care. When the dust settles, our patients will remember that excellent care, not what they read in the newspaper."[114] In the meantime, the *Chronicle* quoted Hunter saying, "We have to get these institutions to quit bleeding and give their parents time to decide what they want to do in coming years."[105]

The Hunter process for reducing losses is their specialty.[110] "The Hunter Group tells you what others do by benchmarking, comparing your expenses with those at comparable hospitals," Larry Shapiro, the pediatrics chair at UCSF, says. "We were way over: 8.2 at UCSF, 7.9 at Stanford, 8.1 for both, while their data say the number is 6.5 for the fiftieth percentile at academic medical centers."[27]

These extraordinary developments appeared to give Mount Zion Hospital a reprieve. Hunter confirmed that the future of that hospital "is the responsibility of the medical school dean and chancellor of UCSF" rather than UCSF Stanford.[114]

On July 30, UCSF dean Haile Debas e-mailed his colleagues, "The future of Mount Zion is completely interlinked with that of UCSF in our academic, clinical, and social mission. We are doing everything we can to keep Mount Zion open as a full service acute care hospital, but realize

---

*Furnstahl returned to the University of Chicago as chief financial officer and chief of strategic development for the hospitals and health system.

†It was an ominous announcement, thought Dr. Ernest Ring, associate dean of UCSF–Mount Zion Medical Center. "The day we got separate accounting, the merger died."[10]

we cannot do this without state support."[102] Debas acknowledged that with the financial services at the south and north campuses operating independently, "A kind of trial separation of the UCSF and Stanford hospitals is already in effect," according to the *Chronicle*.[117]

Bill Kerr agreed when he said a few weeks before he stepped down as chief operating officer of UCSF Stanford, "It's back to premerger thinking at UCSF. We can't afford to be Stanford. Stanford can't afford to be Stanford."[18]

UCSF neurosurgeon Charles Wilson was one of the most ardent supporters of the merger with Stanford when it started and served as a member of the UCSF Stanford board during 1997–98 while Debas was acting chancellor of UCSF. "I became convinced that merging was an economic necessity and would stop competition between Stanford and us. If you weren't merging you'd be missing something. We made money the first year, and everybody was 'high fiving.'" By August of 1999, however, Wilson had changed his mind. "I'm in favor of breaking the merger and getting back under the state. To share the laundry and some contracting is not a merger." Wilson also feared that Stanford would not long continue to accept UCSF's losses. "I think Gerhard [Casper, the Stanford president] will bolt."[7] As he decreased his operating schedule, Wilson, who is universally called "Charlie," indulged his interest in health care administration by completing a master's degree in 1996.[7,118]*

Hunter recommended that the amount of "strategic support," the phrase used on both campuses for the money that UCSF Stanford transfers to the medical schools, be reduced in a phased program over the next four or five years.[25,72] Officials of UCSF Stanford and the medical schools chose not to discuss this subsidy publicly, aware that the supporters of the threatened services at Mount Zion might claim that the hospital favored well-paid faculty and their pet projects over clinical care for poor patients.[72†]

During the 1999 fiscal year, about $120 million flowed from UCSF Stanford to the schools through this mechanism, slightly more than half of it to Stanford.[66] The medical school departments depend on this money for many of their functions and projects, and faculty see reduc-

---

*For more information about this highly skilled neurosurgeon, see the profile of him published in the August 2, 1999, issue of the *New Yorker* in which the author compares his "physical genius" to that of a famous cellist and a popular hockey player.[118] When I interviewed Wilson, energetic and strongly opinionated at 70, he was wearing his scrub suit, having just finished three pituitary resections, his operation of choice.

†UCSF and Stanford are not unique in this regard. Most teaching hospitals do not specify how much they transfer to their medical schools. See chapter 1 for a discussion of how and why teaching hospitals support medical schools.

tions in strategic support as assaults by the hospital on the academic mission. Although difficult to avoid considering while reducing hospital services and discharging employees, the UCSF Stanford board of trustees, constituted as it is, has always had difficulty achieving a consensus about cutting subsidies for medical school programs.[25] One of the forces tending to preserve the merger, Dr. Richard Behrman, an independent member of the board, believes, is the anxiety that support to the schools may be reduced still further if the merger dissolves.[25]

Speculation abounded that the merger was about to unravel. Karen MacLeod, president of the University Professional and Technical Employees, whose union had opposed the merger from its founding, said, "I don't think they would do it unless they were thinking of dissolving."[101]

Another opponent of the merger, San Francisco assemblywoman Carole Migden, said, "Everybody wants to de-couple and end the merger, which I suspect means there's a desire to transfer the costs to the state, which I think is a galling move."[101]

State senator John Burton, also from San Francisco, called for the resignation of Isaac Stein. "He's Chair of the board, and the other guys were only hired help. . . . I would assume that Isaac will probably be getting his hat too."[119]

The Hunter Group's appointment to direct UCSF Stanford was not greeted with universal approval despite Haile Debas's plea that faculty members give them a chance to "turn UCSF around," according to the *Chronicle.*[117]

"The captain of the *Titanic* has finally taken over the ship," said Rose Ann DeMoro, executive director of the California Nurses Association.[112] "The decision to give away this once premier institution to the Hunter Group is disgraceful."[117] DeMoro, who had battled the Hunter Group when it was advising the California-Pacific Medical Center in 1994, added, "These guys are sharks. They circle the water looking for blood, collect huge fees, and then they go back to Florida."[105]

"I am terrified that the Hunter Group is going to be calling the shots at a public teaching hospital," said another union leader. Their "express purpose . . . is to slash and burn and get rid of 2,000 employees."[119]

In an editorial in the *San Francisco Examiner,* Warren Gold, chair of the UCSF Faculty Association and a steady opponent of the merger from its earliest days, claimed, "Rather than listening to faculty, staff, and community members, UCSF Stanford Health Care management is spending $5 million on a consulting firm with a reputation for ruthless cutting to make hospitals more profitable. These consultants have no interest in the university's academic or public service roles." As for the future of UCSF Stanford, Gold wrote, "The merger needs to be dissolved now. . . . The longer we wait before acting, the more difficult it will be to get UCSF back on track."[120]

Mount Zion Decision

On September 23, the UCSF Stanford board, acting on the advice of Lee Goldman,* unanimously decided to close the inpatient and emergency services at Mount Zion Hospital.[121] The losses there threatened "to bring down the entire clinical enterprise," Goldman said.[121] One of the board members voting for the closure was Warren Hellman,[111] whose grandfather, a Mount Zion board member at the time, had contributed to the construction of the Hellman Building, for decades after it opened in 1914, the main structure of the hospital.[122]

The *San Francisco Chronicle* reported that Hellman had tried unsuccessfully to gain the support of California governor Gray Davis, who resisted rescuing the services of a hospital no longer owned by the state.[121] The lack of help from the governor and legislature put to rest, for the moment, the perception at Stanford that UCSF could always turn to the state for succor.[14]

"It seems unlikely that any public agency could be relied upon to appropriate a $50 million annual subsidy to an enterprise the size of Mount Zion," wrote UCSF chancellor J. Michael Bishop.[123]

Closure of some of the services at Mount Zion would "be very difficult, but it was clearly the right business decision," says Catherine Garzio, the UCSF Stanford Clinical Cancer Center administrator at Mount Zion. She wonders, as do others, "Can Parnassus do it by 2000?" and absorb the inpatient surgery and emergency work that would no longer be available at Mount Zion. Her outpatient service faces a similar problem. "These practices lose money, but we feed the inpatient and ancillary services, which are more profitable."[40]

Garzio had the difficult duty, similar to that of other administrators, of keeping her services running effectively as the Hunter-designed reductions in personnel proceed. Although facing uncertainty, she doesn't anticipate being fired. "So I deal with it by concentrating on short-term goals like opening the new clinical building next spring, setting up a business unit approach, and keeping my staff motivated and not jumping ship."[40]

Resignation to the changes at Mount Zion began to replace opposition. "What do you do when there's a hole in the boat?" asks John Kane, a senior UCSF investigator.[98]

San Francisco assemblywoman and Democrat Carole Migden, a

---

*Goldman was speaking on behalf of UCSF in the absence of Dean Haile Debas.

vigorous supporter of the hospital, said, "It seems that the undoing of Mount Zion was based on the private stewardship of a public entity that went sour. What we feared would happen has come to pass. Mount Zion is being dismantled, and its primary mission abandoned."[121]

"Mount Zion was a great idea that never worked," in the opinion of Dr. Ernest Ring, who moved from Parnassus to Mount Zion as chief of radiology in 1993 to help the hospital develop a leading role in San Francisco medicine.[10] Ring, a nationally recognized leader in the field of interventional radiology who had directed his subspecialty at the Hospital of the University of Pennsylvania in Philadelphia and then at the UCSF Parnassus site, hoped to develop in Mount Zion a first-class community hospital on teaching hospital principles. In 1997, just as the merger with Stanford was about to begin, Ring became the associate dean for the UCSF–Mount Zion Medical Center, as the Mount Zion site is called to emphasize its relationship with the medical school.

Ring sees Mount Zion as providing better training in some ways for students and house officers than primary university hospitals that specialize in tertiary care. Experiences at a university-related community hospital like Mount Zion more closely mimic what most trainees will encounter when they enter practice. At hospitals like Mount Zion, they work with first-class clinicians who have treated patients for years in "old-fashioned community medicine."[10]

However, in Ring's opinion, "No one at UCSF took Zion seriously as a hospital." Mount Zion became a "dumping ground" for activities that couldn't be accommodated at the overcrowded Parnassus site. "Moffitt looked down its nose at Mount Zion and saw it as a dingy place."[10]

Ring describes his hospital's peculiar geography. "We're in an area that San Francisco thinks of as a ghetto, though people here don't really know what a ghetto is like" (Ring remembers the much larger North Philadelphia ghetto he knew while working at the University of Pennsylvania). He finds San Francisco a very diverse city with its people crowded into a relatively small space. "The city's constantly being reborn, and since there's only a fixed amount of land it can't sustain pockets of poverty forever. There are billionaires living further up the hill, and even *our* area's becoming gentrified."[10]

Before the financial problems halted development, Ring saw Mount Zion expanding toward the Kaiser hospital two blocks away, "creating a massive medical center." Compared to the facilities on Parnassus Avenue, Ring pictured Mount Zion as a hospital on a "human scale, ideally suited to compete with California-Pacific Medical Center. We could have blown them out of the water."[10]

As for the red ink at Mount Zion, "We never discussed the losses here," says Ring. "Bill Kerr was totally in charge at Parnassus. We had no budget and no authority about financial matters. The old Zion docs saw us as a colony and called us 'occupied Mount Zion.'"[10]

In November, "top San Francisco political leaders," as described by a reporter for the *Chronicle,* made a last-minute effort to "save" Mount Zion by developing a $25 million subsidy,*[124,125] an attempt that did not appeal to UCSF officials. Lee Goldman, as acting vice chancellor for medical affairs, advised directing any additional funds to the support of the San Francisco General Hospital rather than trying to resurrect the inpatient and emergency services at Mount Zion.[125] Its supporters called off the effort a few days later.[126] With staff leaving, UCSF closed the Mount Zion emergency room on November 23 and planned and closed all inpatient beds a month later.[127†]

A letter to the *Chronicle's* editor by Chancellor Bishop, printed two days earlier, made it clear that UCSF was pressing forward with its plans to change the function of Mount Zion Hospital. "While we mourn the loss of what Mount Zion used to be, we cannot ignore what it promises to become," he wrote.[123] Bishop then described how the Mount Zion buildings would house several outpatient services and a new adult urgent care center opening that month. The NIH-sponsored cancer center would flourish and grow with a new outpatient building scheduled to open in the spring of 2000, and radiation oncology and other services would be transferred from Parnassus to Mount Zion soon.[123]

Confirming that a daily census of only 65 patients was "too few to permit the efficient operation of an acute-care hospital," Bishop assured those who still wished Mount Zion could function as it did that the Parnassus hospital, with a daily census of about 350 and a capacity of 440, could more than accommodate the former Mount Zion inpatients comfortably. UCSF would also add 10 emergency beds at Parnassus to treat those patients currently using the Mount Zion Emergency Department, which would be required to close in the absence of inpatient services and a critical care unit.[123]

Local politics being what they are, few if any Mount Zion supporters considered that if UCSF hadn't purchased their hospital in 1990 when it was about to enter bankruptcy Mount Zion would probably have closed then and the community deprived of its services throughout the 1990s.[68]

---

*One reporter suggested that the effort "may be part of [Mayor Willie] Brown's re-election strategy." His opponent was reportedly also working on a solution for Mount Zion.[124]

†Among those who then left Mount Zion was Ernie Ring, who moved to the San Francisco General Hospital as chief of radiology.[10]

"The Second Summer of Hell"

The deadline of October 1, 1999, imposed by presidents Atkinson of the University of California and Casper of Stanford for the committee on the future of the merger to report, passed without one. The universities then charged the leaders of the faculty at both schools to try to resolve the issues. On Monday, October 4, eight chairs from each school and hospital executives met at a hotel near the San Francisco airport. The meeting was chaired by Stanford dean Eugene Bauer and Lee Goldman of UCSF. Despite eight hours of discussion, the group could not develop a plan acceptable to both schools on how to share losses generated by the hospital, a dilemma Goldman describes as "how asymmetric performance [of UCSF Stanford] would affect the faculties and medical schools."[8]

The group tried again a few days later. It met at UCSF Stanford's headquarters — "the last time I was there," says Mary Lake Polan, chair of the Department of Obstetrics and Gynecology at Stanford — and, reaching no decision, it decided to "kick it back to our parents," the presidents of Stanford and the University of California.[38]

"No one trusts generalizations anymore," reports Polan. "The boards and the financial people made mistakes, so we don't trust them." As for the differences between the two groups, Polan says, "We want the financial obligations worked out in advance so that money no longer flows north from Stanford." The Stanford chairs opposed subsidizing UCSF losses and underdeveloped infrastructure any longer, since such support deprives their departments and hospitals of much needed funding. Polan interprets the UCSF preference as "to work at expense reductions and see how it all turned out."[38]

The Stanford clinical chairs then met with Dean Bauer and Mariann Byerwalter, the university's chief financial officer, who was representing Gerhard Casper. Byerwalter presented the financial restructuring formula she and William Gurtner from the University of California had worked out to limit the effect of financial losses at one site or the other. Participants praised the thoroughness with which Byerwalter and Gurtner had done their job and the skill with which Byerwalter presented the program to the Stanford chairmen. The discussion that followed, however, revealed that the plan to limit losses didn't satisfy all the concerns of the faculty leaders.[128] If the merger were to continue, the financial strains might still decrease the amount available to invest in Stanford programs.

One by one, each of the participants gave his or her opinion of what the president should do. The opinions differed, some favoring continuing the merger and others wanting to end it. The split was about even. "It was a very honest, respectful meeting," Polan says. "People said what they believed. No one tried to pressure anyone."[38] It was clear, however, that money was no longer the problem, for the Byerwalter-Gurtner "stop-loss plan" would have protected the school. The trust of the Stanford faculty for UCSF had diminished, and enthusiasm for the merger had vanished.

At about this time, the politicians entered the fray again. State senator Jackie Speier compared UCSF's association with Stanford to that of a battered spouse and said that the relationship had become "abusive."[129] Polan finds the allusion "objectionable" and feels that Speier was "using the 'abusive' metaphor in a trivialized way."[38]

In the midst of this turmoil, two other stories from UCSF briefly distracted attention from UCSF Stanford's troubles. The San Francisco district attorney revealed that a clerk at the UCSF campus, not at UCSF Stanford, had embezzled $4.5 million.[130] In a somewhat more picaresque episode, a UCSF anesthesiologist allegedly stole the credit cards of several of her colleagues and went on a spending spree at Macy's, purchasing dresses and a Ralph Lauren quilt. At a party in the anesthesiologist's new home, the aggrieved colleagues spotted the quilt and alerted the University of California police. At her residence, the police found the items purchased with the stolen cards as well as some jewelry thought to have been taken during a party at one of the doctor's homes.[131]

Two presidents at Stanford shuddered in reflecting what the summer of 1999 had brought. To Kenneth Melmon, president of the Faculty Senate, the arrival of problems "just seemed endless. Everything was wildly out of control."[56]

Gerhard Casper, the university president, remembered the summer of 1997, when politicians almost killed the merger, as the "first summer of hell. Now [1999] we're in the second summer of hell." The current status of the merger has made Casper skeptical about whether public-private mergers such as his could ever succeed. "Public figures still consider it quasi-public, so the people at UCSF worry that they will get punished if they don't do what the politicians want."[49] Stanford and Casper had reluctantly lived with the open discussion of UCSF Stanford's problems for two years.*

In the midst of all this activity, Casper announced, on September 14, that he would resign the presidency of Stanford in August of the next

---

*A Stanford observer commented that the checks and balances of a Democratic legislature and a Republican governor, Pete Wilson, disappeared with the election of Democrat Gray Davis. Now much of the political power in Sacramento, the state capital, favored the interest of unions. "Stanford never understood the highly political nature of UCSF as a public institution and the extent to which UCSF was influenced by politicians and unions."

year. Holding a copy of the Constitution and pointing to the Twenty-second Amendment, the constitutional law scholar said, "If eight years is good enough for a U.S. president, it's good enough for me."[132] He was thus adhering to "Casper's 10-year rule, give or take two years," the term of office he thinks appropriate for those in high academic positions.[49] Observers said that Casper didn't anticipate with pleasure leading another fund drive, which would require his commitment to several more years in the presidency.[25]

How much the problems of UCSF Stanford contributed to Casper's decision to resign at the short end of his rule was a subject of speculation. Although Casper enjoyed almost universal support from the medical faculty, he mused that if anyone wanted to fire him the flow of money to UCSF, a surrogate for the serious morale problems among his colleagues in the medical school, would provide a reason. "Without UCSF Stanford, I would have most likely come to exactly the same conclusion," he says. "On the other hand, it certainly was draining and not the kind of experience that makes you want to go on."[49]

One colleague remembered how much time the Stanford medical establishment, both before and after the merger, Casper's presidency had taken* from an agenda with many other missions for his university.[133,134†] Joseph Martin and he had founded what became UCSF Stanford, and

---

*That so much of Casper's time and energies were devoted to the medical center did not surprise his predecessor, Donald Kennedy. Medical school and hospital affairs took 30 to 35 percent of Kennedy's time, "maybe more," while he was president of Stanford from 1982 to 1992. Kennedy had learned that "medical schools are the primary generator of every possible kind of unresolvable human problem, from disputes over intellectual property to sexual harassment, more than in the rest of the university combined. All other presidents with medical schools say the same."[104] Kennedy perceived a high degree of incivility in many members of the medical school faculty, which he ascribes to their being "hierarchical, high tension, and short of temper because they're sleep deprived."[104] Just a professor again when UCSF Stanford was formed, Kennedy has said that the best move would have been "to be about to merge with UCSF rather than do it!"[104]

Despite the angst medical schools can cause, universities without them, Casper adds, are lesser institutions since they lack faculty working in the medical sciences, such an important element of scientific knowledge and research today. It's the university-owned teaching hospitals, at least in Casper's experience at Stanford, that require so much time and attention from university chief executives.[49]

†In addition to agonizing over his medical establishment, Gerhard Casper's administration improved undergraduate teaching by introducing a series of small seminars for freshmen and sophomores, increased fundraising to more than $300 million annually, and developed a $200 million endowment to support graduate students.[133] By the time his administration ended, the university raised more than $2.5 billion without a formal campaign.[49] Described by the president of Yale, Richard C. Levin, a Stanford graduate, as "a true scholar, a person of really wide learning and wide tastes,"[134] Casper has taught undergraduate courses at Stanford, not something most university presidents do. His commitment to

Martin had returned to Boston before the first, let alone the second, summer of hell began. The merger now seemed in imminent danger of significant change, if not dissolution. Certainly, like Peter Van Etten, Gerhard Casper didn't look forward to participating in the demise of his creation.*

The summer of 1999 had not been an enjoyable season for the leaders of Stanford University and the University of California-San Francisco. The fall would be equally agonizing.

Dissolution

On Thursday, October 28, 1999, Gerhard Casper announced the beginning of the end of UCSF Stanford Health Care. "With great anguish, I have concluded that, in our efforts to find bold solutions to the problems of academic medical centers, we have taken on too much," he wrote to University of California president Richard Atkinson.[135] "We have failed to achieve a new common UCSF Stanford Health Care culture that would provide the wholehearted support needed." At a meeting with the Stanford Faculty Senate, Casper said, "I knew at the beginning of the merger that it was bold and therefore risky [and] would face many obstacles. I'm still not sure that asking for dissolution was the right thing. I only know that I had no alternative than to do so."[135]

Casper made his decision over the three-day period from Sunday the twenty-fourth to Tuesday the twenty-sixth. At a meeting of the UCSF Stanford board on the twenty-second, the chief executives of the UCSF hospitals and the Lucile Packard Children's Hospital told Casper that their staffs were "hemorrhaging and that a decision was essential, that any decision was better than no decision."[49†] The medical schools had still not found a formula to direct the flow of money generated from the physicians' practices and collected for them by UCSF Stanford and had missed the September deadline to complete arrangements for assuming risk from capitated contracts.

---

constitutional law led him to expand benefits to include the domestic partners of university employees. The *New York Times* reported, when he announced his resignation, that faculty members praised Casper for "unifying the university and refocusing it on academics."[134]

*In April, 2000, the university chose John Hennessy, provost and former dean of the school of engineering at Stanford, to succeed Casper.

†Brian May, the chief information officer of UCSF Stanford, explained how the uncertainty was affecting his department. "I've had to outsource the group working on the computer network and hire consultants because we've been losing two to three people per week. No one is going to work for us till the dust settles. Morale is in the tank."[15]

By the next day, Casper was inclined to continue the merger, "to test it over the long term because standing alone would never do." He knew, however, from what his colleagues were telling him, that "I had to resolve it quickly and on solid ground." On Sunday, he decided to "take time out. I cancelled my calendar for Monday and Tuesday, including a development trip to Los Angeles."[49] Casper's ordinarily full schedule would make it difficult for him to do what he thought essential, which was to talk without interruption to people who could help him decide what was best to do.

"Good lawyers ask lots and lots of questions" is the way Casper describes the technique his profession has taught him for resolving troublesome issues. He prefers to do this directly and not through intermediaries. "Until now I had not had much opportunity to talk to smart outsiders, from the business community, for example."[49]

Questioning and requestioning many people is what Casper did on Monday and Tuesday. The negatives began to accumulate. "Given how talent intense this business is and, in the absence of a new culture," a UCSF Stanford culture to replace part of the UCSF and Stanford cultures, "and with people dispirited, I began to think it unlikely that it would work." Casper had always hoped that a common culture was possible, but he was forced to recognize that "When the losses came, there was no chance."[49] Solving the physician income flow dilemma, on which the senior faculty had been working for months, and finding a formula for risk sharing in the absence of a common culture did not seem like goals that could be achieved quickly. Meanwhile, the departure of valuable people and the financial losses would continue.

Casper acknowledges that the fundamental force that concerned everyone was financial. "I didn't fully grasp the extent of the problem at UCSF until David Hunter accounted for the losses in site-specific terms." In analyzing what was killing his creation, the scholar in Casper did not desert him. "It's a Marxist explanation; the economic base overpowers the intellectual superstructure."[49]

As he proceeded toward his decision during that critical week in late October 1999, Casper and his advisers couldn't help but be affected by problems specific to UCSF. They had to calculate whether the financial disaster on the north campus could be quickly repaired, for if not, the faculty at Stanford would continue to object to what some were calling "our subsidizing of UCSF." Whereas Stanford University and its hospital enjoyed stability in their leadership, the same could not be said at UCSF, where some Stanford stalwarts claimed a vacuum existed at the highest levels of its government.

Chancellor Joseph Martin, with Casper the founder of UCSF Stanford, had moved to Boston in 1997, leaving Haile Debas, as acting chancellor, to complete the merger and at the same time direct the medical school. Exhausted by all that had happened, Debas took a long-delayed sabbatical, which coincided with the financial losses, the intense opposition over the Mount Zion solution, and the resignations of UCSF Stanford's top two officers. Lee Goldman, the medicine chair, assumed Debas's responsibilities for the merger, but the faculty did not have the same level of loyalty to Goldman, who had come to UCSF in 1995, that it had for Debas, who had joined the UCSF faculty as chair of surgery in 1987. The new chancellor, Michael Bishop, enjoyed universal respect as a scientist, but he had had little experience in the thickets that character-ized his new job. With the departure of Van Etten and Kerr, the UCSF Stanford management had reverted to the Hunter Group, skilled manag-ers but foreign to the universities and charged principally to reduce the losses, not the sort of assignment that would add to the harmony of UCSF. Furthermore, at the board level the regents from the University of California who were members of the board changed more frequently than did the trustees from Stanford.

Leaning toward dissolution, Casper considering waiting a few weeks in the hope that the problems so far unresolved could be settled. But "I didn't think a solution was likely," and he proceeded to write the letter to University of California president Richard Atkinson, which initiated the termination of UCSF Stanford.[49]

Taking It Apart

On November 19, the Board of Regents of the University of California officially accepted the unanimous recommendation of its health commit-tee to dissolve UCSF Stanford and thereby set in motion the process of ending the merger.[136] Bringing about the separation of the corporation, which had taken three years to construct and had operated for 23 months, would require resolving legal, licensing, and regulatory issues in addition to redistributing assets and personnel.[137]

William Gurtner of the University of California announced that UCSF and Stanford would take over financial liability for their own profits and losses by March 1, 2000, and that UCSF Stanford would be dissolved by April 1.[138] Losses at the UCSF hospitals might continue for as many as three years, Gurtner predicted.[138]

In San Francisco, every one assumed that the University of Califor-nia and the state would welcome back its prodigal.[18] Every political pressure favored bringing the UCSF hospitals home.[20] The unions, which rejoiced at the merger's dissolution, had helped fuel the election of Democrat Gray Davis as governor and produced a large majority in both houses friendly to union measures. Although hospitals these days are rather risky financial investments, current or even prospective losses from UCSF could disappear in the state's immense budget.[20] In the medical school, many faculty, as we have seen, delight in being part of the state system and hold that the relationship helps give UCSF its special character and explains its success.

Presuming that the hospital will become part of the University of California again, the search committee for the new CEO, led by Dr. Stephen L. Hauser, chair of the Department of Neurology, must deal with the university's pay scale, which is no longer competitive for these positions whereas the larger teaching hospitals pay more than $1 million annually. If the CEO is a doctor, however, his or her compensation could be supplemented from the School of Medicine. It seemed unlikely that UCSF would adopt the arrangement used at other academic medical centers where the dean and the CEO of the university hospital are the same person.[12]

At Stanford, the hospitals would return to Stanford Health Services, separately incorporated but tightly linked to the parent university. Then, in December 1999, Gerhard Casper reorganized the leadership by creating the position of vice president for the medical center, the job he tried to fill in 1995 but had put aside to concentrate on the merger of the Stanford and UCSF hospitals. Casper appointed Eugene Bauer, the current dean, to become the vice president with direct responsibility for the operations of the medical center. The senior executives of both the Stanford University and Lucile Packard Children's hospitals will report to Bauer, who will report to the university president. Bauer, in his new role, will also be responsible for most of the functions of the School of Medicine[139]* and will continue as dean until his successor is chosen.[140] The university provost, to whom the dean will report for certain academic matters, including appointments and tenure, appointed the search committee. "The focus of the search," according to Casper's statement, "should be on internal candidates."[141]†

Dismantling UCSF Stanford became the responsibility of a five-

---

*Stanford thereby reestablished the system of governance of the medical center used in the 1960s and 1970s in which the vice president–dean ruled over both the School of Medicine and the Stanford University Hospital.[139]

†Nevertheless, Stanford went outside for its new dean. In December, 2000, the university announced the appointment of Dr. Philip A. Pizzo, physician-in-chief, of Children's Hospital in Boston and chair of the Department of Pediatrics at Harvard, to become dean of the medical school on April 2, 2001.[141a]

member management group,* which developed a plan to transfer specific central services, including contracting, finance, and purchasing, to the sites as quickly as possible. For the time being, information technology and home health care will remain as joint services.

The Packard endowment continued to prompt both UCSF and Stanford University to develop an integrated children's service.[12] However, even this dream seemed likely to dissolve. Talks in January 2000 "broke down over cultural differences and complex issues of governance and operations," Larry Shapiro, the UCSF pediatrics chair, told the *Chronicle*.[138] Deans Bauer and Debas confirmed the separation of their children's services.[116]

Another casualty of the dissolution, which many saw as not that much of a loss, was the attempt to meld the two practice plans, the organizations at each school that process and distribute the clinical earnings of the full-time physicians. The Stanford plan came into the merger as a constituent part of Stanford Health Services, and the UCSF plan joined as a part of the School of Medicine. Managing the two plans as one entity never really came about.[12] Resolving how the funds would flow baffled resolution, and the faculties never agreed on how to share the risks inherent in managed care contracting. The exercise caused much turmoil, which helped to establish the painful undercurrent leading to dissolution.

"No one saw the practice plan problems in advance," remembers Bruce Wintroub, who was charged with consolidating and administering the joint program when he was chief medical officer of UCSF Stanford. Wintroub came to believe that the effort should never have been undertaken, and that the Stanford plan should have been excised from the merger and presumably reabsorbed into the Stanford dean's office.[1]

One unintended result from the agony of UCSF Stanford may benefit each of the campuses. "The managerial and financial problems the merger exposed should help each center know better how to carry out its operations in the future," a Stanford observer suggested and then added, "particularly at UCSF."[142†]

---

*The members include three Hunter Group executives — David Hunter, Brian Goodell, and John Stone, the interim chief operating officer at UCSF — plus Malinda Mitchell from the Stanford University Hospital and Christopher Dawes from the Lucile Packard Children's Hospital.

†This comment is not without justice, notes a consultant. "Bloem [Kenneth Bloem, CEO of Stanford University Hospital from 1989 to 1994] had winterized Stanford, which was more prepared for the decrease in dollars."[142]

The two centers can now focus on solving their specific day-to-day problems, and UCSF can attempt to stop its operating losses. "The faculties and staffs should be reenergized by no longer needing to fight the equity aspect of the merger," Lawrence Furnstahl suggests. In the short run, this activity should improve performance, but longer term, many wondered, will the two centers begin competing with each other for contracts again, allowing the HMOs to choose whichever offers the lower cost?[20]

Released from concentrating on the merger and its problems, faculty members can now concentrate on their primary functions. "Purpose and focus are returning," observed Judith Swain, the Stanford chair of the Department of Medicine. "There'd been no new programs for a year. Suddenly, new ventures seemed to be shot out of a cannon."[53]

Haile Debas also sounded optimistic as he met with his faculty for the first time since returning from his sabbatical leave. Announcing, contrary to some rumors that he might leave UCSF, that he intended to remain as the dean and vice chancellor for medical affairs, Debas told his colleagues, "My millennial wish is that Year 2000 launches all of us and UCSF into happier times and a century full of unprecedented accomplishments."[116]

Not everybody was pleased with the breakup, however, or saw it as good for the two campuses. One of the most unhappy campers was UCSF Stanford board member Warren Hellman, the San Francisco investment banker and University of California loyalist who had championed the merger by "browbeating business leaders, politicians, and regents into accepting it."[111] Deeply distressed, Hellman resigned from the board for a second time, saying, "Stanford throws its hands up and says 'we want out' when they, more than UCSF, had formed it and was running it" with the chair of its board and first CEO coming from Stanford.[111]

Frank Hanley, the pediatric cardiac surgeon at UCSF, also regrets the dissolution.[30] Hanley was instrumental in helping Stanford recruit Michael Black, one of his former trainees, to participate in the interhospital program he directed, which was based at Stanford. Hanley then helped convince the pediatricians in San Jose, a large city nearer to Stanford than San Francisco, to send their children needing heart operations to Stanford rather than to UCSF, as they had been doing. When the merger collapsed, the San Jose physicians, content with the service that Black and the Hanley team had developed at Stanford, might continue sending their patients to Stanford, with the result that the now separate UCSF had lost its San Jose referrals by helping Stanford in the name of UCSF Stanford cohesion.[30]

Post Mortem

Everyone seemed to have an explanation for why UCSF Stanford had failed. Basic to all reasons was that the merger occurred in California.[19] Reimbursement rates in the local health care market, already low by national standards, continued to drop during the life of UCSF Stanford, and the cost of drugs, devices, and supplies rose more than expected. Low unemployment gave valuable employees the opportunity to take other jobs during the turmoil of the merger and made the recruitment of several categories of workers difficult.[72]

The Founding Predicted the Failure

"To sell the merger," a prescient observer says, "the executive management and highest leaders made many promises they could not keep. The promises became the goals."[106]

Getting the support necessary to begin the merger required compromises that quickly came to haunt management and the board. Acceding to the UCSF unions' demands not to lay off any workers, essential to obtaining the state's approval, exacted a terrible price, since mergers, at their beginning, cost money, and unless sufficient reserves are available savings must be instituted at once.

"They needed to take 5 to 7 percent out of the expense base during the first two years. Instead, expenses rose 10 percent" during that period, says Brian Goodell from the Hunter Group, who is assisting with the dissolution of UCSF Stanford and the changes at Mount Zion Hospital.[66] "The merger was no longer profitable by the last quarter of fiscal 1998* and would certainly lose money in 1999," Goodell concluded.[66] Acknowledging the fragile financial situation at the outset and carrying out the cuts Goodell suggests were required would have been unacceptable to the two universities, which almost certainly could not then have gone forward with the merger.[66]

Among the retrospective explanations about the founding were the following:

"No one contemplated a disaster at the front end. You must do this or you get trapped. So when trouble came, no one was prepared."[108]

"The premerger due diligence was horrendous. There shouldn't have been all those surprises."

---

*The 1998 fiscal year ended on August 31, 1998, 10 months after UCSF Stanford began operations.

"We went into the merger with colossal naïvete, like Alice in Wonderland."[98]

"There's a basic problem with the 'merger of equals concept' behind the merger, which produced an obsession with parity. Everybody thinks the others are screwing them. But if they recognize an imbalance, which there is, that opens up even more trouble."[4] Others agree.[143]

"The burning question of the merger negotiators should have been 'Are both sides better off together than individually?' rather than emphasizing whether both sides were coming in equally."[20]

"The inherent dilemma was merging a private and public institution. The dollar problems only exacerbated this."[4]

"If we hadn't had the 'opt-out' clause, would everyone have tried harder to save it?"[111]*

Finally, those who did not participate in the merger's formation asked, "Why didn't anyone see what was coming?"[20]

Structure

Several participants came to wonder whether they had chosen the best structure for the merger. Would a holding company, as was selected by Partners, rather than a whole asset merger, the choice of UCSF Stanford and New York-Presbyterian, have worked better?

"We were too ambitious to accept a holding company and unwilling to face the consequences of a complete merger,"[43] concludes Isaac Stein, who now believes that a holding company would have been the better choice. "The inequality would have been accepted easier" with that form of governance, but "we didn't have the institutional will to do it. We would have pooled the common back office things and contracting. Over time, common clinical programs might have developed. Of course, we still had to deal with two medical schools, not just with one as at Partners."

Stein's conjecture came to pass near the end of UCSF Stanford's life. By the summer of 1999, when management had returned to the two principal sites, the corporation was operating more as a joint venture than an integrated entity.[20]

Isaac Stein has also decided, reluctantly in his case, that the use of Executive Park was ill advised. "Moving people to 3Com was well intentioned but probably unwise. They should have stayed in rented space

---

*The provisions establishing the merger gave both UCSF and Stanford the right to withdraw.

below the radar screen on Welch Road [on the Stanford campus] or Sutter Street [in San Francisco]. Put them in one office and it's noticed symbolically. Lowering the corporate image would have been wise."[43]*

Board member Richard Behrman saw management's priorities as favoring administrative rather than programmatic developments. Consequently, both universities thought that centralizing at 3Com—which led to significant overbuilding—would make the merger effective, even though "they continued to function separately."[25]

Although forming a for-profit corporation was not an option, observers couldn't help comparing the merger to a for-profit transaction. "You can merge everything together and make the tough decisions," says Isaac Stein, whose work involves creating for-profit mergers. "A new culture is created, and the unhappy people leave. There'll be winners and losers." At UCSF Stanford, Stein saw, "we put the parts together but couldn't make the broad decisions because they would cause major disruptions which would never be accepted by the universities and faculties."[43]

Brian Goodell from the Hunter Group would have favored an "intermediate structure between a holding company and a full-asset merger. Each hospital would operate as a 'tub on its own bottom' receiving services from a corporate office." Generally, in Goodell's experience, not-for-profit hospital mergers reduce their costs and centralize more slowly than for-profit entities. In this respect, he sees UCSF Stanford as acting more like a for-profit corporation. The Hunter Group, if called in to administer the hospitals from the beginning, would have forced the UCSF Stanford administration together more slowly and consequently less expensively.[66]

The Leadership

Critics of the merger hold the leadership responsible for not doing the right things and, of what was done, in the words of Stanford dean Eugene Bauer[140] and others,[143] "doing too much too soon."[52] Others, however, came to think that no one could have led UCSF Stanford successfully given the terms of its formation and the deteriorating finances of the health care environment in California.

Management was specifically faulted for hiring too many people

---

*Stein also has more practical objections to 3Com, which was criticized as luxurious, though in reality "They're next to a dump." Besides, the capitalist in him adds, "for whatever it's worth, they're in the same building as some union offices."[43]

and spending too much money too rapidly to consolidate the back office functions. None of this would have aroused opposition if sufficient resources had been available to do it quietly since saving by consolidating was one of the primary purposes of the merger.

Management's not knowing the true financial status of the merger at the beginning was a fatal obstacle, but full understanding of the perilous financial effect of bringing the parties together would have killed the merger before it was born. The underdeveloped reporting facilities, particularly in San Francisco, prevented necessary information from being conveniently available to the executives and the board before expenditures were made.

Although the top officers paid the price of the difficulties by losing their jobs, the configuration of the merger predicted that they would have trouble. "The administrative structure inhibited efficient management. We had one CEO, two deans, two parents, so the CEO couldn't drive it. It was doomed."

"Peter Van Etten's hands were tied, since each of the two partners has veto power. He couldn't really run things. For example, he couldn't pick his number two or number three [chief operating officer or chief medical officer]. They had to be UCSF people to maintain 'balance.' It's like the UN Security Council."[53]

Van Etten himself explains, "The fundamental configuration of the merger was unstable. We have a clinical structure supporting two medical schools, each with different setups. There's an inherent problem in the CEO and the two deans trying to make decisions about the clinical enterprise. The deans' authority is restrained by their faculties [whose interests] may differ from what the CEO thinks is wise."[4]

Contrary to what many thought, the Hunter Group would have preferred that Van Etten and Kerr not leave.[58,66,108] They knew UCSF Stanford as well as anyone and were executing the performance improvement plan that Hunter had developed with Van Etten and Kerr to reduce the operating losses. "We were surprised when they left since we saw them doing what the board had told them to do."[58]

Money

"The merger came about for financial reasons and dissolved for financial reasons," concludes a senior faculty member from Stanford, or, as seen by a UCSF officer, "The trigger was the differential losses, which spooked Stanford to pull out."[12]

The red ink brought forward all the cultural differences between the faculties, the state-private problems, and the geographical distance separating the two medical centers. Eventually, the Stanford faculty came to see UCSF as a "bottomless pit, draining money from their school."[19]

The costs of establishing the merger far exceeded what the founders had anticipated,[52] and they didn't adequately anticipate the effect of losing the financial assistance that the state of California had provided to UCSF when it was a state entity. The disinclination of UCSF to invest in information technology before the merger laid an expensive burden on the corporation as the year 2000 approached and constituted an important source of conflict between the campuses.

"We couldn't understand that so much had to go north," Stanford's Peter Gregory says. "A small 'tax' would have been OK, but not so much of the total.* If UCSF Stanford had not happened, the state would have eventually funded the computer upgrading so vitally needed at UCSF, Gregory assumes.[13†]

In the absence of losses during the first year, UCSF Stanford appeared relatively calm. Hospital volumes were growing, back office functions were coming together, service lines were being organized, clinical integration was beginning, and, most important as it turned out, the public, the legislature, and the press in San Francisco were quiet. The public announcement of the losses at the beginning of 1999 opened the floodgates. All the forces opposing the merger now had something specific on which to base their objections. By the fall, the pressures from the Stanford faculty to stem the flow of money to San Francisco forced Gerhard Casper to call it off.

By August 31, the end of the 1999 fiscal year, UCSF Stanford had accumulated an annual operating loss of $79 million. Both sites lost money, about three-quarters of it at UCSF and Mount Zion and one-quarter at Stanford. With the addition of income from investments, the total loss was $60 million. Without corrective action, losses might reach $218 million by the end of fiscal 2001.[72]

Despite the efforts of the Hunter Group, moreover, the operating losses were continuing as the new fiscal year began. During September,

---

*The California state auditor reported in August 1999 that of the $126 million UCSF Stanford spent for information technology about two-thirds went to UCSF. The premerger business plan estimated that only $25 million would be required at the two sites.[72]

†UCSF faculty also recognized this deficiency. Senior UCSF obstetrician-gynecologist Russell Laros faults the north campus billing and accounting systems, which he describes as "nonfunctional. We tried to move it into a combined system, and no one knew what was happening financially from November 1998 to last spring [1999]. I remember chairmen pleading with Bill Kerr, 'When are you going to give us some data?'"[19]

1999, UCSF Stanford lost approximately $7 million—$4 million at UCSF and about $3 million at Stanford.[74] During October, the losses at UCSF Stanford equaled $10 million.[144] Volumes at Stanford were less than expected, and the near future would bring the unbudgeted costs of dissolution and the loss of the merger's financial advantages. Stanford University might make up some of this shortfall, but, with no model on which to base the estimates, the amount was unknown.[58]

Ironically, the underlying financial status of UCSF Stanford remained strong throughout the tumultuous 1999 fiscal year. On August 31, the corporation had $500 million in cash and investments, $850 million in net worth, and $345 million in debt—a relatively small amount of leverage as hospitals go. During 1999, UCSF Stanford had burned off only $40 million of its initial net worth.[20]

"We started off with a strong capital position, knowing we faced an uncertain future," says Lawrence Furnstahl, the former chief financial officer. "The balance sheet remained strong, so if you still believed in UCSF Stanford we had the wherewithal to finance a turnaround." Furnstahl suggests thinking of the capital in UCSF Stanford as similar to the money raised in a stock offering by a startup company, "which we were. You spend some of the capital to finance the startup losses."[20]

"Why did we only talk about operating losses instead of also mentioning our capital strength?" asks Furnstahl. "To muster the discipline needed to cut costs," he answers. In retrospect, "this may have been incredibly stupid" because it stressed what was weak without balancing it with what was strong. Management also lost credibility because "We let the story, the PR, get out of control. We went too fast from 'we're fine' to 'we're in trouble' but not as much trouble as we said." Furnstahl wonders whether presenting the financial story differently might have given UCSF Stanford more time. "You do all this work, and then you abort it in under two years, less time than it took to create it."[20]

Despite the losses, which, he believes, shouldn't by themselves have caused UCSF Stanford to fail, Michael Abel of Brown and Toland* sees the merger as making "incredible sense financially but not administratively."[69,†]

---

*Brown and Toland is the IPA of physicians from UCSF, California-Pacific Medical Center, and, briefly during 1999, Stanford.

†In the summer of 2000, Dean Debas predicted that the UCSF medical center should take less than two years to reverse its operating deficit.[36] The current losses were running at about $25 million annually, half of the amount many had feared.[36] In the spring of 2000, Mark Laret, director of the University of California, Irvine Medical Center, became CEO of the medical center that William Kerr had led for 18 years.

The Role of the Faculty

Many concluded that an important reason why the merger failed can be found in the inability of the two faculties and the leaders of the University of California-San Francisco and Stanford University to coalesce into a single, new culture called UCSF Stanford. Besides applying to junior and senior professors, the problem also permeated the board of trustees, which "never had time to develop a board culture before the financial crisis hit."[20]

"If there is a failure to be ascribed, it's that UCSF Stanford didn't present a vehicle to which the UCSF and Stanford faculties could transfer their loyalties," Eugene Bauer, Stanford's dean, has concluded.[52]

Christopher Dawes, the chief operating officer of the Lucile Packard Children's Hospital and a member of the UCSF Stanford leadership, says, "With hindsight, we got too far in front of the faculty, which never was brought into it because the benefits of being a part of UCSF Stanford were never made clear."[143]

Gerhard Casper said as much in implying that the faculty had contributed to the failure of UCSF Stanford by not coming together successfully. "I concluded that we could not continue to move forward and then suddenly, three months from now, say, we could not deliver on the risk sharing."[145] The doctors from both campuses could not decide how to share the profits or losses from the managed care contracts their practice plans would produce by the September 1 deadline dictated by the merger agreements.*

"At its core," says Isaac Stein, "the single basic problem was that neither faculty developed a sense of loyalty to UCSF Stanford Health Care. Consequently, the merger only worked if we gave to the faculty and expected nothing of them such as surrendering autonomy or identity." When the losses developed, "all one had was two parties looking to their own interests."† Like others have done, Stein compares the situation to a marriage. "Combining their incomes lets the couple rent a larger apartment, but if one gets sick it falls apart unless there's a deeper commitment." There was not much the board could do about this problem, Stein believes, "absent a merger of the medical schools."[43]

"Rather than pulling together," observes independent UCSF Stan-

---

*David Hunter confirms from discussions with Casper while the Stanford president was deciding whether to abort the merger that he did not "cave in" to the Stanford faculty specifically. "Gerhard believed that the two faculties couldn't do it." Anthropological critics of the faculties compared them to primitive tribes. Hunter adds, in these terms, "Casper couldn't bring the two tribes together."[108]

†Several other observers commented upon the changing reactions of the faculty leaders. "We'll share the profits [1998] but not the losses [1999]" was typical.[143]

ford board member Dr. Richard Behrman, "the primary interest of the faculty and their leaders remained to preserve their own universities." The board couldn't do what was necessary but excused the inaction of the faculty by saying "we're not an academic merger. To make it work, you have to merge academic planning,"[25] which means, fundamentally, combining clinical services, which, as we have seen, made little progress.

The assumption that the faculties were somehow at fault even penetrated the state bureaucracy. A report published by the California state auditor in August 1999, two months before Casper called for dissolution, opined that UCSF Stanford's "failure to achieve its objectives results fundamentally from its failure to fully integrate its two faculty medical staffs and consolidate clinical programs."[72]*

"If the merger means you get more money and don't have to give up anything, that's terrific," is how one of the participants described the way he saw the faculty responding to the merger.

As expected, faculty members objected to being blamed for the merger's failure. "The faculty was enthusiastic at the beginning," says one senior Stanford professor. "When the losses appeared, the tenor changed, until at the end the faculty was at each other's throats. It was lousy management, a lousy board, not the faculty" that scuttled UCSF Stanford. "There was a pervasive sense of distrust, the most important factor dissolving it."

"The financial problems finally caused the dissolution," says another, "not the faculty's boycotting it, as some have suggested."[146]

"The trustee's approach — 'we made the business decision, it's up to you, the faculty, to make it work' — simply makes scapegoats" of them, says a critic of the merger sympathetic to the faculty's point of view.[147]

Ken Melmon at Stanford described how UCSF Stanford created a committee on academic benefits with membership evenly divided between UCSF and Stanford. The group developed what he saw as "startling examples of the academic advantages of the program that would only be accomplished with a successful merger" through a series of suggestions that were unanimously accepted by the two academic senates. The administration rejected the recommendations. It seemed to want "nothing of the faculty in making decisions about money or new programs. The turndown was public and angry. From my perspective, the end was at hand from that moment."[145a]

Doctors at both UCSF and Stanford emphasized that the faculties had never signed on to the consolidation. "We were blamed for failing to

---

*The report also concluded that, while the merger cost money in its first two years, it would likely contribute $90 million in value over the next two years. From these data, Peter Van Etten suggests that "a strong financial case can still be made for the merger."[4]

integrate, but what was wanted was more than we were ever prepared to do in the first place," said a leader from UCSF.[12] An active participant from Stanford concluded, "The faculty never supported it as much as the board and the senior university officials. It put the chairs in a difficult position,"[11] while a chair at UCSF added, "Doctors putting roadblocks in the process was not the problem."[34]

Dr. Michael Abel, the CEO of Brown and Toland, does not agree. Abel believes that "the losses were a convenient excuse for dissolving the merger. It was the physicians who blew it apart." The money seen by Stanford faculty to be flowing from south to north was not the issue, he believes. "Their passive-aggressive behavior convinced the top people to kill it."*[69]

Part of this attitude derives from what a consultant sees as characteristic of some faculty members. "They behave like labor unions, saying, 'How do I keep what I have in place?'"[142]

William Gurtner, who participated in the effort to save the merger in the summer and fall of 1999, agrees. "The faculty's focus was 'what's happened to me.'"[148] At Stanford, the faculty exaggerated the effect of the money they saw flowing north, he believes. "The relative size of the loss was not appreciated. We could not educate the faculty at the south campus what the equity adjustment would be. It was always 'A versus B.'" Like other observers, Gurtner saw the faculties never coming to realize that the "dollar decisions had to be made for the corporation, not for the individual parts." Decisions became emotional rather than logical, he believes.[148]

Looking back from the problems of the fall of 1999, Bruce Wintroub suspects that some of the faculty angst could have been avoided by postponing bringing together the practice plans until about five years after the merger had begun. The organization at Stanford, however, required the integration since the Stanford plan was part of Stanford Health Services, having been transferred out of the School of Medicine to the hospital in 1994.[1]

The Two Cultures:† Stanford versus UCSF

Isaac Stein and Howard Leach, the chair and vice chair of UCSF Stanford, in their official statement after Casper's letter, held responsible

---

*Abel also agrees with those who fault the compromises accepted to complete the merger. "Management should have said at the beginning that we're going into it to take out jobs, not create them. Concession to the union doesn't take advantage of the merger."[69]

†"The two cultures" is cited with apologies to the memory of C. P. Snow, who introduced the concept in 1959 in reference to the differences between the scientific and humanistic communities.[149]

"the very different and complex structures and cultures each of our institutions brought to the new entity."[52]*

"Though UCSF and Stanford were fundamentally compatible — both outstanding research universities — the problems arose because of the differences," explains former Stanford CEO Kenneth Bloem.† "One is a small academic center, the other a large state center, and management is different — tight financial control at Stanford, not so much so at UCSF, where there is state support."[106]

Stanford dean Eugene Bauer confirms what others have observed about the two schools. "Stanford is driven by facts and less by emotions, UCSF by relationships and trust. Stanford's administration is transparent, UCSF's paternalistic."[140] Consequently, the fact that Stanford initiated the dissolution makes sense. The faculty and administration in the south saw Stanford as subsidizing the merger. The San Francisco school would have continued trying to make it work.

Chancellor Bishop of UCSF acknowledged that the impetus for the dissolution had not come from his university. "It was my hope then [from statements he made in July 1999], and remained so to the end, that the merger would allow both UCSF and Stanford to cope with the economic crisis that afflicts academic hospitals throughout the United States."[150]

Now juggling the administrative and public relations aspects of the dissolving merger — rather a far cry from running a research laboratory — Bishop explained in a memo to his colleagues that "the operating losses of the hospitals do not threaten the fiscal integrity of the schools" and that the hospitals, when the separation from UCSF Stanford is complete, will "stand on their own."[74]

William Kerr, the former chief operating officer of UCSF Stanford and later adviser to Bishop, was both surprised and disappointed by the decision to dissolve the merger. "When UCSF agreed to close [the inpatient and emergency services] at Mount Zion," he says, "we hoped that Stanford would accept that we could make the tough decisions that were necessary."[18]

One of the Stanford versus UCSF issues that caused disharmony

---

*Although Stein's service on the board of UCSF Stanford ended with the corporation's dissolution, his university continued to call on him. In June 2000, the Stanford University board of trustees elected him its chairman.

†Those with a historical bent will remember the similarity of the coming of age of Stanford and UCSF medical science. Stanford's occurred slightly earlier, with the transfer of the campus from San Francisco to Palo Alto, and UCSF's a few years later, with some critical recruitments and the replacement of a traditional chancellor who lacked enthusiasm for contemporary science.

was the distribution of the strategic support,[11] funds paid by the hospital to the schools of medicine for services performed by the faculty and used by the departments for academic purposes. Debate centered on achieving absolute equality between the schools for this money, and when Stanford received slightly more UCSF leaders rebelled.

We spent more time figuring how to divide the pie than growing the pie," observed Dr. Norman W. Rizk, director of the intensive care units at Stanford and an officer of the Department of Medicine assigned to help develop the merger.[11]

To confirm its intent to support the schools when the merger was formed, UCSF Stanford, unaware of the losses to come, had pledged to increase by $2.5 million per year for four years[72] the amount of strategic support that the Stanford medical school had been receiving from Stanford Health Services and the UCSF school from its hospitals. With the dissolution and the need to stop the losses at UCSF, strategic support would have to be reduced,[74] as David Hunter had previously predicted would be necessary, putting further financial strain on the schools.*

Summarizing the UCSF Stanford experience, Alain Enthoven believes that "there never was a strong case" for the merger at any time.† He criticizes the high overhead costs of executing the merger, doubts the strength of the argument that combined contracting would have significant value, and emphasizes the state versus private cultural barrier, the inclusion of Mount Zion, "a San Francisco community hospital with serious financial problems," and the separate faculties with their own interests and programs.[151]

A participant affiliated with neither school, observed, "This was a marriage of two parents who couldn't stand each other and were quite different in many ways."[20]‡

---

*Hunter has advised reducing strategic support by $12 million, $6 million for each school, a particularly divisive prospect for the faculties.[72]

†Enthoven is the Stanford health care economist who introduced the term *managed competition* more than 25 years ago.

‡Peter Van Etten summarizes: "Perhaps the biggest failing of UCSF Stanford was that it deterred the leadership at both organizations from addressing the fundamental internal issues that need to be changed to compete effectively. These are issues such as appointment rules, tenure, fundamental changes in business processes, compensation, relations with referring doctors, program development, marketing, establishment of multidisciplinary programs, and improvement of outcomes. So much time was spent trying to make the merger work that we did not focus upon the most critical issues within each institution. Of course, that is usually the case in AMCs [academic medical centers]. It is much easier to battle with the dean, chair, or hospital CEO than with the outside world. The merger, then, rather than helping to provide a solution, became the primary problem."[4]

"A Great Opportunity Missed"

Much of the work done by those trying to make the merger succeed had caused great stress, and at its end many members of the faculty and staff at both institutions would echo the exclamation of Russell Laros of UCSF, "The merger's been a horrible experience for all of us."[19]

Nevertheless, as the faculty and administrators looked back, many wondered whether if they'd done things differently UCSF Stanford would still be standing. As a Stanford faculty member observed, "From 30,000 feet, it looked like such a good idea."[11]

A true believer till the end is Warren Hellman, the investment banker on the UCSF Stanford board, but even he had to concede that "the logic of the merger was flawed. We failed to understand the dynamic between the faculties and were naive about our ability to merge the academic departments." Combining common services "should have worked, but the execution was flawed." Consolidating bidding and contracting "worked better than I anticipated. The merger certainly prevented the further deterioration of rates and may actually have increased them. This activity should have been enough to assure the merger's success."[111]

In 1996, Hellman had chaired the regent's third-party review, which concluded that UCSF would prosper in a merger with Stanford.[152]* During its first year, when UCSF Stanford seemed to be flourishing, Hellman resigned from the board because of other charitable commitments. Two months later, when the financial problems were revealed, he asked to rejoin. "If it's going to fail, I want to help it fail," he explains.[111]

Despite his disappointment about UCSF Stanford, Hellman continues to support the university where he obtained his bachelor's degree.† Two weeks after the announcement of the dissolution, UCSF revealed that Hellman and his wife had given $5 million to support the work of young investigators.[154]

---

*In at least one respect, this is certainly true. Money from Stanford, which might not have arrived without the merger, helped improve UCSF's infrastructure.[153]

†Although born in New York City, Hellman grew up in San Francisco and graduated from Berkeley and the Harvard Business School. Before returning to the Bay Area in 1981, he worked for Lehman Brothers in New York, rising to the level of partner and chair of a Lehman closed-end investment company. He later became general partner of Hellman, Ferro Investment Associates of Boston. In 1984, he and a friend created the firm of Hellman and Friedman LLC, which is primarily engaged in the investment of its own capital. He works from an aerie in an office building near the waterfront with astounding views of the San Francisco Bay and its bridge.

Lawrence Lewin, a consultant who had advised UCSF Stanford early in its creation, believes that Casper had to make an agonizing choice between his faculty, which had come to oppose the merger, "and a good idea." Before the leadership had enough time to fully develop the project, Lewin suggests, "they were hit by two surprises at about the same time — that UCSF needed lots of money to modernize its systems and then the size of the BBA [Balanced Budget Act] cut. Given more time," he wonders, "might UCSF Stanford have succeeded?"[153]

Time is just the treatment that UCSF Stanford needed in Lawrence Furnstahl's opinion. "Much of the current financial crunch could have been avoided if we had only had 18 to 24 months of preparation to get ready."[20]

Gerhard Casper agrees. "We could have worked things out given sufficient time. If the dollar situation had not turned against us, the noise wouldn't be there or at least we wouldn't be hearing the noise."[49] Casper regrets not being able to reduce costs during the first year when UCSF Stanford generated a surplus. Without the pressure of losses, however, "The unions at UCSF would have killed us," he believes.[49]

Members of the Hunter Group, including David Hunter,[108] also regret that the end came so quickly. "We were very disappointed that we didn't have more time to try to make it work," says John Stone. "It was dissolved too soon. We wish people had had more patience." But, Stone adds, whether UCSF Stanford would have eventually prospered and satisfied most people at both universities is "at best a fifty-fifty gamble."[58]

Distinctly not needed in view of the continuing deficits were the unavoidable costs of dissolving UCSF Stanford, the amount of which no one could accurately estimate during the fall of 1999.[58]* Time would be required of the executives, lawyers, accountants, and technical people in disassembling each of the elements that had been consolidated. The financial savings that had finally begun appearing in the wake of the costly back office consolidations would now disappear.

---

*During the last seven months of operation from September 1, 1999 through March 31, 2000, UCSF Stanford lost $127 million, including the costs of taking the merger apart.[154a] The merger lost $49 million during its first two years of operation which began on November 1, 1997. Thus, the total loss for UCSF Stanford during its 29 months of operation was about $176 million.[154a] The hospitals, operating separately after the merger dissolved, continued to lose money. Stanford lost $48 million for the last five months of its 2000 fiscal year which ended on August 31, a particularly difficult period that included a nurses' strike and several accounting adjustments.[154b] Stanford plans on a break-even budget by September, 2001. UCSF expects to lose about $25 million during the fiscal year 2001 which ends on June 30.[154a]

Soon after announcement of the dissolution, management detected a hardening in the negotiating stance of some vendors. Soon the expense budget of $1.5 billion would be halved, and the leverage exerted by the hospitals in San Francisco and Stanford would be less than that for UCSF Stanford.

Administratively, the San Francisco hospitals would have to change the start of their fiscal year from September 1 back to July 1, which is used by the University of California, and reestablish university systems with all the complications attendant on doing in reverse what Lawrence Furnstahl had rushed through for UCSF Stanford two years before.[58]

"It was a great opportunity missed," Bruce Wintroub says. A senior executive for the first three-quarters of its life and a UCSF Stanford enthusiast still, he deeply regrets that "We didn't have the will to stick it out." Wintroub holds that the problems were correctable if only the two owners would have "stayed the course," but "once you lose the will, it's doomed." Both parties, Wintroub believes, failed to lead their faculties sufficiently strongly and consistently. Success depended upon everyone's considering UCSF Stanford "as a marathon, not a sprint."[1]

CHAPTER 8

Conclusions

"The big picture" in the merger scene, suggests Dr. Kenneth I. Shine, president of the Institute of Medicine of the National Academy of Sciences, "is driven by the effort of the teaching hospitals to dominate the market" in their communities. Despite what the consultants say, "saving money by consolidation turns out to be a minor plus. The leaders of academic medical centers are desperate to find out how to get out of the mess they're in."[1]

Shine's analysis, given during the summer of 1998 before the research for this book began, neatly summarizes what 18 months of subsequent study have confirmed. Money can be spent as much as saved in combining hospital functions — UCSF Stanford being the most obvious example — domination of managed care remains an unproven accomplishment supported only by anecdotal data,[2] and combining clinical services for the most part is an unrealized goal. The leaders of teaching hospitals continue to worry about how they can keep their stressed charges whole and functioning.[3]

Merger Mania

"All such mergers should be seen in the context of the merger boom of the past several years," says Victor Fuchs, the Stanford health care economist. "It's a little like an epidemic, an infectious disease. Something gets in the air, and it seems like the thing to do. It's not coincidental that it happened with the stock market boom." Fuchs believes that, given "the control-expenditures mind set," a certain amount of merger activity is to be expected. "The enthusiasts for the merger always exaggerate the amount to be saved."[4]

As consultant Jeff Goldsmith puts it, "A lot of the deals get a life of their own,"[5] or, according to George Vecchione, "People fall in love with deals."[3] Vecchione had participated with David Skinner and William Speck in merging the New York and Presbyterian Hospitals and then became CEO of Lifespan, itself a company of merged teaching hospitals.

The magnitude of the financial problems facing academic medical centers, "which operate so close to the margin, drives people to think of big, bold actions," Kenneth Bloem, the former CEO of the Stanford University Hospital, has found. The merged hospital corporations become so big and complex that close attention to the "nonsexy, day-to-day work" on which management should concentrate gets shortchanged. "The day isn't long enough to do both the big things — the grand, global strategies — and the routine work." As for the faculties, in Bloem's experience, "Academics don't want to bother with this meat and potato stuff."[6]

The enthusiasm for merging teaching hospitals may be decreasing partly in response to the UCSF Stanford debacle. Dr. Jordan J. Cohen, president of the Association of American Medical Colleges, senses that "merger mania seems to have run its course,"[7] and George Vecchione adds, "A chill has come over this."[3]

Governance

In Boston and New York, the hospital boards of trustees, traditionally independent of their affiliated universities, governed the Massachusetts General, Brigham and Women's, Presbyterian, and New York Hospitals. This pattern also characterized the governance of Partners and NewYork-Presbyterian, with university officers or trustees exercising no direct control over the merged hospital boards.

The universities, however, directly controlled the West Coast hospitals before the formation of UCSF Stanford. At UCSF, the state of California owned both the hospital and the school, and the chief executive of both reported to one person, the chancellor of the campus. Although separately incorporated in the 1980s, the Stanford hospital remained tightly linked to the university thanks to overlapping board members and, during Donald Kennedy's tenure, the presence of the Stanford president as chairman of the hospital board.

The different structures of the East Coast versus the West Coast mergers differently involved the deans of the two schools of medicine. At Harvard, deans Tosteson and Martin exercised no formal, direct authority over what Sam Thier and his colleagues in the Prudential Building decided. The deans could concentrate on their academic responsibilities and worry, if they were so inclined, about the losses accrued by the Beth Israel–Deaconess merger and the wealth of problems facing academic medicine in general, a task that many would think is an appropriate occupation for the dean of the Harvard Medical School. In New York, deans Gotto and Pardes participated more fully in what was happening at the NewYork-Presbyterian Hospital, but lacking specific authority and responsibility they could primarily represent only their medical school constituencies.

At UCSF Stanford, however, deans Bauer and Debas participated in the creation of the merger, and later, as members of the hospital board, made vital decisions. This activity put them in what one observer has called a "push-pull position." While assuming a primary role in managing the merger, the deans also had to lead their faculties, which, as the problems mounted, increasingly criticized the organization on whose board they served. For UCSF Stanford to succeed, the deans had to be seen as fully committed to the merger, whatever some of their faculty constituents might have wanted or their private reservations might have been.

Furthermore, the president of Stanford and the chancellors of UCSF created the environment that led to UCSF Stanford and were involved intermittently in the operation of the merger as they also tried, almost in their spare time as it may have appeared to Gerhard Casper, to manage their other academic responsibilities. The presidents of Harvard, Columbia, and Cornell either avoided participating in the problems of Partners and NewYork-Presbyterian or, if they took action, did so quietly and behind the scenes. If either the Boston or New York mergers were to dissolve, the university presidents would not have had to assume the role that fell to Casper, who wrote the letter to the president of the University of California that led to the end of UCSF Stanford.

The fundamental structure of Partners differed from that of NewYork-Presbyterian and UCSF Stanford. The Brigham and the MGH joined together in a holding company, whereas the leaders of the New York and Presbyterian Hospitals and the UCSF and Stanford Medical Centers created full-asset mergers. We have seen how the structure of the California merger came about, in part, so as to be different from that of Boston. "We're not going to be Partners, we see the vision, we can do it right in California" is how one participant described the mantra of the founders there. That enthusiasm — one might call it the hubris of two proud institutions — didn't save UCSF Stanford.

Chastened, several of the leaders of UCSF Stanford now wonder if selecting a holding company structure might have helped it survive and prosper.[8] Would a holding company have allowed more flexible handling of the losses in San Francisco, less intense and expensive consolidation of back office services, and reduced pressure on the skeptical faculty to merge clinical services? This seems doubtful. The primary forces that drove the dissolution of the merger were the deteriorating support of health care in California and the losses at UCSF Stanford. Contributing to the financial problem was the separation from the resources of the state of California of the underfunded UCSF hospitals, which then had to rely on help from meager Stanford surpluses, which later disappeared.

In New York, the dream of consolidating most administrative and clinical services has had to be reconsidered. The plan for a common director of operations for both centers folded when the highly competent New York Hospital executive assigned the job bailed out to take a position with similar responsibilities at a smaller, although similarly renowned, academic institution. Two executives from each of the sites took over, with the primary responsibility of improving operations at the Presbyterian or New York Hospital site.

Which governmental structure is likely to be more effective when teaching hospitals merge? Partners, which operates as a holding company, is stable, and one could reasonably conclude at this point that it is flourishing as much as such institutions can be said to be flourishing these days. Of the two that chose full-asset mergers, UCSF Stanford died and NewYork-Presbyterian lives.

Partners set the pattern as the first of the three to be formed. We have seen why and how its leaders came to choose the holding company approach. Politically, it enabled the merger to occur; governmentally, it proved to be somewhat cumbersome. NewYork-Presbyterian and UCSF Stanford became full-asset mergers, in part because Partners chose otherwise. Did the decisions also reflect geographical realities — Boston, with its affection for history and tradition and its trustees not wanting to interfere with the perceptions of the MGH and the Brigham, versus New York City, with its constantly changing character and trustees who had made their own mergers in business and banking.*

The full-asset mergers at NewYork-Presbyterian and UCSF Stanford permitted the organizations to form one board where there had been two in New York.† Nevertheless, this type of governance has not facilitated the unification of clinical services because of the almost universal resistance of the faculty at the different sites to consolidate. Management and the trustees of each of the mergers discovered this fact of life but not until they had experienced the problem for themselves.

---

*Samuel Thier explains the Partners approach by insisting, "We said this is not a business like a bank."[9]

†In northern California, only Stanford Health Services had a board of trustees before the merger.

It seems unlikely that the form of the merger much affected the combining of clinical services. Partners, as a holding company, established all the efficiencies that the younger, full-asset NewYork-Presbyterian Hospital is attempting and has developed a more efficient, comprehensive system of contracting, marketing, and relating to primary care physicians. The price for the holding company with its multiple boards of trustees is less efficiency and extra work preparing reports and presentations for the meetings between Partners and hospital executives. However, it seems doubtful that the success or failure of the mergers has depended to any significant degree upon what form of governance was chosen.

The UCSF Stanford experience teaches that public governance of one of the teaching hospitals adds a very serious complication. Supported by union leaders, activists for the preservation of Mount Zion Hospital, and disaffected UCSF faculty members, their objections spread by a vigorous press, politicians from the state of California never fully released their charge. Though no longer responsible for funding the UCSF hospitals, they continued to criticize them.

One could charge the Stanford officers with naïvete in not anticipating such a response, despite the politicians' pledge of noninterference wrung from them by the Stanford president. However, Stanford had not experienced this aspect of public ownership and was only familiar with the relatively private, usually calm, reception of the decisions of its governing body. This gracious pattern seemed to apply for more than a year at UCSF Stanford, until the losses appeared and the downgrading of services at Mount Zion Hospital was proposed to help repair the damage. Now all the latent opponents gave vent to their feelings. The public spectacle added to the disharmony at Stanford produced by the financial support of UCSF's underdeveloped infrastructure. No force, no expertise in public relations, seemed able to stem the damnation of the merger.

Only at UCSF Stanford were the faculty practice plans governmentally integrated into the merged hospitals, which was necessary in this case because Stanford had transferred the jurisdiction for its practice plan from the School of Medicine to the hospital three years before the merger. In Boston, the MGH and Brigham plans reside in the hospitals, not yet in Partners, and in New York City they reside at Cornell and Columbia, not in NewYork-Presbyterian.

Combinations of practice plans and teaching hospitals, constituting what have been called "clinical enterprises," have had variable success. Bruce Wintroub, the one-time UCSF Stanford chief medical officer, sees the placement of a practice plan in the hospital as "an awful thing." The director has "a lot of responsibility and no authority since faculty look to their dean" for leadership and not to the practice director.[10]

Parity

Each of the three mergers began, their founders proclaimed, as a "merger of equals." The executives and trustees of each of the six hospitals insisted that without acceptance of this provision merging was impossible. Parity implied that each party came to its merger with equal physical, financial, and intellectual assets and that this premise would govern future relationships. Of course, this couldn't be true. There's no point counting the ways, it's such an illogical hypothesis despite the assumption of its presence in the making of each of the mergers.

At UCSF Stanford, the assumption of parity was one of the requirements of joining that helped to destroy the merger. With losses appearing, the Stanford faculty leaders rebelled at seeing their "more equal" constituency supporting the "less equal" UCSF. When the reality of parity disappeared, the theory of parity remained to curse any possibility of compromise, which was essential to sustain UCSF Stanford. Gerhard Casper understood this and, despairing of any resolution of this dilemma within a reasonable period of time, did what he felt he had to do.

At Partners and NewYork-Presbyterian, so far at least, the absence of parity has yet to be tested. However, if one of the hospitals in the Boston or New York mergers begins to need significantly more support than the other, pressure to preserve the assets of the less demanding unit may follow. Those favoring the mergers hope that the demands of the faculty and staff of the supporting hospital will be insufficient to bring about another UCSF Stanford result.

Headquarters

Partners and UCSF Stanford developed separate corporate headquarters while NewYork-Presbyterian did not. Partners and NewYork-Presbyterian are still alive, and UCSF Stanford is not. Did this choice contribute to success or failure?

Partners adopted a corporate headquarters to avoid favoring one of the founding hospitals or sending a message to other hospitals and physician groups that would later join Partners that they would be subsumed into the MGH or the Brigham. The founders also decided that the new corporation could establish its authority more quickly and begin functioning more efficiently by bringing the leaders of the fused offices together in one place where they could work closely together. The congenial geography of Boston brings the MGH, the Brigham, and the corporate headquarters of Partners relatively close to one another, and the custom of students, doctors, and administrators traveling to and from the MGH and the Brigham, the Harvard Medical School, and the other hospitals in the Longwood area was well established.

The California merger also built a corporate headquarters, but the geography was much less agreeable than in Boston, with significantly greater distances required to travel to and from the hospitals to the 3Com offices near the San Francisco airport. The expenses required to bring the merger into operation in the presence of limited resources from the founding hospitals and a viciously restrictive climate for funding of health care in the state gave the opponents to the merger fuel to press for dissolution. Since part of the resources was spent on creating the corporate structure, and the decisions to spend it emanated from 3Com, the headquarters became a convenient villain for the merger's critics.

The founders of NewYork-Presbyterian deliberately avoided constructing a corporate headquarters. David Skinner, William Speck, and the other managers would run their hospital from within its components, with each of the leaders having offices at both the New York and Presbyterian sites. This solution followed from the basic premise that this merger would have one teaching hospital in two locations. We have seen the practical complications of the NewYork-Presbyterian approach, with executives traveling over many miles of Manhattan's busy streets to manage their duties and meet with their colleagues. However, as long as the basic premise of the merger remains in place, a corporate headquarters would be, as the marketing people say, "off strategy." Time will tell whether the new CEO, Dr. Herbert Pardes, continues or changes this policy.*

In Boston, sustaining the individual characteristics of the Brigham and the MGH were, and continue to be, fundamental precepts at Partners.

The location of the headquarters was not a basic cause of the success or failure of any of the three mergers.

---

*Pardes has, however, replaced the time-honored word *medical* in the titles of the two sites, which are now known as the Columbia-Presbyterian Medical Center, once again, and the New York Weill Cornell Medical Center.

The Boards

Although the boards of trustees of Partners and NewYork-Presbyterian have so far escaped censure, critics pummeled the trustees of UCSF Stanford. Thoughtful analysts of the fate of the merger suggest that its members, as well as the two faculties, helped prevent the development of the new culture that many believed essential for the merger to succeed. Although the hospitals of UCSF and Stanford merged, the new board of trustees never did. The board remained a group of individuals, most of whom represented their own universities rather than the new entity.

On first inspection, this feature might appear advantageous, implying a superior means of cementing the patient care and scholarly interests of the institution. What happened, however, was that whenever critical issues arose most of the members persisted in thinking primarily of how their decisions would affect their universities, where their loyalties continued to reside, thereby relegating UCSF Stanford to third place among their priorities. The independent trustees could not, it appears, transfer the orientation of university partisans to the common venture when called on to resolve, for example, where the financial losses should be assigned or strategic support directed. The majority of the board members continued to emphasize the parts rather than the whole.

Complicating matters further, top university officials on the hospital board would meet privately to decide what positions to insist upon for the benefit and protection of their universities when meeting later as members of the UCSF Stanford board. Management, accordingly, had to focus on the needs of the medical schools and their faculties when it should have been concentrating on running cost-effective hospitals.[11] As one senior UCSF officer put it, "On divisive issues, the members divided along party lines."[12]

Would a board with more outside members and fewer from the universities have saved the day? We'll never know because the constituencies required a balanced UCSF Stanford board for the merger to win approval from the University of California and Stanford. When the losses polarized the faculty, it seems doubtful that a differently constituted board could have produced the new culture that Stanford president Gerhard Casper felt UCSF Stanford must develop for him to have decided to continue the participation of his university.

In New York, the founding trustees of NewYork-Presbyterian, the former board members of the Presbyterian and New York hospitals, despite residual affections for their previous affiliations, were not employees, officers, or trustees of the medical schools or universities, as were most members of the California board. The New York board includes sophisticated businesspeople familiar with medical operations from longtime membership on hospital boards, which was not the case for most of the members of the relatively small UCSF Stanford board. Similarly, in Boston, where the board has now had six years to coalesce, the Partners trustees oversee an enterprise that hasn't yet lost much money. The allegiance of the NewYork-Presbyterian board to the merged company, as at Partners, has yet to be tested by large losses as in California.

Whether or not they are leading a merged company, trustees of university teaching hospitals have had to respond to the greater complexity and size of their charges. Mitchell Rabkin, who as CEO of the Beth Israel Hospital in Boston for 30 years (1966 to 1996) has observed many a board meeting, finds that their traditionally large size interferes with making the rapid decisions now required by the financial stress affecting academic medical centers. "Governance requires smaller, more agile boards," he suggests.[13] Greater use of executive committees allows decisions to be reached without reducing the size of the boards, the membership of which is often allotted to loyal contributors with varying management experience.

The newer members of the boards of some teaching hospitals, some of whom seem more likely to listen with favor to the more grandiose plans of the officers, are what Rashi Fein, professor of the economics of medicine at the Harvard Medical School, calls "dollar people, merger and acquisition types who move money around rather than run things. They seem more interested in hearing about fiscal matters than medical advances."[14]

The Roles of the Faculty, the Deans, and the CEOs

With the making of a hospital merger primarily a business, not an academic, decision, could more than a few faculty members have usefully participated in establishing any of the three mergers studied here? Those who made the mergers and their consultants say no, taking as their model the business world, where a vote of the employees is not a feature of merger negotiations. In the forming of hospital mergers, the risks are high and the details to be worked through are complex. Involving more than a core group in this process is not practical.

Decision making by so few, however, leaves the leaders subject to condemnation from those who oppose the decision. Then, if the venture fails, the critics come out in force, saying "I told you so." The unfortunate case of UCSF Stanford provides a dramatic example of this course. Representatives of the faculties at UCSF and Stanford cried foul when they were blamed for the dissolution. "This was never my deal. Now you're blaming me," they were said to say.

Surely, few employees of a business would speak so freely, but universities are different. Their business is scholarship, which requires the freedom to say and write what one pleases within certain rather ill-defined limits. In a university, custom dictates that the faculty rules. However, this description belies the way medical schools work. The governance of these institutions is only partly democratic or representational and much more hierarchical than is customary among faculties elsewhere in universities. Teaching hospitals operate with more of the characteristics of businesses than of academia; most of the employees work in a traditional top-down culture.

The method of selecting the leadership further reduces the dominance of the faculty since deans and chairmen in medical schools and CEOs of teaching hospitals are appointed and seldom elected.* Nevertheless, deans and CEOs can't ignore the influence of the senior professoriat. To some extent, deans hold their positions on sufferance, for, as we have seen, the same senior faculty cannot only influence what the dean does, but the effective dean must constantly keep aware of what his senior colleagues are thinking. The chairmen, if they act together, can force a dean to retire. This has happened recently. Similarly, hospital CEOs can't ignore the wishes of the senior faculty, for if they lose the confidence of the professors their appointments can terminate if the CEO's boss, usually the trustees but sometimes a university officer as at UCSF, agrees with the faculty.

---

*In medical schools, the chairmen often cling to their jobs for the rest of their active lives. One of the reasons for this tendency is that the position of chairman in academic medicine enjoys significant prestige, more so than accrues to an academic who chairs, say, an English department.

Until recently, the opportunities for building departments or divisions and thereby leaving a legacy to the institution, attracted many physicians with an organizational bent. Furthermore, medical school chairmen, particularly clinical chairmen, are better paid than most of their colleagues and, in the past more so than now, acquired lucrative private practices as a result of being "the professor." One need only refer to the experience of the esteemed William Osler, founder of the Department of Medicine at Johns Hopkins. He accepted the Regius Professorship at Oxford partly to relieve himself of the burdens of a large private practice.[15,16]

Since most clinical chairmen are now salaried, full-time employees, a private practice is less a factor, although large incomes based on practice are still the prerogatives of division chiefs and chairmen of some academic units at famous as well as less well known teaching hospitals. Schools tolerate the inequities these salaries produce because such doctors, usually surgeons or physicians who perform procedures, bring well-insured patients to the hospitals.

Since one of the dean's responsibilities is providing clinical sites at which to train his school's students and postgraduates,* he can't avoid being concerned about the operation of his school's principal teaching hospitals, for if they fail he can't fulfill his educational role. As the condition of teaching hospitals has become increasingly unstable, the leaders of the schools — including those deans to whom the CEO does not report, which is the case in each of the hospitals studied here — find themselves torn between the conflicting plans of the hospital's executives and the wishes of the faculty. At Harvard, the history and governance of the hospitals and the medical school denies the dean the ability to influence hospital policy directly. Similarly, in New York City, Presbyterian and New York Hospitals were and are, as NewYork-Presbyterian, governed separately from the medical schools. In northern California, however, the hospitals were part of the universities, and we have seen how actively the highest officers of the academic establishments participated in UCSF Stanford.

The senior faculty, including deans, department chairmen, and division chiefs, are called on to play important roles in governing medical schools, even though at the leading medical schools they tend to have been appointed because of their academic accomplishments, not primarily for their managerial or business experience.[17]

Senior faculty regularly meet† to work on current issues. The rest of the faculty participates through membership on committees, which nominate leaders of departments, divisions, or programs, advise on the awarding of promotions and tenure, or develop solutions to problems laid before them by the administration or occasionally advanced by faculty members. Wise deans and chairmen consult widely before they institute a new policy that may affect many faculty members. They may refer prospective policies to faculty senates or other organized groups of the professoriat, but these organizations, whose meetings are often sparsely attended, are often debating societies or forums in which the leadership announces the decisions it has reached. The influence of these groups is usually limited, although they can voice opposition, as the chairman of the unofficial Faculty Association at UCSF demonstrates.

---

*Interns and residents are, strictly speaking, hospital employees, but the chairmen and division chiefs, who look to deans not hospital CEOs as their ultimate bosses, recruit them, direct their work, and grade their performances.

†And meet and meet. Recall the complaints of many about the amount of time the mergers have taken from their usual duties.

Allegiance

Altering the allegiances of the members of the high-profile members of the clinical faculties at teaching hospitals remains a goal of trustees and managers. They hope that in time faculty, staff, and board members will come to think of themselves as associated with, for example, the NewYork-Presbyterian Hospital rather than the medical centers of Columbia-Presbyterian or New York Hospital–Cornell. Although this was also a goal in California, UCSF Stanford lasted for such a short time that whatever the planners hoped to accomplish in this regard never had time to develop. Faculty members continued to proudly call themselves Stanford or UCSF people. In Boston, the organizers of Partners recognized that their colleagues would never voluntarily disassociate themselves from the Brigham or the Massachusetts General and deliberately chose the neutral name Partners in recognition of this fact. As Samuel Thier says, "The value of the MGH and Brigham names are too precious to run down."[9]

Interviews conducted for this study suggest that changing such loyalties is exceedingly difficult and not necessarily desirable and that the Partners approach is the most realistic. Academic physicians establish strong emotional ties to the place where they work. Hospitals are only one of those places. Faculty members also attach themselves to the universities that give them their academic titles,[18] as have the doctors at Columbia, Cornell, UCSF, and Stanford. At least the faculty at Partners has only one medical school that claims its loyalty.

In explaining why Partners was still alive and flourishing while UCSF Stanford was dissolving, the dean at Stanford said, "The MGH and the Brigham had formed a less ambitious organizational model that gave faculty members greater opportunity and time to shift allegiances."[19] Given that Partners had had more than five years of experience when UCSF Stanford folded after a life of only 23 months and accepting that the Partners structure was less centralized than that of UCSF Stanford, the evidence is still slim that the loyalties of the Boston faculty have changed. The interviews for this study suggest that the vision of some of the trustees and officers that the faculties in the merged teaching hospitals will in time come to think of themselves as members of the merged corporations rather than the founding institutions is a fantasy unlikely to become a reality. The MGH and Brigham doctors do not think of themselves primarily as Partners doctors, nor do members of the faculty at Presbyterian or the New York Hospital consider themselves to be working for the NewYork-Presbyterian Hospital.

The history of these three mergers, in which each of the hospitals and medical schools enjoy high status, suggests that changing the allegiances of faculties in such mergers is very difficult and not worth the effort. As other academic medical centers consider taking this course, their leaders and consultants should consider this experience.

Finances

Although saving money by consolidating functions always arises when merger talk becomes more than theoretical, at least one of the founders of the hospitals studied here understood the likelihood of this happening. "The proposed merger between New York Hospital and Presbyterian Hospital is not driven by the need to reduce costs," wrote William Speck, then CEO of Presbyterian. "The purpose is to improve patient care."[20]

Speck was prescient in making this statement, although one doubts that he understood before the merger was operating how limited would be the savings from consolidating administrative and financial functions. Review of this aspect of hospital mergers has convinced many observers of the ephemeral nature of "economies of scale," the favorite phrase used to describe the money that can be saved by putting functions together.

"Savings of one to two percent of expenses are more typical" than the higher numbers touted by the merger devotees, according to Scott M. Fassbach, chief research officer at the Advisory Group Company in Washington.[22]* In the experience of Brian Goodell, one of David Hunter's colleagues, "the most successful mergers usually do no better than break even when compared with their separate premerger status."[23]

Converting the information technology systems to accommodate the two entities alone often exceeds $100 million.[5] One of the parties usually comes into the merger with a stronger system — the Brigham in Boston, the New York Hospital in New York City, and Stanford in northern California. The UCSF system was probably the most underdeveloped of all, and UCSF Stanford officials concede that at least $75 million was invested to improve information technology just on the San Francisco campus alone. Enthusiasts contend that whatever was spent would have had to be spent anyway to prepare for Y2K. Nevertheless, the parties entered each of the mergers studied here greatly underestimating the costs.

---

*One consultant called the small amount saved through economies of scale, compared to the revenue base of these immense organizations, "budget dust."[21]

Just putting mergers in place costs money. Consultant Jeff Goldsmith says, "Transaction costs have way outweighed savings" when one includes in the startup costs of converting the information technology systems, activating combined offices, and the lawyers' and consultants' fees. Consequently, Goldsmith believes, "Unless the board can give management a seven-year time horizon," the value of mergers will be difficult to demonstrate. Most of the time, "people want a very fast response and are not prepared for the political fallout," an important cause of the UCSF Stanford failure,[5] whereas $70 million[24] is the minimum cost usually cited to establish a merger. When coupled with the costs of dismantling it, one can see that a great deal of money, which could otherwise have been spent to improve the founding hospitals and the programs of their medical schools, will have been directed into an expensive failure.

Some relief comes from the underlying resources of these historically successful hospitals. All three mergers have significant endowments generating income that could be applied to losses from operations. Although some of these funds can be spent to assure that the entity doesn't lose money, management strives to keep losses from operations to a minimum and even produce a surplus.[25] When income from the reserves must be used to relieve losses on operations, less cash is available to reinvest in the hospitals or for the strategic objectives of the merger such as developing networks or acquiring other hospitals or doctors' practices. Accordingly, "You can't live only on investment income," John Stone of the Hunter Group explains.

However, making money on operations, let alone breaking even, presents an almost insurmountable challenge to the leaders of teaching hospitals, including the ones joined in the three mergers studied here. Useful drugs and devices that better the lives of those who are ill have become increasingly available. Some are very expensive. Yet in Massachusetts, for example, the payers have managed to keep rates essentially flat for the past four years.[9] With costs rising in two digits each year and reimbursement barely increasing, it's not difficult to understand why Partners has had to use some of its reserves to relieve losses on operations for the past two years. As Sam Thier puts it, "It's gotten worse, and there's grave concern. There's a big mismatch between the cost of drugs and supplies with real value for patients and the level of reimbursement, particularly from the HMOs."[9]

The large medical centers have brought whatever muscle they have to bear on the federal government to revise the Balanced Budget Act of 1997, which legislated severe reductions in Medicare payments to hospitals, doctors, and nursing homes.[26] Thanks to the effects of this act, the government's spending on Medicare decreased from 1998 to 1999 for the first time since Medicare's creation in 1965.[26]

However, observers don't see the Congress as a friend of academic medical centers and are pessimistic about receiving long-term relief from that source. Despite some additional support for teaching hospitals in the 2000 budget compromise,[27,28] academic health centers constitute too small a portion of the enormous national expenditure on health care, it is thought, to warrant extensive governmental attention.[29]

Contracting for Managed Care

The possibility of gaining greater control of the local market through size constituted one of the principal reasons for each of the three mergers. Whether this has come to pass is still uncertain. In Boston, the leaders of the Partners monolith, for that's the way the company appears to its competitors, believe that they have been able to negotiate higher rates by convincing the carriers that many of their subscribers will insist on being able to attend the MGH and the Brigham when they get sick. Confirmatory data are hard to obtain.

In New York, the leaders of both NewYork-Presbyterian Hospital and Columbia-Cornell Care have made similar claims, but in Manhattan the limited penetration of managed care makes proof even more difficult to establish. UCSF and Stanford, separately or together, had a monopoly on very few high-end, large-revenue-producing services, and the strength of the merger added little to the number of cases or the prices the insurers were willing to pay. Of course, the short life of UCSF Stanford prevented fully testing the value of this aspect of the merger.[22] Antitrust concerns will probably prevent the two centers from joint action under separate governance.

So far, only PCHI (Partners Community HealthCare, Inc.) has developed a comprehensive, joint, doctor-hospital contracting organization. The presence of only one medical school, traditionally distant from the operations of its teaching hospitals, avoided one of the problems that might have inhibited the formation and function of such an organization.

In New York, Columbia-Cornell Care, representing the universities and their faculties, and the hospital were not able, as of the end of 1999, to combine the contracting function for both doctor and hospital care. Columbia-Cornell Care held NewYork-Presbyterian to blame for this lack of cooperation. The hospital sees such a combination as less likely to obtain contracts than when the hospital acts alone. One suspects that hubris on both sides has contributed to a situation not yet critical because of the relative lack of managed care in many of the traditional sources of patients for the hospital and the doctors.*

Clinical Programs

Reducing costs by combining clinical services immediately appeals to merger mavens unfamiliar with the Byzantine forces that permeate academic medical centers and motivate faculty members. "We do it in industry and banking, why can't you guys do it?" ask board members from the business world and state officials.[11] Although those outside the profession may find the obstacles illogical or the reasons superficial, they are a fact of life in academe, and he or she who pushes will find the wall solidly built. Interviews with medical academics, both those leading their institutions and those in the trenches, demonstrate the difficulty of accomplishing this goal.

Faculty members in clinical departments at American medical schools and teaching hospitals respond more to the forces that connect them to their own organizations than to influences that would link them to another hospital or school through a common entity such as Partners, NewYork-Presbyterian, or UCSF Stanford. Disrupting the pattern is difficult and has been the bane of those building teaching hospital mergers. Well-intentioned but misplaced enthusiasm prompted those forming each of the mergers in this study to expect that "synergies"† would develop as clinical programs and units combined.

Paradoxically, forcing consolidations of clinical services can cost rather than save money. Some doctors with large practices, disgruntled

---

*In the spring of 2000, the universities greatly decreased the size and function of Columbia-Cornell Care. Its three senior officers were relieved, and the number of employees reduced. The change presented "another example of 'managed care-capitation anxiety' not coming to pass," as a P&S chairman explained. With aggressive managed care never reaching New York City, a principal function for CCC had disappeared. Furthermore, with a university official, former P&S dean Herbert Pardes, now the NewYork-Presbyterian CEO, another aim in establishing CCC had vanished. NewYork-Presbyterian Hospital was no longer Columbia's "common enemy" as one of the participants observed. The universities were also not displeased to rein in the cost of the operation originally budgeted for $100 million. By the spring of 2000, about $20 million had been spent.

†Princeton economist Uwe Reinhardt remembers that somebody once compared synergies in hospital mergers to the phoenix, the legendary bird that, according to one account, lived 500 years, burned itself to ashes on a pyre, and rose alive from the ashes to live another 500 years. Neither synergies from hospital mergers nor the phoenix have ever been seen.[30]

by administrative consolidation, will decamp to other hospitals, which will gladly receive them and their patients. The loss of revenue generated by the defection of only a few of these medical high rollers can quickly negate whatever savings are realized by consolidating services.[22]

As we have seen, however, the cause is not hopeless. A few services have come together within the hospitals studied here, usually smaller specialties or those with fundamental financial problems. Consolidations can occur relatively painlessly when a service is strong at one of the hospitals and weak at the other and investing in the weak service seems unwise in this time of limited resources. Although the mergerers emphasize such successes, combinations built on unilateral weakness, small size, or administrative ineffectiveness constitute a minor portion of the clinical services these hospitals provide and consequently reduce only a small fraction of the expenses of these mammoth establishments.

Furthermore, not funding an expensive piece of medical equipment with its attendant staff for both sites in a merger will save some money but, seen as part of the institution's overall financial picture, any reduction in capital expense will be relatively small.[22] Here again, the aims of the faculties to work at "full-service hospitals" conflicts with the economizing goals of the consolidators.

Recognizing the inevitable, executives at Partners and NewYork-Presbyterian have lowered the pressure to consolidate clinical services as service chiefs ask "how does merging services help me do my job better?"[5]

Service lines, by bringing together compatible medical services artificially separated by academic administrative structures, can assist in the marketing of clinical services to HMOs, patients, and doctors and can save money, its devotees explain. Only NewYork-Presbyterian currently favors them. Partners has not adopted service lines, and UCSF abandoned them when its financial troubles surfaced.

To further the service line concept, hospital officials wish that cardiologists and cardiac surgeons would work together organizationally, as should, they believe, neurologists, neurosurgeons, and neuroradiologists and medical, surgical, and radiation oncologists. In practice, these doctors naturally come together, sharing the care of their patients clinically even while they inhabit different administrative configurations. Trying to disrupt traditional academic structures, however, arouses all the turf instincts natural to many academic physicians who have attained top administrative posts. The wise merger leader enters this quagmire with great care.

Sharing what are known as "best practices" provides one potentially valuable goal of merging. Medicine is practiced differently at different hospitals, even among those most highly respected. By studying what is done better at one site, the other can be brought to a higher level of performance.[3] In preparing for the review of the Joint Commission for the Accreditation of Health Care Organizations in 1999, NewYork-Presbyterian energetically applied this principle. Unfortunately, the distractions of the financial crisis in California prevented any significant work toward reaching this goal, which one UCSF faculty member called "an unfulfilled hope of the merger."[31]

Education

Academic physicians love to tell how they work on three-legged stools, juggling their responsibilities for clinical care, research, and teaching. Whereas teaching is the primary activity of many of their colleagues in other schools of the university, this part of the responsibility of most academic physicians occupies the smallest portion of their time. Most are taking care of patients, conducting research, or in a few cases administering their divisions, departments, or schools.

Called "slush money" in the good old days when it existed, excess income from clinical activities formed an important source of support for education. With this resource becoming scarcer, the clinicians must work harder to generate fees to support their salaries and the work of the medical school, which leaves less time and energy for teaching. "There's no more fat left in the budgets to support it," is how one senior UCSF faculty member put it.[31] This is a national problem not specifically caused by the mergers but produced by decreased income that can be used for the care of patients in hospitals, reduced physicians' compensation, and increased requirements for time-consuming documentation.[32] To the extent that the merger itself costs, rather than saves, money, less support will flow from hospital to school, reducing the resources available for teaching and research.

At UCSF Stanford, those clinicians particularly dedicated to student and resident teaching naturally took to blaming the merger for reductions in support for education and increasing pressure to practice more intensely, leaving less time for teaching. To the extent that the expenses establishing and then dissolving UCSF Stanford drove these pressures, the merger could be held at least partially responsible. In conflict with the nationwide effort to decrease the use of expensive hospital beds, "We were even told to increase the number of patients we hospitalized to improve the hospital's finances" notes one senior Stanford faculty member.[33]

Despite all this angst, however, Partners has been able to combine several of the postgraduate training programs for residents and fellows that were formerly separately administered at the MGH and the Brigham. Many, though not all, faculty members see this change as providing more effective training and saving some money. Similarly, a few postgraduate training programs have come together at NewYork-Presbyterian.

Leadership

The toll on the leadership in two of the three mergers studied here should temper the fervor of merger enthusiasts who see themselves surviving in, or succeeding to, top positions. The CEOs of three of the six hospitals lost their jobs because of the mergers, Peter Van Etten and William Kerr because "when the red ink appears, the CEO disappears" and William Speck partly because of problems adjusting to the culture of the other hospital in his merger. It is not difficult to imagine that Kerr would still be CEO of the UCSF hospitals, Speck of Presbyterian Hospital, and Van Etten of Stanford Health Services if their hospitals had not merged. Most ironic is the case of Speck, since it was he, more than anyone at Presbyterian, who led his hospital into its union with the New York Hospital. David Skinner, who left his job as CEO of NewYork-Presbyterian one year before he planned to retire, had to deal during the final months of his tenure with a succession crisis, the departure of several trusted and able senior associates, and a reevaluation by his trustees of the permanence and character of what he had helped to create.

These events do not surprise the professionals who are called in to help resolve the conflicts produced by mergers among senior personnel. Dr. John H. Moxley III, the physician-recruiter who assisted the New-York-Presbyterian search committee, says that "distrust always develops between the top people" who previously headed the constituent parts.[34] "One wants to succeed sooner; the other worries about the guy who's trying to move up." Often, Moxley has found, "This agonizing process can only be solved by their both leaving and the board bringing in a new CEO to move the company forward."[34]

Alter the dissolution, senior university officials at UCSF Stanford wondered whether a wider search leading to the appointment of someone other than those chosen to guide their merger might have produced a more salutary result. UCSF Stanford never had the opportunity to find out. Appointing someone other than Van Etten or Kerr would have been impossible in the political climate that prevailed when the merger was formed. The original choice of Kerr as CEO was dictated by the fact that the chairman of the board was a Stanford man. Kerr was needed "to maintain balance." Then, when Kerr backed away and a CEO was badly needed, Van Etten was there, ready to serve even though his selection violated the Noah's Ark principle thought so important to the merger.

Not only did those at the top of UCSF Stanford suffer. The chief operating officer at UCSF came to grief when Kerr returned to his previous charge as the losses grew. The merger's first and only chief medical officer, although he retained employment at UCSF in his previous job as chairman of his academic department, suffered the pain of discharge from his UCSF Stanford post. The chief financial officer and the senior vice president for strategic development at UCSF Stanford no longer hold their positions. Many of those hired to cement the merger at the executive offices at 3Com left when the dissolution of the merger was completed. Some of those lower in the table of organization let go to return UCSF to solvency might have been retained if the $79 million required to put the merger in place and the costs of the dissolution had not been spent.

The executives in Boston escaped the fate of Kerr, Speck, and Van Etten. The general director of the MGH retired, and the president of the Brigham and later first CEO of Partners planned to do so soon. Samuel Thier, who in effect was appointed to his job from the outside — his tenure in the presidency at the MGH was short — became CEO, with new appointees leading each of the founding hospitals. Thier and Richard Nesson, Partners' first CEO, were good friends and trusted and admired each other. Nesson chose to retire as the founding leader of Partners voluntarily.

Thus, as the twenty-first century began, of the five most senior managers of the three mergers, only Thier was still in place. Twenty-one months had passed from the formal beginning of UCSF Stanford until Van Etten and Kerr departed and only 24 months from the opening celebration of NewYork-Presbyterian before both Skinner and Speck had left.

The CEOs of most academic medical centers are physicians, for it is thought that only they can deal successfully with the faculty members who constitute the staff and the medical school's dean, who is also usually a physician rather than a basic scientist with a Ph.D. and never, of course, a layman. Furthermore, the faculty typically wants a doctor, someone who talks physicians' language, in this position. Many board members, who appoint the CEOs, come to believe that these almost magical organizations need someone with the magic of medicine in his blood to lead the way. Trustees also see doctors, particularly dominating figures like Herbert Pardes, David Skinner, and Samuel Thier, as attractive figures around whom fundraising appeals can be built.

The problem, however, is that doctors who ascend to these heights have not as a rule climbed the ladder that professional hospital administrators scale and have not acquired the nonmedical skills needed to direct such complex organizations.* Nonphysicians labor under the disadvantage of not having gone through what doctors have experienced and may be unable to respond to medical issues as they do. Some doctor-CEOs acquire mentors from the business community and benefit from their advice, as did David Skinner from insurance executive Maurice Greenberg at the New York Hospital. Nonphysician presidents often turn to one or more of their doctor colleagues for vital guidance. Yet whether doctors or laymen do the job better has never been settled. One suspects it is more the person than the profession that makes the difference.

What has this study taught us that might help the CEO of a merger of teaching hospitals to succeed or, more immediately, to retain his job?

1. **Keep your eye on the dollar.** Losses of $1 million per week at UCSF Stanford, more than any other factor, led to the dissolution of the merger only 23 months after it began operating. The red ink cost the top officers and many other employees their jobs.

2. **The same as number 1** with one additional thought. Losses or requirements for capital that are significantly greater at one hospital will not please the leaders and faculty of the other.

3. **Emphasize site-specific management.** Employ the most capable administrators available and charge them to bring the day-to-day management of each of the hospitals as close as possible to the patients and the doctors. Keep in mind that many teaching hospitals are so large that efficient management is very difficult to achieve.

4. **Do not try to create a new culture based on the merger.** Preserve the names, professional reputations, and public recognition of the original hospitals. This presumes that the names and cultures one inherits are worth saving, as are those of each of the six teaching hospitals and their faculties studied here.

---

*A senior UCSF professor put the question of leadership in academics and teaching hospitals even more starkly. "Universities," he said, "are run by business amateurs. Despite the best of intentions, what do deans know about running businesses? We should go to Montgomery Street [the business center of San Francisco] and get professionals. Until recently, most university hospitals have stayed out of trouble because, despite being incredibly inefficient, the administrators had a money machine so they didn't have to be tight managers."

5. **Avoid political conflict with the faculties whenever possible.** Tread carefully when considering the elimination or consolidation of clinical services or the refashioning of academic structures.
6. **Let pragmatism rule over theory.** Do what seems wise rather than adhering ruthlessly to a theoretical construct about the way mergers are supposed to work. Consolidate only those functions that lend themselves best to unified administration.
7. **If offered such a job,** seriously consider doing something else.

Other Mergers

A few other teaching hospitals have taken the course followed by the six hospitals discussed here. Threatened by the possibility that Partners would absorb the Deaconess Hospital and thereby relegate the Beth Israel Hospital to permanent secondary status in the Harvard firmament, among other reasons,[13] the leaders of the Beth Israel merged their hospital with their nearby competitor across Brookline Avenue in Boston. The Beth Israel–Deaconess combination, named CareGroup, then acquired five additional hospitals. Two more of the teaching hospitals that constituted Dean Tosteson's Harvard Medical Planning Group had now come together.

A true merger of both assets and function, CareGroup forced together each of the clinical departments in both former Harvard teaching hospitals under single chiefs. The department directors come from both institutions, and the heads of the large departments of medicine and surgery are both from the Deaconess.[13] Some important clinicians and one entire department from one institution left, in part because of the restructuring, thereby depriving the hospital of important income. "Paradoxically, this did not jeopardize the support of their traditional communities," according to Mitchell Rabkin, a former Beth Israel CEO.[13]

CareGroup continues to lose money despite the consolidations of physical facilities and staffs and "doing everything conventional wisdom says they should do," according to one informed Boston observer, who implies that it is the conventional wisdom that may be at fault. The operating loss of $121 million in 1999 helped to bring down the hospital CEO in November.[35] CareGroup lost somewhat less, $94 million on operations, during 2000. Its principal teaching hospital, Beth Israel Deaconess, lost $50 million on operations.[35a] Although Harvard has traditionally praised the separation of the teaching hospitals from the medical school, the university may have to consider how to help the problems of its neighbor further west on Longwood Avenue.[14]

A less troubled story, also in New England, involves Lifespan, the combination of Rhode Island and Miriam hospitals, the academic centers for Brown University in Providence, and the New England Medical Center, the primary teaching hospital for the Tufts medical school in Boston. Led by George Vecchione, David Skinner's former number two at the New York Hospital, Lifespan is losing less money on operations than in the recent past — about $40 million in the fiscal year ending September 30, 1999, and $34 million during 2000. With the income from endowments, the bottom bottom line at the not-for-profit corporation is positive.[3]

Although Lifespan has not pressed the two schools to merge clinical departments, openings have brought common leadership to two departments. These appointments, which came about when Brown needed chiefs, have been well accepted because the Tufts doctors appointed were well respected in Providence. Vecchione ascribes the relative calm to the 60 miles between the two centers, which, at least in the case of Lifespan, seem to alleviate rather than aggravate potential animosities.[3] In August, 2002, Tufts-New England Medical Center withdrew from Lifespan. The evolution of New England health care from a local business into a regional one never happened, the chief executive of Tufts-New England Medical Center explained. "There has been a perception that we're not Massachusetts-controlled," he told a reporter for the *Boston Globe*. "The most important thing for the financial future of this hospital is our ability to control our own destiny."[3a]

In St. Louis, the merger of the previously separately governed Barnes, Jewish, and Children's hospitals, all teaching hospitals for the Washington University Medical School, with community hospitals in the region as the BJC Health System[36] was making money as 2000 ended. The dire predictions about managed care that helped propel the merger had not invaded St. Louis as predicted. There is little capitated business in the community but mostly negotiated fee for service, which has given the administrators and doctors more time to increase efficiency and reduce length of stay.[37] The corporation's size has improved its ability to negotiate lower rates for services and supplies compared to what the individual hospitals could do previously. As the chief of cardiology puts it, "All the pacemaker companies want their products in Barnes-Jewish," and the manufacturers respond to BJC's purchasing power and the "incredible clout" the hospital exercises in St. Louis.[37]

As neighbors, Barnes and Jewish have long been principal teaching hospitals for Washington University's medical school. Their consolidation has formed in effect a single hospital, which many find has produced a better-run, more user friendly medical center. As at CareGroup in Boston, single directors of departments and services were appointed, almost all from Barnes, the larger and more academic of the two institutions. Also, as at Beth Israel–Deaconess, some doctors at Jewish left, taking business with them, but much of this has been replaced.[37]

As we have found elsewhere, not every professor at Washington University is overjoyed by the merger. As one senior faculty member put it, "financially, they're scraping through, but functionally united, that's a figment of the imagination."[38] Another commented that the merger has done little to benefit the school of medicine. BJC now transfers less money to programs at the school than did Barnes before the merger, but much of this decline is due to the squeezing medical environment and only some to the costs of the merger.[37]

Efforts to combine schools of medicine and their teaching hospitals have failed. The merger of the New York University and Mount Sinai schools of medicine collapsed because of the resistance of the NYU faculty and some of its leaders. The Mount Sinai and Tisch (NYU) hospitals subsequently merged into a corporation called Mount Sinai NYU Health, which operates more like Partners than NewYork-Presbyterian or UCSF Stanford. The new corporation, which was formed on July 1, 1998, quickly and "aggressively," according to Dr. John W. Rowe, the president and CEO,[39] integrated its back office facilities and services with relatively little turmoil. Including the costs of integrating, the consolidations saved $8 million during the first year and may save more in the second. The hospital generated a surplus on operations during 1999 while contributing $30 million for academic development to each of the two schools.

Although some parts of a few programs have been combined, Rowe and his associates have deliberately avoided forcing consolidation of the clinical services. Service lines have been established at the individual hospitals but, as of the fall of 1999, not on a combined basis, which highlights the fact that mergers are not necessary to establish service lines when leaders think them wise. Unlike NewYork-Presbyterian and similar to Partners, Mount Sinai NYU Health has preserved the identity of the Mount Sinai and Tisch NYU hospitals and has not emphasized the corporate entity in its marketing. Focus groups had disliked a facility that they saw as too large and remote. Rowe explains his approach by saying that "It's our merger, not our patients' merger."[39]*

---

*In September, 2000, Rowe left Mount Sinai N.Y.U. to become president and CEO of Aetna U.S. Healthcare, the country's largest health insurer.[39a] By the end of 2001, the two institutions had, in function, though not yet in form, separated from their merger and returned to independent operation.[39b] Early in 2003, Theresa Bischoff, president of the New York University Hospitals Center and, like John Rowe, a enthusiastic champion of the now defunct merger, resigned.[39c]

In addition to UCSF Stanford, two mergers involving academic medical centers have come apart. The most spectacular failure has been the collapse of the Allegheny Health Education and Research Foundation (AHERF), which purchased and then combined the Philadelphia medical schools of Hahnemann University and the Medical College of Pennsylvania and absorbed 14 hospitals, including those owned by the two medical schools, and more than 500 doctors' practices in Philadelphia and Pittsburgh. The corporation extravagantly overspent its resources and went bankrupt, jeopardizing the future of the united school, which was rescued by the city and the state and delivered to Drexel University, a Philadelphia engineering college, to administer. The chief executive of AHERF, whose salary in the 1997 fiscal year was reported to have been $1.17 million, lost his job.[41]*

The Penn State Geisinger Health System, a merger of the teaching hospital in Hershey that trains the students of the Penn State University School of Medicine, a group of upstate community hospitals, and an HMO based in Danville, Pennsylvania, began the process of dismantling their two-year union in the fall of 1999. Although cultural differences were publicly blamed for the dissolution, those close to the scene tell of a problematic leadership structure in which the coequal senior executives differed over fundamental issues.[41]

Informed observers at each of the teaching hospitals studied here and from elsewhere believe that there is a size beyond which these complicated institutions cannot be effectively managed, that bigness becomes a problem that consolidation cannot help. Several doctors and administrators interviewed for this study consider their hospitals even now to be too big to manage effectively. "These places are unmanageable," health care consultant Jeff Goldsmith has concluded. "They're not enterprises capable of focusing their resources and balancing revenue and expenses. So when income drops they don't know what has to be done."[5]

How big is too big is unknown. Health economist Victor Fuchs thinks 500 beds is about the optimum size to deliver the most effective clinical care and that larger hospitals become increasingly less efficient, more costly, and tougher to manage.[4] The leaders at Partners recognize this and maintain separate directors for the less assimilative functions at the Brigham and MGH. In New York, one hospital director continues to administer the immense NewYork-Presbyterian complex as if the Columbia-Presbyterian and New York Weill Cornell sites and the Allen

---

*See the study of the Allegheny debacle by Professor Robert Burns and his colleagues from the Wharton School at the University of Pennsylvania.[40]

Pavilion were one functioning hospital. When and if red ink starts to flow abundantly in New York, will NewYork-Presbyterian return to full-site management?[42][†]

As Harold Luft, the UCSF health care economist, has said, "Mergers are very complicated structures, which people aren't aware of when they go in."[43]

Is the Whole Greater Than Its Parts?

What makes teaching hospitals "great"? Surely, it's not having medical students around to poke the abdomens of private patients, nor is it the often less than ideal creature comforts that these large establishments provide. If you're about to have a normal delivery or are afflicted with a less than major illness, many a patient would rather attend a community hospital, which is easier to comprehend and where the staff's spirit may be more agreeable.

To the public, it's the name of the hospital, redolent with history and medical accomplishment, that wins it a top standing in national surveys. The doctors and scientists, whom the public sees as contributing to medical knowledge through research and advanced clinical care, and the reputation of its medical school help establish the standing of a teaching hospital.

The doctors who practice at teaching hospitals, it is thought, have been more intensely trained and vetted before being appointed to the staffs. If severely ill patients are cared for by a professor, they and their families gain assurance from knowing that they're being treated by one of the most skillful and experienced members of the profession.

Despite the goal of some of the founders to create superb and famous institutions, the combined medical centers so far seem to be almost unrecognized by most people and certainly much less renowned than the hospitals from which they were formed. Patients still choose to be treated at the Presbyterian Hospital in Washington Heights and the New York Hospital on the east side of Manhattan and not at the NewYork-Presbyterian Hospital, a name that confuses citizens, if it means anything at all. Being hospitalized at UCSF Stanford is no longer

---

[†]As 2000 ended, the NewYork-Presbyterian Hospital projected a small profit on operations compared with a loss of $4.9 million on operations during 1999. These results, however, depended upon the hospital's including some income from endowment in its financial reporting for operations, not the accounting practice at Partners or UCSF Stanford. The NewYork-Presbyterian endowments, which total more than $1 billion, produce income that more than adequately covers the operational losses.[42a]

an option, and potential clients of that center will seek care where they have previously received it, at the Moffitt-Long and Mount Zion hospitals in San Francisco or Stanford University and Lucile Packard Children's hospitals in Palo Alto. In Boston, the founders of Partners never assumed that combining the Massachusetts General and the Brigham and Women's hospitals could produce an entity more famous or respected than its constituent parts. "The average person doesn't know there's something called Partners," says Rashi Fein, the Harvard health care economist. "It exists at a different level."[14]

We have seen the difficulty all parties encountered in naming New York-Presbyterian. Was this turmoil really necessary? Probably not. Is the new name, with the absence of space between *New* and *York* and the hyphen, anything more than a linguistic compromise to what must have seemed at times to be an insurmountable dilemma to many at Columbia-Presbyterian and New York Hospital–Cornell? Probably not. Has the name helped to cement members of the faculties and staff that work at the two sites? Hardly. More importantly, has the new name improved the medical care or reduced the expenses of operating the immense structure that is New York-Presbyterian Hospital? We await proof of this.

Some Lessons

One of the most skeptical appraisals about merging within academic medical centers (AMCs) comes from a former participant, who, having long worked in the vineyards, suggests that the mergers may come to be seen as "a phase of AMC development that in retrospect turned out to have been an hubristic delusion of grandeur." To what extent is this discouraging analysis true?

As of the winter of 2000, of the three mergers studied here Partners is a qualified success, New York-Presbyterian a work in progress, and UCSF Stanford a failure. Regardless of how these organizations fared, however, no one could fault the motives of the intelligent, able founders in each case. Although the enthusiasm inherent in creation may have caused them to ignore some of the problems they would face — this was certainly true at UCSF Stanford — the goal for which they worked was critically important: the survival of their institutions in a time of great stress.

Joining with another fine hospital seemed a reasonable method of combating more successfully the economic changes threatening their important institutions. Personal financial gain, so often a factor in the mergers of for-profit companies, was not a consideration. No stock options or appreciation in the value of stock would follow the merging of these hospitals.

However, despite the best of aims and the many skills of the people involved, why did the mergers experience such problems, why did one fail, and why did so many of the CEOs lose their jobs? One reason may be the peculiar character of the institutions they led.

Dr. Michael Bishop, the Nobel Prize–winning scientist who now leads the University of California-San Francisco, agrees. He sees "academic health centers [to be] inherently inefficient even when aggressively managed."[44]

Management authority Peter F. Drucker finds academic medical centers "incredibly difficult to manage. There are so many constituencies, so many purposes."[45]

"Why do these smart people blow it?" asks David Hunter, the consultant whose firm temporarily managed the UCSF Medical Center and the dissolving UCSF Stanford. "It's crazy. They decide we're going to do a merger, but nothing's going to change. No one's going to lose his job." Possibly, it's the industry itself that's the problem. "Tough-minded business people park their brains at the door when they get into health care."[46]

"A merger is not a panacea for anything," warns William Gurtner, the executive in the University of California president's office who supervises the university's teaching hospitals. "If you can't solve it alone," he warns leaders of university teaching hospitals looking for solutions to their problems, "you can't solve it together. Why should something larger necessarily help you do it?" Gurtner, who tried to save UCSF Stanford as a member of the committee charged with restructuring the merger during the summer and fall of 1999, warns that merger makers must not assume that they can enter the world without changing. However, he adds, "Approaching the future does not equal forgetting the past."[47]

Those contemplating the course followed by the leaders of the hospitals studied here should consider whether they and their colleagues are prepared to spend countless hours planning and executing the merger. Although enthusiasm for the venture during its formative and early days damps down complaints of other work left undone, all soon recognize how much the merger distracts people with important administrative and academic responsibilities from doing what they were originally hired to do. "The merger was discussed continuously at meetings, sapping all our energies," says a Stanford senior faculty member.

"They'll meet you to death," warns another, summarizing the complaint of many of his colleagues. In addition to senior members, the need for committee work draws from their laboratories, clinics, and teaching duties some members of the junior faculty, whose academic work is essential for their advancement. A list of committee assignments adds little to the impression their curricula vitae present to committees evaluating full-time candidates for promotion or tenure at competitive universities.

"The burden of proof should be placed on doing something," the consultant Lawrence Lewin advises.[48] When officers of teaching hospitals consider a merger, they should make sure that the following elements are present for such a venture to have a chance of succeeding:[48]

- There must be a compelling case for going ahead based on strategic and cultural considerations.
- The financial justification must be supported by a skeptical, competent, due diligence process.
- The skills at both the executive and board levels must be credible.
- The strategy, the pacing of change, must be right.
- The hospital's traditional supporting community must be maintained.

Alain Enthoven, the Stanford professor who first wrote about managed competition 25 years ago, questions whether academic mergers, whatever their presumed local value, fulfill the broader interests of the country. He suggests that gaining market dominance by joint contracting, even if this were possible, may not serve the public interest because it prevents further reductions in the cost of health care. "I think medical academic centers need to find ways of becoming a part of the solution to America's serious problems arising from rapidly rising health care costs," which price health insurance out of the reach of millions of the uninsured and strain public finances "at every level of government."[49]

Enthoven's charge that academic medical centers should demonstrate, in their decisions, solutions to the nation's health care problems will not, however, relieve the tribulations of the medical and administrative leaders of teaching hospitals, whose profit and loss statements and balance sheets reflect current realities. They realize that their responsibility, first of all, is to ensure that their institutions will continue to perform their valuable work. Each leader must ask what steps should be taken to continue to serve successfully.

- Should we merge with another teaching or community hospital?
- Should we build an integrated delivery system to establish better

relationships with community hospitals and primary care practitioners and keep our teaching hospital busy?

- To what extent can we amalgamate clinical programs, within both our hospital and our network, if we have one, to improve the care of our patients, enhance the education of our students and trainees, and augment the research we perform while at the same time saving money?
- How do we sustain the spirit and creativity of our faculties amid the turmoil these changes produce?
- What else should we do?

Those charged with making their institutions succeed must not be discouraged because one of three attempts to try to solve contemporary problems by merging failed. We have seen the special issues affecting UCSF Stanford, whose able leaders tried to accomplish an extraordinary organizational feat in a state with a viciously stringent level of compensation and with the added complexity of a state-private setting. More promising is the example of Partners, which has accomplished many, though certainly not all, of the clinical, academic, and business aims of its founders, albeit with one medical school to calm the environment rather than two to roil it. At New York-Presbyterian, a new leader is consolidating the work established by the founders, and most there agree that the environment has improved and the likelihood of success has grown.

Merging teaching hospitals is but one of the techniques academic medical centers must use to continue to fulfill their missions. The goal is worth the effort, but no one can now predict which method will best assure the survival and prosperity of these vital contributors to the health of the nation.

References*

Chapter 1. Introduction (1–5)

1. Bodenheimer, T., and Sullivan, K. "How large employers are shaping the health care marketplace." First of two parts. *N Eng J Med* 338 (1998): 1003–7.
2. Mayer, T. R., and Mayer, G. G. "HMOs: Origins and development." *N Eng J Med* 312 (1985): 590–94.
3. Iglehart, J. K. "The American health care system: Private insurance." *N Eng J Med* 326 (1992): 1715–20.
4. Shapiro, S. "An historical perspective on the roots of managed care." *Current Opinion in Pediatrics* 8 (1996): 159–63.
5. Ginzberg, E. "The impact of World War II on U.S. medicine." *American Journal of the Medical Sciences* 304 (1992): 268–71.
6. Bodenheimer, T., and Sullivan, K. "How large employers are shaping the health care marketplace." Second of two parts. *N Eng J Med* 338 (1998): 1084–87.
7. Kuttner, R. "The American health care system: Employer-sponsored health coverage." *N Eng J Med* 340 (1999): 248–52.
8. Ginzberg, E., and Ostow, M. "Managed care: A look back and a look ahead." *N Eng J Med* 336 (1997): 1018–20.
9. Fuchs, V. R. "Managed care and merger mania." *JAMA* 277 (1997): 920–21.
10. Fuchs, V. R. "Economics, values, and health care reform." *American Economic Review* 86 (1996): 19.
11. Iglehart, J. K. "Managed competition." *N Eng J Med* 328 (1993): 1208–12.
12. Iglehart, J. K. "The American health care system: Managed care." *N Eng J Med* 327 (1992): 742–47.
13. Paley, W. D. "Overview of the HMO movement." *Psychiatric Quarterly* 64 (1993): 5–12.
14. Richards, T. "Medicine American style and the growth of HMOs." *British Medical Journal Clinical Research Ed.* 292 (1986): 330–32.
15. Iglehart, J. K. "Managed care and mental health." *N Eng J Med* 334 (1996): 131–35.

---

*Interviews were conducted in person in the city indicated unless identified "by telephone." Page numbers in parentheses indicate where references first appear in each chapter.

16. Robinson, J. C. "Use and abuse of the medical loss ratio to measure health plan performance." *Health Affairs* 16 (1997): 176–87.
17. Michael, E., and Abel, M. D. San Francisco, 11/24/99 by telephone.
18. Iglehart, J. K. "Rapid changes for academic medical centers." Part 1. *N Eng J Med* 331 (1994): 1391–95.
19. Relman, A. S. "Controlling costs by 'managed competition': Would it work?" *N Eng J Med* 328 (1993): 133–35.
20. Lawrence, D. "Why we want to remain a nonprofit health care organization." *Health Affairs* 16 (1997): 118–20.
21. Levit, K., Cowan, C., Braden, B., Stiller, J., Sensenig, A., and Lazenby, H. "National health expenditures in 1997: More slow growth." *Health Affairs* 17 (1998): 99–110.
22. Iglehart, J. K. "Academic medical centers enter the market: The case of Philadelphia." *N Eng J Med* 333 (1995): 1019–23.
23. Iglehart, J. K. "Support for academic medical centers: Revisiting the 1997 Balanced Budget Act." *New England Journal of Medicine* 341 (1999): 299–304.
24. Moynihan, Daniel P. "How medicine became just another product: Teaching hospitals are the latest victims of the war on costs." *New York Times,* 11/27/99, A31.
25. Pear, Robert. "New York's teaching hospitals face sharp Medicare cuts." *New York Times,* 11/24/99, A22.
26. Iglehart, J. K. "Medicare and graduate medical education." *N Eng J Med* 338 (1998): 402–7.
27. Walsh, J. "Stanford School of Medicine." Part 1: "Problems over more than money." *Science* 171 (1971): 551–53.
28. Petersdorf, R. G. "Current and future directions for hospital and physician reimbursement: Effect on the academic medical center." *JAMA* 253 (1985): 2543–48.
28a. Ludmerer, K. M. "Time to heal: America medical education from the turn of the century to the era of managed care." New York: Oxford University Press, 1999, 221–399.
29. Rabkin, M. T. "A paradigm shift in academic medicine? *Academic Medicine* 73 (1998): 127–31.
30. Eisenberg, John M., M.D. Bethesda, MD, 8/7/98.
31. Chernow, Barbara A., and Vallasi, George A., eds. *The Columbia Encyclopedia.* 5th ed. New York: Columbia University Press, 1993, 1504.
32. Iglehart, J. K. "The American health care system: Teaching hospitals." *N Eng J Med* 329 (1993): 1052–56.
33. Goldsmith, J. "UCSF/Stanford: Building a 'prestige cartel.'" *Health Affairs* 18 (1999): 149–51.
34. Petersdorf, R. G. "Academic medicine: No longer threadbare or genteel." *N Eng J Med* 304 (1981): 841–43.
35. Iglehart, J. K. "Rapid changes for academic medical centers." Part 2. *N Eng J Med* 332 (1995): 407–11.

36. Goldberg, Carey. "Teaching hospitals battle cutbacks in Medicare money." *New York Times,* 5/6/99, A1–22.
37. Kennedy, Randy. "New York hospitals braced for cuts." *New York Times,* 5/6/99, A22.
38. "Merger compounded—but did not cause—current campus stresses, says Debas." http://www.ucsf.edu/daybreak/1999/02/25_address.html. 2/25/1999.
39. Herbert, Bob. "Hospitals in crisis." *New York Times,* 4/15/99, A27.
40. Vecchione, George A. Providence, RI, 5/7/99, 11/2/99 by telephone.
41. Andreopoulos, S. "The folly of teaching-hospital mergers." *N Eng J Med* 336 (1997): 61–64.
42. Freudenheim, Milt. "Insurers and uninsured put hospitals in a squeeze: How to collect on stacks of unpaid bills?" *New York Times,* 5/9/99, Week in Review section, 4.
43. Lerner, Wayne M., *Anatomy of a Merger: BJC Health System.* Chicago: Health Administration Press, 1997.
44. Burns, L. R., Cacciamani, J., Clement, J., and Aquino, W. "The fall of the house of AHERF: The Allegheny bankruptcy." *Health Affairs* 19 (2000): 7–41.

Chapter 2. Partners: Formation

1. Golnaraghi, M., and Pisano, G. *Partners HealthCare System, Inc. (A).* Boston: Harvard Business School Publishing, 1997.
2. Blumenthal, David. "Partners HealthCare System (draft case summary)." 1995, 1–24.
3. Blumenthal, D., and Meyer, G. S. "Academic health centers in a changing environment." *Health Affairs* 15 (1996): 200–215.
3a. Blumenthal, D., and Edwards, N. "A tale of two systems: the changing academic health center." *Health Affairs 2000;* 19: 86–101.
4. Mitchell, T. Rabkin, M.D. Boston, 7/23/98, 1/12/00, 11/16/99 by telephone.
5. Boston Consulting Group. Summary of affiliation discussions and associated reference material. Brigham and Women's, Massachusetts General Hospital task force. 1/16/1994.
6. Bray, David M. Boston, 11/20/98, 1/9/00 by telephone.
7. Garland, Joseph E. *Every Man Our Neighbor: A Brief History of the Massachusetts General Hospital, 1811–1961.* Boston: Little, Brown, 1961, 55.
8. Burr, Francis H. Boston, 9/29/98.
9. Tosteson, Daniel C., M.D. Boston, 9/29/98.
10. Carey Goldberg. "Teaching hospitals battle cutbacks in Medicare money." *New York Times,* 5/6/99, A1–22.
11. Pieper, Jay B. Boston, 11/17/98, 12/23/99 by telephone.
12. Kimberly Blanton, "A doctor's heart, CEO's skill: Partners HealthCare chief's passion is driving force behind firm's success." *Boston Globe,* 1/18/98, Business section, C1.

13. Relman, Arnold S., M.D. Boston, 7/23/98.
14. Tosteson, D. C., Adelstein, S. J., and Carver, S. T. *New Pathways to Medical Education: Learning to Learn at Harvard Medical School.* Cambridge: Harvard University Press, 1994.
15. Blumenthal, David. "Partners HealthCare System (draft case summary)." 1995, 2.
16. McArthur, John A. Washington, DC, 11/2/98.
17. Thier, Samuel O., M.D. Boston, 7/24/98, 9/30/98, 12/2/99 by telephone.
18. Lewin, Lawrence S. Arlington, VA, 3/12/99.
19. Blumenthal, David. "Partners HealthCare System (draft case summary)." 1995, p. 3.
20. Austen, W. Gerald, M.D. Boston, 7/24/98, 11/20/98.
21. Nesson, H. Richard, M.D. Boston, 9/28/98.
22. Ferdinand, Colloredo-Mansfeld, J. P. E. Boston, 9/20/98, 11/20/98, 11/24/99 by telephone.
23. Morison, Samuel E. *Three Centuries of Harvard, 1636–1936.* Cambridge: Belknap Press of Harvard University, 1965, 168–70.
24. Beecher, Henry K., and Altchule, Mark D. *Medicine at Harvard: The First Three Hundred Years.* Hanover, NH: University Press of New England, 1977, 29–30.
25. Beecher, Henry K., and Altchule, Mark D. *Medicine at Harvard: The First Three Hundred Years.* Hanover, NH: University Press of New England, 1977, p. 13.
26. Garland, Joseph E. *Every Man Our Neighbor: A Brief History of the Massachusetts General Hospital, 1811–1961.* Boston: Little, Brown, 1961, 51.
27. Beecher, Henry K., and Altchule, Mark D. *Medicine at Harvard: The First Three Hundred Years.* Hanover, NH: University Press of New England, 1977, p. 87.
28. Aldrich, Nelson. W., Jr. *Old Money.* New York: Allworth Press, 1998, 98.
29. Beecher, Henry K., and Altchule, Mark D. *Medicine at Harvard: The First Three Hundred Years.* Hanover, NH: University Press of New England, 1977, p. 168–69.
30. Southworth, Susan, and Southworth, Michael. *AIA Guide to Boston.* 2d ed. Old Saybrook, CT: Globe Pequot Press, 1992, 350.
31. Harvard Medical School, Office of the Dean, 8/10/00 by e-mail.
32. NIH support to U.S. medical schools, fiscal year 1998.
33. Kassirer, Jerome P., M.D. Boston, 7/24/98.
34. "The JIM interview: H. Richard Nesson, M.D." *Journal of Investigative Medicine* 45 (1997): 14–19.
35. Garland, Joseph E. *Every Man Our Neighbor: A Brief History of the Massachusetts General Hospital, 1811–1961.* Boston: Little, Brown, 1961, 10.
36. Ross, Marjorie D. *The Book of Boston: The Federal Period, 1775–1837.* New York: Hastings House, 1961, 148.
37. Bunting, Bainbridge. *Houses of Boston's Back Bay.* Cambridge: Belknap Press of Harvard University Press, 1967, 21.

38. Ross, Marjorie D. *The Book of Boston: The Victorian Period, 1837 to 1901.* New York: Hastings House, 1964, 104.
39. Kirker, Harold. *The Architecture of Charles Bulfinch.* Cambridge: Harvard University Press, 1969, 1.
40. Kirker, Harold. *The Architecture of Charles Bulfinch.* Cambridge: Harvard University Press, 1969, 313.
41. Garland, Joseph E. *Every Man Our Neighbor: A Brief History of the Massachusetts General Hospital, 1811–1961.* Boston: Little, Brown, 1961, 6.
42. McCord, David. *The Fabrick of Man: Fifty Years of the Peter Bent Brigham.* Boston: Fiftieth Anniversary Celebration Committee, 1963.
43. Fulton, John F. *Harvey Cushing. A Biography.* Springfield, IL: Charles C. Thomas, 1946, 335.
44. Aub, Joseph C., and Hapgood, Ruth K. *Pioneer in Modern Medicine: David Linn Edsall of Harvard.* Cambridge: Harvard Medical Alumni Association, 1970, 138.
45. Aub, Joseph C., and Hapgood, Ruth K. *Pioneer in Modern Medicine: David Linn Edsall of Harvard.* Cambridge: Harvard Medical Alumni Association, 1970, 229.
46. Aub, Joseph C., and Hapgood, Ruth K. *Pioneer in Modern Medicine: David Linn Edsall of Harvard.* Cambridge: Harvard Medical Alumni Association, 1970, 228–29.
47. Moore, F. D. "The universities in Cushing's life." In Black, P. McL., and Moore, M. R., eds., *Harvey Cushing at the Brigham.* Park Ridge, IL: American Association of Neurological Surgeons, 1993, chap. 3, 64–65.
48. Mannick, J. A. "Cushing and the Moseley professorship." In Black, P. McL., and Moore, M. R., eds., *Harvey Cushing at the Brigham.* Park Ridge, IL: American Association of Neurological Surgeons, 1993, chap. 4, 76.
49. Fulton, John F. *Harvey Cushing. A Biography.* Springfield, IL: Charles C. Thomas, 1946, 344–46.
50. Fulton, John F. *Harvey Cushing. A Biography.* Springfield, IL: Charles C. Thomas, 1946, 377–84.
51. Blumenthal, David, M.D. Boston, 9/28/98.
52. John Morrissey. "Information Systems, Adding up savings: Hospital, docs reap benefits of computer initiatives." *Modern Healthcare,* 1/19/98, 34.
53. Matheson, David. Boston, 7/22/99.
54. Eisenberg, John M., M.D. Bethesda, MD, 8/7/98.
55. Thibault, George E., M.D. Boston, 11/19/98, 7/22/99.
56. Lee, Thomas H., Jr., M.D. Boston, 11/16/98.
57. Blumenthal, David. "Partners HealthCare System (draft case summary)." 1995, 17.
58. Foreman, Judy. "Merger will require the right blend: Hospitals' cultures may imperil unity." *Boston Globe,* 12/10/93, Metro section, 37.
59. Zitner, Aaron. "The disarming dean: The man behind the MGH-Brigham merger has an aw-shucks style, but don't let that fool you." *Boston Globe,* 12/12/98, Business section, 81.

60. Bailey, Steve. "Harvard's b-school boss to step down: Curriculum revamp approval marks good stopping point, McArthur says." *Boston Globe,* 3/7/ 95, Business section, 39.
61. "Roberts W. Eugene Braunwald, MD: A conversation with the editor." *American Journal of Cardiology* 82 (1998): 93–108.
62. Shine, Kenneth I., M.D. Washington, DC, 7/2/98.
63. Blumenthal, David. "Partners HealthCare System (draft case summary)." 1995, 11.
64. Blumenthal, David. "Partners HealthCare System (draft case summary)." 1995, 7.
65. Blumenthal, D, and Meyer, G. S. "Academic health centers in a changing environment." *Health Affairs* 15 (1996): 205.
66. "H. Richard Nesson." *Boston Globe,* 9/29/98, A22.
67. Braunwald, Eugene, M.D. Boston, 7/24/98, 9/30/98, 11/11/99, 2/7/00 by telephone, 1/2/00 by e-mail.
68. Robbins, Catherine J. Boston, 11/17/98.
69. Chrencik, Robert A. Baltimore, 2/4/00.
70. Golden, Daniel, and Stein, Charles. "MGH, Brigham plan to merge: Consolidation geared to lower costs in anticipation of U.S. health reform." *Boston Globe,* 12/8/93, Metro section, 1.
71. Knox, Richard A. "Hospitals expect merger to save millions: MGH, Brigham super-hospital deal would change face of Boston medical establishment." *Boston Globe,* 12/9/93, Metro section, 1.
72. Gardner, K. "An integrated system grows in Boston." *Hospitals and Health Networks* 68 (1994): 62–63.
73. Blumenthal, David. "Partners HealthCare System (draft case summary)." 1995, 4.
74. Knox, Richard A. "Anatomy of merger reveals systemic ills: Hospital talks shut out Harvard medical dean." *Boston Globe,* 12/16/93, Metro section, 37.
75. Tosteson, D.C. "The Harvard medical group: A vision for the future," 12/1/ 1993.
76. Smith, Lloyd H., Jr., M.D. San Francisco, 6/18/99, 10/27/99 by telephone.
77. "The JIM interview: Samuel O. Thier, M.D." *Journal of Investigative Medicine* 43 (1995): 10–16.
78. Dembner, Alice. "Brandeis president says he'll resign and take MGH post." *Boston Globe,* 12/9/93, Metro section, 15.
79. Dembner, Alice. "MGH makes it official: Thier is widely praised." *Boston Globe,* 12/10/93, Metro section, 40.
80. Knox, Richard A. "Brigham chief leads transition." *Boston Globe,* 12/16/ 93, Metro section, 50.
81. Barlow, E. "Competition among friends." *Harvard Medical Alumni Bulletin,* Summer 1997, 18–30.
82. Dowdy, Zachary R. "H. Richard Nesson, 66, a leader in Boston health care, hospitals." *Boston Globe,* 10/19/98, B5.

Chapter 3. Partners: Development

1. Boston Consulting Group. "Summary of affiliation discussions and associated reference material," Brigham and Women's, Massachusetts General Hospital task force, 1/16/1994.
2. Barlow, E. "Competition among friends." *Harvard Medical Alumni Bulletin,* Summer 1997, 18–30.
3. Boston Consulting Group. "Summary of affiliation discussions and associated reference material," Brigham and Women's, Massachusetts General Hospital task force, 1/16/1994, 150.
4. Matheson, David. Boston, 7/22/99.
5. Haddad, Ernest M., Boston, 11/17/98.
6. Lewin, Lawrence S. Arlington, VA, 3/12/99.
7. "The JIM interview: Samuel O. Thier, M.D." *Journal of Investigative Medicine* 43 (1995): 10–16.
8. Thier, Samuel O., M.D. Boston, 7/24/98, 9/30/98, 12/2/99 by telephone.
9. Thibault, George E., M.D. Boston, 11/19/98, 7/22/99.
10. Colloredo-Mansfeld, Ferdinand J. P. E. Boston, 9/29/98.
11. Buchanan, J. Robert, M.D. Killingworth, CT, 2/9/00 by telephone.
12. Richard A. Knox, "New name, new slant on hospital 'merger.'" *Boston Globe,* 3/22/94, Metro section, 21.
13. Fein, Rashi, Ph.D. Boston, 7/14/99 by telephone.
14. Zane, Ellen M. Boston, 9/28/98, 1/5/99, 7/7/99 by telephone, 1/23/00 by e-mail.
15. John Koch. "H. Richard Nesson." *Boston Globe,* 9/7/97, Sunday Magazine section, 14.
16. Rabkin, Mitchell T., M.D. Boston, 7/23/98, 1/12/00, 11/16/99 by telephone.
17. Robbins, Catherine J. Boston, 11/17/98.
18. Stein, Charles. "Partners HealthCare names vice president." *Boston Globe,* 4/14/94, Business section, 67.
19. Nesson, H. Richard, M.D. Boston, 9/28/98.
20. Blumenthal, David. "Partners HealthCare System (draft case summary)." 1995, 23.
21. Blumenthal, David. "Partners HealthCare System (draft case summary)." 1995, 20.
22. Aiken, L. H., Lewis, C. E., Craig, J., Mendenhall, R. C., Blendon, R. J., and Rogers, D. E. "The contribution of specialists to the delivery of primary care." *N Eng J Med* 300 (1979): 1363–70.
23. Fallon, John A., M.D. Boston, 11/16/98.
24. Potts, John T., Jr., M.D. Boston, 11/20/98.
25. McArthur, John A., Washington, DC, 11/2/98.
26. Lee, Thomas H., Jr., M.D. Boston, 11/16/98.
27. Knox, Richard A. "Hospitals plan $70M link: MGH, Brigham hope information highway leads to an expanded network." *Boston Globe,* 12/26/94, Metro section, 1.

28. Pham, Alex. "Pact would link N. Shore, Boston hospitals." *Boston Globe,* 9/7/95, Business section, 61.

29. Pham, Alex. "'Hm-oh yes we can': Locked in power struggle with health insurers, Partners HealthCare System's goal is to heat HMOs at own game with its hospital network." *Boston Globe,* 6/15/97, Business section, G1.

30. Morrissey, John. "HMOs rule in Boston market, but costs, utilization are high." *Modern Healthcare,* 9/14/98, 56–65.

31. Blumenthal, David. "Partners HealthCare System (draft case summary)." 1995, 11.

32. Syre, Stephen, and Stein, Charles. "Mergers of health care firms often just don't work out." *Boston Globe,* 1/12/2000, D5.

33. Wilmsen, Steven. "Industry group hits Harvard Pilgrim: Suspends ailing HMO's accreditation. *Boston Globe,* 2000, C1.

34. Pieper, Jay B. Boston, 11/17/98, 12/23/99 by telephone.

35. Austen, W. Gerald, M.D. Boston, 7/24/98, 11/20/98.

36. Pham, Alex. "Faulkner joins Partners family: Jamaica Plain hospital affiliates with Brigham." *Boston Globe,* 4/17/98, Business section, E1.

37. Pham, Alex. "Affiliation deal complete." *Boston Globe,* 10/2/98, Business section, C5.

38. Pham, Alex. "Newton-Wellesley agrees to be a unit of Partners HealthCare: Major presence gained in western suburbs." *Boston Globe,* 4/9/98, Business section, D6.

39. Blanton, Kimberly. "Hospital votes to open merger talks: Newton-Wellesley seeks to join with Partners." *Boston Globe,* 9/30/97, Business section, D2.

40. Pham, Alex. "Newton-Wellesley to join Partners HealthCare." *Boston Globe,* 1/27/99, Business section, D7.

41. Pham, Alex. "Partners forms alliance with Vineyard hospital." *Boston Globe,* 8/21/98, Business section, C7.

42. Glynn, Thomas P., Ph.D. Boston, 11/17/98.

43. Markell, Peter K. Boston, 7/22/99.

44. Lagnado, Lucette. "Health care: Jittery hospitals discover bulls can turn into bears." *Wall Street Journal,* 10/26/98, B1.

45. Mongan, James J., M.D. Boston, 11/19/98.

46. Fishman, Mark C., M.D. Boston, 7/19/99 by telephone.

46a. Kowalczyk, Liz. "Partners Healthcare shows gain. Brigham, Mass General perform well, but small hospitals still hurting." *Boston Globe,* 12/16/2000, p. C1.

47. Glaser, John. Boston, 11/19/98.

48. Bero, Cynthia L. Boston, 11/18/98.

49. Gaida, John B. Boston, 11/17/98.

50. Braunwald, Eugene, M.D. Boston, 7/24/98, 9/30/98, 11/11/99, 2/7/00 by telephone, 1/2/00 by e-mail.

51. "The JIM interview: H. Richard Nesson, M.D." *Journal of Investigative Medicine* 45 (1997): 14–19.

52. Zinner, Michael J., M.D. Boston, 7/21/99.
53. Iglehart, J. K. "Managed care and mental health." *N Eng J Med* 334 (1996): 131–135.
54. Gottlieb, Gary L., M.D. Boston, 11/15/99 by telephone.
55. Nathan, David G., M.D. Boston, 11/16/98.
56. Foreman, Judy. "'Jimmy' visits Dana-Farber: Fund's namesake tours institute." *Boston Globe,* 5/22/98, Metro section, B1.
56a. Martin, Douglas. "Einar, Gustafson, 'Jimmy' of child cancer fund, dies at 65." *The New York Times,* 1/24/2001, p. C17.
57. Shaughnessy, Dan. "A mystery story with happy ending: Even Dana-Farber was left clueless." *Boston Globe,* 5/17/98, Sports section, C13.
58. Knox, Richard A. "Doctor's orders killed cancer patient: Dana-Farber admits drug overdose caused death of *Globe* columnist, damage to second woman." *Boston Globe,* 3/23/95, Metro section, 1.
59. "Dana-Farber names president." *Boston Globe,* 9/15/95, Metro section, 47.
60. Knox, Richard A. "3 hospitals form cancer partnership: Dana-Farber, Brigham, MGH will consolidate treatment." *Boston Globe,* 1/17/96, Metro section, 1.
61. Pham, Alex. "Dana-Farber completes joint venture agreement." *Boston Globe,* 7/12/96, Business section, 39.
62. Hsu, Karen. "Harvard, Dana-Farber form cancer research center." *Boston Globe,* 12/10/99, B28.
63. Vennochi, Joan. "Two's company, three's a crowd." *Boston Globe,* 12/9/94, Business section, 77.
64. Samuels, Martin A., M.D. Boston, 7/21/99.
65. Martin, Joseph B., M.D., Ph.D. Boston, 7/22/99, 9/10/99 by telephone.
66. Young, Anne B., M.D., Ph.D. Boston, 10/19/99 by telephone.
67. Parrish, John A., M.D. Boston, 7/21/99.
68. Torchiana, David F., M.D. Boston, 7/22/99.
69. Ausiello, Dennis A., M.D. Boston, 11/20/98.
70. DeSanctis, Roman W., M.D. Boston, 11/18/98.
71. Tosteson, Daniel C., M.D. Boston, 9/29/98.
72. Federman, Daniel D., M.D. Boston, 9/29/98.
73. Ackerman, Jerry. "Partners, Genzyme cut alliance deal." *Boston Globe,* 9/18/97, Business section, C2.
74. Blumenthal, David. "Partners HealthCare System (draft case summary)." 1995, 22.
75. Martin, J. B. "Principles for academic recruitment."
76. Knox, Richard A. "Harvard has gift for med students: $20m shot in arm." *Boston Globe,* 7/17/99, Metro section.
77. Burr, Francis H., Esq. Boston, 9/29/98.
78. Pham, Alex. "North Shore hospitals finalize their merger." *Boston Globe,* 12/3/97, Business section, D9.

Chapter 4. NewYork-Presbyterian: Formation

1. Ferguson, A. Hugh. New York, 4/6/99.
2. Hyman, Allan I., M.D. New York, 1/20/99.
3. Ginzberg, Eli, Ph.D. New York, 11/8/99 by telephone.
4. Lagnado, Lucette. "Sick wards: New York's hospitals merge, cut, and fret as deregulation nears." *Wall Street Journal,* 10/25/96, A1.
5. Solomon, Robert A., M.D. New York, 2/19/99.
6. Rose, Eric A., M.D. New York, 2/19/99, 3/29/99, 12/1/99 by telephone.
7. Speck, William T., M.D. New York, 12/18/98, 4/9/99.
8. Harry J. Bolwell, Vero Beach, FL, 7/1/99 by telephone.
9. Behrman, Richard E., M.D. Palo Alto, 10/7/99.
10. Miller, Edward D., M.D. Baltimore, 2/22/99.
11. Pardes, Herbert, M.D. New York, 12/18/98, 4/5/99, 12/17/99, 8/2/00 by telephone.
12. Shelanski, Michael L., Ph.D. New York, 4/25/99, 11/29/99 by telephone.
13. Lamb, Albert R. *The Presbyterian Hospital and the Columbia-Presbyterian Medical Center, 1968–1943.* New York: Columbia University Press, 1955.
14. Wooster, J. W., Jr. "Edward Stephen Harkness, 1874–1940." *Commonwealth Fund,* 1949.
15. Puchner, Peter, M.D. New York, 2/19/99.
16. Dunlap, David W. "A medical center works on its health." *New York Times,* 10/4/98, Real estate section.
17. Rowland, Lewis P., M.D. New York, 2/19/99, 3/31/99.
18. Betsky, Aaron. *James Gamble Rogers and the architecture of pragmatism.* Cambridge: MIT Press, 1994.
19. Rowland, L. P., Ginsberg, D., Abramson, M., Erlanger, B. F., Turino, G. M., and Yudofsky, S. C. "P&S: An historical perspective." In *The Student Handbook of the College of Physicians and Surgeons, 1982–83.* 171–81.
20. Hogstrom, Harold. New York, 1/22/99.
21. Stevens, Rosemary. *In sickness and in Wealth.* Baltimore: Johns Hopkins University Press, 1999, 323–27.
22. Showstack, J. A. "The social framing of strategic planning in academic health centers," 1997, 1–198.
23. Lagnado, Lucette. "Poison pill: Elite medical centers seemed perfect mates, except to the doctors." *Wall Street Journal,* 3/21/97, A1.
24. Skinner, David B., M.D. New York, 12/17/98, 1/28/00 by telephone.
25. Lieberman, James S., M.D. New York, 6/2/99.
26. Lory, Marc. Manchester, CT, 4/23/99 by telephone.
27. Sparer, Cynthia N. New York, 2/17/99, 1/13/00 by telephone.
28. Vecchione, George A. Providence, RI, 5/7/99, 11/2/99 by telephone.
29. Klein, Arthur A., M.D. New York, 2/18/99, 2/1/00 by telephone.
30. Reuter, L. Frederick. New York, 1/22/99, 11/9/99, 1/28/00 by telephone.
31. Isaacson, Walter. *Kissinger. A Biography.* New York: Simon and Schuster, 1992, 34.

32. Weisfeldt, Myron T., M.D. New York, 12/18/98, 3/29/99, 9/15/99 by telephone.
33. Perales, Cesar A. New York, 1/20/99.
34. Kelly, Robert E., M.D. New York, 2/17/99, 9/21/99 by telephone.
35. Wang, Christopher M., M.D. New York, 4/19/99.
36. Morris, Thomas Q., M.D. New York, 2/19/99.
37. O'Quinn, Marvin. New York, 1/22/99, 11/16/99 by telephone.
38. Flood, C. A. "P&S." College of Physicians and Surgeons of Columbia University, 1989.
39. Mack, John J. New York, 2/24/99, 12/9/99 by telephone.
40. Mundinger, Mary O. New York, 4/12/99.
41. Grusky, Morton H. New York, 1/19/98.
42. O'Donnell, Kathleen D. New York, 1/20/99.
43. Silverstein, Samuel C., M.D. New York, 1/19/99.
44. Tapley, Donald F., M.D. New York, 1/20/99.
45. Leiman, Joan M., Ph.D. New York, 1/19/99.
46. Edelman, Isadore S., M.D. New York, 1/19/99, 10/27/99 by telephone.
47. Saxon, Wolfgang. "Donald Tapley, 72, led Columbia medical school." *New York Times,* 12/16/99, A21.
48. Bickers, David R., M.D. New York, 6/2/99.
49. Rosenthal, Elisabeth. "Leading academic hospital, squeaking by, seeks merger." *New York Times,* 7/8/95, section 1, 1.
50. Morris, Marcia C., Esq. Boston, 3/15/99.
51. Farber, Saul J., M.D. New York, 2/18/99.
52. Coleman, D. Jackson, M.D. New York, 4/7/99.
53. Michels, Robert, M.D. New York, 2/23/99.
54. Fischman, Donald A., M.D. New York, 4/7/99.
55. Thompson, Keith, Esq., New York, 2/16/99.
56. Fein, Oliver T., M.D. New York, 4/8/99.
57. Foderaro, Lisa W. "2 health care giants form joint venture." *New York Times,* 3/10/99, A20.
58. Fein, Esther B. "2 big hospitals pursue a merger." *New York Times,* 1/11/96, B1.
59. "New York hospitals say they are holding talks about merger." *Wall Street Journal,* 1/12/96, C2.
60. Drusin, Ronald E., M.D. New York, 1/21/99.
61. Lewis, Linda D., M.D. New York, 1/19/99.
62. Letter from Jacob Gould Schurman to Nicholas Murray Butler. 1/27/17. Archives of the New York Hospital.
63. Blauer, Joanne. New York, 4/7/99.
64. Farrell, Nancy L. New York, 2/16/99.
65. Gotto, Antonio M., Jr., M.D., D.Phil., New York, 2/18/99.
66. Knowles, Daniel M., M.D. New York, 4/28/99.
67. Kass, Frederic I. "Columbia-Presbyterian strives for quality care." *New York Times,* 7/15/95, section 1, 20.

68. NIH Support to U.S. Medical Schools, Fiscal Year 1999, 02-16-00 http://silk.nih.gov/public/cbz2zoz.@www.med.total.fy99.dsncc.
69. New, Maria I., M.D. New York, 4/5/99.
70. Schwartz, Allan, M.D. New York, 4/6/99.
71. Kligfield, Paul, M.D. New York, 4/8/99.
72. Arenson, Karen W. "$100 million donation set for Cornell medical school." *New York Times*, 5/1/98.
73. Al-Awqati, Qais, M.D. New York, 12/18/98.
74. Pile-Spellman, John, M.D. New York, 6/2/99.
75. Barchas, Jack D., M.D. New York, 6/3/99.
76. Daly, John M., M.D. New York, 2/24/99.
77. Hirsh, David, Ph.D. New York, 4/29/99.
78. Antman, Karen H., M.D. New York, 6/2/99.
79. McGillicutty, John F. New York, 4/28/99.
80. Rosenthal, Elisabeth. "2 more hospitals decide to merge in New York City." *New York Times*, 7/25/96, A1.
81. Pardes, H., and Nathan, C. "The Columbia-Cornell alliance: A strategic response to a changing health care environment. *JAMA* 276 (1996): 1769–71.
82. Nachman, Ralph L., M.D. New York, 12/17/98.
83. Lagnado, Lucette. "New York Hospital head seeks balance in acquisitions to HMOs' growing power." *Wall Street Journal*, 7/26/96, B6.
84. Tenenbaum, Joseph, M.D. New York, 1/20/99.
85. Spivey, Bruce E., M.D. New York, 1/21/99, 4/12/99.
86. Sostman, H. Dirk, M.D. New York, 2/16/99.
87. Larrabee, Eric. *The Benevolent and Necessary Institution: The New York Hospital, 1771–1971*. Garden City, NY: Doubleday, 1971.
88. Strouse, Jean. *Morgan: American Financier.* New York: Random House, 1999, 296–99.
89. Strouse, Jean. *Morgan: American Financier.* New York: Random House, 1999, 689.
90. Loomis, Carol J. "Morgan Stanley Dean Witter: The oddball marriage works." *Fortune*, 4/29/99, 92.
90a. McGeehan, Patrick. "Morgan Stanley official is leaving merged firm." *The New York Times*, 1/25/2001, p. C1.
91. "Hospitals plan merger." *Newsday*, Queens ed., 7/25/96, A23.
92. Sengupta, Somini. "2 hospitals announce completion of merger." *New York Times*, 1/12/98, B3.
93. "The New York and Presbyterian hospital is created." *Dialogue* 19 (January 1999): 1.
94. Lagnado, Lucette. "Top New York medical centers to merge." *Wall Street Journal*, 7/25/96, B12.
95. Moran, Mark. "Smooth sailing for merger of New York teaching hospitals." *American Medical News*, 2/2/98, 9.

Chapter 5. NewYork-Presbyterian: Development

1. Lamb, Albert R. *The Presbyterian Hospital and the Columbia-Presbyterian Medical Center, 1968–1943.* New York: Columbia University Press, 1955.
2. Matheson, David. Boston, 7/22/99.
3. Skinner, David B., M.D. New York, 12/17/98, 1/28/00 by telephone.
4. Morris, Marcia C., Esq. Boston, 3/15/99.
5. Thompson, Keith, Esq. New York, 2/16/99.
6. McGillicuddy, John F. New York, 4/28/99.
7. Burke, Kathleen M., Esq. New York, 4/28/99.
8. Moxley, John H., III, M.D. Los Angeles, 12/3/99 by telephone.
9. Berman, Michael A., M.D. New York, 12/18/98, 6/23/99, 9/21/99 by telephone.
10. Lavan, John. New York, 1/21/99.
11. O'Quinn, Marvin. New York, 1/22/99, 11/16/99 by telephone.
12. Reuter, L. Frederick. New York, 1/22/99, 11/9/99, 1/28/00 by telephone.
13. Martin, Kathryn. New York, 1/21/99, 9/11/99.
14. Schwartz, Allan, M.D. New York, 4/6/99.
15. Tenenbaum, Joseph, M.D. New York, 1/20/99.
16. Hogstrom, Harold. New York, 1/22/99.
17. Lory, Marc. Manchester, CT, 4/23/99 by telephone.
18. Perales, Cesar A., New York, 1/20/99.
19. Corwin, Steven, M.D. New York, 2/17/99.
20. Daly, John M., M.D. New York, 2/24/99.
21. Sostman, H. Dirk, M.D. New York, 2/16/99.
22. Ledger, William J., M.D. New York, 2/16/99, 11/9/99 by telephone.
23. Isom, O. Wayne, M.D. New York, 4/7/99.
24. Knowles, Daniel M., M.D. New York, 4/28/99.
25. Weisfeldt, Myron T., M.D. New York, 12/18/98, 3/29/99, 9/15/99 by telephone.
26. Emond, Jean C., M.D. New York, 4/9/99, 4/29/99.
27. Scalzi, Guy L. New York, 6/3/99, 11/24/99.
28. Steinhauer, Jennifer. "Hospital to form venture with consultants." *New York Times,* 11/9/99, Business Day section, C8.
29. Nachman, Ralph L., M.D. New York, 12/17/98.
30. Lagnado, Lucette. "Top New York medical centers to merge." *Wall Street Journal,* 7/25/96, B12.
31. Crystal, Ronald G., M.D. New York, 4/30/99.
32. O'Donnell, Kathleen D. New York, 1/20/99.
33. Kligfield, Paul, M.D. New York, 4/8/99.
34. Al-Awqati, Qais, M.D. New York, 12/18/98.
35. Kelly, Robert E., M.D. New York, 2/17/99, 9/21/99 by telephone.
36. Shelanski, Michael L., Ph.D. New York, 4/25/99, 11/29/99 by telephone.
37. New, Maria I., M.D. New York, 4/5/99.

38. Beal, M. Flint, M.D. New York, 4/28/99.
39. Leiman, Joan M., Ph.D. New York, 1/19/99.
40. Wolk, Michael, M.D. New York, 2/16/99.
41. Morris, Thomas Q., M.D. New York, 2/19/99.
42. Sparer, Cynthia N. New York, 2/17/99, 1/13/00 by telephone.
43. Dick, Harold M., M.D. New York, 1/22/99.
44. Tapley, Donald F., M.D. New York, 1/20/99.
45. Pardes, Herbert, M.D. New York, 12/18/98, 4/5/99, 12/17/99, 8/2/00 by telephone.
46. Grusky, Morton H. New York, 1/19/98.
47. Lieberman, James S., M.D. New York, 6/2/99.
48. Farrell, Nancy L. New York, 2/16/99.
49. Schley, W. Shain. New York, 2/24/99.
50. Trager, James. *West of Fifth: The Rise and Fall and Rise of Manhattan's West Side.* New York: Atheneum, 1987, 17–18.
51. Smith, Leighton B., M.D. New York, 4/8/99.
52. Fischman, Donald A., M.D. New York, 4/7/99.
53. Coleman, D. Jackson, M.D. New York, 4/7/99.
53a. Miller, Edward D., M.D. Baltimore, 2/22/99.
54. Libby, Daniel M., M.D. New York, 4/8/99.
55. Wazen, Jack J., M.D. New York, 4/27/99.
56. Ferguson, A. Hugh. New York, 4/6/99.
57. Rowland, Lewis P., M.D. New York, 2/19/99, 3/31/99.
58. Gotto, Antonio M., Jr., M.D., D.Phil., New York, 2/18/99.
59. Mack, John J. New York, 2/24/99, 12/9/99 by telephone.
60. Dunlap, David W. "A medical center works on its health." *New York Times,* 10/4/98, Real Estate section.
61. Rose, Eric A., M.D. New York, 2/19/99, 3/29/99, 12/1/99 by telephone.
62. Driscoll, John M., Jr., M.D. New York, 4/9/99.
63. Gersony, Welton, M.D. New York, 4/6/99, 11/15/99 by telephone.
64. Benson, Josh. "Come back, baby docs! Big city-hospital plans to stop pediatric exodus." *New York Observer,* 12/13/99, 1.
64a. Steinhauer, Jennifer. "NewYork-Presbyterian begins work on hospital for children." *New York Times,* 11/17/2000.
65. Perloff, Joseph K., and Child, John S. *Congenital Heart Disease in Adults.* 2d ed. Philadelphia, W. B. Saunders, 1998.
66. Klein, Arthur A., M.D. New York, 2/18/99, 2/1/00 by telephone.
67. Quaegebeur, Jan M., M.D. New York, 2/21/99.
68. Solomon, Robert A., M.D. New York, 2/19/99.
69. Williams, David O., M.D. Providence, RI, 3/18/99 by telephone.
70. Goldberg, Sheldon, M.D. Camden, NJ, 5/25/99 by telephone.
71. Pedley, Timothy A., M.D. New York, 4/9/99.
72. Lagnado, Lucette. "Many financially troubled hospitals haven't been saved by mergers." *Wall Street Journal,* 5/14/99.
73. Morrell, Martha J., M.D. New York, 6/2/90.

74. Lobo, Rogerio A., M.D. New York, 2/23/99 by telephone.
75. Antman, Karen H., M.D. New York, 6/2/99.
76. Barchas, Jack D., M.D. New York, 6/3/99.
77. Leahey, Michael I. New York, 4/5/99.
78. Bickers, David R., M.D. New York, 6/2/99.
79. Ginzberg, Eli, Ph.D. New York, 11/8/99 by telephone.
80. Serfling, G. Aubrey. New York, 2/18/99, 11/1/99 by telephone.
81. Pardes, H., and Nathan, C. "The Columbia-Cornell alliance: A strategic response to a changing health care environment." *JAMA* 276 (1996): 1769–71.
82. Spivey, Bruce E., M.D. New York, 1/21/99, 4/12/99.
83. Mitka, Mike. "N.Y. hospital merger mania." *American Medical News,* 8/12/96, 4.
84. Smith, James P., M.D. New York, 4/30/99.
85. Ascheim, Robert S., M.D. New York, 4/27/99.
86. Hedge, Arthur J., Jr. New York, 6/1/99, 11/22/99 by telephone.
87. Fein, Oliver T., M.D. New York, 4/8/99.
88. Vecchione, George A. Providence, RI, 5/7/99, 11/2/99 by telephone.
89. Rubin, Moshe, M.D. New York, 2/16/99.
90. Puchner, Peter, M.D. New York, 2/19/99.
91. Prager, Kenneth M., M.D. New York, 2/17/99.
92. Lovejoy, William P., M.D. New York, 2/17/99.
93. Rowland, L. P., Ginsberg, D., Abramson, M., Erlanger, B. F., Turino, G. M., and Yudofsky, S. C. "P&S: An historical perspective." In *The Student Handbook of the College of Physicians and Surgeons.* 1982–83, 171–81.
94. Brooks, Andree. "After the recovery room, the recovery hotel." *New York Times,* 5/2/99.
95. Lodge, Henry S., M.D. New York, 4/8/99.
96. Lagnado, Lucette. "Sick wards: New York's hospitals merge, cut, and fret as deregulation nears." *Wall Street Journal,* 10/25/96, A1.
97. Fisher, Ian. "Health commissioner is leaving." *New York Times,* 7/29/98, Metropolitan section.
98. Smith, Randall. "Dean Witter holds its own at Morgan." *Wall Street Journal,* 3/19/99, C1.
99. Blauer, Joanne. New York, 4/7/99.
100. Alonzo, Daniel R., M.D. New York, 4/28/99.
101. Feinberg, David A. New York, 4/30/99, 7/15/99, 10/1/99 by telephone.
102. Finder, Alan. "Koch in stable condition after heart procedure." *New York Times,* 7/2/99, A15.
103. Finder, Alan. "Koch ailment described as moderate heart attack." *New York Times,* 7/3/99, A10.
104. "Koch leaves hospital, heart on the mend." *New York Times,* 7/11/99, New York Report section, 20.
105. Sherman, Marcia. "The man who vanished into his past." *New York Times,* 7/13/99, D8.

106. Greenhouse, Stephen. "Nurses plan strike at Columbia Presbyterian." *New York Times,* 8/5/99, A20.
107. Barnes, Julian E., and Sachs, Susan. "Man killed by police feared his own violent impulses, records show." *New York Times,* 8/3/99, A15.
108. Dao, James. "Bradley misses event for check of heart beat." *New York Times,* 12/11/99.
109. Kelley, Tina. "Artery blocked, Letterman has heart bypass surgery." *New York Times,* 1/15/00.
110. Siegal, Allan M., and Connolly, William G. *The New York Times Manual of Style and Usage.* Times Books, 1999.
111. Benson, Barbara. "NY hospital seizes control: Will put its stamp on merged system." *Crain's New York Business,* 11/17/97.
112. Behrman, Richard E., M.D. Palo Alto, 10/7/99.
113. Speck, William T., M.D. New York, 12/18/98, 4/9/99.
114. Letter to Frank A. Bennack Jr., 3/17/99.
115. Finkelstein, Katherine E. "At a hospital, uncertainty as succession plans change." *New York Times,* 4/9/99, Metro section, B3.
116. Lagnado, Lucette. "CEO crisis roils merger hospital." *Wall Street Journal,* 4/9/99, Marketplace section, B1–4.
117. Hyman, Allan I., M.D. New York, 1/20/99.
118. Lagnado, Lucette. "New York Presbyterian Hospital to open CEO search to end succession strife." *Wall Street Journal,* 4/16/99, B5.
119. Delbanco, Thomas L., M.D. New York, 7/9/99 by telephone.
120. Lagnado, Lucette. "New York hospitals post record financial surpluses amid deregulation." *Wall Street Journal,* 1/25/99.
121. Benson, Barbara. "Serious illness hits NY Presby as merger lags." *Crain's New York Business,* 10/11/99.
122. "America's best hospitals." *U.S. News and World Report,* 7/19/99.
123. Best hospitals 2000. U.S. News & World Report. July 17, 2000; http://www.usnews.com/usnews/nycu/health/hosptl/honroll.htm.
124. Benson, Barbara. "NY Presbyterian bypasses COO in search for new chief." *Crain's New York Business,* 4/12/99.
125. Benson, Barbara. "NYP's internal medicine." *Crain's New York Business,* 12/27/99.
126. "Hospital complex names new leader." *New York Times,* 12/17/99, B14.
127. Benson, Barbara. "NY-Presby picks pres." *Crain's New York Business,* 12/6/99.

Chapter 6. UCSF Stanford: Formation

1. Martin, Joseph B., M.D., Ph.D., Boston, 7/22/99, 9/10/99 by telephone.
2. Casper, Gerhard, Ph.D. Palo Alto, 7/27/99, 11/19/99 by telephone.
3. Van Etten, P. "Camelot or common sense? The logic behind the UCSF/Stanford merger." *Health Affairs* 18 (1999): 143–48.

4. "UCSF Stanford Health Care: The new entity has not yet produced anticipated benefits and faces significant changes." http://www.bsa.ca.gov/bsa/summaries/99128sum.html, Sacramento, Bureau of State Audits, California State Auditor, 1999.
5. Furnstahl, Lawrence J. Executive Park, CA, 7/29/99, 8/20/99 by telephone.
6. Luft, Harold S., Ph.D. San Francisco, 10/5/99.
7. California Public Employees' Retirement System. http://www.calpers.com/, 1999.
8. Fuchs, Victor R., M.D. Stanford, 10/7/99, 11/19/99 by telephone.
9. Korn, David, M.D. Washington, DC, 6/11/99, 1/5/99 by telephone.
10. Blumenthal, David. "Partners HealthCare System (draft case summary)." 1995, 3.
11. Zinner, Michael J., M.D. Boston, 7/21/99.
12. Iglehart, J. K. "Support for academic medical centers: Revisiting the 1997 Balanced Budget Act." *N Eng J Med* 341 (1999): 299–304.
13. Rudd, Peter, M.D. Stanford, 7/27/99.
14. Goldman, Lee, M.D. San Francisco, 6/15/99, 1/3/00 by telephone.
15. Schrock, Theodore R., M.D. San Francisco, 6/15/99, 11/26/99 by telephone.
16. Margaretten, William. M.D. San Francisco, 6/18/99.
17. Andreopoulos, Spyros. Stanford, 10/8/99, 1/13/00 by telephone.
18. Wintroub, Bruce U., M.D. San Francisco, 6/15/99, 11/15/99, 12/20/99 by telephone.
19. Debas, Haile T., M.D. San Francisco, 6/18/99, 8/1/00 by telephone.
20. Bauer, E. A., and Debas, H. T. "The merger of Stanford's and UCSF's clinical enterprises: Impact on education." *JAMA* 276 (1996): 1770–71.
21. Kazak, Don. "A match made in heaven? Two premier institutions plan to unite to remain strong in a hostile health care world." *Palo Alto Weekly,* 10/2/96.
22. Van Etten, Peter W. San Francisco, 6/16/99, 12/13/99, 9/3/99 by telephone.
23. Bauer, Eugene A., M.D. Stanford, 10/7/99, 1/7/99 by telephone.
24. Cohen, Neal H., M.D. San Francisco, 6/16/99.
25. Kane, John P., M.D., Ph.D. San Francisco, 10/4/99.
26. Kerr, William B. San Francisco, 7/26/99, 12/20/99 by telephone.
27. Martin, J. B. "Abrams Lecture: The merger of UCSF and Stanford Medical Centers," 10/7/1997.
28. Simon, Mark. "A doomed hospital merger: Loyalties unravel UC-Stanford marriage." *San Francisco Chronicle,* 10/30/99, A19.
29. Showstack, Jonathan, Ph.D. San Francisco, 6/17/99.
30. Shapiro, Larry J., M.D. San Francisco, 6/18/99.
31. Russell, Sabin. "Stanford, UCSF seek an alliance: Medical schools need to cut costs." *San Francisco Chronicle,* 11/18/95, A1.
32. Kennedy, Donald, Ph.D. Stanford, 10/7/99.
33. Reitz, Bruce A., M.D. Stanford, 7/28/99.
34. Melmon, Kenneth, M.D. Stanford, 7/27/99.
35. Harris, Edward D., Jr., M.D. Stanford, 7/30/99.

36. Wilgoren, Jodi. "Stanford president to resign and teach law full time." *New York Times,* 9/15/99, A18.
37. Swain, Judith L., M.D. Stanford, 7/27/99, 11/15/99 by telephone.
38. Glantz, Stanton A., Ph.D. San Francisco, 7/26/99.
39. NIH Support to U.S. Medical Schools, Fiscal Year 1999, 02–16–00 http://silk.nih.gov/public/cbz2zoz.@www.med.total.fy99.dsncc.
40. Cox, Kenneth L., M.D. Stanford, 10/6/99.
41. Wilson, Charles B., M.D. San Francisco, 6/16/99, 8/3/99 by telephone.
42. Ascher, Nancy L., M.D. San Francisco, 6/16/99.
43. Chrencik, Robert A. Baltimore, 2/4/00.
44. Krieger, Lisa M., and Raine, George. "Suit aims to block hospital merger: Unions charge regents colluded in secret, cite job loss." *San Francisco Examiner,* 6/8/96, A1.
45. "UCSF promises to save 95% of jobs in merger." *San Francisco Chronicle,* 6/15/96.
46. Wagner, Venise. "Panel members say they weren't given enough information on Stanford-UCSF med centers plan." *San Francisco Examiner,* 6/21/96, A4.
47. Russell, Sabin, and Burdman, Pamela. "New doubts surface about UC-Stanford hospital merge." *San Francisco Chronicle,* 7/13/96, A13.
48. Russell, Sabin. "UC regents hesitant over planned hospital merger: Many want power shared 50–50, but Stanford balks." *San Francisco Chronicle,* 7/9/96, A15.
49. Russell, Sabin. "UCSF-Stanford hospital merger faces regent decision: Vote will focus on structure of governing board." *San Francisco Chronicle,* 7/18/96, A17.
50. Russell, Sabin. "UC regents give approval to merger plan: Lt. Governor's idea nixed in favor of private board." *San Francisco Chronicle,* 7/20/96, A13.
51. Krieger, Lisa M. "UC regents seal hospital merger." *San Francisco Examiner,* 7/20/96, A2.
52. Russell, Sabin. "UCSF chief quitting for Harvard job: He's been point man for Stanford merger." *San Francisco Chronicle,* 11/9/96, A1.
53. Boyden, Jaclyne W. San Francisco, 6/18/99.
54. Russell, Sabin. "UC, Stanford OK merger of hospitals: Joint operations to begin in July." *San Francisco Chronicle,* 11/16/96, A1.
55. UCSF history. Chronology of UCSF, 1852–1899. http://www.library.ucsf.edu/sc/hist/chron1.html.
56. Meyer, Kerr C., and Rockafellar, M., N.M. Interviews with Clark Kerr, Ph.D., and Morton Meyer, M.D. Eyewitnesses to UC campus turmoil in the mid-1960s. The Regents of the University of California, 1998.
57. UCSF history. Chronology of UCSF, 1901–1950. http://www.library.ucsf.edu/sc/hist/chron2.htmlhttp://www.library.ucsf.edu/sc/hist/chron2.html.
58. UCSF history. Chronology of UCSF, 1952–present. http://www.library.ucsf.edu/sc/hist/chron3.html.
59. Ramsay, David J., D.M., D.Phil. Baltimore, 1/10/00.

60. Smith, Lloyd H., Jr., M.D. San Francisco, 6/18/99, 10/27/99 by telephone.
61. Krevans, Julius R., M.D. San Francisco, 6/15/99.
62. Edelman, Isadore S., M.D. New York, 1/19/99, 10/27/99 by telephone.
63. Rockafellar, Nancy M., Ph.D. San Francisco, 10/5/99.
64. Abate, Tom. "UCSF on a mission: Satellite campus to serve as nucleus of biotech complex." *San Francisco Chronicle*, 3/1/99, B1.
65. Cushing, Harvey. *The Life of Sir William Osler*. Vol. 1. New York: Oxford University Press, 1940, 269.
66. UCSF School of Medicine. School information. About the school. http://www.som.ucsf.edu/schoolinfo/anout/index.htm. 2000.
67. Martin, Joseph B. Boston, 8/31/99, by e-mail.
68. Rogers, Barbara S., and Dobbs, Stephen M. *The First Century: Mount Zion Hospital and Medical Center, 1887–1987*. San Francisco: Mount Zion Hospital and Medical Center, 1987.
69. Garcia, Ken. "Don't pull plug on Mount Zion: Decisive meeting planned for tomorrow." *San Francisco Chronicle*, 7/22/99, A17.
70. Ring, Ernest J., M.D. San Francisco, 10/4/99.
71. Melnick, David, Esq. San Francisco, 7/9/99 by telephone.
72. Hellman, F. Warren. San Francisco, 10/5/99, 11/23/99 by telephone.
73. Lowen, Rebecca S. *Creating the Cold War University: The Transformation of Stanford*. Berkeley: University of California Press, 1997.
74. Nash, George H. *Herbert Hoover and Stanford University*. Stanford: Hoover Institution Press, 1988, 41–45.
75. Allen, Peter C. *Stanford: From the Foothills to the Bay*. Stanford: Stanford Alumni Association and Stanford Historical Society, 1980.
76. Wilson, J. L. Stanford University School of Medicine and the predecessor schools: An historical perspective. http://elane.stanford.edu/wilson. 1999.
77. Walsh, J. "Stanford School of Medicine, I: Problems over more than money." *Science* 171 (1971): 551–53.
78. Walsh, J. "Stanford School of Medicine, II: Clinicians make an issue." *Science* 171 (1971): 654–57.
79. Walsh, J. "Stanford School of Medicine, III: Varieties of medical experience." *Science* 171 (1971): 785–87.
80. Holman, Halsted R., M.D. Stanford, 7/30/99.
81. Goldstein, Avram, M.D. Palo Alto 10/8/99.
82. Andreopoulos, Spyros. "Stanford-UCSF merger has been tried and has failed before." *Stanford Daily*, 10/18/96.
83. Nash, George H. *Herbert Hoover and Stanford University*. Stanford: Hoover Institution Press, 1988, 127.
84. Kornberg, Arthur. *"For the Love of Enzymes: The Odyssey of a Biochemist.* Cambridge: Harvard University Press, 1989.
85. Kornberg, Arthur, M.D. Stanford, 10/7/99.
86. "Dr. Norman Kretchmer." *San Francisco Chronicle*, 12/29/95, A27.
87. Harrison, Donald C., M.D. Cincinnati, 11/9/99, 11/09/99 by telephone.
88. LaDou, J. "UCSF-Stanford Merger." 1999.
89. Glaser, Robert J., M.D. Palo Alto, 10/8/99.

90. Longmire, W. P., Jr. "The Halstedian influence goes west: Personal and historical remarks." *Pharos* (summer 1999): 19–24.
91. IPS annual report, 1997–1998. http://webdb.aamc.org/findinfo/infores/datarsc/ips/links.cfm. 11/11/1999.
92. Mark, James B. D., M.D. Stanford, 10/18/99.
93. Shumway, Norman E., M.D., Ph.D., Stanford, 7/27/99.
94. Bloem, Kenneth D. Washington, DC, 7/16/99, 11/16/99 by telephone.
95. History of the Palo Alto Clinic. http://pamf.org. 1999.
96. Jamplis, Robert W., M.D. Palo Alto, 9/22/99 by telephone.
97. Andreopoulos, S. "The folly of teaching-hospital mergers." *N Eng J Med* 336 (1997): 61–64.
98. Dzau, Victor M., M.D. Boston, 8/5/99 by telephone.
99. Stein, Isaac, Esq. Palo Alto, 7/28/99, 11/9/99, 12/27/99 by telephone.
100. Esquivel, Carlos O., M.D., Ph.D. Stanford, 7/30/99.
101. Jeffris, Rufus, "Hospital president leaving: Interim board, top officers named to head Stanford Health Services." *Palo Alto Weekly,* 4/15/94.
102. Kazak, Don. "Casper reorganizes med center: Longtime medical school dean to retire next year." *Palo Alto Weekly,* 8/26/94.
103. Kazak, Don. "Stanford names new hospital chief, but top university position remains vacant for now." *Palo Alto Weekly,* 2/10/95.
104. Lane, Alfred T., M.D. Stanford, 7/30/99.
105. Holmes, Edward W., M.D. Durham, 11/10/99 by telephone.
106. "A conversation with Gerhard Casper." *Palo Alto Weekly,* 6/25/97.
107. Kazak, Don. "Two hospitals plan a full merger: Stanford, Packard Children's hospitals hope to wrap up talks soon." *Palo Alto Weekly,* 5/8/96.
108. Kazak, Don. "Packard Hospital approves merger." *Palo Alto Weekly,* 9/11/96.
109. Gregory, Peter B., M.D. Stanford, 7/29/99, 11/18/99 by telephone.
110. Cohen, Harvey J., M.D., Ph.D. Stanford, 7/27/99.
111. Laros, Russell K., Jr., M.D. San Francisco, 10/11/99 by telephone.
112. Abel, Michael E., M.D. San Francisco, 11/24/99 by telephone.
113. Krieger, Lisa M. "Major medical merger in S.F.: Doctors of UCSF and Cal Pacific to team up next year." *San Francisco Examiner,* 9/30/96, A1.
114. Mcafee, Thomas V., M.D. San Francisco, 10/1/99 by telephone.
115. Perry, Patricia E. Executive Park, 7/29/99.
116. Goldsmith, Jeff. Charlottesville, 11/08/99 by telephone.
117. Glazer, Gary M., M.D. Stanford, 7/30/99.
118. Thier, Samuel O., M.D. Boston, 7/24/98, 9/30/98, 12/2/99 by telephone.
119. *UCSF Medical Center/Stanford Health Services Proposed Merger of Clinical Enterprises: Third Party Review.* Oakland: University of California Regents, 1996.
120. Chao, Julie. "Report supports merger of UC, Stanford hospitals, but unions say document ignores important factors that could hurt care." *San Francisco Examiner,* 11/5/96, A3.

121. Showstack, J. A. "The social framing of strategic planning in academic health centers." 1997, 1–198.

122. "Stanford-UC hospitals pick new directors." *San Francisco Chronicle,* 1/9/97, A18.

123. Russell, Sabin. "Medical centers chief named." *San Francisco Chronicle,* 2/14/97, B2.

124. Burdman, Pamela. "New hospital chief bows out: Doubts rekindled about UC-Stanford facilities merger." *San Francisco Chronicle,* 2/19/97.

125. Kazak, Don. "Stanford: CEO named for merged hospitals." *Palo Alto Weekly,* 2/26/97.

126. Lorenz, Elizabeth. "Peter Van Etten: The view from the top." *Palo Alto Weekly,* 8/26/98.

127. Miller, Ronald D., M.D. San Francisco, 7/26/99.

128. Kazak, Don. "Hospital merger under fire: State Sen. John Burton mounts effort to block UCSF-Stanford deal." *Palo Alto Weekly,* 3/19/97.

129. Kazak, Don. "Bill could block hospital merger." *Palo Alto Weekly,* 4/2/97.

130. Kazak, Don. "Officials delay hospital merger: New launch date for Stanford-UCSF is Sept. 1." *Palo Alto Weekly,* 5/2/97.

131. Krieger, Lisa M. "Bills may threaten UC-Stanford merger." *San Francisco Examiner,* 5/22/99, A6.

132. "Assembly OKs bills on hospital merger." *San Francisco Chronicle,* 5/22/97, A24.

133. "Casper: Some meetings will be public — Stanford president defends hospital merger by making pledges for openness." *Palo Alto Weekly,* 5/28/97.

134. "Regents delay hospital merger decision." *San Francisco Chronicle,* 7/10/97, A19.

135. Lucas, Greg, and Burdman, Pamela. "UCSF-Stanford hospital plan nears approval: Most meetings and records of facility must be public." *San Francisco Chronicle,* 8/27/97, A15.

136. Salladay, Robert. "UCSF public access bill progresses." *San Francisco Examiner,* 8/29/97, A4.

137. "The sun shines on a merger." *San Francisco Chronicle,* 8/28/97, A24.

138. Gunnison, Robert B. "Veto for hospital merger bill: Wilson rejects plan for legislative oversight." *San Francisco Chronicle,* 8/3/97, A13.

139. The UCSF and Stanford Health Services: The proposed merger should make the partners fiscally stronger, although the extent of financial benefits is potentially overstated. http://www.bsa.ca.gov/bsa/summaries/97122sum.html. Sacramento, California State Auditor, 97122. 1997.

140. Russell, Sabin. "UC regents approve merger of hospitals: Deal awaits Stanford's expected OK." *San Francisco Chronicle,* 9/20/97, A19.

141. Kazak, Don. "Hospital merger is approved." *Palo Alto Weekly,* 9/24/97.

142. Kazak, Don. "Lawsuit seeks to block merger." *Palo Alto Weekly,* 9/26/97.

143. Kazak, Don. "Merger gets green light from FPPC." *Palo Alto Weekly,* 10/1/97.

Chapter 7. UCSF Stanford: Development

1. Wintroub, Bruce U., M.D. San Francisco, 6/15/99, 11/15/99, 12/20/99 by telephone.
2. Wachter, Robert M., M.D. San Francisco, 6/17/99.
3. Melito, Sean P. San Francisco, 8/27/99 by e-mail.
4. Van Etten, Peter W. San Francisco, 6/16/99, 12/13/99, 9/3/99 by telephone.
5. Showstack, J. A. "The social framing of strategic planning in academic health centers." 1997, 1–198.
6. Showstack, Jonathan, Ph.D. San Francisco, 6/17/99.
7. Wilson, Charles B., M.D. San Francisco, 6/16/99, 8/3/99 by telephone.
8. Goldman, Lee, M.D. San Francisco, 6/15/99, 1/3/00 by telephone.
9. Esquivel, Carlos O., M.D., Ph.D. Stanford, 7/30/99.
10. Ring, Ernest J., M.D. San Francisco, 10/4/99, 12/29/00 by telephone.
11. Rizk, Norman W., M.D. Stanford, 12/2/99 by telephone.
12. Schrock, Theodore R., M.D. San Francisco, 6/15/99, 11/26/99 by telephone.
13. Gregory, Peter B., M.D. Stanford, 7/29/99, 11/18/99 by telephone.
14. Cox, Kenneth L., M.D. Stanford, 10/6/99.
15. May, G. Brian, San Francisco, 7/29/99, 8/29/99 by telephone.
16. Arenson, Ronald L., M.D. San Francisco, 7/26/99.
17. Ramsay, David J., M.D., Ph.D. Baltimore, 1/10/00.
18. Kerr, William B. San Francisco, 7/26/99, 12/20/99 by telephone.
19. Laros, Russell K., Jr., M.D. San Francisco, 10/11/99 by telephone.
20. Furnstahl, Lawrence J. Executive Park, 7/29/99, 8/20/99 by telephone.
21. Perry, Patricia E. Executive Park, 7/29/99.
22. Boyden, Jaclyne W. San Francisco, 6/18/99.
23. Rudd, Peter, M.D. Stanford, 7/27/99.
24. Cohen, Neal H., M.D. San Francisco, 6/16/99.
25. Behrman, Richard E., M.D. Palo Alto, 10/7/99.
26. Cohen, Harvey J., M.D., Ph.D. Stanford, 7/27/99.
27. Shapiro, Larry J., M.D. San Francisco, 6/18/99.
28. Kazak, Don. "Packard Hospital plans own merger: As Stanford Hospital joins with UCSF, Packard merges with Stanford." *Palo Alto Weekly,* 1/2/96.
29. Lane, Alfred T., M.D. Stanford, 7/30/99.
30. Hanley, Frank L., M.D. Stanford, 7/28/99, 1/24/00 by telephone.
31. Reitz, Bruce A., M.D. Stanford, 7/28/99.
32. Rago, Karen A. Stanford, 10/6/99.
33. Ascher, Nancy L., M.D. San Francisco, 6/16/99.
34. Miller, Ronald D., M.D. San Francisco, 7/26/99.
35. Yamamoto, Keith R., Ph.D. San Francisco, 10/4/99.
36. Debas, Haile T., M.D. San Francisco, 6/18/99, 8/1/00 by telephone.
37. Krevans, Julius R., M.D. San Francisco, 6/15/99.
38. Polan, Mary Lake, M.D., Ph.D. Stanford, 10/8/99, 11/8/99, 1/12/00 by telephone.
39. Jacobs, Charlotte D., M.D. Stanford, 11/4/99 by telephone.

40. Garzio, Catherine. San Francisco, 10/6/99.
41. Chrencik, Robert A. Baltimore, 2/4/00.
42. Hall, Carl T. "UCSF cancer program to join top U.S. oncology network: It will be one of select number of centers." *San Francisco Chronicle*, 8/5/99, A17.
43. Stein, Isaac, Esq. Palo Alto, 7/28/99, 11/9/99, 12/27/99 by telephone.
44. Glazer, Gary M., M.D. Stanford, 7/30/99.
45. Serfling, G. Aubrey. New York, 2/18/99, 11/1/99 by telephone.
46. Lehrman, Sally. "Anti-smoking scholar enjoys being a thorn in industry's side." *San Francisco Examiner*, 3/5/95, B1.
47. Glantz, Stanton A., Ph.D. San Francisco, 7/26/99.
48. Shumway, Norman E., M.D., Ph.D. Stanford, 7/27/99.
49. Casper, Gerhard, Ph.D. Palo Alto, 7/27/99, 11/19/99 by telephone.
50. Schindler, Robert A., M.D. San Francisco, 7/16/99.
51. Schevitz, Tanya. "Few UCSF faculty in favor of merger." *San Francisco Chronicle*, 10/15/99, A18.
52. Richter, R. Stanford, UCSF to end merger of med centers. http:/www .stanford.edu/dept/news/report/news/november3/merger113.html. 11/3/99.
53. Swain, Judith L., M.D. Stanford, 7/27/99, 11/15/99 by telephone.
54. Lifsher, Mark. "Snafus plague hospital after merger." *Wall Street Journal*, California ed., 1/14/98, CA1.
55. MacLeod, Karen. San Francisco, 6/15/99.
56. Melmon, Kenneth, M.D. Stanford, 7/27/99.
57. UCSF Stanford Health Care. "Explanation of reduction in profitability and turnabout plan." 1999.
58. Stone, John B. San Francisco, 11/30/99.
59. Workman, Bill. "Health workers at 2 hospitals vote to unionize." *San Francisco Chronicle*, 11/21/98, A17.
60. Abate, Tom. "Job cuts at UCSF Stanford: 2000 positions to be eliminated at hospitals." *San Francisco Chronicle*, 3/30/99, C1.
61. Torassa, Ulysses. "UCSF Stanford merger: One big financial mess." *San Francisco Examiner*, 7/25/99, 1.
62. Schevitz, Tanya. "New setback for hospital—loss soars: Huge UCSF Stanford deficit clouds future of Mt. Zion." *San Francisco Chronicle*, 7/13/99.
63. Russell, Sabin. "Merging off course: Unexpected red ink forces layoffs, service cutbacks at UCSF Stanford Health Care." *San Francisco Chronicle*, 6/17/99, A1.
64. Russell, Sabin. "Angry legislators demand probe of snakebitten hospital merger." *San Francisco Chronicle*, 7/2/99, A20.
65. Torassa, Ulysses. "Lawmakers target UCSF Stanford." *San Francisco Examiner*, 7/2/99.
66. Goodell, Brian, M.D. San Francisco, 10/5/99.
67. "UCSF Stanford pharmacy to close." *San Francisco Chronicle*, 5/8/99, A19.
68. Luft, Harold S., Ph.D. San Francisco, 10/5/99.
69. Abel, Michael E., M.D. San Francisco, 11/24/99 by telephone.

70. Mcafee, Thomas V., M.D. San Francisco, 10/1/99 by telephone.
71. Abate, Tom. "Blue Cross called best plan in California." *San Francisco Chronicle,* 9/24/99, B1.
72. UCSF Stanford Health Care: The new entity has not yet produced antici-pated benefits and faces significant changes. http://www.bsa.ca.gov/bsa/summaries/99128sum.html. Sacramento, Bureau of State Audits, California State Auditor. 1999.
73. Smith, Lloyd H., Jr., M.D. San Francisco, 6/18/99, 10/27/99 by telephone.
74. Bishop, J. M. A message from the chancellor. http://www.ucsf.edu/daybreak/1999/11/03_message.html. 11/3/1999.
75. Wilson, Charles B. "UCSF's mission must survive merger problems." *San Francisco Examiner,* 8/26/99.
76. Epstein, Edward. "Losses threaten S.F. hospital: Mount Zion facility may lose emergency room." *San Francisco Chronicle,* 6/30/99, A14.
77. Abate, Tom. "UCSF Stanford Health Care wants to close Mt. Zion despite cash cushion: Internal e-mail hints UC should scrub merger rather than shut hospital." *San Francisco Chronicle,* 8/3/99.
78. Russell, Sabin. "Merger affects Mt. Zion's fate: Stanford could choose to veto S.F. hospital's pricey overhaul." *San Francisco Chronicle,* 9/17/97, A19.
79. Harris, Edward D., Jr., M.D. Stanford, 7/30/99.
80. Epstein, Edward. "S.F. mayor joins fight to save hospital: Mount Zion operating at one-third capacity." *San Francisco Chronicle,* 7/1/99.
81. Curiel, Jonathan. "Unhealthy report on hospital merger: $11 million loss for UCSF Stanford Health Care." *San Francisco Chronicle,* 5/21/99.
82. Delgado, Ray. "Friends of Mount Zion say 'Keep it open.'" *San Francisco Examiner,* 8/27/99, A24.
83. Brazil, Eric. "Union rally to protest hospital job cuts." *San Francisco Examiner,* 7/13/99.
84. "Don't close Mount Zion without careful study." *San Francisco Chronicle,* 7/23/99, A24.
85. Garcia, Ken. "Don't pull plug on Mount Zion: Decisive meeting planned for tomorrow." *San Francisco Chronicle,* 7/22/99, A17.
86. Torassa, Ulysses. "Inpatient care at Mount Zion in danger." *San Francisco Examiner,* 5/20/99, A1.
87. Melnick, David, Esq. San Francisco, 7/9/99 by telephone.
88. Torassa, Ulysses. "$5 million pledge to save Mt. Zion: Former parent of merged hospitals offers bailout fund in attempt to salvage medical center." *San Francisco Examiner,* 7/20/99, A3.
89. Torassa, Ulysses. "UC regents pass the buck on future of Mount Zion." *San Francisco Examiner,* 7/15/99, A6.
90. Schevitz, Tanya. "Decision delay on Mt. Zion services: UCSF Stanford board reacts to public hearing." *San Francisco Chronicle,* 7/24/99, A15.
91. Abate, Tom. "UCSF births a research center as it amputates an emergency room." *San Francisco Chronicle,* 10/25/99, B1.

92. Gordon, Rachel. "S.F. picked for second UC campus: Regents OK plan to put $800 million biomedical center at Mission Bay." *San Francisco Examiner,* 5/17/97, A1.

93. Newman, Morris. "A $4 billion mix of uses in San Francisco." *New York Times,* 1/9/00, New York Report–Real Estate section, 27.

94. Letter from Joseph B. Martin, 12/9/99.

95. Chernow, Barbara A., and Vallasi, George A., eds. *The Columbia Encyclopedia.* 5th ed. New York: Columbia University Press, 1993, 1626.

96. "City urges UCSF to open campus at Mission Bay: Brown envisions big boost for struggling project." *San Francisco Examiner,* 9/24/96, A2.

97. Levy, Dan. "A campus jewel: UCSF plans first building for Mission Bay location." *San Francisco Chronicle,* 3/19/99.

98. Kane, John P., M.D., Ph.D. San Francisco, 10/4/99.

99. Schroffel, Bruce. San Francisco, 6/17/99, 10/28/99 by telephone.

100. Schevitz, Tanya, and Russell, Sabin. "UC regents stick with hospital: Decision means major cutbacks will proceed." *San Francisco Chronicle,* 7/15/99, A17.

101. Torassa, Ulysses. "UC, Stanford chiefs order review as losses loom." *San Francisco Examiner,* 8/6/99.

102. Debas, Haile T. San Francisco, 8/2/99 by e-mail.

103. Abate, Tom. "UCSF Stanford to rethink '97 merger: Intent may be to keep Mount Zion operating." *San Francisco Chronicle,* 8/6/99, A1.

104. Kennedy, Donald, Ph.D. Stanford, 10/7/99.

105. Abate, Tom, and Schevitz, Tanya. "Top execs quit UCSF Stanford hospitals: Cost-cutting expert takes over as interim boss." *San Francisco Chronicle,* 8/10/99.

106. Bloem, Kenneth D. Washington, DC, 7/16/99, 11/16/99 by telephone.

107. Freudenheim, Milt. "Bitter pills for ailing hospitals." *New York Times,* 10/31/99, Business section, 1.

108. Hunter, David. St. Petersburg, 12/9/99 by telephone.

109. The Hunter Group. www:huntergroup-healthcare.com. 1999.

110. Winokur, Scott. "Hospital fixers' tactics slammed: UCSF Stanford hires 'slash and burn' consultants." *San Francisco Examiner,* 10/4/99.

111. Hellman, F. Warren. San Francisco, 10/5/99, 11/23/99 by telephone.

112. Dougan, Michael. "Layoff fears grip UCSF Stanford employees: New management group is known for heavy cuts at other hospitals it has taken over." *San Francisco Examiner,* 8/11/99, A7.

113. Stark, Karl. "A hired gun for health system's tough decisions." *Philadelphia Inquirer,* 7/20/99.

114. Hunter, David. St. Petersburg. 8/18/99 by e-mail.

115. Perry, Patricia. San Francisco. 9/29/99 by e-mail.

116. Cisneros L. Debas plans to help medical center recover. http://www.ucsf.edu/daybreak/2000/01/20_debas.html. 1/20/00.

117. Russell, Sabin. "UCSF dean says merger overhaul needed." *San Francisco Chronicle,* 8/12/99, A19.

118. Gladwell, M. "The physical genius: What do Wayne Gretzky, Yo-Yo Ma, and a brain surgeon named Charlie Wilson have in common? *New Yorker,* 8/2/99, 57–65.

119. Dougan, Michael. "Consultant takes bigger role at UCSF Stanford." *San Francisco Examiner,* 8/10/99.

120. Gold, Warren. "UCSF-Stanford merger should be dissolved now." *San Francisco Examiner,* 8/12/99.

121. Russell, Sabin. "S.F.'s Mount Zion to shut emergency room: UCSF Stanford board blames hospital's financial losses." *San Francisco Chronicle,* 9/24/99, A1.

122. Rogers, Barbara S., and Dobbs, Stephen M. *The First Century: Mount Zion Hospital and Medical Center, 1887–1987.* San Francisco: Mount Zion Hospital and Medical Center, 1987.

123. Bishop, J. M. "Mount Zion's future remains bright: Community stands to benefit from changes in store." *San Francisco Chronicle,* 11/15/99, A27.

124. Torassa, Ulysses. "Last-minute campaign to save Mount Zion." *San Francisco Examiner,* 11/17/99, A9.

125. Russell, Sabin. "Politicians work on subsidy plan for Mount Zion: $25 million funds package proposed." *San Francisco Chronicle,* 11/17/99, A21.

126. Russell, Sabin. "Mount Zion ER to close on Tuesday: Political leaders fail to get funds to keep hospital going." *San Francisco Chronicle,* 11/20/99, A15.

127. Kim, Ryan. "Mt. Zion ER drops vow to stay open: Will close Tuesday rather than Dec. 23." *San Francisco Examiner,* 11/20/99, A1.

128. Byerwalter, Mariann. Stanford, 10/4/99, 1/6/00 by telephone.

129. Russell, Sabin. "UCSF, Stanford leaders wait to hear from faculty on merger." *San Francisco Chronicle,* 10/1/99, A24.

130. Hatfield, Larry D., and Torassa, Ulysses. "$4.5 million embezzled from UCSF, stunned regents learn." *San Francisco Examiner,* 7/16/99, A6.

131. Van Derbeken, Jaxon. "Credit card fraud suspect invited victims to view booty." *San Francisco Chronicle,* 8/19/99.

132. Workman, Bill, and Simon, Mark. "Stanford's president to step down: Casper leaving post next summer to teach." *San Francisco Chronicle,* 9/15/99, A1.

133. Casper, G. Cares of the university. http://www.stanford.edu./home/stanford/cares/. 1997.

134. Wilgoren, Jodi. "Stanford president to resign and teach law full time." *New York Times,* 9/15/99, A18.

135. Casper, G. Casper letter to UC President Atkinson. http://www.ucsf.edu/daybreak/1999/10/28_casper.html. 10/28/99.

136. Torassa, Ulysses. "Regents formally end merger." *San Francisco Examiner,* 11/19/99, A12.

137. Schevitz, Tanya. "Stanford-UCSF divorce could be lengthy: Separating four hospitals is a delicate operation." *San Francisco Chronicle,* 11/16/99, A17.

138. Schevitz, Tanya. "Jointly run child health services to end: UCSF Stanford grant left up in air." *San Francisco Chronicle,* 1/20/00, A17.
139. Andreopoulos, Spyros. Stanford, 10/8/99, 1/13/00 by telephone.
140. Bauer, Eugene A., M.D. Stanford, 10/7/99, 1/7/99 by telephone, 8/2/00 by e-mail.
141. Casper, G. Gerhard Casper's statement on the restructure of medical center leadership. http://www.stanford.edu/dept/news/report/news/january5/medstatement-15.html. 1/5/00.
141a. Philip Pizzo named dean of medical school. http://www.stanford.edu/dept/news/report/news/december 13/pizzo-1213.html. 12/11/2000.
142. Goldsmith, Jeff. Charlottesville, 11/08/99 by telephone.
143. Dawes, Christopher G. Stanford, 12/3/99 by telephone.
144. "UCSF Stanford reports losses: $10 million in October alone." *San Francisco Examiner,* 12/7/99, C4.
145. Krieger, Lisa M. "Merger needed doctors." *San Jose Mercury News,* 10/30/99.
145a. Melmon, Kenneth, M.D. Stanford, 7/27/99 by e-mail 2/14/00.
146. Blume, Karl G., M.D. Stanford, 11/3/99 by telephone.
147. Andreopoulos, S. "The folly of teaching hospital mergers" [correspondence]. *N Eng J Med* 336 (1997): 1762–63.
148. Gurtner, William H. Oakland, 12/20/99 by telephone.
149. Snow, C. P. *The Two Cultures.* Cambridge: Cambridge University Press, 1998.
150. Bishop, J. M. "UC chancellor's view on failed merger." *San Francisco Chronicle,* 11/10/99.
151. Alain Enthoven. Stanford, 11/6/99 by e-mail.
152. *UCSF Medical Center/Stanford Health Services proposed merger of clinical enterprises: Third party review.* Oakland: University of California Regents, 1996.
153. Lewin, Lawrence S. Arlington, VA, 3/12/99.
154. Schevitz, Tanya. "$5 million grants to UCSF supports young researchers." *San Francisco Chronicle,* 11/4/99, A24.
154a. Russell, Sabin. "$176 million tab on failed hospital merger. Hospitals' bill for merger—$176 million." San Francisco Chronicle, 12/14/2000, p. A25.
154b. Stanford Report. Stanford, UCSF release financial results for fiscal year 2000. http://www.stanford.edu/dept/news/report/news/december 13/audit-1213.html. 12/13/2000.

Chapter 8. Conclusions

1. Shine, Kenneth I., M.D. Washington, DC, 7/2/98.
2. Serfling, G. Aubrey. New York, 2/18/99, 11/1/99 by telephone.
3. Vecchione, George A. Providence, RI, 5/7/99, 11/2/99 and 12/29/00 by telephone.

3a. Liz Kowalczyk. "Tufts-NEMC leaving Lifespan." *Boston Globe,* 8/29/02.
4. Fuchs, Victor R., M.D. Stanford, 10/7/99, 11/19/99 by telephone.
5. Goldsmith, Jeff. Charlottesville, 11/08/99 by telephone.
6. Bloem, Kenneth D. Washington, DC, 7/16/99, 11/16/99 by telephone.
7. Cohen, Jordan J., M.D. Washington, DC, 11/30/99 by telephone.
8. Stein, Isaac, Esq. Palo Alto, 7/28/99, 11/9/99, 12/27/99 by telephone.
9. Thier, Samuel O., M.D. Boston, 7/24/98, 9/30/98, 12/2/99 by telephone.
10. Wintroub, Bruce U., M.D. San Francisco, 6/15/99, 11/15/99, 12/20/99 by telephone.
11. UCSF Stanford Health Care: The new entity has not yet produced anticipated benefits and faces significant changes. http://www.bsa.ca.gov/bsa/summaries/99128sum.html. Sacramento, Bureau of State Audits, California State Auditor. 1999.
12. Schrock, Theodore R., M.D. San Francisco, 6/15/99, 11/26/99 by telephone.
13. Rabkin, Mitchell T., M.D. Boston, 7/23/98, 1/12/00, 11/16/99 by telephone.
14. Fein, Rashi, Ph.D. Boston, 7/14/99 by telephone.
15. Harrell, G. T. "Osler's practice." *Bulletin of the History of Medicine* 47 (1973): 545–68.
16. Bliss, Michael. *William Osler. A life in medicine.* Oxford: Oxford University Press, 1999.
17. Federman, Daniel D., M.D. Boston, 9/29/98.
18. Holmes, Edward W., M.D. Durham, 11/10/99 by telephone.
19. Richter, R. Stanford, UCSF to end merger of med centers. http://www.stanford.edu/dept/news/report/news/november3/merger113.html. 11/3/99.
20. Speck, W. T. "The folly of teaching-hospital mergers." *N Eng J Med* 336 (1997): 1762.
21. Goldsmith, J. "UCSF/Stanford: Building a 'prestige cartel.'" *Health Affairs* 18 (1999): 149–51.
22. Fassbach, Scott M. Washington, DC, 11/15/99 by telephone.
23. Goodell, Brian, M.D. San Francisco, 10/5/99.
24. Krieger, Lisa M. "Merger needed doctors." *San Jose Mercury News,* 10/30/99.
25. Stone, John B. San Francisco, 11/30/99.
26. Pear, Robert. "Annual spending on Medicare dips for first time." *New York Times,* 11/14/99, 1.
27. Andreopoulos, Spyros. Stanford, 10/8/99, 1/13/00 by telephone.
28. Holland, Judy, and Freedman, Dan. "Restoration of Medicare cuts is too late to rescue UCSF Stanford Health Care." *San Francisco Examiner,* 11/12/99, A2.
29. Behrman, Richard E., M.D. Palo Alto, 10/7/99.
30. Reinhardt, Uwe, Ph.D. Princeton, 11/10/99 by telephone.
31. Laros, Russell K., Jr., M.D. San Francisco, 10/11/99 by telephone.
32. Bauer, E. A. "The folly of teaching-hospital mergers." *N Eng J Med* 336 (1997): 1762–63.
33. Holman, Halsted R., M.D. Stanford, 7/30/99.

34. Moxley, John H., III, M.D. Los Angeles, 12/3/99 by telephone.
35. Wilmsen, Steven. "Beth Israel dismisses top official." *Boston Globe,* 11/19/99, D5.
35a. Kowalczyk, Liz. "CareGroup losses hit $105M. Analysts stunned: Brockton move cited." *Boston Globe,* 12/23/2000, Business section, p. G1.
36. Lerner, Wayne M., ed. *Anatomy of a Merger: BJC Health System.* Chicago: Health Administration Press, 1997.
37. Cain, Michael E., M.D. St. Louis, 12/6/99 and 1/2/01 by telephone.
38. Kipnis, David M., M.D. St. Louis, 11/4/99 by telephone.
39. Rowe, John W., M.D. New York, 11/5/99 by telephone.
39a. Steinhauer, Jennifer. "Hospital chief to lead Aetna managed care." *New York Times,* 9/6/00.
39b. Katherine E. Finkelstein. "Celebrated hospital merger a union in name only." *New York Times,* 12/2/01.
39c. Alison L. Cowan. "N.Y.U. Hospitals Center's president to resign." *New York Times,* 1/25/03.
40. Burns, L. R., Cacciamani, J., Clement, J., and Aquino, W. "The fall of the house of AHERF: The Allegheny bankruptcy." *Health Affairs* 19 (2000): 7–41.
41. Reynolds, Herbert Y., M.D. Hershey, 11/24/99 by telephone.
42. Ring, Ernest J., M.D. San Francisco, 10/4/99.
42a. Hogstrom, Harold. New York, 1/22/99, 8/18/00 by telephone.
43. Luft, Harold S., Ph.D. San Francisco, 10/5/99.
44. Bishop, J. M. A message from the chancellor. http://www.ucsf.edu/daybreak/1999/11/03_message.html. 11/3/99.
45. Drucker, Peter F., Ph.D. Claremont, CA, 12/30/99 by telephone.
46. Hunter, David. St. Petersburg, 12/9/99 by telephone.
47. Gurtner, William H. Oakland, 12/20/99 by telephone.
48. Lewin, Lawrence S. Arlington, VA, 3/12/99.
49. Alain Enthoven, Stanford, 11/6/99, by e-mail.

Index

Abel, Michael E., 363, 401, 404
Academic medical centers (AMCs), 437–40. *See also* Teaching hospitals; *and under individual hospitals*
Academic programs, 88–89, 336. *See also* Clinical programs/services; *and under individual programs*
Affiliation agreements, 189–92
African Americans/Blacks, 155, 366
Al-Awqati, Qais, 237
Allegheny Health Education and Research Foundation (AHERF), 434–35
Allegiances, 422–23
Allen Pavilion (Columbia-Presbyterian), 133–36
Alonzo, Daniel R., 237
Alway, Robert H., 293, 294
Alzheimer's research, 105
American Society for Clinical Investigation, 287n
Anderson, Mark, 177–78
Antman, Karen H., 156, 211
Appointments, of medical school faculty, 93–94, 104, 191–92, 234. *See also* Faculty, recruitment of
Arenson, Ronald, 322, 332, 351, 367, 372
Ascheim, Robert S., 220–21, 222, 230
Ascher, Nancy, 275–76, 343, 344, 367
Association of Practicing Physicians, 231–32
Atchley Building (P&S), 227, 228
Atkinson, Richard, 374, 392
AtlantiCare Medical Center, 76

Ausiello, Dennis A., 98, 99–100, 111–12
Austen, W. Gerald, 30, 42–43, 100, 102–3, 111
Autonomy, academic, 23–24

Babies and Children's Hospital, 136, 234, 248; and NewYork-Presbyterian merger, 196–203. *See also* Pediatrics consolidation, NewYork-Presbyterian
Baker, George F., 161, 249–50
Baker Memorial Hospital, 32
Balanced Budget Act (1997), 12, 362, 408, 424
Barchas, Jack D., 211–12, 237–38, 251, 257
Barnes, Jewish, and Children's Hospitals, 433–34
Basic science programs, 152–57, 286, 369–70
Bauer, Eugene, 269, 307, 313–14, 387, 405; and dermatology unit, 340, 350
Beal, M. Flint, 182, 193, 208
Behrman, Richard E., 245n, 383, 398, 403
Berman, Michael A., 173–74, 182, 208, 209, 254; and affiliation agreements, 192; leadership of, 183; recruitment by, 203, 206
Bero, Cynthia L., 86
Beth Israel Hospital, 19, 37, 39, 94, 147; and merger with Deaconess, 88–89, 101, 432

471

About the Author

John A. Kastor, Professor of Medicine at the University of Maryland School of Medicine in Baltimore, was born in New York City in 1931 and grew up in Wilkes-Barre, Pennsylvania. He received his B.A. degree in American history from the University of Pennsylvania in 1953, then served with the U.S. Army Signal Corps and was employed by the National Broadcasting Company before entering New York University School of Medicine, from which he received his M.D. degree in 1962. Dr. Kastor trained in internal medicine at Bellevue and New York University Hospitals and in cardiology at the Massachusetts General Hospital. He was later appointed to the staff at the Massachusetts General Hospital and to the faculty of the Harvard Medical School. In 1969 he joined the Department of Medicine at the University of Pennsylvania School of Medicine, where he became Professor of Medicine in 1976. He was named Chief of the Cardiovascular Division at the Hospital of the University of Pennsylvania in 1977. From 1984 to 1997, Dr. Kastor was Theodore E. Woodward Professor of Medicine and Chairman of the Department of Medicine at the University of Maryland School of Medicine and Chief of the Medical Service at the University of Maryland Hospital. The mechanisms, diagnosis, and management of cardiac arrhythmias are his primary academic and clinical interests. John Kastor and his wife, Mae, a clinical social worker, are the parents of Elizabeth, a journalist, Anne, a general internist, and Peter, a historian.